RESEARCH & RELEVANT KNOWLEDGE

Second printing 2009

New material this edition copyright © 2008 by Transaction Publishers, New Brunswick, New Jersey. Originally published in 1993 by Oxford University Press.

Library of Congress Catalog Number: 2004046063
ISBN: 978-0-7658-0569-0
Printed in the United States of America

Library of Congress Cataloging-in-Publication Data

Geiger, Roger L., 1943-
    Research and relevant knowledge : American research universities since World War II / Roger L. Geiger, with a new introduction by the author.
        p. cm.—(Transaction series in higher education)
    Originally published: New York : Oxford University Press, 1993.
    Includes bibliographical references and index.
    ISBN 0-7658-0569-3 (pbk. : acid-free paper)
        1. Research—United States—History.   2. Universities and colleges—United States—Research—History.   I. Title.   II. Series.

Q180.U5G34   2004
378.73—dc22   2004046063

For Beth Geiger

Contents

Tables

Abbreviations

AAU	Association of American Universities
AEC	Atomic Energy Commission
APL	Applied Physics Laboratory at Johns Hopkins University
ARPA	Advanced Research Projects Agency, DoD
BSP	Behavioral Sciences Program of the Ford Foundation
Caltech	California Institute of Technology
CIA	Central Intelligence Agency
CIS	Center for International Studies at MIT
CIW	Carnegie Institution of Washington
COSPUP	Committee on Science and Public Policy of the NAS
CMR	Committee on Medical Research during World War II
DoD	Department of Defense
FY	fiscal year
GAC	General Advisory Committee of the AEC
GTRI	Georgia Tech Research Institute
HEW	Department of Health, Education, and Welfare
I-Lab	Instrumentation Laboratory at MIT
IDA	Institute for Defense Analyses

IIT   Illinois Institute of Technology

ISR   Institute for Social Research at the University of Michigan

JPL   Jet Propulsion Laboratory at Caltech

MIT   Massachusetts Institute of Technology

NACA   National Advisory Committee for Aeronautics

NAS   National Academy of Sciences

NASA   National Aeronautics and Space Administration

NBER   National Bureau of Economic Research

NDEA   National Defense Education Act (1958)

NDRC   National Defense Research Committee, World War II

NIH   National Institutes of Health

NRC   National Research Council of the NAS

NSF   National Science Foundation

ONR   Office of Naval Research

ORU   organized research unit

OSRD   Office of Strategic Research and Development, World War II

PSAC   President's Science Advisory Committee

Rad Lab   Radiation Laboratory at MIT during World War II
               Radiation Laboratory at UC Berkeley, est. by E. O. Lawrence

RANN   Research Applied to National Needs program of NSF

ROTC   Reserve Officer Training Corps

RPI   Rensselaer Polytechnic Institute

SDS   Students for a Democratic Society

SRI   Stanford Research Institute

SSRC   Social Science Research Council

UC   University of California

USDP   University Science Development Program of NSF

WARF   Wisconsin Alumni Research Foundation

WEAL   Women's Equity Action League

Introduction to the
Transaction Edition

When I originally contemplated a history of American research universities in the twentieth century, my initial plan was to write a single volume. Only well into the writing of what became *To Advance Knowledge* did it become apparent that two volumes would be required. This conclusion emerged initially from the nature of the topic: secondary sources were helpful but incomplete; research in primary sources was essential; and a certain level of detail was necessary to portray the material accurately and interestingly. Once I began the second volume, another good reason became clear. Research universities before World War II and research universities afterward are two different stories. The first is one of a (growing) handful of institutions seeking to advance to world-class standards in basic science and receiving an enormous boost from the great philanthropic foundations. The second is a story of a system of universities impelled forward by the demands and the resources of the federal government, but also guided by their own academic ambitions. *Research and Relevant Knowledge* presents this latter story—how American universities became leading world centers of science and scholarship. Appropriately, it continues the history of these institutions in a different framework from its predecessor.

The history of the major American universities from 1940 to 1990 is an immense subject. As additional publications continue to appear on these institutions and various related topics, it becomes increasingly obvious how much material was passed over or barely touched upon in *Research and Relevant Knowledge* and the abundance of interesting topics that remain to be addressed. Nevertheless, the aim of this volume was always primarily to define and present the outlines of the overall development of universities and research, and only secondarily to illustrate this development with telling examples. This "big picture" has a unifying thread: how American society perceived the value of research universities and made available the resources on which they depend. The consequences—how universities reacted to these opportunities—were strongly affected by this context.

The context for research universities was manifested in a succession of dominant ideologies—distinguishing sets of rationales, expectations, and policies toward academic research—each lasting just over a decade. From 1945 until the early 1990s four major phases of policies and postures dominated the public discourse on research universities. However, there was also an enormous underlying stability and resilience to the system of academic research. So, one might well ask: why the apparent importance of ideologies? Why the underlying stability?

The advancement of knowledge through basic academic research is a notion that is occasionally honored in the United States but not widely understood. Scientists, of course, are well aware of the interconnectedness of research and tangible social benefits, but for much of the population and its political leadership such matters must be accepted largely on faith. Over time, the arguments for supporting academic research may be generically similar, but the public mood for accepting or rejecting such arguments oscillates. Optimism and confidence in the future favor such investments, particularly when they are linked with widely shared national objectives. Public cynicism or defensiveness, conversely, breed doubts about the future and reluctance to invest in it. A favorable climate for academic research thus seemed to be a necessary factor for robust expansion of universities and their research role.

The stability of academic research, in contrast, springs from factors internal to science. First is the inherent expansiveness of science itself. Historian of science Derek de Solla Price sought to demonstrate this in the early 1960s. He calculated that since the scientific revolution of the seventeenth century, scientific production had doubled every fifteen years. Price then argued that such an exponential expansion, which could not persist indefinitely, had probably reached its limits. But he was wrong, at least so far. Judging from real expenditures for basic or academic research, that same pace of growth was maintained in the United States, albeit irregularly, for the rest of the twentieth century.

A second source of stability lay in the usefulness or relevance of scientific discovery. This revelation was the lesson of wartime research; in the postwar era there was no question of foregoing further investigations into radar, computing and electronics, medicine, or—the paradigmatic triumph of pure science—atomic energy. There was a question of where such research might best be conducted. However, universities proved to be indispensable for these demands, and they proved adaptable too. Moreover, scientists knew that relevant knowledge could not be separated from basic research. No matter what the climate, the underlying demand for academic research has continuously grown.

These two dynamics together largely account for four distinct phases of university development from 1945 until the early 1990s—one of the interesting findings of *Research and Relevant Knowledge.*

America's confidence may never have been higher than after the end of World War II. For academic research that confidence was expressed in Vannevar Bush's report, *Science, the Endless Frontier.* Although this idealistic vision was never realized, support for research was continued through wartime channels, and the spirit of the Bush report found expression in the liberal policies of the Office of Naval Research. The onset of the Cold War, and the displacement of wartime academic leaders by a new generation of scientific cold warriors, dampened and challenged this approach. By the mid-1950s the two camps were at loggerheads: one deploring a national science policy dependent on the military, and another wishing to concentrate national investments more specifically on weapons research in government laboratories. This impasse was decisively broken by the shock of Sputnik in 1957.

Sputnik was interpreted to mean that the Soviets were outperforming the United States in science, education, and, of course, space technology. It spurred an unprecedented boost in investments by non-military federal agencies in academic research. This commitment accelerated in the early 1960s, ultimately producing programs to support university development, infrastructure, and graduate education. Medical research shot up as well, inspired more by the national mood than competition with the Soviets. In the middle years of the decade, however, the rate of growth for science funding attenuated as questions about its utility grew more insistent. The *annus horribilis,* 1968, brought an end to the expansion of academic research and anguish over the role that universities had assumed.

For the next ten years universities endured stagnation in research support, the end of enrollment growth in higher education, a crash in the job market for new Ph.D.s, intrusive government regulation, and fiscal distress. Universities largely reacted to student rebellion and public chastisement by withdrawing to the ivory tower. Higher education rhetoric and university actions disdained entanglements with the defense establishment or the corporate world, extolling instead the role of unsullied social critic. Egalitarianism and social justice informed the new zeitgeist as a powerful campus polity sought to enlist the university in such virtuous causes as racial and gender equity, third world liberation, urban revitalization, and environmental preservation. Beneath this tumult basic and useful research proceeded apace. However, by the late 1970s it was becoming increasingly apparent that there was too little research, academic or otherwise, reaching the productive economy.

By 1980 a new social concern ascended in public attention and national priority—economic competitiveness. The lamentable performance of the U.S. economy was blamed in large part on insufficient investment in research by industry and the absence of technology transfer from university laboratories. Federal policies were implemented to encourage technology transfer, and the success of those few universities that maintained close ties with industry now inspired envy and emulation. However, a scientific catalyst clinched the argument, just as Sputnik and the atomic bomb had done in previous eras. Biotechnology manifested its commercial potential in unmistakable fashion. Pure biological research had yielded the tools to transform life itself, with enormous implications for medicine and agriculture. This new paradigm supplied a compelling rationale for investments in academic research, and not just for the life sciences. A fruitful collaboration between academic researchers and industry promised to fuel not only economic development but also new sources of revenue for universities. A vast movement of privatization was underway by the mid-1980s, and it reinvigorated research universities.

Although these developments were taking place while I was writing *Research and Relevant Knowledge*, their historical importance seemed evident. The last sections of this volume accordingly sketch out their early stages. More difficult at the time was dealing with the uncertainty of the future. If the ideologies sustaining research universities since 1945 had been waxing and waning on ten- to twelve-year cycles, another change was due circa 1990. In the event, this volume was completed in the midst of what then seemed to be an ill-defined crisis. In retrospect, it appears that a number of developments conspired to undermine the forward momentum, and the complacency, of research universities. The so-called culture wars in combination with a critique of undergraduate teaching at research universities prompted a barrage of polemical attacks. Financial conditions caused both public and private universities, for different reasons, to cease expansion, hunker down, and devote more resources to undergraduates. A scandal at Stanford over improper charges for indirect costs had huge repercussions in this atmosphere of mistrust. And, mounting federal budget deficits brought a stagnation of federal support for research—and predictions of far worse.

This negative phase of the university ideology, however, was relatively short lived—a little ice age. The buoyant economy of the late 1990s not only engendered optimism, but prosperity in this case had direct links with universities. The boom was driven by high-tech industries—broadband, Internet, biotech—having close ties with university research. Universities were again perceived, and perhaps for better reasons, as drivers of economic growth. In the emerging "knowledge economy" universities were not only key generators of new knowledge, their credentials also appeared to be increasingly necessary for individual success.[1]

The notion of a knowledge economy may be a cliché of the current ideology, but it nevertheless conveys an important message. Its kernel of truth validates the contention of Clark Kerr, Daniel Bell, and others that universities had become central institutions of post-industrial society. This centrality stems from the university's unique role as creator, guarantor, arbiter, and, above all, repository of advanced, expert knowledge. This role is sustained, as I argue in the concluding section of this volume, by a commitment to cognitive rationality. By no means is all new knowledge discovered in universities, but most of it soon finds its way there. Universities serve as the warehouse and distribution center for the most advanced and theoretical forms of knowledge. They have been able to sustain this role, quite simply, because their chief functions of teaching, research, and service all contribute to and draw from this fund of knowledge. These stable and ongoing functions provide the economic base that has allowed them to accumulate and sustain this expertise. By the 1990s American universities had perfected this role more effectively than any others in the world.

How this situation came about is the subject of *Research and Relevant Knowledge*. It was by no means inevitable or foreordained. The central university role of advancing and cultivating learning has been repeatedly challenged. Moreover, it has depended on a complex, evolving relationship between the creators and the consumers of academic knowledge. Accordingly, much of this volume is devoted to what I call the research economy—the sources of funding for university research and the motives behind that support. But universities had to learn how to serve these consumers while preserving internally the conditions of freedom and creativity that spawned this relevant knowledge in the first place. Through trial and error they fashioned an autonomous research role, loosely linked with the academic core. This role was inherently fraught with tension, as the clashes over military research described in this volume show, but it was also a consensual, negotiated relationship that neither side could dominate. This process still persists as universities are presently working out the tensions generated by the commercialization of academic research.

Ultimately, these larger developments were refracted through the experience of individual institutions, which sometimes grasped and sometimes missed opportunities. This study examines eight cases of universities adapting to the changing contexts for research and for higher education at key points in the development of the university research system. These examples illustrate the dialectic forces referred to at the outset of this Introduction. Changes in the research economy and in the prevailing ideology exerted irresistible pressures on universities. Yet those pressures had to be reconciled with the quotidian realities of available resources and ongoing missions. The most successful institutions—the ones continually able to enhance their learning assets—largely managed to harness both processes and to make them work toward that common goal. But the process was an historical one, embodied in specific events occurring over time.

Research and Relevant Knowledge above all set out to describe and to interpret the enormous, disjointed, and often messy history of how American universities developed over the half-century from 1940 to 1990. It will undoubtedly not be the last work on this vast subject. However, it might well remain the only work to encompass this fascinating story in a single volume.

State College, Pa.   R.L.G.
February 2004

Note

1. Developments at U.S. research universities in the current era are analyzed in my subsequent volume, Roger L. Geiger, *Knowledge and Money: Research Universities and the Paradox of the Marketplace* (Stanford: Stanford University Press, 2004).

Preface

American research universities occupy a sufficiently important space in the social order that their study scarcely requires special justification. They conduct about half of the basic research in the United States, train almost all the Ph.D.s and medical doctors, and also graduate about 30 percent of the country's bachelors.[1] They have been heralded as central institutions of post-industrial societies, although other advanced countries have nothing that equals them.[2] Some countries confide basic research to non-teaching academies. Education for the learned professions or even scientific careers can take place under apprentice-like arrangements or in specialized institutions that make no pretense to encompass all knowledge. And the career aspirations of post-adolescents are satisfied in most societies without recourse to higher learning, let alone to teachers who engage in research.[3] The American research universities are by no means unique in combining these multiple tasks; however, they stand alone in the world in terms of their abundant numbers, the variety of their forms, and the extent to which they derive their sustenance from numerous sources. The intent of this study is to begin to elaborate the history of American research universities since the beginning of World War II—the era of their greatest accomplishments.

To study research universities is to address a set of institutions whose central members are obvious, but whose peripheral members are never entirely clear; and to address them from the perspective of their particular role of cultivating, interpreting, and extending knowledge. The subject transcends individual institutions to encompass the university research system—the interactions of all participating and assisting institutions. Also included is the university research economy—the sum of the resources provided to support academic inquiry. The subject is rooted as well in the institutional foundations of universities—in their undergraduate and graduate students, faculty, and facilities. In that sense, this study is about the conditions that surround, sustain, and influence universities in their research role.

This book, although complete in itself, continues and finishes a study of American research universities in the twentieth century. *To Advance Knowledge,* which appeared in 1986, covered the first four decades of the century; the present volume addresses the half-century that followed.[4] Inherent changes in the nature of the subject have made these two works rather different. The earlier study was able to comprehend much of the development of research universities by monitoring just sixteen of them; but after the Second World War far more institutions became meaningful participants in this system. In the 1920s and 1930s universities came to depend on outside support, largely from philanthropic foundations, to meet much of the costs of their research; but afterward the federal government became the foremost patron, and academic research became a matter of public policy. Prior to 1940 universities performed both basic and applied research, although the latter was largely disdained by academic leaders; but postwar universities found themselves in a more ambiguous situation—performing much 'programmatic' research defined by the needs of patrons. The research universities changed as well: in order to accommodate their expanding and changing research role they had to become larger, more complex, more segmented organizations.

The transformation of research universities over the half-century since the beginning of World War II is a subject of vast dimensions. A narrative history can only highlight a tiny, selected sampling of such manifold developments. The material presented in the pages that follow was chosen because it either pertained to occurrences of recognized importance, represented developments experienced widely across universities, or exemplified significant aspects of change. Three distinctly different kinds of topics are treated. Perhaps a third of the text concerns the research economy. Chapters 1 and 6 depict changes in the federal role, while support for academic research from foundations and corporations figures in Chapters 4 and 9. Another third explores different facets of the university research system at strategically important points of development. Finance and the institutional resource base are repeatedly visited; separately organized research units and graduate education, inherent factors in the research process, are principally treated in Chapters 2 and 7. No less important are the climates of opinion prevailing on campuses and the effects produced on internal and external relations—particular foci in Chapters 8 and 10. The remainder of the book consists of case studies of eight institutions during strategic phases of development (Chapters 3, 5, and 9). The experiences of each university detailed here are representative of changes occurring throughout the research system, yet no university is typical. These studies, on one hand, exhibit the rich institutional diversity of the university research system, while also offering a different level of understanding from the system-wide generalities necessarily offered elsewhere.

The research universities have been among the most successful institutions of American society in terms of the expanding scope of their activities, impressive achievements in their major tasks, and high stature relative to international peers. Yet, they have also been subject to a fairly steady stream of criticism. The years

1991 and 1992 were especially trying in this respect. Universities were excoriated for harboring fraud in science, for gouging on indirect cost recovery, for neglecting undergraduates, and for inhibiting academic freedom with a rigid ideological orthodoxy. There was substance to all these charges, but in the main the impressions conveyed were far more misleading than they were accurate.[5] This study too has endeavored to view research universities through a critical lens, but to a different end. It has sought to portray the failings and foibles together with the mundane, incremental, and sometimes striking accomplishments. Moreover, these developments have been situated within a context of the multiple roles that these institutions daily attempt to balance. The chapters that follow strive to depict, accurately and objectively, the evolution of these enduring yet protean institutions as they have evolved during the half-century of their greatest glory and their sorest trials.

A project of this scope and duration could never have been accomplished without the assistance of many individuals and institutions. This volume was begun at the Yale Program on Non-Profit Organizations where it benefited from the encouragement and advice of John Simon and Paul DiMaggio. Since 1987, my work has found a stimulating and supportive environment in the Higher Education Program at Pennsylvania State University. American foundations, which are viewed critically in Chapter 4, have rendered indispensable aid. I am deeply grateful to the Ford Foundation, the Andrew W. Mellon Foundation, the Alfred P. Sloan Foundation, and the Spencer Foundation for their assistance. Particular thanks are extended to William Bowen, James Morris, Peter Stanley, and the late Lawrence Cremin for the interest each took in the substance of this study. The Policy Research and Analysis unit of the National Science Foundation supplied invaluable data and supported a fruitful workshop at Penn State on "Research Perspectives on Research Universities." Martin Trow and Sheldon Rothblatt provided a home away from home at the Berkeley Center for Studies in Higher Education. And, like many other historians, I am indebted to the helpful assistance of staff at the eighteen archives visited in the course of this research.

I owe thanks to the many people who have read parts of this manuscript or supplied me with relevant material. Nathan Reingold, Edward Shils, William Tierney, and Clark Kerr offered useful suggestions on section drafts. Sheldon Meyer has been a model editor—patient, tolerant, offering sound advice when needed. I am particularly grateful to Karen Paulson for carefully reading and editing the penultimate draft; to Vickie Ziegler for providing ongoing encouragement and emotional support; to Jennifer Krohn for assisting with my research and enlightening me with her own; to Dorothy Finnegan, another student from whom I learned; and to Joan Schumacher for being there during the concluding stage. Finally, special thanks to Burton Clark who, when not diverting me to one of his own tantalizing projects, offered valuable comments, continuing friendship, and the inspiration of example.

State College, Pa.   R.L.G.
November 1992

Research and Relevant Knowledge

I

Origins
of the Federal Research
Economy

1. The Organization of Research for War

As the armed forces of Nazi Germany were overrunning Western Europe in June 1940, James Bryant Conant, president of Harvard, was tapped by Vannevar Bush, recently appointed president of the Carnegie Institution of Washington (CIW), to assist in the task of mobilizing American science for national defense. Conant expected that this would involve organizing and constructing government laboratories, and then staffing them with soldier-scientists, such as he and Bush had been during World War I. Bush, however, quickly disabused him of this notion: "we will write contracts with universities, research institutes and industrial laboratories."[1] The manifold implications of this approach were immediately apparent to Conant—it portended the beginning of a new relationship between the federal government and the nation's universities.

In 1916, prior to American entry into the previous World War, the need to mobilize the nation's scientific potential had also been evident. Then, George Ellery Hale had succeeded in prompting the creation of the National Research Council to coordinate the scientific efforts of industry, government and academe. By the time the United States entered the war, though, the military technology of the conflict was well established. The tasks that fell to American science included solving problems of production and supply, refining existing weapons, and developing countermeasures like antisubmarine warfare. Circumstances, moreover, determined that these tasks would be placed under military auspices. Few universities possessed facilities appropriate for large-scale research projects, and immediate battlefield application was the foremost consideration. University scientists capable of contributing to the war effort were consequently inducted into the services, and then assigned for the most part to special labo-

3

ratories. American scientists compiled a creditable record in terms of contributing to the efficacy of the American military effort, but their record for fundamental discovery and invention was comparatively modest, even given the brief duration of American involvement.[2]

After World War I, George Hale and the scientific leadership of the 1920s had been of one mind concerning the proper organization of science. Direction, above all, had to be lodged with the most competent scientists, who alone possessed the expert knowledge to provide leadership in research. Scientific autonomy of this type was best guaranteed, they believed, by relying upon the resources of private philanthropy to support basic research, preferably in universities. To permit government involvement in university research would only bring the intrusion of political considerations and a diminution of the effectiveness of science.[3] This approach succeeded admirably for the research universities during the 1920s. The Great Depression, however, placed severe limitations on this privately based research economy, inhibiting the further expansion of university science. The individuals that Vannevar Bush brought together in the National Defense Research Committee (NDRC) represented a new generation of leadership in American science, one that had emerged during the difficult conditions of the 1930s. Although they too wished to keep scientific choice in the hands of scientists, the possibility of federal support for university research was for them an open issue. They had grappled with the idea since the onset of the New Deal, but no practical arrangements had been worked out for reconciling the twin requirements of public accountability and private expert control.[4] Now, this problem had become truly critical: a massive federal effort in military research seemed imminent, and the fate of the democratic nations of the world might very well depend upon its effectiveness.

Thus, as German armies overran Western Europe, American scientific leaders again confronted the imperative need to organize. Insofar as science was concerned, the United States in 1940 was in a far stronger position than a quarter-century before. Since the last European war both American industry and American universities had vastly increased their capacities for scientific research. In industry, expenditures for applied and basic research had reached $200 million in 1939, up from just over $100 million a decade before and $30 million at the start of the 1920s.[5] Academic science had advanced from an apprenticeship status prior to World War I to full parity with Europe's best in most areas by the early 1930s. Still, the problem of how to realize the full potential of American science was unresolved as Bush and Conant reacted to the deepening world crisis.

Besides Conant, Bush chose as scientific members of the NDRC, Karl Compton, president of MIT, Frank Jewett, director of the Bell Telephone Laboratories, and Richard C. Tolman, dean at Caltech. This group was remarkably close and like-minded. All were distinguished scientists who had advanced to administrative posts. They had collaborated since 1937 as members of the Committee on Scientific Aids to Learning, and they had used that opportunity to discuss informally the international situation and its implications for the United States. All, significantly, were also Republicans who distrusted the enlarged scope of government brought about by Roosevelt's New Deal. In spirit, the Committee's center was MIT. Bush had been Compton's highly valued lieutenant there, rising to a vice presidency. Jewett, a trustee of MIT (and the CIW), had convinced Compton to take the presidency of MIT in order to bring greater emphasis on basic science to its strength in engineering. Compton had been the principal advocate for federal support for basic research during the 1930s. Jewett was the country's spokesman for science in industry. Moreover, his election to the presidency of the National Academy of Sciences (NAS) in 1938 was recognition of the emerging importance of this estate of science. These highly individualistic leaders did not always see eye to eye. Conant and Jewett regarded peacetime federal support for university research with distrust. Tolman and Conant were among the earliest and most outspoken interventionists.[6] As they informally discussed the deteriorating world situation in 1939 and 1940, however, they were of one mind:

> that the war was bound to break out into an intense struggle, that America was sure to get into it in one way or another sooner or later, that it would be a highly technical struggle, that we were by no means prepared in this regard, and finally and most importantly, that the military system as it existed, and as it had operated during the first war, . . . would never fully produce the new instrumentalities which we would certainly need, and which were possible because of the state of science as it then stood.[7]

More ominous yet, they progressively became aware, was the imminent possibility of tapping the awesome energy of nuclear fission. Hence, the crucial importance of reconciling expert direction of defense research by civilian scientists with government funding and ultimate responsibility. Resolving this situation would be the cardinal contribution of the NDRC.

Bush had a model in mind when he first proposed the NDRC. At the time he became head of CIW in 1939, he also became chairman of the National Advisory Committee for Aeronautics (NACA). This committee had functioned during the interwar years as a liaison between civilian science and the military in the field of aviation.[8] Bush's original conception of the NDRC was as a similar kind of intermediary that could coordinate fundamental research in militarily important areas between the Departments of War and the Navy on one side and civilian science as represented by the NAS on the other. Bush was thus proposing to fill what was then a functional void—to initiate and direct research on science-intensive problems that lay beyond the scope of the existing military and naval laboratories, which themselves were then overburdened attempting to perfect existing weaponry.[9] The uniqueness and the importance of this mission undoubtedly were factors in winning prompt presidential authorization, including the power to begin spending emergency executive funds. Bush was thus given a free hand to fashion and to direct the type of organization that he and his colleagues believed would be effective—one controlled by scientists and fully independent for purposes of research. The key element of their approach was decentralization, or what Bush called a pyramidal structure. Each of his civilian appointees became directors of major divisions, and they then established as many specialized sections as they felt were needed. It was at this lowest level, where scientists and engineers worked with representatives from the armed services, that research was actually conducted. Policy, administration and budgetary matters were handled separately. In this manner, the NDRC succeeded in keeping "the exercise of scientific choice in the hands of scientists, who alone were in a position to judge the merits of a given line of research."[10]

The NACA had on occasion contracted out for specific pieces of research, although this was not its usual mode of operation. One of the initial decisions of the NDRC, as indicated, was to rely as fully as possible upon contracts for research with industry and universities. This approach was also compatible with the official neutrality of the United States, as well as the presence in the country of strong isolationist sentiments. By the end of 1940 the NDRC had already let 132 contracts to 32 universities and 19 industrial corporations.[11]

The organization that Bush had devised was revamped the following year, but only at the tip of the pyramid. Its rapidly growing fiscal requirements demanded direct Congressional appropriations. Also, a separate Committee on Medical Research (CMR) was created, which Bush placed parallel to rather than within the NDRC. The result was the creation of the Office of Strategic Research and Development (OSRD), with Bush as director, superimposed over both NDRC and CMR. (The other scientific advisory committee, NACA, continued to operate independently of the OSRD.) After this adjustment, both the organization and the top personnel remained fixed for the entire war. The remarkable results that were achieved under these arrangements have been fully described elsewhere.[12] In part they were facilitated by the flexibility of the organization that Bush had fashioned. Adaptability was no doubt enhanced by the lean, nonbureaucratic and temporary nature of the OSRD, abetted by the close understanding of the individuals involved and their overriding dedication to the cause of victory.[13] As a consequence of this flexibility OSRD projects developed in a highly pragmatic manner. Both the exigencies of war and the possibilities of existing states of knowledge tended to determine the dimensions and dynamics of any particular program. Consequently, there was no single relationship between the OSRD and American universities during the war: there were several different wartime relationships and, more importantly in the long run, correspondingly different postwar precedents.

2. Universities and War Research

The basic relationship between the federal government and universities for conducting wartime research was governed by contracts negotiated according to the principle of no-loss and no-gain. Universities were reimbursed for the direct costs they incurred and also given some allowance for overhead. How much to allow universities for these indirect costs was always a difficult issue since, unlike business firms, educational institutions had no regular manner of accounting for their overhead burden. OSRD eventually settled upon a figure of 50 percent of the project payroll, but other government agencies could and did set their own policies. It took a significant departure from normal federal bureaucratic procedures in order to establish this type of contractual relationship.

The contracts specified that the research itself was what the government was purchasing rather than a final document reporting specific findings. With their obligations defined in this way, scientists possessed sufficient leeway to allow for the uncertainties of the research process. These and other potentially rancorous issues were settled with little difficulty because of the singularity of purpose existing on both sides. Given this cooperative spirit, short and simple contracts could be agreed upon without lengthy negotiations. Some of the early major contracts written by OSRD were only four typewritten pages, and even by the end of the war they seldom exceeded twice that length. Often urgent work was begun immediately and contract terms negotiated afterward.[1]

Given the absolute priority of the war effort, the usual academic tasks of universities were largely displaced for the duration. In matters of personnel, federal authority was all-powerful. Colleges and universities were directly affected by the unrelenting policies of the Selective Service, which ultimately claimed most male students despite university complaints of short-sightedness. With respect to research, the universities soon had to cope with the extensive dislocation of scientific personnel. The system of contract research did not result in many university scientists spending World War II in their own laboratories; for the most part they spent the war in someone else's lab. A large portion of the nation's active physicists, whose expertise was in greatest demand, had relocated before Pearl Harbor. The subsequent acceleration of war research confirmed this trend. These dislocations were only part of the novel circumstances produced by contract research. In general, the larger the research projects, the greater the break with the kind of research arrangements that universities had been accustomed to before the war.

The two largest R&D efforts of the war were the Manhattan Project and the Radiation Laboratory at MIT. In their objectives and development they were almost mirror opposites. The first began as a rather diffuse undertaking, but gradually concentrated an enormous amount of science, engineering, and material resources upon the single goal of producing an atomic bomb. The second began with a single device—a British-designed magnetron, the basis for effective microwave radar—and gradually proliferated into an entire industry with multiple products and applications. Each evolved different relationships with universities.

The quest to build an atomic bomb was touched off by the achievement of fission of the uranium atom in Germany early in 1939. The implications of this discovery were clear to the international community of atomic physicists. A vast number of questions had to be investigated, however, before it could be determined if and how this potential source of enormous energy might be tapped. Research on the physics of chain reactions was immediately begun at Columbia by Enrico Fermi and Leo Szilard. Fermi had just emigrated from Italy after winning the 1938 Nobel Prize in physics for research on neutrons. Leo Szilard, also an immigrant, had years earlier foreseen the theoretical possibility of a fission bomb.[2] Similar investigations were undertaken at Princeton and Chicago, but official support for such work was circumscribed, even after the outbreak of war in Europe.

Research on atomic energy began to intensify in 1940 after it was reorganized under the authority of the NDRC. Bush and the other committee members at this time faced a critical decision: whether or not to commit a substantial portion of the country's finite scientific resources to such a huge and costly effort.[3] The crucial issues were: was an atomic bomb actually possible? Could it be built in time to affect the outcome of the war? And, could the Germans build one? The British felt that the answers were affirmative on all three counts. A special committee under Arthur Holly Compton of the University of Chicago was charged in 1941 with resolving these issues, and it concluded emphatically that such a project ought to be undertaken. Although initially reluctant, the NDRC accepted this judgment and reorganized atomic research in the fall of 1941 for an all-out effort to build an atomic bomb. In January of 1942, A. H. Compton consolidated all theoretical and experimental work on chain reactions at the University of Chicago in the "Metallurgical Laboratory." By December they had attained the first sustained chain reaction in an atomic pile.[4]

As the basic scientific puzzles underlying nuclear fission were solved, one by one, some paramount practical obstacles loomed large. Fission occurred under the proper circumstances principally in the U-235 isotope of uranium, which comprised only 0.7 percent of the naturally occurring element. Isotope separation of this difficulty had never before been accomplished, yet at least several kilograms of pure U-235 would be needed to build a bomb. Two important contributions from E. O. Lawrence's cyclotron at Berkeley pointed a way out of this predicament. Glenn Seaborg in 1941 succeeded in creating the artificial transuranium element of plutonium, which was predicted to have the same fissionable properties as U-235. Then Lawrence managed to separate minute amounts of U-235 by bending Uranium ions in a powerful magnetic field. In an unrelated effort at Columbia, physical chemist Harold Urey was experimenting with a separation process based on gaseous diffusion.[5] At this juncture, in June of 1942, the final decision was taken to launch a full-scale effort to build an atomic bomb with material produced by all of these processes. The laboratory experiments on chain reactions quickly grew into an industrial undertaking of immense proportions. For this reason the entire project was transferred from the jurisdiction of OSRD to the Manhattan District of the Army Corps of Engineers.[6]

The scientific work of the Manhattan Project for its first twelve months continued to be based in universities. The principal research groups were those headed by Lawrence at Berkeley, Urey at Columbia, A. H. Compton at the Chicago Metallurgical Lab, and a theoretical group under J. Robert Oppenheimer, also at Berkeley. In addition, vital experimental data was being accumulated from cyclotron experiments at Minnesota, Wisconsin, Harvard, and Cornell. From mid-1943 onward, however, scientific activity was increasingly concentrated at the Special Weapons Laboratory at Los Alamos, New Mexico. Although the construction and staffing of Los Alamos was done through contracts with the University of California, the Laboratory had a special character that transcended the Academy. Its cloistered staff resembled a huge, multinational physics faculty, which at one point included eight Nobel laureates. The task for which they were assembled was so astronomically expensive that it *could* only be funded by government, and *would* only be funded if it were deemed to be crucial to national interests. Moreover, given the overriding importance of the project, it required security restrictions that were hitherto alien to academic investigations. For the community of atomic physicists, the Manhattan Project constituted a transition to a new research environment—one of far greater permanence than the emergency wartime conditions that gave it birth.[7]

The Radiation Laboratory at MIT was an undertaking of comparable magnitude to the Manhattan Project.[8] At its peak of activity it employed 1200 civilian scientists and technicians, compared with 1400 at Los Alamos; Division 14 of the NDRC, under which it was organized, expended approximately $1.5 billion for radar systems, whereas the Army Corps of Engineers spent $2 billion on the atomic bomb. Had the dimensions of this undertaking been apparent at the outset, radar research too might have been placed under special administration. As it was, circumstances early in the war required the immediate establishment of a crash program in radar research, and MIT, almost by default, was chosen as the location.

Radar was an important topic of military research throughout much of the 1930s in several countries. At the outbreak of the war, however, the effectiveness of existing radar sets was quite limited. No equipment had been devised to generate high frequency wave lengths, which were required to provide accurate resolution with sufficient power to be reflected from distant objects. Early in 1940 the British accomplished this breakthrough with the invention of the resonant-cavity magnetron. In September, while the Battle of Britain was raging, a British delegation brought this device to the United States and successfully demonstrated it at the Bell Telephone Laboratories. The NDRC and its Microwave Committee (Division 14) thereupon resolved to give urgent priority to establishing a civilian laboratory for scientific research on the perfection and implementation of radar. The first choice of the Microwave Committee was to place this facility in the Carnegie Institution of Washington, but it turned out that space there had been preempted by other projects. Arrangements were then sought to use an army airfield, but at the last moment the army made other plans for this facility. Only then did Bush and the Committee turn to Karl Compton to request that MIT accommodate radar research. After being assured that space was available, Compton agreed, and the Radiation (or Rad) Lab—so-called to mask its true purpose—was quickly organized.[9]

MIT was well suited to undertake this task, not just because of its location and its close ties with the NDRC; nowhere in American higher education were the basic scientific disciplines and the applications of science through engineering more closely intertwined.[10] The Institute also had extensive experience in the administration of research contracts. Its Division of Industrial Cooperation had dealt with the problems arising from the conduct of externally supported research for two decades. In fact, the original Rad Lab contract with MIT for $455,000 was the first of the large wartime research contracts with universities. MIT thus became a kind of guinea pig for the OSRD by working out a framework for government-university relations.[11] Nevertheless, there was considerable initial skepticism, particularly among the scientific old guard, about the effectiveness of concentrating large numbers of academic scientists in a single laboratory; and there were rumors early on about dispersing the Laboratory. In fact, the placement proved fortuitous. MIT actually supported the Lab for a short time at an early stage when its effectiveness was in doubt, and its subsequent achievements speak for themselves.[12] More important, the Rad Lab established a precedent for postwar science.

Radar was the most revolutionary technology of the war, in that it substantially transformed every area to which it was applied. The Rad Lab was created at the time of the German night-bombing raids on England, and its most urgent assignments were accordingly to develop an airborne radar set for night fighter planes and a ground set to guide the fire of anti-aircraft guns. The Lab was charged in addition with developing a long-range navigational system. Even starting with the British magnetron, a tremendous amount of research was needed to perfect the basic hardware of magnetrons, antennas, transmitters, receivers, modulators, and wave guides. Then, the more effective radar became, the more potential applications emerged. In addition, the changing military situation during the war created needs for offensive rather than defensive applications. Different groups had to be formed within the Rad Lab to deal with the practical problems of utilizing radar in the aiming and firing of guns, for naval vessels, for airborne systems, for communications, and particularly for aerial bombing. By the end of the war the Rad Lab had, wholly or in part, developed 150 different radar systems.[13]

Radar blossomed into an industry that at once was vital to national security and had important civilian applications. In addition, its development involved the investigation of fundamental questions concerning electromagnetic theory as well as the creation, utilization and effects of high-frequency radiation. There could be little doubt, then, that this research ought to be continued after the conclusion of the war.

The original Rad Lab was at MIT, but not really of MIT. E. O. Lawrence was largely responsible for recruiting the original staff (which in 1940 was a delicate task). He convinced Lee A. Dubridge, dean of the University of Rochester, to take the directorship, and F. Wheeler Loomis, chairman of physics at the University of Illinois, to become his deputy. Division heads were similarly chosen from among the best-qualified available scientists in the country and included I. I. Rabi from Columbia. MIT's own resident expert in this field happened to be called to Washington on another assignment, and only one MIT professor was represented on the steering committee. The Rad Lab nevertheless quickly became rooted in the Institute.[14] It began operating in an existing laboratory and in space created on the roof of another building. The burgeoning personnel soon necessitated the construction of an entire new building—which needed to be doubled in size before it was completed. A nearby building was then purchased, and two more temporary structures were erected. Given these physical facilities, MIT became the logical place to maintain radar research.

Two other wartime university laboratories approximated the general pattern of MIT's Rad Lab. The Applied Physics Laboratory at Johns Hopkins University was created to expedite the development of the proximity fuse—basically a detonator controlled by a radio transmitter within the shell set to explode at an optimal distance from a target. The other major laboratory concentrated research on rockets and jet engines at Caltech.[15] Both these undertakings consisted of numerous projects, involved very large expenditures, and required the services of scientists recruited from many institutions. Their missions were to achieve battlefield deployment in the shortest possible time. These NDRC sections consequently saw through the entire process from basic research through engineering, design, production, and even tactical applications. Most significant for the future was the fact that, like radar, these projects worked with technologies of enduring importance for the military.

The small- and medium-sized wartime research projects developed in a highly pragmatic fashion, and for that reason assumed various organizational forms. Some resembled the large laboratories in that the problems with which they grappled inexorably grew in scope. For example, projects at Harvard involving sonar and countermeasures to radar both expanded into full-fledged laboratories. Work on the complex mathematics of aerial bombing was originally assigned to Princeton and Berkeley, but was later centralized at Columbia in an "Air Warfare Analysis" unit. Special university facilities with military importance were utilized extensively. The differential analyzer at the University of Pennsylvania's Moore School of Engineering was employed almost continuously for calculating ballistics problems. On the other hand, many of the scientific problems that arose during the war required only a single solution. Such a case was the development of RDX, an explosive more powerful than TNT, but at the time too costly and unstable to manufacture. When the desirability of large-scale production of RDX was recognized, the task of discovering a feasible production process was assigned by the NDRC to laboratories at Michigan, Cornell, and Penn State. A solution first devised at Michigan became the basis for actual production.[16]

In these myriad small- and medium-sized wartime research projects the genius of the NDRC organization was apparent. Once the Committee or some other agency determined that a scientific problem was of strategic importance to the war effort it was referred to the appropriate Division. Consideration at one of the regular divisional meetings followed, often including representatives of the NDRC, the services, or other interested parties. An approved project would be assigned to an existing or expressly created section where the appropriate specialists would be set to work. Contracts and other administrative matters were arranged by the Division, subject to the approval of the NDRC and the OSRD.[17] This decentralized structure succeeded, above all, in lodging critical scientific decisions with scientists themselves, who alone possessed the specialized knowledge on which such decisions had to be based. In this respect the NDRC was essentially an ad hoc organization based upon preexisting informal networks within the American scientific community. Accordingly, it depended heavily upon the acumen of those in leadership positions and their contacts throughout the critical networks. The effectiveness of the NDRC on both of these counts has been widely recognized. In addition, the freedom and flexibility with which the NDRC operated is credited with facilitating its mission. These qualities, however, stemmed not only from its decentralized structure but also from the wartime conditions that afforded ample resources with minimal accountability. As a result, the factors that contributed to the NDRC's wartime efficacy were unlikely to endure after the cessation of hostilities.

In another area of small-scale wartime research—medicine—the situation was somewhat different. Much wartime medical research consisted of investigators proposing and undertaking discrete projects in their own laboratories. Medicine was thus the most decentralized and fragmented sphere of wartime research, and it consequently placed a large administrative burden on those who had to coordinate, evaluate, and disseminate this work. This responsibility was shouldered by the Committee on Medical Research, which differed from the organization fashioned by Bush and Conant in one important respect.

In establishing the NDRC, Bush had felt it necessary to make what he called an "end run" around the established institutions for providing scientific advice to the government—the National Academy of Sciences and its affiliate, the National Research Council (NRC). Although supposedly representing the nation's scientific leadership, in 1940 these bodies were heavily weighted with the old guard of the physical sciences, not all of whom shared the sense of political and scientific urgency that lay behind the founding of the NDRC.[18] The situation developed differently in medicine. As the need for war-related medical research became apparent, the Surgeon General directed inquiries through the existing channels of the NRC Division of Medical Sciences. By mid-1941 there were eight major committees and thirty-three subcommittees of the division advising and planning research on aspects of military medicine. When the CMR was created, it did not supplant the committee structure of the NRC, but simply incorporated it. The head of the NRC Medical Division became vice-chairman of the CMR, and the same committees of specialists that had been advising the Surgeon General now acquired the additional authority of recommending OSRD contracts for research projects.[19]

During the course of the war there was little difference in the operations of the ad hoc NDRC committees and the NRC-based CMR committees. But as victory came within sight, and as expectations grew for the rapid dismantling of OSRD, the implications of these different arrangements became apparent. In order to find a means for perpetuating the fruitful wartime relationship between the government and academic scientists, Vannevar Bush found it necessary to propose the creation of a new and controversial entity—a national research foundation (see below). Although he intended that medicine too be included in these arrangements, it would not have been strictly necessary in order to continue federal sponsorship of medical research. Moreover, the wartime accomplishments of the CMR—which included the development of penicillin and important work with blood plasma—promised obvious and far-reaching civilian benefits. In this respect, the medical advances compared favorably with such triumphs of military science as radar, the proximity fuse, and the atomic bomb. The demobilization plans for CMR called for turning uncompleted research projects over to either the military or to appropriate civilian agencies, and the Public Health Service stood ready and eager to inherit much of the well-tuned administrative machinery of the CMR.

World War II marked a decisive shift in the interest of the U.S. Federal Government in advanced scientific knowledge. Henceforth, it would be dependent upon civilian scientists in industry and universities for a substantial portion of the basic and applied research relevant to its many interests. For universities, the commitments made in desperate haste conformed to the four patterns just described. Each left a somewhat different legacy for the postwar period.

Atomic energy was a case *sui generis* that irrevocably united federal interests and academic scientists. There could be no question of the continued postwar development of nuclear physics. Such research demanded, at once, the talents of many of the most skilled university-based physicists, the use of carefully controlled substances manufactured at great expense under government monopoly, and the employment of enormously costly instruments and facilities. Not just the costs, but the stakes involved in atomic research required that decisions affecting this process be made at the highest levels of government. For nuclear physics if for no other subject, the country would have to have a consciously formulated science policy.

It was no less certain that federally sponsored research would be continued on radar, fuses and rocket propulsion. Here, however, policy would be largely determined by the armed services; and the extent of involvement with university scientists was to some extent subject to negotiation and accommodation.

In medicine compelling arguments could be made, illustrated with wartime experience, that continued federal support for medical research would accelerate the flow of benefits to the public. Moreover, the administrative machinery needed for determining whose research might be supported, and why, already existed to some extent in the prewar Cancer Institute and in the wartime CMR committees.

Most problematic of all in 1945 was the last of these four patterns of federal-university research relations—that comprising basic research in non-nuclear physics, chemistry, mathematics, biology, and psychology which had been superintended by the NDRC. Here the federal interest was diffuse and the wartime precedent difficult to replicate. Yet, this was the intellectual territory most central to academic science. How to institutionalize a permanent relationship between the federal government and university research became, after atomic energy, the thorniest issue of postwar science policy.

3. Postwar Federal Science Policy

During the later stages of World War II the idea became increasingly prevalent that the relationship between the federal government and the civilian, largely university-based scientific community ought to be perpetuated in some form after the cessation of hostilities. This general notion, however, came to be expressed through three rather different channels. Within military circles a growing faction sought to establish a permanent means for collaboration with civilian scientific research after the closure of OSRD. Among university scientists involved with the war effort interest focused on an OSRD-like agency to provide federal assistance for postwar research. Among those largely outside of the war research efforts, a kind of anti-OSRD position arose, one that held that postwar federal sponsorship of research should avoid several features of wartime practice. These three views interacted in the shaping of future federal relationships with university research.

Within the armed services, and particularly within those units most closely involved with new technologies, it soon became axiomatic that some liaison with civilian scientific expertise would have to become a permanent part of postwar military operations. The frequently iterated rationale was that the current war constituted a 'close call'; that confrontations in the future would not allow the lead time that the United States had utilized in 1940 and 1941 to mobilize its scientific resources. It was also apparent that future military preparedness would depend upon the results of research at the advanced frontiers of science. Realizing that the services could not themselves operate substantial laboratories for basic research, they sought a means for assuring ready access to civilian science. The prevailing assumption at war's end, and indeed into the postwar years, was that the armed services would have to go to great lengths to make military-related research attractive for civilian scientists. This issue was explicitly addressed in the spring of 1944, and a blue-ribbon committee recommended that a civilian-led Research Board for National Security become the peacetime successor to OSRD. Such a board was soon named, but it never received an authorization to actually function. Instead the whole matter was subsumed in the larger issue of postwar science policy.[1]

The initial impetus for a federal science policy originated with critics of the wartime organization of research and production. Their dissatisfaction centered on the concentration of war production in the nation's largest firms, although an analogous criticism could be made for the concentration of research at a few major universities. From this perspective it seemed that a reorganization of American science and technology was called for in order to utilize the nation's scientific assets for the public weal.[2] The spokesman for this viewpoint in Congress was Democratic Senator Harley M. Kilgore of West Virginia. During the war he introduced two measures to alter the mobilization of science and technology. In 1944, looking beyond the hostilities, he drafted another bill proposing the creation of a national science foundation. This last initiative prompted a reaction from the director of OSRD.

Vannevar Bush too was convinced of the need for a permanent means for assuring the cooperation of the federal government and the civilian scientific community, but only on the condition that the autonomy of science be fully protected.[3] Late in 1944, Bush and several aides arranged to have President Roosevelt solicit his views. In a famous letter dated November 17, 1944, the President praised the accomplishments of OSRD and asked "why the lessons to be found in this experience cannot be profitably employed in times of peace." He then requested Bush's recommendations on four specific issues: the prompt release of findings from secret wartime research; organizing a future program of medical research; what the government might do "to aid research activities by public and private organizations"; and a program for developing scientific talent in American youth.[4] The first and last of the President's points were relatively delimited questions that could be dealt with in straightforward terms. The third, which in a sense subsumed medical research too, was critical for American universities. At long last the federal government was inviting a plan for the general public support of university research. Publication of the letter prompted widespread favorable comment; among scientists it touched off expectations of a hopeful future. As for Vannevar Bush, having created the opportunity to draw a blueprint for postwar science, he would not disappoint.

Bush recruited separate committees to consider each of the President's four questions. The critical matter of aiding research in public and private institutions was under the chairmanship of Isaiah Bowman, president of Johns Hopkins and veteran of the previous decade's efforts to elicit federal support for research.[5] The four committee reports formed the basis for *Science—the Endless Frontier*, but this historic report transcended these documents—indeed, transcended the President's original charge as well. Whereas Roosevelt had foreseen peacetime science hastening practical benefits—better health, new industries, new jobs, and a higher standard of living—Bush responded that such benefits would result from a national policy of encouragement for basic scientific research. *Science— the Endless Frontier*, in fact, constitutes an extended and carefully reasoned justification of the key role of basic science.[6]

The initial premise of the Bush report was that basic research (also called pure or fundamental at the time) was the font of all technological advancement, and that this source was badly in need of replenishment. Using figures gathered by the Bowman committee, he noted that expenditures for research in government and industry, overwhelmingly applied in character, had in 1930 been six times that of basic research in universities; they had then risen to ten times university expenditures by 1940. The war further exaggerated this imbalance by stimulating scientists to exploit existing scientific knowledge in order to fashion countless technological innovations, while also precluding basic research that would add to that stock of knowledge. University-sponsored basic science, he argued, had been unable to provide the needed counterpart to applied research before the war, and all signs indicated that it would also be inadequate in the years ahead. Since the pace of scientific progress would have an important bearing on the health, welfare, and security of the nation, the federal government bore a responsibility to encourage and support such research in the universities. To fulfill this duty Bush advocated the creation of a national research foundation that, much like OSRD, would be under the direction of leading civilian scientists.[7]

Bush presented a strong case. A return to the status quo ante bellum, in which direct support for university research was dependent upon private patronage, seemed likely to cramp the development of American science and squander the scientific momentum generated by the war. There was a widespread predisposition for the general message that Bush promulgated. His report was received warmly by its first recipient, newly installed President Harry S. Truman, as well as by the Congress, the scientific community and the press. The character of the report and its recommendations, however, were not determined solely by the objective situation it described. Its central and informing concept, that of basic research, was pervaded with the values, beliefs and anxieties shared by Bush, the members of his committees, and much of the wider scientific community. Accordingly, basic research was invested with qualities that reflected their preconceptions as much as any past experience or "lessons" of OSRD.

Basic research, it was maintained, was at bottom unpredictable: "important and highly useful discoveries will result from some fraction of the work undertaken; but the results of any particular investigation cannot be predicted with accuracy." It needed to have stable, long-term funding and to be insulated from any outside interference: "free from the influence of pressure groups, free from the necessity of producing immediate results, free from dictation by any central board." In addition, basic science "is fundamentally a unitary thing": "separation of the sciences . . . would retard and not advance scientific knowledge as a whole."[8] These sentiments, in sum, were part of an ideology of basic research, which, as it came to be embodied in the Bush report, had some future consequences for the proposed national research foundation.

Bush was concerned above all with insulating basic research from the vicissitudes of national politics, from the utilitarian orientation that he detected in the Kilgore proposals, and from special interests with influence in Congress. Such concerns were widespread in the scientific community. Both the Committee on Medical Research and the Bowman committee, in fact, recommended far more radical separations between government and science than did the final report.[9] Bush's more moderate plan proposed that a foundation board of scientifically qualified civilians be appointed by the President, and that this board then appoint the foundation director. The foundation board would be fully accountable to the President and the Congress, but the director would be responsible to the board. Under the director, in a pyramidal structure like OSRD's, Bush proposed five divisions: natural sciences, medical research, national defense, fellowships, and publications. Thus, the new foundation would seek to duplicate the broad responsibilities of OSRD, but without even the small representation that the social sciences had managed there. As a general outline for structuring government support for basic research, *Science—the Endless Frontier* was a striking achievement, but it did not turn out to be a blueprint that could be followed in detail.

Legislation for a national research foundation along the lines recommended by Bush was introduced in the Senate by Warren G. Magnuson as soon as Bush's report was released in July 1945. An alternate scheme for a national science foundation (the title soon preferred) was presented by Senator Kilgore. More important than the differences between these two pieces of legislation was the extraordinary consensus supporting the creation of such an entity. The idealism toward science prevailing at the end of the war induced general acceptance of a permanent federal role in supporting scientific research. In hearings 99 of 100 witnesses testified in favor of establishing such a foundation.[10] Most of the matters of overt disagreement were not strictly vital to its initial creation. The populist Kilgore wanted the government to retain all patents resulting from federally funded research—a position that was anathema to Bush and to business in general. This issue, however, called for a larger, government-wide policy. Democrats generally favored some inclusion of the social sciences, unlike Bush and other conservative natural scientists, but this was a subordinate matter that could have been resolved later.[11] The fundamental issue for the future character of the foundation was that of administrative control. Kilgore insisted that the director be appointed by the President and serve at his pleasure, but Bush and his supporters feared that political domination of science might result. These differences soon divided the scientific community, although in an asymmetrical fashion. Isaiah Bowman organized a Committee Supporting the Bush Report to lobby for the Magnuson bill. A rival Committee for a National Science Foundation took the position that establishing a foundation was more important than any of the issues dividing the two sides, thus implicitly accepting the Kilgore proposal.[12] But the ideology of basic research, together with their political conservatism, apparently convinced the Bush faction that no foundation would be preferable to one wrongly organized.

Bush was striving above all else to make the science foundation embody the authority structure of science. He had earlier attempted to convey to Senator Kilgore this distinctive feature of science:

> There is only one sound criterion for estimating the standing and capability of a man of science, and that is the evaluation of the way in which he is regarded by his colleagues in his profession. . . . [These evaluations] should be utilized in the procedure of selecting representative scientists for governmental purpose. . . . It can safely be assumed that men selected for eminence in science by scientists themselves will also generally be disinterested.[13]

What Bush failed to appreciate was that federal support for university research inevitably involved another authority structure—that comprising the responsibility of elected officials for the use of public funds. Budget Director Harold Smith explained the imperatives of this system in his testimony at the Senate hearings:

> an agency which is to control the spending of public funds in a great national program must be part of the regular machinery of government. If the government is to support scientific research, it should do so through its own responsible agency . . . [and] the only effective power of enforcing responsibility is the President's power of appointment and removal.[14]

President Truman fully backed his budget director's position, leaving little possibility of establishing a national science foundation on any other basis while he was in the White House. Bush, who considered himself an astute observer of the workings of the federal government, should have known as much. Furthermore, he was probably the only person in a position to lead the conservative scientists willingly into a constructive compromise that might have reconciled these two systems of authority. For a time he seemed to accept this eventuality, but in the end ideology prevailed.

Early in 1946 a compromise bill was worked out in the Senate which still largely reflected the Kilgore positions, particularly on the responsibility of the director to the President. But acrimony remained in the scientific community, where compromise is not the normal manner of resolving disagreements. As they waited for congressional action the conservatives apparently had misgivings. In May, Bush's aide arranged to have a bill introduced into the House that would have established a national science foundation on Bush's original terms. This maneuver may have been a belated attempt to regain bargaining leverage, but if so it was a grievous miscalculation. The compromise national science foundation legislation reached the floor of the Senate in early July. It was passed after strenuous debate, shorn only of its provision to include the social sciences. When it was sent to the House, however, it had to be reconciled with the Bush-inspired bill. By mid-July it was already late in an extremely busy session. Unable to give the matter sufficient consideration, a House committee tabled the legislation, thereby killing it for the year.[15] There would be other chances for the national science foundation, but they would not be the same as the opportunity that was lost on this occasion.

The summer of 1946 was the critical juncture in the formation of the postwar federal research economy. Developments that had been brewing since the final year of the war rather abruptly crystallized into concrete legislative acts. On July 20, the day after the national science foundation bill was killed, the House passed legislation creating the Atomic Energy Commission. The issue of how the future development of atomic energy would be organized, by far the most prominent science issue before the public, may well have deflected attention from the effort to establish a national science foundation.[16] The AEC directly inherited the programs of the Manhattan Project, including a substantial program of university-linked research. On July 4, Congress created the National Institute of Mental Health within the Public Health Service; and less than two weeks later the Health Service was voted a substantial increase in research funds in order to accommodate the contracts transferred from the Committee on Medical Research. These steps for all practical purposes assured that medical research would not be beholden to a science foundation. The Public Health Service was already organized to support extramural investigations, and both Congress and the public concurred on the need for expanding medical research.[17] Finally, on August 1, Congress without fanfare passed a law creating the Office of Naval Research. ONR, as it came to be known, was the most innovative agency in a determined effort by the military services to establish and utilize permanent contact with the best available civilian science.

The failure to establish a national science foundation as the centerpiece of federal science policy during the propitious immediate postwar climate meant that government relations with civilian science would evolve according to the purposes and dynamics of the mission agencies. Besides the long-established ties between the Department of Agriculture and the Land-Grant universities,[18] four new streams of research support were soon discernible. The Atomic Energy Commission had a broad responsibility for everything related to fissionable and radioactive materials, and beyond that to research in general on nuclear physics.

This included maintaining operations in the vast facilities bequeathed by the Manhattan Project, initiatives for new particle accelerators, as well as sponsored research dealing with all facets of atomic energy. The Public Health Service successfully laid claim to the funding of medical research. And, each armed service inaugurated its own program of support for civilian research. Like the AEC, they perpetuated some large wartime laboratories that were operated under university contracts. But the ONR, in particular, eagerly sought the role of patron to university research. ONR even claimed unabashedly that it was sustaining basic research in the universities until the Congress could agree to establish a national science foundation. Last, and for long least, was the channel that Vannevar Bush had put forth as the mainstream of federal science policy—providing government funds for basic research in the universities. Not until 1950 would the National Science Foundation be created. Then, instead of dominating the federal science matrix, it would inherit the remaining unoccupied spaces.

4. The Postwar Federal Research Economy

The factors that actually shaped the relationship of government and science within the different channels of postwar research bore little resemblance to the considerations that dominated the thinking on science legislation. Common to both were the importance of furthering the scientific advances made during the war and the ineluctability of federal financial support if this were to be achieved. But since no comprehensive organization was enacted, federal agencies took direct measures to sustain the momentum of their wartime investigations. The slow pace of congressional action provided this opportunity, and the considerable funds remaining from wartime appropriations supplied the means.

Disjunctions between wartime and postwar research were actually minor. Through the remainder of 1945 and 1946 the armed services, OSRD, and the Manhattan Project continued to fund research relating to their spheres of responsibility. One thing did change with peace, however: scientists were now free to conduct research where and on what they pleased. Most wished to return to a university setting as quickly as possible. It soon became apparent that the scientists themselves were the critical scarce input to any program of research. Practitioners of the war's most spectacular and arcane field, nuclear physics, were the most sought after; but scientists generally found themselves courted rather than dominated by their new federal patrons. Furthermore, scientific leaders were called upon to advise or consult on virtually all federally funded research programs. The opinions they rendered naturally encouraged federal commitments to basic science, and on terms that fully respected the autonomy of research. An additional dynamic came into play with the postwar realignment of federal agencies. As new responsibilities were allocated and old ones redefined, these units instinctively sought to gain control over basic research in areas relating to their mission. Federal agencies consequently took the initiative to support research and often to woo university scientists. In sum, the prolongation of wartime research funding, the unanticipated strong position of scientists themselves, and the aggrandizement of federal agencies were the factors that shaped federal research policies in the immediate aftermath of war. The failure in the summer of 1946 to establish a considered federal science policy in the form of a national science foundation allowed this pattern to persist without viable alternatives. Circumstances nevertheless shaped the different paths traced by atomic, military and medical research.

Universities in general were slow to realize the possibilities inherent in the federal research economy, but this was not the case among the atomic scientists. Arthur H. Compton, director of the Metallurgical Laboratory and the reactor project nearby at the Argonne Forest Preserve, was determined to convert these facilities into permanent adjuncts to the Chicago physics department. Well before the war was over he had requested Manhattan Project funds for basic research, and made offers of postwar positions to Enrico Fermi, Glenn Seaborg, and others.[1] At Berkeley, E. O. Lawrence always expected to resume the task of constructing the 184-inch cyclotron that had been converted for isotope separation, but by the summer of 1945 the possibilities for building even more powerful accelerators had caused him to significantly enlarge his plans. Given the inevitability of further atomic research, the Manhattan Project had by then established a committee of scientists to consider these issues (naturally including A. H. Compton and Lawrence) which endorsed a substantial program for supporting postwar research. Definite action, however, was for a time deferred until these activities could be transferred to civilian direction. But congressional delays in establishing the Atomic Energy Commission soon compelled General Leslie R. Groves to fill the void. In December 1945 he donated almost $0.5 million worth of Army scientific materials to Lawrence's Radiation Lab and provided nearly that much to assist the construction of particle accelerators. This was soon followed by more than $4 million for operating support and further construction. Support was also provided for A. H. Compton's enterprises at Chicago. A third initiative came from Columbia physicist I. I. Rabi, who was alarmed by the geographical incidence of postwar nuclear physics (particularly Columbia's loss of Fermi to Chicago). Groves advised him to submit a proposal for an East Coast facility while the Manhattan Project was still in a position to provide funding. For this purpose the Eastern universities combined forces to form the Associated Universities, Inc. (originally Columbia, Cornell, Harvard, Johns Hopkins, MIT, Princeton, Penn, Rochester, and Yale). Groves then agreed to fund their projected atomic laboratory at Brookhaven, Long Island.[2] These actions preceded any policy toward atomic research—and fortunately so.

On August 1, 1946, President Truman signed the bill creating the Atomic Energy Commission, but it was not until the end of the year that the AEC was ready to assume its responsibilities. At that juncture it inherited thriving university centers of basic research in nuclear physics at Berkeley and Chicago, as well as a contract with Associated Universities, Inc., to establish an additional national laboratory at Brookhaven. Given the huge and controversial responsibilities of the AEC over atomic weapons, reactor development, and the operations of the far-flung facilities of the Manhattan Project, the formulation of a policy for academic research did not receive the commissioners' immediate consideration. Moreover, the AEC research director was occupied above all with the problems of the applied research and development laboratories, which were faced with depleted staffs, low morale, and deteriorating programs. Los Alamos, for example, held a conference in 1946 in an attempt to persuade university scientists to maintain research connections with the laboratory. The AEC's stance toward basic research was further clouded by the fact that a provision that would have permitted it to make research grants was stricken from the enabling legislation. The sense of the Congress seemed to be that the AEC should confine research support to its own laboratories.[3]

The AEC did not manage to formulate a policy toward basic nuclear research until the second half of 1947. Then it resolved to back the building of the next generation of particle accelerators at Berkeley and Brookhaven.[4] Support for these laboratories, as well as reactor development at Argonne, essentially endorsed the steps initially taken by General Groves. Further interaction with university-based science, however, was largely stimulated by pressure from outside of the Commission.

The AEC's monopoly over the use of radioactive substances carried with it control over the development of several dynamic and exceedingly important scientific fields.[5] Most obvious was the endeavor of nuclear physicists to probe the emerging universe of subatomic particles. By now a cyclotron had become a necessary instrument for any physics department engaged in nuclear research. In an entirely different area, the test reactors of the Manhattan Project held a potential bonanza for biomedical research. The cheap and abundant production of radioisotopes promised to make possible the study of basic biological processes. Radioisotopes were also employed in the study and treatment of cancer. In addition, there was a critical shortage of trained personnel in all areas of atomic research, which could only be remedied through university programs.

Pressures on the AEC for enlarging support for university research became evident in 1947. Universities themselves had begun to submit an increasing number of proposals to the Commission. The matter was then forced further by a request from the Office of Naval Research for the AEC to share the costs of a number of university research projects in nuclear physics. In considering this matter J. Robert Oppenheimer, chairman of the AEC's General Advisory Committee, persuasively argued that AEC support for basic research should be geared to the capacities of university research teams, as the ONR programs seemed to be (see below), and not limited by estimates of the Commission's own internal requirements.[6] Later in the year heightened public consciousness of the dangers of cancer prompted Congress to authorize the AEC to spend $5 million on cancer research. Still, there was a considerable time lag before the Commission could respond to these pressures.[7]

The AEC's stance toward university research was gradually redirected during 1948. By then Shields Warren was directing a new division of biology and medicine. Free of the heavy emphasis on applied work that existed in the physical sciences, he was able to respond to the needs of university biomedical scientists. The Commission also, after a year's delay, consented to the ONR request. Cooperation with ONR was a significant step for the AEC because of the close and congenial relations that ONR had already established with university researchers and because it possessed a capacity for research administration that was absent in the AEC. At the end of the year Kenneth Pitzer, a Berkeley chemist, became the new AEC director of research with the understanding that he would establish closer ties with universities. By this time Warren had already devised an acceptable form of contract for funding university research in lieu of grants. He had also inaugurated a badly needed fellowship program in which the selection of candidates was delegated to the National Research Council. Pitzer was then able to implement these same procedures in the physical sciences. By 1949 the AEC had committed itself to a substantial program of support for university research outside of the system of national laboratories.[8]

By 1950 the AEC was spending $97.6 million for research at nonprofit institutions (mostly universities).[9] Some $80 million was designated for large, self-contained, university-administered laboratories (and included capital costs), while the remainder went for smaller projects. AEC research was exceedingly expensive in terms of facilities, equipment, material, and supporting staff. Nevertheless, in terms of basic research, the AEC's multiple activities were inferior in expenditures only to the second great channel of postwar federal research support—that emanating from the military services.

In the spring of 1946, Army Chief of Staff General Dwight D. Eisenhower circulated a memo "Scientific and Technological Resources as Military Assets."[10] Impressed by the "integration" of civilian and military talents during the war, he intended to make this a permanent feature of postwar military development. Among other things, this implied a

> duty to support broad research programs in educational institutions, in industry, and in whatever field might be of importance to the Army. Close integration of civilian and military resources will not only directly benefit the Army, but indirectly contribute to the nation's security, as civilians are prepared for their role in an emergency by the experience gained in time of peace.

General Eisenhower was facing up to the reality that the Army had become dependent upon "resources"—scientific and technological knowledge—that could be neither incorporated into nor duplicated within the chain of command. The Army would have to devise a permanent means for conducting relations with those crucially important civilian scientists.

With regard to universities, Eisenhower's 1946 memorandum in fact recognized a situation produced by the inertia of war research. The large laboratories continued to conduct a high volume of research despite considerable turnover in personnel. At MIT, for example, the largest contractor for OSRD research, the volume of military research was about the same in 1946 as it had been in 1944, with radar research comprising the bulk in both years. Afterward, the volume of this research expanded regularly.[11] The Army also had need for research on discrete individual topics. After the final shuttering of OSRD in 1947 the Army had to make its own contacts with university scientists. It developed the practice of compiling lists of needed research projects and then circulating them among universities to elicit interest. As the volume of these smaller projects expanded, it allowed some universities, which had been comparatively minor contractors of OSRD research, to become significant performers of military research.[12]

The relationship of the Air Force to university research was similar to that of the Army. The need for permanent access to academic science was recognized before the end of the war. An official scientific advisory group was established in 1944 under the chairmanship of Caltech aerodynamics expert Theodor von Karman. It produced a report in 1945 that emphasized the future dependence of the Air Force on basic scientific research, and the importance of keeping this research under Air Force auspices.[13] For long, however, official Air Force research remained stifled within the command structure without an adequate organization or budget. Extramural research consequently consisted solely of the continuation of wartime projects by various Air Force bureaus.

In 1949–50 the Air Force had $14 million in contracts with about fifty-five universities. Just ten of those institutions received 70 percent of those funds. The Army contracted for $8 million of research with about seventy universities and six of them accounted for half of the total.[14] Besides being concentrated at a few large laboratories, the Army and Air Force almost exclusively supported applied research, closely related to the development and improvement of materiel. From the universities' point of view this "close integration," as Eisenhower had called it, left much to be desired. A good deal of Army and Air Force research was classified; bureaucratic requirements and close scrutiny were bothersome; and reimbursements for overhead expenses, separately negotiated for each contract, were seldom regarded as adequate.[15] This same pattern held for most of the applied research that the various Navy bureaus contracted for, but the Office of Naval Research pioneered radically different practices.

ONR was not a continuation of a wartime precedent, but essentially a new creation, inspired partly by the idealism toward research prevailing at the end of the war and partly by special circumstances.[16] Idealism was exemplified in a group of young naval officers, known as the 'bird dogs,' who were active in planning postwar research and in the early organization and operation of ONR. Above all, they sought to foster a close working relationship with academic science. The unusual circumstances that allowed them the opportunity to pursue that mission on a grand scale included: a protected organizational niche under civilian authority, insulated from the practical outlook of the operational bureaus; relatively bounteous funds, initially from the transfer of wartime appropriations; and a special stimulus to overcome the Army monopoly over atomic research. The first head of ONR, Vice Admiral Harold G. Bowen, had taken an early interest in the possibilities of adapting atomic power for naval purposes, but he had been frozen out of atomic research when the Manhattan Project was formed. The Navy now had an opportunity to regain this lost ground by establishing ties with the demobilized atomic scientists at their home universities. In fact, some 40 percent of early ONR grants went to support nuclear physics, which is why they later sought to share this burden with the AEC.[17]

Given the way ONR construed its mission, cultivating a positive relationship with scientists was as important as gaining the fruits of their research. In the fall of 1945, the 'bird dogs' visited campuses to convince scientists and university administrators of the advantages of doing research for the Navy. To secure cooperation the Navy was willing to assist the research needs of universities and to respect academic research styles. The pitfalls of contracting for research were resolved by devising a single comprehensive university contract to which specific projects could be appended as task orders. ONR also agreed that the research they funded would be unclassified and publishable. Most significant of all, ONR allowed the investigators themselves to initiate proposals. If a proposal was considered to be sound and of interest, ONR would support it without restriction or interference. The anticipated campus opposition to military-supported research failed to materialize, or at least failed to deter institutions. The leading research universities—Harvard, Chicago, California, Caltech, and MIT— quickly signed ONR contracts, and the die was cast. The result of these efforts was that ONR emerged as the ideal patron of science, "the example always to be cited" for enlightened research management.[18]

ONR was structured so that the Navy could rely upon civilian scientists to exercise authority over the content of research. Its top civilian post of Chief Scientist was filled by Alan T. Waterman, who came via OSRD and the Yale physics department. The foremost organizational leaders of American science were recruited for a blue-ribbon Naval Research Advisory Committee, including Karl and Arthur Compton, Warren Weaver, Detlev Bronk, and Lee Dubridge. Twelve specialized advisory panels containing another 125 scientists helped ONR to evaluate proposals. Because of its abundant funds, ONR was able to begin supporting large amounts of research almost immediately after the war's end. By the time ONR received its legislative authorization (August 1946) it had already let $24 million in contracts, which included 602 academic research projects involving 4000 scientists and graduate students.[19] Thus, ONR very quickly became the principal actor in the university research economy. For the rest of the ;1940s it provided approximately $20 million annually for university research.[20] By this juncture ONR was supporting one-quarter of the proposals it received. Still, it managed to fund 1,131 projects in 200 institutions. Moreover, unlike other military and AEC support for basic research, ONR funded small rather than big science. Most of its contracts fell in the range of $12,000 to $40,000 and ran for less than a year.[21] As a patron of research the ONR sought to please as many as possible of its university supplicants.

The outstanding success of ONR as a sponsor of basic research was made possible to a considerable extent by the fact that it was an anomaly within the federal government. Located well down in the Navy organization chart, cloaked in the mantle of national security, it managed to enjoy a degree of autonomy—a lack of accountability to the political process—that the executive branch was resolute in denying to the proposed national science foundation. But this insular position was not likely to endure. ONR historian Harvey Sapolsky has concluded that the golden age of ONR lasted just four years, from 1946 to 1950. After that, as will be seen, ONR had to deal with increasing pressures for relevance to naval needs.[22]

ONR was in a unique position for a military agency, being able both to define its research needs and then to execute a program to fulfill them.[23] Its original mission was defined in vague and open-ended terms—establishing working relations with civilian scientists and supporting basic research of unpredictable future utility to the Navy. The failure to establish a national science foundation gave ONR a further justification as the protector of academic science. Both these rationales buttressed the same policies, but were limited in the long run. In the former case, ONR's capacity to support university scientists depended partly on the vagaries of the huge Navy budget and partly on the internal backing for basic research. The Korean War boosted appropriations for the Contract Research Program (which funded university research) to an annual level around $30 million, but these years also brought pressures for closer relevance to Navy purposes. Sputnik later induced another jump in ONR appropriations, but this too was followed by even closer accountability. During the 1960s ONR provided about $50 million in annual support for basic university research, and another $30 million for applied research.[24] As for being an ersatz NSF, this mission became untenable after 1950, when ONR came under greater internal scrutiny and when the NSF became a reality. Overall, the infusion of ONR funds into American universities undeniably sustained scientific research during a critical transitional period; but ONR was not in a position to implement policies for the balanced development of university science. Support was heavily weighted toward the physical sciences or engineering, and included few funds for 'greasing the wheels' of science. Its criteria for choosing which projects to support, moreover, inescapably included "the probability of ultimate usefulness to the Navy."[25]

ONR's self-anointed role as the savior of postwar academic science generated some controversy among scientists who felt that research should not be beholden to the military.[26] The very success of ONR in pleasing its academic contractors, however, not only deflected these objections but conferred legitimacy upon the military's preponderant role in supporting academic research. Moreover, the high prestige of ONR virtually compelled the other services to follow its example. An Air Force Office of Scientific Research was established in 1951. The same year the Army established an Office of Ordnance Research which eventually became the Army Research Office (1958). Neither of these offices ever matched the magnitude or closeness of ONR's relationship with academic science. The second important precedent that emerged from the experience of ONR was its style of enlightened research management. Besides being utilized for military purposes, these practices would be directly bequeathed to the National Science Foundation.[27]

The third postwar channel connecting the federal government and university research was carved out by the Public Health Service. Although its experience in this realm extended back to the prewar Cancer Institute, the Public Health Service was by no means foreordained for this role. It was distrusted by the academic community of biomedical researchers, who clearly would have preferred a separate research foundation. It was probably the federal agency that stood to lose most from Vannevar Bush's version of a comprehensive national science

trol.[34] A deadlock ensued through 1948. When Truman confounded his Republican opponents by winning reelection, it became clear that his position would have to prevail. Still, science foundation legislation remained captive to Congressional politics until early in 1950. On May 10, President Truman signed the bill that brought into being the National Science Foundation—with a presidentially appointed director and board.[35]

The growth of federal research support in other agencies made the creation of a national science foundation less and less urgent as time passed. The national security argument for supporting basic research lost its force as the services found ways to fulfill their own research needs. The public health interest in basic research, which had been emphasized by Roosevelt and Bush, was completely preempted by the rise of NIH. Additionally, the huge success of the GI Bill precluded any immediate need to expand science training through a program of scholarships. Above all, ONR's posturing as a would-be NSF removed the final argument for specific federal support for basic university research. The vetoed NSF legislation of 1947, in fact, included no appropriations for the proposed foundation: it was assumed that basic research programs would be transferred from other agencies. As late as 1949 the official position seemed to be that perhaps 25 percent of ONR projects would be ceded to NSF, but in fact none ever was.[36] The Navy wished to stay in contact with the scientists it supported. Eventually, however, ONR's posturing made the creation of a science foundation inevitable. Lodging responsibility for basic scientific research within a tertiary office of one of the armed services was a glaring irregularity. If a national science foundation existed in fact, then it was ultimately necessary to create it in law.

The National Science Foundation Act of 1950 founded a minimalist NSF, chiefly concerned with the nurture and support of basic scientific research in institutions of higher education. NSF thus assumed the role that remained officially unoccupied in the federal science matrix. As with the other science-supporting agencies, experience shaped policy rather than the other way around.

NSF owed much to the brief postwar legacy of federal support for university research that preceded its birth. Its first director was Alan T. Waterman, the chief scientist of ONR, and he was joined in his move by other ONR staff.[37] The NSF thus was heir to the congenial style of research management that had been fashioned at ONR. Shortly before his appointment Waterman published a general discussion of "Government Support of Research," based largely on his ONR experience, which clearly foreshadowed the approach that NSF would take. He stressed conducting research at existing institutions, rather than in-house laboratories; he recommended that the supporting agency be staffed with competent scientists, and that they be assisted by panels of outside experts; he favored operating through investigator-initiated proposals; and he advised that administrative requirements be as unobtrusive as possible.[38] A more sympathetic approach to academic research could scarcely have been realistically contemplated. Moreover, Waterman happily accepted a minimalist foundation serving academic science. He well knew his more powerful federal competitors and was willing to concede them their turf.[39] His attitude was generally shared by the National Science Board. Its chairman, James Conant, gave a sharper definition to NSF's mission by drawing the distinction between "programmatic" research which, whether classified as basic or applied, was beholden to the program of a particular agency, and "uncommitted" research—disinterested inquiry, largely arising from the state of disciplinary paradigms—which lay at the heart of the university commitment to advance knowledge.[40] The National Science Foundation was to be the instrument for supporting academic science on its own terms rather than those defined by the mission agencies. Once it was finally created, though, the NSF faced a formidable challenge to win backing in Washington for the importance of the role it had inherited.

The newly created National Science Foundation joined a federal research economy of great size and diversity. The dominant characteristic of that economy, although few commentators were ready to acknowledge the fact, was pluralism of supporters. One significant consequence of that pluralism was that support for university research from several agencies was undoubtedly far larger than would have been the case had it emanated from only one. Bush had foreseen federal expenditures for research in the range of $122 million by 1950.[41] Actual federal research funds were not only more than he envisaged, but different as well. Federal support that year approximated $140 million, but more than 60 percent consisted of large defense-related laboratories.[42] The new, federally based research economy was nevertheless relatively pluralistic and abundant. Its impact, moreover, was soon evident on the campuses of the research universities.

2

Research Universities
in the Postwar Era,
1945–1957

1. From War to Peace to Cold War

Almost a year before the war ended, MIT physics chairman John Slater proposed the creation of a postwar Research Laboratory in Electronics (RLE). His aim was not simply to continue basic research in those fields where the Rad Lab had been active, but also to perpetuate the Lab's cooperative and interdisciplinary style of research. In such a setting, he argued, scientists and engineers could work far more effectively. A postwar laboratory of this kind would thereby supplement the departmental structure of the Institute. Slater's proposal was quickly endorsed by the MIT leadership, who granted the laboratory initial financial backing. Soon the OSRD was able to provide what amounted to permanent support.[1] Thus, among wartime 'producers' of research no less than among its military 'consumers,' initiatives were taken to fashion peacetime sequels to the emergency partnership between the federal government and university scientists.

The initiative begun by Slater at MIT was somewhat precocious, but in other respects it typified the unfolding consequences of the war experience for universities themselves. Many scientists were eager to continue the same lines of research they had pursued during the war, and particularly to investigate some of the fundamental questions that had arisen out of new fields, techniques, or instruments. Some wished simply to get back to 'real research,' but among physical scientists like Slater, in particular, widespread conversions occurred to the wartime style of research—large, multidisciplinary teams of researchers, coordinated assaults upon complex problems, increasingly sophisticated and expensive instruments—in short, Big Science.[2] Such undertakings called for special forms of organization, and additionally could only be sustained by substantial external support. Expectations of continued federal patronage were in the air even before Vannevar Bush's famous report, but universities did not wait for a national science foundation to be formed.

OSRD expenditures for research at universities had been fairly concentrated due to the preponderance of a few large laboratories:

TABLE 1. Universities Having OSRD Contracts > $3 Million[3]

	Contracts	Amount
M.I.T.	75	$116,941,000
Caltech	48	83,452,000
Harvard	79	30,963,000
Columbia	73	28,521,000
California	106	14,385,000
Johns Hopkins	49	10,572,000
Chicago	53	6,742,000
George Washington	2	6,562,000
Princeton	17	3,593,000

The principal contractors generally made commitments for extending or expanding wartime research during the final stages of hostilities. These plans dovetailed, however, with the aspirations of university scientists.

At both Princeton and Harvard, physicists involved in war research sketched ambitious plans for postwar expansion. Both John Wheeler and Edwin Kemble identified nuclear physics as a crucial field of emphasis; both stressed the need to recruit and/or retain top scientists from among those who had shown their mettle in wartime projects. They particularly appreciated the desirability of perpetuating the integration of theorists and experimentalists. Both scientists also warned their universities of the large investments that such plans would entail. At the University of Chicago, Arthur Holly Compton began working toward a greatly enlarged physics department early in the war. These efforts obtained the backing of Chancellor Robert Maynard Hutchins, who established three institutes in August 1945—for Nuclear Studies, the Study of Metals, and Radiobiology.[4] The steps taken to continue electronics research at MIT, similar actions taken somewhat later by Frederick Terman at Stanford, and E. O. Lawrence's aggressive transformation of the Berkeley Radiation Laboratory to peacetime research—all figured in the development of those respective institutions and are described in subsequent chapters.[5] Not every institution could succeed in this game of scientific musical chairs. At Columbia, I. I. Rabi personally took the reins of the physics department in order to direct its postwar redeployment, but key hiring opportunities eluded him, and he soon found himself with five unfilled professorships. Caltech could not address the problem of a severely depleted faculty until after Lee A. DuBridge assumed the presidency in September 1946. Both institutions subsequently enhanced their research capacities, largely by recruiting younger scientists.[6]

The most eminent universities, at least, took a discriminating view of their postwar roles, preferring to forgo links with units engaged in mundane developmental tasks. Harvard was most resolute in this respect. It informed the Navy in 1944 that it did not wish to continue managing an underwater sound laboratory after hostilities ended. This operation was accordingly relocated, and expanded in scope, at a receptive Pennsylvania State College. The University of Chicago similarly withdrew from management of the Clinton Laboratory, an experimental reactor in Oak Ridge, Tennessee, originally used for the production of plutonium. More often, inertia overcame judgment in such matters. Both the Applied Physics Laboratory and the Jet Propulsion Laboratory had contracts with their respective universities that extended beyond 1945. In neither case was the university faculty disposed to perpetuate these ties, but strong advocacy by the leadership of both labs succeeded in preserving them.[7]

The university research system that emerged from the war was the product of mutual need and shared enthusiasm among patrons and performers. At this juncture, however, the performers possessed a distinct advantage. University scientists were the crucial resource, whether for universities attempting to build departments and research programs or for federal agencies wishing to stimulate research in relevant fields. This asymmetry—a seller's market for research—was an important factor, at least until 1950, in shaping a postwar research system that was strikingly congenial to academic scientists even though supported overwhelmingly by programmatic sponsors.

Outside of medicine, federal funds for academic research came almost entirely from the Army, Air Force, Navy, and the Atomic Energy Commission. Support from this 'defense establishment,' moreover, was furnished ostensibly for purposes of national security.[8] These new and tentative relationships assumed a variety of forms, but the underlying conditions favored university scientists. Throughout the defense establishment, considerable skepticism toward university research was often voiced, but for several years a relative abundance of funds and lax accountability gave proponents of research broad scope for action. Their vision, and that of academic scientists who advised them, was in broad terms prescient. Numerous critical fields had been opened during the war in which general advances in knowledge would be likely to produce results of great value to the armed services. This was most obviously the case in electronics and what was then called 'nucleonics' (nuclear and particle physics). Other critical fields, with varying balances of military or civilian potential, included computing, jet propulsion, rocketry, and myriad narrower specialties. In electronics, the open-ended support that was given to special laboratories at MIT and Stanford was a highly effective approach to an inchoate field, producing advances of both applied and basic knowledge.[9] In nucleonics, the organizational interplay was more complicated and, for that reason, indicative of how underlying factors tended to favor universities.

The AEC at its inception inherited commitments to academically linked laboratories at Berkeley, Argonne, Brookhaven, and more tenuously, Oak Ridge. These laboratories were, along with Los Alamos, the centerpieces of its research program. Universities were eager to establish their own programs in this glamorous field, but the AEC originally lacked the authority to offer assistance. ONR quickly stepped into this breach. In just two years it extended contracts to build particle accelerators at eleven physics departments.[10] These commitments resulted from university requests and involved significant investments on the part of those institutions. Similarly, MIT established a Laboratory for Nuclear Science and Engineering with its own seed money, just as it had for the electronics laboratory, before support from ONR materialized.[11] Even with such support, institutions had to expend their own funds to varying degrees for the facilities to house the instruments and for the specialized faculty and staff that used them.

When the ONR faced constraints in its budget in 1947, it asked the AEC to shoulder some of the costs of the nuclear physics program. The AEC initially refused; but the following year, consistent with its gradual accommodation of academic research, it acceded to this arrangement. For 1948 more than $4 million was transferred to the ONR for support of nuclear sciences; two years later the AEC provided $6 million to support about one hundred ONR research projects. By then, the AEC had also established the legal authority and the mechanisms for its own program of support for academic research.[12] These were portentous developments for academic science. The AEC's original aloofness proved untenable in light of the demand for research in this field by university scientists as well as by the Navy. Instead, the AEC became partner to the highly congenial relationship with university science developed by ONR.

By the late 1940s the new federal component of the university research system consisted of three kinds of support. The large laboratories were for the most part continuations or permutations of wartime facilities having, with only a partial exception for Berkeley and Brookhaven, well-defined technological missions. At the other extreme, numerous individual projects, largely basic in nature, were supported by the ONR, the Public Health Service, and to some extent by the AEC. In between, in character and organizationally, lay the support for a variety of critical fields, which was often concentrated in special university centers. From the federal perspective, this support for university research was a small portion of an enormous R&D effort, which was chiefly a legacy of the war. Support for individual projects and critical fields, in particular, represented investments in basic science that were loosely related to this overall effort—options of sort on the cumulating expertise of academic scientists. This was a congenial partnership for academic investigators—predominantly those in physical sciences. Unlike wartime, they were under no pressure to deliver products, but merely expected to advance their fields. With the expectations of patrons and the ambitions of clients in harmony, the initial relationship between academic science and the defense establishment was indeed amicable and fruitful. World events, however, soon altered the tone.

The deepening chill in postwar relations between the Soviet Union and the West crystallized into the Cold War by the end of the decade. The descent of the iron curtain across Central Europe was followed in 1949 by the victory of communist forces on the China mainland and then the detonation of an atomic bomb by the Soviet Union. Each of these developments punctured American assumptions about postwar international relations. The United States reacted early in 1950 with a commitment to develop the hydrogen bomb and plans for a vast rearmament effort. The invasion of South Korea in June of that year confirmed that a new era of military confrontation had dawned. There was some speculation that this emergency called for a remobilization of science through a new OSRD, a prospect that universities generally opposed. Such a step was scarcely needed, however: a network of scientists engaged with defense-related problems was already in place. Only funds and direction were required to focus research on matters of immediate concern for national security. As this was done, the university research system assumed a different cast.[13]

When the defense establishment turned to established university clients for its new needs, it essentially exercised those previously purchased options. Contract research laboratories like JPL and Argonne shifted readily to the production of usable hardware within a relatively short span of time. Academic units were in some cases supplemented with specifically applied counterparts. The electronics laboratory at Stanford, for example, was joined by an applied twin. MIT's Research Laboratory in Electronics was asked to greatly expand its scope of operation. It accepted this challenge without hesitation, and these additional activities were soon hived off as the Lincoln Laboratories, with the former head of RLE as director. At Berkeley, Lawrence first accommodated additional military projects in his laboratory, then launched a new facility at Livermore, which became the locus of most classified projects, including work on the hydrogen bomb.[14]

Most of this applied and developmental activity was both peripheral to the main lines of academic research and also a net addition. In this respect, the congenial postwar arrangements for supporting university research did not so much suffer as they stagnated. Incremental growth occurred in highly programmatic endeavors. In fact, the total picture for university research was mixed. In medicine, the National Institutes of Health were expanding according to their own dynamic, and in 1951, the long-heralded National Science Foundation began operating, albeit without significant funds to disburse. Both sources would add support for academic research during the peak years of Cold War fervor (1950–57). This Cold War esprit was soon ascendant at the AEC (see below). With respect to research, its principal effect was a vast expansion of the national laboratory system, including consecrating Livermore as the second weapons lab.[15] Support for academic research by the AEC failed to grow during these years, and researchers were vexed by rigid secrecy requirements, but support did not decline. The single area where academic research clearly suffered was in the support that had come from ONR.

As the Office of Naval Research came under closer scrutiny from the Navy in 1950, it had to find explicit and plausible connections between sponsored research and the naval mission. Inevitably, its contribution to basic academic research contracted. ONR remained the unit of the armed services with the closest and thickest ties with academic science, but it would never again be the generous, liberal patron that it was from 1946 to 1950.[16] Its new approach instead was concentrated heavily upon critical fields. Emmanuel Piore, Waterman's successor as chief scientist, in 1954 defined three kinds of research relationships. First, and clearly meriting major backing, were areas of vital importance to the

Navy that had little relevance to other parts of the nation's scientific community. Examples of these were oceanography, fluid dynamics, the chemistry of explosives, applied mathematics, and research on the Arctic and the upper atmosphere. Second, and deserving support in cooperation with other agencies, were areas vital to naval technology and operations that were also important for other patrons of research. These included solid-state physics, meteorology, electrochemistry, statistics, microbiology, and areas of psychology. The third area Piore referred to as "listening post activity," meaning that connections with naval technology were remote but that awareness was warranted because of the potential for future relevance. This was the kind of research commitment that ONR had made liberally during its early years, but now it deserved only "modest support . . . in balance with the rest of the effort."[17] Piore's classification could be extended to characterize the posture of the entire defense establishment toward academic research during the Cold War years. The emphasis, and hence the growth, was on programmatic support for critical fields.[18] Listening-post activity related to basic academic research was maintained, and was fairly extensive in such fields as nucleonics, but remained a lesser priority during years of relatively tight budgets.

In addition to altering the flow of research funds to universities, the onset of the Cold War affected research universities through two related phenomena. The first was a series of events that altered the leadership and emphasis of federal science at the highest level. The second, under the rubric of McCarthyism, comprised impositions on higher education stemming from the surge of anticommunism that swept the country, fanned by politicians on various levels out of both patriotic and self-serving motives. Both phenomena were played out on the national stage. Universities and research thus constituted, from a national perspective, relatively minor theaters. For universities, however, these developments did much to define the context in which they operated during the Cold War years.

That civilian science and military technology had become firmly joined during World War II was understood by all involved. The terms of their interaction were nevertheless defined by a multitude of specific arrangements in the years that followed. Vannevar Bush had originally proposed the placement of defense research under civilian leadership in a national research foundation. In its absence, the Research and Development Board was established by the National Security Act of 1947 as the highest advisory body for defense science.[19] Bush served for two years as its initial chairman and he was succeeded by his OSRD partner Karl T. Compton, president of MIT. Besides this central group, each of the services had recourse to civilian expertise through scientific advisory committees and additional panels for evaluating weapons systems. Then too, perhaps the most important administrative post in defense science was occupied by a civilian, Alan Waterman, chief scientist at ONR. At the AEC—a civilian agency but chiefly concerned with weapons development—scientific expertise was embodied in the General Advisory Committee. Its membership was drawn mainly from wartime scientific leaders, including J. Robert Oppenheimer (chairman), James Conant, Lee Dubridge, Enrico Fermi, and I. I. Rabi. Through the 1940s, then, military technology was developed with the advice and cooperation of independent civilian advisers. With regard to national security, the views of civilian science advisers were usually as close to those they advised as had been the case during the war. No one contemplated what might happen when opinions diverged.

Such a fissure began to open in 1949, provoked in parts by communist aggressiveness, the loss of the American nuclear monopoly, and the inner momentum of weapons development. The specific issue was whether or not the U.S. should launch a crash program to build a fusion or hydrogen bomb—the 'Super' as it was then called.[20] As a means of reasserting nuclear superiority and an apparent answer to the manpower advantage of communist forces, the hydrogen bomb had great appeal to politicians and certain interested parts of the armed services, particularly the strategic bombing contingent of the Air Force. Many civilian scientists embraced this same outlook. Besides being deeply patriotic, some also felt the additional lure of possibly participating in this scientific challenge. Chief among this latter group were Edward Teller, E. O. Lawrence, and most of Lawrence's Berkeley associates—some of whom were now in the advisory apparatus. The contrary position was more subtle. Although not fully apparent in 1949, the technical feasibility of an H-bomb had become almost assured. There were reasons nevertheless to deplore an all-out program to develop one, as well as the very reliance on such a weapon that would surely result. Building weapons solely because they were technically feasible was a dangerous precedent, a sure route to an uncontrolled arms race. A device 1000 times more powerful than the Hiroshima bomb had no foreseeable tactical application. Having the H-bomb would thus tend to displace calculated military strategy with a design for Armageddon. This negative position was endorsed by the entire General Advisory Committee (GAC) and then shared by four of the five Commission members, but in January 1950 President Truman bowed to overwhelming political pressure and approved the development of the 'Super.' The premonitions of the opponents about the arms race and an annihilation strategy would prove accurate; but then, in a sense, so too did the arguments of the victorious proponents.[21] A powerful animus nevertheless developed after the fact against those who had ostensibly broken ranks on a national security issue.

Among the dissenters, who represented the old guard of the science elite, Conant was most unreserved in his opposition, but Oppenheimer was regarded, inaccurately, as the decisive influence on the position taken by the GAC. Conant was the first to be rebuked. In April 1950 he was proposed as sole candidate for election to the presidency of the National Academy of Sciences, honorifically perhaps the foremost position in American science. A revolt from the floor, however, placed in nomination and then elected Detlev Bronk, president of Johns Hopkins. The insurrection was led by Berkeley chemists, who were strongly behind building the H-bomb. It was supported by other members of similar persuasion. The episode was a considerable embarrassment to the president of Harvard, and signaled the end of Conant's active involvement in nuclear policy.[22]

Oppenheimer's retribution was longer in coming and more far-reaching. In

1954, while McCarthyist hysteria still gripped the country, he was subjected to a celebrated 'trial' which resulted in the lifting of his security clearance and hence banishment from the community of active nuclear scientists. Oppenheimer was distrusted because of prewar association with leftists; but one of the chief arguments used to demonstrate his unreliability, if not outright disloyalty, was his failure to support the 'Super.'[23]

The battle over the hydrogen bomb was fought in the advisory apparatus of the federal government, high above the mundane activities of academic research. These events nevertheless signified a palpable change in the research environment. The old guard of World War II leaders quickly disappeared from the GAC and other influential advisory positions. Conant withdrew from involvement, Fermi resigned, Dubridge left when his term expired, as did Oppenheimer, who was merely a seldom-used consultant at the time of his trial. Their replacements were, inevitably, scientists with lesser or more recent leadership credentials who also tended to be dedicated cold-warriors and vociferous advocates of weapons development. With advisers such as these, the defense establishment had little to fear from the civilian input to its R&D effort.

The academic science community in general was less easily controlled. The changing of the guard at the advisory level was accompanied by a pervasive unease. Most scientists undoubtedly accepted the reality of the Cold War and perhaps also the unpleasant necessity of the arms race. There was widespread dissatisfaction nevertheless with the elaborate security precautions imposed on much research, in the form of secrecy and classification requirements, and on researchers as well, in the form of security checks and clearances.[24] Opinion was more polarized on the mortification of Oppenheimer. Here, the scientific community generally felt, the new leaders of federal science had gone too far, acting more out of vindictiveness than concern for security. Whatever acrimony existed in the university research system, however, remained at manageable levels. Academic scientists were able to accommodate themselves and their work to the Cold War environment as readily as they had to postwar conditions. Those wishing to participate in weapons-related activities had abundant opportunity; those wishing to avoid such commitments could for the most part find a congenial alternative in basic research. As long as investigators were engaged in pure science, most reasoned, it mattered little who might be supporting them, or why. After the sense of crisis that pervaded the early 1950s began to wane, scientists and academic leaders became increasingly comfortable emphasizing a division of labor that stressed the university's commitment to disinterested basic research and ignored the special laboratories of the defense establishment. This distinction was made all the more plausible by the concentrated nature of most defense research. Thus, as will be seen in Chapter 6, by the late 1950s the university research system was at once heavily implicated in the research economy of the Cold War and increasingly wishing to disassociate itself from those very entanglements.

A similar ambivalence surrounded the involvement of universities with McCarthyism.[25] The unreasoned, near-hysterical fear of communism that gripped the country from the late 1940s through the mid-1950s gave rise to a variety of practices that have been grouped under this rubric. Faculty were required to sign loyalty oaths or disclaimers of communism as a condition of employment; special committees of Congress or state legislatures conducted hearings designed to expose and purge individuals with past communist associations or current leftist sympathies; colleges and universities took this process one step further through their own investigations and the imposition of sanctions against those who did not cooperate with the government committees; and constitutional rights and academic freedom were ignored by laws forbidding allegedly tainted individuals from teaching. To tie all these actions to Senator Joseph R. McCarthy, whose demagogic reign lasted from 1950 to 1954, is somewhat misleading. First, the phenomenon itself had broad popular backing. Most states, for example, enacted legislation or conducted hearings of this sort. Second, where prolonged controversies ensued, as over the California Loyalty Oath, other powerful political agendas became intertwined with strands of ostensible anticommunism.[26] Thus, although there was some capriciousness in the timing and nature of attacks on particular campuses, the intimidation of McCarthyism was a pervasive and long-lasting phenomenon.

McCarthyism was essentially imposed on universities from outside. Its exploitation of popular fears of communism, simplistic conflation of liberal ideas and subversive acts, emphasis on past rather than present behavior, and disregard for individual liberties, let alone academic freedom, were all antithetical to the academic ethos—the principles that universities publicly espoused. But universities were part of American society too; many academic leaders were zealous in their own opposition to communism, and institutions could scarcely ignore the foremost concerns of the government and the public on which they depended. Thus, legislative investigations of university teachers were invariably followed by subsequent internal examinations. In general, the more dependent an institution, the more likely it was to assist rather than resist McCarthyism. Private institutions with strong academic traditions were probably compromised least, while public institutions with weak traditions were most likely to join in persecuting the accused.

The first McCarthyite purge of university faculty took place at the University of Washington.[27] A committee of the state legislature scrutinized the faculty in 1948 to uncover subversives. It identified ten candidates, who were then subjected to further investigation by a university committee. The latter body determined that the suspects had violated no university rules and recommended their retention. President Raymond Allen, himself an ardent anticommunist, chose instead to fire three faculty who had refused to testify to the legislative committee, and to place on probation three others who had declined to identify former associates. The readiness with which the university presumed wrongdoing and prescribed punishment was striking at this relatively early date. At this same juncture, by way of contrast, President Hutchins of Chicago addressed a similar legislative red hunt in Illinois by defending academic freedom and directly challenging the simplistic notions of the inquisitors.[28] Such principled stands by university leaders virtually disappeared after 1950 when Senator McCarthy escalated the entire red-baiting phenomenon.

University teachers were intermittently harassed by anticommunist investigations, but in 1953 they became the principal target of congressional committees. More than one hundred faculty were then subpoenaed, and at least thirty of them lost their jobs as a result.[29] Research universities by this point were largely wary of the entire phenomenon, seeking to protect themselves and minimize damage to their faculty and their image. They nevertheless tended to have little compunction about sacrificing irregular or even nontenured teachers, but they generally sought to protect established professors. At the University of Michigan, three faculty members invoked their First and Fifth Amendment rights before the House Committee on Un-American Activities in 1954. Two were subsequently dismissed by President Harlan Hatcher, even though a special university committee had recommended that one of them be retained.[30] Both Harvard and MIT chose to protect, in a fashion, professors of certifiable left-wing pedigree caught in the McCarthyite web. Dirk Struik of MIT spent five years under suspension, with pay, until charges against him were dropped; and Wendell Furry of Harvard was slapped on the wrist with three years of probation. However, both institutions also found cause to discharge other individuals.[31] In these and other similar cases, universities basically chose to make fine-grained judgments about an individual's loyalty, integrity, and degree of misconduct rather than resist the entire process. These decisions were also shaped, inevitably but silently, by considerations of expediency. According to Ellen Schrecker, the historian of academic McCarthyism, Cold War patriotism nevertheless outweighed expediency in shaping university behavior.[32] Universities did not condemn on principle these unwarranted violations of individual rights and academic freedom.

The worst features of McCarthyism began to wane after 1954. The Senator and his outrageous tactics were discredited that year, and subsequent court decisions diminished the powers of Congressional inquisitors to have uncooperative witnesses prosecuted. The House Committee on Un-American Activities continued to subpoena witnesses into the 1960s, and laws remained in force in virtually every state requiring loyalty tests and ostracizing former communists. The principal impact of McCarthyism in higher education was nevertheless felt by those individuals who were accused or interrogated. Some careers were completely destroyed, many others disrupted for years.[33] More pervasive and insidious were the incalculable effects of intimidation, which encouraged acceptance of the status quo and avoidance of politics.

The impact of McCarthyism on institutions was far more muted. For a time, certainly, life on particular campuses was disrupted when local faculty were investigated. One of the most serious and prolonged controversies occurred at the University of California over a required loyalty oath and the policy of barring communists. While it raged, from 1949 to 1952, it was assumed to be highly inimical to academic development. Some faculty were fired, others resigned in protest, and recruitment suffered as offers of appointment were refused. But the

predicted eclipse of the university's reputation never occurred. Quite the opposite happened, as will be seen in Chapter 3.[34] The University of Illinois, on the
other hand, was not so fortunate. Its rapid postwar academic development under
President George D. Stoddard (1946–53) was derailed amid charges that the new
regime was soft on communism. Here too, ideological battles were confounded
with other divisive factors, especially the conflict between the old and new
guards during a period of rapid change. The result was the alienation and departure of many of the distinguished faculty recently recruited and ultimately a
slower pace of academic development for the university.[35]

By the latter years of the 1950s, prevailing academic sentiment tended to separate McCarthyism from the Cold War which had made it viable. Universities
freely condemned the excesses of the McCarthy years and rationalized their own
actions as defensive. At the same time, they remained fully engaged with the
ideological mobilization that had accompanied the anticommunist crusade. Relevant academic disciplines were significantly affected. The whole field of international relations and area studies was shaped during these years. Scholars who
were unsympathetic with American foreign policy and American allies were
largely purged during the McCarthy years. More important though, these fields
grew enormously during the 1950s through close cooperation with government
agencies and support from sources that backed the American role.[36] History too
was enlisted to inculcate American values, the solidarity of Western Civilization,
and an internationalist perspective.[37] McCarthyism per se may have been a
lamentable pathology of the Cold War, but universities had fully internalized
and projected the partisan view of world affairs that fueled its remarkable energy.

The ready conversion of research universities from wartime to peacetime to
Cold War conditions reflected subtle changes in their nature that contemporaries largely failed to appreciate. Idealistic spokesmen were accustomed to regarding them as unitary organizations, highly insulated from society, principally committed to the unfettered pursuit and dissemination of truth. Postwar research
universities, however, were increasingly compartmentalized institutions, pene-
trated to varying degrees and in various parts by external influence. They had to
look to both society and government for the financial resources to support their
core academic functions. At the same time, research became an increasingly
autonomous activity, shaped by the sources that supported its insatiable needs.

2. The Burdens of Finance

As the federal research economy was forming during the late 1940s, the program
having the most immediate impact on higher education was the GI Bill created
by the Servicemen's Readjustment Act of June 22, 1944. Some 15 million veterans of World War II were offered the opportunity to continue their education
at government expense. Approximately two million chose to do so by attending
a college or university. At the peak of the resulting influx, 1947, almost as many

veterans were enrolled in higher education as there had been students just a decade before. All told, enrollments doubled from 1938 to 1948, with veterans providing the bulk of the increase.[1] As enlightened social policy, the GI Bill can hardly be faulted. It eased the dislocations of demobilization, rewarded those who had served their country with the opportunity for a better future, and constituted a massive investment in human capital that would pay dividends for years to come. Less significant for American society, perhaps, were the effects of the GI Bill on universities. A hectic half-decade of severe overcrowding, year-round operations, and the predominance of mature, serious students followed its enactment. Married-student housing became a new fixture at most universities; and adolescent campus customs, like freshman beanies, were summarily abandoned. In addition, the forced over-enrollment of the period made "the uncritical acceptance of largeness . . . a major legacy of the GI Bill."[2] These visible and striking institutional changes were nevertheless superimposed upon more fundamental trends that shaped university development during two turbulent decades of Depression, war, and postwar adjustment.

The forces acting upon American higher education were evident in the shifting relationship between the public and private sectors. By the beginning of the 1930s, enrollments in public colleges and universities had grown to a rough parity with those in the private sector, and institutions in both were enjoying an unparalleled degree of prosperity.[3] The onset of the Great Depression then brought considerably greater hardship to tax-supported state universities than to highly endowed private institutions. Comparative conditions began to reverse after 1935. The continued fall in interest rates and the contraction of voluntary support kept the private universities under fiscal pressure for the remainder of the decade. At state universities, however, higher enrollments and public programs supporting students and new construction permitted renewed expansion. By 1939 the public sector had grown to claim 53 percent of total enrollments before wartime disruptions once again restored a rather artificial parity.

These fundamental prewar trends continued after 1945, even though the impact of the GI Bill temporarily smothered their effects. As the veterans claimed nearly every available college opening, the rough parity between the two sectors persisted until the beginning of the 1950s. At the same time, the financial effects of this influx gave considerable respite from prewar penury for both types of institution. At private universities, where student tuition covered a large proportion of instructional costs, over-enrollment provided extra revenues that more than made up for additional costs. State universities were even more fortunate because the Veteran's Administration paid the out-of-state tuition rate for all GI Bill students, thus considerably swelling tuition revenues. By 1948 the Veteran's Administration was paying 56 percent of student fees in private universities and 67 percent in public ones. At the University of California, for example, revenue from student fees reached $12.6 million in 1947–48—five times what it had been in 1937 and twice what it would be five years later. The University of Wisconsin received an additional $10 million from extra veteran tuition.[4]

During the years of the GI Bill the underlying financial trends continued to

favor public institutions and to hinder private ones. The private universities suffered from the persistence of low interest rates, despite inflation that raised prewar price levels by 70 percent in a decade (1940–50). Under these conditions it
made little sense, for donors or donees, to make major efforts to augment
endowment. The state universities meanwhile used these years to lay the foundation for an expansive future. Government fiscal policies during the war had
encouraged states to keep taxation at high levels, even though there was little for
them to purchase. As a result some states, notably California, emerged from the
war with reserves that could be devoted to higher education. State universities
were able to invest heavily in new facilities, hire additional faculty, and raise salary schedules. Capital spending in the public sector during the postwar decade,
for example, ran 50 to 80 percent higher than at private institutions.[5]

The changing economics of the endowed private research universities, even
those richly endowed, were evident at Yale:

Yale Income	1937–38	1947–48	1957–58
From endowment	$4,056,000	$4,508,000	$6,647,000
From student fees	2,164,000	5,195,000	9,028,000

In real terms, Yale's income from endowment lost more than a third of its purchasing power in the decade spanning World War II. To compensate, substantially greater funds had to be derived from student tuition. Even with higher
charges, Yale's real income declined 9 percent (1938–48).[6]

The situation at Yale merely illustrated one facet of a more pervasive postwar
malaise for American private higher education. Although financial problems
were considerably mitigated by the tide of veterans enrolling after 1945, private
colleges and universities nevertheless faced the future with considerable apprehension. The report of the President's Commission on Higher Education (1947–
48) reflected the bleak prospects for private higher education. While projecting
an expansion of higher education based on a doubling of enrollment rates of
college-age cohorts by 1960, the Commission presumed that this expansion
would take place in public institutions. Private colleges and universities, it
implied, would at best retain their existing clientele.[7]

The underlying weaknesses of the private sector, as well as the absence of governmental sympathy for its plight, elicited some positive steps from among its
traditional supporters. Late in 1947, the Rockefeller Foundation set up an
Exploratory Committee on Financing Higher Education and Research. As a
result of its report the foundation, joined by the Carnegie Corporation, sponsored a full-fledged inquiry by a Commission on Financing Higher Education. In
three years of work (1949–52) the Commission produced two reports and nine
special studies. While by no means partisan, it took particular care to explore
those issues affecting the health of the private sector.[8]

The two basic financial problems facing private institutions were the inability
to increase income in line with rising prices and the lack of capital for purposes
of expansion, improvement, or income. As Yale's finances illustrated, the 1940s
marked a watershed in the economics of endowed universities. Whereas endow-

ment provided 29 percent of the income of all private universities in 1940, by 1950 that figure had fallen to just 16 percent.[9] The endowments of private universities were crucial to their commitment to advancing knowledge. To a great extent endowment income upheld high standards in student recruitment through financial aid, supported the extra costs of a large and prestigious faculty, and subsidized undertakings like graduate education or instruction in esoteric fields, which could not be supported by student charges alone. The private universities financed their basic operations as best they could during the late 1940s through increased student tuition, considerably assisted by overenrollment; but they were limited by what the market would bear. The Eastern institutions charged tuitions of $400-450 in 1940 and $600-650 in 1951. Although these increases failed to match inflation, it was still widely feared that "private colleges will soon be forced to admit only the economically privileged."[10] Tuition charges at these schools nevertheless continued to rise, and by 1955 approximated real prewar levels.

The loss of purchasing power by private universities was in part absorbed by their faculties, whose salaries failed to keep pace with inflation. In fact, academic salaries fell well behind price increases during the war, and then were unable to recoup that loss in the ensuing decade. In the early 1950s college teachers were scandalously underpaid. The private research universities, which had formerly set the standard for the profession, struggled to maintain salaries at sufficiently competitive levels to attract and retain top scholars. The following schedule of minimum salaries at two leading research universities, public and private, illustrates this situation:

TABLE 2. Minimum Academic Salaries at Two Research Universities[11]

	State University		Private University	
	1940	*1950*	*1940*	*1950*
Professor	$4,200	$7,200	$7,500	$8,500
Assoc. professor	3,300	5,700	5,000	6,000
Asst. professor	2,700	4,500	3,600	4,500
Instructor	2,000	3,900	2,400	3,000

The private university's incremental advances were woefully inadequate (13-25% vs. 72% inflation), and it had lost its salary advantage over the state university at all but the full-professor rank. Yet at the senior levels salaries were still probably sufficient to maintain an excellent faculty. The private universities generally adapted as best they could to their straitened circumstances. The expanding base of university knowledge nevertheless called for additional commitments, which were difficult to make without additional capital.

Fund-raising and capital-spending were constrained at private universities by several factors. A postwar truism (which was not true!) held that there were no more huge personal fortunes of the kind that had previously yielded great capital gifts. Foundations too, by and large, seemed no longer capable of assisting universities through capital grants. Their own endowments had suffered the same fate as those of the universities, and, as will be seen in a later chapter, they generally adapted to diminished real income by seeking strategic opportunities for grants. Hopes were high for some time that industry would be able to enlarge its philanthropic role substantially, and that it would be especially attracted to the mission of providing succor for private universities.[12] These expectations, however, went largely unrealized. Direct corporate gifts to universities remained comparatively modest, even after all question of their legality had been cleared away. Firms that did give to universities tended to favor those institutions offering identifiable benefits. This tendency was also evident in the far larger contributions of businessmen themselves. Two of the rare capital campaigns of the late 1940s were conducted by MIT and the Harvard Business School, and they succeeded largely due to gifts of this kind.[13]

Private research universities for the most part had to depend upon voluntary support from a broad spectrum of sources. Few were able to mount capital campaigns during the 1940s, and the Korean War then introduced new elements of uncertainty that inhibited fund-raising for several more years. Still, the situation was not entirely bleak. If postwar voluntary support was well below what universities felt they needed, it exceeded what they had received during the Depression and the war. The following figures provide an index for the fluctuations of this irregular phenomenon. Immediately after the war, giving was barely higher than it had been during the difficult years of the late 1930s. After a substantial improvement, it remained mired on a plateau for the six years spanning the Korean War. Only after 1955 would giving surpass in real terms the levels reached at the end of the 1920s, a quarter of a century earlier:

TABLE 3. Voluntary Support for 28 Universities, 1928–1954 (1967$)[14]

	In Millions of Dollars
1928–31 (avg.)	168
1936–1940 (avg.)	90.6
1945–46	108.6
1946–47	91.3
1947–48	92.2
1948–49	129.4
1949–50	138.6
1950–51	136.2
1951–52	135.8
1952–53	132.4
1953–54	138.8
1954–55	157.8

For private universities dependent upon philanthropy, this pattern meant a prolonged scarcity of new capital. They were able for the most part to continue existing operations, but the resources for additional undertakings had to be sought in the research economy. Such funds, naturally, reflected to varying degrees the preferences of sponsors rather than the unfettered choices of universities themselves.

Perhaps it mattered little for the development of American science if the private universities waned while the state universities waxed. Indeed, if one accepted the viewpoint of the President's Commission on Higher Education—that most of the resources for the expansion of higher education would have to come from the federal government—then perhaps publicly controlled institutions might even be the more appropriate vehicle. This view was contested vigorously by private universities and by their traditional supporters in foundations and industry. Some of their arguments merely reflected the political idioms of the era; for example, the assertion that privately controlled institutions protected freedom against the threat of imminent federal control.[15] Self-interest aside, one can still discern the special importance of the role played by the private research universities and the predicament they faced at this juncture.

American universities had risen to scientific parity with their one time European mentors during the interwar years on the basis of a privately funded university research system.[16] Foundations, and to a lesser extent industry and individual benefactors, had provided funds for university research projects; the universities themselves, largely through the aid of voluntary support, provided the infrastructure on which that research depended. The private research universities, particularly the most affluent half-dozen, naturally led this development. But their very attainments forced other universities, state and private, to seek to emulate the high standards that they set. All these efforts taken together had the effect of mobilizing resources for university research from a great diversity of sources—college alumni, business corporations, philanthropists, as well as those few state governments wishing to maintain first-class universities. The American university system derived its strength not just from the leadership of its top universities, which in fact was often myopic, but from the decentralized competition of many good universities, the diversity of their distinctive achievements, and the pluralism of the sources supporting them.

For academics formed within this system, the persistent financial weakness of the private universities after the war seemed to pose a grave threat. Not only was the existing academic leadership at peril, but so were competitiveness, diversity, and pluralism too. These qualities might be submerged in a system dominated by tax-supported institutions. Without the goad of independent competition it seemed unlikely that state universities would by themselves seek to raise academic standards. Moreover, for all their recent progress, the state universities too faced an uncertain future.

By 1950 the special conditions favoring state universities had largely run their course. Construction from the Public Works Administration and the wartime reserve funds had been completed, and the windfall of veterans' fees was coming to an end. Henceforth, university development would once again depend upon the wills and the whims of state legislatures. The outlook in this respect was not auspicious. The federal government now claimed the great bulk of the nation's tax dollars, and state responsibilities for highways, welfare, and aid to localities

seemed to be growing more rapidly than those for higher education.[17] But
macro-economic trends such as these actually had little meaning in light of the
great variety of conditions across the forty-eight states.

Before World War II only five state institutions stood forth as research universities by virtue of the quality of their faculty and the quantity of their graduate
education and research. Four of them were in the Midwest—Illinois, Michigan,
Minnesota, and Wisconsin—and the fifth was California. After the war this pattern tended to persist, with the universities of the Midwestern states and California remaining strongest, and only perhaps Washington and later Texas bidding to join this group. Each case was somewhat different. Support for the
University of California benefited from the widespread recognition of Berkeley's
scientific accomplishments, the determination to raise the Los Angeles branch
to the status of a distinguished university, and the general postwar economic
growth of the state. In the Midwest, the most dramatic steps to increase university funding and research occurred in Illinois. Indiana's two universities
advanced to merit inclusion with the research universities. Michigan suffered
from budgetary constraints throughout the 1940s and Wisconsin continued to
be precariously financed, but both remained strong in research. The University
of Texas had a special source of capital in the revenues from extensive oil lands.
At the University of Washington the war triggered aspirations for first-rate status. The state's investment included funds for establishing a medical school, and
extra veterans fees were devoted to future building.[18] Despite such conspicuous
progress, even in 1950 only a dozen state universities, by generous count, nearly
monopolized nonagricultural research in the public sector, and their total effort,
furthermore, was less than the research activities of the dozen largest private universities. Despite the eclipse of the privately funded university research system,
research support remained skewed toward privately controlled institutions.
Both state and private universities nevertheless faced the same fundamental conditions.

The American university was in essence organized as a teaching institution.
The core of support—whether student fees, state appropriations, or income
from past gifts—was predicated upon this instructional role. For this reason,
funding explicitly designated for research was derived through different channels
and was accounted for in a special category—variously called 'separately budgeted,' 'externally supported,' or 'sponsored' research. Such funds tended to flow
to the universities possessing the greatest capabilities for conducting research.
The central organizational problem for the American research university was
thus how to transform resources provided for the educational mission into a
capacity to perform research. The key factors were faculty, graduate education,
and the facilities needed for research. To attract productive scholars and scientists universities had to offer above-market salaries and reduced teaching loads:
they had, in short, to pay faculty more to teach less. High-ability graduate students increasingly had to be recruited and supported as well, and they in turn
claimed a disproportionate share of the instructional resources. Libraries, laboratories, equipment, work space and supporting services were inputs to graduate

education and research of which universities never had enough. Finally, the intellectual configuration of a research university needed to respond, quite irrespective of its teaching burden, to the changing terrain of academic knowledge. This imperative created, above all, steady pressure for expansion into new specialties and emerging subfields. Taken together, the infrastructure supporting the research capacity constituted a costly form of overhead to the university's central teaching role. Yet, the more ample this infrastructure, the greater the university's potential for advancing science and scholarship.

From this perspective the basic predicament of the postwar research universities is evident. The emergence of the postwar federal research economy yielded unprecedented funds for the direct support of research. At the same time, the persistence of adverse financial conditions inhibited the development of an underlying research capacity, especially in the private universities, but to a significant degree in the state institutions too. The result was unbalanced development.

This imbalance was perhaps most evident in medical schools. As the Yale medical director complained, by 1950 funds for medical research were available in abundance while the nation's medical schools were running an annual deficit of $10 million. He blamed this situation not just on the federal government, but on trends in private philanthropy as well. The tax system had driven the 'venture capital' for higher education into small and inefficient foundations which then imitated their larger counterparts by attempting to support medical research. When this occurred, "a million dollars [capital] became $35,000 [income] overnight." Moreover, research grants were not paying the full cost of research. He estimated that the actual rate of overhead expense at the Medical School to be 25 percent; yet Yale was receiving only the equivalent of 5 percent in reimbursements. Establishing professorships in burgeoning fields like biophysics and microbiology seemed more important than funding research projects on specific topics. "The greatest need now," he concluded "is for funds to support the core of the educational program, the faculty and staff."[20] Indeed, the same could be said for the research universities in general during the decade following the war. The influx of unprecedented amounts of support for numerous kinds of programmatic investigations caused research to expand with little relation to the university's academic core.

3. Organized Research in Postwar Universities

Separately organized, separately financed research has been a feature of American universities since their emergence in the nineteenth century. The special arrangements for this separateness, in fact, are a confirmation of the primacy of the teaching mission. The first explicit organized research units were created to accommodate the requirements of large and costly instruments (observatories) or collections (museums). Both demanded the ongoing attention of a staff of specialized personnel in addition to the expertise of a professor/director. The extraordinary expenditures created by these activities were generally met through a permanent endowment.

Not until after World War I did new possibilities appear for organized university research. The Stanford Food Research Institute established by the Carnegie Corporation in 1919 was dedicated to studying a class of problems not bounded by a physical instrument or collection. Still, here too it was the initial endowment gift that made the institute possible. At this juncture, separate research funds were assumed to be bound to particular institutions. When the National Research Council catalogued such funds, for example, it accordingly did so by university. Most of the philanthropic support during the 1920s continued to be university-specific.[1] Some foundation programs, like the Laura Spelman Rockefeller Memorial's support for social science at the University of Chicago, underwrote the research activities of regular departmental faculty. In addition, foundations began to provide general support for university research in the form of grants for 'fluid' research funds at particular institutions. Not until the 1930s did foundation funding for specific research projects become common. By World War II, American universities were somewhat accustomed to the phenomenon of separately organized research and had already shown remarkable flexibility in devising appropriate institutional structures. Afterward, such a context would prove fertile for further proliferation of organized research.

The emergence after the war of the federally dominated research economy vastly increased the magnitude of funds available for university research. But these funds were not a pure windfall for the research universities. To a large extent federal research funds represented a different relationship between the patron and the performer of research. The myriad arrangements that the universities devised to administer and employ these funds were shaped as much by the nature of this relationship as by the nature of the research.

As Harvard president James B. Conant noted with dismay, the bulk of the funds available to support research were 'programmatic' in character. University research, on the other hand, had traditionally been of an 'uncommitted' nature.[2] Conant quite rightly emphasized the motivation underlying support for academic research rather than the nature of the research itself. Ideally, academics were inspired to do research by the state of knowledge in their field—what was known, what needed to be known, and what could feasibly be discovered. They endeavored to contribute to the corpus of knowledge in their discipline; their contributions would, in turn, be evaluated by the appropriate disciplinary community, and professional recognition and reward for the investigator would result. Such research was essentially disinterested: the concern of the investigator was with the validity of the knowledge contribution, not with whatever use might be made of it.[3] The initiative for programmatic research, on the other hand, typically came from the funder, and was predicated on the probability that the investigator's knowledge contribution would, at least in the long run, have utility for the sponsor. The first pattern was more likely to involve basic research, and the second, applied—but not necessarily. The basic-applied axis of research was by no means coextensive with the disinterested-interested axis. It was the latter continuum that corresponded with the activities underlying the proliferation of organized university research, especially that supported by the defense agencies.[4]

The different arrangements for sponsored research in postwar universities could be located on this disinterested-interested continuum. At one end lay research conducted within the context of academic departments without need of supplementary organization. Such a situation approximated the academic model outlined above in that the research topics emanated from disciplinary paradigms. At the opposite extreme were the federal contract laboratories, which were entirely the creatures of their respective sponsoring agencies. Research performed in these units, irrespective of its academic content, was funded solely because of its utility for the sponsoring agency. In between these two extremes were the various centers, institutes, programs, or bureaus—there was no standard nomenclature—that comingled the academic aspirations of university faculty with the utilitarian interests of funders. Two points on this continuum became populated by relatively common types of research units. Here the generic term *centers* will be used for units that facilitated largely academic research outside of departments. Somewhat further removed from departments, *institutes* accommodated research that was more strongly oriented toward the interests of sponsors.[5] The campus impact of the burgeoning postwar research economy varied according to these four possible arrangements for externally sponsored research.

For university scientists and scholars during the second quarter of the twentieth century, the most congenial research support generally took the form of foundation grants for 'fluid' research funds. Usually designated for one particular area, like the social sciences, such funds were often distributed internally by a faculty committee, and otherwise had no strings attached. This ideal of unrestricted support became increasingly elusive after the war. The Carnegie Corporation gave such free funds to the Harvard Laboratory of Social Relations, and the Ford Foundation later provided faculty grants-in-aid without restrictions.[6] But the trend in grant-making was in the direction of focus and accountability. As will be seen in Chapter 4, most foundations found it necessary to concentrate their finite grant funds upon delimited objectives in order to achieve perceptible results. The fluid research funds available were clearly inadequate for the enlarged aspirations of natural scientists.

Immediately after the war the only federal program capable of assisting individual faculty to conduct nonmedical research of their own choosing was that of the Office of Naval Research. The key feature was the ONR's willingness to fund investigator-initiated proposals, and thus to support research inspired by disciplinary paradigms. Research funds from ONR thus became the closest approximation to uncommitted support available from the federal government. Still, some faculty had difficulty forsaking the prewar ideal of complete research autonomy.

As late as 1948 Berkeley physics chairman Raymond Birge objected that if the work of a project could be specified in a detailed budget and the findings foreseen in advance, then the endeavor was development rather than basic research.

Birge furthermore felt that such contract research threatened to smother the kind of fundamental investigations that universities ought to harbor.[7] In the natural sciences Birge's concerns would soon be considered antediluvian, but these attitudes lingered longer in the social sciences and humanities. A survey of behavioral scientists at Harvard found one who felt that applying for external research support implied "a certain type of research output, a prescribed palpability"; and another concerned with preserving freedom of choice in research and avoiding having "to choose 'quick and certain' experiments."[8] Also common was the allegation that patrons, generally foundations, were only willing to support projects involving team research or quantitative methods, thus neglecting the 'lone wolf' type of scholar. Of course, it could be argued that the favored approaches were precisely the ones that required outside assistance; but still the sense of intradepartmental equity somehow seemed endangered.

This latter problem was one of several delicate personnel issues thrust upon the universities by the proliferation of organized research. Supported faculty might have less time to commit to teaching and administration, and might also benefit from perquisites like summer salaries. Policies had to be formulated that would preserve equity within departments, while also respecting the intellectual freedom of faculty members to pursue their own research—and grants. As research transcended departmental boundaries, however, exceptional arrangements were increasingly needed.

A *center* was described by Harvard president Nathan Pusey as "an administrative device for assembling scholars from different disciplines and departments around a shared interest. Centers are means for facilitating interdisciplinary assaults on complex fields of investigation." The proliferation of these entities was to his mind testimony to the manner in which the search for new knowledge was "now pursued increasingly in areas which fall outside the traditional boundaries of earlier delimited fields of study" (i.e. disciplines).[9] In more prosaic terms, the distinguishing features of *centers* were that their participants largely remained rooted in established departments; the research undertaken was, like departmental research, predominantly academic in nature; but the enterprise was sponsored by outside agencies out of nonacademic or practical interests in these "complex fields of investigation." *Centers* essentially conducted academic research that was supported for ulterior motives. The tensions inherent in this dual orientation were evident in their operations.

The Russian Research Center at Harvard could be considered prototypical. The Carnegie Corporation took the initiative in creating the Center in order to focus greater academic attention on the Soviet Union. Given the importance of the Soviets in the postwar world, it reasoned that more and better information about them was urgently needed. The Corporation was particularly interested in having Harvard make such a commitment, since its preeminent stature would legitimate the field.[10] After some informal contacts set the stage, a pilot program was begun in the fall of 1947. A five-year grant of $75,000 allowed full operations to begin early in 1948.[11]

The Russian Research Center was set up to be exclusively a research organization. Participating faculty continued to carry on their teaching responsibilities within their respective departments. Its Executive Committee represented the departments of Social Relations, Government, History, Economics, Law, and Slavic Languages. The members of the Center—faculty on part-time assignment, postdoctoral research associates and graduate fellows—were drawn predominantly from the first three of those departments. The Center's primary objective was to enhance intellectual understanding of the Soviet Union, specifically by enlarging the body of academic knowledge, disseminating that knowledge to the scholarly and educated public, and training additional scholars in this field. The Center also had an abiding commitment to interdisciplinarity—to provide new interpretations and new methodologies by bridging disciplinary boundaries.[12] Such a mission produced tension along two separate axes: between academic knowledge and ulterior purposes, and between interdisciplinarity and departmental ties. Nor were these tensions peculiar to the Russian Research Center; they were rather inherent to an extradepartmental unit with extra-academic goals. The manner in which these tensions evolved at the Russian Research Center indicates the general evolutionary course that *centers* seemed to follow.

Early publicity from the Center clearly emphasized its external mission: "to study Russian institutions and behavior in an effort to determine the mainsprings of the international actions and policy of the Soviet Union." This sentiment echoed the expectations of the Carnegie Corporation that the Harvard Center would "bring expert knowledge to the aid of those officials who must conduct day-to-day negotiations with the Russians."[13] Probably the closest it came to furthering these nonacademic objectives was an extensive Refugee Interview Project supported by the Air Force Human Resources Research Center. Whatever its usefulness for the Air Force, the data from this undertaking were nevertheless utilized at the Center for a number of scholarly monographs. By the end of its first decade, the practical mission of the Center was only ritualistically invoked, whereas it became almost strident about the academic nature of its activities. The Center claimed not to engage in directed research and not to hire professional staff for prescribed investigations, while stressing rigorous adherence "to the standards of scholarship of the accepted disciplines."[14] This emphasis was clearly preferred by the Harvard faculty.

Basic to the existence of *centers* was the reality that the crucial function of evaluation remained lodged with academic departments. They bore the chief responsibility for recommending promotion, awarding tenure, and certifying Ph.D.s. This fact of life was reflected in the Russian Research Center. Tenured members, who had attained eminence in their own fields, felt free to dabble in those of their neighbors; but junior faculty perforce had to be mindful of those "standards of scholarship of the accepted disciplines." As a result, interdisciplinarity remained an elusive ideal. A review committee noted that the Center could not itself make appointments, and thus could not directly recruit top figures in the field; it was weak at the intermediate, pre-tenure level, where career considerations made disciplinary criteria paramount; and graduate students and postdocs remained closely bound through departments to the reward structures of their respective disciplines.[15] One review committee member concluded that the Center had done a "superb job . . . in creating an atmosphere of mutual tolerance," but "the opportunities for interdisciplinary use of concepts and of ideas have been largely neglected or overlooked."[16]

One commitment that the Russian Research Center quite consciously set out to fulfill was that of enlarging the literature in this field. The first ten years of work produced 34 books and 350 articles or book chapters.[17] Some of these writings pertained rather narrowly to a single discipline, and some helped to fill out the corpus of what soon became the curriculum for Russian Studies. Moreover, given the difficulty facing Americans who wished to study the Soviet Union during these years, most of this work would not have been done without explicit institutional encouragement. Nevertheless, given relatively secure funding and the persistence of departmental hegemony, the Center's work gravitated toward the academic/disciplinary objectives to which faculty were predisposed. In this respect the history of the Russian Research Center foreshadowed the development of area studies centers generally in American universities.

This process has been termed the "academic enclosure" of area studies and their centers: "it was not that international studies academics . . . set out to make international studies a wholly academic enterprise, but rather in their zeal to advance international studies within the university, they consistently neglected the needs of the enterprise outside the university." Instead of providing training in foreign affairs for future businessmen, teachers or civil servants, these scholars reproduced more academics; instead of broadening public understanding of international problems, they communicated among each other.[18] At the centers in which these programs were lodged, conditions favored the displacement of the original motives of sponsors by the underlying academic goals of scholars. This drift was not confined only to area studies centers, but rather was inherent in the constitution of *centers*. The dynamics change, however, as one moves along the continuum away from departmental research and toward *institutes*.

The salient feature of a university *institute*, viewed as an ideal type, is the closer nexus between the nature of research performed and its utility for sponsors. In some cases, direct interest is such that if one *institute* would not perform the research another would be found that could. More often, given the inevitable entrepreneurship of ongoing *institutes*, research contracts expressed both the needs of the sponsor and the distinctive research capabilities of the *institute*. The fecundity of the research programs of individual professors was responsible for the creation of some *institutes*, whereas others resulted entirely from external initiatives. Universities agreed to host *institutes* for a mixture of reasons: to retain the loyalties of key faculty; to acquire specialized facilities; to provide services to state or federal government; or to enhance institutional prestige. The fact that externally supported *institutes* imposed a comparatively small financial burden—generally space and overhead expenses—was also a factor. *Institutes* were particularly valuable for providing graduate students with opportunities for training, employment and dissertation topics. They could also have pronounced effects in enhancing the research capabilities of faculty. In both of these situations, though, the benefits tended to be limited to the small group directly concerned with that particular specialty. Given the importance of the research results to the sponsor (as opposed to research for academic recognition), *insti-*

tutes were often led to employ nonfaculty professionals as full-time researchers. More than any other characteristic, the presence of professional researchers distinguished *institutes* from *centers*. Often the director too was a full-time, non-teaching appointee. The *institute* staff might thus be significantly removed from academic departments and the imperatives of academic evaluation. University oversight was exercised rather indirectly through an executive board or advisory committee.[19]

The incorporation of survey research into universities after the war provides a good example of institute dynamics. The principal units all had extraacademic origins and were products to some extent of new federal interests. As large organizations, virtually self-financed, and difficult to incorporate within existing administrative controls, such institutes presented new problems to university administrators. The inescapably applied character of their work often distanced them from colleagues in related academic departments.[20] The result was that several lines of tension affected their development.

The Michigan Institute for Social Research (ISR) developed out of a wartime survey unit of the Department of Agriculture headed by Rensis Likert. After the war he sought affiliation with an academic institution in order to investigate basic scientific problems of survey research. His group was accepted by Michigan on a trial basis in June 1946, and quickly made permanent as the Survey Research Center. The Regents instructed, however, that the Center was to be financially self-supporting from the proceeds of grants and contracts, and that it would "impose no burden upon the general funds budget of the university."[21] A year and a half later it was joined by another migratory research group, the Research Center for Group Dynamics, which aimed to study group life scientifically in natural and laboratory settings in order to address social problems. Established at MIT in 1945, it had been forced to find a new home after the death of its founder. In 1949 the two centers were officially amalgamated within ISR.

With no support from the university, ISR depended on performing quantitative social research for industry, foundations, and especially the federal government. In 1946, a series of annual surveys of consumer finance was initiated for the Federal Reserve Board; problems of organizing and managing human activity were studied for the ONR; and attitudes of people living near large atomic facilities were surveyed for the AEC. During the early years, virtually all of the Survey Research Center's revenues came from federal contracts. Somewhat later, General Motors commissioned a report on public perceptions of the role of large corporations. The Institute inaugurated an ongoing analysis of voting behavior with the support of the Carnegie Corporation, and began an extensive data-gathering project, the Detroit Area File, at the behest of the Ford Foundation.

By 1950 the ISR budget had climbed to over $800,000, and the Institute itself had established a national reputation for leadership in survey research techniques. Because ISR received no direct support from the University, it was permitted to retain the overhead on the contracts it received. These funds soon accumulated to a sizable reserve that could be employed flexibly to further the Institute's research role—a luxury few other research institutes enjoyed. During the 1950s it gradually acquired some permanent institutional support. Staff were paid for any teaching or service they performed, and the university accepted responsibility for the directors' salaries.[22] Still, the nature of ISR's status caused some discomfort. It complained that reliance upon short-term contracts to perform specific pieces of research precluded long-range planning or the development of an integrated program. Nor could it provide for activities related to research, like publication or conferences.[23] In other words, ISR manifested a clear proclivity to move toward a more academic posture, but was held rather tightly to its applied mission by the character of its support and its lack of articulation with university departments.

Despite the inherent separateness of externally funded institute research, the degree of closeness or remoteness from departmental/academic research constituted an important variable in the nature of an *institute*. For example, the Columbia Bureau of Applied Social Research (f. 1944) was in roughly the same business as ISR during the late 1940s, yet it managed to fulfill a dynamic role as an adjunct to the Columbia sociology department.[24] The initial mission of the Bureau—marketing research for the publishing and communications industry— was of dubious academic respectability. And for good reason. According to the Bureau's early director, these commercial studies "provide data and experience. But it takes alot of work and time to 'sell' them; and often in order to complete them, the staff has to neglect other work which has higher scientific priority."[25] In time, however, individuals managed to use this institutional base for their own academic purposes. As a result, during its postwar heyday (c. 1948–58) the Bureau contributed substantially to the development of academic sociology.

The Bureau has been described as the organizational expression of the intellectual commitments of Paul Lazersfeld, its founder and sometime director.[26] The status and the academic tone of the Bureau was also heightened by the close involvement as an associate director of Robert K. Merton, the star of Columbia sociology. Younger faculty, like the prolific Seymour Martin Lipset, contributed greatly to the Bureau's output. These members of the sociology department, in particular, succeeded in imposing an increasingly academic cast to the Bureau's work. Lazersfeld, above all, projected onto specific research projects his own deep commitment to the discovery of fundamental explanations of social phenomena through mathematical analysis. In this manner some rather mundane research questions were elevated into classic sociological studies. Also significant was the involvement of sociology department graduate students in the work of the Bureau. Training was a major objective of the Bureau and reinforced the concern with fundamental explanation and methodology. Seminars spontaneously formed to ponder issues emerging from current research. Graduate students worked and reworked the Bureau data sets to produce, singly or in combination with their teachers, numerous monographs.[27]

The interaction between the Columbia sociology department and the Bureau of Applied Social Research in its heyday produced an evanescent burst of creativity that significantly enriched the discipline. Their relationship nevertheless remained at all times problematic. Lazarsfeld himself was deeply concerned with the nature and the potential of university research institutes. He conceptualized two antithetical types. A "faculty research facility" (analogous to *centers*) which basically served to facilitate the research projects of faculty. Research topics would depend entirely upon the interests of individual faculty, and thus little coordination or continuity of research could be sustained. Lazarsfeld was a proponent of a second type—autonomous research units having their own directors and staff. He sensed, however, that their effectiveness was continually inhibited in the American university by the precariousness of external funding and by the hegemony of departments. The Bureau of Applied Social Research, he felt, was forced to function in part as a faculty facility even as it aspired to be an autonomous general-purpose research unit.[28]

Over the long term, in fact, the ambiguity of the Bureau's mission tended to preclude continuity in its research. During the most creative period, the unifying theme of the Bureau, in terms of work and community, was the preoccupation with developing new methodologies of applied social research. This spirit breathed intellectual excitement even into sponsored projects. By the end of the 1950s, however, the major innovations had not only been accomplished, but were being widely replicated at other institutions. They could no longer provide a theme for unifying and extending the Bureau's work.

Continuity was further obstructed by the Bureau's unequal relationship with the sociology department. The department (and other Columbia social science departments as well) had no incentive to gear its hiring to the content or the style of the Bureau's research. Thus, when a dynamo of Bureau energy like Seymour Martin Lipset left Columbia, no appointment was made to sustain the momentum in political sociology. Bureau staff who developed expertise in particular areas were in fact often lured away by academic appointments elsewhere, since the department could not be induced to offer competitive appointments. The Bureau was thus a shifting kaleidoscope of personnel and interests, and its patterns of research were influenced by external patrons.[29]

In retrospect it became apparent that the *institutes* that cleaved most closely to their stated purposes were those that specialized.[30] Some specialized in research techniques (the analogue for the natural sciences being *institutes* built around a scientific instrument). Michigan's ISR would fit this pattern, as would the National Opinion Research Center at Chicago. Steady work was required to support a permanent professional staff. For example, ISR conducted analyses of every national election since 1948. Other *institutes* specialized in subject matter (here the natural science analogues are probably most abundant in biomedical sciences, where stable funding has long been available).

The closest that the Bureau came to subject specialization occurred in the 1960s. As the federal government became the predominant funder of Bureau research, several clusters developed, each oriented toward different aspects of social policy. This development fragmented the Bureau into distinct groups with few shared interests and little need for interaction. In addition, as the work of the Bureau was increasingly oriented toward policymakers in federal agencies, it became more estranged still from the Columbia sociology department.[31] Eventually, the unsatisfactory nature of this relationship prompted reorganization.

The Bureau was absorbed into a more comprehensive Social Science Research Center intended to serve all the interested departments—explicitly the kind of "facility" that Lazarsfeld had wished to avoid.

Lazarsfeld's powerful advocacy of social research institutes nevertheless served to illuminate the dynamics of these units. The type of general-purpose research institute that he favored would seem to lie between the ideal types of *centers* and *institutes,* and thus would experience considerable tension between the value system of departments and disciplines, on one side, and the services demanded by external sponsors on the other.[32] For a classic *institute,* like ISR, priorities are clearer: while there is a common proclivity for staff to make small contributions to university instruction by teaching graduate students, the ultimate goals of the unit are derived from its specialized mission and the external support it garners.[33] The influence of the client becomes even more dominant at the programmatic extreme of the organized research spectrum.

At *federal contract research laboratories* the sponsors paid the full costs and determined the general objectives and work plans of the units. The universities, as contractors, largely provided managerial services. In their internal operations as research organizations these laboratories resembled federal or industrial laboratories more than university research units. In fact, one might legitimately ask why they operated under university contracts at all.

Each of the contract laboratories was a special case, so that circumstance largely accounted for university affiliations. As explained above, most were simply continuations of wartime arrangements. For the government this relationship carried certain advantages for the retention and treatment of personnel. For universities, the contract laboratories cost nothing and brought handsome management fees. They also strengthened one particular facet of a university's research capability. The relationships between universities and laboratories were nevertheless inherently problematic from the outset.

The Applied Physics Laboratory at Johns Hopkins was a case in point.[34] Its director, Merle Tuve, wanted the laboratory to be closely integrated with the university after the war in order to preserve the tight, fruitful coupling of science and technological development. The university could neither make such a financial commitment nor induce its departments to appoint the numerous Lab personnel. Instead, an arm's-length arrangement was worked out: the university gave Lab scientists appointments on campus in a new Institute for Cooperative Research, but in return insisted that the Lab eschew the actual production of weapons. The true nature of this relationship became apparent soon afterward. The Lab found it necessary to assert control again over the production of the guided missile system it had designed, and the university, with little leverage over the Lab, had no choice but to acquiesce. Contract research centers danced more to the tunes of their federal paymasters than those of their nominal university managers.

Still, the contract research centers were not merely creatures of their military patrons. The history of the Jet Propulsion Laboratory (JPL) at the California Institute of Technology reveals pervasive tensions on both sides of this relationship.[35] The Lab was justified to the trustees immediately after the war for usual reasons: it would uphold the international reputation of Caltech in the fields of aeronautics, and jet propulsion; it would maintain at no cost a large base of scientific and engineering expertise; and it would conduct significant amounts of basic, unclassified science. All this proved true, although the last point was sometimes in doubt. But the JPL in fact had little interaction with Caltech, and there was always a sizable faction among the faculty who regarded it as incompatible with the school's academic mission. The patrons—first the army and then NASA—for their part found the relative independence of JPL to be a source of various irritations. Their attempts to assert greater control over the laboratory, just like those of Caltech, were partially effective at best. In the long run, the organizational self-interest of the Lab itself largely prevailed. JPL preserved its special mission and its special status; Caltech never seriously entertained the possibility of relinquishing its ties to JPL in aeronautical and space sciences, nor of forgoing its management fee.

The incompatibility of the laboratories and their university sponsors was rooted in the highly applied nature of their work. The JPL, for example was primarily an engineering culture, while that of Caltech was strongly scientific. At the Applied Physics Laboratory only about 5 percent of expenditures were regarded as basic research.[36] The classified nature of most research created a further barrier to academic linkages. The exceptions were the large particle accelerators funded by the AEC. Scientists at these facilities conducted basic research, but they were supported for reasons that were scarcely disinterested. It was a truism of postwar science policy that the atomic bomb had been made possible by the fundamental discoveries of the interwar years. Who could say if the study of mesons would not be as valuable as the study of neutrons had been? Thus, the most expensive scientific instruments to build and to operate, designed for one of the most basic kinds of scientific research, possessed a compelling national security rationale for public support.[37]

When measured in dollars, the postwar federal contract laboratories carried great weight in the university research economy. In 1951-52, twenty-four such laboratories consumed 47 percent of federal research expenditures at nonprofit institutions;[38] however, a great deal of this research was peripheral—in location and in character—to the main university research effort. Some laboratories were (like the Applied Physics Lab) located far from campus; the topics investigated were usually of interest to only a handful of faculty and graduate students; and the classified nature of much research placed it outside of academic communication channels. The sphere of research dominated by the federal patron was actually even greater than would appear. The contract laboratories were a shifting category.[39] In addition, other large concentrations of defense-related research of essentially the same character existed at a number of universities. The Willow Run laboratories of the University of Michigan, for example, conducted more classified research in the early 1950s than all the sponsored research on the rest of the Michigan campus. For Cornell, the Aeronautical Laboratory in Buffalo occupied an analogous position. And, as will be seen in the next chapter, several large laboratories at MIT worked almost exclusively with Defense Department funds.[40]

4. An Autonomous Research Mission and Its Discontents

The postwar proliferation of organized research units, and their equivalents, signified a new departure for American universities. Previously, research had with few exceptions been linked with the basic teaching mission in that those who performed research were predominantly teaching faculty members, assisted by their graduate students. Henceforth, research at a growing number of institutions would evolve into a separate and autonomous role. Universities would have been unlikely to reach this state of affairs on their own, but after the war experience they felt duty-bound to perpetuate the role of performing government-sponsored, mission-oriented research. Even on those campuses where faculty committees weighed the perils and the prospects, sufficiently flexible guidelines were invariably approved to permit organized research to grow according to the availability of federal support—not its appropriateness to academic goals.[1]

An autonomous research mission fit awkwardly into an organizational structure that was predicated on instruction. Academic departments were the basic organizational units, and they defined their purpose in terms of teaching students. Similarly, the entire financial structure of the university was erected for the purpose of supporting academic activities. The extreme looseness of this structure allowed for many anomalies and incongruities; but an autonomous research mission raised difficulties that were too glaring to fit within this system.

Research personnel presented one such problem. The University of California, for example, faced the situation where organized research units were offering scientists far larger salaries than teaching departments could afford. The university was consequently induced to establish a parallel system of appointments and compensation for research personnel (1952). Research appointees were denied, however, many of the prerogatives of regular faculty, thus according them a form of second-class citizenship.[2] Other universities sooner or later established similar arrangements.

Financially, the most serious problem pertained to overhead costs. The government accepted the responsibility of paying the total costs of large defense projects, and when these were calculated according to a formula adopted in 1947 the indirect cost component equaled 40–45 percent of salaries and wages. Other agencies took the view that in funding "academic" types of research, particularly investigator-initiated proposals, the universities ought to bear some of the expense. In practice, the Public Health Service settled on 8 percent of project costs for overhead, NSF in 1951 announced an overhead rate of 15 percent, and the AEC bargained over each project. The private foundations generally paid no indirect costs. The research universities frequently and forcefully made the case that, in the aggregate, organized research was often a net drain upon university resources. Reimbursement rates were raised during the 1950s, indicating the gradual acceptance of the universities' view. The issue has been perennially divisive, depending as it does upon fine distinctions of accounting; but there can be no doubt that it was particularly troubling to the strapped private universities at this juncture.[3]

Finally, the overall process of administering and accounting for research grants became so large and complex that separate administrative structures had to be put into place. One by one, under various titles, universities established offices of grants and contracts to oversee this process. These offices, however, could do little more than standardize procedures of solicitation, accounting and reporting. The essence of the process—the research itself—remained beyond their ken. All of these were practical matters that, with varying amounts of controversy, gradually received practical solutions. Behind them lay some less tangible but more troubling misgivings about the new research role that universities had assumed.

At the conclusion of World War II universities accepted the necessity for a permanent federal role in the support of university research. Five years later, as the impact of the Cold War began to dominate the research economy, university leaders began to express misgivings about the results. The continuum of organized research, extending from the projects of individual faculty to the federal contract research centers, carried consequences or implications that were disquieting to the accustomed academic regimen. The concerns can be grouped under the general rubrics of distortion, displacement, dependence and domination.

Distortion of university research.   In arguing for the creation of a national science foundation, Vannevar Bush had warned that, unless counteracted, applied research would tend to drive basic research out of the university.[4] The preponderance of 'interested' funders in the postwar research economy seemed to threaten, at least, that academic investigators might foresake the puzzles of disciplinary paradigms in order to pursue problems of their patron's choosing. A particularly egregious example of distortion was presented by classified research, the results of which were withheld from the body of academic knowledge. James B. Conant, in a widely noted statement, declared in 1947 that no secret research would be conducted on Harvard's campus. Conant's policy was endorsed in principle by most other research universities, but rarely followed in practice. For one thing, there were several degrees of classification. In certain fields, particularly those supported by the AEC, security restrictions were impossible to avoid. MIT even taught a classified course in nuclear engineering.[5] Classified research was often conducted in separate, deliberately isolated wartime facilities, which were sometimes officially designated to be 'off-campus.'[6] Finally, another kind of distortion was caused by the preponderance of federal research funds in the natural sciences. Foundations attempted to provide compensatory support for the social sciences, but there too the incidence was skewed (see Chapter 4). As a result, two classes of faculty became evident on campus—those who had the advantages of being associated with organized research units, and those who did not.[7]

Displacement of other university functions.   The review committee of the Harvard Russian Research Center was critical of the fact that senior faculty devoted one-half of their time to the Center, but that their departments received no compensation for the corresponding loss of their services.[8] This point illustrates a situation that could be generalized considerably. The hypertrophy of research in certain areas inevitably demanded faculty time commitments that had to be made at the expense of other activities, notably undergraduate teaching. Long reluctant to make additional appointments on the basis of external research support, universities tended to juggle their several missions with the awareness that research now carried more weight.

Dependence upon external research support. The chemistry chairman at Rochester has provided an account of his department's dependence on outside funds (1950), most of which came from federal sources. These funds paid 35 percent of the department payroll, bought 42 percent of its equipment and supplies, supported ten of eleven postdocs and most of the advanced graduate students. This situation too might be generalized. By 1950 funds for organized research were an integral part of the operations of departments in the physical sciences and could not be replaced by institutional resources should the need arise. His objection might also have echoed through university science departments: "the ever present uncertainty about the continuation of funds . . . conspires to make the life of the Department Chairman and of many of his faculty members miserable."[9] From the universities' point of view, raising research funds was a process over which they had little control. It depended overwhelmingly upon the relationship between the investigator and the patron. Universities were thus dependent in their research role upon short-term grants and contracts, which precluded prudent planning.

Domination by the federal government. University attitudes toward the federal patron were colored by the onset of the Cold War and Korean War, which portended the permanent militarization of university research.[10] McCarthyism followed, projecting a tangible threat of ideological domination.[11] Against this backdrop the interlude of disenchantment with the federally dominated research economy becomes understandable. The final report of the Commission on Financing Higher Education reflected widespread ambivalence. While recognizing that "the nation has vastly benefited from the strengthening of basic science made possible by this federal aid," the Commission nevertheless "reached the unanimous conclusion that we as a nation should call a halt at this time to the introduction of new programs of federal aid to colleges and universities."[12] They reasoned that the independence of institutions of higher education stemmed from diversity and competition within the system, and that these qualities would be lost "if higher education is subject to further influence from the federal government." Federal power would eventuate in federal control; and "direct federal control would in the end produce uniformity, mediocrity and compliance."[13]

The premonitions of the Commission, of course, did not come to pass in the 1950s.[14] More interestingly, the entire litany of worries about sponsored research had little impact upon the evolution of the university research system. Organized research activities on campus burgeoned, despite lingering concerns about negative effects. As late as 1959, for example, a closed meeting of the leading private universities formally stated their opposition to the distortion of research objectives, the displacement especially of undergraduate teaching, the loss of administrative freedom that dependence had brought, and their vulnerability to federal domination.[15] Why, then, had they failed to act upon these concerns?

Research itself was the domain of individual faculty members. Universities were structured to create the conditions for research and to evaluate the results, but faculty themselves retained an inviolate intellectual sovereignty over the substance of their research and over the areas of expertise that they were charged with teaching. Universities did in fact erect elaborate procedures for overseeing research arrangements, which generally included written approval from department heads, deans, and offices of grants and contracts. But while these procedures could lay down guidelines, they could not effectively make judgments about distortion, displacement, or dependence. When a faculty member and a funding agency could agree upon the desirability of a research project, unless a flagrant breach of university policy were evident, universities were obliged to accede.

Take the case of the Cornell Aeronautical Laboratory in Buffalo. The assumption of control of this facility by the university, at a some financial risk, was arranged by the Engineering dean for the virtually exclusive benefit of the School of Aeronautical Engineering. The Cornell historian writes that "if the acquirement [sic] of the laboratory had been put to a Faculty vote, it would certainly have been rejected."[16] But the aspirations of aeronautical engineering were at issue, not the misgivings of the rest of the faculty. The possible award of an AEC computing facility provides another illustration. When interested universities were invited to comment upon the plan all but one were highly critical of the terms offered by the AEC. Yet, all of these same universities overcame their objections and submitted proposals for the facility.[17] When the acquisition of resources for research was at stake, it would seem that research universities could not say no.

The proliferation of organized research, then, reflected both the program-driven needs of sponsors and the aspirations of individual academics. The complicity of universities in this process was unavoidable. If universities wished to retain the loyalty of their most productive faculty, they had to respect the intellectual sovereignty of faculty in their fields. In practice, this invariably implied accommodating research projects that faculty arranged. Universities controlled this decentralized process only after the fact.[18] Thus, in the first decade of the postwar era organized research grew in a highly irregular fashion, but by about 1955 organized research was clearly the norm. In fact, the more organized research units a university engendered, the higher their scientific eminence was likely to be. By then the dynamics of the university research system—rules, tactics and strategies—were becoming increasingly evident to all the players. During this formative decade, however, institutions were compelled to adapt, each in its own fashion, to the new conditions created by the postwar research economy.

3

The Development
of Universities
in the Postwar Era

The aftermath of World War II was a time of fluidity in the university research system. Institutions that had conducted large amounts of wartime research were best positioned to exploit the unfolding opportunities of the new federally dominated research economy, but their success was by no means foreordained. A great scramble for personnel occurred as scientists who had relocated for wartime research decided between returning to their former institutions or accepting another offer. Assembling research teams with proven credentials was a highly competitive endeavor that required the commitment of substantial institutional resources. So too was the effort to arrange large-scale support from new federal agencies. In these uncharted waters, commitments to undertake organized research were made hastily; somewhat later the consequences of these haphazard arrangements began to be apparent. Universities then confronted, each in its own fashion, the consequences of a transformed research role.

The Massachusetts Institute of Technology not only housed the largest amount of war research on and around its campus, but was also among the most aggressive institutions in laying the basis for its continuation. The University of California had at its Berkeley campus an insuperable advantage over other institutions in the person of E. O. Lawrence and in the makings for the world's largest particle accelerator. Its dominance in nuclear physics consequently paved the way for a phenomenal growth in both the quantity of research and the quality of academic departments. Not every institution was prepared for the new postwar climate. Yale felt at once the urge to participate, the fear of being left behind, and deep misgivings about assuming an autonomous research role. Its grudging and prolonged adaptation represented a third pattern for coming to terms with the postwar research environment.

1. The Massachusetts Institute of Technology

When the MIT physics department evaluated its needs after a decade of postwar development, it stressed that "a healthy and vigorous research program . . . is the key item. . . . On this research program depends the quality of *everything* else that the physics staff undertakes."[1] Accordingly, MIT set its priorities with research on top, followed in order by the education of physicists and service to the rest of the institution. In microcosm, the attitude of the physics department mirrored what had become the postwar philosophy of MIT as a whole: research was paramount, and the other functions of training scientists and engineers, and of serving industry and government, were in a sense downstream from this central and overriding commitment. Like other research universities, MIT expressed a preference for conducting fundamental research rather than applied or developmental work; but in an engineering milieu those terms were interpreted loosely. In practice, MIT had comparatively few qualms about the nature of the research that it would conduct. Whatever research topics the faculty found interesting would, besides creating new knowledge, enlarge the Institute's resources in terms of income, manpower, and equipment. In turn, these contributions would facilitate MIT's educational and service missions. With this outlook, MIT was able to exploit the potential of the postwar research economy more fully than any other university.

Given its traditions, MIT was well suited for this role. Throughout the twentieth century it had been the country's premier engineering school, even allowing for the achievements of Caltech, its smaller clone on the West Coast. Under the leadership of Karl Compton (1930–49) emphasis had been placed on bolstering this strength in engineering with greater emphasis on basic science, particularly physics; but on the eve of World War II, 80 percent of MIT students still enrolled in the Engineering School (1939), and the Institute preserved its close relationship with industry.[2] Research at MIT received a tremendous impetus from wartime research contracts. The amalgamation of physics and electrical engineering in the Radiation Laboratory not only proved to be extraordinarily productive, but also demonstrated the complementarity of basic and applied research. This combination was what MIT wished to exemplify. The continuation of this type of research in peacetime in the Research Laboratory of Electronics (RLE) was thus a natural, but also a fateful step.

The RLE, as will be seen, was far more than just another organized research unit. Its style, internal dynamics, and multifarious achievements epitomized postwar MIT. It was hardly accidental that two former directors advanced to become MIT presidents. The RLE budget when added to other research contracts helped to make MIT's postwar research budget of $8.3 million dwarf its academic budget of $4.7 million (1946–47)—a relationship that would not change.[3] Nor did this represent, as did many other large federal research contracts, activities sequestered in remote or restricted locations. RLE united the institution's two most vigorous departments and was central to its vitality. At MIT research really was the principal activity.

The proliferation of organized research units testifies to this orientation. A census in 1978 identified sixty-five such units that had been created since World War II, thirty-six of which were still in operation. They were described as evolving devices "for dealing with the disorderly conditions produced by massive additions to the body of learning, rising demands for the immediate application of knowledge in the public interest, and the availability of a great deal of money."[4] Each of these facets of organized research—the knowledge base, sponsors' demands, and the availability of support—is important for appreciating the role of research in the development of MIT.

Given the worries prevalent at research universities about dependence and displacement, it is noteworthy how MIT's relatively uninhibited approach to research funding turned this situation to advantage. Because research at MIT financially outweighed education, research was able to shoulder a good share of the costs of running the institution. As early as 1947–48, MIT was charging to its research contracts $1 million of a total academic payroll of $3.8 million. The same year research contracts in excess of $13 million yielded more than $2 million for overhead. It soon became evident, in fact, that contract research could more than pay for itself. In the physics department, for example, the actual salary budget increased in the postwar decade (1946–56) from $400,000 to $600,000, but the amount charged to the academic budget decreased from $400,000 to $200,000. In the same interval the charges for general expenses and special departmental research remained constant at an arbitrary $17,000.[5] The department during these years expanded from thirty-four to forty-eight regular appointments, the majority of the additions being full professors. In a given semester 70 percent of them might be engaged in classroom teaching.[6] In short, MIT was able to cultivate one of the country's largest physics departments—highly eminent as well—while actually lightening the burden on its treasury.

The abundance of federal research contracts probably gave postwar MIT more flexibility in terms of operating income than other private universities. Significantly, it employed this to raise faculty salaries to levels prevailing at leading East Coast universities—something that MIT had never been able to manage in the past. It also continued to benefit from its traditional close ties with industry. In 1947 MIT made a special appeal to oil companies for support of research in the new Laboratory for Nuclear Science and Engineering. In return for access to the Lab and its findings, plus other considerations, six major companies promised $600,000. These arrangements were broadened into an Industrial Associates Plan that brought in more than $1 million annually by the mid-fifties.[7] The limiting factor in the postwar development of MIT was not operating income, but capital with which to underwrite its expanding activities. Here, too, MIT was somewhat more fortunate than its peers. It was one of the few research universities able to undertake a capital campaign before the Korean War, which brought it $25 million (1949–50).[8] In financial terms, then, MIT took advantage of "the availability of a great deal of money" for sponsored research, and entered the 1950s in enviable fiscal condition. But inevitably this rapid expansion raised questions about the overall development of the institution.

During the late 1940s a faculty committee undertook an extensive educational survey of the Institute to assess its current state and future directions. The committee's report, named for its chairman, Warren K. Lewis, set a number of guidelines for development.[9] An exercise of this nature typically becomes an occasion for affirming and expressing the preponderant academic values of the faculty. The Lewis Report recommended, in effect, that the prosperity of the Institute, based as it was upon programmatic research, be utilized to achieve several important academic goals. The Report was critical of excessive vocationalism, and wished to commit the Institute to a broader educational mission. It urged the Institute to elevate the social science and humanities departments to the status of a school, thus becoming more like other universities. Concerned about the postwar growth, it advised that expansion be limited by the ability to attract high-caliber students. At the same time, it emphasized that new commitments ought to be made selectively, in fields where MIT could clearly excel—specifically areas that could benefit from an environment of science and technology.

The Lewis Committee exhibited the same academic proclivities with respect to sponsored research. It was naturally mindful of the great contribution that research was making to the educational mission of the Institute. MIT's numerous state-of-the-art laboratories simply would not have existed without outside sponsorship, and the bulk of MIT's graduate students derived financial assistance as well as contact with real-life problems by working in these labs. Still, the Report asked that "some reasonable balance should be achieved between commitments to sponsored research and to the fulfillment of [MIT's] normal obligations as an academic institution." It particularly warned against the over-commitment of faculty time, the undertaking of extensive development or design work to the detriment of fundamental research, and the persistence of large projects after their scientific potential had begun to wane. The Report particularly stressed that research should not be accepted solely to generate income for the institution.[10]

In order to avoid these dangers, the Lewis Report urged that the administration be vigilant in its role as research manager, evaluating the contribution of new or ongoing research projects to the educational mission of the Institute. It acknowledged, however, the inescapable reality of the postwar research economy: "in the final analysis, the scope and character of sponsored research at M.I.T. is determined by the faculty." Research relationships were voluntarily entered into by individual faculty, who considered them to be the most productive use of their time and the Institute's facilities. Thus, "faculty policy on sponsored research is the aggregate of these individual judgements."[11] In effect, then, the university administration was to oversee and to assure the academic respectability of a research policy that was determined primarily by sponsors' demands and faculty interests. In this situation faculty and sponsors together possessed a decisive leverage over an institution. This was all the more the case at MIT, where research predominated, where the sponsor was in most cases the Department of Defense, and where the official stance toward sponsored research was permissive.

Sponsored research made a powerful contribution to the growth of academic knowledge at MIT, while also producing a cornucopia of technological achievements for sponsors. Confining sponsored research within the academic guidelines recommended by the Lewis Committee, and outwardly favored by the administration, consequently proved difficult. This tension was evident in the histories of some of the principal teaching and research units.

The Research Laboratory of Electronics.   The RLE has assumed a legendary stature among organized research units. Jerome B. Wiesner, RLE Director (1952–61) and Institute President (1971–80), called it "an almost ideal research environment"; and found it to be "a unique and wonderful experience to spend a major part of [his] adult life and perhaps the most enjoyable period of it in this atmosphere."[12] The conditions that engendered such reverence were no doubt the freedom to pursue basic research questions wherever they might lead, the assurance of secure and ample funding, and the intellectual dynamism produced by the confluence of seminal work in several complementary fields. The RLE clearly was more than a continuation of wartime research.

RLE inherited facilities and equipment from the wartime Radiation Laboratory, along with a broad mandate to study phenomena associated with microwave radiation. Most crucial, however, were the liberal terms by which the joint services (ONR, the Air Force, and the Signal Corps) provided support. Initial annual support of $600,000 was given for the RLE to allocate as it saw fit for basic research and graduate education in this general area. In return, the services wished "to maintain close liaison between the military and the frontiers of electronic science and engineering"; and to have "a laboratory from which the military services can draw competent technical help at critical times . . . a research facility that can grow rapidly to meet a specific need."[13] Although a later generation would consider this to be a Faustian bargain, it was not so regarded at the time. MIT scientists and administrators became accustomed during the war to assisting the U.S. military in the defense of the country and accepted this assistance as a patriotic duty. They did not have to wait long for further opportunity.

Unlike the aloofness that characterized the relationship between ONR and most academic research, the services continuously utilized their access to RLE for assistance with military projects. From the outset the joint-services contract was supplemented by the continuation of classified research from the Radiation Laboratory. But soon the services had new needs to meet. In 1946 the Navy requested that the RLE develop a guidance system for the Meteor missile. According to one participant, "after much soul-searching, it was recognized that this was, indeed, an advanced engineering project, that both applied research and advanced development were required in its execution, and that it had many attractive features for engineering pedagogy."[14] Perhaps this was the case, but it also would have been difficult for MIT to say no to one of the RLE's principal sponsors. This pattern would become familiar: ingrained patriotism and plausible rationalizations invariably led to the acceptance of military programs.

The RLE was closely, although not officially, involved in a series of "Summer Studies" that MIT organized for the military. These were ad hoc groups of scientists assembled to consider intensively some broad area of concern. The conclusions that were drawn, not surprisingly, often called for additional, extended research projects. The availability and flexibility of RLE then facilitated the accomplishment of these tasks. The RLE became one of the central knots in a tangled skein of relationships between MIT and the military.[15]

The outbreak of the Korean War created conditions for increased military utilization of the RLE, as foreseen in the original agreement. In 1950 the Pentagon asked RLE to double its budget in order to accommodate applied military research projects.[16] Part of this additional work was connected with the beginning of an Air Force effort to design and build an early-warning strategic radar system. At the same time, an ad hoc group (Project Charles) was formed to consider the feasibility of this project and the desirability of MIT's undertaking it. The dimensions of this undertaking proved so massive that the creation of a separate organization was recommended. Accordingly, in 1951 the Lincoln Laboratory was established as a federal contract laboratory administered by MIT. Many of the military research projects at RLE were then transferred to the Lincoln Laboratory, and in fact the RLE director moved there as well. This mitosis would seem to have swung the balance at RLE back toward more fundamental research. In many ways, however, the two laboratories were joined in a single effort. Some graduate students pursued research at Lincoln, and Lincoln staff earned advanced degrees at the Institute; RLE and Lincoln spawned some sixty electronics firms; and Lincoln also became an ongoing sponsor of RLE research projects.[17]

The segregation of military hardware development from more academic types of research nevertheless helped to preserve the special qualities of the RLE. For some time thereafter the preponderance of support came from the joint services contract and was allocated at the discretion of the director. Over time the specific projects would become a larger part of the budget and the work, but the latitude allowed by the basic contract was the key to the intellectual dynamism of the RLE. A separate study would be needed to describe how the many lines of inquiry progressed, branched, or intertwined. Five distinct research groups existed at the Lab in 1946, ten in 1951, twenty-two in 1956, and thirty in 1961. By this last date eighteen of those groups belonged to a separate Division of Communication Sciences and Engineering (est. 1958) that had evolved from just one of the 1946 groups.[18]

To the extent that there was a common element to the multifarious activities of the communications groups it emanated from mathematician Norbert Wiener's seminal work on information and communication.[19] By the time his basic concepts were presented to the public in *Cybernetics* (1948), they had already become familiar within the RLE. Wiener himself played an active role in nurturing the implications of communications theory by holding seminars in his home and by personally kibbitzing on projects that caught his interest. These implications were relevant to a spectrum of topics ranging from the immediately practical to the highly theoretical. Among the former were applications of statistical communications theory to problems of military communication, to the theory and design of electric circuits, and to the building of MIT's pioneering digital computer. Applied to the way humans communicate, these theories posed fundamental questions for understanding the architecture and functioning of the brain (neurophysiology), brain-speech interconnections (communication biophysics), and the nature of speech and language. It was the investigation of this latter domain that gave rise to MIT's renowned linguistics department. Research in this area during the early 1950s focused on problems of speech analysis and machine translation that were closely related to engineering applications. After Noam Chomsky joined MIT and the RLE in 1955, the emphasis shifted to the study of syntax and the elaboration of a new approach to linguistics. Recognition of the importance of this work was quite rapid, and in 1961 a graduate program in linguistics was launched. Thus, in a decade and a half, this single research track cultivated in the RLE blossomed into a full-fledged department with an international reputation.[20]

The conclusion one active participant drew from the experiences of RLE was "that military support of university research can be extraordinarily fruitful for both parties."[21] Indeed, besides the case of linguistics, innumerable examples could be cited of RLE contributions to the academic development of MIT, with the physics and electrical engineering departments being the principal beneficiaries. RLE was an asset to teaching as well. In its first dozen years it engendered almost six hundred student theses.[22] The academic success of RLE, however, was facilitated by the hiving off of most weapons work in the Lincoln Laboratory. Where this kind of arm's-length relationship did not exist, the academic value of defense-sponsored research was more dubious.

The Center for International Studies (CIS).   The CIS differed appreciably from the *centers* characterized in Chapter 2. Like other MIT research units, it was created to meet the knowledge requirements of the federal government. Although interdisciplinarity was an early goal, it actually became mother to the department of political science. And, even though 'academic enclosure' of sorts was its eventual fate, the CIS long remained closely linked to the extra-academic mission of its sponsor.

In 1950 the State Department asked MIT for advice on overcoming the jamming of Western radio broadcasts into the Soviet Union. This initial seed, when given suitable academic cultivation, gave rise to an ad hoc study group (Project Troy) for the investigation of international communications. The group's report recommended the establishment of a permanent research organization by Harvard and MIT devoted to science and public policy. The entity that emerged more than a year later—the CIS—differed considerably from the original conception. Harvard declined to participate, leaving it solely an MIT enterprise. The State Department also withdrew, to be replaced as sole sponsor by the Central Intelligence Agency. The new Center was to be devoted to research aimed at solving "long-term problems of international policy which confront decision makers in government and private life."[23]

In fact, MIT was an odd place for the federal foreign policy establishment to turn for assistance since it possessed no programs in area studies or international affairs. Its few political scientists were located in a larger department of "economics and social science," where paramount importance lay with the former. Apparently, MIT was chosen for its pliability to government purposes, rather than for any intrinsic capabilities. The fact that the person chosen to direct the Center, Max Millikan, was returning from a position with the CIA lends credence to this supposition.

In only four years the new Center burgeoned into a substantial operation employing between seventy and eighty people. At the core were about six MIT faculty. They were supplemented by a revolving research contingent of postdocs, visiting faculty, and foreign guests.[24] All the social science disciplines were represented, but the center of gravity was clearly in political science. By 1956 the political scientists were reorganized as an autonomous section within the economics department. In 1962 they became a separate department with a graduate program, although still largely an emanation of the Center. The principal foci of CIS activity were economic/political development, communism, international communications, and military/foreign policy. Besides its core support from the CIA, the Center received foundation grants and government contracts for specific studies, as well as consistent assistance of diverse sorts from the Ford Foundation.

The close connections between the Center and the CIA caused certain misgivings in the MIT administration. As early as 1953 Provost Stratton warned that the kind of information-gathering that the Center was undertaking would inevitably implicate MIT in political decision-making. In 1956 President Killian expressed his concern over the foreign operations of the Center, and instructed Stratton to stay fully informed.[25] These concerns seem to have prompted the Center's Visiting Committee to pose some sharp questions at their next meeting. How could the Center reconcile its government support with the sponsorship of supposedly objective scholarship by researchers abroad, or with the objective analysis of U.S. policies? How could it justify the close relationship with people in government and the use of classified information in light of its academic mission of advancing knowledge? Director Max Millikan defended the Center, stressing the importance of its contribution to the government and the scrupulousness of its internal procedures. People in government were unable to perform the kind of in-depth analysis being done by the Center, and yet they needed this sort of information. In order to have contact with these 'operations' people, Center personnel had to have security clearances and access to classified material. Studies undertaken abroad or analyses of U.S. policy, he claimed, were undertaken only with private sources of funding, and thus were not compromised by CIA sponsorship.[26]

Millikan's explanations seem less than convincing in retrospect. Yet if one accepted, as MIT generally did, the validity of the overriding purpose of assisting the U.S. government, then it became difficult to find fault with the particulars of the Center's operations. The Visiting Committee and the administration basically accepted Millikan's version of the Center's activities, even though they were sensitive to the incompatibility of aspiring, on one hand, to contribute to the academic literature on international relations, while also advising the government on the conduct of foreign policy. Their temporizing solution was to recommend the academic strengthening of the Center through the recruitment of additional staff, and to hope for the attainment of stable long-range financing—ex the CIA.

The strains inherent in the Center's dual role became increasingly untenable as the political climate changed during the 1960s. Apologetics for American foreign policy, for which the Center became known, were received far differently during the Vietnam War than they had been during and after the Korean conflict.[27] Reliance upon CIA funding was cut back in 1963, and then terminated entirely in 1965. An $8 million grant from the Center's most generous benefactor, the Ford Foundation, aided the transition. In fact, throughout the 1960s the type of academic drift that the MIT administration had hoped for to some extent took place. The death of Max Millikan at the end of the decade and a subsequent reorganization of the Center largely confirmed this development. Thus, the CIS belatedly underwent the same type of 'academic enclosure' experienced by area studies centers elsewhere.[28] In addition, the Center developed a flourishing political science department where there had been none before. But it should also be recognized that, by virtue of its birthright, *raison d'état* took precedence over academic inquiry in the CIS; and MIT was only able to extricate itself from this uncomfortable situation with delay and difficulty. Nor was this the only case.

The Instrumentation Laboratory (I-Lab). While many research units owed their existence to the efforts of academic entrepreneurs, the phenomenal growth of the Instrumentation Laboratory qualifies its director, Charles Stark Draper, as the most successful entrepreneur in the annals of academe. The individual, the crucial importance of this field, and the accommodative policy of MIT all contributed to this feat.

Draper's I-Lab was in many respects a unique organization before the war, but the legacy of war research gave it a permanent importance. During World War II a series of computing gunsights were developed there that greatly improved the ability of gunners to hit rapidly moving targets. The need for such work was never-ending, and after the war the I-Lab had all the research work it could accommodate. Draper's chief postwar activities nevertheless shifted to inertial guidance systems.[29] Over the course of time such systems became progressively more vital components of ships, aircraft, nuclear submarines, ballistic missiles, and ultimately spacecraft. Draper himself was a perfectionist of enormous energy and capability. He preferred to create entire systems and to oversee all phases of his projects, from design, through engineering, to development. This was the style of the wartime labs, and Draper consciously perpetuated it within the department of aeronautical engineering. Having risen from student to professor at MIT before the war, Draper was a Tech old-timer who commanded great respect.[30] No one was likely to object as he found additional applications for his specialty on projected weapons systems. The number and size of I-Lab projects inexorably expanded, as did the overhead that accrued to MIT.

Within a decade of the end of the war, the scope and the importance of the I-Lab had given it a special status. Provost Stratton regarded it as

> one of several projects under MIT management which are of such critical national significance as to transcend our own, local, institutional interests. Therefore, decisions affecting the growth and administration of these projects must rest on factors other than those which govern the conduct of most academic research.

Once again, *raison d'état* became the paramount consideration. For although Stratton believed that Draper's work on inertial navigation "may well be the key to our whole guided missile program," he was not pleased with the academic development of the aeronautical engineering department.[31]

The problem stemmed largely from the fact that Draper dominated both the department and the laboratory and tended to concentrate upon a restricted range of topics. Although the I-Lab, with its huge contracts, made a significant contribution to the department's budget, facilities, and teaching role,[32] Stratton feared that the department itself was losing ground to those at Caltech, Stanford, and Cornell. Additional recruitment of top-notch people was needed, but this was virtually impossible given Draper's hegemony. Meanwhile, in the comparative isolation of the I-Lab, Draper had developed a cohort of faculty to his own liking, who were "almost completely unknown to the administration and to the Engineering Faculty."[33] But Draper's laboratory was too important to the nation to disrupt for reasons of "local, institutional interests." By 1960 the I-Lab budget had grown to $20 million—the same as that for regular organized research for the rest of the institution. It soon took another quantum leap when the I-Lab assumed major responsibilities for the Apollo space program. The I-Lab budget was in excess of $50 million by the end of the decade when arrangements were finally made to spin it off as an independent nonprofit corporation—the Draper Laboratories.

A determined protest movement and prolonged negotiations were necessary before the reluctant Draper agreed to this last step.[34] By this time the operations of the I-Lab were of the same order of magnitude as those of the Lincoln Lab, located seventeen miles away in Lexington. In terms of work, the federal contract research center was actually closer to academic research than was the I-Lab.[35] In fact, the Lincoln Laboratory had spun off a separate nonprofit corporation in 1958 (MITRE) in order to shed tasks similar to those routinely performed in the I-Lab. The inappropriateness of administering a multimillion-dollar development project as an appendage of an academic department was widely apparent by the time that its connections with MIT were severed.

Developments in CIS and the I-Lab have been followed beyond the immediate postwar decade to reveal how fundamental features of their makeup caused conflicts with their ostensible academic mission and ultimately brought difficulties to MIT. One school of thought, which was prominent in the late 1940s and ascendant on campus two decades later, held that such problems were inherent in military sponsorship of university research. On the other hand, the experiences of MIT could be, and in fact were, used to make a powerful case that such sponsorship achieved its principal goals: stimulating significant advancements of academic knowledge, producing tangible applications beneficial to both sponsors and society, and making positive contributions, financially and materially, to the research capabilities of the Institute.[36]

The Lewis Report expressed a full list of sensible caveats concerning military sponsored research, and these were frequently echoed by MIT administrators. Yet in some cases the Institute clearly transgressed its own avowed principles. Why, then, did a seemingly fruitful relationship between the Institute and its research sponsors sometimes wobble off course?

The answer begins with MIT's role during World War II. The wartime research achievements first reflected, and then validated, a devotion to national service. This ideal was endorsed with uncritical enthusiasm by President Karl Compton and his successor James R. Killian, Jr.[37] Postwar military-sponsored research, especially in the RLE, led to results that were scientifically even more satisfying. This combination of national service and scientific success engendered some secondary effects that reinforced commitments to this path of development. Financially and academically, government research programs buttressed the standing of the Institute. Prominent scientists, furthermore, acquired strong personal identifications, not only with certain lines of research, but with the underlying missions of project sponsors. This was not true for just Charles Draper and Max Millikan. In 1954, for example, President Killian coauthored a paper with the director of the Lincoln Lab urging the building of a comprehensive radar system for the defense of the North American continent.[38] There was a virtual absence, furthermore, of any negative feedback.[39] It thus became increasingly unlikely that MIT could give precedence to academic values when they seemed to conflict with national service.

The agencies that established working relationships with MIT were encouraged by their experiences to utilize these ties for their own purposes. This tendency was furthered by the general drift of the military component of the research economy. The extremely liberal policies of the immediate postwar years were motivated by the desire to establish regular access to academic science. Once these lines of communications were open, the services moved on to increasingly applied military research after the onset of the Cold War. Then too, after the initial technological breakthroughs, the perfection of systems of radar or computers or inertial navigation depended upon proportionately more developmental work and proportionately less basic scientific work. Both these tendencies were reflected within MIT by a perceptible loss of vitality within research units. The evidence for the three units just discussed points to a gradual diminution of the kind of creative interactions that characterized their early years. Over time they became more like umbrella organizations for numerous, discrete, self-contained projects.[40] As these patterns became entrenched, there may well have been diminishing intellectual and pedagogical returns from military research.

The difficulties that military research eventually posed for MIT were long in developing, but these problems should not be allowed to obscure the most salient feature of MIT's role in the postwar research economy. MIT blazed the trail for government sponsorship of university research, both in the era of the NDRC and in the postwar years. The fruitfulness of this relationship for both parties resulted in large measure from some distinctive characteristics of MIT—its powerful combination of science and technology and its willingness to accept research as the preponderant institutional role. MIT's success was not lost on other research universities. A decade into the postwar era they had all to some degree explored the pathways that MIT had blazed. But others, for the most part, declined to go the entire route. MIT would continue to hold the distinction of being the research university most involved in serving military and industrial patrons.

2. The University of California, Berkeley

At a 1952 gathering of academic luminaries, Harvard Provost Paul Buck asked, as a conversational gambit, which university was likely to displace UC Berkeley from its place among the top six American research universities? Although there was no consensus answer, the incident is memorable because of the general acceptance of the premise of Buck's question: that Berkeley was about to lose its esteemed rank and sink in the academic hierarchy.[1] The reason for this dour prognosis was understood. The entire University of California had been wracked with controversy over the Board of Regents' 1949 decision to require all UC faculty to sign a loyalty oath and the subsequent firing of 31 faculty who had refused on principle to do so (1950). While this conflict ran its ugly course for the next two years, it seemed unlikely that the university would be able to avoid significant defections from its existing faculty, let alone recruit distinguished additions. Yet, these events did not set the course for the university. When a systematic ranking was done at the end of the decade, Berkeley not only rose, but emerged as the challenger of Harvard for preeminent status among American universities. In spite of occasional adversity, Berkeley was the outstanding academic success of the postwar era.[2]

Three general factors stand out in the rise of Berkeley. First was a decided commitment to academic distinction that pervaded the campus. Second was a generally favorable financial environment that allowed such ambitions to be pursued. The third, a wild-card of sorts, was the fortuitous presence of E. O. Lawrence and the spectacularly successful Radiation Lab.[3] The rise of Berkeley was nevertheless scarcely foreordained. Besides the political storm over the loyalty oath, the university also had to navigate the uncertainties of a vast expansion and transformation into the hydra-headed UC System. In the end, however, these factors too tended to reinforce the commitment to academic distinction.

At the conclusion of World War II, Robert Gordon Sproul had already presided for fifteen years over the Berkeley-based higher education empire called the University of California. Besides the home campus, it included an agricultural unit at Davis, a medical school in San Francisco, a fledgling liberal arts college in Santa Barbara, a growing southern branch in Los Angeles, and, among its

research appendages, a marine biology station in La Jolla. Not an academic himself, Sproul was particularly sensitive to the outward manifestations of university
success. As he regularly took to the hustings around the state, he described the
university's accomplishments to illustrate how deserving it was of public support. Perhaps surprisingly, achievements in research were high among its selling
points. Besides the tangible benefits from discoveries in agriculture or medicine,
the prestige of academic distinction also appealed to California pride and latent
resentment of Eastern cultural hegemony. Encouragement of research and backing for academic advancement in general thus became axiomatic to Sproul's
leadership. Specifically, he intervened decisively to assist, and thus to retain,
renowned scientists like Lawrence. Sproul also contributed toward building a
highly qualified faculty by closely scrutinizing recommendations for appointments and promotions. Over time, the academic standing of Berkeley departments steadily improved, and expectations of high standards became widespread. By the end of the 1930s California had arguably emerged as the premier
state-supported research university (helped in part by the Depression woes of
Michigan and Wisconsin). Yet the university was still in no position to compete
for top scholars with the leading private institutions in terms of salaries, facilities,
or working conditions.[4]

In the fall of 1943 Sproul wrote to the heads of each of the university's units
asking them to consider how they would implement "drastic" budget cuts that
might be forced by a postwar economic crisis.[5] Instead, the University of California turned out to be one of the most financially fortunate state universities.
Instead of an economic collapse, the West Coast experienced sustained postwar
growth and prosperity, which provided the underpinnings for generous state
appropriations. From 1946 to 1951, they increased by an average of 24 percent
per year. During these same years, by virtue of enrolling the largest number of
veterans, the university became the foremost beneficiary of the liberal tuition
provisions of the GI Bill. In 1946–47, for example, it received $11.5 million
from student fees, a sum that exceeded the combined instructional budgets of
Berkeley and UCLA. In terms of real spending per student, the Berkeley instructional budget grew by 56 percent from 1946 to 1950, and then another 45 percent in the next four years.[6]

While the academic core of the university was thus swelling, so too were its
facilities. California had been one of the states that set aside sizable reserves of
wartime tax revenues for capital construction in the postwar period. Although
almost half of the university's existing buildings had been funded by private
donations, the next phase of construction was financed by public funds. The
immediate postwar plans called for spending $60 million for projects through-
out the university by 1950. When that date arrived, the state building program
had already committed more than twice that amount to construction. Some $25
million of this total was spent at Berkeley, a substantial portion to augment facilities for the physical sciences.[7]

Although these figures indicate an impressive material strengthening of the
university, they also reveal California moving with somewhat greater decisive-
ness along a path taken by most other states.[8] Another dimension to UC finance,

however, was probably unmatched at any other state university—the general availability of funds for discretionary use and the availability of state funds for research as well as educational purposes.

Sproul had originally earned his position through his mastery of all the details of the business of running the university. As president he maintained a great deal of actual decision-making in his own hands, particularly in matters concerning the Berkeley campus. This degree of control seems to have allowed Sproul a certain freedom of maneuver in financial matters. After the war, funds for discretionary use were secured from the overhead payments on federal contracts. Instead of being applied toward actual running costs, these funds were set aside by the Regents in a special fund. The units receiving the federal contracts seem to have been given special consideration in allocations from this fund; and a large part of it was cycled through self-liquidating projects for other purposes. Overhead reimbursements were thus employed in a flexible and timely fashion for strengthening research capacity.

By 1954 this special fund had mounted to $13.6 million when its existence was challenged by the governor. The university was, after all, being paid twice for the same thing. The Regents, nevertheless, were reluctant to eliminate the fund, citing its importance for augmenting the quality of the university. As a result of this strong stand a compromise was reached. Half of the fund was used to offset state obligations, and the other half was retained in the (now-named) Regents' Opportunity Fund. Significant resources thus continued to be available to bolster the university's research role. For example, in the 1960s this Fund was used to create institutes for the creative arts and the humanities—areas in which organized research units could not ordinarily be sustained through outside grants.[9]

These last examples underscore the university's willingness to devote its own resources to research-related ends. California was in fact the first university to establish a regular faculty research fund in 1915. This fund continued to operate in the postwar period, although by then the vast bulk of faculty research was supported from outside sources. Of crucial importance in the postwar era was the willingness of the university to underwrite organized research units. Such commitments helped to make Berkeley into the country's most fertile breeding ground of organized research units, and the initiator of the acronym, ORU.[10]

As explained in Chapter 2, every ORU has its own individual story. The Institutes for Industrial Relations (1945-) and the Institute of Transportation (1947-), for example, were created by the legislature with an eye to providing specific services to the state. A number of units emanated from Berkeley's primordial ORU, the Radiation Lab. And others were started under a variety of circumstances to facilitate faculty research. By the mid-1960s there were at least forty ORUs at Berkeley alone (131 in the entire University of California) making it the nation's most prolific campus in this respect. Perhaps a more important statistic, which goes far toward explaining the large number of ORUs, was that at this juncture state funds accounted for 29 percent of ORU income. California accepted the desirability of providing "core support" for university ORUs, in large part because this support helped to garner additional funds from outside sources.[11] State support of organized research also tended to have a crucial effect upon the character of the ORUs.

In terms of the continuum from disinterested academic research to interested patron-dictated research (Chapter 2), California's liberal subsidization of ORUs gave them the freedom to take a more academic orientation—to be less dependent upon producing findings for external sponsors. The university's policy from the beginning of the postwar era was to encourage basic research intended to advance the frontiers of knowledge, and to eschew, insofar as possible, applied or developmental work.[12] The university, in other words, endorsed the inherent proclivities of faculty for disinterested research. In doing so, it advanced academic prestige as a laudable end in itself. A remarkable consensus thus prevailed among faculty, administration, regents, and even important external constituencies that Berkeley should strive to be one of the country's finest research universities. Still, achieving the most highly rated graduate programs required more than will and wealth. That additional factor—call it success itself—was the crucial contribution of the Radiation Lab.

With the celebration of VJ Day, Ernest O. Lawrence's Radiation Lab was about to enter the third phase of its brief existence. When Lawrence won the Nobel Prize for Physics in 1939, just eight years had elapsed since the building of the first cyclotron. Only since 1936 had the scale of activities, supported by private funds, grown to the point that his laboratory became a separate entity. This first phase of the Rad Lab—creation under a charismatic leader—culminated in 1940 with a Rockefeller Foundation grant of $1.4 million to build 100 MeV cyclotron with a 184-inch magnet. The second phase might be called 'ordeal by battle,' as the Rad Lab and its key personnel were totally mobilized for war. The 184-inch magnet was employed in isotope separation, and the other cyclotrons were utilized for, among other things, the discovery of the first man-made elements—neptunium and plutonium.[13] While the Rad Lab itself employed 1200 workers in 1944, its prewar cadre of young physicists largely dispersed during the war to projects at MIT, Chicago, and ultimately Los Alamos. They nevertheless returned to Berkeley as quickly as possible because it was the most suitable place to pursue high-energy physics. And they returned—not as they left— as conquering heroes. Through their wartime achievements Lawrence's epigone had earned the right to fiefdoms of their own in the form of specialized research groups. Thus in its third phase the postwar Rad Lab assumed the likeness of a 'feudal monarchy': Lawrence largely conducted external relations with the university, the federal government, and private patrons, while his barons exercised suzerainty over their respective machines, staffs, and cognitive territories.[14]

The university, for its part, took the steps that were needed to ensure the return of these scientists and the reconstitution of the Rad Lab. Glenn Seaborg, the discoverer of plutonium, provides a case in point. A Berkeley Ph.D. in chemistry (1937), he worked as a research assistant in the department and the Rad Lab for two years, then was made an assistant professor before being summoned in 1942 to the Metallurgical Lab at Chicago. At the end of the war the University of Chicago attempted to retain him, offering a princely academic salary of

$10,000. Lawrence and Chemistry chairman Wendell Latimer, however, prevailed upon Sproul to elevate Seaborg directly to a full professorship, to increase university support for chemistry, and to bring Seaborg's Chicago assistants to Berkeley as well. In addition, Lawrence promised to find outside funding for Seaborg's laboratory.[15]

The scientific ambitions of E. O. Lawrence, in combination with his great personal prestige and his extensive connections, assured the proliferation of the Rad Lab's postwar research program.[16] One objective was to get the 184-inch magnet cyclotron in operation as soon as possible, a project entrusted to Robert Thornton; from Luis Alvarez came a proposal for a linear proton accelerator utilizing radar equipment developed during the war; and from Edwin MacMillan came plans for a novel electron synchrotron. Together with Seaborg's nuclear chemistry lab, these four major undertakings would be the core of the Rad Lab program in the immediate postwar period. But this was not the full extent of Lawrence's empire: there were additional research groups, and their influence extended further into the science departments. Both these aspects of the Rad Lab—its contributions to atomic physics per se, and its *rayonnement*—were important for the development of the university.

The benefits to the university of Lawrence's achievement were palpable. Atomic physics was far and away the most exciting scientific field in the postwar era, and Berkeley was the indisputable leader. Not until the next generation of accelerators was built would there be significant competition. Despite the distinguished history of the university, this was the first occasion in which it demonstrated undisputed national and international leadership. It was a heady experience, made all the more satisfying by virtue of the boost it gave to West Coast pride. Physics set an example and a standard for the rest of the university—an achievement to be emulated.

The core divisions of the Rad Lab set the intellectual pace with the most spectacular discoveries. From 1945 to 1947 Seaborg's group grew from 21 to 43, Alverez's group from 9 to 37, and MacMillan's group from 6 to 12. Seaborg identified transuranic elements number 97, 98, and 101 (Berkelium, Californium, and Mendelevium); the 184-inch cyclotron produced the first man-made pions early in 1948; and MacMillan's synchrotron quickly followed by discovering the existence of the neutral pion. In keeping with its leadership, Berkeley quickly became the country's foremost producer of physics Ph.D.s.[17]

Other groups within the Rad Lab grew and prospered as well. By 1947 there were 72 engineers working in an electrical and mechanical engineering group. Besides building and caring for the machines, they also undertook projects of their own. Other research groups were organized around work on the older cyclotrons: medical physics, theoretical physics, radiation-counting techniques, cloud chambers, and nuclear-emulsion detectors. Wendell Latimer supervised a laboratory for high-temperature chemistry, and Melvin Calvin headed a unit on bio-organic chemistry.[18] In the Donner Lab (f. 1941), organized separately from the Rad Lab, E. O. Lawrence's brother John led a research team in medical physics. Perhaps the best example of how Rad Lab achievements spilled over into other areas of the university is provided by Calvin's group.

An organic chemist, Melvin Calvin in 1937 joined a Berkeley department dominated by G. N. Lewis and other physical chemists.[19] He had no direct ties with the Rad Lab before the war, and worked on the rather peripheral problem of waste disposal for the Manhattan Project. His links with Rad Lab personnel were chiefly social. At the Faculty Club during the war he had discussed with both Lawrence brothers his hopes of pursuing research utilizing the radioactive carbon-14 (discovered in the Rad Lab in 1940). According to his recollections, Ernest approached him the day after VJ Day to ask if he would be interested in starting a carbon isotope lab to produce compounds for medical research. "Don't worry about the money," Lawrence added characteristically, "I'll take care of that, you just do the science." E. O. Lawrence wished to secure radioactively tagged compounds for his brother John and his associates to use in research and cancer therapy in the Donner Lab. Calvin was willing to do such mundane work as the price for the opportunity to undertake his own project, unraveling the chemistry of photosynthesis. Only E. O. Lawrence could have confidently promised *both* external funding and access to tightly controlled radioactive substances.[20]

With Lawrence's backing, Calvin had few worries about raising money or justifying his research program. He defined the research objectives of the chemical biodynamics laboratory in an intuitive, open-ended manner that allowed him maximum freedom to pursue his complicated puzzle. Ten years were needed to decipher the sequence of chemical changes involved in photosynthesis, but the effort earned Calvin a Nobel Prize. In the meantime, the laboratory grew enormously. By 1974 it possessed a budget of $3 million and a payroll of one hundred. A worthy understudy to Lawrence, Calvin became an academic entrepreneur in his own right.

Calvin found ample scientific justification for the expansion of his chemical biodynamics laboratory. Large-scale operations gave him the freedom to pursue scientific questions without having to worry about immediate results. Any diminution in his financial base of grants and contracts was tantamount to a loss of this freedom, a loss of opportunity for discovery.[21] With this attitude Calvin was naturally zealous in maintaining personal control over the laboratory. This attitude resulted in continual tension between the lab and the chemistry department—a common situation for this type of ORU. Calvin was unable to secure academic appointments in the department for the chemists in his laboratory because, he alleged, such positions would have given the lab a base independent of the department. As it was, he had to depend upon the department for his status in the university, and the price was to share the largesse of his lab. About one-third of his lab budget supported other department members, whose research program Calvin could not directly control. Calvin resented this intrusion, and the department resented his relative autonomy. When a new chemistry building was planned in 1957, Calvin bristled that he had not been allocated sufficient space. A phone call to the chairman of the Kettering Foundation secured a pledge of $300,000 toward a separate building. Identical commitments were then arranged from NIH, NSF, and finally the California Regents, making possible the construction of Calvin Laboratory in 1962. In sum, by capitalizing upon a unique opportunity made available by Lawrence and the Rad

Lab, Calvin was able to advance markedly the reputation and research base of organic chemistry at Berkeley.

Calvin was philosophical about his great opportunity to undertake basic research on photosynthesis, saying that one had to pay society's price for the privilege of pursuing one's own goals.[22] This was certainly Lawrence's approach as well: he financed Big Physics first by serving medicine and then by making weapons. In this respect research at Berkeley was consistent with the programmatic circumstances that characterized the postwar research system as a whole. Berkeley's distinctive good fortune, however, was in possessing programs like Calvin's and Lawrence's that had huge payoffs in terms of fundamental research at the cost of manageable commitments to sponsors. Berkeley's conscious preference for basic research was further abetted by explicit financial backing for research, particularly in the ORUs, from state and university sources. As a result, Berkeley succeeded more decisively than any other postwar research university in laying claim to the academic high road. In contrast to MIT and Yale (see below), for example, Berkeley managed to have both a concentration on fundamental kinds of investigations and a plethora of ORUs. This combination would ultimately place it in an insuperable position when the research system began providing substantial amounts of resources for disinterested inquiry.

Berkeley's academic development made great strides in the years immediately after the war. Building a preeminent university, however, was an incremental and unceasing process. The momentum established in these early years, in a sense, made possible the stages that followed. The specific features of those stages were nevertheless determined by a concatenation of events that emerged from the University's darkest hour—the period of the oath controversy.

The conflict that began as a kind of melodrama with the imposition of a noxious and otiose oath upon the UC faculty, soon developed into a protracted and demoralizing struggle that brought little credit to either side. In the opinion of its chronicler, "the controversy had been mostly a futile interlude in the life of an otherwise highly productive intellectual community."[23] By 1952, when the California Supreme Court ordered the non-signers reinstated (provided they sign an oath that was now required of all state employees!), the predominant attitude of Berkeley faculty members was to put the controversy behind them and to repair the damage done to the university. The struggle heightened, in particular, faculty concerns for self-government, terms of employment, and academic freedom.[24] At this same time, the Regents implemented a reorganization plan that established separate academic heads for the principal university branches. These two developments were linked in the person of Clark Kerr.

At the height of the controversy Kerr had delivered a severe criticism of the oath to the Regents.[25] He thus became strongly identified on campus as a defender of academic freedom. The faculty shortly thereafter voted to nominate him as their choice to become Berkeley's first chancellor. Installed in 1952, Kerr vigorously defended free expression, thereby managing to assuage fears of the loss of academic freedom at Berkeley. He contributed to restoring the morale of the faculty, as well as allaying the misgivings of potential recruits, but beyond this the powers of the chancellor were limited. Sproul had never wished to relinquish control of the Berkeley campus, and in his accustomed manner he kept most significant matters under his personal control. It took several acrimonious confrontations behind the scenes for Kerr to obtain a modicum of administrative authority. Lacking the power to approve anything, because all actions required Sproul's endorsement, Kerr could only say no. He used this negative authority systematically to upgrade the Berkeley departments. A second outlet open to Chancellor Kerr was to impose some order on the development of the campus through academic planning. Both these endeavors aided Berkeley's academic rise.

Kerr brought to the chancellorship a determination not just to make Berkeley an excellent state university, but to excel in the national arena as well. In the backlash from the oath controversy, Kerr found strong backing for academic improvement among the faculty, particularly in the powerful Academic Senate. He consequently received full cooperation from these quarters for the sometimes draconian measures he employed.

In the mid-1950s large numbers of the faculty recruited during the postwar crush were due for promotion. Kerr evaluated every dossier for appointment or promotion to tenure, professor or overscale. To raise the academic standing of the university it was necessary to be exceedingly rigorous in these evaluations. For a time, 20 percent of the recommendations that had passed all other hurdles were refused. In imposing these high standards he received the backing of the deans, the Academic Senate, and ultimately President Sproul. In some cases it was necessary to place departments in receivership; at other times review committees were used to recommend strategies of improvement. Kerr's implicit benchmark was a standing of sixth or higher nationally: departments that attained this level were left to manage their own affairs; those that did not invited some form of intervention. Each year Kerr chose three or four departments upon which to focus improvement efforts. The underlying expansion of the university gave him considerable leeway to utilize new appointments in order to enhance quality.

As chancellor, Kerr intensified a process of building eminent departments that was well under way. A good illustration may be found in sociology—as dramatic a turn-around as occurred there. Prior to 1946 Berkeley had no sociology department at all. Instead it possessed a Department of Social Institutions that had been created by a renegade historian, Frederick J. Teggart, for the historical and comparative study of ideas and institutions. Even before the war, as Teggart approached retirement, Sproul had pondered what to do with this anomaly. He was advised by outsiders to convert it to sociology, but within the department there was a live antipathy toward the very idea of sociology.[26] When Sproul was able to address this situation after the war, he renamed the department, which consisted entirely of Teggart's former students, "Sociology and Social Institutions" and placed it in receivership under Edward Strong of the philosophy department. Strong informed the administration of the need to appoint empirical sociologists, using a common Berkeley argument: "research projects in the social sciences are now in a favorable position to receive financial support from the SSRC and other foundations. . . . To get anything we must have something to offer." This course was followed. Although two additional historical/comparative scholars were also added in the 1940s, appointments of young sociologists predominated. By the time Herbert Blumer was brought from Chicago to head the department (1952), the balance had already swung from social institutions to sociology.[27]

Blumer was clearly supposed to extend this progress further. He drafted a five-year "Plan of Development" for the department that indicated the desirability of seven new positions. During the course of the 1950s the department made a succession of outstanding appointments on both the junior and senior levels. As it expanded, the legacy of Social Institutions was gradually smothered (the name was dropped in 1960). ORUs supplied a key element in the department's development. The 'real' sociologists who were hired in the 1940s were assisted with one-third appointments at Clark Kerr's Institute of Industrial Relations; and Blumer hired Charles Glock of Columbia's Bureau of Applied Social Research in order to establish a similar unit, the Survey Research Center. By 1961 the department included the directors of three ORUs, and was undoubtedly receiving an ample share of external research support. In reputation, its rise was meteoric. By the mid-fifties it was considered to rank sixth nationally, and less than a decade later it was judged the most distinguished in the country.[28] That this achievement spanned the eras of Sproul's autarchy and Kerr's chancellorship and presidency suggests the continuity of aspirations at Berkeley.

In addition to department building, the second contribution of Kerr's chancellorship was plotting an ambitious future for the campus. Upon assuming office, he found a mushrooming program of construction that had not been coordinated with any vision of Berkeley's academic development. He appointed a planning committee early in 1954, and by 1957 they produced "An Academic Plan for the Berkeley Campus."[29] The Plan was predicated upon Berkeley rising from a 1954 enrollment of about 15,000 to a ceiling of 25,000 in 1965. Envisioning the further development of junior colleges in California, the Berkeley enrollment was projected to be predominantly upper-division (11,000) and graduate (8000). Largely for this reason, a substantial lowering of student/faculty ratios was foreseen. Taken together, these two effects called for a doubling of the Berekely faculty from 1055 to 2110. The Academic Plan, then, was a maximal statement for the academic development of Berkeley. It stated that the Berkeley faculty should be comparable in quality with the other top universities (namely Harvard, Yale, Columbia, Chicago, and Michigan); and it foresaw, like them, the recruitment of graduate students on a national scale (a daring commitment for a state-supported institution). In keeping with the emphasis on fundamental inquiry, the core academic departments were those slated for the greatest expansion.[30] Remarkably for a plan that proposed maximal feasible goals, the targets of the plan were substantially met or exceeded by 1965.

At the time the Academic Plan was being formulated, the Berkeley departments were being rated by faculty around the country as second in overall rank. At the time of its realization, another such rating was in progress that would judge them to be the most distinguished. During this interval, Clark Kerr succeeded Sproul as president (1958). His successor as chancellor of Berkeley was Glenn Seaborg, who described his basic policy as getting "as many distinguished faculty to come as possible."[31] In a typical example of the way in which academic distinction becomes reinforcing, he created a special Committee on the Humanities to bring them up to the level of the sciences. Kerr's signal achievement as president also contributed: the adoption of the California Master Plan in 1960 guaranteed the university's privileged place in higher education's division of labor in the state.[32]

The academic development of Berkeley under the Kerr presidency occurred in an era of undreamt of prosperity for higher education, and for the research universities in particular. Berkeley was nevertheless ideally suited to benefit from the awakened appreciation for academic science. The initial advantage in nuclear physics, the relative abundance of resources during the postwar era, and the consistent academic leadership of Sproul and then Kerr, backed by the Berkeley faculty—all provided an incomparable base for Berkeley's rise to preeminence in the post-Sputnik years. The extraordinary result was that Berkeley became the paragon of academic distinction among public institutions—the epitome of what American research universities aspire to be.[33]

3. Yale University

When A. Whitney Griswold became the 17th president of Yale in 1950, he received some contradictory counsel from two of his principal deans. Edmund W. Sinnott, head of the Sheffield Scientific School and new dean of the Graduate School, advised him that the graduate school "is the very core of the university." There great scholars labored "solely for the advancement of human knowledge. And . . . on the attainment of that great goal depends the rest of human progress. . . . [T]o help carry it forward is the most important task of a university." The redoubtable dean of Yale College, William C. Devane, was less philosophical: without deprecating the alumni of Yale's graduate and professional schools, he emphasized that "they will not be as important people to Yale or the nation in the future as the graduates of Yale College. To illustrate this point in the national scene one needs only to look at the rosters of government, industry and business. To illustrate it for Yale one needs only to analyze the source of gifts to the Alumni Fund. This is a crass and brutal judgement," he added, "but it needs to be made."[1] As antithetical as these positions might appear, anyone who had been at Yale as long as DeVane and Sinnott, and Griswold too, had internalized both these points of views. Leading Yale in the postwar era meant striving for academic eminence *and* serving the crucial alumni/undergraduate constituency.

By most objective measures Yale emerged from the war in enviable condition. A 1946 evaluation of academic departments conducted by the AAU placed Yale ahead of Harvard, California, and Chicago with the highest average rating.[2] In terms of wealth, Yale's $115 million endowment was second only to that of Harvard. Yet, Yale's standing on both these counts concealed cause for disquiet.

In terms of purchasing power, the income from the Yale endowment lost 28 percent of its value between 1940 and 1947. Even as late as 1954 it was 9 percent below that of 1940 in real terms, while the student body had grown by 50 percent. Highly endowed universities like Yale depended on such income to support instruction. New undertakings usually required additional endowment or, more difficult still, a redeployment of expenditures.[3] Yet, expansion was imperative in the postwar environment. Developments at Yale during the postwar decade thus took place against the backdrop of continued difficulty in obtaining additional secure income. As the great wave of GI Bill students subsided, Yale faced persistent budgetary deficits and an impending "era of retrenchment." As late as 1952–53, for example, a financial shortfall prompted a freeze on promotions.[4]

Academically, Yale could not afford to be complacent about its high standing. The departments in which it received the highest possible rating were, with the exceptions of history and physiology, small and less conspicuous: anthropology, art, geology, German, linguistics, Oriental studies, and philosophy. Those in which its relative standing was lowest were the three crucial fields of chemistry, physics, and economics, as well as sociology.[5] Moreover, Yale had not figured significantly in wartime research, and had in fact lent many scientists to projects elsewhere. Yale thus stood at an inherent disadvantage in the emerging postwar research economy, made all the worse by its lack of standing in the physical sciences.

President Charles Seymour was sufficiently concerned about this situation to seek an evaluation of the state of Yale science departments in 1945, and he was apprised of the need to improve them before Yale fell hopelessly behind.[6] Efforts to rectify this situation, however, were at this time limited to making a few additional appointments. Possibilities for modernizing outdated laboratories or facilitating research in other significant ways were delayed by financial constraints and the general malaise of Seymour's last years.[7] But the president was also restrained by his own predilections for the other side of Yale. He found it "deplorable," for example, that faculty promotions in the medical school were heavily based upon productivity in research. In his final presidential report he stressed the necessity of reestablishing superior teaching as a primary factor in faculty promotions.[8] At the presidential level, Yale was not attuned to the dynamics of the postwar research economy.

Yale's relative weakness in science also stemmed in part from some basic features of the institution. The anachronistic division between Yale College and the Sheffield Scientific School had inhibited the science departments during the interwar years. The chemistry building dated from 1923, and the physics building from 1912. Except for medicine, the sciences suffered from inadequate space. Yale scientists were also expected to carry a teaching load comparable with that of their colleagues in the social sciences and humanities, which was far heavier than that borne by scientists at other leading research universities. The problem was aggravated by the general aversion toward science of Yale's prep-school clientele. About half as many undergraduates majored in science at Yale (10–11%) as at similar universities.[9] The problem was thus a longstanding one that made it difficult for Yale to improve its relative position in rapidly advancing fields like physics.

As early as 1940 the physics department was frustrated in just such an effort. In an unusually explicit planning document the department's standing and resources were compared with its competition at other research universities.[10] While it was felt, perhaps too optimistically, that the department had been steadily turning out very sound graduates and had a high reputation, its research results had not been as "spectacular" as other institutions. (Yale had been virtually left out of the development of nuclear physics.) And although its reputation was "on the upgrade," it needed one additional physicist "of outstanding accomplishment," as well as the development of the younger faculty, in order to "rise rapidly toward the top." The department received authorization to search for a "star" who might lead such a transformation. An opportunity soon came with the arrival in this country of emigrant Nobel Laureate Peter Debye. Yale made a serious attempt to woo Debye from his temporary post at Cornell, but he finally decided to remain in Ithaca. The mobilization of war research quickly followed, and Yale was soon concerned about having sufficient instructors to teach its physics courses instead of recruiting renowned researchers.[11]

From a postwar perspective Yale's 1940 effort seems both modest and clumsy. Modest, in that Yale envisioned rehabilitating the standing of the physics department by adding just one physicist over the next decade. The clumsiness stemmed from Yale's apparent unfamiliarity with the market for top physicists. Yale had originally sought to offer a salary of up to $7500. Debye was ultimately offered $10,000, plus other emoluments; but Yale essentially matched the Cornell offer instead of bettering it. Moreover, Debye seems to have decided for Cornell while Yale was still clarifying the terms of its offer. Decisive action on Yale's part might have improved the chance of success.

After the war the physics department faced the same problem of recruiting an outstanding atomic physicist in an even more competitive market. The department this time succeeded in bringing in Gregory Breit from Wisconsin in 1947. Breit was a productive, highly regarded theoretical physicist with extensive experience in wartime research, including the Manhattan Project. Arriving with a team of seven assistants, he brought the style as well as the substance of postwar physics research to Yale. But this scale of operation, in conjunction with Breit's difficult personality, soon engendered friction within the department. By 1949 disagreement reached the point that Breit and his group demanded an autonomous institute. In a compromise, Breit was given greater authority as chairman of a newly formed Research Committee in Theoretical Physics. Other stormy periods followed, but Yale managed to placate its temperamental star.[12]

Breit brought five ONR task orders with him to Yale. The departmental total for that year was just six task orders, worth $230,000. To these were soon added a series of contracts with the AEC. Breit's arrival thus marked the beginning of organized research on a large scale in the Yale department. Chairman William W. Watson was quick to perceive the problems associated with this development: the specter of federal control, the slanting of research interests, the distasteful duty of conducting classified research (some of Breit's projects). But he also concluded that federal research support was "absolutely essential."[13] The physics department soon showed the effects of national trends. For example, by 1952 two-thirds of the physics graduate students were working as assistants on research contracts, making it quite impossible to reduce enrollment as the provost wished. By the same date the department was expanding, in part through complicated appointments allocated by fractions to its regular budget, AEC contracts, and the Brookhaven Laboratory. Soon Watson, who had formerly feared the impermanence of federal support, was advocating making regular faculty appointments on the basis of research funds.[14]

Provost Edgar Furniss recognized that the postwar research environment was predicated upon expansion into new areas of knowledge and new investigative techniques. Such expansion required outside sources of funds, but at the same time universities had to create a research capacity with their own funds in order to attract such support.[15] The development of physics at Yale exemplified the difficulty of this circular process.

Despite the rapid progress of organized research, the physics department in 1952 was still, according to its chairman, "lagging behind all the universities with which we are inevitably compared in every scholarly pursuit." Yale was then trying to "climb into the 'major league' of physics departments operating high-energy particle accelerators." It had just signed a contract with the AEC for the construction of a linear electron accelerator and was negotiating another for a heavy ion accelerator. To make a case for such an award demanded a commitment of Yale resources; success would require additional expenditures. As Chairman Watson explained,

> to obtain ... funds from a government agency ... we must have staff members demonstrably able to design, construct and operate such machines ... The University must also be willing to provide a site and the basic building.[16]

Just to play in the major league was an expensive commitment, and not necessarily a popular one. Dean Devane acidly commented that the university freeze on promotions (1952–53) had been imposed in order to be able to afford the new physics laboratory.[17]

By this juncture, only seven years from war's end, the Yale physics department had clearly transcended its former state. It was now driven as much by the imperatives of the research economy as by the instructional needs of the university. Chairman Watson pledged that "we shall do our best to keep our activities in balance"; but he also recounted difficulties of reconciling instruction and research, and of maintaining disinterested basic research alongside that funded by the military.[18] Furthermore, the status of the department was anything but secure. In 1956, with a new physics building and both accelerators operating, conditions in the department appeared to be much improved. Shortly thereafter, however, the first public rating of university departments since the 1930s appeared. Yale physics was ranked a poor eleventh. The only worse showing for Yale was the marginal department of geography.[19]

The plight of the Yale physics department seemed paradoxical. Yale had spent extravagantly to meet the department's needs, and even sacrificed to do so; it was now annually conducting more than $1 million in sponsored research ($1.8 million in 1958–59), a substantial fraction of the Yale total. Yet, Yale had not kept pace with the explosive growth of physics in other research universities. Watson wrote President Griswold that he needed even more resources, especially full professors. Yale had only seven, whereas higher ranking departments had from twelve to twenty. Moreover, he argued, as he had previously, such appointments could be made on soft money: "under the existing national situation, a high caliber physicist will always attract enough outside funds to go a long way toward paying his own salary."[20] But Griswold had already embarked upon a different approach. With growing doubts about the leadership and the accomplishments of the science departments, he appointed a President's Committee to undertake a critical reappraisal of Yale's entire effort in the sciences. It would eventually conclude, among other things, that Yale did indeed need more physicists, but that it should circumscribe its overall effort. Rather than trying to compete with larger departments, the committee advised that Yale concentrate on those specialties in which it could excel.[21]

The Yale economics department pursued quite a different strategy of development than did physics and was also affected differently by the Yale milieu. Instead of seeking established stars, it initially improved itself by finding, hiring, and retaining excellent junior appointments. Moreover, this strategy not only brought an increase in its research capabilities, but also a rise in its national standing.

The stages of this process are clearly discernible. In the years immediately after the war Yale economics faced a highly competitive market for faculty. Although Yale lost a few valued members, department chairman Kent T. Healy was acute in his judgments and aggressive in recruitment.[22] At least five appointments were made on the assistant and associate professor level who would long be credits to the department. Healy emphasized that personnel would be "the key to whatever success the department may achieve" (1948). By this date it was already apparent that the young appointments were more productive than the full professors, and "contributed to an important degree to pull up the professional standing of the economics department at Yale."[23] At this critical juncture, Healy embarked upon a prescient course of action. Anticipating that his rising stars would be aggressively recruited by other universities, he conducted a campaign to alert the administration to this possibility. He deliberately planted the suggestion that outside offers should be matched, even if doing so meant promoting people more rapidly than Yale's accustomed languid pace. Healy stressed this theme until he relinquished the chairmanship in 1951. Whether or not his urging was the decisive factor, the outcome he sought was achieved. The promising economists that he had recruited were promoted and retained. In addition, the rising prestige of the department facilitated the further recruitment of additional recognized scholars.

The new chairman, Lloyd G. Reynolds, was immediately faced with an extraordinary crisis. William F. Buckley's God and Man at Yale appeared in 1951 and, in a kind of oblique McCarthyism, charged that the department was a hotbed of collectivist thinking. This rather wild accusation aroused an intense protective reaction. Some members rebutted Buckley directly in print. Elaborate analyses of the introductory texts were made to disprove Buckley's charges of bias. Reynolds sought to forearm the new president for possible confrontations with alumni by supplying a confidential summary of the political views of each department member. Reynolds carried the counteroffensive to the alumni himself, moreover, by explaining the professional character of the department and the discipline in numerous presentations.[24]

By placing the economics department under a national spotlight Buckley inadvertently assured that it would receive special consideration both inside and outside of Yale. Several Yale benefactors made gifts for fellowships that allowed Yale to attract first-rate graduate students. The department also secured university backing to make five significant professorial appointments (1950–53). By 1953 Reynolds could claim that the economics department had truly arrived:

> We have been "averaging up" over the course of time. The Department now stands higher than ever before in national reputation and influence. A significant indication of this is that all the appointments which we offered this year [five] were accepted with alacrity.... We have been visited by sixteen leading economists from universities in all parts of the world; Yale has definitely been added to the traditional Columbia-Harvard-Chicago circuit.[25]

This type of testimony is in some ways more telling than national rankings. In addition, the department conducted more than $150,000 in sponsored research. For the remainder of the decade it was able to build upon this firm foundation. Reynolds would soon boast that the department's graduate students were among the best in the nation, despite considerable competition. In 1955 the department received an unanticipated boost when the Cowles Commission, an endowed institute specializing in quantitative economic research, decided to move from Chicago to Yale. Reynolds's optimistic assessment of the department was vindicated when the Keniston ratings appeared at the end of the decade: Yale economics was ranked third behind Harvard and Chicago.[26]

The rise of the Yale economics department provides a striking success story in the perpetual competition for academic distinction, but it is balanced to some extent by the disappointment in physics. In Yale's other postwar 'problem' departments, chemistry was able to raise its standing considerably, while sociology registered little progress at all.[27] Clearly, the fate of departments hinged upon individual actions and personal circumstances that were only partly under the sway of university policies. Yale's overall standing in the Keniston survey was a strong fourth—hardly a decline from the somewhat anomalous rating of 1946. Remarkably, Yale's stature remained high despite its deep-seated distrust of many features of the postwar research economy.

For a modern university president, A. Whitney Griswold had an unusually rigid conception of his institution's proper role. In giving due recognition to the importance of Yale College, Griswold became one of the country's foremost advocates of the liberal arts tradition. Excellence in scholarly and scientific research, in his view, were complementary to liberal education as long as such activities were focused upon fundamental academic topics. Accordingly, Yale had no business undertaking applied research or providing services for external constituencies. Yet, the postwar research economy was essentially predicated upon such programmatic activities. Other university presidents would argue that no meaningful distinction could be made between research commissioned for disinterested or interested ends, but not Griswold: he sought academic purity and took steps to attain it. One of the distinctive features of his tenure was the banishing of institutes. At the same time that organized research units were pro-liferating at other research universities, Griswold was purging Yale of them. The first casualty was the Institute of International Studies; also killed were smaller units studying alcoholism and primate behavior. In a similar spirit of eliminating the merely useful, he abolished the undergraduate nursing school, the department of education, and reduced the school of engineering to departmental status. The research units that were tolerated had to be, like the Cowles Foundation, closely integrated with academic departments—and named something other than 'institute.'[28]

Griswold's treatment of the Institute of International Studies was an egregious breach of academic mores. Joseph Willits of the Rockefeller Foundation, which supported the Institute, found his action "amazing"; Princeton economist Jacob Viner, a member of the Institute's Board, regarded it as "stupid administration."[29] Shortly after assuming the presidency, without any consultation, Griswold informed the Institute that the University would withdraw financial support, that it should confine itself to the study of politics, and that it would be integrated into the political science department. This decision stemmed from both a personal animus against the Institute, with which he had once been affiliated, and a deep conviction against what he called "programmed research." Griswold believed strongly that the best academic work was accomplished by individual scholars working within disciplinary traditions—a position that was dubbed 'departmentalism' at Yale and that contributed toward the marginal status of the Institute. He also alleged that scholarship at the Institute was of poor quality, certainly lower than in his day.[30]

Griswold's opinion was not shared by the academic community in international relations. Willits rated the Institute among those producing the highest quality social science research, and other universities quickly expressed interest in adopting it. A proposal from Princeton proved most attractive. Princeton's attitude was totally opposite that of Yale: it sought to coordinate the Institute with teaching units without altering its character, and Princeton offered to support it with institutional funds which would then be matched by the Rockefeller Foundation. According to Willits, Princeton offered the kind of effective organization and management for research that was appropriate for the postwar era: it was "trying to merge the advantages of good teaching and good research," and "will offer a setting of much greater potential effectiveness for the Yale Institute than Yale has been able to offer."[31]

Griswold was at least somewhat chastened by the negative publicity that this incident generated. Willits charitably expressed the hope that the experience would help him to become a great president of Yale. While Griswold never altered his views on programmatic research, he did alter his tactics. The department of education, for example, was eliminated through slow strangulation.[32] But if Griswold was out of harmony with the postwar research economy, he combined that outlook with a fierce regard for academic excellence. His instincts served Yale well in the cultivation of some distinguished departments, but were counterproductive in precisely those fields where extradepartmental research units were prevalent.

Griswold shared the prevailing conservative distrust of federal sponsorship of university research. He seems to have bowed to the inevitable in areas like physics and medicine; however, there was no institutional encouragement at Yale for faculty to seek outside research support. As a consequence, academic entrepreneurship, which played such a vital role in expanding research at other universities, was somewhat suspect. Nor were research ties with private industry welcome. Griswold had appealed to private corporations to aid independent universities with voluntary support, but he rejected out of hand the possibility of cultivating quid-pro-quo relationships with industry.[33] Taken together, these factors constrained the development of certain fields at Yale. Engineering was allowed to languish; and without the fruitful interaction between physics and engineering that existed elsewhere, the scope of Yale physics was narrowed as well. Empirical social research was little encouraged, and international studies eventually had to be reconstituted on a more palatable basis.[34] How then, one might well ask, did Yale remain as eminent as it did?

In the humanities (rated second overall in the Keniston survey) Yale possessed superb facilities, including several special library collections. During this era about half of each Yale class majored in English, history, or American studies, which provided an ample base for sustaining these large and prestigious departments. In the social sciences (rated fifth) the emergent economics department was joined by strong departments of psychology and anthropology that, ironically, had benefited from the former presence of the Institute of Human Relations.[35] In the biological sciences (ranked seventh) the faculty of arts and sciences departments were complemented by research-oriented units in the medical school. The latter, with considerable autonomy from the rest of the university, became an early and major participant in the research economy. By the mid-fifties 50 percent of the medical school's budget came from soft money, including 40 percent of regular faculty salaries.[36] In the physical sciences (ranked eighth), strong departments of chemistry, geology and mathematics compensated somewhat for the weakness in physics.

Yale's inherent strengths, combined with Griswold's concern for quality in pure research, clearly produced an array of distinguished departments. Beneath the surface, however, there were growing indications that aloofness from a substantial portion of the research economy was not a viable approach for the long term. Quite aside from the fact that the Keniston rating method was highly favorable to Yale (the humanities were heavily overweighted; only traditional disciplines were included; and engineering was left out), it would seem that 'departmentalism' had its own pernicious effects.

By the end of the 1950s Yale began to lose scientists to other institutions at an alarming rate, while experiencing difficulty in its own recruitment.[37] This problem was in part the stimulus for the President's Committee, mentioned above, that undertook a critical review of the natural sciences and mathematics. They concluded that at least five departments were guilty of orientations toward "older" sets of problems, to the comparative neglect of emerging fields.[38]

The committee report signaled the beginning of a far-reaching reorganization of the sciences at Yale. Its most important features need only be noted here. A new divisional administration was created, which, in order to remedy past laxness, was given oversight of all appointments and promotions to tenure positions in the science departments. The departmental structure in the biological sciences was substantially reorganized, and key new appointments were made in physics and chemistry. An inquiry into the state of the engineering school resulted in its incorporation into the undergraduate faculty of arts and sciences.[39] Also significant was the emergence of new leadership in key positions: economist John Perry Miller became dean of the Graduate School and future president Kingman Brewster, Jr., became provost (1961).[40] Yale would not completely efface its predilection for the academic high road, nor would it lose its distinctive character as a research university; but during the 1960s it would gradually shed the parochialism of the 1950s and become integrated, with decreasing reluctance, into the research economy.

MIT, UC Berkeley, and Yale exhibited startlingly different organizational cultures and modes of adaptation to the postwar research economy. For MIT, the assumption of an autonomous research role prompted no serious misgivings. It aggressively sought research opportunities and willingly accepted in consequence the obligation to further the programmatic ends of its sponsors. Berkeley too fell readily into acceptance and cultivation of a separate research role, but there the intellectual compass pointed in a somewhat different direction. Programmatic research and ORUs were essentially means for the attainment of the higher tacit goal of building academic distinction. This last value was cherished equally at Yale; the official university position, however, was that programmatic research was a diversion rather than a means for its achievement. Yale thus disdained autonomous research, despite its presence in the great collections of Sterling Library, the medical school, the physics department, and elsewhere.

In spite of these vivid contrasts, the leading research universities still possessed more similarities than differences, and had more in common with each other than they had with the numerous institutions that awoke more tardily to the imperatives of the postwar research system. MIT, Berkeley, and Yale sought after and coveted the same economists or chemists, and they financed their research with grants from the same agencies. The requirements for a successful academic career, as described by a newly appointed psychologist at Yale, were the same as for a physicist at MIT or a chemist at Berkeley:

... initiating and sustaining a research program. In subtle and not so subtle ways, the unverbalized message was, "you were not brought here because you are a nice guy or a good teacher. You were brought here because we think that you can do worthwhile research, and don't ever forget that."[41]

At the departmental level, especially at the top departments, the culture was that of the academic disciplines, and the highest value was placed on contributions to the advancement of knowledge. The relative abundance of funds in the research economy reinforced disciplinary cultures. To have a successful and well-supported research program was the highest form of faculty power and freedom, as was evident in the careers of Charles Draper, Melvin Calvin, and Gregory Breit. The research universities, for all their diversity, projected a single and powerful model. The attractiveness of this model for universities of lesser stature became increasingly apparent as the nature of the postwar research system unfolded. Standing by ready to assist this process, as they had in the 1920s and 1930s, were the great American philanthropic foundations, which now had to adjust their mission to the overweening presence of the federal government.

4

Private Foundations
and the Research Universities,
1945–1960

The development of American research universities during the 1920s and 1930s had depended on private funds for the support of academic research. The most salient features of this era were 1) the private character of these funds, principally from foundations and wealthy individuals; 2) the stewardship of these resources by individuals drawn from the leading universities, private industry, and public life, coordinated through intermediate institutions like the National Research Council; and 3) an avowed commitment to backing the best possible science, which generally meant recognized scientists at the foremost research universities.[1] The federally dominated research economy that emerged after World War II was partly superimposed over these earlier arrangements and partly displaced them. Change was most profound in the natural sciences. For example, when the Rockefeller Foundation made the final grant to complete the 200-inch refracting telescope at Mount Palomar (1948), it marked the last Big Science project to be supported entirely with private funds. Henceforth, extensive and expensive scientific undertakings would be the responsibility of government, and the physical sciences generally would look to Washington for succor. Some fields of chemistry continued to attract the interested patronage of private industry, and some foundations remained committed to supporting biomedical science; but the private portion of the research economy in general inexorably adjusted to the preponderance of federally supported science.

There were clearly manifold opportunities in the postwar university research system for enlightened philanthropic patronage. But foundations were constrained by limited resources and confronted with abundant possibilities for benefiting mankind. Prior to 1955, most foundation endowments suffered from the same financial constraints that afflicted the endowed universities. During the last half of the 1930s total foundation grants in the United States had averaged $80 million annually; from 1945 to 1952 that average climbed to just $102 million, but was worth 25 percent less in real terms. In addition, major donors willing to match foundation grants were few. This gloomy picture was considerably brightened after 1950 by the appearance on the national scene of the Ford Foundation. Within a few years its grants were triple those of the Rockefeller Foundation and the Carnegie Corporation combined. Its total of $66 million in 1953, in fact, constituted 40 percent of all foundation giving that year. Moreover, the majority of Ford grants during its first decade of activity were directed to colleges and universities.[2]

Foundation support for research universities in the postwar era basically flowed toward three broad objectives. The first of these comprised the medical and health fields. The impetus for this giving came as much from the stipulations of original donors as from careful assessment of opportunities for scientific advancement. Indeed, it was noted in Chapter 2 that medical school administrators would have preferred general support over grants for research. In the years immediately after the war about half of medical research was privately supported, but, with the expansion of NIH, the federal government was outspending private donors 2:1 as early as 1950.[3] Medical research supported by foundations contributed some important pieces to the complex mozaic of biomedical research, but that vast topic lies beyond the scope of this discussion.

The second channel of foundation support consisted of a broad range of activities that contributed directly or indirectly to strengthening the system of university research. Such commitments provided support for graduate education or postdoctoral fellowships; support for learned or professional organizations, like the National Academy of Sciences and the Social Science Research Council (SSRC); the sponsorship of studies of timely issues facing universities (finances, sponsored research); or grants for the strengthening of university resources that complemented research (libraries, faculty fellowships). In addition to these important and ongoing concerns, the major foundations acted both formally and informally to advance the quality and effectiveness of research universities per se. The program of the Ford Foundation, in particular, was the first in a generation to address this task.

The third general area where foundations had a significant impact was the study of human affairs—the social and behavioral sciences. Here, above all, the foundation goal of bettering mankind and the university mission of studying mankind met full face. Moreover, foundations and research universities were for long the principal actors in this arena without the overbearing presence of government.[4] Foundation efforts to advance the social and behavioral sciences not only played a role in the internal development of research universities but also constituted an important episode in the evolution of those disciplines.

The sections that follow focus first upon the attempts of major foundations to advance and shape the social sciences and then on similar efforts to strengthen institutions as research universities. In both undertakings foundation officers attempted to formulate desirable ends and devise programs to achieve them, only to be frustrated to a considerable extent by the intractability of the research universities themselves. In both arenas much was accomplished, although not necessarily what had originally been intended.

1. Foundations and Academic Social Science

The two foremost supporters of academic research before 1940, the Carnegie Corporation and the Rockefeller Foundation, both had residual interests in the social sciences. During the latter part of Frederick P. Keppel's long presidency of the Carnegie Corporation (1922-41) about one-fifth of university research grants had gone to this area, but such grants dried up almost entirely during the war. The Rockefeller Foundation inherited a bold and extensive program in the social sciences when it absorbed the Laura Spelman Rockefeller Memorial in 1929, but these commitments too had attenuated by the end of the 1930s. Still, the Foundation maintained a relatively stable commitment of about $2 million in annual grants by the Social Science Division before and after the war. A good part of these funds, however, was directed to foreign institutions, reflecting its worldwide vision; while domestically the Foundation continued to underwrite the activities of operating social science research agencies (particularly the National Bureau of Economic Research (NBER)).[5] For the Rockefeller Foundation greater commitment to academic social science meant shifting the emphasis of an ongoing program. For the Carnegie Corporation it required a searching appraisal of philanthropic opportunities and the shaping of a new program.

The Carnegie Corporation.   At the end of the war the Carnegie Corporation lacked an overriding sense of purpose. For two decades Keppel had steered a consistent and fairly unimaginative path. His immediate successor died in office (1944) having known only the wartime emergency. The presidency was then thrust upon Devereaux C. Josephs (1945-48), an investment banker who directed the Carnegie offspring, the Teachers' Insurance and Annuity Association. Josephs was a neophyte as a philanthropoid, but he was fortunate to have capable assistants in Charles Dollard and John W. Gardner (who would become, respectively, the next two presidents of the Corporation).[6] As they worked together to formulate a meaningful program, Dollard articulated the essential challenge facing foundations in the shadow of the new federal role:

> the problem of the foundations is no longer whether the project is good, but whether foundation support is the critical factor in its inauguration or continuation. There are respectable projects which would absorb ten times the income of all foundations put together. What we have to look for is not merely fertile ground but ground which will remain unbroken unless we turn the first shovelful.[7]

Another critical consideration was added by Gardner, who advised that "the Corporation should never forget that its most precious asset will be its sense of direction." This meant keeping "unshakably in mind the range and pattern of our objectives ... and our basic strategy for attainment of those objectives." Finally, Josephs articulated what was to be the operating philosophy: to aim primarily at facilitating the critical developmental stage of ideas or activities, rather than provide continual support of ongoing enterprises—"the influence of the Corporation will be lost if we support undertakings too long after the developmental stage."[8]

In their own fashion, the officers of the Carnegie Corporation articulated some basic principles of effective foundation philanthropy: a programmatic orientation to determine fields of interest; intervention at strategic moments; and limited duration of commitments. Foundations in the postwar era had to plan carefully and focus their activities judiciously if their grants were to make a significant impact. Given the myriad possibilities that existed in the turmoil of the immediate postwar period, it is noteworthy that so much of the Carnegie Corporation program came to embrace universities and social science.

During the first seven months of 1946 the officers of the Corporation met regularly in order to establish that crucial sense of direction. They finally resolved upon several general areas of emphasis. Of these, Education, International Relations, and Social Science would claim the bulk of the Corporation's grants for the ensuing decade. Another, strengthening citizenship, accounted for grants in citizenship education and American Studies, but did not amount to a consistent program. Education, although the rubric listing the largest number of grants, turned out over the years to be fairly diffuse. International Relations and Social Science became the principal substantive foci of Corporation activity until 1955.[9]

John Gardner formulated the most coherent rationale for supporting international relations. In keeping with current concern over American isolationism, he argued that the peace of the world now depended upon the development of a "sagacious and consistent foreign policy" by the United States. For American leaders to carry out such a policy required that their actions be understood and supported by public opinion. The problem was thus "to educate 130,000,000 people," which made the educational system the crucial arena for spreading knowledge of world affairs. Teachers and other opinion leaders would have to be educated at the undergraduate level. This undertaking called for the training of a cadre of university teachers, which, in turn, necessitated augmenting the knowledge base and increasing the number of experts in these fields. Academic expertise thus became the prerequisite for attaining the other objectives. Gardner therefore concluded that the focus of Corporation actions "will inevitably be the graduate schools of our institutions of higher education."[10] Here was a circumscribed area in which foundation support could be the decisive factor.

The Carnegie Corporation program in international affairs, as it evolved, devoted considerable support to the study of international relations, and lesser amounts to promote international exchange; but the bulk of these grants went to initiate area study programs in major universities during the late 1940s. The centerpiece of this program, and the most generously funded (23% of area studies commitments) was the Russian Research Center at Harvard.[11] Similar units were supported elsewhere to encourage the study of Japan at Michigan, Southeast Asia at Yale, the Near East at Princeton, and South Asia at Penn. Some of these centers built upon existing strengths; in the case of Harvard the Carnegie Corporation's intention was to attract top social scientists to the subject. In other cases it strained somewhat to achieve worldwide coverage. In this last category, many grants were made on what appeared to be a tenuous notion of proximity: responsibilities for Latin America were divided among several Southern universities (Texas, North Carolina, Vanderbilt, and Tulane); Scandinavia was confided to Minnesota and Wisconsin; Columbia took Europe; the University of Washington, Soviet Asia; and McGill University in Montreal received support for Arctic Studies.[12] Since these grants were predominantly for purposes of research and the training of scholars, they reflected fairly directly Dollard's rationale for supporting international studies. Such clarity of purpose and action was more difficult to achieve in general social science.

For Carnegie president Devereaux Josephs the underlying motivation was to discover "how the social sciences can be put to work." Behind this impulse lay a perception, born no doubt from recent events, that the power of modern governments to guide and control the "social machinery" had grown, and that this seemed to require a corresponding increase in knowledge about society. His concern was "with getting this knowledge into circulation, and with seeing that those who acquire social leadership have useful knowledge in a form which they can understand."[13]

Josephs's understanding of this issue seems to have been influenced by a candid assessment of the field made by Robert T. Crane, recently retired director of the SSRC.[14] Crane impressed upon Josephs the ineffectiveness of most efforts to extract practical knowledge directly from the social sciences, and emphasized instead the utility of both focusing upon long-range problems of modern society and seeking to improve the efficacy of social science research. From his position at the organizational center of academic social science, Crane had reached some surprisingly pessimistic judgments about the field. He described universities as "primarily pedagogical institutions," without "effective research organization," where social researchers found "paltry" support and worked "under almost medieval conditions." Universities nevertheless held unequaled advantages in their broad coverage of social issues, the disinterested nature of their research, and the integration of training with actual research. Crane's assessment, in fact, recapitulated Beardsley Ruml's conclusions of two decades before: the necessary precondition for achieving useful social scientific knowledge was to strengthen basic social science within the universities.[15]

The Carnegie Corporation in the 1940s did not have, relatively speaking, the kind of assets that Ruml possessed in the 1920s, and American social science had become a far larger and more mature entity to modify. Although a comprehensive program for studying "the role of the social sciences in modern society" was formulated, actual grant-making was shaped considerably by opportunities in the field. Three general thrusts were discernible. Support for strengthening the social sciences was largely channeled into the SSRC—an expedient, though unimaginative, course of action. Second, in accordance with the prevalent belief that applied social knowledge would only result from interdisciplinary investigations, backing was given to Harvard's department of Social Relations as well as to interdisciplinary units at Minnesota and North Carolina. Third, the Corporation funded some research on enduring practical problems like race relations (Chicago) and voter behavior (Michigan Survey Research Center).[16]

In area studies and the social sciences the Carnegie Corporation identified two malnourished and cognitively underdeveloped fields in postwar universities. The former, however, proved far more tractable than the latter given the means available. After the first series of grants the Corporation reevaluated its policy toward area studies and decided to continue supporting only the more successful programs. The hallmarks of success were aggressive leadership, the backing of university leaders, and a willingness by faculty to transcend disciplinary boundaries.[17] Perhaps the model in this regard was the Michigan Center for Japanese Studies. In this particular field cross-disciplinary cooperation was readily attained because cultural and linguistic investments tended to overshadow disciplinary ties. The university, for its part, had buttressed the Center by appointing Japanologists to several departments.[18] The other conspicuous achievement was Harvard's Russian Research Center, where the cascade of publications obscured for a time the organizational weaknesses described in Chapter 2. The programs at Penn, Princeton, and Yale were also renewed. The abandonment of the other area studies programs indicated disappointment with their results. At Columbia, for example, the Corporation grant for European Studies was used to launch some new courses and organize seminars, but "no tightly integrated program" emerged.[19] Still, as a whole the area study program produced some enduring achievements. When the Corporation withdrew from area studies in the mid-fifties, its progeny found more bounteous support from the Ford Foundation, which laid claim to the field.

In the social sciences it was much more difficult to point to solid attainments, particularly ones achieved through foundation initiatives. In part this frustration stemmed from the original assumptions of the Social Science program. By 1949 a degree of disillusionment with interdisciplinarity was already evident in Charles Dollard's observation that "a great deal of time is wasted in premature attempts to produce very large 'syntheses' or 'integrations' of the social science fields."[20] His judgment was validated to some extent by the department and the Laboratory of Social Relations at Harvard. For all its ambitions and accomplishments, the social relations approach failed to achieve such general results. The Corporation remained committed to cross-disciplinary work, especially with regard to partial syntheses aimed at specific problems, but reached a policy decision to cease supporting such work for its own sake.[21]

The obstacles to "putting social science to work" were even greater. The logic behind this goal should have favored supporting established research institutes, which were more likely than departmental researchers to formulate researchable questions and to provide empirical data as answers. In fact, the greatest assistance the Corporation could render to units like Michigan's Institute for Social Research turned out to be provision of support for their academic proclivities, such as perfecting research methodology. By 1955, with John Gardner as president, the Corporation backed away from even this type of support.[22] Robert Crane had originally advised the Corporation to concentrate its efforts in a limited area of the social sciences, an approach that requires some in-house expertise. Lacking that, actual grants in the decade after 1945 did not focus upon any single problem area for more than a few years.[23]

Almost by default, then, the Carnegie Corporation was thrown back upon a strategy of strengthening social science largely by working through the Social Science Research Council. Indeed, the Corporation was a consistent benefactor of the SSRC, and at one point the most effective postwar contribution to social science was identified as an SSRC administered program of fellowships for young social science faculty.[24] This and other programs of the SSRC undoubtedly furthered the development of university social science, but in an incremental manner rather than through the decisive intervention originally envisioned. This discrepancy between aspiration and realization was not experienced by just the Carnegie Corporation. It paralleled the contemporary experience of the Rockefeller Foundation and prefigured the subsequent efforts of the Ford Foundation.

The Rockefeller Foundation. While the Carnegie Corporation sculpted a postwar policy *de novo*, the Rockefeller Foundation Social Science Division had considerable continuity of leadership and program. Its director since 1939 was Joseph Willits, formerly dean of the Wharton School at Penn and director of the NBER, who had thus been a central figure of prewar economic research. He administered a program that had been a mainstay of social science research since the 1920s. Economics naturally loomed large in the grants of the Division. Willits too was jarred by the war, however, and particularly by the advent of the nuclear age. As he reevaluated the Foundation's role in the postwar world, the themes he decided to emphasize were similar to those selected at Carnegie: the encouragement of international peace and social adjustment within nations.[25] The clearest manifestation of the former concern was the establishment of the Russian Institute at Columbia. Unlike Carnegie's subsequent research-oriented Harvard Center, this unit was originally intended primarily to train Russian specialists, largely for government work. In general, though, the foundation chose to support the field of international relations, where it had been active since 1929, rather than area studies. Under the rubric of social adjustment, programs were conducted in both economic research and the functioning of American political democracy. In spite of Willits's initial postwar enthusiasm for applied social research, grant-making in the Social Science Division was characterized more by stability than by the Carnegie concept of strategic—and temporary—intervention.[26]

From his prewar experiences, Willits had a keen appreciation for the realities of the social sciences in American universities. He could at times echo the prevailing consensus about the general inadequacy of social science training and the weaknesses of practitioners.[27] But when confronted by the charge that the field had no scientific basis (also a frequently bruited opinion) he once responded by listing thirteen locations where conditions existed for fruitful social scientific research.[28] Interestingly, all were special programs or organized research units, with the sole exception of the heavily patronized Chicago department of sociology. Willits was in fact mindful of the obstacles to departmentally based social science research, and even contemplated making this issue the focus of a major Division program.[29]

Instead of a separate program, the bolstering of academic research in the social sciences was implicit in the role Willits assumed. He consciously sought to provide guidance to university leaders for improving the conditions for research in the social sciences, and by doing so he exerted considerable influence behind the scene. It was through Willits's office, for example, that the relocation of the Yale Institute of International Relations to Princeton was negotiated. Having virtual veto power over the move, Willits favored Princeton because of its enlightened approach to research in this field.[30] In the case of his former university, Penn, Willits tried to enlist the new president, Harold Stassen, to the cause of research. He explained to Stassen how Penn's paucity of grants was a result of its narrow focus on teaching and lack of concern for research. He furthermore told Stassen exactly what steps might be taken to rectify this situation.[31] Willits thus actively utilized his position and his grant-making power to further the model of the research university.

The stability of the Rockefeller approach was evident in 1949, when a budgetary tightening forced the Social Sciences Division to reexamine its basic policies. After prolonged consultation with his staff, Willits resolved upon a set formula: 35 percent of the Division budget would be devoted to basic research to develop a science of social behavior; 35 percent would support applications of social science to social problems, including international relations; 10 percent would be reserved for fundamental moral and philosophical issues underlying social science; and 20 percent would underwrite the Division's longstanding backing of training, fellowships, and grants-in-aid.[32] In theory, this policy committed the bulk of Foundation social science funds to discipline-building; but in practice grant-making tended to confirm a pattern of supporting separate research institutes. These units, in Willits's mind, were the loci of the most scientific work in the social sciences; and they, of course, were best positioned to produce applicable social knowledge.

A major redirection of social science policy did not occur until after Willits's retirement in 1954. His successor was then faced with markedly different circumstances within and outside the Foundation. Externally, he could not ignore the fact that the "Ford Foundation had moved into the social sciences in a large way financially." Within the Foundation, a far-reaching policy change was made to favor problems of underdeveloped countries, and this emphasis was to be reflected in the programs of all the divisions.[33] Under Willits's hand the Social Sciences Division expended the bulk of almost $30 million to support academic social science in the United States. The discipline of economics, where Willits felt the U.S. had become preeminent in the world, was a major beneficiary. So too were the principal research institutions associated with universities. Beyond that, this support was diffused into the social sciences through the Foundation's own programs and those of the SSRC. By the mid-fifties, however, the Rockefeller Foundation, like the Carnegie Corporation, was willing to cede the patronage of academic social science to the new colossus of American philanthropy.

The Ford Foundation and the Behavioral Sciences.   With the death of Henry Ford, Sr., in 1947, almost 90 percent of ownership in the ailing Ford Motor Company passed to the Ford Foundation, making it potentially, and soon actually, the world's largest philanthropic entity. To create a national foundation commensurate with these assets meant devising a program "to advance human welfare"—in the words of the charter—without the guidance of established traditions or organizational experience. This daunting task was complicated first by the magnitudes involved. The Ford Foundation was virtually compelled to make grants of great size that held potential for great impact. Moreover, its grants were sure to be made in the full glare of public scrutiny. Second was a problem of leadership, which was acute at the beginning and only gradually assuaged over time. The Foundation trustees had less than full confidence in the first three presidents and were often divided among themselves. The fractious politics of the board in turn affected the direction of the Foundation. Finally, the initial years of Foundation operations coincided with the height of McCarthyism in the country. The polarization of political discourse that occurred during these years created an added difficulty for programs purporting to bring change to American society, a difficulty further aggravated by hostile Congressional investigations of foundation activities.[34] Despite the controversy that swirled around and about the Foundation, its actual programs were largely shaped by a competent and dedicated staff. The Ford Foundation invested heavily, although not exclusively, on the intellectual frontiers that had been charted by the Carnegie Corporation and the Rockefeller Foundation. In addition, it was able to do what no foundation since the 1920s had been capable of—making significant capital grants for both basic institutional strengthening and special purposes. Thus, from the mid-fifties to the early sixties the Ford Foundation became the most significant external arbiter of the development of university research outside of the natural sciences.

The modern Ford Foundation traces its intellectual birthright to a study committee of independent consultants chaired by H. Rowan Gaither, Jr. (1948–50), which surveyed the philanthropic landscape immediately after the death of Henry Ford, Sr. The committee rejected medicine as being well served by the NIH, and bypassed the natural sciences as likely to be supported by the federal government and the new NSF. It focused instead upon what were basically social concerns. Its report, which was adopted as the official program of the newly constituted foundation, designated five emphases: the establishment of world peace; improving the economy; the strengthening of democracy; problems of education; and furthering what was originally termed the scientific study of man and later called the behavioral sciences.[35] It was not coincidental that this list encompassed the postwar programs of the Carnegie Corporation and the Rockefeller Social Science Division. The fundamental problems that both had seized upon immediately after the war had by the late 1940s become widely appreciated. These concerns now became embodied in functioning divisions of the new foundation. Four of them would develop and proliferate over the years into myriad programs and activities, while only one of these seminal programs would be terminated—the effort to build the behavioral sciences.

Once in operation, the Ford Foundation touched nearly every facet of American higher education, but its greatest immediate impact was undoubtedly felt in the social sciences and in the research universities. The International Division quickly became the mainstay of area studies and international relations. The program on Economic Development assumed the Rockefeller mantle as the chief patron of research in economics.[36] The section that became most intimately involved with university social science, however, was Program V—the so-called Behavioral Sciences. This neologism was chosen for reasons peculiar to the situation. It was thought desirable to avoid the word 'social,' which might carry connotations of socialism or social reform. At the same time, there was a wish to include psychology as the most scientifically mature of the 'human' sciences. Political science and economics were less concerned with 'behavior,' but they were well covered in other programs. The behavioral sciences as defined by Ford, then, came to center on psychology, social psychology, anthropology, and sociology, but did not actually exclude any of the social sciences.[37]

The Behavioral Sciences Program (BSP) sprang from the same perception of the social sciences that had motivated the other two foundations. The central objectives were "to acquire scientific knowledge of human behavior and to apply such knowledge to human affairs." But in order to have any expectation of attaining these goals an anterior effort had to be made to advance and develop these subjects technically—to make them more scientific. At Ford the critique of the current state of the social sciences was more thorough and explicit. It also seemed to carry two somewhat different messages. The first was that the social science disciplines were not yet fulfilling their basic mission: there was insufficient integration of theory and empirical data, and little cumulation of knowledge; too few highly qualified individuals were recruited into the social sciences; and the training of future researchers was sadly deficient. A second set of criticisms, however, implied that the existing organization of the social sciences was an obstacle to progress: cooperative work was largely lacking; departments were isolated from one another; and overspecialization seemed rampant.[38] The divergence between these positions was not specifically addressed by the program officers, although it carried far-reaching implications about what kind of programs the Foundation might sponsor to advance the behavioral sciences.

The BSP began with an impressive list of specific topics on which it hoped to promote research and derive applicable knowledge. Although these were never entirely forgotten, most of the applied, or problem-specific work of the Foundation came to be concentrated in the other divisions. Thus the BSP tended to focus on its distinctive mission of technical advancement, which it defined as, 1) increasing the number of "competent behavioral scientists"; 2) making the content of the behavioral sciences more scientific; 3) improving methods of investigation; and 4) developing institutional resources. Or, put more simply, the BSP "tried mainly to build up the basic resources of the behavioral sciences—in ideas, in methods, in men [sic] and in institutions."[39]

In seven years of existence the BSP made grants of almost $43 million: of this total, $13 million belonged to a rather special project in mental health, and almost $10 million was committed after termination to conclude various initiatives. According to Ford's own internal reckoning, 37 percent of these funds went for "men" (training); 28 percent for ideas (basic research); 20 percent for institutional resources; and only 1 percent for methods. The remainder (14%) was accounted for by applied research.[40]

The downfall of the BSP had little to do with this pattern of grant-making. Rather, it reflected political anxieties among the trustees, who never fully grasped the recondite notion of building social science. They could unite behind the general aims of the Program, but particular grants were frequently divisive.[41] Rowan Gaither was the true godfather of the BSP from the days of the Study Committee, and while he was president of the Foundation (1953–56) the behavioral sciences were fairly secure. But when ill health forced him to step down, the avoidance of controversy became the watchword under his successor, Henry T. Heald (1956–65). The BSP was promptly shuttered, albeit with some generous terminal grants intended to forestall recriminations. Program director Bernard Berelson was not mollified. He regarded the decision to terminate "hurtful" to both the field and the Ford Foundation. Specifically, he was disturbed that the Foundation's large presence in this area had induced both the Rockefeller Foundation and the Carnegie Corporation to withdraw. He also felt that applied social studies of the kind that predominated in the other divisions skimmed the cream off these fields, and that it should be replenished through support for basic research.[42] Although he strongly supported the Program and felt that there was a great deal more to accomplish in this area, Berelson did not defend all of the actions it had taken.

In a Five-Year Report on the BSP (1956) Berelson offered a critical evaluation of its accomplishments. Most interesting are his assessments of the grants he considered "particularly good" and those he found "particularly disappointing":[43]

Particularly Good

Establishing the Center for Advanced Study in the Behavioral Sciences
Program in Law and the Behavioral Sciences at the University of Chicago
Programmatic support of good men (see below)
Research in mental health
Institutional development: Johns Hopkins & MIT
Individual grants-in-aid

Particularly Disappointing

Program of university surveys
Inventories of knowledge in the behavioral sciences
Interdisciplinary research and study
Summer training sessions (under the SSRC)

A pattern is evident in Berelson's lists. The disappointments seem to be associated with the original, rather ambitious Foundation aims for reforming the behavioral sciences; the successes largely buttressed existing practices in the disciplines.

One of the earliest, and perhaps most central, discomfitures of the BSP concerned promoting the notion of "behavioral sciences" to universities. It quickly became apparent that the currency of the term was due to the assets of the Ford Foundation rather than the inherent attractiveness of the concept. In 1953–54, grants were given to launch "thorough reviews of the state, the problems, and the needs of the behavioral sciences" at Chicago, Harvard, Michigan, North

Carolina, and Stanford.[44] These surveys consisted of self-studies by faculty committees at each university supplemented by reports from visiting committees. The stated purpose was to promote the development of institutional resources, and particularly to aid graduate education, but there was obviously a more subtle agenda: universities adopting the behavioral sciences approach might expect financial assistance from the Foundation. The results were uneven. The home committee at Chicago was deemed to be derelict in its task; while Harvard produced a polished report of 500+ pages which it published and distributed. Nevertheless, even this impressive effort failed to strike the right chords as far as the BSP was concerned. The report that met with most favor was that from Stanford, in part because it proposed major innovations, especially a "Behavioral Sciences Research Institute" and special professorships.[45]

The disappointment, from the Foundation's point of view, was that none of the surveys started from a fundamental reevaluation of the nature and actual state of the behavioral sciences. Instead,

> the Surveys tended to concentrate on means of attracting Ford Foundation support but to resist specifying its purposes ("free," "fluid," or "program" funds), to concentrate on adjustments of the status quo but to avoid fundamental reorientation. They tended, that is to say, to concentrate on tactics and organizational arrangements for development within existing frameworks.[46]

Some token grants (by Ford standards) were eventually awarded "for development and improvement of work in the behavioral sciences," Stanford and Harvard being most favored and Chicago (at least in this respect) neglected. Most important, however, Berelson concluded that university social science could not be reformed in this manner.[47]

The BSP also attempted to foster cooperation between the humanities and the social sciences with its "interdisciplinary study and research awards" (1953). The judgment here was essentially the same—that fruitful relationships spanning the humanistic and social scientific realms could not be brought into being through such monetary inducements. This conclusion, together with the experience from the surveys, seems to have caused a reassessment of the backing given to interdisciplinarity. Although the concept was attractive in theory, implementation created problems, especially with personnel. If top figures were persuaded to participate in interdisciplinary ventures, their absence from the disciplines might retard the advancement of basic social science. Also, given the inherent advantages of the disciplines in recruitment, there was likely to be a deterioration in the quality of personnel in interdisciplinary programs over time.[48]

In a similar vein, one of the BSP's particular successes also represented a partial reorientation of its original purposes. The Center for Advanced Study in the Behavioral Sciences at Stanford was intended to be a major instrument in upgrading the quality of behavioral scientists. It was modeled after the Institute for Advanced Study in Princeton, where a corps of permanent appointees, a contingent of distinguished annual visitors, and carefully selected postdocs collaborated on advanced topics in a variety of fields. Crucial to the original conception of the Center was the notion of training an elite group of the most talented postdoctoral social scientists, who might thereby "avoid the intellectual dilution which derives from the presence of lesser qualified people" in university programs.[49] Under the Center's first director, Ralph Tyler, however, the idea of training students was abandoned almost from the outset. In practice, the ideas of interdisciplinary collaboration and of developing model programs for the behavioral sciences were eclipsed as well. The Center became primarily an academic retreat, providing chosen social scientists with ideal conditions to accomplish their work. As such it became a valued institution for individuals and the profession. But its realization was a less bold innovation than the original concept.

After a few years of operation the BSP had moved a considerable distance from its original critique of the social sciences. The coordinator of the Surveys program articulated the emerging attitude when he argued that the quality of individuals was the key element in the advancement of the behavioral sciences, and not, by implication, organizational innovations. He accordingly advocated putting grant money into the hands of individual scientists to be used as they saw fit.[50] Indeed, most of the successes on the BSP scorecard reflect this approach. "Programmatic support of good men" (1956–57) provided substantial grants for eminent scientists "to do the things they most want to do, without much attention to the 'project-like' characteristics of the proposals and, in fact, with the intention to eliminate the contrived aspects of some projects." "Individual grants-in-aid" (1953, 1956–57) provided small amounts without strings to facilitate the research programs of individual faculty. And the Center, as it developed, enhanced the productivity of already productive individuals.[51]

This shift signified a new assessment of university social science on the part of the Foundation. Although the objectives of the Foundation and those of university social scientists were not identical, there was a considerable amount of overlap. But in the tug-of-war of defining and pursuing these objectives, it was the academics that pulled hardest. By the last years of the BSP, it had largely swung around to accepting the academic status quo and to strengthening the social sciences on their own terms.

There is no single explanation for this development. In part, the original BSP critique of the social sciences was unduly pessimistic about actual conditions, and too ready to embrace the chimera of interdisciplinarity. (It must also be borne in mind, however, that this critique was the rationale for intervention in the first place.) In part, American social science was far more vigorous by 1956, and much less in need of reformation, than had been the case at the end of the 1940s. In the main, however, the social sciences evinced a powerful inertia of organization and doctrine. Organizationally, they were deeply rooted in university departments and directed by a superstructure of associations and the SSRC. These organizations were run by a large and changing oligarchy of representatives who fairly faithfully reflected their respective disciplinary communities. Intellectually, the cumulation of knowledge within the paradigms of the established disciplines was a sufficiently challenging and elusive goal for the great majority of active researchers. Inevitably, the Ford Foundation discovered that it was easier to accelerate momentum along established paths than to change the direction of social science development. In this respect, the experience of the BSP foreshadowed the entire relationship between the Foundation and the universities.

The incidence of social science support.   The termination of the BSP did not appreciably lessen Ford Foundation spending on the social sciences. Economics and international programs, in particular, received increasing support after 1957. At the Carnegie Corporation and the Rockefeller Foundation grants for social scientific research after this date reflected the programmatic emphases that each had chosen—education and then social issues for the former, and third-world development for the latter. The end of the BSP in the same year as the launch of Sputnik marked the end of the postwar era in American social science. No comparable foundation program for the systematic development of the social sciences would henceforth be attempted.[52] The organization and epistemology of social scientific research were no longer problematic. Instead, patrons of research showed a confidence they had previously lacked in using the social sciences to address specific issues. Also after 1957, federal support for academic social science became significant; no longer were social scientists solely dependent for resources on the major foundations. Finally, within the disciplines a crescive momentum became evident as graduates of the leading programs carried the latest theories and methods to departments across the country. The great investments in academic social science by these three foundations during the postwar era most certainly contributed to the maturation of American social science.

Support for academic social science accelerated greatly in the twelve years following the war, largely due to the expanding activities of the Ford Foundation. Grants from the three foundations to the leading universities (Table 4) rose from $4.5 million in 1946-49 to $43.6 million in 1955-58.[53] Ford grants accounted for no less than four-fifths of the grants in the last period. The universities listed in Table 4 are the seventeen largest recipients, and their total grants represented a substantial part of the support given to social science in these years. These universities also constituted a large fraction of American social science. With minor exceptions, they were the highest ranking universities in the social sciences, and they awarded almost half of the Ph.D.s in anthropology, economics, political science, and sociology. These same foundations were also the mainstay of the Social Science Research Council, which, unlike the foundations, disbursed its funds in small parcels for grants-in-aid, fellowships, workshops, and conferences. SSRC expenditures directly supported the ongoing activities of the social science disciplines, largely in universities.

The three foundations followed similar courses of action in supporting university social science. Wickliffe Rose's 1920s dictum of "making the peaks higher" seems no longer to have been fashionable in philanthropic circles, yet that was the course these foundations took.[54] Almost half (48%) of these funds went to the 'Big Three' universities in social science—Harvard, Columbia, and

TABLE 4. Foundation Support for University Social Science, 1946–1958 (Totals, Ph.D.s Awarded, Relative Rank)[55]

	Support		Ph.D.s 1950–56		1957 Ranking	
	$000	%	No.	%	Rank	Score
Public Universities:						
Michigan	4,380	5.1	110	2.2	6	928
California	3,941	4.6	134	2.7	4	995
Minnesota	1,892	2.2	140	2.8	7	580
North Carolina	1,706	2.0	101	2.0	19	205
Illinois	1,079	1.3	16	0.3	13	315
Wisconsin	987	1.2	264	5.3	10	409
Private Universities:						
Harvard	17,530	20.5	107	2.1	1	1,311
Columbia	12,216	14.3	317	6.4	3	1,002
Chicago	11,714	13.7	438	8.8	2	1,061
Yale	6,206	7.2	139	2.8	5	933
M.I.T.	5,322	6.2	43	0.8	not included	
Stanford	4,777	5.6	66	1.3	8	520
Cornell	4,005	4.7	195	3.9	9	488
Princeton	3,705	4.3	79	1.6	11	407
Pennsylvania	2,966	3.5	165	3.3	14	314
Northwestern	1,705	2.0	78	1.6	15	299
Johns Hopkins	1,626	1.9	51(est.)	1.0	16	267
Totals	85,647	100.0	2443	49%		

Chicago. More remarkably, the totals received by the private universities correspond almost perfectly with their 1957 rankings in social science. Foundation giving-patterns naturally differed for public and private universities. Support for programs in public institutions almost never included capital gifts, while favored programs in private universities commonly did, contributing to the higher totals. There are only two significant anomalies in the correspondence between rank and amount of support. North Carolina was particularly favored as a Southern university and a regional center of social science research; and MIT's large total resulted chiefly from support by the Ford Foundation for the Center for International Studies. (In fact, the unusual nature of the CIS, noted in the previous chapter, is underscored here.)

The bias in foundation patronage toward the universities that subsequently were ranked highest can be viewed as either cause or effect. It stemmed directly from the initial foundation policies. Where the objective was advancing the knowledge base of the social sciences, support was naturally directed to the leading figures in the top departments. Where the objective was applied social knowledge, the foundations sought those who could most effectively perform the needed studies, which again favored organized research units in the leading universities. Much of this latter type of support, particularly Ford grants, went to professional schools, especially those of business and law. There the disparity in research capacities probably favored the Big Three even more decisively than in social science departments.[56] At the time, departments favored by foundations had insuperable advantages. Longer term, the Ph.D.s trained in these research-enriched environments populated expanding social science departments at other universities. Securing social science grants became a two-sided process. Universities could, and did, take measures to make themselves into more attractive and more likely recipients. Nevertheless, during the postwar era (1946–57) foundation grant-making rather faithfully reflected the distribution of research capacities in the social sciences.

Of the 'Big Three,' Harvard was clearly preeminent in the social sciences and related professional fields, and Chicago and Columbia were roughly comparable in support and rank. All three institutions employed the same formula for success—multiple centers of academic strength in the departments, ORUs, and professional schools. Harvard's economics department was the unchallenged leader in its field both before and after the war. In the department of Social Relations—itself a bold departure—Talcott Parsons was orchestrating the elaboration of a general theory of action intended to comprehend all facets of social systems. The Laboratory of Social Relations under Samuel Stouffer conducted empirical work on group behavior. The Russian Research Center was the prototypical area studies unit, with the most generous funding of its ilk, and it was joined by research units devoted to Far East Asia and International Affairs. The Harvard Business School was one of the few with a developed research capacity. It was led, furthermore, by Dean Donald K. David, a powerful trustee of the Ford Foundation who was not reluctant to wield his influence on behalf of his school.[57]

Chicago and Columbia possessed the same elements to a somewhat lesser degree. They were, besides Harvard, the other two preeminent centers for the development of sociology, and both had distinguished economics departments. Columbia had the Bureau of Applied Social Research, and Chicago the National Opinion Research Center. Columbia cultivated international relations more intensively, while Chicago probably conducted more research in its schools of law and business. But, like Harvard, they presented foundations with a multitude of opportunities for supporting social science research.[58]

The next three universities in the social science rankings, on the other hand, differed significantly from one another. Berkeley was a rapidly rising star in the academic firmament at the time the Keniston rankings were made, and this momentum was reflected in a rapidly rising volume of grants. As previously noted, Berkeley was aware of the possibilities of foundation support and was determined to take the steps required to claim its share. This was accomplished primarily by building up the basic social science departments, and secondly by augmenting their research capacities with related ORUs.

Michigan had a more stable grants record, largely as a result of the Institute for Social Research and the Center for Japanese Studies. But, as the origins of those units would suggest, its activities were more the result of happenstance than design. Michigan's venerable president, Alexander Ruthven (1930–50), was critical of organized research and its effects on the university. By the early 1950s Michigan had attained a balanced and distinguished social science program without the kind of premeditation evident at Berkeley. The self-survey sponsored by the Ford Foundation identified a reluctance to compete in the national arena for top social scientists. The Visiting Committee took issue with this attitude and encouraged the University to raise its sights. Foundation encouragement in this case seems to have helped Michigan to attain a prominence in the social sciences that it had not independently sought.[59]

Yale, despite its lofty ranking, seems to have forgone an opportunity to play an even larger role in the development of the social sciences. Its prewar ORUs, the Institute for Human Relations and Institute of International Relations, were ideally situated to perform the kinds of investigations that the foundations were eager to fund. Yet neither sought grants aggressively, and both fell victim to the prevailing disdain for organized research. Yale possessed leading departments in both economics and psychology (both ranked 3), but it repeatedly failed to address its acknowledged weakness in sociology. Yale was first slow to perceive, and then overtly hostile toward, an emerging research environment in which departmental quality and external support for organized research were mutually reinforcing. It consequently failed to keep pace with Chicago and Columbia, which, given Yale's resources, would have been a reasonable expectation.[60]

Seventh-ranked Minnesota attained only five-eighths of the ranking score and less than half of the funding of sixth-ranked Michigan. This difference attests to a rapid falling-off in relative departmental strength.[61] Below the top six universities, the capacities for social science research were increasingly thin and spotty until the very end of this era, and these conditions were reflected in foundation grant-making. It would be unfair to disparage the social sciences at these universities; many talented individuals and some quality programs existed. In addition, most of these schools were engaged in, or about to initiate, significant upgrading efforts. Foundation support often figured prominently in such developments, as at Stanford, MIT, and North Carolina. Foundations also deliberately cultivated areas of local strength, such as population studies at Princeton and applied economics at Penn's Wharton School. In the case of area studies, the foundations largely implanted new academic specialties. The distribution of social science capabilities would broaden rapidly after 1960; but during the postwar era most universities, in contrast to the Big Three, offered foundations few opportunities for investing in the social sciences. If anything, the foundations probably strained to find worthy projects beyond the charmed circle of the leading institutions.

While foundation programs clearly aided the institutional development of the social sciences, the underlying purpose was to further their intellectual development. Results in this realm are more difficult to assess, but a few conclusions are evident. In promoting area studies, the foundations created centers of expertise at major universities that had not previously existed, and could not have been sustained without external support. Later it would appear that they overinvested in these programs and largely lost sight of the original objectives.[62] There can nevertheless be little doubt that these programs produced a sizable scholarly literature on world affairs. The foundations also performed a valuable service by supporting university-based social-science research institutes like ISR and BASR. Here the chief contribution was providing resources for work of a predominantly academic nature, which relieved the pressures of doing applied studies and permitted a closer integration with social science departments. The substantial support that was directed toward law and business schools most likely had mixed results: it undoubtedly induced a greater involvement in research than would otherwise have been the case in these professionally oriented units, but overall results did not seem commensurate with original expectations.[63] In all these cases, foundation patronage helped to create new bodies of knowledge that were, for the most part, academic rather than practical in nature.

Programs intended to achieve an interdisciplinary synthesis of knowledge about society and human behavior brought more doubtful results. Superficially, it seemed both plausible and compelling to attempt to integrate the sociological understanding of social structure, the anthropological conception of culture, and knowledge of personality derived from clinical psychology and psychoanalysis. In fact, the most concerted effort of this type, that at Harvard under the leadership of Talcott Parsons, is generally considered to have fallen short of expectations.[64] The paradigms of each field were far from established and in combination failed to produce a scheme upon which social scientists could agree or make the basis of further investigation. In a similar vein, the substantial foundation investment in applications of the techniques of clinical psychology to the behavior of groups was in the long run disappointing. Some of this work eventually found its way into the literature on management, but small group theory failed to become a major component of American sociology.[65]

The foundations eventually swung around to supporting social science on the terms preferred by academic practitioners—unrestricted support for "good men," investigator-initiated projects, research institutes, and graduate training—support, in sum, for the best departments as conventionally defined. Given the limited research capabilities in the social sciences, the strategy of 'making the peaks higher' seems to have been appropriate. It rather quickly promoted more scientific approaches in these disciplines. Longer term, however, it did even more: it unified these disciplines into national entities, rather than collections of rival schools, and it soon produced additional peaks. Berkeley sociology is a case in point. It achieved preeminent status through judicious recruiting from peak departments, notably Chicago and Columbia. The result was a unit that reflected all of the currents of American sociology rather than those of one particular school.[66]

The Berkeley sociology department, like most of the other entities that were indebted to foundation patronage, was a single institutional manifestation of a ferment of ideas too broad and deep to analyze here. Instead, an oblique view of this ferment can be had from one systematic attempt to identify the major twentieth-century advances in the social sciences and to correlate them with the conditions under which they were made. The exercise itself was inherently controversial and inescapably imprecise, but the cogency of the conclusions arises from the sum of the examples.[67]

A heavy preponderance of advances from 1930 to 1965 came from the United

States. The majority were produced by teams, rather than individuals. Both of these trends seemed to be strengthening. More than three-fifths of advances since 1930 required "large amounts of capital, particularly for survey research and large-scale tabulations." Most advances occurred in large cities and/or university centers; nearly two-thirds of the advances since 1930 were interdisciplinary in nature; and more than four-fifths were stimulated by practical demands or considerations. In response to their critics, the authors distilled their main findings:

> what seems to have worked best were small teams in large places—a spatial concentration of stimulation and support, a plurality of persons, organizations, and initiatives, and some communication with the world of practical needs.[68]

In the most general terms, regardless of original intent, foundation policies toward university social science in the postwar era largely fulfilled this prescription.

2. Foundation Support for University Advancement

In the mid-1950s the condition and the capacity of the nation's educational system became a widespread concern. Such issues, and particularly their implications for colleges and universities, were reflected in the programs of the major foundations. Carnegie Corporation president John Gardner articulated this new outlook in his 1956 annual report—"The Great Talent Hunt." He underscored the importance of highly educated workers for contemporary society, and foresaw a doubling or trebling of American higher education in the coming two decades. These realities by themselves translated into many possibilities for foundation activity: assisting talented individuals to educational attainments commensurate with their abilities; promoting the needed expansion of graduate and professional education; counterbalancing the trend toward narrow specialization with programs of liberal education; and sustaining "a very small group of first-line institutions" that trained the "highest echelons of professional, scientific and scholarly talent." Such a program would inescapably require "maintaining the standards and the vigor" of the research universities.[1]

President Henry Heald of the Ford Foundation was mindful of the same concerns. He declared unabashedly "that the strengthening of American higher education is one of the primary means by which the Foundation pursues its objective of advancing human welfare."[2] Only the Ford Foundation, in fact, possessed the assets that could materially affect the financial constraints of private colleges and universities. Three programs of capital grants for universities addressed this problem from 1956 to 1966 (Table 5). The motivation for each of these programs was somewhat different: the first was intended to assist the better-quality private institutions and, implicitly, encourage others to emulate them; the second was motivated by external considerations and assisted all private colleges

TABLE 5. Ford Foundation Capital Grants to Universities 1955–1966 ($000)[3]

Program	Accomplishment Grants 1956–57	Endowment Grants 1956–57	Challenge Grants	Yrs.	Match	Total	Endowment Mrkt.— 1957
Chicago	1,379	3,621	25,000	1965	75,000	105,000	175,276
Columbia	778	4,223	25,000	1966	75,000	105,000	138,758
Cornell	1,585	2,557				4,142	84,000
Harvard	1,497	3,503				5,000	458,000
Johns Hopkins	637	1,026	12,000	'60–62	24,000	37,663	84,368
Northwestern	1,899	3,060				4,859	114,000
Penn.	1,460	2,353				3,813	57,486
Princeton	1,468	2,367				3,835	116,955
Stanford	1,380	2,225	25,000	1960	75,000	103,605	94,700
Yale	1,638	3,362				5,000	256,623
10-Univ.	13,721 (27%)	32,154 (15%)	87,000 (25%)				
Other Challenge Grants Universities							
Brandeis	329	531	12,000	'62–64	36,000	48,860	32,730
Brown	767	1,235	12,500	'61–64	25,000	27,002	5,284
Denver	—	871	5,000	1960	10,000	15,871	51,153
Duke	1,127	1,816	8,000	1966	32,000	43,943	37,647
Emory	597	963	6,000	1966	24,000	31,560	55,008
New York U.	1,143	3,857	25,000	1964	75,000	105,000	48,388
Notre Dame	1,177	1,898	12,000	'60–63	24,000	37,075	10,425
Southern Cal.	—	1,761	14,000	'62–64	42,000	57,761	27,307
St. Louis	780	1,256	5,000	1965	15,000	22,036	30,597
Tulane	878	1,414	6,000	1964	12,000	20,292	50,905
Vanderbilt	556	897	15,000	'60–66	52,000	58,453	56,419
Washington U.	876	1,412	15,000	1965	45,000	62,288	

and universities; and the third was originally an attempt to increase the number and strength of private research universities.

The Accomplishment Grants Program was intended to assist private institutions and to strengthen the academic profession. It disbursed $50 million to institutions that had made progress in raising faculty salaries above the abysmal postwar levels. The entire roster of private colleges and universities was evaluated according to regional standards, and one-fifth (126) of them was selected for grants. The likely influence of these grants, however, was largely overwhelmed by the subsequent decision to award faculty endowment grants to *all* accredited private colleges and universities. This latter program was a direct consequence of the decision to separate the Foundation from the Ford Motor Company.

In 1955 the Foundation announced that it would begin to sell its 88 percent holdings in the now-thriving Ford Motor Company. When a market valuation was placed on these privately held shares, the world's largest foundation became considerably larger. The Foundation's assets had been valued at $580 million and its grants totaled $66 million (FY1955). Then, in January 1956, it sold approximately 22 percent of its holdings of Ford Motor for $642 million. By 1960 the Foundation would show a net worth of $2196 million and award grants of $163 million.[4] By way of comparison, the Ford grants that year exceeded those of the National Science Foundation.

The move to diversify the Foundation portfolio was called for by the incompatability between the nature of its assets—equity in a firm in a cyclical industry—and its philanthropic mission of advancing human welfare. The decision was in all likelihood hastened by the pressures that hostile Congressional investigations placed upon Foundation activities.[5] Moreover, the Foundation was regularly assailed by conservative journalists and politicians. Under these circumstances, the trustees had little inclination either to enlarge the scope of Foundation programs or to invite additional controversy with new undertakings. They chose instead to dispense with some of this new wealth in an expeditious manner. Before any stock had actually been sold, the Foundation announced grants of $210 million to private colleges and universities, $198 million to nonprofit hospitals, and $90 million to private medical schools (not included in Table 5).

The higher education grants were made to 630 private colleges and universities—the entire population of four-year accredited institutions. Each grant was based on the size of the undergraduate instructional budget for the previous year, and the funds were to be used as endowment for faculty salaries for at least ten years. The endowment and accomplishment grants together seem to have been limited to $5 million. Despite this cap, the private research universities did well: the ten leaders from Table 5 received 27 percent of all accomplishment grants and 15 percent of the endowment funds.[6]

In foundation circles the great Ford capital distribution of 1956–57 has often been dismissed as mindless philanthropy.[7] From the viewpoint of the recipients, however, these grants were not only welcome but also large enough to have a significant budgetary impact. For half of the leading universities, the accomplishment and endowment grants represented more than 3 percent of current endowments. Even at a wealthy institution like Yale, Ford gifts were meaningful: out of gifts to permanent funds of $12.4 million in 1956–57, $9.1 million were given by the Ford Foundation through these and other programs.[8] The Ford Foundation of this era consistently tilted its programs to benefit private institutions and research universities, thus favoring private research universities on both counts. Moreover, unlike the bulk of external funds that flowed into the research universities, Ford endowment and accomplishment grants, and occasionally other Ford gifts too, were for core university purposes. The Ford Foundation by itself was a significant factor in the financial revitalization of the private universities.

The Ford capital grants of 1956–57 occurred at a turning point in the financial affairs of the private research universities. Foundations, and preponderantly the Ford Foundation, spearheaded a dramatic expansion of voluntary support for these universities.[9] From this juncture into the mid-sixties, foundation grants constituted more than a third of total gifts to the major private universities. Perhaps more remarkably, foundation gifts to just ten major universities in 1960 comprised more than a third of all foundation giving to higher education.[10] In part, this abundant support was a product of the natural operations of existing programs; in part, the principal private universities were selected to lend salience and legitimacy to foundation causes like area studies or business education; and occasionally these institutions were consciously singled out for assistance in their own right. The largest undertaking of the latter type was the Ford Foundation program of Challenge Grants (originally called the Special Program in Education: Table 5). In this effort the Foundation initiated what soon became a national effort to expand the number of the research universities—endorsing, in effect, the primacy of this model.

The Challenge Grants were initially a response to the concentration of research support among the "recognized national and international leaders," as well as to the relative disadvantage of private universities compared with their growing public counterparts. The Foundation made the thinking behind the program quite explicit:

—that the continuation of the established dual system of publicly and privately supported higher education is essential to the welfare of the nation.
—that the Foundation most appropriately performs its role in society when it supports primarily privately supported higher education.
—that regional peaks of excellence in privately supported higher education are essential to nationwide vigor and growth, overall academic and institutional freedom, and broad equality of educational opportunity.[11]

The first two assumptions were articles of faith that justified the Foundation's particular solicitude toward the private sector; the last was the chief rationalization for Challenge Grants.

Although the program was subsequently broadened to include liberal arts colleges, its principal focus was on universities. Grants were made to sixteen universities and sixty-eight colleges, but the universities claimed 64 percent of the funds. As a condition of receiving $222.5 million, these sixteen universities agreed to raise an additional $641 million. What the Foundation sought to accomplish was chiefly to build upon existing academic strengths—"strong schools or departments" and "a tradition of scholarship or evidence of seeking to establish it"—and concommitantly to develop the financial wherewithal to sustain high-quality academic programs. The Foundation chose the candidates it wished to consider on the basis of leadership, strategic importance to their region, fund-raising potential, and commitment to academic improvement. It then worked closely with the institutions in formulating a plan of development. The Foundation intended to have considerable influence in determining the objectives of each plan, but the ensuing grant would then be essentially free funds to be employed as the university saw fit. The matching requirements were crucial to the program objective, not just for the money itself, but because it forced these universities to enhance fund-raising capabilities.[12]

The initial grantees exemplified the aims of the program. Johns Hopkins, the original American research university, was comparatively underdeveloped aside from its renowned medical school and the Applied Physics Laboratory. Its undergraduate college had not produced sufficient loyal and wealthy alumni, and as a national institution it had not cultivated close ties with local benefactors. The Foundation also resuscitated the venerable dream of providing the academic leadership that had always been absent from the capital region. Vanderbilt was a perennial candidate of foundations for nurturing academic excellence in the South. Notre Dame, the Catholic university having the largest endowment, was selected to provide academic leadership to that sizable, but somewhat insular, segment of American higher education. The University of Denver was a new and rather unlikely candidate for research university status, but it was virtually the only private possibility in the Mountain States region. Stanford was already well along in its rapid ascent among research universities, which will be examined in the next chapter. As the first university chosen for the Challenge Grants Program, Stanford epitomized the criteria. In fact, the Stanford example may well have been the true inspiration for the Challenge Grants Program.[13]

The criteria for qualifying to be a Challenge Grant university were multiple and subjective. As the list was expanded over time, it appeared that any large private university might hope (or scheme) for this bounty. Five of the next eleven universities chosen were located in the New York, Chicago, or Boston area, which cast doubt upon the goal of improving regional balance. When Columbia and Chicago were favored in 1965–66, presumably for being urban, it seemed that the established research universities had now become eligible. Clearly, one of the difficulties that the Challenge Grants Program confronted was the growing throng of candidates clamoring for preferment.[14]

The grants themselves were unquestionably a boon to the recipients. Besides the academic development they facilitated, the processes of planning and fund-raising left positive legacies. The Foundation too could regard this program as a success. It had been extended in 1965 and 1966, and a further renewal was contemplated in 1968. The assessment of conditions in the private research universities on that occasion provides some insight into the changes that had occurred during the years the Challenge Grants Program operated.

In 1960 it could confidently be stated, "that only the Ford Foundation, among the foundations of our time in our society, can provide support in sufficient amounts over a sufficiently sustained period of time to stimulate a major advance in the development of dispersed peaks of excellence"; but the outlook was otherwise in 1968. A program of similar impact would cost far more, and thus curtail other foundation support to higher education. Moreover, several federal agencies had followed in the wake of the Ford Foundation by establishing science development programs to encourage more universities to become active in research. The Ford program, it was now feared, might be "dwarfed" by these federal initiatives.[15] (See Chapter 7.)

On the other hand, "a general expansion of the scale of giving to private universities and colleges" during these years had accomplished one of the major aims of the program. Certainly it no longer needed to be demonstrated that institutions "can greatly expand the scale of their support"; in fact, there was now "a tendency to make fund-raising a chronic, perennial matter, maintained at new levels by permanent, enlarged development offices."[16] In encouraging more aggressive norms for fund-raising, the Challenge Grants Program had hastened this phenomenon, one of the most significant financial developments of the decade for private research universities. But this achievement also weakened the case for continuation. Recommended instead was "a quiet decision to maintain a special interest in those institutions among the original sixteen which can now be considered to be particularly good bets for further development."[17]

Who might these be? Brandeis, Notre Dame, and Vanderbilt were deemed likely candidates; with less conviction, so were Emory and Washington–St. Louis (jointly supported); and with more qualifications, Tulane. Stanford was singled out for special attention, even though it was a frequent recipient of grants from regular Foundation programs. On the other side of the ledger, though, little seemed to have been altered at Johns Hopkins, Columbia, or Chicago; and Southern Cal, Brown, Duke, and NYU disappointed Foundation expectations.[18]

The decision not to renew the Challenge Grants Program was one increment in the gradual withdrawal of Foundation patronage from the specific commitment of strengthening private research universities. Viewed retrospectively, this mission had been accomplished. However, universities themselves still harbored high ambitions for further academic development, and were in fact entering a new era of financial stringency largely caused by those ambitions (see below, Chapter 8). The private research universities had largely succeeded in expanding their resource base and their research capacity; and the foundations, especially the Ford Foundation, had been in the forefront in assisting this achievement. After 1960 the private research universities' gargantuan share of higher education philanthropy slowly and steadily shrank as more and more institutions adopted the same fund-raising techniques. At the same time, the relative contribution from foundations toward supporting these universities declined in similar fashion. Both the share of total gifts to private research universities from foundations, and the share of total foundation support for higher education given to leading private research universities declined regularly for the next three decades.[19]

TABLE 6. Foundation Gifts, Percentage of All Voluntary Support

	1956–57	1965–66	1975–76	1985–86
To ten leading private research universities (from Table 5)	49.3	33.4	27.4	20.8
To all U.S. colleges & universities	25.0	20.2	15.4	15.0

American foundations, and particularly the Ford Foundation, affected the postwar development of research universities in three specific areas. They first supported the social sciences before appreciable federal resources were made available. They then attempted to strengthen the private research universities financially and academically so that those institutions could support high standards and thereby exert a positive influence on the academic system as a whole. Third, in a program discussed in Chapter 7, foundation support beginning in 1957 had a major impact on the stimulation of graduate education. In all these endeavors, foundations were to some extent countering the decided programmatic emphasis of the postwar research environment. Although the original foundation programs in social science had their own programmatic tilt, the eventual course was to support quality social science research as defined by academics themselves. In providing institutional support, the foundations gave backing to conventional academic standards. The same was true in graduate education, where support was provided for the most talented college graduates to pursue Ph.D.s in the leading departments.

Taken together, the separate actions of the major foundations lent powerful backing by the mid-fifties to a particular model of what a research university ought to be. It was not the MIT model of an institution devoted to programmatic research for industry or the Pentagon; nor was it, like Yale sometimes appeared, an ivory tower aloof from the research economy. Rather, the normative model of an American research university was embodied in the postwar development of Berkeley; in the tacit, although somewhat idiosyncratic, academic leadership of Harvard, or the cultivation of academic strength that Joseph Willits perceived at Princeton. The essential traits were increasingly evident to all concerned: the striving for academic distinction as measured by the peer ratings of departments; the placing of increasing emphasis on graduate education; and an abundance of research activity, both within and surrounding the basic disciplinary departments. The largest sums in the research economy were still being absorbed by the laboratories devoted to programmatic research for the defense establishment. But it was becoming increasingly apparent by the mid-fifties that academic distinction would be rewarded with research support. Moreover, the corner was about to be turned. After Sputnik, the nexus between academic distinction and research-related support of diverse kinds would become the dominant note of the research economy.

5

University Advancement
from the Postwar Era
to the 1960s

The abundance of federal support in the postwar research economy clearly redounded to the advantage of those universities with substantial research capacity already in place. For the most part, they were the prewar research universities, but any institution with extensive programs in engineering or physical science could achieve some participation. For an institution to improve its qualitative standing was nevertheless a far more competitive task. The two foremost examples of such upward mobility were Stanford and UCLA. Stanford was a charter member of the research university club, but in the quarter-century after World War II it managed to rise from near the bottom of that group to a position near the top. UCLA had advanced during the interwar years from beginnings as a teachers' college to university status as part of the "southern branch" of the University of California. After the war, however, it became the only new institution to join the ranks of the prewar research universities. The University of Pittsburgh provides an instructive counterpoint to these two California success stories. Pitt sought to accomplish the same objectives and made notable progress, but ultimately saw its ambitions frustrated. Together these cases provide insight into the variegated institutional base of the university research system during the transition from the comparatively restrictive postwar conditions to the lush environment of the 1960s.

Although UCLA and Stanford are quite different as institutions, they share similarities in their postwar development. Both universities had virtually no wartime research on their campuses, and both managed initially to become postwar participants through a few large, defense-related projects. The goal of building academically distinguished departments was prominent in the thinking of administrators on both campuses, but actual progress during the 1940s and early 1950s was sporadic and not always visible. Both institutions began to develop rapidly in the mid-1950s, and thus were poised to take advantage of the conditions that followed Sputnik to advance and consolidate their positions as leading research universities.

In the rise of Stanford and UCLA—and in that of Berkeley as well—a "California factor" was clearly at work. The increased accessibility of the West Coast through air travel, the benign climate, and the deep attachments individuals formed for those settings—all contributed intangibly to academic development. Even more important was the relentless prosperity of the state. Around 1960 California became the most populous state in the union, and it has been consistently among the wealthiest states as well. For higher education this prosperity meant, simply, that resources were potentially available in abundance. Tapping these burgeoning resources and utilizing them to build academic distinction were the challenges facing Stanford and UCLA. For each institution, academic development was a prolonged process involving foresight, commitment, and occasional good fortune.

1. Stanford University

When Stanford welcomed its first students in 1891 it possessed, at least on paper, the largest endowment of any American university as well as nearly nine thousand acres of land adjoining Palo Alto. During the next half-century, however, the university had difficulty first realizing the full value of its wealth, and then augmenting it in keeping with the university's growth. Founding president David Starr Jordan (1891–1913) managed to build a well-respected institution, despite having to endure the earthquake of 1906, legal challenges to the endowment, and the protracted domination of the mercurial Jane Lothrop Stanford. Ray Lyman Wilbur, during his long presidency (1915–42), sought consistently to bolster Stanford's academic strength. With few active benefactors, however, the university was not able to profit fully from the boom of the 1920s, but suffered from the effects of the Depression of the 1930s.[1] When J. E. Wallace Sterling became the university's fifth president in 1948 he took the reins of an institution that had had "to adjust its physique to a kind of chronic malnutrition." Stanford was not very selective in terms of students or faculty, and its reputation was to some extent riding on the past. Sterling perceived Stanford to be on a kind of plateau—a rather high plateau, to be sure, but one from which it must either rise with the other research universities or be relegated to the status of a respected regional institution.[2]

Sterling was determined that Stanford would take the upward path to greater national stature, and he was eloquent in conveying this vision to others. He stressed the basic theme that Stanford was destined to fulfill the role of the leading comprehensive private university on the West Coast. In order to realize that destiny, Stanford would need academic leadership to overcome the torpor of existing departments and to recruit faculty members with established reputations. Such efforts, in turn, would demand substantial additional financial resources. Much of the responsibility for bringing about such changes rested at this juncture with the president himself. Sterling importuned the Stanford alumni for financial support and he personally traveled about the country interviewing prospective faculty.[3] He soon became an adept fund-raiser; while recruitment responsibilities devolved upon deans and department heads. Even as Sterling began these efforts, developments in electrical engineering were laying the basis for the kind of changes that Sterling wished to effect.

Stanford's renowned achievements in electronics are associated with the career of Frederick E. Terman, who was chairman of the department of electrical engineering before the war, dean of engineering afterward, and provost of the university from 1955 to 1965. He was not only a gifted scientist—a pioneer in the field of radio and electrical engineering—but he also possessed astute insight into the workings of the academic system. As a Stanford insider, he shared Sterling's vision of the destiny of the university, as well as the concern over its current condition. Terman also felt that he himself understood the steps that needed to be taken.

Frederick Terman was the son of the renowned psychologist, Lewis Terman, who chaired one of Stanford's more distinguished departments. After receiving a Stanford degree in engineering, he disregarded the conventional wisdom that engineers should seek practical experience, and instead followed his father's advice to pursue theoretical training. This path led Terman to MIT where he took a Ph.D. under Vannevar Bush. He thus became, like his mentor, one of the few figures in the country working along the frontier between electrical engineering and physics. From the time Terman joined the Stanford engineering faculty in 1927, he foresaw that the way to advance his field was through collaboration with other basic scientific disciplines. During the 1930s Terman developed the department of electrical engineering, created some notable inventions, and established himself as an authority in radio engineering. World War II created opportunities for further scientific and academic advancement.

Terman spent the war in a key position as director of the Radio Research Laboratory at Harvard, which developed radar countermeasures and thus employed similar devices as the Radiation Laboratory at MIT. In addition, Harvard of the James Conant era made an indelible impression. Terman noted how the leaders of Harvard thought through their problems: they anticipated situations that the institution might face, and thus were prepared to make critical decisions on the basis of long-range rather than momentary considerations. This was the case with postwar research, which Terman no less than the leaders of Harvard foresaw as likely to have a decisive impact on universities. Terman learned from acquaintances that the Harvard Corporation had discussed these possibilities and concluded that the university would decline to operate laboratories of the wartime type—those engaged in secret work, segregated from campus, and employing a staff of professional researchers. Instead, Harvard would endeavor to recruit the best scientists and allow research programs to form around topics of their choosing. MIT, in Terman's eyes, took the opposite tack, basically continuing its huge wartime operations. Terman concluded that Stanford should be guided by the Harvard approach: he "was quite willing to bend a little more than

Harvard would have . . . because [Stanford] was hungrier than Harvard, but [he] wasn't prepared to go nearly as far as MIT . . . . They weren't gaining anything by going that far."[4] Moreover, the Harvard approach was more conducive to Terman's long-range goal for Stanford, which he articulated as early as 1943— "a position in the West somewhat analogous to that of Harvard in the East."[5]

The postwar building of scientific research at Stanford began modestly, but early, with the authorization to establish a Microwave Laboratory in January 1945.[6] Terman anticipated that Stanford would have an edge in this area because of the prewar invention of the klystron (a microwave generating tube). He and Stanford president Donald Tresidder had originally expected to attract industrial support for research, but in 1946 the Office of Naval Research began awarding contracts for such work. The following year additional contracts for military-sponsored research were consolidated with some of the ONR work, and these activities formed the kernel of the Stanford Electonics Research Laboratories. By 1950 Stanford was performing almost $500,000 of electronics research for the Department of Defense—about one-quarter of the university's total research expenditures. At this juncture the Korean War greatly expanded these activities. When the Navy dangled the prospect of large contracts for classified, applied research in this area, Terman felt that Stanford could not refuse. Stanford had achieved a research program in electronics second only to that of MIT; to allow these research contracts to go elsewhere, he told President Sterling, would mean forfeiting that position. Accordingly, Stanford added an Applied Electronics Laboratory, which was soon conducting over $1,000,000 of research by itself.

There proved to be little difference between the work of the two electronics laboratories, and they were accordingly merged into the Stanford Electronics Laboratories. Classified or no, Stanford engineers felt that their work in electronics involved fundamental scientific questions and was closely integrated with the academic mission of the university. This contention was not special pleading, but rather reflected the reality of the particular scientific territory they were exploring—the interstices of physics and electrical engineering. Building more powerful and sophisticated microwave tubes may have solved important problems for the Navy, but it also contributed to the linear electron accelerator with which Robert Hofstadter earned a Nobel Prize for exploration of the interior of the atom. This same matrix of research yielded the Nobel Prize-winning work by Felix Bloch on nuclear magnetic resonance, as well as the equipment that made possible UHF television broadcasting. Electronics research at Stanford created capabilities for path-breaking fundamental research, while also retaining the engineering nexus between science and technology. Electronics at Stanford consequently established close linkages not just with the Department of Defense, but with industry as well.

Close ties with private industry played a contributory role in the advancement of science at Stanford, particularly in electronics.[7] The electrical engineering department had entered into a cooperative venture with Sperry Gyroscope before the war and been rewarded with a stream of royalties on the klystron.

The microwave laboratory had been established at the end of the war as part of a larger strategy of renewing that kind of industrial connection. As the lab developed, federal contacts quickly became dominant; but even so, prototypes developed in the Stanford laboratories eventually had to go into production, which called for a close interaction with industry. Terman explicitly urged his faculty to establish ties with industry in order to bring this about. Over the long run these relationships were highly beneficial to Stanford, although not chiefly through the normal channels of industry-sponsored research and patent royalties.

The booming electronics industry gave rise to numerous new firms, many of which were started by people who had developed devices in the Stanford laboratories. Because these entrepreneurs worked with the same technologies and wrestled with similar scientific problems they cultivated continuing relationships with those labs. These links in time led to somewhat self-interested philanthropy. The Varian brothers, Russell and Sigurd, had helped to invent the klystron with Stanford professor William W. Hansen. In 1948 Varian Associates was incorporated. The chief technical interests of the firm centered on klystrons, linear electron accelerators, and nuclear magnetic resonance instruments—all Stanford products.[8] Varian Associates also became the first tenant in the Stanford industrial park. Terman brought together William Hewlett and David Packard, thus contributing to the founding of their phenomenally successful firm. They later donated part of the building for the Applied Electronics Laboratory (the first of many large gifts). More generally, Terman noted that the high technology firms that had located on Stanford land provided more money in gifts to the university than in lease income. In addition, these firms paid double tuition for their employees to attend engineering classes; and beginning in 1957 they contributed annual membership fees to belong to the Stanford Industrial Associates Plan.[9] The creation of the Stanford Research Institute was originally envisioned as yet another means for strengthening ties with industry. This separate, nonprofit corporation performed more practical kinds of services that did not fit with the academic research programs of faculty.[10] The connections that evolved between Stanford and private corporations thus became sustaining relationships for both parties.

What clearly had emerged by 1950 was a triangular nexus between electrical engineering at Stanford, the Department of Defense, and the electronics industry. For Stanford, this development was the entering wedge into the postwar research economy. Electrical engineering was the first department to seek and sign sizable research contracts, and the success of the whole electronics complex gave Stanford a well-defined niche.[11] This place was largely secured with indigenous personnel and products at a time when Stanford was in a poor condition to compete for scientific stars. Success in electronics gave Stanford salience within the research community, and contributed toward bolstering the finances of the university as well. More important, like other advanced technologies that emerged from World War II, electronics had a huge future in which Stanford would fully participate. In the 1960s programs flourished in 'second or third generation' microwave technologies like solid state electronics, lasers, and materials research. In these latter applied fields Stanford managed to duplicate the "unusually smooth blending of academic, military, and corporate interests" that had originally characterized research in electronics.[12]

Stanford's initial achievements in scientific research after the war were owed in part to Terman's skills as an electrical engineer, partly to his acumen as an academic entrepreneur, and in large measure to the fortuitous circumstances that emerged in the field of electronics. Terman was riding the wave of the future in a critical field. The situation facing President Sterling elsewhere in the university was less promising. In many areas no traditions existed on which to build, and Stanford had meager resources with which to compete in the tight postwar academic marketplace. Academic advancement for the rest of Stanford during Sterling's early years was a more grudging process.

The Stanford that Wallace Sterling assumed direction of in 1948 was for the most part a placid and intimate place. The majority of students and faculty were located in the College of Humanities and Sciences, where academic departments were both autonomous and insular. All decisions with appreciable budgetary impact were made by the president; when department heads wanted authorization to hire new faculty, for example, they phoned up "Wally" to get his OK.[13] Personnel decisions were so informal that official policy was uncertain at what point tenure was achieved.[14] If Sterling was to fulfill his intention to "build a faculty not merely of good men but of the best men," there was much that had to be changed.[15]

In his initial year as president (1948) Sterling asked each department head to prepare a five-year statement of the department's "projected hopes and plans," and this request was repeated in 1955. In the interim, Stanford's dealings with the Ford Foundation stimulated additional self-assessment in the behavioral sciences.[16] According to these documents, economics was one of the stronger departments, but lacked the resources to realize its potential in research. It confessed to being unable to accomplish any of its 1949 goals, remaining at the same level of staffing and coverage. History was a far weaker department, but it managed some progress. As late as 1954, history described itself as merely a "service department" and was deemed to have little potential for graduate education. Just two years later, though, it reported widening faculty recruitment to national scope and raising standards for graduate students. In general, the picture that emerged by 1955 was of perceptible improvements in quality, but little progress in terms of additional appointments or significantly larger departmental budgets.

Even with the help of the Ford Foundation, upgrading the behavioral sciences proved difficult. The committee that planned the deployment of Stanford's 1951 research grant found faculty capable of research lacking in sociology and anthropology. When the 1955 Ford grant provided for the hiring of a senior sociologist, Stanford needed three years to induce a major figure to accept the position. Stanford's self-study of the behavioral sciences had called for the establishment of a research institute in the behavioral sciences—a recommendation strongly backed by the visiting committee. Stanford subsequently deleted this from its final proposal to the foundation, in effect forgoing that portion of the subsequent grant, because a sufficient research base had not yet been established.[17]

Insofar as the Stanford departments advanced academically before 1955 they did so by bringing in a relatively small number of scholars of national standing to fill key positions: Kenneth Arrow in economics, Robert Sears in psychology, or Albert Bowker in statistics.[18] These individuals provided the nuclei around which strong departments later formed. Of particular importance, these scholars possessed the 'national' outlook on their respective disciplines that the Stanford departments needed to internalize. The visiting committee for the behavioral sciences, noting that such a national perspective had often been lacking in the recruitment of faculty, urged new procedures to rectify the situation. By 1955 this factor was beginning to change decisively, yet another obstacle barred the path to the national arena. As the visiting committee also pointed out, "Stanford's salary scale falls substantially below that of state universities with which Stanford competes in the Pacific area and very much below that of five large privately controlled institutions in the Middle Atlantic and New England regions."[19] Meeting Stanford's ambitious goals depended upon expanding its financial resources.

Wallace Sterling obtained an excellent vantage point for viewing Stanford's financial situation when he served as a member of the Commission on Financing Higher Education (1949-52). In keeping with a Stanford preoccupation, he took particular interest in the issue of corporate contributions. It was then widely felt that business firms had a special responsibility to support private institutions of higher education, in part to counter the possible effects of the growing federal presence.[20] A close working relationship with business and with businessmen would be one hallmark of the presidency of this former history professor. Even more important would be Stanford's relationship with foundations.

Prior to World War II, Stanford had been one of the weakest of the private research universities in attracting voluntary support, but under Sterling its rise was meteoric. In his first ten years of office Stanford vaulted to a position second only to Harvard in gifts received. The pattern of giving reflected the support for a rejuvenated Stanford. Sterling began his presidency by canvassing the Stanford alumni. He found enthusiasm for the future of the university, but this did not translate into copious gifts. Alumni giving at Stanford in fact remained well below the national averages until the end of Sterling's presidency. Corporate contributions also lagged the averages, even after they were doubled in 1957 by establishment of the industrial associates plan. Instead, Stanford received a substantial amount of its voluntary support from gifts and especially bequests from very wealthy individuals. Sterling was obviously adept at appealing to the most affluent stratum of Bay Area society, individuals who predominantly owed their fortunes to commerce and industry. Thus, Stanford's ties with industry seem to have been rewarded most lucratively through the generosity of individual businessmen.[21] This giving was complemented, and in fact stimulated, by the special relationship that evolved between Stanford and the Ford Foundation.

Sterling was closely involved with the modern Ford Foundation from its inception, when he sent Rowen Gaither four pages of reactions to the founding

Report. Sterling was forthright in his recommendations, viewing matters from the Foundation's perspective:

> universities are more inclined to seek support for sporadic ideas, good men in estab-
> lished fields (both of which are commendable), than to approach upon Foundations
> for support of a program, or parts thereof, which is carefully worked out in terms
> of the particular university's own resources and facilities; and . . . Foundations do
> not adequately insist on the latter as a fundamental prerequisite for Foundation sup-
> port.[22]

Sterling's judgment was appreciated in the Foundation and became a factor in awards to Stanford. When the university received its first significant grant in the behavioral sciences, William McPeak wrote Sterling:

> Wallace you may be pleased to hear that our advisors gave Stanford a much higher
> rating in the behavioral sciences because of you and their expectations of you and
> not alone because of the university's previous accomplishments.[23]

This particular grant was portentous for Stanford. Up to this point the university could hardly be considered an obvious candidate for the Foundation's objective of building the behavioral sciences (it could boast strength only in the psychology department built by Lewis Terman). Yet, Ford Foundation patronage contributed importantly to Stanford's academic advancement. Another significant boost in this same area occurred when the Center for the Advanced Study in the Behavioral Sciences was located at Stanford. The land for the Center was offered on Sterling's initiative, and the transaction was undoubtedly smoothed by his relationship with the Foundation. The Center, in turn, proved to be an asset to the behavioral sciences at Stanford. It largely assured Stanford's inclusion in the behavioral sciences self-studies and subsequent grants. This program caused the participating departments to scrutinize themselves and formulate their goals at a particularly crucial moment—just as additional resources were becoming available. A few years later Stanford's special relationship with the Ford Foundation helped the Stanford Business School in a similar foundation program that propelled it into the front ranks.[24]

The solicitude of the Ford Foundation toward Stanford should not be construed simply as favoritism. The university's studied efforts at self-improvement were entirely congruent with the kinds of changes the Foundation was attempting to induce in colleges and universities generally. Stanford's clear sense of its destiny implied a set of definite goals which spurred the kind of introspection and planning that appealed to Foundation officers. In a curious manner, thought processes in the university and the foundation sometimes mirrored each other. In the self-studies sponsored by the Program on Behavioral Sciences, for example, Stanford came by far the closest to fulfilling the expectations of the Foundation. This situation would be repeated at the end of the decade in a much more auspicious way when the Ford Foundation decided to support the general strengthening of private research universities.

The year 1955 marks a kind of end of the beginning to the postwar advancement of Stanford. Afterward, income from all sources increased in an ascending curve. Additional unencumbered funds were derived from the development of Stanford's land into an industrial park and commercial space. Further assistance came from a succession of large grants from the Ford Foundation. In another auspicious development, Frederick Terman was named to the new post of provost of the university. There, more intimately involved with academic affairs than the president could ever be, he attempted to transpose his approach to engineering to the entire university. The decade of his provostship witnessed the transformation of Stanford.

Sterling had searched for an imposing figure to oversee academic development, but he could hardly have done better than his own dean of engineering.[25] By the time Terman became provost, he had fully elaborated a philosophy for advancing Stanford. First, emulate the best. In engineering his reference point was MIT, where, he would only concede, research was more extensive but not higher in quality. For Stanford as a whole, the ideal was Harvard. Measuring Stanford against such standards produced a relentlessly critical mindset. One dean recollected that Stanford administrators were incessantly engaged in criticism during these years; that they perpetually discussed the problems and weaknesses of departments even though considerable progress was being made.[26] Second, rigorously evaluate all appointments and promotions. As provost Terman attempted to assess the merits of the members of each department. His files contained exacting judgments: e.g. "very good teacher; good at research—but not really outstanding"; "disappointment—bright but doesn't produce"; "out of line—low."[27] Third, the key to academic prestige lay in building upon strength—creating what he called "steeples of excellence." Such an approach meant striving for renown in a limited number of fields, rather than seeking broad coverage. Furthermore, the fields chosen had to be significant in themselves: "what counts is that the steeples be high for all to see and that they relate to something important."[28] This last element of Terman's strategy, in particular, required the active engagement of the university administration.

As provost, Terman functioned as the chief academic officer of Stanford with budgetary responsibility.[29] His office was charged with assuring the continuity and coherence of university policies across the schools and with the determination of budgetary needs. Most important for Terman, the office represented an independent point for the evaluation of appointments and promotions—the ultimate gatekeeper for the faculty. In his first years Terman estimated that he was returning one-half of the recommendations for further justification, and ultimately rejecting one-third.[30] He thus acted much like Clark Kerr had as chancellor of Berkeley. The provost also represented an independent point for the appraisal of academic needs, which gave Terman the opportunity to put his 'steeples' strategy into effect. The Stanford faculty numbered 427 in 1955; 575 in 1960; and 824 when Terman stepped down in 1965. By then, he had passed judgment on the great majority of them.

The Terman legend is so firmly fixed at Stanford that it begs critical scrutiny. Terman himself estimated that building the Stanford faculty took some twenty years, and that the effects of this gradual process became increasingly evident during the decade in which he was provost. According to former dean of

Humanities and Sciences Robert Sears, the department heads deserved the real credit for advancing Stanford's stature. In departments like history and psychology this was probably the case; but on different occasions, chemistry, biology, political science, and economics needed steering from above—more likely from the dean than from the provost—to spur them to incorporate emerging specialties.[31] Sears also contended that Terman did not understand the humanities, nor care to. This shortcoming, combined with his fixation on excellence, seems to have produced one of the uglier episodes of his tenure.

Philip H. Rhinelander was brought to Stanford from Harvard in 1956 to become dean of the College of Humanities and Sciences. For several years he worked closely with Terman to advance those departments. By 1961, however, Terman had lost confidence in the dean. In a meeting with Sterling, he presented a damning bill of particulars: Rhinelander was alleged to be mentally unstable, unable to make decisions, dishonest, capricious, egocentric, and disloyal to Stanford. These charges were quite implausible. Rhinelander, to his credit, showed good sense by resigning when confronted with Terman's hostility. The contemporary explanation for the resignation was that the two men had disagreed over budgets. Terman's files from that era, however, indicate a persistent desire to have the provost more actively involved in appointments. In particular, Terman wanted to be brought in at the stage when searches had been narrowed to a short list, rather than merely approving or disapproving after a candidate had already been selected.[32] Such an extension of the powers of the provost would have intruded into the customary sphere of departmental authority. (Terman's recommendation was in fact never adopted.) But such a wish was consistent with the man. Confident that he knew what was best for Stanford, Terman wanted the authority to make decisions to be in his own hands. Rhinelander's opposition to such autocracy appears to have been the cause of his abrupt discomfiture.[33]

Terman's position on building 'steeples of excellence' also implied centralization of authority and planning. Indeed, after stepping down he authored reports that recommended all new or vacant senior positions be re-allocated by the provost so that they might "contribute to the height of an important steeple."[34] As provost, though, Terman had opposed as "too rigid" the establishment of long-range plans, since they might have constricted his own freedom of action. A time nevertheless came when it became necessary to 'think through' rigorously Stanford's likely future course.

By the end of the first decade of Sterling's presidency Stanford's annual budget had tripled and the pace of expansion was clearly accelerating. The trustees of the university expressed some concern at this juncture about the upward spiral of expenditures. In addition, a recently completed study of the organization of the university had been critical of the absence of any long-term planning that could relate Stanford's educational goals and priorities with its fiscal needs.[35] In this respect Stanford was no different from other research universities of the era. All generally felt that progress would best proceed by taking advantage of opportunities as they presented themselves, rather than by deliberately planning. But the disquiet of the Stanford trustees apparently provided a powerful stimulus.

Sterling instructed the top officers of the university to prepare a document outlining the future financial needs of the institution. Their report, "Stanford's Minimum Financial Needs in the Years Ahead," was presented to the board on October 10, 1959.[36]

The report dispelled any notion of heedless spending at Stanford; instead the message was conveyed that the university had not only made great strides, but had gotten more for its money than had peer institutions. Terman set the stage by describing what had already been accomplished. The selectivity of undergraduates was now approaching that of the Ivy League, and in certain fields Stanford competed with the top schools for graduate students; several academic departments were among the best in the country, and the university had truly attained national visibility. But Stanford's goal should be, according to Terman, to establish itself "on a par with the best institutions in the East, and as *the* outstanding institution in the West—not even excluding the University of California at Berkeley."

The vice president for finance, Kenneth Cuthbertson, next showed that Stanford's resources did not match that aspiration: on a per-student basis its regular income was about half that of Harvard, Yale, and Princeton. The actual consequences of this highly relative penury were then detailed for most aspects of the university's operations—the schools of humanities and sciences, business, engineering, and the graduate school; the library, financial aid for undergraduate and graduate students; student services, physical plant, and other operations. In this exercise the consequences of Stanford's limited income were apparent. Faculty salaries at Stanford were now "reasonably good," but an "adequate top" was lacking to recruit and hold the most outstanding scholars. Substantial increases in the number of faculty were called for to accommodate a growing number of graduate students, to build selectively upon certain 'steeples,' as well as to rectify some areas of weakness, like the humanities and business. Levels of student aid were clearly inferior to the competition; library resources were inadequate; etc., etc. . . . The final exercise attempted to fix a price for these manifold "minimum needs." Current trends in income from all foreseeable sources were extrapolated to 1965 and 1970 in order to establish what the shortfall would be. The total additional funds required to meet Stanford's minimal needs were computed by adding, 1) the amounts included in the income extrapolations; 2) the amounts required to cover the shortfall; and 3) needed capital spending. By this calculation, the amount of new money that would have to be raised through voluntary support equaled $155 million.

The report was given a vote of confidence by the trustees. They not only endorsed an effort to meet those minimal needs, but generally wanted to see them exceeded. Before anyone had time to elaborate the plan in greater detail, or to contemplate the massive fund-raising work that would be entailed, Stanford received an unexpected call from the Ford Foundation requesting a meeting with President Sterling and the university officers about an undisclosed matter. What occurred at the meeting has been described by Cuthbertson:

When we finally settled down after the small talk, one of the foundation's officers said to the president that they had been giving some consideration to a program of

large general support grants, and asked whether Stanford had done any thinking
about where it wanted to be in the next ten years. You can imagine our smugness
and their surprise when the president excused himself, and came back in less than a
minute with the copy of the presentation we had so recently made to the board of
trustees.[37]

This was the inception of the Ford Foundation's Challenge Grants Program,
described in the previous chapter, and Stanford fit its prescription perfectly in
terms of private control, regional considerations, high ambitions, and proven
leadership. This was hardly surprising: all of these themes had been repeatedly
stressed in Stanford's communications with the Foundation throughout the
1950s. Stanford's long-range planning merely completed the picture. If the ultimate purpose, in a sense, was to replicate Stanford, then Stanford's carefully formulated plans seemed to prove to the Foundation that challenge grants were the
means to achieve that goal.

In September 1960 the Ford Foundation announced an unrestricted grant of
$25 million to Stanford, with the only condition being that the university raise
$75 million in matching funds. Together these sums represented about four
times Stanford's non-research operating budget, more than had been raised
through gifts in the 1950s, or about three-quarters of its endowment. Stanford
had reformulated its financial goals for the decade, and projected a figure of
$346 million in new money that would be required to meet its objectives. $100
million of that would come from tuition and land development, and the rest
from voluntary support. For the last, Stanford had to reorganize its disjointed
development efforts, which had been fragmented among different 'associates'
plans and the alumni organization. The first objective was to fulfill the matching
requirement for the Ford grant, but the momentum of giving clearly needed to
be sustained thereafter. In the event, these goals were comfortably met: for the
decade (1961–70) Stanford received gifts worth $278 million.[38]

The Ford grant and its attendant fund-raising campaign are credited with
accelerating the development of Stanford by about a decade. The early 1960s
were undoubtedly propitious years for research universities generally, but Stanford managed to launch its efforts sooner and to carry them further than most
other institutions. Real instructional expenditures per student approximately
doubled from 1959 to 1965, eliminating much of the Stanford disadvantage vis-
à-vis Harvard, Yale, and Princeton. These funds had an enormous impact at the
departmental level. Dean Robert Sears has recalled a great eagerness on the part
of the faculty at the end of the 1950s to improve the quality of the university.
The resources for accomplishing this became available at the beginning of the
1960s. During those years his school was receiving budget increments allowing
for 5 to 7 percent annual raises (generous for that era), plus $200,000 to
$400,000 in additional funds for new positions.[39] From 1959 to 1965 the uni-
versity averaged fifty new faculty positions a year—an increase of 60 percent.
These new positions were filled for the most part with senior appointments, carefully selected to bolster the prestige of the university. In fact, Stanford 'raids' on
other university faculties became notorious in those years. Some schools and

departments greatly exceeded their projected growth. The business school, for example, became a magnet for gifts. Dean Ernest C. Arbuckle had foreseen in 1959 raising his budget from $750,000 to $2 million by 1970, but by 1967 it already stood at $3.4 million.[40] Of greatest importance, however, was what these funds accomplished. Dean Sears regarded the availability of funds to be the single most important determinant in building quality: money purchased quality, which in turn attracted more money with which to build additional quality in terms of faculty, students, and research support.[41]

A measure of the quality of the Stanford faculty may be had by comparing the standing of its academic departments in the rankings done in 1957, 1964, and 1969 (Table 7). In the first of these Stanford had five departments ranked among the top ten, seven ranked between eleventh and fifteenth place, and six not

TABLE 7. Rankings for Stanford and UCLA Departments

	1957	1964	1969
Art history			
Stanford	nr		11*
UCLA			good
Classics			
Stanford	15	nr	4
UCLA			good
English			
Stanford	15	6*	6*
UCLA	14	14	12*
French			
Stanford	nr	11*	8
UCLA	nr	11*	17*
German			
Stanford	nr	13*	5*
UCLA	13	20*	18*
Linguistics			
Stanford			good
UCLA	nr	11	2*
Music			
Stanford	nr		10*
UCLA	12		10*
Philosophy			
Stanford	nr	10	11*
UCLA	10*	11	8*
Spanish			
Stanford	nr	nr	17*
UCLA	nr	5	9*
Anthropology			
Stanford	14	10*	9*
UCLA	8	6*	7*

TABLE 7. Rankings for Stanford and UCLA Departments
          (*Continued*)

	1957	1964	1969
Economics			
Stanford	5*	6	7*
UCLA	16	16	14*
Geography			
Stanford			
UCLA	6	7*	10*
History			
Stanford	15	7*	5*
UCLA	nr	12	12
Political science			
Stanford	13	7*	6*
UCLA	12	13	12*
Psychology			
Stanford	5	1*	1
UCLA	nr	11*	10
Sociology			
Stanford	nr	11*	15*
UCLA	11	11*	8
Biochemistry			
Stanford		2*	2*
UCLA		17*	11*
Botony			
Stanford	14	9*	11
UCLA	12	11	14*
Developmental biology			
Stanford			2*
UCLA			good
Microbiology			
Stanford		7	8*
UCLA		26*	18*
Molecular biology			
Stanford			4
UCLA			13*
Pharmacology			
Stanford		12*	1*
UCLA		nr	16*
Physiology			
Stanford			good
UCLA		12*	7*
Population biology			
Stanford			9*
UCLA			16
Zoology			
Stanford	14	4	3*
UCLA	8	8	12*

TABLE 7. Rankings for Stanford and UCLA Departments
(*Continued*)

	1957	1964	1969
Astronomy			
Stanford			
UCLA	nr	nr	11*
Chemistry			
Stanford	15	5	3*
UCLA	10	9*	7
Geology			
Stanford	6	7	4*
UCLA	14	10	7*
Mathematics			
Stanford	9	6	6
UCLA	nr	15*	14
Physics			
Stanford	6	5	5*
UCLA	nr	19*	19
Chemical engineering			
Stanford		10*	4*
UCLA			adequate+
Civil engineering			
Stanford		5	4*
UCLA		good	good
Electrical engineering			
Stanford		2	2
UCLA		19*	10*
Mechanical engineering			
Stanford		3	2
UCLA		17	11*

* = ties

nr = not ranked

ranked. Just seven years later, in a more comprehensive ranking, Stanford had eighteen departments in the top ten (eight of these in the top five), five ranked from eleven to fifteen, and three not ranked. By 1969 Stanford had advanced to having sixteen departments ranked among the top five. Even taking into account all the caveats concerning rankings of this type, Stanford's achievement was remarkable—easily the best relative improvement of any research university. Moreover, when scrutinized in detail Stanford's achievement becomes more, rather than less, impressive. Terman's admonition to build in important areas appears to have been followed. Stanford's advancement by 1969 was most apparent in the largest and most competitive disciplines: English advanced from 15 to 6; history from 15 to 5; psychology from 5 to 1; and chemistry from 15 to 3. Other central disciplines—mathematics, physics, economics—remained fairly stable with rankings near 6. In addition, Stanford did quite well in some dynamic fields not included in the 1957 study: electrical engineering was 2, biochemistry, 2; molecular biology, 4; microbiology, 8; and pharmacology, 1.

The student body at Stanford was transformed as well, in keeping with the growing stature of the institution. Frederick Terman, interestingly, felt that investments in undergraduate education did not pay and urged instead that resources be concentrated on graduate education, where national reputations were forged.[42] This approach was only partially followed. Undergraduate education continued to be the principal reference point to higher education for American society. Accordingly, it was emphasized in the plans that Stanford presented in connection with fund-raising appeals. Specifically, the university sought to increase further the selectivity of incoming freshman, to augment financial aid to the point that admissions could be need-blind, and to bolster the residential character of undergraduate education. More generally, curricular changes were called for to accommodate students with greater academic capabilities and to bring them into closer contact with increasingly eminent faculty.[43] The center of gravity nevertheless shifted toward graduate education during these years. From 1959 to 1967 Stanford added just 650 additional places on the undergraduate level, compared with 2200 new places on the graduate level. A bare majority of undergraduates remained (52%). Graduate students were far more expensive to educate, and thus their growing proportion corresponded with the rapid rise in instructional costs. Moreover, those working toward Ph.D.s required substantial amounts of financial support. In both academic and professional fields, Stanford managed to extend greatly its drawing power and its selectivity.[44]

Given the progress in faculty building, Stanford was able to participate fully in the explosive growth of the research economy during the 1960s. Essentially, Stanford utilized the substantial resources raised from private sources to build its research capabilities, and these capabilities in turn attracted federal research dollars. By 1966 Stanford was receiving the third largest total of federal R&D funds (after MIT and Michigan) not including the Stanford Linear Accelerator. The sources of these funds reflected both the academic distinction that Stanford had attained and the relevance of much of its research to technological application. That is, Stanford was one of the leading recipients of funds for pure science from the National Science Foundation and second only to MIT in funding from the Department of Defense and NASA.[45] In general, Stanford consistently received a much larger proportion of its research funds from the federal government than the national averages.

At the end of the 1960s Frederick Terman felt that Stanford had not yet attained its goal: it had become a very good university, but still below the best. Stanford was now close enough, however, that a few additional steps would bring it equal to Berkeley, Harvard, and MIT.[46] Terman himself, however, was no longer able to guide those steps. He had retired from being provost in 1965 after orchestrating academic development during the university's most dynamic decade. Wallace Sterling withdrew in 1968 after presiding over two decades of breathtaking transformation. Their departures signaled the end of an era in more ways than one. The Stanford that took the final steps to academic preeminence would be different from the one they had led.

The rise of Stanford could not have been accomplished without extremely good fortune—the patronage of the Ford Foundation, the discovery of the klystron as an entree into electronics research, or the robust economy of California and the Bay Area. But each of the external factors was complemented by an internal, organizational capability that permitted Stanford to capitalize on these opportunities. Sterling's ability to project the accomplishments of Stanford made the school a more attractive object of philanthropy. Terman was extremely aggressive after the war in building electronics research and courting federal backing. Later, this same aggressiveness would secure an important federally supported center for materials research for Stanford, after initially having been passed over; and this episode was followed by the prolonged, successful campaign to win funding for the $100 million Stanford Linear Accelerator—the largest single authorization for academic science to date.[47] The high ambitions fostered by the Stanford administrators also made the university's aspirations dovetail so closely with the objectives of the Ford Foundation. This last factor was fundamental to Stanford's achievement.

In terms of university governance, postwar Stanford had a somewhat autocratic character. The top administrators instinctively sought to keep information and initiative in their own hands. For example, when a 1958 study was commissioned on the reorganization of the university, they discussed the findings frankly among themselves, but declined to share them with faculty or trustees because they were "too negative."[48] Terman's attack on a recalcitrant dean has already been described. Basically, the provost and deans exerted great influence over departmental matters by stacking search committees, through the authorization of new positions, and ultimately by the veto of personnel recommendations. In this way the exceedingly optimistic goals of Sterling, Terman, and others were projected throughout the institution.

Such high ambitions were widely shared among the faculty, but some professors inevitably found themselves crowded or threatened by Terman's steeples. When opposition occurred, Terman dealt with it in a fairly ruthless manner. Sterling, on the other hand, was far more affable than the provost and tended to remain above the fray. Terman was largely responsible for forcing the political science department to adopt a greater emphasis on behaviorism, which was an approach more conducive to foundation support. In a similarly motivated move, Terman contravened the biology department's choice of a chairman in order to achieve greater emphasis on biomedicine and biochemistry. The losers in these encounters felt that departmental autonomy, broad coverage, and undergraduate teaching were sacrificed for the cause of greater research funding and enhanced national prestige.[49]

Two significant changes took place in the organization of the university during the Terman era. The 1958 reorganization study was commissioned because too much of the university's business was being conducted from the president's office. In an effort at decentralization, three vice presidencies were created—for business, finance, and the provostship. This move consecrated Terman's authority as provost, while also freeing Sterling to concentrate on the external relations of the university, especially fund-raising. Thus, in the last phase of his presidency, Sterling had little to do with internal affairs, which had not been the case for the first decade of his tenure.[50] The second change did not occur until the end of Sterling's presidency, but it opened the way for lessening administrative autocracy and providing faculty with a more effective voice in university affairs. Throughout Stanford's history the faculty had expressed themselves through the Academic Council to which all regular faculty belonged. In 1968 this unwieldy body of more than 800 was supplemented by an elected Faculty Senate. In practice this represented a shift in influence from a small group of senior faculty who were well known to Terman and Sterling to the faculty as a whole. The departure of the autocrats was thus accompanied by the timely creation of a body capable of more democratic decision-making.[51]

The new structure at Stanford would soon be sorely tested. Even as Stanford was entering the front ranks of American universities the consensus that had undergirded its advance was showing signs of erosion. Particularly at issue was one of the fundamental components of Stanford's success—the synergism between basic and applied research. The increasingly eminent physics department, for one, sought to confine itself to pure research. When the linear accelerator was finally approved, the department greeted it more as a threat to their autonomy than as an opportunity to advance science. The department obstructed collaboration with the accelerator laboratory by attempting to impose a quota on the number of academic appointments and graduate students that the accelerator could receive.[52] A more general, and more ideological, conflict soon became evident over the conduct of classified military research, and also over the ties with the private Stanford Research Institute. These issues were part of a national movement, as will be seen in Chapter 8. But for Stanford, *nouveau arrivé*, they posed the question of whether or not the university still needed to be hungrier, and bend standards further, than Harvard.

The future character of the university was also an issue raised by the change in the environment for research universities to one of no- or slow-growth. By the end of Sterling's tenure Stanford was near its optimal enrollment, voluntary support had leveled off, so had the availability of federal research funds, and it was beginning to incur a series of budget deficits. The great expansion was over. During that long period of growth Stanford had raised its standing by recruiting to its faculty large numbers of distinguished scientists and scholars. This process would slow considerably in the years ahead. For Terman slow-growth called for a more rigorous application of the steeple principle. All senior staff positions should be controlled and allocated by the administration in such ways as to maintain and enhance the steeples. A corollary of this approach would imply a fairly cold-blooded treatment of junior faculty, few of whom would have much chance for tenure. Terman looked once more to the Harvard example, where, he argued, "Conant's ruthless system" had demonstrated that restrictions imposed on a stable faculty could lead to the highest level of quality.[53]

Many of Terman's recommendations for personnel would become inevitable given the static conditions that overtook Stanford and other research universities. The distinguished departments that he had helped to build, however, would no longer submit to the degree of central direction that he continued to advocate. Rather, Stanford's continued advance in the academic hierarchy would depend more upon the sense of destiny that Terman and Sterling had done so much to instill. In a new era and with a different kind of leadership, Stanford continued to progress, employing variations of its old formula: research for government, service to industry, patronage from the private sector, and unquenchable ambition.[54]

2. The University of California, Los Angeles

UCLA is the youngest of the leading research universities.[1] Its predecessor was merely a normal school when adopted by the Regents of the University of California in 1919. It was elevated to the status of a college in 1923, receiving authorization to offer a four-year course in arts and science. Early in the next decade the campus became the center of the "Southern Branch" of the university, which included La Jolla and Santa Barbara. Soon, despite the protests of the California Taxpayers Association, it was accorded the right to offer graduate work. During these years the campus grew under the uninspiring direction of Provost Ernest Carroll Moore, who was terrified both by suspicions of communists on campus and by the power of Los Angeles business leaders off campus.[2] For all practical purposes, however, the campus was run by President Robert G. Sproul as a part of his "one university." Despite the inherent awkwardness of being some 400 miles from the locus of authority, these arrangements largely sufficed until the end of World War II.

As a component of a larger system, UCLA existed in a complex organizational universe that had three distinct centers. The conduct of everyday academic affairs was confided to the Los Angeles campus, although all significant decisions were subject to approval from the university offices in Berkeley. There, the president and the business office were responsible for the budget and university policy. All, in turn, were subject to the oversight of the University Board of Regents. This apparent hierarchy was actually a kind of triangular relationship because the regents played a direct role in the advancement of the Southern Branch.

Behind the rise of UCLA was the rise of the city of Los Angeles and its environs to become the second largest metropolitan area in the country. As the population increased, so did the political clout of the region in the state legislature and among the regents of the university. A powerful group of 'southern regents' emerged, who steered the development of UCLA at every major step. Foremost among them was Edward A. Dickson, regent from 1913 until his death in 1956 and chairman the final eight years. Dickson was instrumental in having a branch of the university established in Los Angeles, and thereafter remained closely informed about developments on campus. On numerous occasions he exerted his influence on behalf of UCLA.[3]

University president Robert Sproul has been accorded considerably less admiration in Los Angeles than in the north. He certainly was not opposed to the development of UCLA—quite the contrary. Yet, for a number of reasons he was the person who often seemed to impede its ambitions. First, Sproul's highest priority was clearly to establish the standing of Berkeley as a world-class university. Second, political considerations, for which the president was responsible, sometimes weighed against UCLA. For example, an agreement was struck for a time with the president of the University of Southern California that UCLA would establish no graduate schools or departments in competition with those at USC. Third, Sproul's insistence upon the unity of the university, and particularly the concentration of all decision-making authority in his own hands, was not only cumbersome but increasingly detrimental to the functioning of the Southern Branch. Finally, Sproul is remembered more for saying 'no' to UCLA than for approving the resources that actually built the campus. But Sproul was a politician and a pragmatist; when the balance of power shifted to favor greater development in the south, he acceded. In the end, however, he remained committed to the supremacy of Berkeley, and that attitude was ingrained even more strongly throughout the university administration.[4]

The business office and its head, James Corley, were particularly resented in Los Angeles. Corley scrutinized the aspirations of UCLA with the unsympathetic eye of an accountant. In retrospect, Corley would justify his actions by saying that he was just following orders—that Sproul and the regents were not willing to move as rapidly to develop UCLA as its proponents wished. But in fact Corley's decisions appeared to obstruct the establishment of a research presence on the Los Angeles campus.[5]

Beyond the administration, UCLA had to contend with the august faculty of Berkeley itself. Preoccupied with enhancing their own distinction, Berkeley professors had slight regard for their 'country' colleagues in the south. Berkeley always assumed that it was better and deserved greater resources. In sum, during the first phase of its postwar development the relations of UCLA with the university administration and the Berkeley campus were a source of frustration. By the end of the 1950s, however, this relationship would turn into the institution's greatest asset.

The frustrations were experienced most acutely by the head of the UCLA campus. Lacking the authority to make an appointment or to set a budget, the UCLA provost constantly had to defer to Sproul. Clarence Dykstra assumed the office of provost in 1945, and as former president of the University of Wisconsin, chafed under these conditions. He had high ambitions for UCLA, but was powerless to act on them. His difficulties in dealing with Sproul, it was widely believed on campus, were a factor in bringing on a fatal heart attack in 1950.[6]

The UCLA deans were in a somewhat better position. They at least exercised considerable authority within their respective schools, while for budgets, appointments, and buildings they dealt directly with Sproul. The responsibility for the academic development of UCLA from the war until the end of the 1950s thus lay predominantly with the deans, many of whom were appointed during Dykstra's tenure. The deans of the professional schools were largely recruited from other universities—Stafford L. Warren came from Rochester to start the medical school in 1947; Neil H. Jacoby was lured from Chicago in 1948 to direct the business school; and Llewellyn Boelter came from Berkeley in 1944 to head the school of engineering. The basic academic disciplines, on the other hand, were presided over by indigenous UCLA products. Most senior of them was Verne O. Knudson, who directed graduate studies from the founding of the college (1924–58) and briefly became chancellor (1959–60). Paul A. Dodd played an important role in the recruitment of faculty as dean of Letters and Science (1946–61). And Gustave O. Arlt first assisted and then succeeded Knudson as graduate dean (1958–61).

The UCLA deans not only presided over their respective spheres, but together constituted a kind of oligarchy that was chiefly responsible for conducting the affairs of the campus. On two occasions they were formally in charge: after Dykstra's death UCLA was led for more than two years by a committee of deans consisting of Dodd, Knudson, and Warren, and at the end of the 1950s, another interregnum was bridged by Dodd and Knudson. Throughout this period the Deans' Advisory Committee was the most important body for discussing and deciding campus policies. The deans of the professional schools brought to UCLA a determination to raise their schools up to high national standards, while the insiders in Letters and Science represented the best of the pre-war faculty. Knudson, for example, was a respected physicist in the comparatively old-fashioned field of acoustics. These deans worked steadfastly and consistently to upgrade the academic quality of the UCLA faculty. They also had another trait in common: all were on social terms with some important southern regents.

Regent Edward Dickson befriended these deans and entertained them regularly at his home. Officially, members of the university were supposed to communicate with regents only through the president. Dickson, however, sought out the deans on social occasions and questioned them in detail about current developments on campus. This direct channel of communication was obviously useful to both parties.

The pressure exerted by southern regents like Dickson, and later Edward W. Carter and Edward Pauley, was critical for surmounting the latent resistance of the university administration and furthering the development of UCLA. Their close involvement had drawbacks as well.[7] The southern regents were highly successful businessmen with decidedly conservative political outlooks. They could not comprehend, for example, why faculty members might object to having to sign a loyalty oath. Occasionally their intrusions created problems. The appointment of Dale Coffman of Vanderbilt as founding dean of the law school (1946–56) showed distinct signs of regental intervention. Coffman turned out to be a poor administrator, but in addition he was a rabid anticommunist and a vocal antisemite. Such opinions apparently caused no qualms with his friends among the regents, but they were an embarassment on campus. Some felt that Coffman took advantage of his regental connections to protect his position. As administrative problems in the law school mounted, a decanal committee was finally appointed to investigate. In a difficult decision, the committee recommended Coffman's dismissal from the deanship in 1956.[8]

An irreducible element of politics tinged the triangular relationship between campus, university, and regents. These influences were nevertheless superimposed over the incremental growth and maturation of the institution. UCLA enrolled 10,000 students before the war; in the early 1950s, after the departure of the GIs, enrollment had grown to 15,000; and by the end of that decade it reached 20,000. While student numbers only doubled in these two decades, the regular faculty grew from 220 to over 900. Graduate-level students comprised only one in eight in 1940, but numbered one in three by 1960. These changes reflected the transformation from a teaching institution to a research university. The nature of this transformation, however, can only be glimpsed within the individual schools and departments.

Initially, the most significant contributions to sponsored research at UCLA came from the establishment of the medical school. Stafford Warren, who in 1947 accepted the challenge of building one from the ground up, was from the outset determined to have a large, first-class school. His aspirations considerably over-reached the original commitments made by the governor and the university administration. To realize these high ambitions, Warren had to be as adept at politics as he was at science.

In 1946 Warren had been a medical adviser to the Bikini atom bomb tests. His specialty, radiological medicine, was critically important for the development and use of atomic energy, and it led to close relations with the Atomic Energy Commission. He brought a team of researchers to Los Angeles from Rochester, expecting from the outset to establish an active center of research. Almost immediately he was offered a large research contract by the AEC. The university was quite reluctant to provide the facilities required, but when Warren threatened to begin the project in a tent, Sproul committed enough funds for a temporary structure. This was the beginning of the UCLA medical school, which had a quasi-permanent research laboratory well before any students were enrolled.[9] Warren would have to repeat this performance, at one point using commitments toward cancer research from NIH to leverage new facilities out of the university. In this way the availability of federal research funds not only propelled the development of the medical school, but also provided the entering wedge for research on the UCLA campus.

Warren had to secure more than just research funds, however, to build the kind of comprehensive medical school that he envisioned. When he was appointed by the governor to establish a state commission on radiological defense, he used the opportunity to build a "political machine" for the medical school. He had learned by accompanying Sproul on one of his tours of the state the importance of building community support. Accordingly, Warren took to the road himself in order to heighten public awareness of civil defense and to link it with the UCLA medical school. He later estimated that he showed his films of the 1946 atomic tests to more than one million Californians.[10] Warren succeeded in building considerable community backing for the medical school, which in turn was a great asset when it came to battling the university administration.

Corley and the business office for long resisted the growth of a research presence in the UCLA medical school. At the university medical school in San Fran-

·cisco, research was largely financed through special endowments and cost the state very little. Corley was consequently opposed to the establishment of a costly research faculty in the south. On one occasion he prevailed upon the regents to refuse an electron microscope for UCLA that would have been wholly paid for by NIH, the pretext being the future expense of maintenance. Nevertheless, by basing the development of the school on the procurement of federal research and training grants, UCLA was able to advance despite such obstruction.[11] Once the medical school was firmly established, its development was inextricably linked by the politics of the university with that of the senior medical school in San Francisco. Warren consequently began to cooperate with his counterpart in San Francisco, taking turns in submitting major requests.[12]

The medical school under Warren and the Atomic Energy Project associated with it became the chief center of research at UCLA until at least the mid-1950s. In 1958–59, the school's $3 million in sponsored research represented 60 percent of the campus total. Warren later recalled that until the early 1950s research simply was not contemplated in most departments outside of the physical and biomedical sciences.[13] By building a nationally visible medical school, Warren actively contributed to changing the culture of the campus. In some ways this was an even more difficult process in those academic units that dated from the prewar UCLA.

The first teaching of business subjects on the Los Angeles campus was aimed at training high school teachers of shorthand and typing. The "College of Commerce" (est. 1935) added accountancy to the curriculum. When Neil Jacoby became dean in 1948 he inherited this legacy, replete with typing and shorthand labs, eleven faculty, and 1350 students. Coming from the Chicago of Robert Hutchins, Jacoby had no sympathy for such vocationalism. He aspired to create a school of management that would "educate the business leaders of Southern California." In two decades as dean that is precisely what Jacoby did.[14]

To attain his objective, Jacoby had to expand the intellectual scope of the school while restricting its pedagogical responsibilities—to teach more subjects on a more advanced level to fewer students. Accomplishing this required vastly greater resources and also involved the school with boundary disputes with the economics department. The development of the school was nevertheless strongly supported by regent Edward Carter, himself a Harvard MBA. Edward Dickson too deplored the teachers' college legacy, and he backed Jacoby's efforts to fashion a high quality business school. With such support, the needed resources were forthcoming, and the milestones of academic development passed swiftly. In 1950 the school limited itself to upper classmen; the faculty grew to 44 by 1952, thus effectively overgrowing the teachers of the old regime; graduate degrees were first offered in 1953; and the graduate school of management formed in 1955. The last half of the decade saw the institutionalization of research in the school, including its own 'division of research' which after 1956 freed the faculty from having to work through other less hospitable organized research units. A large grant from IBM followed, which created the Western Data Processing Center, a pioneering application of computers to business research. These growing research activities helped to attract a Ford Foundation grant at the end of the decade that established yet another ORU, the Western

Management Science Institute. This evolution culminated in the mid-1960s, when undergraduate education was phased out entirely in order to conform with the pattern of other leading business schools which taught only on the graduate level.[15]

This serial listing of accomplishments should not obscure the difficulties that Jacoby had to surmount in order to carve a niche for the school within the university and gain support outside. Attempts to raise funds among the Los Angeles business community, for example, were not uncontested. Jacoby proposed an aggressive 'Business Research Associates Plan' that would have centralized fundraising for all the area's business school at his own school. Understandable complaints from the University of Southern California eventually caused President Kerr to quash the plan.[16] On the other hand, the orientation of the UCLA business school toward serving the Los Angeles business community meant that it faced comparatively little hindrance from Berkeley in its development. Moreover, this situation would seem to hold for the professional schools at UCLA in general: their nexus with the professional communities of Los Angeles was the principal stimulus to their vigorous development.[17] The achievements of Jacoby and Warren were thus not exceptional; UCLA, far more than Berkeley, was dominated by its strong professional schools. The academic departments were far more affected by the overweening presence of Berkeley.

One of the strongest departments in the College of Letters and Science was chemistry. Before the war it had a reputation as a good teaching department that conducted small-scale research. Following the war the department found itself unable to recruit established chemists for want of sufficient salaries or reputation, and was thus forced to develop indigenously. The department chairman, William G. Young, built a reputation in organic physical chemistry (he synthesized Vitamin A); and he was able to establish a research group of national stature in this area. Young was the first member of the UCLA faculty to be elected to the National Academy of Sciences in 1950, and he was soon followed by coworkers Saul Winstein (1953) and Donald Cram (1956). They continued pioneering research in this specialty, for which Cram was recognized with the 1987 Nobel Prize for Chemistry.[18]

The building of the department of chemistry was nevertheless a slow, cumulative process. Unable to lure stars, Young instead brought in large numbers of instructors on three-year appointments. They were carefully scrutinized, and only the best were retained. Young felt that the application of "very high standards" for promotion and tenure was the chief reason why chemistry "finally ended up as a very strong department." Also noteworthy is the fact that Young had the opportunity to encourage such standards throughout the physical sciences: he became divisional dean for this area in the College of Letters and Science, and thus was in the key position for screening all departmental recommendations.[19]

The chemistry department made few appointments on the professorial level before the 1960s. One exception, Willard Libby, came to the department from the AEC in 1959—just in time to collect a Nobel Prize for his discovery of Carbon 14 dating. At the time of his arrival Libby was unimpressed with the general state of academic development at UCLA, but he regarded chemistry as the best department at the university.[20] His arrival, however, occurred at an inflection point. Libby himself brought very large research grants from NASA and the Air Force into the programs on planetary physics. Chemistry was soon given the resources for top-level talent searches in the 1960s. For the most part, though, chemistry and other UCLA departments that achieved national recognition during the 1950s were built internally.

In the fall of 1952 Raymond B. Allen became chancellor of UCLA—the counterpart of Clark Kerr at Berkeley and a potential successor to the venerable Sproul. Allen had been president of the University of Washington where he had, among other things, energetically purged suspected communists from the faculty—a deed surely not unappreciated by the California regents.[21] Allen was genuinely committed to the academic development of the campus, but he, like Kerr, found the powers of the chancellor to be limited. The UCLA graduate division, for example, bypassed the chancellor completely and reported directly to Sproul; and budgetary authority remained with the university offices in Berkeley.

With its titular head far removed, UCLA continued its pattern of collegial governance during the 1950s. Allen worked closely with the council of deans, and in the large College of Letters and Science a committee of the divisional deans operated in the same manner. The Academic Senate also played a crucial role: its Budgetary Committee had the responsibility of forming committees to evaluate senior-level appointments and promotions. The workings of these successive layers were generally effective in enhancing academic standards at UCLA, largely because they were manned with a sense of conscientious duty by the better scientists and scholars among the UCLA faculty. Typical of the esprit de corps, one professor later recollected about the Budget Committee that it was "a rewarding experience to make judgments about what's central to a university—the kind of people you bring in."[22]

Collegial governance could generate a steady pressure for academic betterment, but was less likely to yield the kind of determined quest for excellence that Frederick Terman spurred at Stanford. At worst, collegial control combined with local loyalties and the insularity of being within a multicampus university could produce complacency. This trait was evident in the mid-1950s when Allen asked his deans to estimate the stature of their respective schools. Paul Dodd's response was far too optimistic: his "rough estimate" of the standing of the departments in Letters and Science placed them *all* in the top ten.[23] The Keniston rankings that were done only three years later gave a rather different picture (see Table 7). These rankings placed UCLA 14th nationally—hardly a discreditable showing, but still inferior to most prewar research universities. Considering its origins, though, UCLA had risen to national prominence in a strikingly short time. Important questions nevertheless remained to be answered about setting even higher academic goals and securing the autonomy to pursue such goals.

The matter of the future course of UCLA very quickly came to a head. The context was the increasingly specific planning efforts that stretched from 1953, when the legislature commissioned the *Restudy of the Needs of California in*

Higher Education, to the adoption of the Master Plan in 1960.[24] In light of a huge projected increase in the demand for public higher education and the planning of new campuses, the two principal campuses of the University of California were asked in 1957 to prepare statements about their future plans and needs. When these reports were formally considered by the regents' Committee on Educational Policy, the element of complacency that had crept into the UCLA administration was suddenly exposed.

Committee chairman Edward Carter found the contrast between the Berkeley and UCLA reports disturbing. The former was already an eminent university, but the whole tone of its study was "one of self-examination—very critical—aimed at up-grading the character of Berkeley." If put into effect, he presciently observed, Berkeley would be "challenging Harvard for first place ten years from now." UCLA was, on the other hand, "a less distinguished university. . . .

> It has grown rapidly, of course . . . but we have there at the present time almost one-fourth of our students studying applied arts and business, the intellectual contents of which are certainly less rigorous than other departments. It seems to me the UCLA objectives merely extend to 25,000, with pretty much what we are doing now. I would guess it was prepared by the present administrators who feel they are doing pretty well and are content to do the same. I don't feel a real attempt to up-grade the Los Angeles campus . . . that if this is followed Los Angeles will be[come] one of the first ten universities in the United States.

Chancellor Allen took refuge somewhat lamely in "regional interest and the land-grant tradition"; but this was grist for Carter's mill:

> We are going the route of the Big Ten land-grant great middle west universities at Los Angeles. At Berkeley we are going the route of Harvard, Yale, Columbia and Chicago.[25]

The challenge thrown to the UCLA administration was clear. First, they were being told to jettison the more vocational residues of the past—physical education, home economics, and undergraduate business.[26] With the expansion and diversification of higher education in California, these were not subjects that a research university need teach. UCLA's future should lie with upper-division studies in the academic disciplines and especially graduate-professional work. Second, UCLA needed to apply to itself the critical self-examination that was evident at Berkeley, and, above all, to set a higher standard for emulation. Still, the message was difficult for Allen to grasp. Essentially an administrator, he lacked the intuitive knowledge of what the highest academic standards really meant. He directed, for example, that sets of catalogues from the four top universities named by Carter be acquired and distributed at UCLA because these were "symbols considered important by the Regents."[27] Although Allen had never been given the actual reins to lead UCLA, he failed when put to the test to demonstrate the ambition and imagination to advance the institution. It was the death-knell of his chancellorship.

By 1957 Allen was a "beleaguered chancellor" and not only because of his limited academic vision. Besides disappointing Regent Carter on the issue of planning, Allen had alienated regents on two other issues. The long investigation and dismissal of Coffman, who had backers among the regents, had been a painful process. The Pacific Coast Scandal of 1956, which involved payments to football players by the UCLA coach, was also damaging. Allen first sided with alumni in support of the coach ('everyone did it') and then took the opposite position at the behest of Sproul. In addition, Allen apparently never fit into the social set of deans and regents which was so important for the informal governance of UCLA.[28] The following year Clark Kerr was named to replace Sproul as president of the University, the position that Allen had coveted. Kerr's recommendation to replace Allen as chancellor of UCLA was supported by the regents with near unanimity.[29]

The Kerr administration took the helm of the University of California as the academic plans for Berkeley and Los Angeles were being digested. In the summer of 1958 the regents adopted a statement of policy on this matter that had been formulated by Carter's committee and duly weighed by the Academic Senates and all parties concerned.[30] The two campuses were officially accorded the same elite role: to have all work "grounded in research and in the intellectual disciplines"; to give primary emphasis to "excellence in research and instruction"; to restrict enrollment to the number of students that can be given "high quality instruction"; and to place emphasis on upper division and graduate teaching. Both institutions were projected to halt their growth at 25,000 students, with an eventual target of only 6000 in the lower division. Most important,

> plans for the future and budget allocations for the Berkeley and Los Angeles campuses shall be based on the principle that the two campuses should be comparable in size and have equal opportunities for developing programs which, although not identical but rather complementary, are of equivalent quality.[31]

This was a mandate for UCLA to emulate Berkeley—the clear dawning of a new era. Moreover, it was given with the clear understanding that the financial backing required for this kind of heroic exertion would be forthcoming from the regents.[32] The year 1958 was the beginning of a revolution for UCLA and for the University of California.

Having endured the discomfort of being chancellor of Berkeley under Sproul, Clark Kerr understood the need for decentralization. Almost immediately he began to delegate authority for budgetary and personnel decisions to the branches, and in a short time the chancellors became for the first time largely sovereign over their respective campuses.[33] At this same time, Raymond Allen announced his resignation and was replaced on an interim basis by Verne Knudson. In 1960 Franklin D. Murphy, University of Kansas chancellor, assumed the post.

Although he was chancellor for just eight years (1960–68), Franklin Murphy is held in the same esteem as a university-builder at UCLA as Sterling and Terman are at Stanford. These, of course, were years of breathtaking development at all the research universities. Also, the important political decision to accord UCLA equality in principle with Berkeley preceded him. These years nevertheless mark the transformation of UCLA into a mature research university, and Murphy's contribution was by almost all accounts substantial.[34]

Symbolically, Murphy conveyed to the campus a sense of its own separate identity. He insisted that the institution be referred to as UCLA, rather than as a branch of the somewhat amorphous University of California. Murphy's most pointed confrontations with President Kerr concerned matters of increased autonomy for UCLA and honorific recognition for the chancellorship. He also sought to utilize alumni, athletics, and residential life to create a sense of loyalty and focus like that found in more established universities. More tangibly, during his tenure the campus received an enormous infusion of resources. Murphy acquired a reputation locally for going to Berkeley or Sacramento and 'pounding the table' to demand what UCLA was entitled to. However, parity of treatment was conceded when he accepted his position, and he never subverted the university administration by going behind its back.[35] In fact, Murphy had little to complain of during these expansive years. When he took office the basic instructional budget for UCLA, including the medical school, was $2 million less than that of Berkeley (which had no medical school). UCLA consistently gained ground until its instructional budget *without* the medical school approximated that of Berkeley by the late 1970s. Also, during the early 1960s there was more new construction at UCLA than at any other campus of the university.[36]

The governance of UCLA changed markedly during the Murphy years. First, the oligarchy of deans in the College of Letters and Science came to an end with the retirements of Knudson, Dodd, and Arlt. The powerful traditions of the Academic Senate remained to ensure a strong collegial voice, but the upper administration was no longer dominated by this experienced and close-knit group. With them as well went a good deal of the back-door access to the regents. Instead, Murphy was able to fill both these roles. Making good use of the powers that had now devolved upon the chancellor, he was known as the person to see in order to get things done, whether it be cutting through red tape or reversing previous decisions. This last trait, in fact, tended to undermine the position of his vice chancellor (the counterpart to the provost at Stanford). Murphy quite properly became the principal figure for securing and mobilizing the support of the southern regents. A contemporary described him as "a virtuoso in utilizing the strength of Los Angeles to get what he wanted."[37] The administrative style that Murphy imposed ultimately brought a significant change in the nature of the institution. UCLA became more insulated from the politics of the university and those of the regents, and as a result grew more bureaucratic—in the best sense of that term. The internal operations of the university became more autonomous and more governed by established procedures; and the influence of the Los Angeles community was exerted more diffusely through an increasing volume of voluntary support.

The process of building academic distinction at UCLA was fundamentally different from that at Stanford. Even as its resources were rapidly increased, UCLA continued to recruit faculty predominately at non-tenured ranks. During Murphy's first five years as president, regular faculty positions increased by 320, or about a third. Two hundred of those positions were at the assistant professor level, and one hundred were full professors. Senior appointments, when they were made, were employed at UCLA primarily to rectify weaknesses, to compensate for losses, or to rehabilitate problem departments.[38] This leveling-up approach is probably more typical for state research universities, where public expectations support the offering of a broad spectrum of programs; but it represents the antithesis of the 'steeples' principle employed at Stanford. The leveling-up approach would also seem to produce more modest results.

The 1965 Cartter study of departmental quality brought disappointment to Murphy and UCLA.[39] For all its exertions, UCLA had not significantly bettered its showing on the 1957 rankings (Table 7). UCLA's most highly rated departments were Spanish, Anthropology, and Geography—hardly the most competitive or salient fields. Clearly, relative progress became increasingly difficult as an institution neared the top. This showing apparently caused Murphy to reevaluate hiring practices, and to adopt a modified 'steeples' approach. He now sought to assemble core groups of scholars who could achieve national standing. The strong chemistry department, for example, was given two additional full professorships.[40] 'Steeple' building, however, may be an inherently difficult commitment for public universities to maintain, given their broad responsibilities. In the early 1970s, when expansion ceased and austerity budgets were imposed, UCLA reverted to an approach to faculty allocation that was based almost entirely on student enrollments.[41]

There were other disappointments on UCLA's developmental path. The intention of shifting the balance of enrollments decisively toward upper division and graduate work was simply not realized. The following enrollment figures from the UCLA Academic Plans show the projected and actual changes:[42]

TABLE 8. Actual and Estimated Enrollment at UCLA

	Actual 1961	1962 Est. for 1970	1967 Est. for 1972	Actual 1972
Lower division	6,232	6,000	5,880	8,063
Upper division	6,467	9,500	8,035	10,163
Master's/professional	3,973	6,500	7,095	7,366
Doctoral level	2,202	6,000	3,990	2,884
Totals	18,874	28,000	25,000	28,476

Lower division enrollments increased instead of diminishing, and doctoral students attained only a fraction of their intended growth. Planning in itself was obviously no panacea. The plan, for one thing, ignored the historic centrality of the undergraduate college. Murphy's efforts to create traditional loyalties at UCLA in terms of alumni, athletics, and residential life were in fact testimony to this reality, and may have been a wiser course. On the doctoral level, there is no gainsaying the fact that the addition of only 682 students during a decade of burgeoning graduate enrollment represented a disappointment for UCLA's academic aspirations. During the 1960s, at least, the basic disciplines at UCLA failed to rival the academic distinction of their counterparts and theoretical peers at Berkeley.

UCLA nevertheless definitively entered the ranks of the major research universities. It was one of the institutions that benefited most from the post-Sputnik boom in federal research spending. By 1963 it was among the top ten recipients of such funds. The life sciences continued to lead the proliferation of organized research, but they were no longer exceptional in this respect.

Edward Carter, back in 1957, had been oddly prescient about UCLA as well as Berkeley: the university that emerged from the 1960s bore a closer resemblance to the public research universities of the Midwest than to its sister campus in the north. The rise of UCLA brought a secure place in the second tier of research universities—those with distinguished departments in a large number of fields, but few nationally leading ones.[43] In addition, whereas Berkeley seemed oriented predominantly toward international communities of scientists and scholars, UCLA shared with other state universities a decided regional orientation. It had numerous ties with the entertainment industry, for example, and further linkages were provided by vigorous professional schools and one of the most extensive systems of extension education. Thus, to a large extent, the elements that were responsible for the postwar rise of UCLA continued to fuel its development. Being a part of the University of California, and especially achieving parity with Berkeley, assured a relatively generous resource base. Continued success in the federal research economy vindicated and sustained the research role that it sought. Finally, growing regional support provided, at first indirectly through the state and later more directly through gifts, additional resources for development. UCLA's renewed progress since the late 1970s is testimony to the continuing efficacy of this formula.

3. The University of Pittsburgh

On July 18, 1955, the University of Pittsburgh announced that Edward H. Litchfield would become its twelfth chancellor. His appointment came "at a critically important time in the University's history," according to the chairman of the board, because "the trustees have set forth new goals, which, when realized, will place the University of Pittsburgh among the leaders of the world's great universities."[1] Ten years later, almost to the day, Litchfield resigned from the chancellorship broken in health and diminished in reputation, the academic accomplishments that he had engineered endangered by a fiscal morass that was also his doing. The meteoric career of Edward Litchfield could be the stuff of Greek tragedy: he was a man of extraordinary abilities as an academic, an administrator, and a businessman, yet he brought about his own downfall through a fundamental flaw in character. At issue here, however, is not the man, but the institution he sought to develop—the relative disappointment of the ambitious plans for the academic advancement of the University of Pittsburgh.

In spite of considerable postwar development, Pitt in 1955 was an unlikely candidate to become one of the "world's great universities." It was essentially an urban service university, largely oriented toward commuting students—a 'trolley-car college' it would later be called. Sixty-four percent of the 20,000 Pitt students came from surrounding Allegheny County, and about the same proportion attended part-time. There were dormitory accommodations for only 164 students. Just 56 percent of the faculty held Ph.D.s, and a disturbing number of those were from Pitt itself. Faculty members were expected to teach fifteen hours of class per week. Instructional expenditures were well below the per-student average for eastern private colleges. Since the end of the war Pitt had granted 773 Ph.D.s, but more than 60 percent of them were in the high-volume fields of education, psychology, and chemistry. The university's most notable accomplishment before 1955 was the reorganization and modernization of its medical complex. It was here that most of Pitt's $2 million of research was conducted, and also where Dr. Jonas Salk brought acclaim to the university in 1954 by perfecting a vaccine against polio.[2] Except for this last distinction, Pitt in 1955 was a middling American university, perhaps somewhat above the median, but not by much. The most promising factor for its aspirations were the members of the board of trustees. They represented the great industrial and financial fortunes of Pittsburgh, were behind the emerging 'Pittsburgh Renaissance,' and had bankrolled the development of the Health Center. If the trustees wished to build a first-class university in Pittsburgh, they probably could tap the resources required.[3] In Edward Litchfield they appeared to have a leader suited for this task.

The new chancellor was just 41 years old at the time of his appointment. He had earned a doctorate in political science at the University of Michigan before the war, and held administrative posts in occupied Germany afterward. He joined the Cornell School of Business and Public Administration as a visiting professor in 1950, and rose to become dean just three years later. In his short tenure there Litchfield converted the school to a graduate-level unit, doubled its enrollment, and made it self-supporting. He founded the *Administrative Science Quarterly,* the principal journal in this field, and also became the executive director of the American Political Science Association. Litchfield's activities transcended the academy. He founded and presided over the Governmental Affairs Institute in Washington, a nonprofit corporation that worked closely with the State Department, and he became an active board member of three major industrial corporations. These extra-academic commitments continued after Litchfield became chancellor, and required that he spend part of each week in Syracuse, New York, and Washington. A tireless worker with prodigious energy, Litchfield did not overtly shirk his responsibilities in Pittsburgh; however, the multiple roles that he continued to fill were part and parcel of the hubris of the man.[4]

Litchfield's academic specialty—ironically—was administration. He propounded the then novel view that administration was a unified field of expertise that transcended the conventional boundaries of business, government, universities, and nonprofit organizations. Before his arrival at Pitt, the university had been essentially managed from the chancellor's office.[5] Litchfield devised an elaborate administrative structure that included as many as eight vice chancellors, in addition to a large presidential staff. It made the university decidedly top-heavy with administrators, but Litchfield's philosophy was to set the direction at the top and to delegate authority over actual operations. Besides, the administration was in this case intended to lead the academic revolution.

Litchfield brought to Pitt a well-articulated plan for academic advancement that emphasized the centrality of the academic disciplines. In numerous forums he argued that the disciplines provided instruction in the liberal arts for under-graduates, advanced training and research at the graduate level, and basic knowl-edge to serve the needs of the professional schools.[6] Litchfield attempted to real-ize this scheme in his organizational chart by creating a vice chancellor for academic disciplines—in effect, a provost who supervised the divisions of humanities, natural sciences, and social sciences. A separate school of liberal arts, another for general studies (part-time and non-degree students), and some of the professional schools all drew their teachers in part or in whole from these divisions.

Litchfield realized that Pitt could only achieve its goal of national prominence on a selective basis, and for that reason adopted an equivalent of Terman's 'stee-ples' approach. The favored areas at Pitt were sometimes called "spires of dis-tinction." He sought to take advantage of what he called "cluster organizations" (institutes, centers, programs) in order to achieve flexibility and integration of disparate fields. In particular, Litchfield sought "to gain national prestige in a very short time." Thus, in order to raise the prestige of the disciplines as a whole Pitt considered it a "tactical necessity" to "give special support to certain parts of programs which can most quickly gain national eminence."[7] This sense of haste permeated the university during the Litchfield years.

Indeed, progress was swift from the moment Litchfield assumed the chancel-lorship. Faced with the overwhelming task of transforming both student body and faculty into the mold of a research university, he attacked the most critical matters. He immediately raised faculty salaries, reduced teaching loads, and introduced sabbatical leaves. In conjunction with these steps, a rigorous evalu-ation was undertaken of the existing faculty. For three years a succession of administrative committees scrutinized the performance and potential of all non-medical faculty: 202 of the 660 did not measure up to the new standards and were discouraged from remaining at Pitt. By 1962, 121 of them had departed. By that date also, the faculty had increased to 972, with more than half of them being Litchfield-era appointees.[8] The goal of attracting distinguished faculty was significantly abetted by a $12 million grant from the A. W. Mellon Trust to advance the basic disciplines (1958). The ten distinguished professorships that this money supported, in addition to doctoral and postdoctoral fellowships, were decisively important in allowing Pitt to start building 'spires of distinction.'[9]

Fashioning a student body appropriate to a research university was a problem of larger dimensions. Tuition was raised by 43 percent and entrance standards stiffened. These changes took a toll on the part-time students, who nevertheless still made up approximately half of Pitt's enrollment. The number of freshmen from the top 20 percent of their high school class increased from one-third in

1956 to two-thirds in 1962. Average S.A.T. scores rose by 89 points. By acquiring local properties and converting them to dormitories, Pitt was able to house more than three thousand students on campus by 1963. Even more significant was a shift in emphasis toward graduate education. With the proliferation of professional schools and the encouragement of graduate study in the disciplines, Pitt's proportion of graduate/professional students rose from under a quarter in 1955, to a third in 1960, and to two-fifths in 1965.

Litchfield opportunistically expanded the physical facilities of the university. He acquired a neighboring hotel, apartment buildings, a municipal hospital, and even the Pittsburgh Pirates baseball stadium. He also planned or actually constructed a succession of major academic structures. By 1962 he claimed that an additional $100 million of university property had been added or was under construction.[10]

The Litchfield program caused expenditures at Pitt to climb steeply while, until 1962, enrollments were falling. The size of the faculty was doubled, and the average salary was doubled as well. The growing research budget covered part of this payroll, but the instructional budget for the university nevertheless nearly tripled. The shift to graduate/professional education was also expensive, requiring greater faculty resources as well as substantial student aid. Pitt was largely successful in attracting benefactions to finance buildings and acquisitions, although it had to resort to a tuition surcharge to fund the first dormitory project, in effect mortgaging future revenues. More onerous were the requirements for maintaining the additional space. All these factors together rapidly escalated expenditures. The Wells Committee, a special body sponsored by the Ford Foundation to investigate the cause of the crisis at Pitt, reported with some amazement that expenditures per student doubled from 1957 to 1961.[11] Somehow income needed to rise at that same vertiginous pace.

The unfolding of the financial crisis at Pitt has been admirably depicted in a recent history of the university.[12] In brief, the initial tuition hike permitted the university to operate comfortably within its budgets for the first two Litchfield years. A small deficit in 1958–59 grew to almost $2 million the next year, half of which could not be covered in current accounts. Litchfield responded by presenting a detailed financial plan to the trustees. A $10 million loan would assist the university through two years of rapid development and then be repaid with the surpluses that would occur after 1962. Litchfield's plan was confidently adopted, but the deficits for the next two years ran nearly $2 million more than had been forecast. Worse, there was no surplus for 1962–63. Litchfield surprised the trustees by proposing an additional loan of $5 million in January 1963, and under the circumstances they had little choice but to accede.

At this point it was fully evident that the university was in a state of crisis and that decisive action was imperative to restore financial equilibrium. The trustees created a Budget and Audit Committee to monitor the university's finances more closely, but merely discovering the dimensions of the problem was time consuming and the chancellor was of little help. Pitt's finances thus deteriorated further during this process. The deficit for fiscal 1963 was finally reckoned at $3.4 million. Litchfield was repeatedly told to bring expenditures into line with the university's income. In May 1964 he reported that there would be a small surplus for that year. In October, however, a deficit of $4.5 million was reported. The crisis now approached a scandal and could no longer be concealed from the public. During the first part of 1965 the administration and the trustees worked frantically to keep the university fiscally afloat, but with the current accounts running about $25 million in the red, short-term palliatives could accomplish little. At the height of the crisis, in May, Litchfield suffered a mild heart attack. Two months later he submitted his inevitable resignation.

During those frantic months the notion had taken hold that salvation could only be attained with an infusion of public funds. This idea was not as novel in Pennsylvania as it might have been in another state. The Commonwealth of Pennsylvania had been providing nearly $5 million annually to the university to aid programs in the public interest.[13] When it became clear that the university's private benefactors would not underwrite past profligacy, the state became the last resort. An appeal was made in June 1965 and the Commonwealth responded with a special appropriation of $5 million to allow Pitt to weather the next two years. The search for a more comprehensive solution to Pitt's financial woes ineluctably pointed in the same direction. The following summer legislation was passed that converted the University of Pittsburgh into a "state-related" institution. Pitt's headlong quest to become the equal of the leading private universities ended with an ignominious crossover to the public sector.

The inescapable question raised by Pitt's debacle is, how could a major university allow its finances to slip entirely out of control? Other research universities in the 1960s found that pressures to spend exceeded their capacities to increase revenues, but none even approached the dimensions of the disaster at Pitt. The Wells Committee provided one kind of answer by identifying the major factors that lay behind the cost spiral. The committee flagged several questionable practices, such as financing dormitories with a tuition surcharge and inordinate administrative overhead. Increasing the proportion of graduate/professional students was inherently costly, but these costs seemed even higher at Pitt than at other research universities. One of Litchfield's pet innovations—the trimester system—turned into a major fiscal liability. Few undergraduates wanted to attend full-time during the summer, which made this semester quite costly to the university. But 70 percent of the faculty were given twelve-month contracts, considerably escalating salary costs. In general, the committee found the faculty and facilities at Pitt to be greater than needed for the number of students at the university.[14]

Deeper than these specific items lies another kind of failure—administrative incompetence. The administrative apparatus installed by Litchfield simply did not work well; it lacked the essential feedback of information that could provide a basis for intelligent adaptation. This failing was most grievous in financial matters. The budget was prepared by the vice chancellor for planning and development, but was never reviewed by the treasurer and comptroller who monitored revenues and expenditures. The budget was consequently divorced from reality, as became apparent during the crisis. Even when the trustees intervened, it took them many months just to gain a reasonably accurate picture of actual conditions.

At a deeper level still are the personal shortcomings of Edward Litchfield. He was responsible for making the administrative structure function, and he better than anyone else should have known the true condition of the university. But Litchfield seemed incapable of facing up to anything short of success. When it became apparent that the ambitious goals he had set might have to be abandoned or postponed, Litchfield refused to confront the facts. Instead, he dealt with crucial issues obliquely, or worse, in the case of budgets, through wishful thinking. For example, on the vital matter of having adequate enrollments, he wrote the vice chancellor for academic disciplines in the spring of 1963: "I think you were going to make a study to see whether or not we were letting our academic levels get ahead of what we could secure from the market."[15] Later that year he proposed forming a committee of his inner group (which apparently never met) to determine "some really thoughtful academic ways of thinking about new methods of achieving present objectives at lower costs."[16] These were both matters that should have been addressed long before. Rather than deal with problems, Litchfield invariably preferred to plunge ahead. He was still devising new programs the day his heart attack forced his withdrawal.

The rise and fall of Edward Litchfield and the obvious maladministration tend to obscure some fundamental questions about the development of Pitt as a research university. Was its original goal of becoming a major research university feasible? How far did Pitt actually advance? Could Pitt's goals have been pursued more effectively? Or conversely, did Pitt advance farther and faster during the Litchfield years than would have been possible through orthodox means?

The Wells Committee made a systematic effort to determine the qualitative attainments of Pitt's academic programs, but came to the cryptic conclusion, "that the University has made more progress than its detractors will admit, but less than its most ardent admirers assert."[17] Indeed, Pitt presented a mixed picture. In terms of research funding, the university made great strides. In the mid-sixties Pitt was around 23rd in the country in the amount of federal research funding received. About 70 percent of these funds came from NIH for biomedical research, the area that was most highly developed before Litchfield arrived. Pitt also succeeded in becoming a regular recipient of funding from two new federal agencies, NASA and the Agency for International Development. It fared worse (34th in 1964; 43rd in 1966) in attracting funds from the NSF, which probably reflected academic quality across the sciences more accurately.[18]

The Wells Committee had access to the as yet unpublished findings of Allan Cartter's "Assessment of Quality in Graduate Education." It accorded Pitt a national ranking in just one department—philosophy was ranked eighth. This department was the most successful 'spire' erected at Pitt. Fortuitous circumstances had permitted Pitt to recruit an outstanding cluster in the philosophy of science. These individuals had been assisted by the establishment of the Philosophy of Science Center (1960), and the result had been a department of national standing. The other side of this accomplishment, however, was that none of the other departments at Pitt were regarded highly enough to be rated as 'strong.'

Most social science departments, for example, were rated as 'adequate plus'; chemistry and physics, which Pitt considered among its best departments, were rated 'good,' or somewhat above the median.[19] In some cases recognition was belated. One potential 'spire,' anthropology, was ranked 13th in the 1969 ratings. But for the most part the 'spires' at Pitt failed to gain national renown "in a very short time."

On close examination, Litchfield's vaunted strengthening of the academic disciplines was decidedly spotty. According to Charles H. Peake, the vice chancellor for this area, the effort to develop 'spires' meant that,

> the advancement of the few was made at the expense of the many. As a consequence most of the 28 Departments remained inadequately staffed. This discrimination was accepted because the chairmen were assured that their respective Departments would soon share in the quality buildup.[20]

One indication of the lack of depth in these departments was the continued use of more than one hundred part-time faculty. Teaching at Pitt was thus done by a combination of recognized scholars, part-timers, and also large numbers of teaching fellows. What constituted 'adequate staffing,' however, goes to the very heart of this matter.

As the chief recruiter for senior appointments, Charles H. Peake was regarded as the architect of Pitt's advancement during the Litchfield era. But a key trustee also accused him of being one of the causes of Pitt's reckless spending. Allegedly, Peake could convince the chancellor to approve any new appointment that would contribute toward the goal of national recognition. Peake himself, however, presented quite a different account. As his statement above would indicate, he felt that the disciplines were always starved for resources. He later complained, in particular, that Litchfield's favor shifted to the professional schools:

> new schools were established, expensive graduate professional programs were staffed and subsidized, a professional quadrangle and a professional classroom building were planned. . . . Since funds were limited, the development of the staffs of the disciplines virtually ceased.[21]

An examination of the instructional budgets only partially corroborates Peake's contention. The funds spent by the academic disciplines increased by 131 percent from 1956 to 1963, with fairly steady increments of growth. The budgets for the non-health professional schools increased somewhat more rapidly by 160 percent. By this last date both schools and the health professions all had budgets of comparable magnitudes. Peake charged, however, that the academic disciplines with their third of the budget were expected to teach 70 percent of the university credit hours.[22]

Pitt at the end of the Litchfield era was a heterogeneous institution. A number of new schools and programs were staffed with young, ambitious scholars and heavily oriented toward research. In the academic disciplines the contradictions were glaring: the recent, research-minded appointments largely set the academic tone of the departments, but they also had to face the exigencies of higher education at Pitt—fairly large teaching responsibilities, much of it basic in nature, and inadequate resources. In general, uniform high standards were not achieved across the university as a whole. But this was to be expected in an institution in transition—a transition that in terms of its original aims was never completed. In a sense, then, Pitt's 'great leap forward' was a truncated experiment. Perhaps its most positive result was to instill a sense of excitement and high ambition. This esprit was crucially important in sustaining the university through its crisis and aftermath. The Pitt faculty was adamantly opposed to any backsliding in the matter of quality, and remained committed to future advancement.[23] In another sense, the experiment at Pitt ran long enough to draw some definite judgments. Compared with other advancing institutions, Pitt during the Litchfield era evinced at least three shortcomings that precluded the realization of its ambitions.

First, Pitt failed to develop a broad base of support. Litchfield made recriminations during the crisis that the business moguls of Pittsburgh had failed to live up to an implicit obligation to provide the resources for Pitt's rise to greatness. The real problem was that the Litchfield administration did not extend its search for support beyond these few individuals. The Wells Committee found that the university's relations with the community "ranged from 'poor' to 'fair'"; and that its relations with alumni were "particularly bad." The university did not launch a fund-raising drive aimed at alumni until *April 1965,* and then it was bungled badly. In June, Litchfield wrote his vice chancellor for planning and development:

> your development people simply don't know Pittsburgh. . . . I think it is imperative that we get at least one person in who knows the community thoroughly, who is socially acceptable in the most 'social' circles, and who can do all the things that we simply can't do with a hired staff brought in from the outside.[25]

This revelation occurred a decade too late.

Pitt did not lack for success in raising funds. The total for voluntary support during the Litchfield years was near $80 million. Pitt was the only university in this fund-raising league that consistently derived the majority of its gifts from foundations. These were largely Pittsburgh foundations, which again underlines the narrow base of support. One consequence of this limited base was that Pitt's voluntary support did not expand over time.[26] Another difficulty was that much of these funds were directed toward the Health Center. It conducted the only fund-raising drive of the Litchfield years, and the Center's continued development was strongly supported by the Pittsburgh plutogens. Pitt was also crowded by its neighbor, the Carnegie Institute of Technology, which conducted a $22 million capital drive from 1957–60.[27] Yet these were all compelling reasons why Pitt needed to develop other sources of support.

Early in 1963, Litchfield had conveyed this same message to one of his vice chancellors: now that Pitt was attaining national stature, it "therefore need[ed] to look for support outside the Pittsburgh area."[28] He was specifically thinking of appealing to the Ford Foundation for a Challenge Grant. He suggested that Pitt administrators visit the Foundation, and that perhaps there were connections that might be exploited through the trustees. This seemingly reasonable message in fact betrayed the failings of the Litchfield regime: 1963 was a late date to get to know the Ford Foundation.[29] The university seemed unaware that the way to impress the Foundation was to put one's own house in order. Even more to the point, this kind of fund-raising was a responsibility that the chancellor could not delegate.[30]

This last episode exemplifies as well the second shortcoming of the Litchfield administration—what might be labeled provincialism. For a university that purportedly aspired to a national stature, the Pitt administration showed little awareness of conditions among its would-be peers or in important centers of the research community. Individual scholars at Pitt were naturally embedded in their own disciplinary networks. But the administration that was supposedly leading the academic advancement was deficient in this respect. Litchfield's ignorance of the Ford Foundation was unconscionable in light of what the Challenge Grants program might have done for Pitt. Late in 1962 he instructed Charles Peake to give materials research a high priority because "the whole field is going to get quite a play." Three years earlier the Ford Foundation and the Department of Defense had begun investing in this field.[31] In 1964 Litchfield had high hopes that Pitt might be included in the NSF Centers of Excellence program, quite unaware that the university's financial chaos would preclude consideration of its proposal.[32]

This inability or unwillingness to view Pitt from the perspective of other research universities was closely related to its third shortcoming, overconfidence or the absence of self-criticism. The ability to evaluate realistically the relative merits of individuals, programs, and departments was an inescapable element in the advancement of Berkeley and Stanford, and to a lesser extent UCLA. The dominant note at Pitt, on the other hand, was the touting of progress that had been achieved. Litchfield was naturally the chief cheerleader. There was a facile quality to the quantitative documentation of academic progress that he frequently recited; in particular, he provided no meaningful context in which to evaluate such accomplishments as the attraction of thirteen Woodrow Wilson fellows.[33] Once again, Litchfield's congenital aversion to facing unpleasant facts served the university badly.

There can be little doubt that the Litchfield administration in its early years gave a tremendous impetus to the academic advancement of Pitt. It was after this initial spurt that it failed to do the things that were needed to sustain forward progress. If Pitt had built more slowly and more solidly at that stage the university might have accomplished far more. Pitt's crash occurred during the years when American society was devoting more copious resources to research universities than ever before. There was good reason, nevertheless, that Pitt found its share inadequate. The Wells Committee concluded philosophically that "it takes time, judgement, dedication, money and good luck to build a great university."[34] Pitt's shortfall of money and luck was a direct result of haste, poor judgment, and insufficient dedication.

When Pitt became a state-related university in 1966, it resolved problems for both the institution and the Commonwealth of Pennsylvania. For Pitt, the state provided a lifeline out of its financial morass without resorting to some equivalent of bankruptcy. For the state, the university supplied a means for filling an embarrassing shortage of places for reasonably priced higher education in western Pennsylvania. Tuition was immediately reduced by two-thirds, and the demand for undergraduate places at Pitt surged.[35] Pitt became a different kind of university: henceforth its academic superstructure would be supported by the teaching of large numbers of undergraduates. The proportion of graduate/professional students receded back below one-quarter, where it had been when Litchfield arrived.

The transition was not an easy one for the university. As it slowly straightened out its financial affairs, Pitt learned the meaning of retrenchment sooner than other American universities. A full decade was needed to expunge the deficits of the Litchfield era. During that time the appropriations from the state assured the continuation of most academic programs, and also gave reason for hope to the majority of the faculty who did not wish to abandon Pitt or its aspirations. During these years, then, Pitt was largely able to consolidate the many additions and innovations of the Litchfield years. But little forward progress was evident. In the mid-seventies Pitt was performing about the same amount of sponsored research (in current dollars) as in the mid-sixties. Even with substantial subsequent increases, Pitt was 42nd in research expenditures in 1989.[36] Nor is it likely that Pitt increased its academic ranking. The 1982 *Assessment* found Pitt to be below the top thirty universities—in a range where precise rankings have little significance. Indeed, the pyramid of research universities in the 1980s was larger and broader than it was in the early 1960s. The position that Pitt currently occupies would lie in the middle statum, among many other universities that are active in research and genuinely excellent in some areas. Its overall transition since World War II is thus somewhat typical of American universities in general. For Pitt, however, the journey was more dramatic and the outcome something of a disappointment.

Although universities develop for the most part incrementally, the years from the mid-1950s to the mid-1960s were momentous for Stanford, UCLA, and Pitt. Each institution was substantially different by 1965 from what it had been a decade earlier. For Stanford, the decade of Frederick Terman's provostship was the decisive phase in a continuous process of development. The Litchfield era at Pitt, on the other hand, was marked by discontinuities at both its beginning and end. At UCLA, an official commitment to higher academic standing, following on earlier progress, emerged in 1957 and then persisted for a decade through the chancellorship of Franklin Murphy. The similar chronology here is closely related to the sameness of their aspirations. Results, however, varied.

For Stanford and UCLA, the ultimate success of their commitments was heavily dependent on two other achievements. They both established significant bases of research in programmatic fields during the postwar era. In each case, electrical engineering at Stanford and the medical school at UCLA, programmatic research had important synergistic effects of fertilizing more basic subjects and fostering a research culture within the institution. Their second achievement was to develop a wide foundation of external support that both endorsed and underwrote academic advancement. The relative shortcomings of Pitt in both these respects are glaring. Its Health Center, which provided the original locus of research, was not appreciably integrated with the rest of the university, and for some purposes served as a rival to the other schools. Nor was Pitt able to expand upon the generosity of a few local magnates to develop support among alumni and national foundations.

Each university made a commitment to academic advancement that was unusually strong for the mid-fifties. These actions reflected a larger shift of sentiments across universities which preceded decisive changes in the research economy. In a funding environment still weighted heavily toward programmatic research, all three institutions put basic research in the disciplines and academic prestige foremost. These priorities were set despite possessing strengths in more programmatic areas that might well have been emphasized. Instead, they responded to different sorts of stimuli that were encouraging commitments to academic distinction. In part, such signals were emanating from the private foundations, as described in the previous chapter. It will be seen in the next chapter that similar messages were coming from the nascent National Science Foundation, although not yet accompanied by compelling sums for support of research. The importance of these actions soon became evident. Universities that successfully embraced the ascending ideal of basic research were destined to thrive under the new conditions about to emerge from the transformation of the research economy.

6

The Transformation
of Federal Research Support
in the Sputnik Era

1. The 1950s Research Economy and the Rise of NSF

The university research economy of the early 1950s was an odd configuration. It was a product not of necessity, like wartime research organization, nor of design, as Vannevar Bush had vainly proposed, but rather of a succession of largely unrelated and uncoordinated developments in disparate cells of the federal megalith. These arrangements reflected the widely varying needs, powers, and resources of the several federal agencies. Not surprisingly, when this system was viewed from the performers' perspective—from its consequences for science and universities—it appeared to be disturbingly incoherent. Despite the unprecedented sums of money now directed to academic research, there was widespread apprehension about the nature and the future of the university research system.

Concern arose, above all, from the preponderant role of the armed services, supplemented by the Atomic Energy Commission, in the funding of university research. In the immediate postwar years these agencies had either extended wartime arrangements or gone to considerable lengths to enlist the continuing cooperation of academic scientists. After Cold War rearmament was in full swing, however, the defense establishment capitalized on its initial investments in academic science. Growth after 1950 occurred overwhelmingly in applied or highly programmatic projects. The Pentagon and the AEC accounted for 76 percent of federal funds for academic research, or 87 percent if Federal Contract Research Centers were included.[1] By no means all of these funds bore the taint of military ends. Still, by the end of the Korean War university spokesmen were increasingly voicing concern over the preponderance of programmatic funding in federal support of university research.

Harvard president James B. Conant, who had articulated the distinction between programmatic and uncommitted research, now warned that the "pendulum [was] in danger of swinging too far toward organized programmatic research."[2] According to Merle Tuve of the Carnegie Institution, "most of the work classed as research and development and carried out in universities is actually development work directed toward specific goals. Even the basic research which is supported is defined as to general area and given a project description in advance."[3] MIT provost Julius Stratton warned "that new patterns of research are emerging that will be difficult to reconcile with the true spirit of the university" and that "if . . . we strive to contain the widening scope of research entirely within the framework of our large universities, we shall end by changing their character and purpose."[4] For Tuve, these changes were already under way. University administrators in their clamor for research contracts and overhead reimbursements seemed to regard "their organizations simply as industrial corporations," which he considered "a tragic confusion of social purpose."[5]

As for the university's proper calling—basic, or uncommitted, or unfettered research, in this somewhat idealistic view—it was handicapped by the ascendancy of the military research agenda. Insufficient federal funds were being made available for basic research, which was conventionally lauded as the font of future technological progress. On campus, fears were prevalent that basic investigations were being squeezed out by the abundance of programmatic funding. There was also considerable concern, tinged perhaps with some nostalgia, that the freedom of individual scientists to follow their own curiousity had largely disappeared.[6] Specifically, military dominance over basic research was deplored. Caltech president Lee A. DuBridge called it "an anomalous and precarious situation to have the future of basic research hang by the thread of continued appropriations to the military agencies, or of their continued interest."[7] By 1953, this same critique was heard from another source as well. The fledgling National Science Foundation added its none-too-disinterested voice in favor of greater civilian sponsorship of basic university research.

The creation of the NSF in 1950 was at best a tepid endorsement of the notion of public support for basic academic science.[8] The foundation was actually charged with undertaking three different kinds of activities. Least controversial were the tasks of 'greasing the wheels of science,' which had been largely neglected because of the fragmented nature of federal research support. This included supervising international cooperation and exchange, maintaining a register of scientific personnel, and awarding graduate fellowships. Only the last of these activities represented a potentially significant ongoing expenditure. The central charge to the NSF was to support basic scientific research, but the original legislation also included the phrase "and to appraise the impact of research upon industrial development and the general welfare." The implication seemed to be that the NSF was also obliged to demonstrate the usefulness of undertaking basic research at all. The NSF's third group of functions related to the government's own overall scientific effort: namely, developing "a national science policy"; assisting upon request the research activities of the Defense Department; and evaluating the scientific research undertaken by other federal agencies.[9]

In reality, each of these sets of activities reflected expectations that were at variance with the nature of the new foundation. The authority to formulate national science policy, it was soon apparent, required a far more lofty standing in the executive branch than the deliberately insulated NSF could possibly claim. Assisting the DoD was a risible goal, given the disparity in resources. The intended role in evaluation reflected the desire of the Bureau of the Budget to gain some measure of control over the presumed waste and duplication in federally supported research. But for the NSF to do this presupposed a capacity to intrude upon the normal responsibilities of other, far more powerful agencies. This particular charge was a troublesome element in the early history of the NSF, since it implied efforts of coordination and evaluation that the foundation was neither inclined nor equipped to handle.[10]

The NSF in the flesh was in fact considerably closer to the image long advocated by the academic community than was the NSF on paper created by Congress. That is, the foundation from its inception regarded as axiomatic that its primary role was the support of basic scientific research and graduate education in the nation's colleges and universities. The twenty-four-person National Science Board, which governed the foundation, was dominated by university scientists and administrators. It contained ten university presidents and vice presidents, including such formidable figures as James Conant, Lee DuBridge, and Detlev Bronk. Presidents Dollard of the Carnegie Corporation and Chester Barnard of the Rockefeller Foundation were obvious friends of the academy. Only the three corporation presidents were outsiders who might possibly harbor doubts. The man chosen to direct the new foundation, Alan T. Waterman, had already demonstrated as Chief Scientist at ONR that the federal government could fund university research without compromising the integrity of scientific inquiry. Princeton-educated, protégé of Karl Compton, long a professor of physics at Yale—Waterman fully shared the values of the academic science community.[11] This meant, above all, that the foundation would adhere in the main to a policy of supporting the best possible science—that most likely to contribute to the advancement of fundamental knowledge. The NSF from its inception was thus first and foremost patron of the research universities.[12]

The preferred role of the new foundation was not one that could be readily grasped by the Congress or the country. The NSF thus had little alternative but to enter the lists in the debate over the nature of federally supported research: to plead the case for the efficacy of basic scientific research and to warn judiciously of the dangers attending the predominance of programmatic support. Waterman himself became the principal spokesman for the virtues of basic research. Most of the foundation's early annual reports contained invocations to this ideal, and his numerous speeches, often reprinted, consistently addressed this same theme.[13] Other opportunities were exploited as well. When the foundation published its first compilation of federal research expenditures, it concluded the factual summary by raising pointed policy questions: "Is it desirable . . . that such a large portion of funds for research and development at nonprofit institutions should be administered by agencies whose interests are primarily military? . . . What are the long-run implications of the Government's emphasis on applied research and development in contrast to basic research?"[14] The refrain became familiar, but the case was not easily made.

The challenge faced by the inchoate NSF was to create a niche for itself within a federal research establishment that was already largely elaborated. Nor were conditions propitious. The foundation began its life during the blackest hour of the Korean emergency. It attempted to grow during years of pervasive stringency in the federal budget. The atmosphere was poisoned further by the anti-intellectual pall of McCarthyism. Typical of one influential point of view was Secretary of Defense Charles E. Wilson's crass characterization of pure science (what proponents would call 'basic research'): "if successful, it could not be of any possible use to the people who put up the money for it—that made it pure."[15] Under these circumstances it was all too easy for the same elements in Congress that had held the foundation hostage before 1950 to dismiss the entreaties of Waterman and his allies for greater support for basic academic science.

Part of the price of securing passage of the National Science Foundation Act had been acceding to a $15 million ceiling on appropriations. The first full NSF budget (FY1952) that was submitted to Congress tactfully requested $14 million. The majority of these funds was to have been used to support research, and accordingly, in his written justification and in his testimony at the Hearings, Waterman reiterated the standard rationale for supporting basic science. Apparently unimpressed, the House Appropriations Committee reduced the NSF request to just $300,000, and this sum was subsequently endorsed by the full House. The NSF was treated more sympathetically in the Senate, after some exertions by its backers, but its final appropriation for 1952 was $3.5 million—just 25 percent of the administration request.[16]

This first budget episode testified to the real resistance that stood in the way of gaining acceptance and resources for the NSF's principal *raison d'être*. It also set a pattern for the following years. A presidential budget request of $15 million for 1953 yielded a congressional appropriation of $4.75 million; a $12.25 million request for 1954 brought the foundation $8 million. In 1956 the foundation finally exceeded the former ceiling with a regular appropriation of $16 million; and in 1957 it received its first relatively generous budget of $40 million.[17] Progress was slow, but the NSF gradually asserted its role.

From 1952 through 1958 the NSF distributed $59 million in research grants and almost $18 million in graduate and postgraduate fellowships. Given its accelerating growth, more than half of those funds were disbursed in the last two fiscal years. If the penury of the foundation in its initial years represented a relative failure to win acceptance of its case, the increases that followed constituted a relative success. One source of confusion was removed in 1954, when an Executive Order realistically defined the NSF's role within the federal science effort. The foundation was declared to be "increasingly responsible for providing support by the Federal Government for general-purpose basic research"; while at the same time it was deemed important and desirable that other federal agencies continue to support basic research "in areas which are closely related to their missions."[18] In essence, this pronouncement resolved the implicit conflicts over research turf and defined the NSF's primordial mission.

During these years the NSF managed to expand and develop its chosen niche in part by adapting to the conventions of the capital. The rationale for basic research was commonly made more politically palatable by being tied to national security and the need to stay ahead of the Russians. The foundation also showed its willingness to do the bidding of Congress, undertaking for example a program of summer institutes for science teachers as an implicit quid pro quo for more funding for basic research. By 1957 the foundation even managed to begin supporting 'Big Science' projects in astronomy.

The fledgling NSF comprised a minor component of the federal research economy. Its growth was nevertheless indicative of an inchoate trend. From the end of the Korean War, federal support of university research moved tentatively in the direction advocated by the critics cited above: that is, programmatic research tended to stabilize in universities even while activity increased in federal contract research centers. Greater support for basic science grew upon small bases in NSF and NIH. By 1958 their share of the total had risen to 35 percent of federal support. More important, these changes betokened the beginning of a more fundamental transformation in the nature of university research. In 1954, according to official bookkeeping, basic research constituted 64 percent of on-campus academic R&D (i.e. excluding agriculture and contract centers), and four years later it had risen to 74 percent.[19] During this interval the federal contribution to these totals remained roughly constant, which indicates that other funders were increasing support of basic research as well. Despite these favorable trends, arguments were made with increasing vehemence that support for basic scientific research in the nation's universities was inadequate. In sum, a dozen years after the end of World War II, the state of academic science was at once relatively prosperous, discontented, and directionless. Conditions were ripe for change.

2. Sputnik

The postwar era for the university research system ended on October 4, 1957, when the Soviet Union launched a satellite into orbit around the earth. From the moment that the Soviet achievement was announced, the psychology and assumptions undergirding scientific research in the U.S. began to change. Interestingly, *Sputnik I* was an astonishing development only for the uninformed. The Soviets had given forewarnings of their intentions; and the United States was proceeding, without great haste, toward launching of a satellite of its own in conjunction with the International Geophysical Year. But those who were uninformed of, and unprepared for, Sputnik included the Congress, the press, and the American people. They all tacitly perceived what the Eisenhower Administration wished not to acknowledge: the United States was in a race for space with the Soviet Union, and it was losing.[1]

In many ways the American rocket programs before Sputnik exemplified the weaknesses of the postwar research system: namely, the predominance of programmatic military purposes over the goal of advancing science; a parsimonious attitude toward the funding of basic scientific research; and a failure to realize that the competitiveness of American science rested on a complex infrastructure for graduate education and academic research. Initially, all three of the armed services had proposed their own rocket and satellite systems. After a review, a questionable decision was taken to confide the IGY satellite project to the Navy program. It did not receive a top priority, however, precisely because it was labeled as basic science—without foreseeable military applications! In addition, there was little sense that the United States needed to compete. Scientific leadership of the world had fallen into the lap of the United States as a result of World War II, and the assumed superiority of American institutions seemed to assure that it would remain there. All of these factors would be held to account in the public clamor that followed Sputnik.

The launching of the Soviet satellite immediately provoked prolonged national soul-searching. Any hopes that the Soviet accomplishment might be dismissed or forgotten were dashed by the launch of the much heavier *Sputnik II* just one month later. As both the press and the politicians took up the themes of Soviet strengths and American weaknesses, it became apparent that far-reaching measures would be required to address the crisis. A purely pragmatic response might have noted that Sputnik was essentially an engineering achievement, and that existing American efforts to accomplish the same goal had been impeded by the organizational rivalries and ponderous management practices of the armed services. These factors were addressed; but public discourse came to be dominated instead by the conviction that the United States had to improve itself internally in order to meet the Soviet challenge.

For Senator Lyndon Baines Johnson, Sputnik constituted a second Pearl Harbor for the United States. It also offered a golden opportunity for him and fellow Democrats to attack a heretofore popular President—to wrap their own political program in the American flag. For the party in the White House, it was difficult to be critical of the state of the nation. Instead, the crisis was used to rationalize prior convictions. Vice President Richard Nixon, for example, asserted that Sputnik betokened increased conflict with the Soviets for the allegiances of Third World countries; and a secret executive report on the implications of Sputnik dourly advocated a massive national program of fallout shelters. But Johnson and the Democrats were able to formulate a more far-reaching domestic policy agenda. In addition to the obvious need to extricate the space program from the internecine competition of the armed services, they found two other responses, in effect, ready made: the well-honed arguments of the nation's scientific community that the United States had been neglecting basic research; and an equally well-developed argument that the country needed to increase the capacity and effectiveness of its educational system. In a comparatively short time after Sputnik was in orbit, it became apparent that "Space, Education, and Science" would be the main thrusts of America's response.[2] Each had an impact on the research universities.

Space. The National Aeronautics and Space Administration was legislated into existence on October 1, 1958—almost a year after the launching of *Sputnik I*.[3] In a number of ways the problem of reorganizing the nation's space effort resembled that posed by atomic energy after World War II. In both cases the scientific fields contained almost limitless capacity for basic research; they also necessitated huge and costly investments in technology; and they possessed the potential for providing significant benefits for mankind. These considerations argued for civilian control over the space effort and open scientific disclosure of investigations and findings. On the other hand, the technology of space exploration, if not space itself, was of undeniable importance to the security of the nation. A continuation of the substantial and secret military activity in this area was thus inevitable.

In light of these similarities, it is not surprising that the new space agency bore some resemblance to the Atomic Energy Commission, created twelve years earlier. Both were under civilian direction, but whereas the AEC had the obligation of serving both civilian and military users of atomic energy, NASA was to be the public and peaceful side of the American space effort. The military services would continue with their own secret programs for rockets and satellites. This dichotomy helped to promote an affinity between NASA and the scientific community. Indeed, the passage of the National Aeronautics and Space Act of 1958 was widely viewed as a victory for civilian science. The expansion of human knowledge was proclaimed as one of the underlying purposes of the agency, and scientists had played a prominent role in formulating the legislation. To be more accurate, however, the interests of the scientific community on this occasion benefited from a conjuncture of political forces. For the immediate future that conjuncture would continue to underwrite the prosperity of American science.[4]

NASA quickly became another mission agency with significant involvement in the university research economy—a sixth channel of federal funding for academic science. NASA's predecessor, the National Advisory Committee on Aeronautics, was a focused, conservative agency that conducted most research in-house. Academic research was a minor component of NASA's burgeoning expenditures; but as the agency's budgets peaked above $5 billion in the mid-sixties, the roughly 2 percent that found its way to universities was a significant amount. By 1965, NASA contracts constituted 9.4 percent of federal R&D obligations to universities, and 17.5 percent to university-run contract research centers.[5] Moreover, NASA's research funds were spread fairly widely across the research universities. The effort at MIT, largely associated with Charles Stark Draper's department (see Chapter 3), was by far the largest single concentration, but by 1966 NASA was awarding more than $1 million in contracts to 36 different universities. NASA deliberately sought to support a broad range of academic research in what it called the space sciences. In fact, NASA in the early 1960s found itself in a position much like ONR after the war: as a neophyte agency it had to buy its way into academic science in order to have ready access to the expertise it would need (see pp. 188–90).

NASA's funding peaked in the mid-1960s, and subsequently its resources were devoted more closely to maintaining its extensive facilities and developing the hardware for manned space flight. By 1983, for example, NASA's contribution to academic R&D had fallen below 2.5 percent of the total. The bubble of NASA spending for academic research thus coincided with the mid-sixties surge from other federal sources, adding fuel to what was by then an overheated research economy.

Education.   Sputnik did not create a crisis in American education—rather, the problems that the United States faced in the late 1950s originated with the American servicemen who returned to their families after World War II. Sputnik did play a role, however, in overcoming the reluctance of the federal government to deal with a maturing baby boom that was on the verge of becoming a student boom.

The difficulties facing elementary and secondary education were the paramount educational questions for federal lawmakers in the mid-1950s. The inadequate financial base for building additional classrooms and staffing them was one major preoccupation. Consideration of these issues was also tinged with Cold War concerns—that precious intellectual talent was being wasted by those who did not continue their schooling, and that the United States was not producing sufficient numbers of scientists and engineers. Meaningful federal initiatives to deal with the problems confronting the schools were obstructed by such highly divisive issues as public aid to parochial schools and segregated schooling in the South. Nor did the prevailing fiscal austerity permit large new programs.

Higher education faced similar difficulties and also similar constraints. An effort to air these was begun in 1956 with the appointment of a presidential task force, the Committee on Education Beyond the High School. As the Committee deliberated in 1956 and 1957, three salient issues emerged: the desirability of extending more widely the opportunity to attend college; the critical need, in light of the rising demand for college teachers, to raise the abysmal levels of faculty salaries; and the need to provide financial assistance for the construction of additional facilities to accommodate the projected enrollment boom. The first of these might have been ameliorated by a program of federally supported scholarships or need-based student aid; the second would require additional institutional revenues; and the third suggested federal assistance for financing capital expenditures. The obstacle to any of these actions was a deep-seated aversion in the Congress and the Administration to federal intrusion into education. An additional impediment was a reluctance to spend. It was an inauspicious omen when Congress cut the initial appropriation for the Committee, and later terminated funding altogether before it had completed its deliberations.[6]

Amid these cross-currents, uncertainty reigned about what the federal government might do for higher education, or if it could do anything at all. The presidential task force, for example, in the end endorsed aid for construction over a program of scholarships, and that course also seemed to be the preference of the higher education community. But the administration leaned in the direction of student aid. Sputnik resolved the uncertainty about whether or not the government would take action: within a year the National Defense Education Act of 1958 was signed into law.[7]

Judged in relation to the needs of American higher education and the possibilities for alleviating them, NDEA was a tentative measure at best. It offered loans for college students (partially forgiven for those who became teachers), fellowships for graduate students, and support for languages and area studies. The real significance of NDEA, rather, was that it broke the stalemate that had been blocking federal financial assistance for higher education. NDEA itself was greatly expanded in subsequent years. It was followed in five years time by federal assistance for the building of college and university facilities, and then by other forms of categorical aid. Last would come the programs of need-based student aid aimed at widening access to higher education.

As its title would indicate, NDEA was prompted by the peculiar attitude of national insecurity and inadequacy that prevailed after Sputnik. Congress declared that federal action was required by the existence of an "educational emergency"; federal assistance was being provided "to help develop as rapidly as possible those skills essential to the national defense."[8] This rationale implied that the federal investment should be directed toward the best intellectual talent (graduate fellowships) and toward programs of research and teaching in somewhat esoteric fields that could not otherwise support themselves (languages and area studies). The original NDEA, and more particularly its subsequent extensions, thus principally aided research universities.

A second breakthrough was required to establish a federal responsibility toward widening access to higher education. This step did not occur until Lyndon Johnson occupied the White House. In the deliberations that preceded the Higher Education Facilities Act of 1963, "the national defense rationale of federal higher education policy receded, and the goal of equal educational opportunity began to emerge."[9] The latter goal indeed came to predominate in the higher education legislation associated with President Johnson's Great Society programs, and it became virtually the sole concern with the Education Amendments of 1972. Federal involvement with higher education, through the Office of Education in any case, shifted during the 1960s from a concern for specific attainments, which were congruent with the aspirations of the research universities, to preoccupations with the social incidence of higher education, which had far different implications for the allocation of resources.

Science.   At the time Sputnik was launched, the pluralist system of government support for university research was fully operational, save for the imminent addition of NASA. It was thus possible to increase the nation's commitment to reseach almost immediately by simply augmenting appropriations within existing channels of support. This in fact was done. But the way in which research funding was increased resolved a long-standing ambiguity about the federal role in the postwar university research economy. The reaction to Sputnik, at bottom, resulted in an endorsement of the case for disinterested academic research. As the consequences of this commitment were worked out over the next ten years, the place of university research in the national system was transformed.

TABLE 9. Indicators of Change in University Research[10]

	Gross National Product	National Basic Research	% GNP	Total Univ. R&D	% GNP	Basic Univ. Research	% Nat. Basic Research	Federal % Univ. Research
1953	364,900	441	.12	255	.07	110	25	43
1960	506,500	1,197	.24	646	.12	433	36	67
1964	637,700	2,289	.36	1,275	.20	1,003	44	79
1968	873,400	3,296	.38	2,149	.25	1,649	50	77
1986	4,291,000	14,163	.33	10,600	.24	7,100	50	67

Sputnik superimposed upon existing expansionary tendencies, gave a powerful impetus to university research that carried onward for about ten years. The principal results were that the character of university research was, in the aggregate, altered; and the place of university research in the total national R & D effort was significantly enlarged. From 1953 to 1968 national spending for basic research approximately tripled as a proportion of GNP, as did total university R&D. The universities also doubled their share of basic research performance to half of the national total (about where it was in 1990). As Table 9 reveals, these trends were evident from the mid-fifties—before Sputnik; but the gains after Sputnik were produced by ever-larger absolute increments of research funding, provided overwhelmingly by the federal government. These commitments thus reflected widespread public support for science, refracted through the political process. They brought about a shift in the university research system from a predominance of programmatic, often applied, research in the early fifties to a marked preponderance of disinterested basic research by 1968.

The post-Sputnik transformation of university research took place through growth. The former programmatic relationships between the military and university laboratories largely remained in place; they simply were overgrown and overshadowed by burgeoning commitments to basic research. This growth fell into two discernible stages. Table 9 shows that the increments of expansion were approximately the same for 1960-64 and for 1964-68. The percentage change was thus less for the second period, and after 1968 growth ceased entirely. The acceleration and then deceleration of growth in the research system during the post-Sputnik decade had a political analogue. The increased national prominence of academic science, and its increasing share of national resources, resulted in a corresponding salience in the national political process.

3. The Politics of Academic Science

The measures taken by the federal government in the years following Sputnik permanently altered the research universities by enlarging the dimensions of academic research and by making the conditions of that research unavoidably more dependent on government. From the viewpoint of the nation's capital, however, the research universities were a small wheel within a somewhat larger wheel labeled 'science,' which revolved according to the dynamics of more pressing national and international issues. The space race, the alleged 'missile gap,' and issues of armaments and disarmament were the matters that brought scientists further into the corridors of power after 1957 than ever before. There, the question of the development of academic science was but one, and by no means the most pressing, of their concerns. These academic scientists and statesmen nevertheless shared the long-standing concern with the inadequate funding of basic research and the dearth of support for research universities. Within a few short years, they succeeded in redefining these issues, thus setting the context for determining federal policies.

The first organizational response by the White House to the launch of Sputnik was the appointment of a special assistant to the President for science and technology (11/3/57). The post was entrusted to James R. Killian, president of MIT—a certified statesman of science (although not an actual scientist) who had previously served the Administration in a number of official tasks. A Science Advisory Committee had existed since 1951, but it reported to the Office of Defense Mobilization and was too distant from the President to have appreciable influence. It was thus more than symbolic when this group was expanded and elevated to become the President's Science Advisory Committee (PSAC). Killian was elected to be its chairman, further assuring access to the President.[1] This close relationship proved congenial to Eisenhower himself, who found the scientists to be a relatively disinterested source of information compared with the politically charged advice he received on most major issues. The relatively high degree of influence was also due to the make-up of the PSAC and what they were asked to do.

Killian found his fellow PSAC members to be familiar types. Almost all had been "tested in the crucible" of weapons research and development during the war, generally at MIT's Radiation Laboratory or with the Manhattan Project. Since that time they had been continually involved with federal science activities in a variety of capacities. As a result, "they had considerable political savvy and knew how to find their way around government."[2] Seven of them were nominally university professors, although such men as Hans Bethe and I. I. Rabi were wide-ranging scientific statesmen as well.[3] Like Killian, ten members held executive positions: four of them were in the federal government and six were more or less outside (that is, they headed organizations that worked closely with the government and/or with government funds). The remaining five were executives from industry. Killian thought it important for establishing harmonious relations with the President that these men did not harbor political ambitions. Not that they should: they already were the senators and governors of science—central leaders in the government of federally sponsored research.

The PSAC members found themselves in a situation that resembled their wartime service. They were asked to serve their country during a critical time, in which the national interest seemed axiomatic and scientific and technological expertise was crucial for accomplishing well-defined national goals. Three problems were of overriding importance: launching an effective space program; formulating a coherent strategy for the missile program; and reassessing the strategy for nuclear deterrence based upon massive retaliation—a perilous doctrine now that the Soviets too had the capacity to retaliate massively. PSAC members discussed these and other matters generally among themselves, but the actual expert work of the Council was done through more specialized panels. As many as 200 scientists manned these panels during the Eisenhower Administration. Most were focused on specific aspects of the issues just listed, but one panel was dedicated to "basic research and graduate education."[4]

The views of PSAC on this last subject fairly faithfully reflected the arguments in favor of basic research that had been propounded throughout the 1950s. Alan Waterman was in fact a member of the committee, making it all the more certain that PSAC thinking was congruent with the positions already articulated by NSF.[5] Once the new organizational machinery to deal with the critical matters of space and defense was put in place, PSAC was able to focus on formulating national policies toward basic research and higher education. The committee essentially argued for an explicit policy that would recognize basic research as a national resource and a federal responsibility. They felt that the predominance of programmatic research in federal science support was distorting the national research effort; yet economic progress and national defense ultimately depended upon basic research. Since universities lacked adequate resources for this task, greater public support was indispensible; and such support needed to be provided through long-term, flexible arrangements that assured the freedom of individual investigators.[6] These views, while reasonable, were different from most other scientific advice proffered by PSAC. Based upon neither analysis nor empirical evidence (beyond anecdotes), this conception of basic research emanated from an interrelated system of beliefs—an ideology of basic research.

PSAC was in a strategic position to articulate and recommend to the government measures that were implicit in the ideology of basic research. It began by publishing two rather modest reports. "Strengthening American Science" (1958) appears somewhat conservative in retrospect, but probably stated the case for academic science as forcefully as was prudent at that juncture. It explicitly condemned the programmatic nature of most federally sponsored research ("the most impractical thing that can be done in designing and directing programs of scientific research is to worry overmuch about how 'practical' they are"). The report cautiously recommended improving this situation through a more careful organization of the federal research effort, most notably through a "Federal Council for Science and Technology," which was subsequently created. The Report specifically foresaw squeezing intramural federal research by rigorously reviewing the activities and procedures of federal laboratories. Just the opposite was advised for extramural (i.e. academic) research. Scientists in universities, it advised, should be given more freedom and more general support to pursue basic research. The Report was also somewhat old-fashioned in reserving leadership to private philanthropy for sustaining the research universities themselves.[7] In "Education for the Age of Science" (1959) PSAC addressed the problem of enlarging and improving science education at all levels. This document called for much greater national spending for education, and also foresaw the need for more and stronger research universities.[8]

The ideology of basic research received a notable consecration that same year, when the National Academy of Sciences, the American Association for the Advancement of Science, and the Alfred P. Sloan Foundation sponsored a "Symposium on Basic Research." Two hundred and fifty statesmen of science—PSAC members and their ilk—gathered at the Rockefeller Institute for Medical Research to present and applaud a succession of platitudes about the importance of basic scientific research.[9] More remarkable, this occasion was further dignified by the presence of President Eisenhower, who traveled to New York City to address the celebration. The proponents of academic research were no longer crying in the wilderness. If any one item signaled the new cogency of their message it would be the announcement at the Symposium by the frugal Eisenhower that he would recommend federal financing of the $100 million Stanford Linear Accelerator.[10]

The national mood was clearly edging toward greater acceptance of the case for academic science when PSAC produced a much bolder statement of what role the federal government ought to play. A panel chaired by Glenn Seaborg, then chancellor of the University of California at Berkeley, produced "Scientific Progress, the Universities, and the Federal Government" (1960). The Seaborg Report, as it is known, was the credo of the ideology of basic research.

The Report began by asserting in exceedingly strong terms four propositions. 1) Scientific research should be regarded as an investment: "simply in terms of economic self-interest our proper course is to increase our investment in science just as fast as we can, to a limit not yet in sight." 2) Basic research and graduate education "*belong together* at every possible level." 3) Strengthening academic science was of "absolutely critical importance to the national welfare, and hence inescapably a responsibility of the federal government: "either it will find the policies—and the resources—which permit our universities to flourish and their duties to be adequately discharged—or no one will." Finally, 4) universities themselves lacked the means to support science: "thus partnership between the university and the national government is the indispensible basis for first-rate university work in science."[11] The implications of this partnership were spelled out in the recommendations of the Seaborg Report. For the government simply to contract for research services was from this point of view unacceptable. It had a responsibility to aid the entire endeavor of university research. The Report specifically called for a substantial enlargement of graduate education through federal fellowships; the building of university faculties through more flexible forms of federal support; the encouragement through federal stimulus of new fields of research and education; federal support for the expansion of university facilities through matching grants; and of course greater support for research itself. In a timely and potentially popular recommendation, the Seaborg Report called for a doubling of the number of "first-rate academic centers of science"—from about fifteen or twenty to "thirty or forty in another fifteen years." More generally, however, the report favored the interests of those fifteen or twenty established research universities. It advocated sticking closely to the best-science procedures, such as peer review; and it wanted any new research centers to be closely linked with universities. Appearing three years after Sputnik and just days after the election of John F. Kennedy, the Seaborg Report provided a blueprint for the great expansion of federal support for academic science that would occur during the first part of the 1960s—the authority repeatedly cited to justify those programs.

From the end of the Eisenhower Administration through the Kennedy years, the Executive Branch was the most influential locus for what was soon referred to as the "scientific establishment," and thus the most important platform for propagating the ideology of basic research.[12] The Presidential Science Advisor was the lynchpin of this establishment, or what might more accurately be called an "intricate structure of interlocking relationships."[13] He came to preside over an expanding advisory empire that included PSAC itself, the Federal Council for Science and Technology (1959), and the Office of Science and Technology (1962). Implementation of actual programs for academic science nevertheless depended upon the actions of the Congress. A far more unwieldy enterprise than the executive branch, Congress was also more resistant to accepting direction on the basis of specialized expertise. Its relationship with the scientific establishment was consequently slower to develop and less close in character.

Not that Congress failed to respond to the Sputnik crisis: it too considered structural changes to be necessary in order to meet the new scientific and technological challenges. The Senate created a new standing committee on Aeronautical and Space Sciences, while the House established a similar body on Science and Astronautics. Both these committees were largely preoccupied with space issues initially.[14] There was also some congressional interest in establishing a cabinet-level Department of Science and Technology, which would have been open to greater congressional influence than the science advisory structure in the White House. This dubious plan, which was largely opposed by the scientific establishment in and out of government, was finally put to rest when the Office of Science and Technology was established in the Executive Office.[15] Congress did not develop its own internal sources of scientific advice until the latter half of the decade, when the Science Policy Research Division was developed in the Library of Congress. Until then, Congress had to rely to some extent on the same members of the scientific establishment that advised the Executive Branch.

The "intricate structure of interlocking relationships" that comprised the scientific establishment existed more outside than inside the federal government. These overlapping networks tended to center upon the National Academy of Sciences and its operating arm, the National Research Council. Both the statesmen and the most eminent practitioners of science belonged to one or the other: through the NAS they had ready access to the rest of the nation's top scientists; and through the NRC they could contact scientific leaders throughout industry and government.[16]

The way in which the outlook of the scientific establishment actually reached lawmakers during these years can be seen in the activities of the NAS Committee on Science and Public Policy, known as COSPUP. This committee consisted largely of the senior statesmen of the Academy and reported directly to its president; it was regarded as "the apex of the Academy's power structure."[17] COS-PUP was brought into being and then chaired by George Kistiakowsky, who had succeeded James Killian as Presidential Science Advisor to Eisenhower. He foresaw its function as providing scientific advice to congressional committees as well as working with the science planners of the executive branch. Indeed, during its heyday any report endorsed by COSPUP was "assured privileged access to the top-level science advisory groups in the executive branch."[18] But, partly because of these close ties, its relationship with the Congress did not blossom to the same extent.

COSPUP was designed in part to respond to strains in the relationship between the federal government and academic science that became evident around 1963. Apprehension within the scientific community prompted the NAS, through COSPUP, to undertake and publish a comprehensive review of federal support for academic research, which it described as a sequel to the Seaborg Report of 1960.[19] Concern in Congress, primarily with the acceleration of federal expenditures for research, caused the House Committee on Science and Astronautics to appoint a Subcommittee on Science, Research, and Development. The Academy volunteered to share its expertise in these matters, and as a result COSPUP was instructed to prepare a report for the House Science Committee that would address the questions: "what level of Federal support is needed to maintain for the United States a position of leadership in basic research . . ." and, "what judgment can be reached on the balance of support now being given by the Federal Government to various fields of scientific endeavor, and on the adjustments that should be considered. . . ."[20]

These were the questions that the scientific establishment had been answering, implicitly, since at least the time of Sputnik. The COSPUP report, *Basic Research and National Goals*, predictably called for more research funding and for the balance to be shifted in ways favorable to higher education. The actual report consisted of some fifteen essays, each written by a member of the COSPUP panel and each reflecting somewhat different facets of the original questions. A consensus was nevertheless apparent on the issues crucial to academic research. Several contributors urged that a distinction be made between "big science" and "little science." The latter, which was virtually synonymous with basic academic research, needed substantial increases in funding—the figure of 15 percent compounded annual growth was generally accepted. Just as important, the panelists wished to disassociate the needs of academic research from the high, and potentially unpopular, costs of big science. Beyond this, there was wide agreement on two points: that the present system had worked very well to assure the ascendancy of American science, which implied that it needed only more resources, properly distributed, to perpetuate this success; and second, in effect to implement the first point, that the National Science Foundation deserved much greater funding and a much larger role in determining the course of American science.[21]

The second principal activity of COSPUP during these years was to give Congress and the executive branch even more explicit advice on federal support of science. This was done through the commissioning of studies of the present state and needs of specific disciplines. Four such studies appeared during the halcyon period (1962–66), covering ground-based astronomy, chemistry, physics, and plant sciences; another six studies were completed by 1974. These studies were at once expert and thorough descriptions of these fields, conveying past growth trends, the current state of knowledge, and likely future requirements. They were also political documents designed to present their disciplines in the best light to the appropriate federal agencies.[22]

Each discipline presented itself as not only deserving of greater support, but also as suffering from comparative neglect. When the prevailing assumption of a 15 percent compounded rate of annual growth was taken as the norm, relative neglect was not difficult to demonstrate. The physics committee thus complained that their discipline had received under half of its expected increment for the previous two years, and asked that its funding be increased by 21 percent for the next four years in order to catch up. Each field had its own special case. Ground-based astronomy justified its existence in relation to newly feasible space-based instruments, and presented needs for working facilities for double the number of astronomers within a decade. The plant sciences asserted that the expansion of basic research in this area was essential to the health of the nation's agriculture, and detailed an itemized bill that worked out to $1.492 billion over the next ten years. Chemistry presented the most elaborate case, arguing that because it was not the special ward of any one federal agency it had been neglected by all. Its essential needs for additional research support, and especially increasingly expensive instrumentation requirements, now dictated that federal funding should rise from $50 million in 1964 to $120.9 million in 1968.[23]

Precisely what the effect of COSPUP's efforts were on federal funding of academic science is impossible to isolate. The COSPUP imprimatur, together with the wide influence of Kistiakowsky, nevertheless assured these reports of close attention at the highest levels of the federal science structure. There the atmosphere was receptive. Both the PSAC and the NSF, for example, tended to agree with the main contentions of the chemistry report. No doubt this was one factor influencing NSF to more than double its support for chemistry from 1964 to 1968 and add a budget line for chemical instrumentation.[24] Still, a broader perspective is called for to appreciate why the scientific establishment was able to further the ideology of basic research so effectively in the years after Sputnik.

The President's Science Advisor and PSAC, COSPUP and the National Academy of Sciences—these were the most salient points from which the leaders of the diffuse scientific community expressed their conception of what academic science could contribute to the country and what the country ought to contribute toward supporting academic science. If the content of this message remained fairly constant during these years, the receptivity of official Washington evolved with time. The Seaborg Report, which coincided with the election of President Kennedy, represented a kind of fulcrum in the changing attitudinal climate of the capital and the country. Two years before the report, the scientific establishment still assumed the posture of insurgents, declaiming the dire consequences of the predominance of programmatic research and the absence of programs to support the universities themselves. Two years afterward, the emphasis had changed. The statesmen of science now premised their advocacy on the overall efficacy of the plural federal system of research support, while urging piecemeal changes and increased resources in order to make it even better. The change in the stance of the scientific establishment reflected changes in the ways the federal government had dealt with these matters.

Scientists had little or no real power in Washington. Their ideology was received as favorably as it was in the federal government for a combination of reasons. On one hand, it mirrored many of the realities besetting academic research at the end of the 1950s. From another perspective, it was undeniable that the ideology of basic research became linked with other, more politically potent goals. Sputnik joined this ideology to a more comprehensive set of assumptions that posited worldwide leadership for the United States in military and scientific affairs. During the 1960s, the case for academic research also furthered the broadly accepted goal of expanding higher education. Factors such as these are virtually impossible to disentangle in the protracted process of formulating and authorizing legislative programs. Rather, the best evidence that the scientist's ideology held sway in Washington during the first part of the 1960s comes from the results themselves—from the multitude of actual measures taken to advance academic science.

4. Federal Support and the Golden Age of Academic Science

With the scientific community providing a chorus of encouragement, the university research economy was expanded along the lines recommended in the Seaborg Report—namely, that a far greater investment in basic research was vital to the national interest, that it should be made in universities, that they would as a result require additional forms of assistance, and that the federal government bore the responsibility for supporting these measures.

The growing federal commitment to academic research during the post-Sputnik era can be separated into two roughly equal stages. The years from 1958 to 1963 saw precipitous rates of increase as the initial reaction to Sputnik was followed by the high ambitions of Kennedy's New Frontier, which prominently included a concern for international scientific preeminence. Federal spending for academic research rose from $456 million in 1958 to $1,275 million in 1964. This increase represented a doubling of national effort—from 0.1 to 0.2 percent of GNP. These quantitative changes brought a qualitative transformation. Basic research, which was estimated to comprise 62 percent of academic research in 1958, rose to 79 percent of the total six years later. Just as recommended, the commitments of the federal government fueled this expansion: of $819 million in additional support for academic research over this interval, federal sources provided $722 million—8 of every 9 new dollars. Moreover, this new federal support was decidedly less programmatic in character: 59 percent of it came from the 'disinterested' funders, NSF and NIH.[1]

During the second stage of the post-Sputnik expansion (1963–68), growth continued at a declining rate and the material prosperity of academic science reached a peak. But the atmosphere gradually cooled. Having become accustomed to the new abundance, scientists adjusted their sights upward, as was evident in the COSPUP reports. But at the same time increasing resistance emerged in Congress to both spiraling appropriations for science and the ideology of basic research upon which they were premised. It was during these years, nevertheless, that the government acted most generously toward supporting the infrastructure of academic science. Overall, this half-decade is characterized best by the extremes that were attained in academic science—the highest percentage of basic research (79% in 1964); the highest percentage of federal funding (74% in 1966); the highest proportion of GNP (0.25% in 1968)—as well as the secular peaks that were reached in total real expenditures, (1968) those from federal sources (1968), and real appropriations for the NSF (1966–68).[2]

Within a decade a university research system that had been encumbered by a predominance of programmatic sponsorship was transformed into one with a striking bias toward disinterested basic research. In retrospect these years would appear to have been a new golden age for academic science. The change had come about in a typically American way—through differential growth. Funds continued to flow through the five channels of postwar federal support, and NASA constituted an additional sixth channel; but the greatest change came from the unprecedented growth of NSF and, on an even larger scale, NIH. The altered climate of expectations nevertheless affected all channels to some extent. The vast federal commitment to academic science of the post-Sputnik decade, when examined in closer detail, resolves into the individual histories of these several channels.

The National Science Foundation.   The mission of the NSF was precisely that promoted by the ideology of basic research, and the scientific establishment accordingly envisioned making NSF "a much larger agency than it is now—so large that it can eventually become the 'balance wheel,' or even the main 'umbrella,' for the support of basic research."[3] When this wishful ideal was expressed in 1965, the foundation was supporting about 14 percent of federally sponsored academic research. But its actual importance to research universities was considerably greater.

As one of the immediate reactions to Sputnik the NSF budget was raised from $40 million to 130 million (FY1959), and the first budget of the Kennedy Administration (FY1962) brought its appropriation to twice that figure. Overall, the foundation's appropriations increased by a compounded annual average of 20 percent until reaching $480 million in fiscal 1966. Looking backward at this steep ascent, it is difficult to appreciate that these increases were the product of annual struggles. Alan Waterman, with his fervent belief in the foundation's mission, advocated even greater increments. The White House generally requested hefty increases, but these proposed budgets were usually first chopped by the parsimonious House, and then restored by the more magnanimous Senate.

NSF itself, as soon as it entered the era of large budgets, aspired to expand its range of activities. At the heart of the NSF was its support for awards to individual investigators. Such grants were the sustenance for 'small science' and basic research—funds for individual investigators across university science departments. As early as 1955, though, the National Science Board approved foundation involvement in building and operating 'big science' facilities. Facilities that were subsequently created for astronomy, oceanography, and atmospheric physics also provided places for university scientists to work. Then, larger appropriations allowed the foundation to begin practicing what it had long preached—providing support to academic science outside of specific research projects.[4]

The shifting balance of NSF activities from the beginning to the peak of the post-Sputnik era can be discerned in the following figures:[5]

	Little Science	Big Science	Graduate Fellowships	Institutional Support & Equipment
1960 ($mil.)	57	8	13	12
(%)	63	9	14	13
1966	158	59	44	97
(%)	44	16	12	27

'Big science' represented a number of discrete commitments of different types. Facilities like the national observatories were stable, long-term obligations for NSF whose capital needs might vary considerably from year to year. The "national research programs" included both long-term (Antarctic program) and fixed-term commitments. Of this last type, the 1966 NSF budget included $17 million for Project Mohole—the wonderfully named, but ill-conceived plan to drill a hole through the Mohorovicic discontinuity in the earth's crust. This misadventure was in the process of drawing the foundation into an exceedingly costly engineering effort—a subterranean NASA—until it was summarily terminated by Congress that same year. NSF's uncritical enthusiasm for this project cast suspicion on the judgment of the scientific establishment: perhaps scientists could not say no to any potential research project.[6] More typical and more telling of NSF's role during these years were its programs for institutional support, because they addressed the most ambiguous area in the federal relationship with universities.

The NSF had consistently felt that it should assist universities with more than just the direct costs of research. This attitude reflected the fact that excellence in scientific research depended upon the research capacity of universities, which was largely financed through institutional funds. The relationship between internal research capacity and the award of external research funding inescapably overlapped. Some types of research were predicated on expensive facilities or instruments, while smaller equipment was routinely included in research grants. In addition, federal agencies at this time paid universities an additional 15 to 20 percent to cover the indirect costs of doing federally sponsored research. Still, there was no common agreement about how far the federal government ought to go in supporting the research capacity of universities. A second dimension of this issue surfaced with the Seaborg Report and gained in importance thereafter. Because research capacity depended so heavily upon internal resources, it was the chief factor undergirding the concentration of research support in relatively few universities. Any effort to broaden the number of research universities and the national research effort had to address the issue of bolstering university research capacity.[7]

Alan Waterman had been eager to have the NSF provide direct assistance to universities, but such measures were scarcely feasible until the end of the 1950s.[8] A program was begun in 1959 that aimed at buttressing institutional support of science by offering funds on a matching basis for renovating and equipping "graduate research laboratories." The foundation moved more boldly in this direction the following year with a program of direct institutional grants. Universities were to be given a sum equal to 5 percent of their research grants from NSF, up to $50,000, to use as they saw fit for any scientific activity. Both programs were seen as efforts to supply "the universities with money for a general strengthening of their science departments as opposed to supporting only specific projects."[9] The institutional grants may have been tantamount to a higher rate of indirect cost reimbursement, except that they were earmarked for science. The formula was in fact adjusted, first to increase the minimum grants to a more meaningful level, and then to raise the maximums. Overall, institutional grants were weighted toward aiding smaller performers, and thus intended in part to deflect the ubiquitous suspicions of elitism that dogged the foundation.[10] Even so, established research universities benefited disproportionately from the larger programs that funded research facilities. Institutional grants received funding of $1.5 million in the FY1961 budget, but that figure was multiplied tenfold by the mid-sixties. Funding for graduate research facilities began at the level of $2 million in FY1960, and fluctuated between $16 and $28 million through the mid-sixties. These two programs were then eclipsed in size by a new form of institutional aid.

The foundation was sensitive to congressional disapproval of the concentration of research funding in a relatively small number of institutions. The recommendation of the Seaborg Report calling for a doubling of the number of first-rate research universities was welcomed by NSF not just because it addressed this sore point, but also because it sought to do so in a manner consistent with the best-science convictions of the scientific establishment—namely, by raising the research capacities of second-tier institutions so that they might merit greater direct research support through regular channels. Discussions of this notion began soon afterward within the foundation, and in 1962 the National Science Board authorized the formulation of a program to work toward this end.[11] It took time for this concept to gain acceptance, and the first awards were not made until 1965. The "University Science Development Program" (USDP) was intended "to accelerate improvement in science" by identifying institutions with "the greatest possibility of moving upward to a higher level of scientific quality," and by awarding them funds "in accordance with carefully developed plans" designed permanently to enhance specific science departments.[12] The fortunate institutions were carefully chosen according to their existing scientific strengths, the proposed five-year plans for science development that they submitted, and the university's ability and willingness to support science development with internal funds. Most of the grants fell in the $4 to $6 million range over five years. Thirty-two institutions were designated as recipients of these awards during 1965–68. The program continued to make smaller grants through 1971. The USDP by itself disbursed $177 million, and the derivative programs another $54 million.[13]

The Science Development Program represented a subtle extension of NSF's assumed responsibilities toward academic science—from supporting research, to supporting institutions doing research, to supporting the aspirations of institutions wishing to do more research. Moreover, it was an exceedingly delicate task for a federal agency to award these prizes selectively, on the basis of its own subjective judgment of merit, to just a handful of institutions. That this course was possible during the mid-1960s was testimony to the ascendancy of the ideology of basic research—to the political consensus that continued to provide largely uncritical backing to the expansion of academic science. The Science Development concept, in fact, made this expansion more palatable politically by promising to spread the bounty of federal research funding. For that reason it quickly expanded both within and outside the NSF.

The foundation aggressively championed this goal, bringing it to the attention of other science-supporting agencies through the Federal Council on Science and Technology. President Lyndon B. Johnson was not blind to the fact that the science development program promised to bring about greater geographic and demographic dispersion of federal research funds. This goal was elevated to a government-wide policy in September 1965 when the President issued a directive instructing all federal agencies to "contribute to the improvement of potentially strong universities" by establishing programs similar to the USDP.[14] Specific programs were quickly established for this purpose by NASA, NIH, and the Department of Defense (see below).

Within the foundation it proved both politically popular and, because differences between grantees and rejectees were often minimal, consistent with the developmental rationale to create additional kinds of science development grants in order to aid a wider circle of recipients. The USDP was soon supplemented by a Special Science Development Program, which consisted of somewhat smaller awards to eleven institutions that did not quite fulfill the requirements for the larger grants. A still more focused program was inaugurated in 1966 to further development in selected science departments at still weaker institutions. All told, 73 grants of this last type, averaging about $600,000, were made to 62 institutions. Yet another variant on this theme followed—the provision of funds to colleges for science improvement. Looking only at the university programs, more than one hundred institutions ultimately benefited from science development funding. They represented a substantial part of the universe of institutions, below the established research universities, that were significantly involved with federal research.[15] What began as a highly selective program soon provided something for almost everyone.

The science development programs at NSF were constrained by the foundation's budgetary difficulties after 1968, and then terminated by President Richard M. Nixon in 1971. An extensive survey was conducted shortly thereafter to assess what the impact of the program had been. The investigator found an overall pattern of favorable results, but was not always able to detect discernible changes on quantifiable indicators.[16] The opinions of those at NSF who had been involved in the program were more strongly positive. Besides accelerating science development in the affected departments, NSF also felt that important intangible effects had been spawned by the grants: the benefits to institutions from being induced to plan; the raising of aspiration levels; and the stimulus felt by some nonrecipients.[17] The generally favorable effects of disbursing $230 million to university science departments can hardly be doubted, and they will be considered in the next chapter in connection with changes in university rankings. For the NSF and for public policy, however, a more vexing question was the relative value of such undertakings compared with direct support of research.

In 1965 the NSF was subject to an extensive review, both sympathetic and critical in spirit, by a special subcommittee of the House Committee on Science and Astronautics.[18] This episode is conventionally regarded as a step in the gradual disenchantment of Congress with the pieties of the scientific establishment.[19] Such an interpretation, however, allows the hint of future developments to overshadow the dominant themes of the moment. If anything, this juncture was the high-water mark for the ideology of basic research. There was hardly a cavil about the assumptions undergirding the role that NSF had assumed—about its becoming the "balance wheel" of national science, about the necessity of 15 percent growth rates, or about its expanding role in assisting university development. The final judgment of the subcommittee was that NSF should in fact be enlarged, but enlarged in ways that made the foundation somewhat uncomfortable. The legislative results of this review were not enacted until 1968, and thus reflected a good deal more than what was said at the 1965 hearings. The most important alteration was the specific inclusion of applied research in the mission of the NSF. This sentiment reflected a change in the national mood that had become magnified since 1965. Some doubt had arisen about the heretofore unquestioned benefits of basic research, but more importantly the country seemed to be faced with mounting problems that presumably needed to be addressed through science. This additional mandate was not in itself exceptional: the phenomenal growth of NSF had been accomplished in part by adding tasks like teacher institutes, institutional support, or Mohole. But in 1968 one crucial factor had changed: there was no additional funding to support additional foundation roles.

In the fiscal year following its congressional review, the still-favorable view of the NSF was evident in an appropriation rise of $60 million, from $420 to $480 million. But the peak had been reached. FY1967 brought an identical appropriation, and 1968 was only slightly larger in current dollars. In real terms, the NSF appropriations did not surpass the 1966–68 plateau until 1985.[20] The reasons for NSF's fall from favor, and indeed that of university research in general, will be considered in due course. A glance ahead to these leaner times, however, reveals some fundamental features of NSF's role in the research economy.

Although the NSF budget has fluctuated considerably in real terms, awards to individual investigators for basic research showed greater consistency. From 1963—i.e., after the large initial post-Sputnik increases—to the late 1980s these grants exhibited a real compounded growth rate of better than 3 percent.[21] This task, together with sustaining big-science research in astronomy and geosciences and providing certain science facilities, remained the true core of NSF activities. During the exceedingly prosperous mid-sixties, individual research grants fell to a relative low point of just 42 percent of foundation science support, but during the leaner early 1980s, they rose as high as 68 percent. From this perspective, then, the developments of the 1960s stand out more clearly.

NSF throughout its history has been above all the patron of basic research. When this mission was emphasized as a national goal and given substantial uncritical support, the foundation tended to expand its interpretation of what this mission comprised. By 1967, for example, it was devoting a full quarter of its scientific funds to institutional support.[22] This kind of assistance was expensive and had no clear boundaries, as the burgeoning of the science development programs testifies. When basic research was devalued as a national commitment and NSF budgets shrank, this type of peripheral program became vulnerable and ultimately untenable. The inherent expansiveness of the NSF mission of promoting basic research was ultimately contained through fiscal means in reaction to a changing climate of opinion, but even then the foundation was largely able to protect its core commitments over the long run.

The post-Sputnik decade witnessed the rise of NSF in a double sense. In 1958 the foundation accounted for less than 7.5 percent of federal funds for academic research; a decade later it supplied more than 15 percent. This latter share of the federal responsibility for federally supported science, moreover, would remain stable in the years that followed. For a time NSF surpassed the Department of Defense as the second largest funder of academic research (1972–81). Thus, although the NSF never advanced to the dominant role of 'balance wheel,' it did significantly increase its presence in the research economy. Second and perhaps more important, NSF largely set the tone for the entire expansion of academic science. It most forcefully articulated the ideology of basic research; it also was the most aggressive agency in implementing measures that reflected that outlook. Finally, it succeeded to a large extent in influencing other federal agencies to act in a similar manner. NSF thus provided scientific leadership throughout the 1960s, even though its weight in the system was considerably overshadowed by its sister agency in the funding of disinterested research, the National Institutes of Health.

The National Institutes of Health. NIH, as a sibling of NSF, was not only older and larger but it also differed in its *raison d'être* and the dynamics of its growth. NIH was ostensibly a mission agency. As the research arm of the Public Health Service it was dedicated "to improve the health of the people of the United States through the conduct of researches, investigations, experiments, and demonstrations relating to cause, prevention, and method of diagnosis and treatment of diseases."[23] Although this charge encompassed numerous possible courses of action, from the 1950s onward NIH chose to pursue its mission very largely through the sponsorship of basic research. In this respect, NIH embodied the interests of the biomedical research community in much the same way that NSF represented the natural scientists generally. The important difference, however, was that NIH had little need to beat the drums for the value of basic research and its unpredictable future payoffs. Rather, the expectations that research sponsored by NIH would cure disease or alleviate suffering was the force that impelled a rising tide of funding for basic biological and medical science. The Congress was most susceptible to this allure. In the late 1950s, when concern was highest for establishing a science advisory capacity in the White House, a smooth working relationship already existed between the NIH and the Committees of the House and Senate that controlled their appropriations. The Presidential Science Advisor, as a consequence, had almost nothing to do with the health sciences.[24] Due to the nexus between Congress and NIH, the growing prosperity of biomedical science began before Sputnik and was sustained through and beyond the post-Sputnik decade.

The rise of NIH to become the paramount funder of academic science spanned the directorship of Dr. James A. Shannon (1955-68). In contrast to the director of NSF, the head of NIH probably held less power internally, but played a more crucial role in conducting the external relations of the agency.[25] Congress appropriated funds for each of the Institutes separately, which gave them some autonomy in their operations. But Shannon as director assumed the key role of assuring liaison with Congress. From FY1947 to FY1954 the NIH appropriations grew from $8 to $71 million. While this was an impressive rate of growth, less than $18 million was allocated in the latter year for university research. By this juncture, however, the groundwork had been laid for a larger NIH role. Already eight separate Institutes were operating. They had emerged from the confusion of responsibilities with NSF and other mission agencies as the predominant supporter of biomedical research. The American Medical Association had ceased to fear federal spending in this area, and leadership had emerged in Congress pressing for greater federal initiative in fighting disease. The first NIH budget of the Shannon years (FY1957) saw funds for extramural research more than double to $85 million.[26]

While Shannon was director a potent coalition existed between the medical research lobby, the congressional committees that controlled funding, and NIH itself.[27] Compared with the proponents of the ideology of basic research—established scientists for the most part with ties to the National Academy of Sciences—the medical research lobby was remarkable for consisting chiefly of lay persons and for having close political ties with Congress. The individual accorded greatest credit in organizing this lobby was Mary Lasker, the wife of an advertising executive who became involved in health-care issues in the early 1940s. Working with her husband until his death in 1952, she was able to mobilize talents in public relations and fund-raising. The Laskers assembled a network of like-minded wealthy individuals and health-care leaders. Their faction gained control of and rejuvenated the American Cancer Society, as they renamed it, and turned the Society into an advocate for research. The Laskers themselves established a family foundation which they used as a reservoir of funds to promote the cause. Their ultimate concerns embraced health care generally, but medical research was an especially crying need.

In the late 1940s the Laskers focused their activities on promoting federal support for medical research through the National Institutes of Health. Mary Lasker soon became adept at manipulating the levers of congressional influence to advance this goal. She hired a full-time lobbyist to help secure passage of the act creating the National Institute of Mental Health (1946); she established personal entree to several key Congressmen, and ultimately to the White House; she was able to mobilize her network to give sympathetic testimony before congressional committees; and she rewarded friends of medical research in the Congress where it counted most—with campaign contributions and opportunities for favorable publicity. In 1947 Mary Lasker mediated between the Congress and the NIH to set in motion the events that created the legislation for the National Heart Institute (1948). From that juncture, the basic structure for expanding the NIH medical research empire was in place.

Combating disease was a popular cause in the Congress against which few votes were likely to be cast. The issue confronted annually was, nevertheless, how much should be spent for this estimable purpose? Here the medical research lobby served as a consistent goad for greater fiscal exertions. Budget setting for most federal agencies was a winnowing process: estimated needs for the coming year were reduced first at the department level, and then by the Bureau of the Budget, before appearing in the President's budget recommendations. These recommendations were often lowered further in congressional committees before a final figure would be voted. During James Shannon's tenure the NIH budgets were different. The subcommittees responsible for these appropriations, with the encouragement of the medical research lobby, consistently raised the not-ungenerous figures forwarded by the President. The process included summoning the heads of the individual institutes to testify, discovering their original estimates of need, receiving assurances that such funds could be productively spent on medical research, and then restoring the deleted funds, and sometimes more, in the interest of the nation's health. During two decades (1948–68) Congress raised the proposed budgets for NIH on sixteen occasions, and even the reductions, during war years, were comparatively minor. Appropriations for medical research ratcheted upward at an accelerating pace.

Shannon inherited a NIH budget of $98 million, of which 64 percent was obligated for grants (FY 1956). For the next five years the average annual *increase* in the NIH budget was $96 million, and for the next six years the average rise was $156 million. The portion devoted to grants expanded to 81 percent. NIH surpassed the Department of Defense as the largest single funder of academic research around 1960. By 1965 it was larger than the next two sources combined and three times the size of NSF.

By the mid-sixties it had become commonplace to view the NIH as "a

National Science Foundation for the basic biological sciences."[28] This was in fact an apt description, particularly for human biology. It was not, however, the role with which Shannon sought to have NIH identified. He explicitly conceded that NSF should function as the balance wheel—"providing for the stability, vigor, and balanced growth of academic science." NIH, on the other hand, had "a health and not a science mission."[29] But NIH in practice took an exceedingly long-range view of its responsibilities. It not only commissioned vast amounts of basic research, mostly through large numbers of comparatively modest grants, but it also provided for many of the attendant needs of the biomedical wing of the academic research community. The NIH may have had little reason to employ the ideology of basic research to justify its support of academic science, but it operated in ways consistent with that ideology.

NIH resisted classifying the investigations they supported as either applied or basic research. When viewed from the underlying motives of the investigators, Shannon estimated that this support was two-thirds applied, but when judged by scientific character it was predominately basic. According to the bookeeping criteria employed by NSF, however, the actual role of NIH in academic science during the mid-sixties was overwhelmingly in support of basic research. Federally funded research in medical schools, 89 percent of which came from the NIH, was considered to be 87 percent basic. The NIH funds that went to other university departments (about three-eighths) were undoubtedly skewed toward basic research to at least the same degree.[30] One marked effect of the rise of NIH, then, was to shift the spectrum of academic research toward the high proportion of basic research that was attained in the 1960s.

To accomplish its goals in research NIH had to provide support as well for greatly expanding the infrastructure upon which medical research depended. Until the mid-1950s, at least, the finances of university medical schools were in a parlous state, but Congress expressly forbade NIH from aiding medical education per se. Instead, assistance was directed toward activities related to medical research. Its first initiatives were aimed at expanding the number of trained medical researchers. A fellowship program made awards to individuals wishing to pursue the Ph.D. Training grants made to departments were considerably more generous allowances to be used for salaries and academic support for graduate students, postdoctoral fellows and faculty acquiring research skills. Substantial funds were allocated to these two programs. During the mid-fifties they cost almost one-third of the amount expended on external research grants, and in the early 1960s more than 40 percent of that figure (see below). Viewed from another perspective, the NIH fellowship program alone was comparable in size to that of NSF (c. $50 million) during the last half of the 1960s, but the NIH training grants were additionally about three times that magnitude. Federal funds for training scientists were thus heavily concentrated in the biomedical fields.

In 1956 Congress authorized NIH to offer matching grants for capital costs for health research facilities. Such support was vitally needed if universities were to expand their research capacities in the health sciences. An additional—political—consideration was the desire to achieve more equitable geographical distribution of medical research spending. This program received appropriations of $30 million for its first six years and then $50 million for another five years before being phased out. In 1964, for example, capital expenditures for research facilities at medical schools comprised about one-fifth of the national total for higher education, and NIH provided 43 percent of that figure ($45.5 million).

The same year that NSF began its institutional grants NIH launched a similar program. The funding came from the NIH research budgets, and the grants were designed to assist "health-professional schools" with funds they could employ for any purpose related to health research. Typically, these funds were used for supporting students or young scientists, for seed money for future projects, to purchase shared equipment, or for 'crash' projects too urgent for the funding process. Each school was automatically eligible for a $25,000 base grant, with additional funds being based by formula on the amount of external research funding. By 1965 the NIH general research support program had a budget of $44 million, which made it four times larger than NSF's institutional grants program. The largest single award that year was almost $600,000.[31]

The single area of science support in which NIH was later and smaller than NSF was science development. Whereas the NSF Science Development Program was a somewhat delayed response to the recommendations of the Seaborg Report, NIH created its Health Sciences Advancement Program after President Johnson's 1965 policy directive on this matter. In light of the magnitude of direct and indirect institutional support already provided by NIH, the health sciences had a broad and well-funded academic base by the mid-1960s. There was comparatively little need to create additional centers of research.[32] The NIH Advancement Program accordingly adopted a supplementary goal of encouraging the development of the health sciences at institutions having "considerable strength in related fields of science." This rationale was undoubtedly behind awards to such relatively established programs as Cornell (Ithaca), Purdue, and Rice. All told, only eleven universities were given these awards, and the average grants were about $2.5 million, or just half of those made by NSF.[33]

The funds indicated in Table 10, which represent a substantial portion of the NIH budgets, for the most part were expended in universities. NIH, in effect, assumed responsibility for the entire enterprise of university medical research—training scientists and supporting facilities as well as providing the direct costs of research. Indeed, the large amounts spent on producing the manpower for medical research stand out in the NIH budgets. This is not to imply that NIH

TABLE 10. NIH Appropriations, 1956–1967 ($ millions)

	1956	1960	1964	1967
Total appropriations	98	430	974	1,413
Research grants	46	215	540	722
Training/fellowships	17	90	219	285
Institution support	—	30	99[c]	117[c]

[c] = estimated

shouldered the entire burden: universities found themselves compelled to raise vast sums in order to keep their research capacities abreast with the steep rise of available grants. Those that could afford the investment, however, were largely assured that research and training would be amply supported.

NIH thus provided a cornucopia of resources that transformed American medical schools. The training of medical practitioners in the American scheme of things had not always been complementary to the conduct of research. Prior to World War II, those medical schools connected with major universities performed significant amounts of research, but many medical schools were scarcely involved in research at all. By 1954, when the federal government was supporting one-half of the research in medical schools, research still remained concentrated: just 13 institutions expended more than $1 million, and they constituted 50 percent of the total. In 1966, however, 88 institutions received more than $1 million from NIH alone; and the 13 largest recipients garnered only 32 percent of the total.[34]

By the end of the 1960s at least three salient developments characterized the reformation that had taken place in American medical schools. First, as research came to dominate the make-up and activities of the preclinical departments, the major medical schools became more like research institutes than teaching institutions. Second, cadres of medical researchers were now to be found in the majority of medical schools where they had not existed previously. And third, graduate study for the Ph.D. became a major undertaking of many medical schools. As a result, the link between graduate education and research that characterized science departments elsewhere in the university became a permanent feature of American medical schools.[35] These changes were fully evident in the rapid transformation of the population of medical schools. The number of scientists employed there mushroomed from 15,600 in 1958 to 50,000 in 1965. Full-time faculty grew from 9600 in 1958 to 23,000 in 1968, even though the number of medical students increased by only 20 percent—from 30,000 to 36,000. The contingent of graduate students grew far more rapidly, reaching almost 10,000. Medical faculty in the basic sciences at the end of the 1960s, a prominent study concluded, bore "a one-to-one relationship to the total number of graduate students."[36]

The largesse of the NIH spilled predominantly, but not exclusively into medical schools. The magnitude of the funds disbursed by NIH made it a major factor in neighboring disciplines as well. NIH was the largest single supporter of academic chemistry (1964), providing one-fifth of research funds. The National Institute of Mental Health, which was separated from NIH in 1967, was an important factor in the social and behavioral sciences. Together NIMH/NIH provided 47 percent of federal support for sociology and 41 percent for psychology. On the other hand, the medical schools were not entirely wards of NIH. In 1964 they received 28 percent of their research funding from other sources.[37]

The same disillusionment with basic research and desire for greater practical results that affected the role of NSF in the late 1960s had an impact on NIH as well. In addition, the remarkably effective coalition responsible for its rise unraveled. The most zealous congressional advocates passed from the scene; James Shannon retired in 1968; and the redoubtable Mary Lasker shifted with the national mood. President Lyndon Johnson was among the first to demand that research results be translated more rapidly into disease treatments; and in the once pliant Congress the aura surrounding NIH was broken by a report that charged it with poor management.[38] But unlike NSF, disenchantment with the mission of NIH meant a reduction in its rate of growth, not its scale of operations. Testifying before Congress in 1965, James Shannon predicted that health-related research in the U.S. would reach $3 billion by 1970. Although this figure was not reached until 1971, few projections beyond those years of heady growth were so close to the mark.[39]

NIH budgets become somewhat confusing to interpret after 1967 due to the excision of NIMH, delayed obligations, supplemental appropriations, and reserves. The rate of growth slowed, inevitably, but the flow of grants continued to mount by more than $100 million every year but two from 1965 to 1971. Following this stretch, President Nixon's premature 'war against cancer' fueled another substantial advance.[40] Even when measured in constant dollars, the NIH growth curve registered only a hiccough for 1970 and 1971 in its otherwise steady ascent. The relative prosperity of NIH was evident in the fate of its programs for supporting the infrastructure of the health sciences in the universities. Capital funds for research facilities were cut severely after 1968, while allocations for training and fellowships were reduced by about a quarter. The program for general research support (actually a component of the research budgets) nevertheless continued undiminished. Hard times were less hard in the health sciences.

Overall, the result of the ample funding of NIH was that the American medical school by the end of the 1960s had become a distinctive enterprise:

> scientists in the preclinical departments can remain *au courant* with the advancing edges of biological, physical, and social sciences, translate these for their clinical colleagues, and collaborate with the latter in both clinical research and relevant fundamental research that are also part of the education of graduate, medical and postdoctoral students.... Findings can be both tested and then immediately put to work for the benefit of patients in the same institution.[41]

Even if one discounts this somewhat idealized view, the rise of NIH during the post-Sputnik era fixed the medical schools as the most research-intensive academic component of universities.

The defense establishment: AEC, DoD, and NASA. The university research sponsored by these three federal agencies was tied to their respective missions in a far more explicit manner than that of NIH. All three possessed huge R&D budgets in which spending for Development dwarfed those for Research; and they looked to the universities for just a small, but important, contribution to their science and engineering efforts. These agencies were responsible for 84 percent of federal R&D expenditures at the end of the 1960s, but their share in the sponsorship of university research had been in a steady decline. The most dra-

TABLE 11. Federal Agencies, Support for University Research 1958–1964 ($ millions)[42]

	Total	DoD	AEC	NASA	NSF	NIH	Other
1958	219	91	33	—	16	72	7
1964	866	198	67	44	126	401	28

matic changes occurred following Sputnik, despite the net addition of NASA to the system. In an increase of almost $650 million, the defense establishment accounted for $185 million (29%), while NSF and NIH were responsible for $439 million (68%). This trend would continue for another decade. For the Department of Defense, in particular, these developments signified a transformation of its role. From being the predominant funder of university research in the postwar era, it increasingly faced a problem in the post-Sputnik years of sustaining its ties in a university system that had progressively less incentive to perform programmatic research.

NASA and the AEC have often been lumped together with the DoD because many of their activities are substantially linked with the nation's defense effort. They are also similar in their administrative patterns and relationships with industrial firms.[43] In their relations with academic science, however, both similarities and differences existed. The similarities encompass three areas. It was vitally important to their own large science and engineering operations, first, to have access to university scientists working on the frontiers of basic research. The need here was both to keep internal scientists abreast of the state of their fields, and to be able to turn to expert help for research questions that transcended internal capabilities. Having ready access to university scientists when needed required the long cultivation of these relationships, as was clearly foreseen by the ONR after World War II. Second, there were certain kinds of research, central to the agency mission, that either could not or would not be performed by university scientists on their own. Each agency consequently had the responsibility to provide the facilities, special instruments, and/or research support to see that these investigations would be conducted. Third, their large internal requirements for science and engineering manpower required the continual recruitment of university-trained and university-based individuals.[44] Beyond these functional similarities, the experiences of these agencies with academic science differed markedly during the decade of the 1960s: the AEC exhibited the greatest stability with only moderate growth; NASA, as a newcomer, had to create a niche for itself in the university research system; and Defense was challenged to adapt to a diminished role and an increasingly unreceptive academic community.

The stability of the role of the Atomic Energy Commission derived primarily from its highly specialized mission. Its chief responsibilities were atomic weapons, reactors, and high-energy physics, but it also was concerned with particle physics in general and radioactive isotopes. In 1964 the agency had a budget of

$2.4 billion, and about half of that was spent on research, development, and education. Less than 10 percent of the total budget went for basic research, and just 23 percent of that subtotal went to universities. The AEC was nevertheless more important for the funding of academic science than that figure—or the slightly different total for expenditures given above—would indicate. Much of its support for high-energy physics, which was a university-linked endeavor, was provided through the system of National Laboratories. The Lawrence Radiation Laboratory at Berkeley and the Brookhaven National Laboratory, operated by a consortium of universities, by themselves constituted capital investments of $241 million and had operating budgets of $73 million (1964). These operations represented the epitome of Big Science—experiments conducted by teams of researchers, assisted by a small army of supporting staff, employing expensive materials and equipment.[45] University scientists also utilized portions of the facilities at the even larger installations at the Argonne, Oak Ridge, and Los Alamos laboratories.[46]

The construction of giant particle accelerators was the facet of the AEC's academic role that generated the greatest notoriety during the 1960s. In 1962 a three-year political deadlock was resolved in favor of building the $100+ million Stanford Linear Electron Accelerator. The next year, however, ten years of wrangling ended in the rejection of an accelerator proposed by the Midwest Universities Research Association. This last episode had major repercussions for the federal funding of research by raising the issue of geographical distribution in an acute way. The midwestern physicists were eventually mollified when the National Accelerator Laboratory (now Fermilab) was sited in Weston, Illinois.[47] Beneath the turbulence that swirled around these hundred-million dollar decisions, there was considerable continuity in the AEC's support of university research.

As explained in Chapter 1, the AEC inherited a closer relationship to university research than had been foreseen in its enabling legislation. There was always some latitude in the terms of this cooperation—some discretion on the part of the AEC in the degree to which it would support universities for the minor part of its mission to which they contributed. During the early years of the AEC, the General Advisory Committee was predisposed toward cultivating basic research in universities. Under the chairmanship of Lewis Strauss, who engineered the removal of Oppenheimer's security clearance, the AEC's relations with university scientists deteriorated.[48] But an entirely different disposition characterized the agency after 1961, when Glenn Seaborg assumed the chairmanship. Throughout the 1960s he affirmed the views of the 1960 Seaborg Report, namely, that universities were the most fitting place for basic research.[49] The AEC under Seaborg was thus fully in accord with the prevailing consensus on the ideology of basic research.

Seaborg's conviction that "graduate education and the process of basic research belong together" obviously favored universities. During 1964 the AEC supported 514 research contracts that brought funds to 150 colleges and universities. Columbia, with $4.7 million, recieved the most, and D'Youville College's $4000 was the least.[50] The research supported by the AEC was more capital-intensive than that of any other agency, and this fact helped to account for its unique procedures. The AEC awarded research funds solely through contracts, which it negotiated separately with each performer. It was the usual procedure to ask the performer to assume some of the costs for each project. Setting terms for small research projects would ordinarily be perfunctory, but it took a year of negotiations with Princeton to settle arrangements for undertaking fusion research.[51] The AEC continued the practice of using negotiated contracts even after it received authorization to make grants in 1958.

Glenn Seaborg expressed wholehearted support for the principle of building additional academic centers of excellence, but he felt that this goal should only be pursued through supplementary funding: existing programs aimed at supporting the highest quality work and should not be altered. The AEC went as far as offering training grants in nuclear engineering to under-enrolled programs, thus encouraging the growth of graduate education at up-and-coming institutions. But it was the only major agency that did not follow the President's directive to establish a science development program. The AEC did help those institutions that would help themselves. For example, when Texas A&M expanded its physics staff and obtained $3 million in state and private funding, the AEC awarded them a like amount to build a cyclotron.[52]

The scientific commitments of the AEC remained, above all, centered on its extensive system of national laboratories. During the 1960s it expended a minor portion of its large budget to nurture research and graduate training in universities in those fields for which it was responsible. The directness and the continuity of this relationship bred extremely close relations between the AEC and nuclear scientists. This closeness largely worked to the advantage of the agency when it came to imposing its own strict requirements for security, secrecy, and loyalty.[53] The result was relatively stable and long-lived research relationships within one of the most politically volatile of scientific fields.

NASA possessed the most narrow mission among all the research-funding agencies, but this did not prevent it from cultivating a wide involvement with university research. Several reasons account for this. The prodigious engineering feat of sending men to the moon and back demanded additional knowledge on myriad specific subjects, from behavioral biology to planetary science. Moreover, the massiveness of this effort placed an additional burden upon the nation's already strained system of scientific research and training. NASA sought not only to fulfill its immediate research needs, but also to strengthen academic science in those areas where its activities were concentrated. An additional, although unpublicized, consideration was undoubtedly operating. As a newcomer to the university research system, NASA had to purchase access to top-quality academic science. Programmatic support was less likely to accomplish this, outside of special areas; thus the price became general support for areas relevant to space science.[54]

NASA became a major participant in academic science in fiscal 1963 when its obligations to universities soared from $30 to $87 million. The following year, when outlays to universities rose to $108 million, NASA devoted about $42 million to project research, another $27 million to special development projects, and $37 million to what it called the "Sustaining University Program." This latter program supplied institutional support in the general area of space-related science and engineering. About half of these funds consisted of grants for the training of graduate students, while the remainder was split between support for the construction of research facilities and unrestricted funds for research. From fiscal 1963 through 1967 the Sustaining University Program comprised a third of all NASA obligations to universities—almost $40 million per year. This figure nevertheless represented less than one percent of NASA's budget. After 1967 support for academic science went almost exclusively to project research. All told, from 1962 to 1971 the Sustaining University Program alone disbursed $225 million to more than 170 colleges and universities.[55] This sum was only slightly less than the total NSF funding of science development programs, and reached far more institutions.

The Sustaining University Program supplied institutions with support of an exceedingly liberal kind. The training grants, which usually gave a graduate student full support for three years, were allocated to institutions, thereby encouraging the dispersion of talented graduate students and the wide development of programs. Construction funds created laboratories that were otherwise lacking for the study of space-related topics. And research grants could be used to recruit distinguished scientists to work in space science. Nobelist Willard Libby at UCLA, for example, received approximately $800,000 per year in unrestricted support. One innovation of the Program was 'step funding,' which assured continuity to NASA projects. The initial grants were for two years of support spread over three years; each subsequent year of support was then allocated over a three-year period.[56] The Sustaining University Program buttressed core academic functions despite the agency's mission of accomplishing specific projects.

To rationalize this liberal support NASA curiously resorted to a favorite argument of academics in pre-Sputnik days: namely, that the heavy burden of project research had the potential of distorting the basic educational mission of universities. The Sustaining University Program thus was intended to counter to some extent the effects of NASA's extensive programmatic research agenda.[57] The large training component of the Program was designed to compensate for the huge demand that NASA placed on the nation's scientific manpower—5 percent of all scientists and engineers in the mid-sixties. In addition, when President Johnson called for greater dispersion of research funds, the NASA Program was well suited to contribute toward this end. Most of the established research universities received funding from the Program, but the agency concluded that its "'seed grants' have been most successful in stimulating productive, space-related research in universities which are not among the present leaders." Such universities, recipients of relatively large grants from this program, would include Arizona, Georgia Tech, Purdue, Maryland, RPI, Pittsburgh, Rice, and Texas A&M.[58] Support for these schools in fact antedated the President's directive, which would suggest that, although NASA sought to establish beach-heads at the established research universities, its large needs and late start forced the agency to take a broader approach in cultivating ties with academic science.[59]

The military, because of its needs during World War II, was the grandfather of all federal support for academic research outside of agriculture. The emergence of special agencies for nuclear, medical, and basic scientific research progressively removed a major portion of these responsibilities from the armed services, and created the pluralist federal research system. For its part, the Defense Department in the years before Sputnik was inclined to circumscribe even further its involvement with academic scientists. But the Sputnik crisis abruptly reversed this drift: research at the DoD was substantially reorganized, and for a time larger sums were made available to support basic research. But the DoD only partly and belatedly shared the emerging ideology of basic research. The latent schism between its mission and the predilections of academic scientists grew more pronounced as time passed. Eventually, the fundamental issue that had troubled university scientists since the war—should the military be a major funder of academic science?—was explicitly addressed.

The repercussions of Sputnik reverberated through the Pentagon in the form of legislation creating the Advanced Research Projects Agency (ARPA, later DARPA) and establishing the office of the Director of Defense Research and Engineering. The Director was the principal science advisor to the Secretary of Defense, and also responsible for coordinating R&D among the services. According to the first incumbent, this office stabilized the organization of science and technology in the Pentagon after a succession of postwar administrative shuffles. Besides enhancing the standing of research, it helped to overcome the interservice rivalries that had plagued the missile development programs. The director also gave Defense a strong and singular voice in the numerous interagency bodies concerned with science and technology.[60]

ARPA, which reported to the Director of Defense Research and Engineering, was organized immediately after Sputnik to do what the armed services apparently could not do individually: organize research on complex technological challenges of broad scope and significance.[61] It harkened back to the much-admired model of the wartime OSRD. A relatively small staff conducted no in-house research, but was charged with mobilizing the efforts of the best existing scientific talent and focusing them on areas of potentially valuable technology. The difference was that ARPA was designed to have the vision to identify and address generic technologies that would pay off, if at all, in the medium-to-far future. ARPA was first assembled to pick up the pieces of the several missile programs, but that task was soon ceded to the newly created NASA. ARPA was thus left with the responsibility for general, high-risk topics that transcended the interests of the individual services.

As a new entity in the economy of academic research, ARPA was somewhat anomalous in the post-Sputnik environment. It was avowedly programmatic when the balance was shifting toward disinterested research; it also emphasized interdisciplinary work in the face of the hegemony of the disciplines; and some of its more imaginitive projects generated controversy among a public increasingly disturbed by the war in Vietnam and the military's emerging "Dr. Strangelove" image. One of the most successful ARPA ventures was the initiation of interdisciplinary laboratories for materials research at a dozen universities (1961). This action, as intended, inaugurated sustained research in this field. In a similar move, ARPA contributed to the development of computer sciences in the 1960s by supporting work on graphics and software. Unlike materials science, which the agency ceded to NSF in 1972, ARPA remained active in this field and became the principal supporter of research on artificial intelligence. More controversial were its forays into the social sciences, particularly its attempt to know the enemy better by modeling social systems.[62] ARPA, like the early ONR, was an ideal funder of academic research. It could act quickly with a minimum of paperwork; it provided long-term support for those fields it wished to stimulate; and it supported research in a manner that ceded control to investigators. ARPA thus added a new element to the university research economy, one that would be praised some two decades later for being proactive, flexible, and focused on future needs.[63] But ARPA became controversial and unpopular in the late 1960s, and partly for that reason, it tended to pursue the bulk of its work through government and private laboratories rather than universities.

The episode that reveals most clearly the disjunction between the ascending ideology of basic research and the descending stature of the military in academic science was Project Hindsight. From 1963 to 1967 the Director of Defense Research and Engineering sponsored this elaborate effort to measure the role of research in the creation of major technological innovations—weapons systems, to be exact. The project sought to determine the economic value of these innovations in relation to their predecessors, and to identify the nature and sequence of "research events" of the previous twenty years that were incorporated in the innovations. The results, reported late in 1966, were scarcely welcome to the basic research community. About 9 percent of the relevant science events consisted of applied or directed science, and just 0.3 percent were the result of basic/undirected science. The balance of events, then, were technological in nature. This finding seemed to undermine the prevailing belief that basic research was the fount of technological progress. On the other hand, Hindsight validated the DoD's approach to R&D. It found that "the approximately $10 billion of DoD funds expended in the support of science and technology over the period 1946 to 1962 . . . has been paid back many times over"; and that "the traditional DoD management policy of keeping applied science and technology closely related to the needs of systems and equipment in development . . . is basically sound if one wants an economic payoff on the 10-year (or shorter) time scale." By its own lights, Hindsight provided "a strong, factual demonstration that recent mission-oriented science and technology are a good investment in the short run"; but it was unable "to demonstrate value for recent undirected science."[64]

The immediate motives for undertaking Project Hindsight lay with the embattled position of research within the DoD as well as congressional criticism of that research effort.[65] Its effect nevertheless was to provide a rejoinder to the ideology of basic research. The conclusions were foreseeable from the methodology of the study—its focus on complex engineering projects, its short time-frame, and its counting of equally weighted research events.[66] The NSF clearly felt the challenge, and quickly countered with a study of its own—Project TRACES—which employed a different method and, not surprisingly, concluded that basic academic research was (longer-term) the chief factor fostering technological advancement.[67] Little matter: more harmful for academic science than the findings of Hindsight was its timing. The conclusions were publicized just months after President Johnson had announced that the time had come to extract more applications from the nation's investment in basic research.[68] Hindsight probably changed few minds, but it was grist for the mills of those who were becoming disillusioned with the hypertrophy of basic research. The project diminished the mystique of academic science, but contributed little luster to the Pentagon alternative.

The kinds of activities that Hindsight endorsed represented the vast bulk of military R&D, but were atypical of the DoD's ties with university research. Both ONR and ARPA, for example, supported basic academic research that was not closely linked with technological development, and there is little reason to suspect that they erred systematically in doing so. These offices valued access to academic science and took steps to maintain it under increasingly trying circumstances.

At the same time that Hindsight was being publicized, the DoD was establishing a science-development program for universities. Interestingly, two years earlier it had told Congress that such a program was unnecessary. It noted that the "traditionally strong universities" could not handle all of the department's research needs, and that much of its support consequently went to the next tier of institutions, strengthening them in the process. It furthermore took the position that a university's own resources, not federal funds, were the key to developing centers of research excellence.[69] The inauguration of Project THEMIS, then, seemed to betoken a greater appreciation of the need to improve and broaden the department's access to university science. THEMIS distributed almost $95 million in three-year block grants to nearly one hundred institutions before it was terminated by Congress in 1971. It differed from the programs of other agencies in that almost all of its grants were of similar size—$700,000 to $900,000—and they were given to institutions that were well down the research university hierarchy. The grants themselves were fairly narrowly focused on specialty areas, where neophyte institutions might develop niches in the research system. The awards also appeared to favor states and institutions that were less inclined to hold anti-military views.[70]

As opposition to the Vietnam War grew, hostility was aimed at the campus manifestations of the DoD—principally the Reserve Officer Training Corps and defense research, but also THEMIS. The DoD was faced with the problem of preventing the antiwar movement from disrupting the ties with academic science that it had cultivated for a quarter-century. After some provocative incidents, the Director of Defense Research and Engineering enjoined his staff to "take all necessary actions to preserve our mutually beneficial relationships with the academic research community during this period when there are potentially divisive pressures."[71] These pressures affected the DoD's role on many university campuses. Several federal contract research centers were divested from university sponsorship; many universities banned classified research and some even threatened to cut all ties with the DoD.[72]

Such actions, however, affected the spirit more than the substance of the department's relationship with universities. The use of contract research centers was being reduced before the anti-war movement, and changes in their sponsorship scarcely affected their operations. Less than 10 percent of department-supported academic research (4% of actual contracts) were classified, and that portion was conducted by a handful of institutions; and faculty resolutions to proscribe all contact with DoD never became university policy. Despite this poisoned atmosphere, university faculty members sent increasing numbers of research proposals to the DoD.[73] The decisive change in relations between universities and the DoD came from neither party, but from Congress.

Opposition to DoD research on campus became salient at a point in time when it was increasing only moderately and when the DoD was slipping toward third position among federal supporters of university research. Particularly conspicuous and controversial was support for research in the social and behavioral sciences. Confronted with the conundrum of fighting against guerilla warfare, spawned by political and social revolution, the DoD in the 1960s felt a need for greater knowledge about foreign countries and basic social and political conditions. To a far greater degree than in engineering, expertise in these fields was concentrated in universities.[74] Pentagon patronage in these fields was perceived by critics to be inherently biased toward existing U.S. policies and against social change in developing countries.[75] Even more troubling was the unbounded nature of such military curiosity. In 1968 antiwar Senator J. William Fulbright conducted hearings on this matter. He was alarmed by a recommendation that the DoD expand its spending for social science research on the pretext that it "must now wage not only warfare, but 'peacefare' as well." The Director of Defense Research and Engineering testified that social science research was needed by the Pentagon because "the political, economic and cultural activities of a nation are intimately intertwined with military efforts." The Senator responded, "in effect then you are taking full responsibility for everything."[76] The following year the Congress acted to constrain the apparently unbridled scope of Pentagon research.

A rider to the Military Authorization Act for fiscal 1970, supported by Senator Mike Mansfield, stated that no DoD funds were to be used to support research unless it had "direct or apparent relationship to a specific military function or operation."[77] Mansfield's explicit intention was to challenge the role that the DoD had assumed since World War II. He could find no "rationale that dictated that the Department of Defense should be the principal sponsoring agency for much of [federal] research"; and he intended to "close out a second and a backdoor National Science Foundation which has grown up in the Department of Defense."[78] The implementation of the Mansfield principle across the services was somewhat inconsistent, and its actual impact was masked by other factors.

According to the Senator's own figures, 3 percent of the DoD contracts and 4 percent of academic support were affected. At the same time, far greater cutbacks were attributed to budget tightening. The Mansfield Amendment was softened considerably the next year by making the opinion of the Secretary of Defense the determining criterion of relevance. It nevertheless had its desired effect. Hostility in Congress as well as the antiwar movement and budget tightening all combined to end the Pentagon's role as a 'backdoor NSF.'[79]

From 1969 to 1975 real DoD support for basic research in universities declined by more than 50 percent. As a proportion of total federal support for academic research, DoD funding declined from 34 percent in 1960, to 15 percent in 1970, and then to just 8 percent in 1975.[80] This was one issue on which the antiwar movement seemed to prevail. There were a number of ironies, however, in this apparent achievement.

The extensive sponsorship of academic research by the Pentagon raised a number of fundamental issues which were generally not addressed by opponents.[81] The abuses against which Senator Mansfield inveighed were less prevalent at the end of the 1960s than any time since World War II, except perhaps in the social sciences. The systematic rationalization of the DoD under Robert McNamara had progressively suffocated basic research with centralization, mission relatedness, and, worst of all, cost effectiveness.[82] Indeed, the relative decline of defense research would suggest that the university research system had for some time been growing progressively less influenced by the military at the time the Mansfield amendment was passed. It was not the actual nature of this relationship, but the polarization that had occurred in the country and on campuses that made even the attenuated presence of military-sponsored research intolerable at this juncture.

Harvey Brooks argued at the time that it would have been unrealistic to believe that the existing level of support for academic science could have been achieved without the efforts of the military and the stimulus of the Cold War. Yet, it was legislated that the military should no longer fulfill that role. Senator Mansfield specifically asked that most funding of basic research be turned over to "the agency set up for this sole purpose"; and Brooks estimated that NSF could have assumed the military's responsibilities toward academic science with a 50 percent increase in its budget.[83] Nothing of this sort occurred. The resources available for academic science declined at NSF just as they did at the Pentagon.[84]

For the research universities, the decline in DoD support for academic science could not have come at a worse time. The phenomenal growth of the 1960s had passed its apogee, and the stagnation of the 1970s was settling over them. Moreover, the effect of the Mansfield amendment was to terminate those Pentagon programs that were most beneficial to academic science, such as Project THEMIS.[85] Programmatic research funds, on the other hand, were unaffected. For that very reason, neither was the Pentagon's supposedly nefarious influence over academic research. DoD domination of university research, insofar as it existed, was always concentrated in specific departments and specialties. In aeronautical engineering, parts of electrical engineering, optics, underwater acoustics, and numerous other specialties the DoD consistently supported research that would not otherwise have been performed. This kind of support cemented long-term relationships and a degree of influence that substantially affected the units concerned.[86] The developments of the 1960s called into question, and ultimately rejected, the other role of the DoD, which had been pioneered by ONR and intermittently practiced by ARPA and Project THEMIS—that of contributing to the disinterested pursuit of academic knowledge.

American higher education experienced two great revolutions during the 1960s. The nation chose to make a sizable increase in the public investment in academic science of all kinds. Similarly, American society chose to implement policies at the federal, state, and local levels that would substantially increase the proportion of young people attending college. As objects of national purpose, priority, and policy, each revolution enjoyed approximately ten years of ascendancy. For university research, the consequences of Sputnik were palpable in 1958, and continued to unfold until 1968. As a federal commitment, furthering access to higher education first became an explicit legislative goal in 1963, and remained a high priority through 1972, when the final programs were put in place for a comprehensive federal system of need-based student financial assistance. The five years in the middle of the 1960s when both these revolutions overlapped appear in retrospect to have been the golden age for research universities.

The research revolution fell into two roughly equal halves. From 1958 to 1963 federal support for university research rose at a vertiginous pace. These quantitative changes were accompanied by new programs in the principal federal agencies supporting research and a reorganization of the structure governing federal science. With academic scientists installed in the President's Science Advisory Council and scientific issues occupying the forefront of public concern, science during this period held greater influence in Washington than in perhaps any other era.[87] The values and axioms of the ideology of basic research emanated outward from the NSF and the National Academy of Sciences. For the first time the federal government was committed to supporting the advancement of knowledge largely on the terms favored by scientists themselves.

The ideology of basic research remained for the most part in the ascendancy for the next half-decade, but its comfortable assumptions were repeatedly jostled by other preoccupations. Scientists carried less weight with Lyndon Johnson, who was preoccupied first with the domestic agenda of the Great Society, and later with his tragic blunder in Vietnam. Johnson reportedly asked the members of his Science Advisory Council, "what can I do for grandma?" But this sort of advice was beyond their ken.[88] Johnson's solicitude for grandma, and that of Congress as well, gradually introduced two new elements into the matrix of academic research.

The first was an explicit concern for the geographical distribution of federal research funds. Johnson confronted this issue during his first days in office in the matter of the proposed particle accelerator for midwestern universities. The perennial interest of the Congress in where federal dollars are spent was soon piqued. Legislation began to be written in ways to promote greater dispersion of

funds. The 1964 expansion of the NDEA allocated additional graduate fellowships to institutions instead of individuals; The NASA authorization for the following year admonished the agency that "consideration be given to geographical
distribution of Federal research funds whenever feasible."[89] Hearings were held
in the summer of 1965 by the Senate Labor Committee on this issue, and in
September there came definitive word from the White House. Federal research
funds were, according to the President, "still concentrated in too few institutions in too few areas of the country." He intended "to find excellence and build
it up wherever it is found so that creative centers of excellence may grow in every
part of the country."[90] The science-development policies that have just been
described were partly the result of this new policy. The agencies, however,
became acutely mindful of the scrutiny of the Congress in their other funding
decisions.

The second new element was the concern that the national investment in basic
scientific research should yield near-term benefits in applications. Here too, Congress and the President moved in tandem. The congressional review of NSF,
which began in 1963, was determined to introduce applied research to the foundation's mandate. Then in 1966, President Johnson signaled that the time had
come to seek greater returns from the public's investment. In a meeting with the
directors of NIH, he instructed them to formulate plans for translating biomedical research into "specific results in the decline of deaths and disabilities."[91]

These developments were duly noted by contemporaries. Donald Fleming
claimed that federal laboratories and research contracts were becoming a scientific pork barrel. Daniel Greenberg argued that a new politics of science had
emerged, replacing the old, elitist politics of science that had become untenable
in the presidency of Lyndon Johnson.[92] But change in the pluralistic and decentralized university research system was ponderously slow. Efforts to distribute
research funding more widely, especially the science development programs,
remained consistent with the prevailing ideology of basic research. They sought
the same goal as the Seaborg Report—more centers of excellence—and they did
not challenge the fundamental principle of allocating support to what scientists
themselves determined to be the best science. Moreover, by aiding the development of institutions, these programs were consistent with the purposes of the
other, expansionary revolution taking place in higher education. The push
toward applied research, on the other hand, was in fact effectively resisted until
the research revolution had run its course. Only after 1968 might it be said that
funds were directed to applied research at the expense of basic research.

During the golden age from 1963 to 1968 the research universities benefited
from three thrusts of federal policy. Direct spending for academic research crept
upward in decreasing increments until the apogee was reached. At the same time,
the programs that were transforming the federal commitment to expanding
access to higher education, lodged with the Bureau of Education, greatly
expanded the support available for graduate and undergraduate students and for
capital expansion.[93] The third thrust consisted of the policies just mentioned—
those programs that provided institutional support for established and would-
be research universities under the guise of science development. These latter pro-

grams constituted a recognition of the importance of institutional research capacity for the conduct of academic science. They also represented the most extensive federal commitment ever made for this purpose. But this kind of support was fragile: it became the foremost casualty of the changing political environment.

After 1968 a new politics of science definitely did prevail. The mystique surrounding the ideology of basic research soon vanished. At the same time, the drive to extend access to higher education, which remained a preoccupation for at least another half decade, came to emphasize the nontraditional and disadvantaged students who were more marginal to research universities. In the new atmosphere, science development programs were particularly vulnerable.[94] Eventually, it was decided that the federal government would aid institutions through their students instead of their scientists. Still, the most important outcome was that the main fruits of the revolution in academic research were preserved. Federal funding, and indeed the total value of research performed in universities, entered a decade of stagnation in real terms. But the general level of research activity that had been attained during the post-Sputnik decade was maintained. The American polity rejected the ideology of academic scientists, but not their science. The cessation of growth in the academic research enterprise had a practical justification. Those programs had been sufficiently effective that the essential rationale for the revolution in academic research had finally disappeared. No longer was American science in danger of being eclipsed by the Soviets; no longer was academic science concentrated in just fifteen or twenty universities; and no longer did graduate programs need to be expanded in order to counter the shortage of faculty and researchers. These changes, brought about by the revolution in the national commitment to university research, had wrought a revolution on university campuses as well.

7

The Golden Age on Campus:
The Research Universities in the 1960s

1. The Evolving University: Contemporary Perceptions

The twin revolutions, in access to higher education and in academic research, provided an underlying dynamic to a far-reaching transformation of American higher education during the 1960s. At the start of the decade two of every ten 18-24 year-olds were students, and at the end that figure had risen to three. Given the larger population of young people, this widening participation translated into increases of 119 percent in undergraduates and 147 percent in graduate students—together the largest enrollment increment for any decade in enumerated history. More remarkable, American colleges and universities made qualitative progress even while they expanded. Research expenditures grew by 261 percent; regular faculty expanded by 139 percent; and general and educational expenditures rose by 250 percent.[1] The research universities, staid and conservative in their role as guardians of academic standards, were in the forefront of some of the most dramatic changes. Besides performing the bulk of academic research, they pioneered an enlargement of university roles, the ascendancy of graduate education, the specialization of the curriculum, and an alteration of faculty roles. As more institutions entered the ranks as certified research universities, these patterns spread. Eventually, as the Zeitgeist changed, the research universities were first again in enduring financial crises, experiencing the student rebellion, and harboring challenges to the values of rational inquiry for which they ostensibly stood.

These momentous developments were keenly scrutinized by contemporaries. The Sputnik crisis greatly stimulated writing on higher education. The first part of the 1960s saw the first appearance of complete data on university research from the NSF and blue-ribbon assessments from the National Academy of Sciences. At the end of the decade the student rebellion brought forth untold volumes of commentary, while the systematic analyses sponsored by the Carnegie Commission produced the most comprehensive depiction of the American system of higher education that it is ever likely to receive.[2] Still, these were difficult times for clear observation. If the heady expansion and the ideology of basic research occluded the view during the first part of the decade, the political polarization of the later 1960s distorted perceptions more seriously. The best of contemporary writings nevertheless document both the conditions and the anxieties of research universities in the 1960s.

In academe as well as government, a key concern in the aftermath of Sputnik was the effect of federal programs on the nation's universities. Although this subject was no longer novel, a new note was struck in three separate projects which sought to establish empirically the actual state of the relationship. The first of this genre by Charles V. Kidd included a survey of deans and department heads that was begun before Sputnik; in the second, sponsored by the Brookings Institution, Harold Orlans sampled 36 colleges and universities; then in 1960, the Carnegie Foundation organized self-studies of federal relations at 26 campuses.[3] Quite independently these studies converged on the same major conclusions. Each witnessed to the inescapable fact that federal support since World War II had substantially enhanced the scope, vigor, and quality of graduate education and university research in the natural sciences. In addition, the weight of evidence seemed to exorcise many of the bogeymen associated with the federal-university relationship since the war—specifically the concerns over distortion, displacement, dependence, and domination that were discussed in Chapter 2.

The persistent fear that demand from federal agencies for applied and developmental work would distort university research had not been borne out by the end of the 1950s. Instead, Kidd noted, "a remarkable process of mutual adaptation" had occurred between federal agencies and university scientists. Furthermore, the pendulum seemed to be swinging away from programmatic research, and universities seemed comfortable about the kinds of investigations being conducted by their faculty.[4]

The displacement issue was more complicated. Universities were loath to admit that they did not lose money by conducting government research, thus consuming resources that might have been employed for other purposes. In the long run building research capacity undeniably claimed substantial university resources. But the Princeton self-study (for the Carnegie Foundation) noted that the incremental indirect costs of conducting research tended to be less in the short run than the compensation for indirect costs that universities received from some federal agencies. On a related issue, both Kidd and Orlans suspected that the expansion of research had adverse consequences for undergraduate teaching; but the Princeton study pointed out that reduced teaching loads—another effect associated with greater research—ought to improve classroom instruction. On balance, even though research had caused universities to expand certain activities, there was little hard evidence that anything else had been crowded out.[5]

Without doubt, universities had become dependent on the federal govern-

ment for the support of research and graduate education, but negative consequences stemming from that dependence remained hypothetical. The alleged
uncertainties of the project system were moot: large-scale research projects
tended to have considerable stability, while in other areas the volume of individual project grants produced the same effect. The nightmare of university business
officers, that these funds might suddenly be withdrawń, was nothing more than
that. As a result, universities overcame their reluctance to use research funds for
faculty salaries in practice sooner than in theory. Orlans found the growing
acceptance of this practice to be "astonishing." It was also unavoidable if universities were to staff classrooms in fields like physics or medicine where faculty
members were heavily engaged in sponsored research. In other departments, universities clung weakly to the somewhat qualified principle of not hiring tenured
faculty on 'soft' money.[6]

In these years concern was still voiced that federal support would bring federal
domination and control. Kidd, however, underlined the fact that fifteen years of
federal support for university research had not brought this result. Orlans worried that the threat still existed, but his pessimism was uncharacteristic for the
early 1960s.[7] Universities by then not only trusted the federal patron, but were
looking for additional forms of patronage.

In a third major area of agreement, these studies seemed to converge on the
universities themselves as the principal source of vulnerability in the research system. The problem was essentially financial. It was exceedingly costly to develop,
maintain, and augment a significant research capacity; and the resources for this
purpose had to be generated largely by the institutions themselves, whether
through gifts or state appropriations. This situation had two consequences.
Major research universities felt themselves to be under constant fiscal pressure
to find additional resources for these purposes. And, because some succeeded
better than others, such financial constraints were the reason for the high degree
of concentration of university research.[8] After Sputnik this concentration was
increasingly regarded as unhealthy and limiting. In this respect, sentiment on
campus dovetailed neatly with the thrust of the coeval Seaborg Report. It also
mirrored the growing support for additional kinds of federal aid for higher education. Overall, these reports favored general forms of research support by the
science-funding agencies, institutional aid that would relieve the fiscal pressures
on universities, and programs that would increase the number of universities
capable of conducting first-rate research.[9]

A half-decade after the Sputnik revolution commenced, Clark Kerr offered an
exegesis on the new phenomenon that he called unabashedly the "federal grant
university." Federal aid had been a 'good thing,' he averred, and more and different forms of federal aid would be even better. But Kerr also expressed an
awareness of the evanescent and unstable nature of the contemporary situation.
Those very issues that had worried the academy since the emergence of the postwar system he summarized as "intuitive imbalances," produced by the uncoordinated actions of different actors in federal agencies and universities. He judged
the current moment, however, to be a fulcrum in this development. With the
imbalances identified and scrutinized, as in the preceding studies, forces had

been set in motion that would seek through bureaucratic means to achieve greater balance among regions, universities, disciplines, and institutional activities. As a result, he concluded, "we are in the midst of a vast transformation of university life and none of us can be too sure where we really are going."[10] By the end of the post-Sputnik decade, just a few years later, appraisals were already being made of where this transition had taken the research universities.

By 1968 a new consensus had emerged. The principal focus had now shifted from what government had done or might do to universities to what they were doing to themselves.[11] The active agent behind these developments was none other than the research process itself, stimulated as it had been by federal largesse. The very proliferation of research, specialized academic knowledge, and graduate education seemed to have overwhelmed the organizational and financial ecology of these institutions. The emerging sentiments toward research universities now wished to hold them to account for their apparent excesses.

Christopher Jencks and David Riesman called one facet of this phenomenon the "Academic Revolution" in a book of that title. By that phrase the authors meant the decades-long process by which the academic profession, led by faculty in the research universities, had attained virtual autonomy over the conditions of their own existence. The result was an "academic imperium" by which they exercised hegemony over the values, the curriculum, and the institutional life of much of the rest of American higher education. The former consensus, which had applauded the expansion of research and its associated values, struck the authors as "appallingly complacent." Their own views were nuanced and not always consistent, as they freely admitted, but nevertheless expressed the growing sentiment that academic research had to a considerable extent lost touch with both the concerns of the real world and the intellectual needs of students.[12]

Jencks and Riesman depicted academic scientists and scholars as constituting just another self-interested profession, narrowly preoccupied with the internal matters of their own disciplines. To this end, they had shaped the graduate schools of arts and sciences into rigid disciplinary categories, which then exerted influence downward onto undergraduate education. At the leading institutions in the country, "university colleges" had adopted the goals, specialized curriculum, and pedagogical style of the graduate schools. While this approach benefited some small portion of students, the majority of undergraduates suffered from the depreciation of teaching, fragmented or esoteric courses, and the discouragement by the academic imperium of alternative models. Nor was all well at the graduate level: the authors regarded the graduate academic departments as "for the most part autotelic. They resent even being asked whether they produce significant benefits to society beyond the edification of their own members."[13] Jencks and Riesman advocated reforms aimed at broadening the corpus of academic knowledge and inducing academics to communicate with extramural constituencies; but they were not sanguine about such possibilities.

Another element of the emerging consensus was that the insatiable appetites of research universities had outstripped their financial resources. This perception could be invoked by critics to argue that universities ought to reform and restrain themselves, or by sympathizers who believed that the government ought to provide further aid so that they might extend their activities. Whether evidence of failure or accomplishment, the financial strains were apparent by the last half of the decade. In 1966, for example, the Carnegie Corporation felt that conditions warranted a comprehensive study of higher education finance. This need was the impetus for establishing the Carnegie Commission on Higher Education, and finance was indeed the first topic it addressed before embracing a far larger agenda.[14]

One of the Commission's first publications was an analysis of research university finances by William Bowen, provost and later president of Princeton. He began by establishing the long-term record on costs per student at three private universities. These costs had doubled in each postwar decade, and indeed had increased at this same rate in other 'normal' periods. The reason that cost increases in higher education exceeded those in the economy at large Bowen attributed to the basic technology of the enterprise. In university teaching there were scant opportunities for growth in productivity, yet such growth elsewhere in the economy spurred increases in the standard of living that had to be matched in university salaries. The result was a steady real rise in the costs of higher education. This situation had been exacerbated for research universities by the relative increase in graduate education, which was inherently more costly. Bowen then extrapolated university income and expenditures for the next decade using reasonable estimates based on postwar trends. The results showed an income shortfall of between 30 and 40 percent by 1975. Clearly, for these universities to remain in the fast lane of development, additional sources of fuel would be needed. For Bowen, anything less was unthinkable for the private research universities about which he wrote.[15]

While these two works depicted macroscopic trends in the university research system, a third contemporaneous volume by Jacques Barzun, provost of Columbia, elucidated how the day-to-day activities of major research universities conspired to produce these results. The institution that Clark Kerr judged aborning five years before had, according to Barzun, now emerged as a distinctive entity—the new American university. A beehive of frenetic activity, this new university was engaged in a perpetual, headlong rush to satisfy the desires of faculty, students, donors, patrons, surrounding communities, and the public at large. The very conjuncture of these manifold activities produced apparent contradictions: the proliferation of courses led to a flight from teaching; and burgeoning incomes produced an ineluctable poverty. Like the sorcerer's apprentice, the research universities in their golden age seemed about to be overwhelmed by the forces they had unleashed.[16]

In order to manage its swollen affairs, the new university had vastly expanded its administrative structure. Even then, the control exercised by the administration remained tenuous, chiefly because individual faculty members wielded substantial autonomous power by virtue of their academic stature and the potential demand for their services from other institutions. Their bargaining leverage assured that the administration would minister to their ambitions: all research possibilities would be accepted, some of the 'essential' new faculty would be hired, most new specialized courses would be approved, and teaching loads would be bid down. These faculty did not necessarily disdain teaching, but the structure of incremental demands upon their time made by scholarly activities, research patrons, and the administrative work of university and department meant that "students come last." Another incremental process produced crescive expansion of the university's financial obligations. Entrepreneurial faculty had to be appeased, research grants did not cover their full costs, additional students cost more than they were charged, and even gifts left the universities with expenses, such as building maintenance, over and above the amounts received. Reconciling these obligations with uncertain flows of revenue made the preparation of budgets, even when systematized within the new administrative structure, akin to "trapeze work."[17]

In order to cope with the shortcomings of the new university, Barzun offered essentially normative recommendations, as indeed did the other authors.[18] As historical evidence, however, what they described is of greater interest than what they prescribed, for their advice foretold little of future events. The issues that they identified, on the other hand, were fundamental to the development of research universities. The decade of the 1960s had witnessed monumental progress in the growth and dispersion of research funding, the competition for institutional prestige, and the expansion of graduate education. It was precisely the achievements of these years that provoked the crisis that confronted research universities at the end of the decade.

2. Changing Patterns of Research and New Research Universities

Growth provided opportunity for the research universities in the post-Sputnik era—so much so that it became an imperative felt throughout the university sector. The established prewar research universities were pressured by their faculties to take advantage of the new abundance by expanding departments, facilities, and graduate programs. For the second tier of universities, conditions now permitted the emulation of more prestigious models. Beyond them, particularly among newer, expanding state institutions, it was possible to enhance academic status by establishing doctoral programs and attracting funds for research. The research university ideal was a powerful magnet during these years: it not only embodied those academic traits held in highest esteem, but also encouraged behavior that was richly rewarded by the university research economy.

The research university ideal was well understood in American higher education. It was evident, with minor variations, in the development strategies of Stanford, UCLA, and Pittsburgh; and the same goals were pursued in other institutions, sooner or later, with varying degrees of determination and success. At bottom, the behavior that propelled this ideal was embodied in the incentives of individual faculty and departments. In such matters as the numbers, qualifications, and accomplishments of faculty, most institutions were able to make substantial absolute improvements during the 1960s. But gaining ground on their competitors—rising in the university hierarchy—proved a more difficult task.

The three most relevant measures for comparing research universities are the level of research expenditures, the quality of the faculty in the eyes of their peers, and the prestige and size of doctoral programs. These factors are strongly inter-related. They are also composites—aggregations of the grants received by professors or the reputations of individual scholars. The realities behind these factors vary across departments, as does the relative standing of units within a university. Despite such variation, each research university is also characterized by a more fundamental kind of unity derived from its traditions, leadership, and resources. This overall institutional character is generally more enduring than that of individual parts.

When the Seaborg Report called for a doubling of the number of "first-rate centers of academic science,"[1] the meaning of that phrase was assumed to be evident. In fact, it concealed one of the principal ambiguities of the university research system. The identity of the existing first-rate centers was apparent: the open question at the time was which institutions might join the anointed as future research universities.

At the time of Sputnik, the sixteen established prewar research universities still occupied the top of the academic prestige hierarchy.[2] (cf. Table 16) The only new campus to join this august company was UCLA; the only member in danger of slipping out was Johns Hopkins, which remained quite small outside biomedical fields. In the second tier of universities, those recognized for academic strengths were Indiana, Northwestern, Ohio State, Duke, and New York universities, as well as the universities of Washington (Seattle) and Texas. Beyond these 24 institutions, the relative achievements or potential of other would-be research universities was difficult to judge.[3]

These same prewar research universities, plus UCLA, received the largest amounts of federal research funding at the beginning of the 1960s. All except specialized Caltech were among the top twenty recipients. Their dominance in terms of research funding, however, was less certain and less enduring than their academic prestige. The relationship between overall academic standing and the amount of research funding was actually rather loose. Departments in the humanities and social sciences made appreciable contributions to institutional reputation, for example, but received comparatively little outside funding. The bulk of research funds was directed toward biomedical sciences, engineering, physical sciences, and agriculture. It was not unusual for universities to house special programs in a single area that considerably inflated their funding totals. Research expenditures for individual institutions thus reflected the disparate emphases of federal agencies. Overall, however, the dominance of the leading universities was waning with time.

From the immediate postwar era to the present, a secular process of increasing dispersion of university research has been underway, as the following figures indicate:[4]

TABLE 12. Federal R&D Obligations to Ten Largest Recipients (%)

1952	1958	1968	1978	1988
43.4	37.0	27.7	22.7	21.5

In general, university research capacity has consistently widened over these four decades, although the processes at work have not acted uniformly. The decline from the extreme concentrations following the war was the result of the continual development of additional major research universities, as well as the receding prominence of large Pentagon projects, some of which were reclassified. After Sputnik, federal policies explicitly and implicitly encouraged greater dispersion. More research funding, a rising supply of trained researchers, and the expansion of faculties—all assisted ambitious universities to increase sponsored research. Science development programs and institutional support provided additional and more direct incentives. As a result, a substantial portion of the overall lessening of concentration in research occurred in the post-Sputnik decade.

A more detailed picture of the changing patterns of distribution in the university research system shows that the twenty-five universities receiving the most federal research funds experienced an overall decrease in research share, with the largest performers suffering the greatest relative loss (Table 13). The gains registered by those institutions in positions 26 and lower were spread rather evenly. On the whole, this pattern can be partly explained by the relative abundance of research funds, which made it far easier for large numbers of institutions to obtain grants and contracts. These new entrants to the system *ipso facto* lessened the concentration. Indeed, the share lost by the ten largest performers roughly equals that gained by smaller research performers in positions 51 and lower. In addition, the 'new' money injected into the research system tended to be distributed more widely than the 'old' programmatic funds. For example, the ten universities receiving the most research funding from the Department of Defense claimed 40 percent of its total, but the corresponding figure for HEW was 26 percent (1968).

Interestingly, the changed shape of the research hierarchy does not correspond with the transformation envisioned in the Seaborg Report. The contingent of new research universities might have been expected to occupy places 16

TABLE 13. Federal R&D Obligations by
Institutional Strata (%)[5]

Strata	1963–64	1972–73	+ / −
1–5	19.27%	16.00%	−3.27
6–10	12.39	11.21	−1.18
11–15	9.23	8.64	−0.59
16–20	7.31	6.76	−0.55
21–25	5.42	5.37	−0.05
26–30	4.56	4.69	+0.13
31–35	3.78	4.15	+0.37
36–40	3.39	3.64	+0.25
41–45	3.09	3.28	+0.19
46–50	2.68	2.90	+0.22
51–	28.88	33.36	+4.48
Total	100.00	100.00	0.00

to 35, but these ranks showed no gain at all in research share. Instead, the research funds lost by the leaders seemed to go to the small performers—those hardly likely to become the next "first-rate" centers. The evolution of the research university system thus seemed to contravene one of the central policies of the 1960s.

The institutional development programs of the Ford Foundation and the science development programs of the various federal agencies all had the same essential purpose of strengthening and broadening the research base of American universities.[6] The different programs varied widely, however, in their approach and their incidence. The Ford Foundation Challenge Grants Program aimed at strengthening institutions as a whole and was limited to the private sector. It allowed the greatest latitude for use of the funds, and also required substantial matching funds. NSF sought for the most part to enhance core scientific departments on the premise that these were the key to developing research capacities throughout an institution. Like Ford, NSF also looked for strong institutional commitments toward these same ends. NASA and the Department of Defense sowed their seed money most widely in order to gain access to academic scientists and to initiate research programs that met their special needs. All together, these programs injected over $800 million into universities, a sum approximating the total federal support for academic research in 1963 (Table 14). The peak of these commitments occurred from 1965 to 1968, when the Ford Foundation efforts were concluding and the largest federal programs were in full operation.

Some of these programs have been evaluated individually,[7] but there has been no effort to estimate the extent to which they collectively achieved their intended results. One possible answer is provided in Table 15. There the share of total federal research funding for 1963–64 and 1972–73 is compared for 36 developing institutions that receive more than $6 million from these programs. (Some first-tier research universities also qualified for development funds, owing to the diverse criteria of these different programs.) These 36 universities contain most of the institutions from which the new generation of research universities could be expected to emerge. The performance of fourteen other comparable

TABLE 14. University Development Programs of the 1960s[8]

	Years	Amount ($000)	Number of Recipients
Ford Foundation Engineering Dev.	1958–66	48,539	20
Ford Foundation Challenge Grants	1960–67	197,500	15
NASA Sustaining University	1962–71	221,473	175
NSF: University Science Dev.	1965–71	179,590	32
NSF: Special Science Dev.	1966–71	11,937	11
NSF: Departmental Sci. Dev.	1967–71	42,688	62
Dept. of Defense: THEMIS	1967–71	94,490	82
NIH: Health Sci. Advancement	1966–74	26,250	11
Total	1958–74	822,467	216

TABLE 15. Universities Receiving >$6,000,000 in Science Development Funds: Change in Research Share 1963-1973[9]

Institutions	Grants for Dev.	Share 1963-64	Share 1972-73	% Change
Private Universities				
Washington U.	*35,829	0.93%	1.29%	24%
New York U.	*34,108	1.92	1.29	−33
Vanderbilt	*24,626	0.48	0.58	21
Case Western Reserve	24,625	0.81	0.77	− 4
U. of Southern Cal.	*24,469	0.92	1.13	22
Notre Dame	*18,902	0.25	<0.20	<−20
Duke	*15,052	1.04	1.01	− 3
Brandeis	*14,275	0.30	<0.22	<−27
Brown	*13,692	0.67	0.42	−37
Tulane	*11,153	0.68	0.40	−41
Rochester	8,488	1.09	1.00	− 8
Denver	*8,133	0.52	0.21	−60
Illinois Inst. Tech.	7,597	0.63	0.29	−54
Emory	*6,759	0.35	0.43	12
Rensselear Poly. Inst.	6,701	0.33	<0.18	<−45
Poly. Inst. of Brooklyn	6,408	0.47	0.15	−68
State Universities				
U. of Virginia	11,912	0.43	0.44	2
U. of Florida	11,808	0.71	0.70	− 1
U. of Arizona	11,250	0.54	0.60	8
Indiana	11,085	0.76	0.38	−50
Purdue	10,940	0.87	0.92	6
Florida State	9,995	0.38	0.28	−26
U. of Maryland	9,967	1.16	0.65	−44
U. of Colorado	9,807	0.79	1.09	38
U. of Pittsburgh	9,319	1.12	0.77	−31
U. of Iowa	9,024	0.64	0.68	6
U. of Oregon	8,845	0.63	0.33	−48
Colorado State	8,608	0.34	0.61	79
U. of Washington	8,529	1.64	2.50	52
U. of Kansas	7,902	0.50	0.49	− 2
N. Carolina State	7,706	0.39	0.41	5
U. of N. Carolina	7,428	0.58	0.85	47
Michigan State	7,132	0.54	0.65	20
U. of Texas	6,934	1.51	0.84	−44
Texas A & M	6,668	0.45	0.59	31
Georgia Tech	6,468	0.29	0.33	14

*Includes Ford Foundation Challenge Grants

Degree of Change	−30+%	−30−10%	±10%	+10−30%	+30+%
Private institutions	7	2	3	4	0
Public institutions	5	1	7	2	5
Other institutions†	4	3	0	5	2

†Institutions of the same type receiving <$6,000,000.

institutions is given at the bottom of Table 15. Judging from the results, the collective wisdom of these different programs appears to have been highly fallible. Out of 36 institutions, twelve are among the most dismal performers from the early sixties to the early seventies, suffering declines in their share of research in excess of 30 percent; another three show moderate declines (− 30–10%); ten show little change (± <10%); six show moderate increases (+ 10–30%); and just five show considerable relative growth (+ > 30%). On balance, this group performed worse than institutions with comparable research programs that received less than $6 million in development funds.

The comparison made here between science development programs and subsequent research funding is necessarily crude. Science development aid may have assisted the departments to which it was directed without having a noticeable effect on total research funding. Also, several of the unimpressive performers would later improve their research stature considerably—notably Arizona, Texas, and Georgia Tech. Still, when one considers that these 36 universities received 55 percent of the science development funds, and that the results were somewhat worse than might have been expected from using a dart board for selection, it seems likely that the university research system was changing in ways that had not been anticipated by these programs.

A depiction of the relation between the overall quality of institutions and changes in the quantity of research during the 1960s is given in Table 16. There the changes in research share given in the previous table are portrayed for a wider sampling of universities. The quality strata reflect contemporary perceptions.[10] The first level consists of the top tier of prewar research universities plus UCLA. The next group contains those that were closest to the top institutions in terms of strong departments. The third level consists of the strongest emerging, or would-be research universities; while the fourth level contains similar, but somewhat weaker, institutions. Those schools that had notable programs only in engineering are listed separately, although they generally correspond with level four. These 63 institutions include 32 of those listed in Table 15, the 16 prewar research universities, and the 14 significant research performers from Table 15 receiving under $6 million in development funds. Once again, the universities that might have been expected to become the next research universities (Levels 2 & 3) largely experienced declines in their research shares. Clearly, factors other than relative position in the academic hierarchy affected academic development.

The institutions that increased their research share substantially were all publicly controlled. The strongest of this group academically were the universities of Washington and North Carolina. By the mid-sixties Washington had become a true heavyweight in research expenditures, while North Carolina, with little in engineering or the physical sciences, received most of its funding for medical research. UC Davis had emerged by this date as another potent arm of the University of California, while Colorado and Utah were advancing as regional research universities. Texas A&M was also expanding its research activities, mostly in engineering and agriculture.

The institutions showing a moderate increase in research share were split between the public (7) and the private (6) sectors. Among the privates, however,

TABLE 16. Change in Research Share, 1963–64 to 1972–73, by Quality Level of Graduate Faculties (1964)

Degree of Change	−30+%	−30−10%	±10%	+10−30%	+30+%
Level 1 (17)	Chicago Columbia Illinois Michigan Princeton	Berkeley Harvard Penn UCLA	Cornell Johns Hopk. Minnesota Stanford Yale MIT, Caltech	Wisconsin	
Level 2 (11)	Brown Indiana NYU Texas	N'Western Ohio St.	Duke Purdue	Wash. U.	N. Carolina U. of Wash.
Level 3 (13)	Iowa St. Oregon Pitt Syracuse	Brandeis Rutgers	Iowa Kansas Rochester Case Western	Mich. St. Penn St.	UC Davis
Level 4 (12)	Maryland Tulane		Florida Virginia	Emory Oregon St. Rice SouthernCal Vanderbilt Yeshiva	Colorado Utah
Engineering (10)	IIT Brookl. Poly CarnegieTech RPI Tennessee		NC State	Arizona GeorgiaTech Missouri	Texas A&M
63 Insts.	20	8	16	13	6

four received research funds almost exclusively in biomedical fields (Washington U., Vanderbilt, Emory, and Yeshiva). Southern California also had a large medical school, although Rice did not. Four of these private schools were beneficiaries of Challenge Grants from the Ford Foundation (Table 15)—the only such recipients to show gains in research share. Among public institutions, Wisconsin was the single established research university to advance its reputation and research support. At the second level, Penn State and Michigan State showed promise as advancing institutions, although the latter was stronger at the time. The remaining three public institutions—Arizona, Missouri, and Georgia Tech—were not at this time major performers of research.

The private sector was overrepresented among those losing the greatest research share (12 of 20). Princeton and Chicago retained their eminence despite relative reductions, but Columbia's reputation was slipping noticeably. The small private engineering schools as a group were the greatest losers of research share, most likely because of the diminished role of research funding from the

Pentagon. The remaining five private universities all had narrowly based research programs, and they found it difficult to keep pace with other universities. The woes of Pitt, which forced it to become a public university, have been detailed in Chapter 5. The weakness in the public sector, on the other hand, was somewhat less than it appeared. Illinois, Indiana, and Texas all suffered from divesting medical schools, and Michigan shed a facility for defense research; however, changes in their research shares would have been negative in any case. Of the others, Oregon once appeared to be a rising university.

The data on changes in institutional research shares provide a snapshot of the development of the university research system for a single ten-year period. This span of time was nevertheless fateful for research universities. The first half-decade represented the second leg of the post-Sputnik expansion, while the next five years was characterized by consolidation of previous gains and adjustment to leaner times. During the initial period, research-linked institutional aid was more readily available than anytime before or since. Federal support for academic research doubled in current dollars during these years, so that an institution had to double its intake of these funds just to maintain its relative position. The majority of the institutions discussed here enlarged their enrollments, their faculties and their incomes; but it was difficult to get ahead. Three major trends of this era help to account for the pattern of changes in research share.

First, the continued dispersion of research funding was produced by a combination of public policy and institutional response. In Washington, as indicated in the previous chapter, the impulse of federal agencies to spread widely both research funding and research-linked aid was partly a self-imposed mission and partly a response to increasing pressures emanating from Congress and the White House. But it meant that the policy implied by the Seaborg Report of selectively building up a handful of institutions was not politically feasible. This may not have been too much of a loss: the Ford Foundation's attempt selectively to strengthen institutions had not met with great success. The alternative approach that was followed, however, produced the results seen above: science development programs touched 216 institutions (Table 14); and the 63 strongest research universities (Table 16) on balance saw their share of the federal research economy diminish. Less visibly, federal encouragement of dispersion encouraged large numbers of smaller institutions to emulate the research university ideal. The desirability of this course was called into question when these policies were terminated and research funds stagnated.[11]

Second, the federal policy that most shaped the pattern of academic research was the vast expansion of biomedical research by NIH. At the beginning of the 1970s more than half of federal research funds were devoted to the life sciences. Universities with research-oriented medical schools benefited from this "NIH effect." A good number of the universities that increased their research share, then, were capitalizing on the growth of biomedical research, and conversely, universities without medical schools were less likely to increase their relative shares.

The third trend was the greater development of public as opposed to private universities. This result stemmed from basic differences between the two sectors.

Few private institutions embraced the expansion of research as an end in itself. They tended to be more sensitive to enhancing the prestige of both their graduate programs and their undergraduate colleges. They also possessed limited financial resources with which to absorb the substantial overhead costs associated with research. Private universities consequently tended to limit their growth—in enrollments, in faculty, and indirectly in research commitments. Public higher education, on the other hand, expanded vastly during the 1960s. Almost every state created or developed at least one additional institution as a research university. This process will be examined in the following section; but generally, rapid enrollment growth and the infusion of large amounts of resources gave developing public universities unparalleled opportunities to advance in the university research system.

In the post-Sputnik environment, funding for research was, relatively speaking, the least constrictive input to the research process. Somewhat more difficult to obtain were competent scholars and scientists to perform research. In even shorter supply were highly qualified graduate students who were destined to become the next generation of university researchers. Most problematic in the long run was the institutional funding base that was required to initiate and sustain qualitative improvement. In the quest for quality, the university research system of the 1960s was shaped by these constraints as well as by the comparative abundance existing in the research economy.

3. Academic Quality and Institutional Development

The fact that some universities are better than others, Bernard Berelson remarked, was "a fact of life in graduate education that, like other facts of life, is seldom discussed openly, even though it is of crucial importance."[1] Such reticence was due to the controversy inherent in the subject. The two principal objections to assessing the quality of departments or institutions were that it could not be done accurately, so that the results would not be valid, or that it should not be done at all, because it created invidious distinctions. As a result, few efforts have systematically addressed this central 'fact of life' of American universities.

The first explicit classification of colleges and universities was done by the Bureau of Education before World War I, but it provoked angry complaints and was never published.[2] When Raymond Hughes privately conducted and published the first regular ranking of academic departments in 1925, his study aroused both interest and criticism. In 1934 he repeated the survey under the auspices of the ACE, but this time only listed departments as either distinguished or adequate in order to deflect complaints.[3] The AAU conducted a rating after World War II, but some universities refused to cooperate. The results were never published and apparently have been lost.[4] Recent efforts, like *An Assessment of Research-Doctoral Programs in the United States* (1982), bear the scars of past controversy. Although its statistical techniques were state-of-the-art, the authors were nevertheless defensive about rating academic programs at all, and refrained from listing departments by rank. Afterward, opinion swung back to the position that no useful purpose would be served by updating the quality rating of American universities.[5] This attitude stands in marked contrast to the 1960s, when improving graduate education was a national priority and qualitative evaluation was seen as contributing to that end.

The academic ratings done by Heyward Keniston in 1957 were the first to appear in a quarter of a century.[6] They were undertaken as part of an internal review of graduate education at the University of Pennsylvania and were consequently limited to the institutions with which Penn wished to compare itself. The Keniston ratings nevertheless fulfilled an important need and were widely utilized. But their narrowness was also apparent. The American Council on Education soon filled this lacuna by asking Allan Cartter to conduct the first of the comprehensive peer assessments of the quality of university departments.[7]

The importance of the Cartter study corresponds with the reasons that inspired it. First was the broad coverage: more than 4000 respondants evaluated 1663 departments in 106 universities. All but the most marginal producers of Ph.D.s in arts, sciences, and engineering (29 disciplines) were thus included. For the first time administrators, department heads, and faculty throughout American universities could judge their relative standing.[8]

Second, to avoid the well-known criticisms of other ratings, Cartter sought to perfect the techniques of subjective, reputational assessment. To clarify what was being judged, respondents were asked to rate the quality of both faculty and graduate programs; to identify bias, the responses were compared by region and by type of respondent (department head, senior and junior faculty); and for consistency the results were measured against other departmental ratings where they existed. In all these tests the study demonstrated a high degree of reliability. Although one might cavil with individual findings, there could be little doubt that these ratings reflected the informed opinion of university faculty.

Third, given the rapid evolution of American universities in the mid-sixties, the study provided an up-to-date evaluation of the status of departments. The need for such information had by then come to be regarded as axiomatic. Moreover, the sponsors of the study did not want the results to become 'written in stone.' They planned from the outset to conduct a sequel study within five years. In due course, the Roose-Anderson *Rating of Graduate Programs* appeared in 1970.[9] The Cartter study thus injected a new element into the underlying competition for academic prestige. Now the funders of research and science development programs had reliable indices of the relative strengths of programs. On the university side, administrators and department heads had ammunition with which to argue for greater resources, whether to counter weakness or to build upon strength. The fact that a second evaluation was in the offing could hardly help but accentuate the sense of competition. These studies had the unmistakable effect of focusing even greater attention onto graduate education and research.[10]

The Roose-Anderson study, when it appeared, showed significant positive changes in the departments that had been rated five years earlier. Thirty percent of the departments registered appreciable absolute increases in their scores, while just 7 percent declined. The physical sciences and engineering were the most uniformly positive, with just 2 percent backsliding. The biological sciences showed the most mixed results (13% declining). The percentage of advancing departments, however, was generally consistent across disciplinary groups.[11] In all likelihood, this improvement reflected the increased resources that had been devoted to building departments and expanding research capacities. In that respect the interval between the two studies (1964–69) constituted just one segment of a longer evolution. On the other hand, some of those resources were devoted to the establishment of new doctoral programs, predominantly at the less mature universities. These programs typically entered at the bottom of the status ladder, 58 percent being rated in the lowest category.

The rankings were predicated on the assumption that academics understood and recognized the nature of academic quality; but just what factors determined this quality was a critical matter. Allan Cartter specifically addressed this question in his study.[12] Some factors, like the number of fellowship holders choosing a particular department, were reflections of reputation. Others, like strong neighboring departments and good libraries, were similar products. The single causal factor that he explored was the high cost of achieving and maintaining quality departments. A direct correspondence existed between average faculty salaries and overall institutional ratings. It clearly required good salaries to attract and retain eminent faculty. How universities managed to meet these costs, though, was more complicated.

The crude data on institutional income that Cartter examined revealed two groups among the highly rated (25) universities. The private universities tended to be small and to have relatively high income per student; the larger state universities achieved eminence with lower per-student income, but these ratios were still generally higher than those at less distinguished public institutions. Cartter hypothesized that when enrollments exceeded the equivalent of 20,000 undergraduates economies of scale were possible in the attainment of quality; that is, additional students could be given high quality education at a lower unit cost. For the less distinguished universities, however, such economies of scale were not apparent. Enrollment growth seemingly could result in additional resources for qualitative improvement, but there was no certainty that it would.

Universities followed different paths—out of choice and out of necessity—as they attempted to maximize prestige within the research system, to expand their incomes, and to meet obligations to their several constituencies.[13] The data offered in Tables 17–20 cover several of the key variables related to the prestige and research capacity of four universities over more than two decades.[14] Graduate enrollments and number of Ph.D.s awarded are indicative of the size of graduate programs. The peculiar dynamics of graduate education will be examined in the next section, where it will be apparent that size is strongly associated with quality (Table 21). The percentage of graduate and professional enrollments indicates the mix of pre- and post-baccalaureate teaching. No optimal mix is apparent, but some base of undergraduate education was needed to support the faculty who taught graduate students. Full professors, in particular, were the

TABLE 17. Princeton, 1955–1977

	Graduate Enrollment	Percent Graduate	Ph.D.s Awarded	Full Professors	Instruction $/Student (1967$)
1955	520	14.9	101	140	1130
1959	758	20.4	118	165	1400
1962	956	23.4	167	178	n/a
1967	1543	32.4	215	238	2023
1972	1421	25.4	262	266	2075
1977	1501	24.7	223	284	2341

critical scarce input to research and graduate education. Their numbers and their salaries reflected the quality level that each university could afford. Faculty salaries and departmental expenses generally were the chief components of the instructional budget. This was the core expenditure of universities and the one most indicative of the costs of quality that Cartter had attempted to measure. Instructional expenditures are expressed here in constant dollars on a per-student basis. This figure reflects a different mix of activities at each institution. As with all these data, relative change over time is most revealing, and comparisons of the extent of change among institutions are more meaningful than comparisons of any absolute numbers.

Princeton traditionally placed a preponderant emphasis on its undergraduate college, and owed its affluence to the generosity of those alumni. It cultivated a small, efficient, and prestigious graduate school, which before the war was limited to 250 students. Afterward, Princeton consciously decided to expand graduate education in keeping with the growth of sponsored research.[15] Graduate enrollments tripled in the twelve years after 1955, while the undergraduate college grew by just 10 percent. The growth in graduate education helped to drive an increase in the cost of education at Princeton: the number of full professors grew by 70 percent, and the instructional spending per student by almost 80 percent.

TABLE 18. Stanford, 1955–1977

	Graduate & Prof. Enrollment	Percent Graduate & Prof.	Ph.D.s Awarded	Full Professors (n/i med.)	Instruction $/Student (1967$)
1955	2358	32.2	168	161	706
1959	3157	37.5	197	210	1181
1962	3871	40.5	261	295	1828
1967	5386	47.6	498	353	2756
1972	4961	43.4	557	394	3266
1977	5199	44.4	460	450	3161

TABLE 19. Michigan State University, 1955–1977

	Graduate & Prof. Enrollment	Percent Graduate & Prof.	Ph.D.s Awarded	Full Professors (n/i med.)	Instruction $/Student (1967$)
1955	1635	10.5	137	221	862
1959	3638	18.6	145	256	959
1962	5048	20.0	210	412	903
1967	10025	24.2	423	653	944
1972	9993	22.4	633	842	1071
1977	11317	23.9	504	921	1001

The rapid expansion of the mid-sixties and its attendant costs forced Princeton in time to reevaluate its policies. In a major decision, it decided to expand the undergraduate college by admitting women (see Chapter 8). Graduate education was deliberately scaled back in the early 1970s, although the momentum of growth in Ph.D.s and professorial appointments continued. In keeping with this reduction, growth of research funding was well below average (Table 16). Princeton maintained its financial position, with some difficulty, during the early 1970s, and was modestly stronger by 1977. Princeton was above all a conservative institution: it sought to keep its relative position in the prestige hierarchy, while also preserving the character and the stature of its undergraduate college. To accomplish these ends it had to expand greatly during the post-Sputnik era, and then adopt a protective strategy to preserve the financial strength on which its attainments rested.[16]

The rise of Stanford has already been described, at least in its initial phases. The figures given here show the underpinnings of its substantial advancement. In 1955 it was twice the size of Princeton, but had only a few more full professors. Graduate enrollment grew from under a third to almost half of the student body by 1967. Undergraduate enrollment grew modestly during this period, as Stanford sought to raise the prestige and selectivity of its undergraduate college as well. The rise in instructional spending was meteoric, reflecting the success in

TABLE 20. University of Arizona, 1955–1977

	Graduate & Prof. Enrollment	Percent Graduate & Prof.	Ph.D.s Awarded	Full Professors (n/i med.)	Instruction $/Student (1967$)
1955	354	6.2	7	120	506
1959	1456	13.6	17	210	560
1962	2300	14.6	40	293	581
1967	3856	18.0	154	396	658
1972	5481	20.6	212	610	865
1977	6531	22.6	232	596	1063

fund raising. These funds allowed Stanford to hire additional full professors to build its "steeples of excellence." The momentum of Stanford's advancement continued into the 1970s, despite a leveling of graduate enrollments. Instructional spending, however, plateaued during the middle of the decade, before again growing in the 1980s.

John A. Hannah, the longtime president of Michigan State University (1941–69), held an unwavering belief that his institution should provide services to the community and educational opportunities to the largest possible number of people.[17] In implementing this philosophy, Hannah endured the barbs of academic purists like Robert Maynard Hutchins, who ridiculed a degree course in Packaging. But this approach eventually made Michigan State a university of over 40,000 students—one of the largest in the country. It also put Michigan State at the center of the explosion of graduate education. By 1970 it was the sixth largest producer of Ph.D.s in the country. Unlike the other large producers, which were all prewar research universities, its doctorates were concentrated in applied and professional subjects. The university departments with the highest national standing, like Hotel and Restaurant Management, tended to be in those areas; but few of its departments in arts and sciences achieved national rank.

Michigan State was nevertheless perceived to be an advancing and promising research university in the 1960s. It relied predominantly on growth to build its faculty and its graduate programs. Real spending per student increased only modestly from the 1950s to the 1970s, so more students, predominantly undergraduates, were required to generate the income for more faculty. But the course of development that Hannah pursued made it difficult to navagate the transition from quantity to quality. Professorial salaries were well below those of the established research universities, which meant that the university could recruit few academic stars. It hired instead chiefly at junior levels. The continued growth in full professors thus represents the effects of the promotion pipeline rather than determined faculty-building.[18] Given the Michigan State belief in service and access, its graduate enrollments were sensitive to market fluctuations. Even at the peak of the boom in graduate study, only 45 percent of the Michigan State graduate students were full time, and that figure declined thereafter. If only full-time students are considered, Michigan State was 85–90 percent undergraduate. The stagnation in relative expenditures that affected Michigan State in the 1970s was typical of the public research universities of the Midwest. A combination of a soft regional economy and the rationalization of state funding formulae put a cap on spending levels at these institutions.

The University of Arizona, in contrast, was an institution that continued to advance through the 1970s, and for that reason its development will be examined in the next chapter. As a public university Arizona too relied on enrollment growth for the resources to build departments. Its pattern of development indicates how crucial the golden-age conditions of the 1960s were in providing the initial impetus that allowed it to become a research university. In this respect, Arizona was one of the principal beneficiaries of the dispersion of research funding. More important, though, the steady expansion of graduate education, professors, and expenditures permitted increases in academic quality. Just as Michigan State exemplified the stagnation of midwestern universities, Arizona typified the flowering of the Sun Belt states in the 1970s.

These four patterns of development are only partially representative of the experiences of research universities. If similar statistics were compiled for other research universities, they would reveal almost endless variations in timing and emphasis on the basic themes just described. Private universities wished to cultivate selective and prestigious undergraduate colleges, but allowed greater relative expansion of their graduate programs. They were far more sensitive than their public counterparts to the financial consequences of these programs, and as revenues leveled off, they were the first to begin cutting back. Public universities all depended in part on the growth of undergraduate education to build the academic departments that sustained graduate education and research. When their campuses could expand no further, they tended to behave somewhat like private institutions by emphasizing graduate programs.[19] The public universities as a whole nevertheless tended to be sensitive in their actions to student demand, which remained strong even after funding for research and graduate education passed its peak.

Both public and private universities sought in their own individual ways to enhance the absolute quality of their faculty and programs, which is what mattered for everyday life on campus. Institutions also sought improvement relative to their peers when that was possible. The figures given in the previous tables indicate that absolute improvement should have occurred. Universities generally experienced real increases in expenditures that outpaced growth in enrollments. These greater resources permitted them to hire more faculty with better credentials and preparation, as well as to provide them with assistance for research and scholarship. Thus, the real improvements in university departments reported by the Roose-Anderson Report should have come as no surprise. These gains represented the culmination of developments begun in the 1950s. Certainly since Sputnik, universities found it rewarding to augment and improve their research capacities. Only at the end of the 1960s did changes in the research economy call that axiom of the university research system into doubt. The actual adjustments that this required were in most cases prolonged and incremental. Graduate education, however, was the part of the university most attuned to continued growth. As the most sensitive barometer of conditions in the system, its reactions to the changing climate were most dramatic.

4. Graduate Education in the 1960s

American universities produced about 3000 earned doctorates per year on the eve of World War II.[1] After the dislocations of the war and its aftermath, that figure rose rapidly to a plateau of just under 9000 doctorates in the mid-fifties. The size of doctoral cohorts then climbed steeply, reaching another plateau above 33,000 in the mid-seventies. The 34,790 degrees awarded in 1973 were not surpassed for half a generation.[2] The pre-Sputnik level of doctoral awards was recognized as inadequate for the needs of the academic profession, but the level reached in the 1970s, it was equally apparent, was excessive. Conditions surrounding one of the Academy's slowest processes evolved with disconcerting speed.

Even before Sputnik the country faced a shortage of qualified college teachers. One reason was demographics: by 1957 the baby-boom cohorts had already filled the nation's elementary schools and the enrollment boom of the 1960s could readily be foreseen. A second reason was the limited number of faculty with doctorates—the desirable qualification for teaching at the college level. A survey in 1953 estimated that just 40.5 percent of college teachers possessed doctorates, while roughly 30 percent of new entrants to the profession had their final degree. These facts were publicized in biennial reports from the National Education Association (1955–65) and gave rise to the conviction, which persisted into the late 1960s, that a crisis was at hand: a vastly larger number of doctorates were thought to be needed to avoid a decline in the quality of college instruction.[3]

More doctorates and more teachers were undoubtedly needed, but the sense of crisis was overdone at first, and then persisted far too long. Bernard Berelson had made a dispassionate assessment of this question in his 1960 study of graduate education and concluded that the talk of crisis was "unwarranted and misleading."[4] Berelson argued that the universities would produce a sufficient number of doctorates without major changes in their programs, and he further pointed out that the higher education system had considerable freedom of maneuver to adapt to the existing supply. This view was consistently ignored, however, in favor of the crisis consensus. A second challenge was offered by Allan Cartter in the middle of the decade.[5] Cartter found that educational standards, as measured by college teachers with doctorates, had not been deteriorating at all—by the early 1960s the proportion had risen ten percentage points, surpassing 50 percent. The statistics supporting the crisis view, it seems, were ignoring the substantial number of new teachers who completed their doctorates *after* taking an academic post. In addition, non-degree holders exited college teaching positions at twice the rate of those having doctorates.

Cartter argued this case for several years as "a missionary for what . . . seemed like a radical point of view," but he had little success in shaking the consensus. During these years, though, the numerical relationships began to shift. Doctoral awards were increasing by double-digit percentages, while birth rates had already turned down. In 1970 Cartter was able to demonstrate conclusively that universities would soon graduate more doctorates than could possibly be absorbed into the academic profession. Even then, the expansionist mentality that had been induced by fears of faculty shortages died hard. Coeval projections foresaw from 50,000 to 77,000 annual doctoral degrees awarded by the end of the 1970s.[6]

Throughout the 1960s, the shortage of college teachers provided a powerful incentive for individual universities to do well for themselves by doing good for the country. Establishing or expanding doctoral programs raised the prestige of an institution, allowed it to recruit and retain better faculty, encouraged research, qualified it for special forms of federal aid, and, especially for state schools, justified appeals for increased resources. As long as taxpayers were willing to foot the bill, there were few negatives associated with entering the doctoral lists.

Expansion had in fact been occurring ever since the war. In 1949 just over 100 regular universities awarded doctoral degrees. By 1970, after doctorates had expanded almost sixfold, the number of doctoral institutions had doubled. At least 35 universities conferred their first doctorates in the 1950s and 45 more in the 1960s.[7] Many of the new postwar entrants were graduating a significant number of doctorates by 1970: e.g. the University of Utah (first Ph.D. 1947), 248 in 1970; Florida State (1952), 286; Southern Illinois (1959), 129. They and others like them were clearly important contributors to the rise of doctorates from the 9000-degree level in 1958 to the 33,000 plateau in 1972. Many other institutions would fall somewhere between Arizona and Michigan State (Tables 19 and 20) in raising their doctoral production from very low levels to hundreds per year. The prewar research universities, however, remained the volume producers: Berkeley, Columbia, Illinois, and Wisconsin all produced over 800 doctorates in 1970—nearly 3 percent of the total for each.

Institutions sought to address the shortage of doctorates in other ways. Since it was college teachers who were needed, suggestions were made throughout the decade to supplement the research-oriented Ph.D. with other kinds of doctoral degrees. Various doctorates for college teachers were proposed, and introduced at some institutions; but the concept was flawed and the timing was wrong. The notion of a teaching doctorate presupposed a separate market for faculty who would do no research. While many such positions actually existed in American higher education, it was somewhat demeaning to label them as such. By the end of the decade, when criticism of the research emphasis of the Ph.D. was highest, Ph.D.s were in ample supply. Teaching doctorates, which presumably required less time and effort, could scarcely compete with Ph.D.s in a unified market. Little actually came of this initiative, which was widely touted as a national policy, but resisted at the departmental level.[8]

While the higher education community was preoccupied with the number of doctorates, the research community was perpetually concerned with the quality of doctoral education. The quality issue extended beyond the ratio of teachers with Ph.D.s; it focused on who the future faculty members were and where they were trained. One persistent worry of the late 1950s was that the most able college graduates were not being attracted to graduate study. Another was that, due to the proliferation of graduate programs, a decreasing proportion of doctorates were emerging from the strongest programs. Berelson, for example, had shown that whereas the top fifteen universities of 1925 had graduated 76 percent of the doctorates, their share had declined to 43 percent in 1957 and was obviously headed lower.[9] Both the Ford Foundation and the federal government addressed these qualitative concerns by increasing support for graduate students.

The Woodrow Wilson Fellowship Program had evolved after the war, assisted by several foundations, to support first-year graduate students. In 1957 a Ford Foundation grant boosted the awards from 200 to 1000 recipients. Since the objective was to identify and support the most able students, Woodrow Wilson Fellows were chosen through a national process of nomination and screening. Because of more plentiful support in the natural sciences, the fellowships were concentrated in the humanities and social sciences. The awards were worth $2200 and could be taken at a university of choice. The institution was given an additional $2000, three-quarters of which was earmarked for further fellowship aid. Thus, Woodrow Wilsons were plums, financially and honorifically, for both the recipients and the schools at which they chose to study. Their expansion through Ford Foundation funding added appreciably to the number of 'free-choice' awards that were given to the country's most promising graduate students through national competitions.[10]

Federal programs for supporting graduate education were initially motivated by anxiety about international scientific competition, and thus were also shaped by qualitative concerns. These programs were expanded in two distinct stages. After Sputnik, the National Defense Education Act created fairly generous three-year fellowships for students destined for college teaching or international studies ($1500 per year, $4500 total). The National Science Foundation also used its increased funding to provide more fellowships to the extent that it was able. Federal fellowships outside of the biomedical fields, however, remained circumscribed into the early 1960s. These efforts received a new impetus from a 1962 Report from the President's Science Advisory Committee: "Meeting Manpower Needs in Science and Technology." This document argued, in essence, that federal programs like NASA were making great demands on the supply of highly trained (i.e. doctoral) engineers and physical scientists, and that the government must therefore accept the responsibility for expanding this supply without any dilution of quality. It accordingly recommended increased federal support for graduate education through both fellowships and facilities.[11] Steps were duly taken to formulate such a program in 1963, but they were not implemented until the Johnson Administration. NDEA was expanded; the NSF added a large program of traineeships; and NASA entered the field with fellowships aimed at producing 1000 doctorates per year. Overall, federal support for graduate education rose quickly to a peak in 1966–67, and then remained at a high level until 1970. The increase in the number of students supported was substantial. The NSF, for example, funded 845 predoctoral students in 1956, 2749 in 1962, and then 8156 in 1967. Overall, the number of students supported by federal fellowships and training programs reached 60,000 in the 1966 and 1967 academic years, compared with approximately 15,000 just five years before.[12] The nature of this kind of support was just as important as its incidence.

Federal agencies had to deal with two issues as they extended support for graduate education. The award of free-choice fellowships to highly qualified applicants allowed these recipients to matriculate at the leading departments in their fields. As they did so, the distribution of academic talent was skewed to an even greater extent than would ordinarily have occurred. In 1957, for example, Harvard received twice as many NSF fellows (129) as Berkeley and MIT; 2.5 times Caltech and Chicago; three times Princeton, Wisconsin, and Stanford; and four times Illinois, Columbia, Michigan, Cornell, and Yale. A similar pattern was repeated with Woodrow Wilson Fellows.[13] As both a political and a practical matter, measures were clearly called for to assure that additional funds would be spread more widely. For NDEA fellowships a maximum limit for a single university was set. The research agencies took a different tack by linking graduate student support with research funding through 'traineeships,' which were awarded to the university rather than the student up to a maximum number. By 1966, traineeships outnumbered fellowships by better than two to one for NSF, NASA, and NIH.[14] This approach assured that federal support for graduate education would reach a broad range of universities.

A second issue was the commitment to maintain quality in graduate education despite the huge expansion. This concern was the rationale for these same federal agencies to add "cost of instruction" grants of $2500 to their fellowships and traineeships. In addition, institutions with federally supported graduate students became eligible for various types of institutional support for facilities. These provisions not only injected additional resources into graduate education, but also provided institutions with lucrative incentives to establish or expand such programs. All together, this outpouring of federal funding shaped graduate education during the 1960s.

Doctoral education has been perhaps the most anarchic area of American higher education. Although most universities organized graduate divisions in order to standardize and monitor the requirements for the doctorate, actual programs of study remained largely the province of individual academic departments. They were responsible for admitting, for advancing, and predominantly for supporting their students.[15] Although departments were perpetually concerned with standards—indeed, the entire process was built upon successive evaluations—they had a proclivity for numbers too. A critical mass was needed for a viable graduate program, and more was usually better. Departments consequently tended to be liberal in their admissions criteria. Keniston, for example, deplored the fact that most departments at Penn accepted nine of ten applicants (1957), and urged that efforts be taken to raise the quality of the graduate student body. This same condition, accompanied by the same sentiment, existed widely across American universities. The top graduate schools at the end of the 1950s, Berelson found, were admitting about half of their applicants, but elsewhere the system was essentially open: "everybody who wants to get into graduate school does get in."[16] To improve conditions, for individual departments or the system as a whole, both more applicants and more support were needed.

The vast majority of full-time doctoral students in the U.S. required some form of financial support. In fact, the limitation of such funding was undoubtedly a factor in the leveling off of doctoral awards from 1954 to 1958. Berelson reported that 75 percent of full-time doctoral students were receiving a stipend, and 92 percent of recent degree recipients in the arts and sciences had been supported.[17] These were the favored ones: a poll of part-time students or those who had discontinued their studies would have revealed a paucity of support and a reservoir of potential full-time students.

Graduate students were principally supported by fellowships, research assistantships, and teaching assistantships. According to Berelson's rather liberal estimates at the end of the 1950s, each of these components was then supporting somewhere near 25,000 students.[18] In the first category, there were approximately 11,000 national fellowships supplied by NSF, NIH, NDEA, and the Woodrow Wilson Foundation. Dedicated university funds supported a like number of graduate students, and the balance came from a variety of smaller public and private scholarships. The number of research assistants was by and large a function of research funding, particularly from federal agencies. Teaching assistants, on the other hand, carried a portion of the instructional burden, so that their numbers depended partly upon undergraduate enrollments.

The general rise in federal research funding should have brought about at least a doubling of research assistantships in the 1960s, but the data are uncertain. As for teaching assistants, their numbers actually rose more rapidly than enrollments from the late fifties into the mid-sixties, at both public and private universities, which suggests that the supply of graduate students was as important a factor in this growth as the demand for lower division teachers. Even the most prestigious state institutions took advantage of this resource: more than 40 percent of the lower division courses at Berkeley and Michigan in the early 1960s, for example, were taught by T.A.s.[19]

The abundance of support for graduate students made possible the extraordinary leap in doctorates, as intended, but it also shaped the contours of graduate education. Table 21 provides a revealing profile of graduate study at the height of the boom. The fourteen disciplines portrayed there are from engineer-

TABLE 21. Graduate Enrollment and Support by Departmental Quality Level in 14 Disciplines,* 1968[20]

Roose-Anderson Rating	Number Depts.	Enrollment		Percentage			
		Avg.	Total	Fellows	R.A.s	T.A.s	Other
4.0–5.0 (distinguished)	92	141	14,297	40	27	16	17
3.0–39 (strong)	201	92	21,566	33	25	22	20
2.5–2.9 (good)	174	66	12,719	30	23	28	19
2.0–2.4 (adequate +)	210	53	11,869	30	16	31	23
1.5–1.9 (adequate)	153	47	7,560	27	15	30	28
0.0–1.4 (marginal)	111	30	3,549	24	11	36	29
not rated	260	38	8,132	25	18	33	24
Total	1201	66	79,692	32	21	26	21

*Chemical, civil, electrical, & mechanical engineering; chemistry, geology, mathematics, physics; anthropology, economics, geography, political science, psychology, sociology.

ing, social and physical sciences—primarily fields supported by the NSF. Graduate student support was more ample in the biological sciences, and less available in the humanities. These disciplines, then, are broadly representative. What they show is both the persistent effects of quality in graduate programs as well as the results of the enlarged quantity of graduate support.

The regularity of the relationship between departmental quality and graduate education is striking. The better departments are larger and support more of their students through fellowships/traineeships and research assistantships. The weaker departments are smaller and rely more heavily upon teaching assistantships and "other" forms of support. This last category would include students supported by foreign governments or the GI Bill, self-supporting master's degree students, or finishing students who had previously been supported.

Unlike undergraduate colleges, bigger was better for most graduate departments during the 1960s. The best departments attracted many free-choice fellowship holders, as well as having fellowships and traineeships of their own to dispense. The wealthier schools had a particular advantage. Princeton, for example, was able to support 71 percent of its graduate students with fellowships. One-quarter of these awards came from its own dedicated funds and were devoted exclusively to the humanities and social sciences.[21] Under such conditions, the strongest departments could enroll an optimal number of graduate students, which in most cases was relatively large. Numerous graduate students served the interests of research-minded faculty: they created a need for specialized graduate classes; they facilitated research as assistants; and as future researchers they enhanced the reputation of the department and their mentors.

The research universities had become accustomed to competing for the best graduate students in the postwar era; the new abundance of support now allowed them to do so largely with federal funds. One result was to accentuate the process by which the top departments monopolized the most promising students. It became commonplace for the better departments in well-funded fields to limit their intake of graduate students to the number that could be supported. This practice produced a form of internal stratification among graduate students, which is evident in Table 21: the most favored students held fellowships and the next group served as research assistants. Teaching was thus relegated to the department's weaker students or made a required—and often resented—obligation. The strongest departments were able to accommodate two-thirds of their students as fellows or research assistants.

The manner in which the system as a whole adapted to the mushrooming of graduate education is also evident. The abundance of support in some respects attenuated the effects of stratification: there was sufficient funding in the system that support and talented graduate students were spread widely across institutions. Very roughly, the strongest 40 percent of departments (2.5 + in Table 21) enrolled 60 percent of the graduate students, and the weakest 60 percent had 40 percent of the students. But even this weaker group managed to support more than 70 percent of their students. They relied more heavily on teaching assistantships, to be sure, but still had a preponderance of fellowships and research assistantships. The abundance of federal support for graduate study, together with the mechanisms that dispersed this support fairly widely, fueled the growth of graduate study at all levels of the system. The number of applicants to graduate schools increased because there were more college graduates to apply, especially by the late 1960s, and because the national mood during the decade placed a high value on postgraduate studies in basic disciplines. But although the growing tide of graduate students allowed the established departments to become much more selective, it also permitted the proliferation of new and expanding programs. As a result, graduate study in the U.S. remained open to all comers.

All of the factors just reviewed portray a robust state of health for graduate education in the 1960s, but it was not so regarded at the time.[22] Increasing criticism was directed at the hegemony of departments, which, it was alleged, inhibited specialization, interdisciplinary approaches, or applied learning, while also preserving outmoded requirements. In part, such dissatisfaction reflected the fact that the conditions and expectations surrounding graduate education were changing more rapidly than departmental curricula. But there were palpable problems as well, chief among them was the inordinate time actually taken to complete Ph.D.s outside the natural sciences. This problem also clearly retarded the goal of producing more qualified college teachers. A second troubling condition, closely related to duration, was the high rate of attrition in graduate programs in these same areas. This situation, however, was assumed to contribute to the maintenance of high standards, and thus was seldom identified as a 'problem.'[23]

On the surface, it was somewhat surprising that increased support for graduate students did not appear to lessen the time to the doctorate. In fact, the bulk of this support was weighted toward beginning graduate study rather than ending it. Universities competed for students through offers of initial stipends; and even the most generous fellowships were limited to three years of support. Financial aid was difficult to obtain for the final stage of completing a dissertation, but ABDs (all but dissertation) were hotly recruited for regular teaching positions. As a result, many completed their degrees while teaching full time, which delayed their doctorates for several more years. The problem was largely confined to the humanities and social sciences, where the average duration of graduate study was seven and one-half years beyond the bachelor's degree (compared with just over five in the natural sciences).[24] This was a conspicuous target for reform. Two separate efforts to grapple with this issue—one academic and the other practical—illuminate conditions in graduate education in the 1960s.

Writing at the end of the 1960s, David Breneman proposed a model of faculty and departmental behavior toward graduate education that was based on conditions then existing at Berkeley.[25] The model was predicated on the double function that doctoral students serve in the life of departments: as inputs they helped to generate resources with which to build departments; and as outputs they contributed to the prestige of departments and their faculty. It was generally recognized that the education of doctoral students consumed more effort than that of undergraduates, and was commensurately rewarded in departmental allocations. A larger population of graduate students yielded further benefits in advanced classes to teach and graduate assistants. Departments consequently had strong incentives to expand their recruitment of graduate students as long as qualified applicants were available. The constraint they faced was on the output side. Only those Ph.D.s who were placed into other strong departments conferred prestige upon their mentors. Producing too many doctorates, and seeing them forced to accept employment in undistinguished, non-research institutions, would soon diminish the reputation of a department and its members. Thus, a department might be motivated simultaneously to have a large number of doctoral students and a small number of actual graduates. This situation was precisely what Breneman found in the humanities and social science departments of Berkeley.

The behavior exhibited by these departments was both perverse and rational. Even during the 1960s, the market for faculty at other research universities was thin. Over two postwar decades (1947–67), Berkeley produced 4.1 percent of all Ph.D.s, and 7.1 percent of the total graduated by the top twenty universities (the schools dominating the high-prestige market). By the end of that period, 47.5 percent of Berkeley Ph.D.s had been placed in prestigious academic settings, 40 percent in neutral ones, and just 12.5 percent in places connoting negative prestige.[26] These admirable results were achieved with humanities and social science departments graduating somewhere between 15 and 30 percent of their entering graduate students. If they had been more productive, their results would certainly have been worse. A tripling of Ph.D.s—approximating the efficiency of the chemistry department—would have meant that Berkeley graduates needed to claim about 20 percent of the high-quality faculty openings in the country.

Not only was attrition high in these Berkeley departments, it was also delayed. Non-graduates averaged three to four years of study, thus assuring the department of large graduate enrollments and a limited output. This result was accomplished, perhaps without conscious design, by the structure of the programs: breadth requirements that spanned the entire discipline; language requirements (the English Department required Latin or Greek); ambiguity or lack of information about relative achievement and prospects for completion; relatively late attrition points (written and oral examinations); and severe expectations for the dissertation. Each of these hurdles was justified on its own supposed merits, but such requirements were readily dispensed with elsewhere where departments lacked a vested interest in limiting the number of graduates.

Berkeley represented an extreme case; its rate of attrition was the highest among leading universities.[27] As a state university, Berkeley possessed large departments and an implicit obligation to remain somewhat accessible. The funding formula by which the Regents weighted doctoral students as 3.5 times a freshman or sophomore was also factored into departmental behavior. And, having newly arrived at the top of the academic pyramid, the Berkeley departments were particularly sensitive to nuances of prestige. These departments consequently epitomized the incentives for long duration and high attrition, but this pattern of behavior was repeated elsewhere. The attrition rate nationally for highly qualified doctoral students was roughly 75 percent in the humanities, 70 percent in the social sciences, and just 40 percent in the natural sciences.[28]

The chemistry department had similar inclinations for high graduate enrollments and high national prestige, but faced a different demand for its doctorates and established a different pattern for graduate education. Many chemists found employment in industry, which for purposes of prestige was a neutral outcome. The chemistry department could thus have a high output of Ph.D.s while making limited claims for academic placements. And it did. Chemistry admitted more doctoral students than humanities or social science departments and graduated better than 75 percent. It occupied a comparable share of the national market, and had an excellent record in placing its graduates. Moreover, attrition occurred much earlier, during the first or second year. For chemistry professors, an unsuccessful student was a waste of their own valuable laboratory space, whereas the resources utilized by humanities students, like library collections, were costs to the university. Chemists consequently promoted efficiency through the design of their program, which reversed the delaying mechanisms described above.[29]

The connections between markets for graduates and the nature of programs seemed to be borne out by the economics department, which was evolving away from the social science pattern and toward that of chemistry. A considerable increase in the demand for economics Ph.D.s in academic and nonacademic settings lay behind this movement. The department streamlined its program around 1960, not without some bloodletting, by greatly reducing the breadth requirements and no longer requiring two foreign languages. The examinations were narrowed and related more closely to course work, while progress toward the dissertation was regularized. As a result, economics fell between chemistry and other social sciences in terms of attrition and time to completion.

A third, and apparently anomalous, pattern of behavior was evident in another Berkeley department. The Botany Department had grown only moderately in terms of graduate students and faculty, and apparently preferred that course. It admitted only the number of students it felt it could accommodate, and hoped to see them all earn Ph.D.s. The crucial difference underlying the behavior of the Botany Department seemed to be that it was secure in its prestige. It was rated number 1 by the Cartter Report, which implied that, unlike the major disciplines, this field could be adequately covered by just sixteen faculty members. Botany chose not to grow, having little to gain from greater size and much to lose in terms of collegiality. This type of behavior could be found elsewhere among relatively secure departments. The Princeton Graduate School as a whole, for example, wished to remain relatively small and to have a high graduation rate. It consequently regularized graduate student progress and encouraged dissertations of moderate length. Princeton managed to graduate more than half of the students entering doctoral programs in the humanities and social sciences, and had the lowest average time to the doctorate.[30]

These examples demonstrate that the same basic motivations of faculty and departments could produce widely differing patterns of behavior and development. The graduate schools could set general requirements for all departments, even admissions quotas, which were later imposed at Berkeley; but such steps did little to inhibit individualistic behavior. One reason was that enhancing prestige, whatever its undesirable incidental effects, was an inherent goal of research universities as well as of their faculty members. This shared purpose was just one of the reasons why graduate education proved so recalcitrant to reforms.

The supposed incoherence and inefficiency of graduate programs in the humanities and social sciences was a particular concern of McGeorge Bundy when he assumed the presidency of the Ford Foundation in 1966.[31] Influencing the foundation's thinking on this matter was Bernard Berelson, who had concluded in his 1960 study that additional funding targeted at completion of the doctorate was the key to shortening this process.[32] A foundation program was hastily formulated and adopted in 1967. It called for establishing a four-year doctoral program as the accepted standard—two years of course work after the bachelor's degree, usually followed by one year as a teaching assistant and another to finish a dissertation. To achieve this goal the foundation awarded grants to ten of the leading research universities (as determined by the Cartter ratings) over seven years so that they could offer four years of continuous support to graduate students in the humanities and social sciences.[33] In addition, the foundation harbored the expectation that the stimulus of streamlining degree programs would induce further reforms, and thus produce more coherent programs. The grants, about $4 million per institution, were to be supplemented by institutional funds, and the universities were left with considerable discretion in achieving the four-year goal. Their plans accordingly varied in approach: Yale, Princeton, and Stanford opted to provide four-year support packages to all new students in these areas; Wisconsin sought to reduce reliance on teaching assistantships for three-quarters of its students; and Michigan dedicated these funds to helping just 40 percent of relevant students during their third and fourth years. However employed, the grants did not accomplish their principal purpose.

Over the course of the program, the length of time required for doctorates at the ten universities, with few exceptions, increased rather than declined. A subsequent evaluation sponsored by the Foundation could not "point to a single university where the program was a clear success": the hypothesis that duration was related to financial support, it concluded, "was simply wrong."[34]

Students clearly did not relish the opportunity for more efficient graduate studies. From their point of view, the importance of completion with distinction outweighed other considerations.[35] But several other developments affected the situation. Federal support for fellowships began to decline shortly after the inception of the Ford grants (as did the Woodrow Wilson Fellowships, from which Ford withdrew support). The intensification of the Vietnam War made graduate school a safe haven for some from the depredations of the draft. Most significantly, the market for new college teachers softened rapidly. Given a shortage of academic jobs, it seemed better to acquire stronger qualifications than to acquire them sooner (although this was usually a mistaken perception, given the burgeoning surplus of applicants). These conditions probably reinforced an

inherent dilatoriness in graduate study that made assured support in itself conducive to inefficiency. In short, students no longer had much incentive for quick
entry into the academic labor market or for cutting corners on their degree programs.

Faculty in the humanities and social sciences, who ultimately controlled the
pace and content of graduate study, never really endorsed a shorter degree
course. Those subjects that required mastery of foreign languages or sojourns in
distant places were deemed by their expositors to call for more than four years'
apprenticeship. In more ruminative subjects, like literature or philosophy, faculty thought it desirable that there be ample time for, well, rumination. Perhaps
only in quantitative areas of the social sciences was the mastery of needed skills
in four years' time attainable. These recalcitrant faculty were not necessarily
throwbacks to an earlier era. In refusing to accede to foreshortened doctoral
programs, university faculty were upholding the traditions of a research degree
to which they and their institutions were committed. They were also, as was evident in the Berkeley case, protecting the prestige and market position of their
departments by restricting output.[36] In addition, the comparison with the natural
sciences, which strongly influenced the impulse to reform, was misleading. Students in the laboratory sciences were brought to the research front much sooner
than their counterparts in the slow subjects. Prospective academicians in the natural sciences then routinely took positions as postdocs after their degrees. All
told, their professional apprenticeships were probably *longer* than those of social
scientists and humanists.

Officers of the Ford Foundation later complained that the universities had not
embraced the goals of its program, but had cynically taken the money as a form
of general support.[37] Due to the abrupt implementation of the program, each
university had in fact largely integrated the Ford grant into its existing structure
of graduate support. This approach virtually guaranteed that nothing of consequence would be changed. Then, as other fellowships began to disappear, the
Ford funds became a badly needed replenishment for income lost from other
sources. In the parlance of philanthropy, leverage did not work in this case. But
the foundation bore much of the blame: it had not formulated and stipulated
guidelines that would have compelled these universities to greater exertions
toward reform. Moreover, this was not the only flaw in the conception and
implementation of this program.

The effort to reform graduate education was the Ford Foundation's last major
program aimed specifically at helping the research universities.[38] It was also the
most 'elitist' of those programs, in the sense of that term current in the late
1960s. The program principally aided ten of the wealthiest institutions (eight
more universities were later given considerably smaller grants).[39] Bernard Berelson had argued, no doubt correctly, that any successful reform of graduate education would have to be adopted first by the most prestigious institutions. But
other institutions could only hope to emulate these affluent institutions if federal
support for graduate education continued to expand. This assumption was soon
belied by events. As a result, the program had the actual effect of increasing the
advantage of these leading universities in the competition for the top academic

talent. At one time this approach might have been justified as "making the peaks higher!" By the time that the program was in full operation, however, elitism was in bad odor, both in the Ford Foundation and beyond its walls. One consequence was that officers of the Foundation neither believed in the program, nor did they attempt to monitor it rigorously. More important, the notion of excellence that the foundations had long upheld came to be increasingly on the defensive throughout the university research system.

During the course of the 1960s graduate education expanded greatly but changed very little. The solicitous attention that it received from well-meaning patrons assured that the faculty would remain in control of the process and that the established research universities would continue their hegemony over the most crucial inputs. The vast expansion of graduate education in terms of support and participation assured that the research university ideal would be projected far beyond the institutions at the top of the academic ratings. By the end of the decade, however, this still-thriving enterprise was besieged with doubts.

Amazingly, the crisis in graduate education that the United States faced after Sputnik had been addressed so swiftly and massively that scarcely a decade later another crisis emerged of almost inverse proportions. The traditional patterns of graduate study that had been enthusiastically emulated now seemed ill-fitted for new subjects, new students, or the newer graduate institutions. The spirit of the graduate school seemed to be exerting a baneful rather than enlightening influence on the undergraduate college. The prestigious graduate programs that universities had scrambled to establish now constituted an increasingly onerous financial burden. Finally, the products of these programs, so desperately sought up to then, were suddenly in oversupply. The ills afflicting graduate education, however, were part and parcel of a more general crisis that now gripped the research universities.

8

Dissolution of a Consensus

1. The Student Rebellion

Just as the Fall semester was about to open at Berkeley in 1964, the Dean of Students informed student organizations that the sidewalk area in front of the campus could no longer be used for political purposes. Prior to this directive, the university had tolerated groups of every political stripe manning tables there for recruitment, fund-raising, speech-making, and leafleting, even though such political activity was proscribed on university grounds. The ban on these activities touched off a spiral of events that engulfed the entire campus for the rest of the year. Student defiance of the order and the subsequent disciplining of students led to the coalescence of the "Free Speech Movement." Demonstrations, arrests, and sit-ins were followed by negotiations, the formation of special committees, faculty attempts at mediation, and an eventual falling out between the two sides. A strike ensued, which forced a tentative accommodation, but the former stability could not be regained. The chancellor of the Berkeley campus was soon replaced and President Clark Kerr, castigated from left and right, found himself unable to escape the polarizing effects. In 1967 he too fell victim to the continuing turmoil, dismissed by the Regents at the behest of Governor Ronald Reagan.

The events of the Free Speech Movement at Berkeley have been recounted numerous times.[1] Yet, there is nothing in the issues themselves to suggest why this controversy assumed the proportions it did; why it polarized and ultimately paralyzed the country's foremost public research university; or why seemingly reasonable individuals were so powerless to resolve the crisis. Commentators accordingly analyzed underlying conditions—the structure of the University of California, the political culture of Berkeley, or the nature of the student estate.

But although these and other factors helped to shape the crisis at Berkeley, they could not explain why this type of crisis was replicated on campuses across the United States, and indeed the world.

The student rebellion in the United States drew its energy from three sources of discontent: opposition to the war in Vietnam, on which campus opinion tended to lead the nation; the civil rights movement, where universities followed in the wake of the struggle in the South; and the universities themselves—their procedures, organization, and curriculum, especially where these bore some connection, however remote, with the first two issues. The combination of national and local concerns imparted a powerful dynamic to events. The intense passions and moral fervor of the antiwar and civil rights movements were transferred to relatively mundane university matters. These feelings intruded, for example, into normal university measures to discipline students who ostensibly had been unruly in a noble cause. Accustomed to their traditional posture as guardians of reason and reasonableness, universities were repeatedly unnerved to find themselves morally outflanked. Moreover, the tenor of student protest evolved far more rapidly than the capacity of universities to learn from previous discomfitures.

For three years after the Free Speech Movement, the antiwar movement dominated campus discontent, gradually developing from debate to direct action. By 1966 demonstrations and minor sit-ins were occurring widely to protest the complicity of universities with the Selective Service System and the presence on campus of Dow Chemical Company, the manufacturer of napalm. The following year larger and more boisterous demonstrations provoked arrests and 'police brutality,' which caused strikes at Berkeley and Wisconsin, and varying degrees of disruption elsewhere.[2]

The Spring of 1968 saw an explosion of disruptive protests at campuses across the country, but the disturbance at Columbia in April and May signaled a new phase of the rebellion. The planned construction of a gymnasium on the edge of Harlem gave radical students a symbol for linking the university and the existing power structure with social and racial issues. The radicals seized five university buildings and occupied them for several days with considerable backing from other students. The administration was compelled to call in police to remove the protesters by force. In this drama, enacted before the nation's media, the script may have been spontaneous, but the plot was premeditated.

The most radical faction among the demonstrators, whose spokesman was Mark Rudd, regarded university issues as mere pretexts for launching a revolution against American society. Such goals soon drew radicals away from universities, and ultimately into terrorism. Henceforth, there were individuals on and around campuses who accepted the appropriateness of violence to further their cause.[3] In a second development at Columbia, black students followed the precedent of the civil rights movement and the new doctrines of black power by separating their organization and demands completely from those of white radicals. Subsequently it would be black student movements, no longer seeking civil rights but exceptional programs, that would provoke some of the most serious campus disturbances. Soon thereafter, black students brandishing guns traumatized Cornell, demands of black students precipitated a strike at Harvard, and the Black Action Movement temporarily disabled the University of Michigan.[4] In 1970 the rebellion reached a violent and ignominious culmination with a fatal terrorist bombing at Wisconsin and the murder by duly constituted authorities of six students at Kent State and Jackson State.[5] In just a few short years the student rebellion had profoundly affected the outlook and behavior of research universities, particularly undermining their confidence in their distinctive mission.

The Berkeley Free Speech Movement produced in a serendipitous way a form of confrontation that transformed student politics.[6] The bumbling actions of the University of California administration provoked students to respond with tactics learned in the civil rights movement: civil disobedience and nonviolent resistance, especially the sit-in, accompanied by a set of demands to be met. As used in the civil rights movement, these tactics generally had attainable goals. The strategy was to make acceptance of the goals—desegregation, minority hiring—less onerous than enduring continued demonstrations and the attendant adverse publicity. This calculus was one that an individual business could make. Transferred to the vastly more complicated organizational world of the university, with its multiple internal constituencies and diffuse centers of power, the goals of confrontations became broader in scope, more complicated to implement, and correspondingly less attainable.

In the simplest terms, most campus crises consisted of three kinds of student demands. At the kernel of the crisis was the rectification of some immediate grievances—freedom of political activity, banishing Dow Chemical Company, eliminating defense research, or blocking the Columbia gym. These became linked, however, with far more sweeping reforms that were either beyond the power of the administration to grant or required considerable time and negotiation to accomplish. Finally, there was always the issue of forgiving students for their righteous misbehavior—amnesty, dropping charges, or otherwise abnegating the disciplinary process. All together, the loose interconnectedness of these disparate issues and their general association with popular positions created widespread sympathy with the student cause on campus (although these feelings failed to carry through to the general public). This combination of elements confounded those charged with resolving the crises.

After the Free Speech Movement, the pretexts for campus disorders often appeared to be trivial or contrived. The psychological overkill applied to these issues was in fact inherent to the tactic. The object of wrath symbolized a transcendent evil. The university response then became crucial. By provoking forceful intervention to protect the unfortunate symbol, or to end a demonstration, the university created the second-order issues of police brutality, punishment, and amnesty. These issues could sometimes be used to escalate the protests. If the protesters could then disrupt the functioning of the university, they acquired real bargaining leverage. At this point, more general kinds of demands could be made concerning the nature of the university and how it should be changed.

The administrative structures of American universities generally proved incapable of withstanding these kinds of pressures. Universities were, above all, consensual communities. Authority over day-to-day affairs was diffused broadly throughout the institutions. Especially in research universities, individual faculty had extensive autonomy over their own and their departments' activities. At the other extreme, ultimate responsibility for basic policies was lodged far above with trustees or regents. Procedures to discipline and punish were designed to deal with individual miscreants who violated consensual norms. The formal authority of university administrators thus depended on the maintenance of consensus. The new style of confrontation was effective precisely because it shattered the tacit acceptance of the status quo. When university administrators had to resort to coercion, their moral ascendancy was lost. The weight of student opinion swung over to the insurgent victims, and faculty tended to blame the administration for the disorders that ensued.

Once impaired, the formal authority of university administrations was difficult to reassert.[7] The different constituencies of the university (faculty, teaching assistants, students) advanced claims of their own, and external groups (alumni, the press, legislators) exerted unaccustomed pressures to influence campus decisions. Different theories of decision-making were advocated and acquired plausibility. The faculty, in particular, were thrust into the forefront of prolonged crises. Some individuals displayed courage in defusing volatile situations; and when order prevailed, faculty committees often worked out sound policies for dealing with contentious issues. But in the heat of confrontations, they tended to be ineffectual: faculty were badly divided among themselves, and when they could agree it was generally to advocate leniency toward protesters.[8]

Institutions that were capable of maintaining a semblance of internal coherence and consensus were able to weather confrontations with radical students with minimal damage. Burton Clark called this the "importance of moral capital," and it largely accounted for the relative stability of such campuses as Princeton, Yale, and Chicago.[9] Elsewhere, more often than not, universities experienced what Edward Shils decried as "the hole at the center of university government"—an absence of authority that deprived university administrations of the means or the backing to deal with student demands.[10] Eventually, universities learned to cope with student demonstrations through crisis management, lengthy negotiations, and usually concessions. But during the last years of the sixties the research universities underwent substantial changes under a rush of events over which they had little control.

The student rebellion touched colleges and universities of all kinds across the United States, but insofar as it focused on institutional issues the target was implicitly the research universities. The *Port Huron Statement,* original manifesto of Students for a Democratic Society, had accorded universities unique importance. Universities were part of a system of dehumanizing institutions that dominated American society; but they were also places where a liberating dialogue could be initiated, where people might be able to participate in decisions affecting their lives, and where education and knowledge might be made relevant to social, political, and economic realities.[11] Throughout the subsequent history of the student rebellion, these themes were never far below the surface. During confrontations and crises, however, students tended to invoke three general issues that fundamentally concerned the universities: that specialized disciplinary knowledge was irrelevant, particularly for undergraduates; that the multiversity, broadly speaking, was dysfunctional as an institution and that universities should sever all links, including research, with the Department of Defense. These concerns were often shared by others of more moderate persuasion, but the student rebellion moved them into the forefront.

Before the student Left was visible or audible, the notion that basic features of the research universities were detrimental to undergraduate teaching was most often made by conservative commentators.[12] Evidence was hardly lacking. The relative growth of graduate education, *ipso facto*, meant that many professors had less contact with undergraduates. Larger numbers of faculty permitted the offering of more specialized disciplinary courses, which were increasingly remote from the interests and the intellectual backgrounds of ordinary undergraduates. Clearly, the evolution of the research university since the 1950s had reduced the weighting of undergraduate education in the equation of university activities. Beginning with the Free Speech Movement, students too began to complain of this comparative neglect. For the remainder of the 1960s the supposed deficiencies of undergraduate teaching and the inappropriateness of the specialized disciplinary curriculum became clichés of the student movement, the backdrop for more immediate grievances.

If teaching and curricular issues were never the foremost issues in actual confrontations, they were issues taken seriously by the accused. Many of the faculty at Berkeley, it was reported, "acknowledged the essential justice of the students' case against the multiversity and . . . confessed their own not-so-small contribution to the malaise."[13] The administration responded by establishing a commission to investigate the state of education at Berkeley. This same pattern was repeated at most universities in the years that followed. Committees of varying scope and composition were charged with evaluating the complaints made by disaffected students, scrutinizing the educational process, and recommending reforms.[14]

In general, these efforts at reform had some positive effects. After two decades of hectic development, which heavily emphasized noninstructional elements, time was overdue for focusing some critical thinking upon the university's educational role. It could not but help, for example, to make teachers more sensitive to the instructional needs of students. Certainly the casual denigration of undergraduate teaching in time became publicly unacceptable. Innovations like student evaluations of classes now gave teachers a further reminder of their pedagogical responsibilities. The much-maligned teaching assistants also received some attention and occasionally some organized guidance.[15] The overall thrust of reform, however, was aimed at the content and the form of course offerings, and here results were more equivocal.

The curricular reforms of this era were all permissive in a double sense. Given the context of the student rebellion, any stiffening of requirements or standards was inconceivable. Instead, requirements for general education courses or foreign languages were dropped or diluted. The supposed tyranny of the grading system was diminished as students were given the option of taking courses on a pass-fail basis, and in some cases failing grades were no longer recorded. New mechanisms were put in place for establishing courses outside of departmental frameworks. And, students were given the latitude to undertake independent studies or to design their own majors. Overall, students acquired substantially greater freedom to make their studies more challenging, more relevant to current affairs, or simply easier.

On a deeper level, the permissiveness that was now enjoyed by students was an extension of the very logic of the postwar research university. The "academic imperium" described by Jencks and Riesman in the *Academic Revolution* consisted of the devolution of authority to the departments and their faculty.[16] With the reforms, the disaffected were incorporated into this system. Now they too could design specialized courses that suited their own purposes. These courses would be interdisciplinary in nature and focused on real-world problems instead of disciplinary puzzles, but they were still essentially theoretical in their approach. Such courses were entirely in keeping with the capacious nature of the research university, which could assimilate interdisciplinary studies as readily as disciplinary specialties. As a result, the curricular reforms reinforced the very characteristics against which they were directed. If the failing of the research universities was the lack of coherence and consensus in undergraduate education, the new offerings brought appreciably greater incoherence and dissensus. Specifically, gifted and academically motivated students could now more easily study advanced material on their own, just like fledgling graduate students. Those who sought relevance in the curriculum were now given theoretical treatments of foreign and domestic issues, not material connected with the world of affairs and of work. (A movement toward occupational relevance would develop in the 1970s.[17]) Attempts to remedy anomie through special living arrangements—experimental or residential colleges—tended to attract the most disaffected students, often creating centers of the counterculture where anomie was an admired condition. For the average university student, the reforms of this era produced a college education with less direction, less rigor, and less overall coherence. They constituted a second-order fragmentation of the curriculum, superimposed upon the earlier fragmentation brought about by disciplinary specialization. In some cases, where the new courses were politically inspired, they detracted from the university's role as a place of serious intellectual work. Overall, genuine educational benefits for undergraduates stemming from these curricular innovations would be hard to demonstrate.

When Clark Kerr set out to provide a candid depiction of the nature of the multiversity, with its inherent and profuse inconsistencies, he could have had little inkling that he would shortly be hoisted on his own petard. The Free Speech Movement took Kerr to be the villain of their drama—the arch-technocrat who had fashioned a university dedicated to serving the existing power structure of capitalist society; turning its hapless students into cogs of the machine.[18] Whereas the preceding critique had focused on pedagogy and curriculum, the attack on the nature of the multiversity, at least internally, centered on organization and governance. Here too, the students' critique was shared by more contemplative observers.

By the latter 1960s, the American university was widely perceived to be in a troubled state. Burton Clark reached the conclusion that "the multiversity has indeed lost its balance," due to the divergent interests of its inhabitants. Faculty increasingly pursued their professional careers, which had the effect of channeling their energies into their disciplines and departments. A separate "administrative class with interests and ideologies of its own" promoted growth and efficiency internally while maintaining the institution's ties to outside groups. These separate forces had produced a drift toward an impersonal, degree-centered university. They created institutions of massive size that could offer little in the way of personal fulfillment or intellectual development to the students whom they ostensibly served.[19]

In the minds of alienated students, the ills of the multiversity stemmed above all from its bondage to other dehumanizing institutions of American society. Certainly evidence was readily available to link the university with capitalism and the state. The California Board of Regents, it was noted, amply fulfilled C. Wright Mills's conception of a conservative 'power elite.' Clark Kerr trumpeted the university's central and indispensable position in the "knowledge industry." In words that discontented students could only regard as chilling, he asserted that "the university and segments of industry are becoming more alike . . . . The two worlds are merging physically and psychologically."[20] Seen in the proper context, Kerr and other spokesmen were pointing with pride to the university's increasing usefulness to society. Student rhetoric, however, turned this notion on its head to demonstrate university subservience to outside interests. This kind of inversion was even more dramatic when directed toward the university's relations with the federal government. Services that formerly had been proudly rendered to assist in the defense of the nation were now seen as evidence of complicity in sustaining the Cold War. The escalation of the Vietnam War in 1965 gave immediacy to such allegations: "corporate liberalism," under the banner of anticommunism, was labeled as a source of oppression throughout the world. The university, which students claimed was oppressing them, was seen to be part and parcel of that larger system.[21]

Within these broad parameters the politics of the student Left varied considerably among campuses, among groups on a given campus, and over time. By 1968 an extremist faction had appeared, dedicated to opposing 'racism' at home and American 'imperialism' abroad. According to Mark Rudd, the student movement was no longer interested in "dorm rules, or democratizing student governance or any of that bullshit."[22] Yet, it was on just those kind of mundane issues that the student rebellion had an appreciable impact on universities.

One of the hallmarks of New Left thought was the notion of "participatory democracy"—that individuals ought to be able to take part in the decisions shaping the social institutions that affected their lives. From the Free Speech Movement onward, students pressed for inclusion in the decision-making structure of their universities. The existing forms of student government were dismissed as ineffectual—"sandbox government" it was called at Berkeley. Students demanded more—nothing short of representation in real power centers of the university. University administrators were initially cool to this notion. The 1966 Report at Berkeley, for example, merely called for the establishment of "effective channels of communications" with students.[23] As student demonstrations grew in magnitude and ferocity, however, more savvy administrators realized there was far more to fear from disruption than from participation. Inexorably, students representatives were added to departmental and university-wide committees, allowed to attend the meetings of official bodies, and even appointed as trustees. This strategy of "cooptation," as radicals derisively termed it, had two things working in its favor from the university's point of view. First, where students would cooperate in good-faith, both sides had much to learn from each other. Second, the premise of the students' demands was largely faulty. The university by its very nature did not possess power centers where momentous decisions were made to shape student lives or assist corporate liberalism. Rather, power was diffused widely and subtly throughout the institution. Students in fact found themselves privy to the tedious meetings by which consensus was maintained, vested interests defended, and the different components of the university incrementally adjusted to one another.[24] These humdrum activities provided little scope for gaining publicity or raising the consciousness of the uninitiated. Once the ardor of rebellion began to cool, students either ignored participation in governance or entered into it responsibly. Their presence, however, did not change the character of American universities.

Students were far more successful in asserting control over the decisions that shaped their lives outside the classroom. Universities rather quickly chose to retreat rather than resist the abandonment of parietal rules and the whole notion of *in loco parentis*. Jencks and Riesman used the fashionable metaphor of guerrillas challenging a colonial regime to describe the situation. It may have been the most militant among the students who actually challenged the constraints that universities sought to maintain, but they were supported by the rest of the student population. Administrators had little will, and faculty even less, to enforce these rules upon their recalcitrant subjects. Only outsiders continued to believe that parietal rules could and should be enforced. The guerrillas thus succeeded merely by sustaining a relentless pressure.[25] In fact, institutions would have had to relax their rules in any case. Their authority over students was challenged in the courts throughout the 1960s and progressively eroded. By 1968 *in loco parentis* as a legal principle was virtually moribund.[26] Overall, the last half of the sixties witnessed a revolutionary emancipation of students from parietal rules at campuses throughout the country. This triumph, at least in the short run, did little to further education. If anything, the license in personal behavior achieved by students accentuated the distance between student and faculty cultures and contributed to the demoralization of intellectual life.

In comparison with the relevance of university courses or the structure of the multiversity, the issues surrounding university ties with the Department of Defense were both more tangible and more fruitful of symbols for mobilizing protests. In the early years of the antiwar movement 'evil' recruiters (from the armed services, CIA, or defense contractors) supplied the pretexts for demonstrations. By 1967 the student movement had become far more ideological. University research links with the DoD became the focus not just for protests and demands, but for demonstrating that the university was inextricably part of the military-industrial complex.[27]

When student radicals sought to attack military research on campus, they paid little attention to the individual projects of departmental faculty. The large Contract Research Centers, which were remote from campus and employed their own staff, were also difficult to target. Most often students opportunistically seized upon a symbol capable of crystalizing opposition to the war and the Pentagon. Faculty sentiment at the major research universities was decidedly opposed to war, and consequently unsympathetic with many of these undertakings, particularly those well removed from regular faculty research activities. Faculty thus became important allies of the students in opposing military research.

One inviting target was the Institute for Defense Analyses. IDA, as it was known, was a think tank for the Army and Navy created in 1956, which operated under a governing board of twelve research universities. There was little actual substance behind this formal arrangement: IDA conducted most of its research with a large in-house staff and made use of academic consultants individually. It nevertheless valued its university ties for providing access to academic experts and a degree of independence from the military brass. Both these qualities allowed IDA on occasion to function as a voice of reason against some of the wilder extrapolations of the arms race.[28]

IDA became a focal point of protest at Chicago, Princeton, and Columbia, each a member of its governing board. IDA was most visible at Princeton, where it conducted highly secret, but scarcely malevolent, research on communications codes in a building leased from the university. An SDS sit-in there in October 1967 forced the university community to review this relationship. Faculty opinion largely sided with the students in opposing secret military research, and a committee formed to investigate the issue recommended that ties with IDA be severed.[29] At Columbia, SDS discovered the IDA issue only after a faculty group had been wrongly informed by the Dean of the Graduate Faculties that no connection with the university existed. With the university thus embarrassed, SDS chose to emphasize IDA during the 1967–68 school year as a means to radicalize students and oppose the war. IDA became its principal target in the Spring of 1968—at least until the gymnasium issue presented itself—even though a faculty committee had already recommended the termination of university sponsorship. IDA in fact resolved this issue for itself that same year by reconstituting its governing board as individual members rather than university representatives. But Chicago, Princeton, and Columbia severed all ties nonetheless.[30]

In some cases research units specializing in defense work were willing to cut ties with universities in order to avoid having committees of students and faculty intrude into their affairs. At Columbia, for example, the Electronics Research Laboratories chose independent nonprofit status as the Riverside Research Institute (1967), and the Hudson Laboratories, a Navy contract research center, was moved into the U.S. Naval Research Laboratory (1969).[31] Research for the Pentagon in the social and behavioral sciences was particularly unwelcome on campus. In 1969, under pressure from student protesters, both American University and George Washington University divested off-campus research units of this kind sponsored by the Army.[32]

If the military-industrial-university complex hypothesized by student radicals existed anywhere, it would be in the largest performers of DoD research, the top three of which were MIT, Stanford, and the University of Michigan. They owed this status to large, specialized, semi-academic laboratories that had been nurtured and shaped by Pentagon research contracts. In each case a substantial portion of this research was driven off campus by student protests.

At the end of the 1960s, MIT was the Defense Department's largest nonprofit research contractor and also the largest performer of university research. The close integration of basic science and engineering at the Institute had generated a high volume of research for federal agencies and industry since World War II. In addition, its two 'special laboratories' had evolved massive research programs, almost exclusively for the DoD. Funding for the Lincoln Laboratory was $67 million in 1968–69, while that for the Instrumentation Laboratory was $56 million. The latter figure approximated the funding for all other Institute research projects.[33] As a technological university, MIT was spared initially from the excesses of student radicalism, but there was nevertheless growing concern among scientists themselves about the implications of military research. This concern focused particularly on the I-Lab directed by Charles S. Draper. His penchant for pursuing projects from conception through to production and deployment had made the Lab an anomaly even at a technological university (see Chapter 3). Its mushrooming growth during the 1960s had already caused the administration to have misgivings, but it drew the ire of the peace movement because of its role in developing MIRV warheads for Navy Poseidon missiles. These separately targeted missile heads were regarded as a destabilizing factor in the arms race.

Separate groups of graduate students and faculty at MIT united to organize a "research stoppage" on March 4, 1969, to protest the war and to emphasize the social responsibility of scientists. This action, and the debate that it provoked, forced the administration to deal with the question of military research at the special laboratories. The political positions of the insurgents ranged from moderate opposition among the faculty, radical opposition in the graduate student group, and an extremist faction that emerged in the undergraduate splinters of SDS. In the main, they did not seek to separate the special labs from the Institute, but rather, in what might be regarded as either a tactic or a pipe dream, to convert them to civilian, socially constructive research. The desirability of moving in this direction was endorsed by a panel convened by President Howard Johnson. Agreement dissolved, however, when it came to implementing such a change. A consensus probably existed that MIT ought not to be involved in the actual development of weapons systems. But student leftists wanted the redirection of laboratory work to serve as a political statement—a repudiation of the military and all it stood for.

Charles Draper, on the other hand, was publicly critical of any university oversight over I-Lab research. He was backed by the Lab's nearly 2000 employees, who saw their livelihoods threatened if university peace activists were to decide which projects the Lab could accept. Instead of reconciliation, MIT's policy caused the issue to become more divisive and distracting. SDS kept the issue roiling through a series of disruptive demonstrations, while the I-Lab found that continued uncertainty about its status was hampering its ability to conclude contracts. In addition, the existence of projects that might have permitted conversion to civilian research soon proved chimerical. In May 1970, President Johnson announced that because MIT could not manage the I-Lab under the type of supervision that it had imposed the previous year, the Lab was to be spun-off as an independent nonprofit corporation.[34] The decision pleased no one: the peace activists lost an opportunity to strike a blow against the military; MIT became purer, but also poorer; and the new Charles Stark Draper Laboratory harbored bitter feelings over its expulsion. MIT nevertheless resolved an issue that had badly distracted its activities.

The student movement against military research at Stanford in 1969 represented the state of the art in terms of ideological sophistication, tactics, and effectiveness. There had been little student protest at Stanford before 1968, despite occasional visits by missionaries from Berkeley. The first determined sit-in occurred shortly after the Columbia crisis.[35] Disruptive activities by student radicals escalated thereafter until the university experienced the worst violence in its history in the wake of the 1970 invasion of Cambodia. In between, Stanford became the locus of the most concerted campus campaign against military research.

The initial target of student activists was the Stanford Research Institute (SRI), the second largest independent research institute in the country. SRI actually had little connection with the university except for its governing board, which consisted of the Stanford Trustees. It was described as "a loose confederation of entrepreneurs" who had to generate research contracts to maintain themselves and their staffs. Originally established to provide research assistance to West Coast industry, by the end of the 1960s it derived 70 percent of its contracts from the federal government, 50 percent from the DoD.[36] In the Fall of 1968 activists began publicizing SRI involvement in classified research related to chemical and biological warfare, as well as counterinsurgency in Southeast Asia. The general revulsion toward these types of research caused the matter to become a campus-wide concern. A faculty-student committee was quickly appointed to review the Stanford-SRI relationship. As was usually the case, differences grew sharper as student charges and demonstrations kept attention focused on the issue. The kinds of research performed by SRI made it a particularly insidious organization to student radicals: "a strategy center and intellectual staging area for the penetration of private enterprise in developing countries."[37] Their goal was consequently to assert university control over SRI in order to nullify that role.

The issue came to a head in April 1969 when student activists, in a surprise tactic, occupied the Applied Electronics Laboratory—an on-campus unit that conducted considerable classified research for the DoD (see Chapter 5). After a nine-day sit-in, the university responded by granting major concessions to the demonstrators: most classified research would be phased out and procedures to review contracts with the military would be established. At this same time, the committee that reviewed the Stanford-SRI relationship reported its conclusions. A majority favored complete separation (accompanied by a covenant proscribing objectionable kinds of research). A minority took their cue from the "control SRI" slogan and advocated integration with the university. This combination of events sent a chill through SRI itself. With university opinion clearly sympathetic with the growing numbers of radical students, SRI operations would have been severely affected by any degree of university control (which was the point). The head of SRI reported that half his staff would quit if university control were imposed. The Stanford Trustees quickly resolved the matter by voting to cut the connection between the two institutions.[38]

The student rebellion had a palpable effect upon relations between the DoD and American universities. It was undoubtedly a factor in the decline of Pentagon support of academic research from a high of $279 million in 1969 to a low of $184 million just five years later. In this respect, student demonstrations complemented the Mansfield Amendment, passed in 1969 (see Chapter 6). There was an unintended symmetry between these two developments. The Mansfield Amendment deprived universities of the most congenial kinds of support from the DoD, those unrelated to military purposes. Student protesters excised the least congenial forms of research, those which were most immediately linked to military ends. The former dollars, unfortunately for universities, disappeared; but the latter funds continued to be expended in different institutions, or more commonly in the same units without university affiliation. What, then, had been accomplished by the protestors and their occasional victories?

Wolfgang Panofsky, director of the Stanford Linear Accelerator and a critic of classified research on campus, perceived a dilemma in this apparent success: "on the one hand we deplore that the Defense Department is isolated from outside sources of information while at the same time we decry that people in the universities are too involved in Defense Department secrets."[39] Panofsky's dilemma stems from a particular conception of the university that required it to be unsullied by contact with the DoD. This conception was in fact shared by the great majority of liberal-minded faculty at major research universities by the end of the 1960s. Student radicals may have regarded the university as a base or an instrument in their crusade against American society, but the broad consensus on campus preferred to see the university as an ivory tower. This predilection arose from the prevailing liberal sensibilities of the faculty—an underlying hostility to external authorities, an uncritical sympathy for the causes championed by students, and a penchant for reasoning in absolute, moralistic terms.[40] Panofsky's own views were fairly typical: a university, he felt, "should exercise collective moral restraint as to what kind of work it advances."[41] Similar sentiments were embodied in the research policies that emerged from confrontations over military research.[42]

As a result of the turmoil of the late 1960s, a general consensus formed that universities best exercised their social responsibilities by remaining apart from and morally superior to the society of which they were a part. This notion was significantly fostered by, and represented a compromise with, the campaign of student activists against military research. It also expressed the assumptions of politically active students, the majority of liberal faculty, and even those members of Congress who voted for the Mansfield Amendment. In this sense, the ivory tower view tended to supersede the image of what might be termed the 'amoral, technocratic multiversity' attributed to Clark Kerr. To appreciate the consequences of this shift, one has to take into account the intense political and intellectual polarization that existed in this era. The Vietnam War and domestic racial issues were such that individuals were compelled to take one side or the other. Reasoned exchanges of differing opinions on these issues became extremely difficult—more so on campus than off. In this atmosphere, the moral judgments of the socially responsible university were inherently tendentious and coercive. The convictions of the university activists were elevated over the rights of those individuals who held contrary views. There was no concern, for example, for the academic freedom of individuals who wished to engage in 'immoral' research at the I-Lab or the Applied Electronics Laboratory, or many other similar units. The rights of students to enroll in ROTC was never weighed on the same moral scales with the right to have black studies programs. Criticism of government and industry was now considered more virtuous than the service roles that universities had cultivated with some pride in the postwar era.

The prominence of these new moral sensibilities did not have a dramatic impact on day-to-day life in the multiversity. The business of the university for the most part muddled along in its multifarious compartments relatively unaffected by the hyperbole generated by any particular issue of the moment. Indeed, as explained above, the entire student rebellion produced changes of small consequence in curriculum and university organization, and affected the most peripheral defense-related research. But the summed result of the student rebellion produced a more pervasive change in the atmosphere of university life—in the way that universities thought of themselves, responded to internal demands, and presented themselves to the public. Henceforth, a university polity standing outside of the formal structure of university governance would play a powerful role in determining the course of institutional change.[43] This polity consisted of politically active groups of students and, increasingly, politically motivated faculty. Their actions were predicated upon a conception of the social responsibilities of the university. They thus advanced evolving versions of the tendentious moral agenda of the late 1960s. Their power, which came to be well understood by university administrators, derived only partly from the threat of resurrecting the confrontational tactics of the 1960s; recourse was more frequently made to public opinion and the courts. The existence of an active and aggressive university polity thus added a new and complicating factor to the governance of universities. The implications of this development for the research universities transcended any of the specific issues that were involved. Universities would henceforth have to struggle to defend their unique role, to adapt to the changed priorities of American society, and to find the massive resources that were required to fulfill their mission.

2. The Financial Crisis of the Research Universities

Before the student rebellion had subsided, the research universities were confronted with a mounting crisis of an entirely different sort. Throughout the 1960s they had been engaged in a desperate scramble to increase income as rapidly as expenditures, but by the end of the 1960s this race began to be lost. The leading private universities—Columbia, Cornell, Harvard, Princeton, Stanford, and Yale—each faced deficits in their operating budgets that averaged more than $1 million.[1] The financial travail of the public research universities was slower to develop, but similar in result. The ubiquity of this predicament and the stature of those affected indicated that it was not due to imprudence, but rather stemmed from the nature of research universities, from behavior patterns acquired during the golden age, and from the onset of altered conditions at the end of the decade.

During the post-Sputnik decade, the expenditures of research universities increased at a remarkable rate. Taking random examples, from 1958 to 1966 'Education and General' spending rose 119 percent at the University of Washington, 130 percent at Cornell, 140 percent at Michigan, and 172 percent at Penn.[2] These increases were basically generated by internal factors—growth in enrollments, faculty, and the volume of research. Most conspicuous among the expanding budget categories were faculty salaries. Larger graduate programs and more research both called for increases in the number of faculty, and salaries rose as well. The AAUP set a goal of doubling the level of faculty salaries in the decade of the sixties, Overall increases for the first seven years ranged from 5 to 7 percent—not far off that pace.[3] These salary advances occurred against an underlying inflation rate of less than 2 percent and 2.5 percent annual productivity growth in the economy.[4] Faculty salaries, in other words, received a premium due to excess demand for college teachers and the need to redress the low salaries prevailing since the war. But actual salary budgets had to increase still more. Promotions and job changes, which were rapid in these years, boosted individual salaries by more than the averages for stationary faculty. William Bowen detected a long-term 7.5 percent annual rate of *real* increase *per student* in instructional costs, which consisted largely of faculty salaries.[5]

A second source of increased expenditures, seldom mentioned in the plaints of university leaders, was the rising cost of administration. As another long-term trend, administrative costs grew more rapidly than those for faculty. The profusion of university tasks described by Jacques Barzun, alluded to earlier, simply required additional administrative staff.[6] In addition, the same forces that drove faculty salaries also operated for administrators. A third factor, or group of factors, driving up costs could be grouped under 'overhead.' Each new building, even if subsidized by government, represented ongoing charges for maintenance and operation. Although these growing expenditures were caused by internal factors, they were only loosely under the control of institutions. Academic aspirations in combination with the relative abundance of resources propelled expenditures upward.

Both public and private universities experienced the same pressures on costs, but they differed in their sources of income. In an era of burgeoning public spending for higher education, the private sector was at a comparative disadvantage. Private universities benefited from public funds for research, graduate education, buildings, and graduate fellowships; but their core budget had to be funded through the income from student tuition, endowment earnings, and gifts. Through the first half of the 1960s conditions were generally favorable in each of these categories.

The most prestigious private universities of the Northeast generally charged the highest tuition, creating in effect a ceiling price for private higher education. This level of tuition represented the increasing needs of these institutions constrained by what their peer institutions charged. During the 1960s these ceiling tuitions rose moderately in real terms initially, and then more steeply after 1964:[7]

Ceiling Tuition Fees, Private Research Universities, 1959–1971 (1967$)

1959	1964	1967	1971
$1469	$1711	$2017	$2334

The overall real increase of 59 percent in twelve years represented less than the 7.5 percent rate of annual increase in costs per student detected by Bowen. It does, however, reveal that a substantial part of the increasing real expenditures of private research universities were paid for by their students. In fact, their vulnerability stemmed from the difficulty of raising other forms of income at a comparable rate.

From the end of the Korean War through the mid-sixties, the stock market moved steadily upward with only minor setbacks. The value of university endowments increased handsomely, but because the yields on stocks and bonds were low, increases in income from endowment were less bounteous. During the same period, total gifts to higher education rose steadily too, with private research universities, as always, among the largest beneficiaries. Gifts were most often earmarked for specific purposes, but private universities tended to place some portion of these funds, typically one-third, into permanent endowment to augment future income. Income from endowment and gifts was the chief basis for enhancing the research capacity of private universities, but the very limitation of these income sources placed a constraint on expansion for private universities. They generally preferred to raise the quality of their programs through greater emphasis on graduate education and higher per-student expenditures. Public universities, meanwhile, increased income by accommodating more students, faculty, and programs (see Chapter 7).

The funding of public research universities varied from state to state, but the bulk of income everywhere in this era came from state appropriations.[8] Income from student tuition typically accounted for 10 to 25 percent of this amount. The years from Sputnik to the early 1970s witnessed a huge expansion of the public commitment to higher education. Measured against national personal income, nonfederal appropriations rose from the level of 0.4 percent in 1957 to

0.96 percent in 1972.[9] During the 1960s these appropriations quadrupled. An increasing portion of this spending went to enlarge state colleges, build branch campuses, and finally to provide a system of community colleges; but substantial funds were reserved for research universities. The latter, for example, received 54 percent of all state appropriations to higher education in 1968.[10] The financial buoyancy of state research universities was translated into greater effectiveness in the research economy as measured by changes in research share (see Table 16).

In the late 1960s the financial environment became decidedly less congenial for the endowed private universities. The stock market made a secular peak in 1966 that was not surpassed in real terms for two decades. Giving to higher education after 1965 went into a ten-year slump.[11] Financial difficulties would reach the public sector somewhat later and for different reasons, as will be seen in the next section. Specifically, it became harder for private institutions to increase revenues even as the costs faced by research universities continued to escalate. Worse yet, increasing costs in this period were driven more by external than by internal factors.

After 1967 the underlying rate of inflation rose to the unaccustomed level of about 5 percent, which placed upward pressure on salaries for faculty and other employees.[12] Rising price levels were always a serious problem for universities because revenues could not be increased with the same rapidity. Noninstructional costs also increased disproportionately. Between the mid-sixties and the mid-seventies universities ceased to be protected enclaves of the economy and instead were forced to comply with the same federal legislation concerning employee benefits and occupational safety as other large employers. Fringe benefits more than doubled as a percentage of salary, further inflating payrolls. When the Arab oil embargo tripled energy prices in 1973, university budgets absorbed another blow.

Federal spending for academic research reached its apogee in 1967 and 1968, but the fall-off in this case posed a manageable problem. Funding for sponsored research declined only modestly in real terms, and given the nature of research universities, research not funded was research not done. More hardship came from the sharp cutback in the other funds that assisted university research efforts. Such funds totaled more than $1 billion in 1967, but in the next nine years they declined by more than 70 percent in real terms.[13] These programs had subsidized such vital components as fellowships, equipment, and facilities. Universities had expected this type of federal support to increase, but instead these costs had to be absorbed as federal funds were withdrawn. The change was auspicious. For a decade after Sputnik universities benefited financially by expanding research and graduate education, largely because of this generous ancillary support; but after 1967 this was no longer the case.

To these external causes of rising costs must be added some additional factors that were internal to the universities but scarcely avoidable. Technological advances required that substantial investments be made in modernizing the university infrastructure, such as purchases of telephone equipment, television studios, and especially computers. New programs to assist minority and low income students also required funds. These latter initiatives were a consequence of the transformed expectations about access to higher education, especially to elite institutions. Substantially higher provisions for student financial aid at private universities were the result. Henceforth, part of the increases in tuition would be lost to the student aid budget.

Finally, university costs continued to rise because of the inherent inertia of expansion. Commitments were made well in advance for buildings and staffing which incorporated assumptions of rising income. The research universities had acquired a growth mentality during the fat years of the 1960s which was not easily eradicated. The financial problems listed here impinged gradually on the research universities. It was common to excuse the revenue shortfalls or budget deficits as temporary consequences of short-term economic dislocations. Instead, the basic causes of escalating costs continued to worsen: inflation rose to double digit levels after the 1973 oil embargo; costs for noninstructional items soared; federal programs continued to be scaled back; and the costs of recruiting and assisting disadvantaged students expanded. It became a common assumption that additional forms of support would have to be forthcoming from the federal government in order to maintain quality and access in American higher education, especially the private sector.[14] But in this hope too the private universities would be disappointed. Thus, financial conditions deteriorated more rapidly than universities were able to adjust to their predicament.

These circumstances affected each institution somewhat differently, but the experience of Yale University well illustrates the changing fortunes of private universities during these years. Although it had the second largest university endowment, Yale endured all of the difficulties just discussed. The evolution of its income over two decades is summarized in the following figures:[15]

TABLE 22. Yale University Income, 1955–1975 ($000,000)

	1955	1959	1963	1967	1971	1975
Investments	7.5	11.1	15.4	22.0	30.4	33.8
Tuition & fees	8.6	12.3	15.7	19.9	27.4	40.5
Net income	21.7	33.0	48.6	89.9	128.2	171.2

The first row represents the income from investments that was used for expenses, the second all income from students, including room and board, and the third the total income available for operations—the totals include income for sponsored research (which equals expenditures), gifts for current use, and revenue from other operations. Most remarkable is simply the expansion of scale: income quadrupled from 1955 to 1967, with little inflation, and then nearly doubled again by 1975. For most of the first decade of this growth, Yale's financial performance was solid. Investment income, the relatively inelastic source, increased faster than student charges. Yale operated with a balanced budget from 1956 to 1963. In the next two years, however, expenditure growth caused by "highly competitive conditions," especially for faculty, caused deficits which mounted to $1.3 million. Costs at this juncture were rising at an 8.5 percent annual rate, while income was growing by only 7 percent. There was no single cause for this disparity: faculty salaries increased in line with income, but expenditures for general administration, physical plant, and the libraries rose at twice that rate.

These years marked the beginning of the administration of Kingman Brewster, Jr. (1963–77), and aspirations ran high. The new president placed particular emphasis on establishing competitive faculty salaries and increasing research support in the humanities and social sciences. For Brewster, Yale's needs thus came first, followed by considerations of cost and then revenue. He accordingly detailed an "Educational Deficit"—that is, "what it would cost to do those things Yale considers of vital importance to do but cannot afford to do."[16] The challenge was to increase income sufficiently to do those vitally important things.

Additional revenue was thus the only thinkable solution, and Yale's endowment of nearly $500 million was its principal income source. A process was begun to overhaul and rationalize the management of the endowment in order to realize a greater return from the long-running bull market in common stocks. This meant investing more heavily in growth stocks rather than the high-yielding securities traditionally favored by endowed institutions. A second goal was to make endowment's contribution to operating expenditures stable and predictable by basing it on a set formula that would smooth out market fluctuations. A "university equation" was created that allowed Yale to spend some of the gains on its portfolio along with the yield from dividends and interest. The actual gains of the previous year were not the basis for these expenditures, but rather an historical average of the appreciation over previous years. Yale took two other steps to boost investment income. It confided the management of its portfolio to a specially created, quasi-independent firm of professional money managers. President Brewster also announced a ten-year fund-raising effort, although not an official campaign, the proceeds of which would be devoted largely to increasing the endowment.[17]

The Yale Plan was highly regarded in university financial circles as an imaginative way to deal with tightening budgetary constraints. In particular, it showed conservative universities how to capitalize on the bull market in stocks that seemingly had no end. Unfortunately, the years when the plan was formulated and implemented in fact marked the final phase of the secular postwar bull market. The structure of the Yale Plan, furthermore, assured that the university would be spending its theoretical "realized gains" even when it was experiencing losses. Initially, though, the plan served its purpose. The amount of endowment actually spent was raised by about one percentage point, which by itself produced an extra $5 million for spending. During the next several years Yale showed only modest deficits, but then the shortfalls began to mount. The 1970 budget was in the red by $1.75 million, 1971 by $2.57 million, and the following years promised to be even worse. Given inflation and the instability of financial markets, it was no longer possible to be hopeful about additional income. This time Yale had to reduce expenditures. "Clearly," President Brewster announced, "we do not have the means to keep up the recent momentum of improved quality in everything in which we are currently engaged."[18]

The leaders of Yale concurred that there "should be a redesign of Yale which would give a lower expense base."[19] Implementing this notion nevertheless took time. At the end of the 1970–71 year the university allowed 75 faculty members to depart without replacements. The redesign called for a 10 percent reduction in academic spending for 1971–72, and then a further 10 percent reduction over the following two years. In addition to this retrenchment, the second budgetary crisis had two notable consequences for Yale. The need to scale back operations in line with resources forced the university to adopt more rigorous measures for internal planning.[20] Now the same kind of rationalization that had previously been applied to the management of the endowment would be imposed upon the internal management of the university. Second, in order to find additional revenue the university had no other recourse than tuition—"the most substantial controllable source of increases in income" in the words of the treasurer. The last year in which tuition was not increased was 1968. For the next six years it was annually hiked by an average of more than 9 percent (versus inflation of about 6 percent). The problem facing Yale was the stagnant nature of other sources of funds: income from endowment and expendable gifts were both flat during these years, and overhead from research leveled off with the scaling back of federal funding. These developments reduced the budgeting process, according to the treasurer, to "one essentially of studying the requirements for additional compensation of the faculty, staff and employees and of making an enlightened judgment in regard to increases in rates of tuition."[21]

During the first half of the 1970s Yale was in a financial vise due to stagnant sources of income and inescapable increases in cost. The results of this squeeze can be summarized with just a few figures. From 1970 to 1974 (FY), Yale's spending increased by $31.7 million (but adjusted for inflation this represented a *decline* of 1.4%). Of this amount, $15.3 million went to increase salaries and wages (including a new union contract for hourly employees). Largely because of inflation, $15.9 million went for items that universities would prefer not to spend their funds on—utilities, insurance, office expenses, and employee benefits (largely health care and mandated contributions). The categories that did not increase were those central to university purposes—fellowships, books, supplies, equipment, and maintenance. In short, the payroll barely kept up with inflation, academic support was eroded, while nonacademic expenses consumed more than half of new funds. The Yale deficit was brought under control, but in the process, as Brewster admitted, "there have been real qualitative losses."[22]

The years of financial crisis brought enduring changes to Yale in terms of the balance of its activities, its sources of income, and its posture toward American society. These changes, furthermore, were representative of similar forces at work at other research universities. The most important of these changes consisted of a persistent, incremental scaling back of the commitments made during the post-Sputnik era. At Yale this development was, oddly enough, intertwined with the special issue of admitting women to Yale College. The same situation was faced by Princeton, where actions were taken somewhat more deliberately and implications were elaborated more clearly.

The idea of undergraduate coeducation gained ground at both Princeton and Yale after 1965.[23] Originally both schools thought in terms of establishing a coordinate relationship with an established women's college, similar to the Harvard-Radcliffe or Brown-Pembroke relationships. Yale even received an anonymous gift to examine the possibility of merging with Vassar. This far-fetched idea was seriously studied in 1966–67, but enventually dismissed by the Vassar trustees (who decided instead to admit men). Lacking a plausible partner, Princeton established a committee to investigate the feasibility of coeducation. The possible ramifications were studied far more thoroughly than at Yale and a strongly positive recommendation was returned in 1968.[24] Yale too, after its false start, was by now all but committed to coeducation. The overriding issue in the deliberations of both schools was still the recruitment of men. Each feared that it was increasingly losing good students to coeducational schools, and was even more fearful that additional students would be lost if the other became coeducational and it did not. These institutions had evolved strongly meritocratic admissions procedures since the 1950s, and maintaining the high quality of incoming freshmen was an overriding institutional priority. By the Fall of 1968 the die was cast; each school scrambled to commit itself, independently of the other, to admit women for the following academic year.

The deliberations of the Princeton committee were predicated on the admission of women as 1000 additional students. The report included a detailed analysis of the financial implications of such a step. Its conclusion was that Princeton had "the opportunity to make an extraordinarily good educational investment." The new students would contribute substantial amounts of tuition income, but, because of the expansion of the 1960s, they would require few new faculty: "the very large recent growth in the graduate program has inevitably meant that, at various places in the university, an educational capacity has been created which is not now fully used, some of which could be applied to an increased undergraduate body."[25] This was a rare confession for a research university. The efforts of the 1960s to build departments by establishing critical masses of scholars for purposes of graduate education and research had created a faculty that was seriously underutilized for instruction. This shoe fit Yale no less than Princeton. For both schools the admission of women allowed them to have larger and academically more talented undergraduate student bodies while also alleviating their financial burdens with additional tuition.[26]

The psychological aspects of the transition to coeducation were so paramount that they have largely obscured a more fundamental restructuring away from high-cost graduate education. Both Princeton and Yale added more than 1000 undergraduates between the Fall 1968 and Fall 1975, while graduate education was slightly reduced. In the same years, the number of faculty rose (in anticipation of more students) and then fell (due to budget shortfalls). Princeton added 11 senior positions and 36 junior positions in the first two years of coeducation, but then reduced positions by 2 and 11 over the next five years. Yale's situation was more severe. It added 25 senior and 11 junior faculty in the first two years, but then lost three senior and 55 junior positions by 1975.[27] Both schools protected their prestige by maintaining senior faculty, but sacrificed assistant professors.

Few other universities had the same luxury of increasing enrollment without diluting their recruitment pool, but the same kind of restructuring nonetheless occurred elsewhere. Graduate education was scaled back in light of the growing surplus of Ph.D.s and shrinking support, while additional undergraduates were admitted in order to make better use of faculties grown large during the 1960s. The additional income from tuition was also welcome. In this way the preponderant emphasis on graduate education of the post-Sputnik era was gradually attenuated.

The second enduring change caused by the financial crisis affected the basic sources of income at private universities. The increasing dependence on tuition revenues at Yale, which began in 1969, continued for at least twenty years. This trend was partly due to persistent difficulties with investments. The Yale endowment lost value in real terms throughout the 1970s; however, it then rose steadily during the 1980s. The burden of finance was nevertheless shifted toward student charges. In 1967 income from tuition (without room and board) approximated 73 percent of investment income, but in 1987 it amounted to 190 percent of such income. In terms of what students actually paid, tuition roughly doubled in real terms from 1968, the last year of no increase, to 1989. Through two decades of tuition increases, Yale remained committed to meritocratic admissions without regard for an applicant's ability to pay. The university has also been continually apprehensive about how its students would meet these rising charges.

As tuition increased, Yale like other private universities had to raise the amounts of student aid provided out of its own funds. It thus netted less than 100 cents of each additional tuition dollar—the price of maintaining the best possible applicant pool. In the midst of its budget crisis, Yale attempted to find additional ways for students to pay for their education. It imposed a $500 increase in student fees without any corresponding addition to student aid funds, and proposed a novel loan plan to bridge the difference. The "Yale Tuition Postponement Option" allowed students to defer payment (i.e. borrow) up to $800 each year, to be repaid with interest as a percentage of future income. It was thus the first income-contingent loan plan offered in American higher education. Within three years, 40 percent of Yale freshmen were participating—a rate that made the plan too costly.[28] The Yale plan was then abandoned and reliance placed instead on federal loan programs.

The long-anticipated additional federal financial assistance to hard-pressed colleges and universities came in the form of the Educational Amendments of 1972. By this juncture, broadening access to higher education was the only public purpose that could justify additional outlays. The aid was accordingly channeled to students instead of to institutions, as the universities had hoped. Direct aid subsidized low-income students, while less indigent students qualified for federally subsidized loans. Of the two forms of aid, loans assumed greater importance for the research universities. Along with institutional student aid, loans became another source of funds undergirding the steady rise in tuition. Yale's individual solution to its own financial straits thus anticipated a major national trend which allowed more of the burden of financing higher education to be shifted to students.

The third enduring consequence of the financial plight was to encourage a gradual drift away from the ivory-tower aloofness that had been the natural accompaniment of the Academic Revolution, reinforced in a perverse way by the otherworldliness of the student rebellion. This change first affected states of mind, but it also produced tangible developments. As university leaders, in particular, wrestled with the problem of expanding revenues they became increasingly willing to come to an accommodation with other elements in American society.

For Yale the constituency most needing to be mollified was the alumni. As early as 1970, when the outlook was in many ways bleakest, President Brewster specifically addressed Yale graduates about their role in sustaining the university's traditions. The state of their ties to alma mater became a crucial matter in mid-decade, when Yale sought to alleviate its financial problems through a carefully orchestrated fund-raising effort. The "Campaign for Yale" set a goal of raising $370 million between 1974 and 1977, two-thirds of which would be earmarked for endowment.[29] As campaigns go, this one was a struggle. It was launched when the miserable economy of the 1970s was at low ebb, and it had to surmount the cultural gulf that separated Yale of the 1970s from the institution that wealthy graduates had known. The Campaign belatedly reached its stated goal, but perhaps more importantly, this sustained effort to repair relations with alumni laid a foundation for more successful fund-raising in the next decade.

Associated with the Campaign was another significant step in Yale's rapprochement with the extramural world. The School of Organization and Management—Yale's version of a business school—opened its doors in 1977. Kingman Brewster was sufficiently within Yale traditions to reject the notion of an ordinary business school as too vocational—too close to what Whitney Griswold had labeled the 'service-station' concept of a university. But Brewster was deeply committed to developing a fruitful interaction between social science and social praxis, including the professions. In this vein he had shepherded the creation of the Institution for Social and Policy Studies as an interdisciplinary unit where social science could be brought to bear on a number of policy areas.[30] The new School of Organization and Management continued this tradition, being linked with the social science departments. It was explicitly intended to train professionals for careers in public and nonprofit, as well as private, enterprises. This initiative was also congenial to many alumni, who had expressed willingness to support business studies at Yale. In this step too, Yale was in the forefront of a national trend toward a greater weighting of professional education.

The second decade after Sputnik was a difficult one for Yale and for all of the research universities. The forebodings of President Brewster about qualitative decline, however, do not seem to have been borne out. The rating of faculty done at the end of the 1970s showed Yale to be even stronger than ten years earlier when the crisis began.[31] Many sister institutions could not make that claim. The important point is that the research universities proved surprisingly resilient during a prolonged period of financial distress. In a sense, the enormous investment that had been made in the first decade after Sputnik sustained the academic enterprise to a considerable extent through another decade of successive frustrations. But it would not be accurate to conclude that little had been lost. The combined impact of the student rebellion and the financial crisis stopped the forward momentum of research university development. More seriously, it created subtle but lasting impediments to the pursuit of their essential mission.

3. A Deeper Malaise

For most of the 1960s American universities were largely able to set their own course. What society demanded of them were the tasks that they preferred to perform. With alacrity they undertook the challenges of extending basic scientific knowledge and training increasing numbers of researchers. In the aftermath of the student rebellion and the onset of the financial crisis, however, this general social endorsement of their activities evaporated. Those immediate traumas were displaced by a deeper malaise which stemmed from the dissonant signals that research universities now received from American society. For higher education, access had eclipsed the advancement of knowledge as the nation's first priority. In research, findings applicable to immediate problems were demanded, while current rhetoric disparaged traditional scholarship in academic disciplines. This changed outlook affected the special status that research universities long held. The federal government no longer felt compunction about intruding into internal university matters, and state governments increasingly denied distinctive treatment to their flagship institutions. On campus, universities had to deal with groups actively committed to engaging the institution in social and political issues. Instead of setting their own agendas, the research universities of the 1970s were placed in the position of defensively shielding their fundamental purposes against unsympathetic or hostile critics.

The great wave of student protests that had welled up in the late 1960s crested first in 1968–69, and a second time in the Spring of 1970, but its energies then dissipated.[1] After 1971, campus radicalism ebbed considerably, but a residue of activism and sympathy for the Left remained. Henceforth, student demonstrations lacked the kind of overriding issues that could mobilize great crowds of students, polarize the university community, or close institutions. But like aftershocks of a major earthquake, they were unsettling because they recalled past disasters and portended future ones.

Once the inciting effects of the Vietnam War passed, student discontent became preoccupied with campus issues or campus manifestations of national issues. Rallies and demonstrations became more prevalent than confrontations, and students began to work through organizations of their own devising to alter conditions that affected their own lives. Some of the issues remained the same. Protests were sporadically staged against campus appearances of the still-despised C.I.A. or armed services. The presence of Marxist and radical perspectives in the curriculum, won during the student movement's heroic era, occasionally had to be defended en masse. The situation of blacks on campus became a persistent source of tension and potential conflict, largely stemming from the fulfillment or nonfulfillment of concessions previously wrested from university administrators. On a few campuses Hispanics too demonstrated for recognition and their own programs. Almost everywhere, the role of women became a contentious issue. By mid-decade, in a newer note, tuition hikes and financial issues became a frequent source of protest.[2]

Students in the 1970s increasingly turned to local activities and worked through and around existing authorities. 'Public Interest Research Groups' became one popular means for heightening student influence. At many activist campuses, student groups induced the dining halls to boycott lettuce and grapes to assist the unionization of farm workers. Seeking to extricate themselves as much as possible from the capitalist system, students organized food coops, tenant organizations, and student-run book stores. In sum, in the aftermath of the student rebellion university campuses harbored broad sympathies for most causes of the Left and backed those sentiments with actions; but these issues only infrequently brought students into the streets. Studies conducted at Harvard, in fact, showed student political sympathies to be almost as far to the Left in 1974 as in 1969, but for most confrontation held decidedly less allure.[3]

One legacy of the student rebellion was a pervasive sense of egalitarianism on university campuses. According to Lewis Mayhew, the fundamental features of universities had been challenged: "rationality and intellectuality, meritocracy, selectivity, collegiality and shared authority, campus autonomy, professorial expertise and training, and the primacy of professors in instruction and evaluation—all were called into question by the 1970s."[4] These things could be challenged with simplistic slogans, but only defended through patient and nuanced analysis.[5] A pronounced skepticism lingered among students toward these foundation stones of the academic authority structure.

Universities were of two minds concerning egalitarianism. The university community fervently supported the universality of scientific knowledge, and hence the equal rights of all to participate in education and learning. Authority in the university, on the other hand, was based essentially on the possession of knowledge and produced unequal, hierarchical relationships. To be a member of the academic profession is to spend much time making judgments about the intellectual performances of others—grading students, evaluating colleagues for promotion, criticizing the manuscripts and proposals of others in the field, and reviewing published work. For students, higher education has traditionally meant acquiring learning to achieve advantage in the workforce.

The attitudes prevailing in the wake of the student rebellion tended to undermine the legitimacy of these fundamental processes. Where faculty adopted the manner and dress of students and conducted nonauthoritarian classes, they generally eschewed rigorous grading as well. Where social goals were confounded with professional judgment, predominantly in the humanities and social sciences, political values colored the evaluation of professional work. Many students found it difficult to reconcile their relative privilege and potential career advantages with their egalitarian values, which produced the sad and wasteful phenomenon of the ideological drop-out. None of these phenomena was crippling in itself, but together they created an ongoing tension in the daily lives of universities between authority based on knowledge and pervasive egalitarian sympathies. Objectivity and value neutrality could no longer be assumed; instead substantial portions of the university community embraced a politicized view of their activities.

For the generation of university presidents who took office during and after the campus crises, a prerequisite for survival became the ability to operate within this new politicized context. Often presidents were chosen for their apparent rapport with students during the time of troubles. A second desirable attribute, stemming from the other crisis facing universities, was an ability to handle the mounting financial problems. For these reasons, it was common to promote presidents from within the institution who were already familiar with the existing problems and personalities. Provosts, in particular, who dealt intimately with both faculty and finances, were often tapped. Whatever their origin, the new presidents of the 1970s needed the same attributes: a fluency in the language of academic egalitarianism and a capacity to deal with students in an open and non-authoritarian manner. Above all, they placed pragmatism above principle in dealing with dissent. In practice this approach usually meant appeasement rather than resistance in response to student pressure. This posture was understandable given the circumstances, perhaps the only feasible course.

The consensus that normally undergirded the authority of university presidents could no longer be taken for granted in the early 1970s. Faced with a polity that was easily offended and readily mobilized for protest, it was imperative to prevent any escalation of conflict that might directly test the limits of authority. Police intervention was to be avoided in order to preclude provoking the latent antipathies of the bulk of the students, and especially to avoid involving the faculty. The least damaging approach tended to be a kind of tactical appeasement, in which demonstrations were allowed to persist until enervation set in. Concessions were freely made in matters that universities could live with, such as not purchasing lettuce, but seldom where vital interests were at stake. For example, the many protests against tuition hikes and economy measures that occurred in the mid-seventies were entirely ineffective.[6]

The new style of leadership had no better exemplar than Derek Bok, who assumed the presidential mantle of Harvard from Nathan Pusey in 1971. Bok was associated with the liberal side of the divided Harvard community: on the litmus test of Harvard politics, he had opposed calling in police to eject protesting students from Massachusetts Hall in 1969. He was perceived to be adept at crisis management, but once in office Bok's talent proved to be crisis avoidance. His evasiveness dismayed even students, who were accustomed to having rigid principles against which to rail. When demonstrators again occupied Massachusetts Hall, demanding that Harvard sell stock in Gulf Oil because of the company's operations in Angola, Bok tolerated the sit-in for a week until the protesters left of their own accord. He also long ignored the outrageous harassment by SDS of a professor who had written on inequality, although in the end Bok explicitly deplored those acts. A student editorial charged him with making "cosmetic concessions which divide and pacify the constituencies he must manipulate. . . . He adjusts Harvard just enough to take the initiative away from those demanding changes, makes the minimum effort necessary to blur the issue."[7] This complaint might be a formula for campus leadership in the new era.

Bok, in fact, consistently got the upper hand against the internal adversaries of academic authority. The most radical student factions soon discredited themselves through such tactics as breaking windows, which the university community found repugnant. The Harvard Black Studies Program was a particularly egregious case of academic appeasement (which Bok inherited) since it gave undergraduates a voice in choosing faculty. These arrangements progressively lost support and were reformed by the faculty in 1972 along lines of accepted practice.[8] Bok not only survived the crises of the 1970s, but went on to complete two decades of distinguished leadership of the country's oldest, wealthiest, and in many ways most prominent university. He also became a spokesman on how to navigate through the minefields of a politicized campus.

In *Beyond the Ivory Tower: Social Responsibilities of the Modern University* (1982), Bok set out in his own distinctive dialectical style to resolve the lingering challenge first posed by the student rebellion. He started on page one with Clark Kerr's notion of the multiversity—the thesis of a traditional, supposedly neutral university devoted to learning and service. The antithesis was provided by the moralistic critique of student activists—that the university inherently upheld the vested interests that controlled American society. The resolving synthesis offered by Bok was the socially responsible university, which "must constantly address moral issues and ethical responsibilities in all [its] relations with the outside world."[9]

Bok's intricate arguments addressed the principal moral issues that had been thrust upon universities since the late 1960s. He made a fundamental distinction between the academic and nonacademic responses of universities to social issues. For the former, he advocated preferential admission of minorities "exercised with care and judgment," but he opposed preferential hiring of minority faculty as dysfunctional and wrong. The university's moral purview over research, Bok concluded, extended chiefly over that supported by its own funds, but was quite circumscribed where sponsored research was concerned. The most critical issues for the socially responsible university nevertheless concerned the nonacademic actions advocated by internal groups. Here Bok's language proffered sympathy to the activists' goals but few substantive concessions. He felt that universities were only justified in taking political positions when their vested interests, academic or institutional, were at stake. He judged the divestiture of stock for political reasons to be ineffectual compared with the exertion of shareholder pressure. Boycotts too were inappropriate. How then did the socially responsible university express its moral and ethical vigilance? Its administrators were to address such concerns directly, and seize the initiative on "ethical issues *before* they emerge from the pages of the campus newspaper." It would teach moral reasoning to students and encourage individual engagement in assisting the socially disadvantaged and furthering social causes. Above all, the socially responsible university would convey sensitivity and earnestness toward the causes its constituents espoused.[10] By doing so, additionally, it would protect and preserve its own academic prerogatives.

Beyond the Ivory Tower articulated a practical approach to administering universities still seething with constituents who had little regard for academic norms and values. Essentially it advocated embracing the views of the university's adversaries, at least in part, in order to dispell the more awkward or impractical consequences. This point of view was far from being a cynical strategy; it was rather an imperative stemming from a new overriding consensus. By the early 1970s the ideology of basic research had been displaced throughout much of higher education by an ideology based on egalitarianism and social justice.

Dominant ideologies affect universities by placing differential valuations on the multiple ongoing tasks that higher education performs. Out-of-favor activities are usually acknowledged as necessary, but are hedged about with reservations and caveats; favored activities are supported in absolute terms with scant worry about qualifications. Although always assuming the posture of insurgency, an ascendant ideology is like a bandwagon in full regalia. It represents convictions already internalized at many campuses, and it also serves as a powerful goad to the laggards, the wavering, or the holdouts. The ideology of basic research received its clearest articulation three years after Sputnik, and was ascendant for at least five more years. The timing for the ideology of egalitarianism and social justice was similar. Doctrinal statements appeared three years after the apocalypse of 1968, and these sentiments colored the actions of universities for most of the decade of the seventies. One of the sharpest presentation of this viewpoint was made by an independent task force, chaired by Frank Newman, which was funded by the Ford Foundation and reported to the Secretary of Health, Education and Welfare. The Newman Report exemplified the prevailing conviction that virtually everything in higher education needed to be reformed. Simultaneously, similar views were formulated by a group of renowned scholars and major university presidents. This second report, from the Assembly on University Goals and Governance, indicated the degree to which research universities themselves endorsed this outlook, even though it depreciated their distinctive mission.[11]

Negatively, the reports were critical of the traditional patterns of undergraduate and graduate education—the forms in which the research universities excelled. The Newman Report attacked the "academic lockstep" by which students proceeded directly from high school to college to graduate school. In calling for an education that was less academic and more integrated with experience, it urged students to delay entering college, to stop-out or attend part time, and to work before contemplating graduate study. This advice was coupled with animadversions on the power accorded to university credentials in hiring, and a decidedly sour depiction of the academic disciplines.[12]

This last criticism inevitably pointed toward the graduate schools, which trained the teachers who taught the 'narrow' and 'irrelevant' courses. Given the crisis in graduate studies depicted in Chapter 7, overspecialization, the hegemony of disciplines, and poor completion rates presented easy targets. In this light, it seemed desirable to urge graduate students to focus greater effort on practical or applied endeavors. To counteract the alleged bad influence of the graduate schools, both reports recommended breaking the monopoly of the Ph.D. for faculty positions and appointing instead some teachers drawn from the realm of praxis (a suggestion that could only worsen employment prospects for new Ph.D.s).[13]

The research role was also subtly discounted by asserting that teaching should be recognized as the foremost university mission. From this perspective it was a short step to recommend that universities avoid research commitments that did not directly contribute to education. Research was further demeaned by allegations that much current disciplinary research was trivial or motivated solely by faculty self-interest.[14] Such strictures testify to the suspicion into which the research role had fallen.

On the positive side, the reports first advocated equalizing conditions for minorities and women. They endorsed special efforts of recruitment, preparation, and institutional adaptation in order to raise the enrollment levels of blacks. Such efforts had begun in the mid-sixties, but the participation rates of blacks still remained below national averages. At the beginning of the 1970s a revolution of expectations by and for women was in full swing. The key issues of equal standards for admission to graduate schools, equal pay with male colleagues, and greater recruitment to faculty positions were all endorsed by the reports. Beyond these matters, support was expressed for greater institutional variety, which in effect criticized the past domination of the research university model. Finally, the reports urged that universities place greater emphasis on teaching and seek more interaction with the outside world.[15]

The elements of the new consensus consisted of notions that in themselves could scarcely be opposed. Sentiments in favor of better teaching, broader recruitment, or relevance represented qualities or outcomes that were desirable in their own right and were to some extent legitimate counterweights to the previously dominant emphases. In spirit and sometimes in practice, however, they contradicted the natural propensities of research universities. In everyday operations choices had to be made. Growing fiscal problems made it difficult to sustain existing programs, let alone find funding for new initiatives. Leadership too was constrained. Universities could not simultaneously move aggressively to expand research capacity and also fulfill the new social agenda. At some point these two goals appeared to conflict. To accept or reject the new ideology, however, was no longer solely an internal matter. In important respects it was forced upon the universities by the federal government.

During the 1960s, federal civil rights laws were aimed at ending discriminatory practices in industry and particularly in the South. Universities were not originally subject to this legislation, and efforts to increase the representation of blacks on campus were solely an institutional matter. The situation changed abruptly when discrimination on the basis of gender was forbidden, and when civil rights law was extended to include higher education. By Executive Order No. 11375, issued by President Johnson and effective October 1968, every federal contract had to include nondiscrimination language, and contractors found to be out of compliance were required to survey their employment practices and develop a plan of affirmative action to rectify the situation. Within a few years, the entire panoply of federal civil rights legislation was altered to encompass sex discrimination and to apply to higher education.[16]

At the time Executive Order 11375 was issued, the Women's Equity Action League, or WEAL, was founded by Bernice Sandler, a staff member on the House Education Committee who had extensive contacts in Congress. WEAL sent letters to campus groups across the country apprising them of the implications of the Order and offering assistance in formulating complaints. These complaints soon flowed into the Office of Civil Rights in the Department of Health, Education and Welfare, numbering more than two hundred by the Fall of 1970. All colleges and universities having federal contracts were affected, but in fact the research universities were a special target. As Congresswoman Martha Griffiths pointed out, "women comprise 40 percent of the faculties in teachers colleges, and about the same in junior colleges. But in the prestigious private and state universities the percentage of women is much less."[17] Harvard was one of the first universities to be investigated; Michigan became a test case for achieving equal pay for women; and Berkeley eventually established one controversial model for affirmative action plans. The major research universities were congenial targets as well because of the strength of the local polities supporting this cause. The case against Michigan was prepared by the investigative work of a group of students and university employees; and when Harvard resisted the claims of HEW to review "all university records," 1400 people signed a petition calling for an affirmative action plan.[18]

Indeed, it seems unlikely that higher education would have become the chief focus for attacking discrimination against women without the presence of extensive campus support for this cause. The potency of the movement derived as well from the zeal of the bureaucrats charged with enforcing the regulations. Often new to their position (HEW tripled the number of 'contract compliance investigators' in 1972), unfamiliar with the higher education 'industry,' and committed to a literal interpretation of equality—the federal regulators set about imposing affirmative action without regard for academic customs of hiring and promoting faculty.[19] The regulators became for a time a force unto themselves. When the Secretary of the Treasury—former Harvard College dean John Dunlap—was urged to mollify these regulations, for example, he objected that such a change would outrage his own bureaucracy.[20]

What the regulators undertook was no less than a feat of social engineering. They set out to transform the gender and racial composition of college and university faculties that had largely been recruited over the previous quarter-century—during times when social norms about the education and careers of women had been decidedly different, as had the educational attainments of minorities. Unlike most regulation, this effort was not designed to bring a minority of violators into line: *every* university was guilty of not conforming to the new standards. For the first half of the 1970s, negotiations between universities and regulators proceeded amidst considerable confusion. Neither the institutions nor HEW knew precisely what standards were to be enforced. For a time it appeared that some of the principal research universities would have to forfeit all federal funding; but this 'death penalty' was never invoked and women's groups, for their part, complained of lax enforcement. Another recourse was the courts. Women and minorities were progressively given extraordinary leverage for launching lawsuits against universities. The eventual result by the latter part of the decade was that all the major universities had adopted affirmative action plans: the counting of women and minorities became an institutionalized preoccupation.[21]

For federal officials there was a delicious irony in this turn of events. Having endured vilification from campus radicals and, all too often, faculty just short years before, they had now seized the moral high ground: the federal government had become the champion of social justice in the form of equality for women and minorities, and the universities appeared to be evading social responsibilities.[22] But more than irony was involved in this turn of the tables. The government, especially the Congress, pressed its newfound moral superiority over universities with a succession of further intrusions into academic affairs. For example:

Title IX of the Education Amendments of 1972 supplied a blanket prohibition against gender discrimination in educational programs and activities. When put into practice its principal effects were, first, to assure that women would have equal access to and treatment in all graduate programs; second, to force institutions to provide numerous activities, especially athletics, for women on a comparable basis; and third, to provide easier recourse to litigation in cases of alleged discrimination in employment.[23]

In research, the government panicked in response to rather uninformed public fears that experiments with recombinant DNA would produce dangerous new life forms. Strict regulations that would have stifled the entire field were originally proposed, but complaints from scientists eventually prompted revisions. In an additional crusade against largely imagined abuses in research, HEW established cumbersome bureaucratic procedures for all research involving human subjects.[24]

Another needless intrusion into university affairs was created by the so-called "Buckley Amendment" which, by opening confidential files to students, greatly complicated record-keeping and undermined the candor of academic recommendations.[25]

Then, the Health Professions Education Assistance Act of 1976 usurped university control over student admissions by requiring that medical schools enroll transfer students who had studied abroad (having failed to gain admission to an American school). This appalling piece of special-interest legislation provoked the single successful example of principled opposition: a few schools placed their federal funding at risk by refusing to accede, and the most coercive features of the law were rescinded.[26]

These examples sketch out a clear pattern of federal disregard for university autonomy in the 1970s. As some approving commentators blandly put it, "the fact that the political institutions of society have felt it necessary to impose a system of regulation on the universities implies a judgment that higher education, like business and the professions, cannot be trusted to serve the public interest on its own initiative."[27] This 'judgment' constituted an extraordinary reversal of the historic relationship of trust between universities and American society. Sociologist Nathan Glazer characterized the government's new stance as "adversarial regulation."[28] It proceeded from the conclusion that universities were guilty of violating the public interest; it required institutions to submit vast documentation in order to incriminate themselves; and the penalty for noncompliance was in theory the same no matter what the transgression—the withholding of all federal funds. The peculiar effectiveness of this approach stemmed from the mutual reinforcement of three forces: the zeal of the regulators, who extended their requirements beyond the generally phrased intent of congressional legislation or Executive Orders; the well-organized and committed special interests on campus, always ready to exert pressure; and the courts which provided backing and enforcement to the regulatory web.

Federal regulation of universities, and particularly affirmative action, remained a contentious issue throughout the 1970s. In the 1980s the adversarial nature of this relationship lessened somewhat, but the regulations continued in force and, more significantly, universities remained strongly committed to the basic goals of affirmative action. Even two decades after the regulatory onslaught began, no summary judgment of its overall impact is possible. Traditionalists believed that federal meddling with the inner workings of universities produced irreparable harm. Proponents of women's rights generally felt that the government allowed universities to drag their heels, and that more should have been done. University leaders vociferously endorsed egalitarian goals while also seeking to protect their own freedom of maneuver from restrictive procedures.[29] The practical effects of these policies, however, were fully evident.

The hiring of faculty was undoubtedly the most sensitive area for universities. They were committed to selecting the most qualified individuals for faculty positions, but federal civil rights law was based on minimum necessary qualifications for employment.[30] The affirmative action plans that were negotiated pledged universities to reach certain numerical goals in terms of gender and race without specifying exactly how such goals would be attained. In the early years of draconian threats and confused enforcement, there can be little doubt that 'goals' were interpreted as quotas and that reverse discrimination against white males was rampant. Harvard, for example, was informed by an HEW official that the next person hired in the History Department had to be a woman. In this case a call from Derek Bok to the Secretary of HEW ultimately attained a more flexible guideline.[31] Few other administrators had such recourse. Taken together, affirmative action plans committed colleges and universities to hiring more faculty from protected groups than were actually available.[32] The pressure to find well-qualified candidates that met affirmative action goals consequently became intense.

In response to this pressure, university administrators at first tended to adopt procedures that would force departments to hire women and minorities. Sometimes, white males were only considered if and when no affirmative action candidate could be found. Occasionally, institutions would declare internally that for the time being they would hire only women or minorities. A few majority candidates had promised positions withdrawn because they did not contribute to the numerical goals.[33] Somewhat later, approaches that were less blatantly discriminatory became almost ubiquitous: slots were created in specialties pertaining to minorities or women; or, institutions established a pool of positions that would only be awarded to departments identifying acceptable affirmative action candidates. These tactics decreased the global number of positions for which majority candidates could compete, but they did not discriminate against any individual applicant. From the departmental perspective, such tactics provided incentives in the form of additional positions, and reduced the possibility of weak appointments caused by pressure to hire in thin markets. Given the inducements, departments often appointed minority and women candidates who had not yet finished their doctorate in preference to majority candidates with Ph.D.s, a practice which, by increasing the difficulty of launching an academic career, was sometimes a disservice to all concerned.

The critical issue was to what extent affirmative action requirements skewed the selection of university faculty. In general, the most egregious departures from academic norms tended to occur at non-research institutions, where administrations were stronger and departments weaker. The research role of universities was buffered from adverse effects by three factors: where departments had the autonomy to uphold academic standards, as they did in first-tier institutions, weak appointments were unlikely to occur and even less likely to stay on; the departments where most funded research occurred were comparatively unaffected because of the scarcity of affirmative-action candidates in engineering and the natural sciences; and the top institutions generally had the pick of the most promising scholars from the limited pool of well-qualified minorities and women. The research universities were on the whole quite resistant to any externally imposed lowering of standards. They nevertheless internalized the goals of affirmative action and went to great lengths to find suitable women and minority faculty.

The impact of affirmative action at research universities was thus to a considerable extent self-imposed. The chief contribution of the Office of Civil Rights was to require each university to draw up an affirmative action plan with goals and timetables. If universities were realistic about the size of the availability pools, their plans might not produce terribly onerous obligations. Berkeley is a case in point. When its plan was finally approved in 1975, after three years of negotiations and a short funding freeze, it was regarded as a model for major universities.[34] Berkeley followed the most current federal orders to the letter. It treated each of its departments individually, comparing the percentages of minority and women members with those for the pool in each field. As a result of this procedure, the deficiency of minorities in most departments was a small fraction of one position and required no action. Women were better represented in the availability pool, and goals were set accordingly. Out of 75 departments, 31 established goals for women, 1 for African Americans, 2 for Asians, and none for Hispanics and Native Americans. The timetables established by Berkeley were exceptionally long—up to sixteen years for nontenured faculty. This was because of little projected turnover: 81 percent of the Berkeley faculty were tenured and no enrollment growth was foreseen. Few Berkeley departments were thus required to hire persons of a specified type. But there was pressure nonetheless. The Berkeley plan was roundly criticized by partisans of women's and civil rights.[35] Vigilance by such groups created a constant goad for the hiring of women and minorities.

Other universities followed the same procedures, but less mechanistically. Many stretched to extend their hiring goals. Princeton, for example, interpreted fractional deficiencies within a department as justifying the appointment of an additional minority faculty member. Michigan established goals for some departments that were not deficient and overall targets for minorities that were unrealistically high.[36] The ascendant egalitarian ideology and local coalitions of activists induced universities to go beyond the legal minimum in implementing affirmative action. President Richard Lyman of Stanford no doubt expressed the consensus view of the desirability and correctness of these goals in spite of the awkwardness of the requirements for implementation. He believed "that federally enforced affirmative action was necessary, if the *de facto* exclusion of blacks and people with Hispanic surnames and American Indians from the higher reaches of American colleges and universities was to be ended [and furthermore] that it has done more good than harm in the university."[37] It was this internal conviction of the correctness of affirmative action that ultimately propelled university policies. Once affirmative action plans were filed and accepted, federal regulators had little further involvement. The mandatory campus offices of affirmative action, although in theory invested with formidable powers over appointments, largely shuffled the mountains of paper that these requirements generated.

The entire spate of federal regulations imposed on higher education in the 1970s, and particularly affirmative action, had three demonstrable results. They saddled universities with new administrative costs at a time when they were generally in a parlous financial state. Whole new offices had to be created and staffed, the volume of paperwork to be processed grew enormously, positions and salaries had to be upgraded, and universities were dragged into costly litigation. Some of these expenditures were inevitable as higher education was included in the universe of large employers; some undoubtedly rectified unwarranted discrepancies in treatment; but some still constituted an unproductive diversion of resources.

In a second perceptible effect, the requirements of affirmative action completely transformed the process by which faculty were selected. The practices that prevailed up to 1970 were little different from those depicted in *The Academic Marketplace* of 1957. They depended heavily on informal networks of scholars and were strongly influenced by the prestige hierarchy of institutions.[38] Now openings had to be publicly advertised and efforts taken to seek out minority and women candidates. Searches became large, costly, cumbersome affairs. On the other hand, the choosing of faculty also became more open and competitive.[39] While this last result was clearly welcome, its achievement was somewhat tarnished by the surreptitious side of these policies.

Affirmative action, finally, accomplished its immediate purpose of increasing the number of women and minorities on university faculties. During the decade of the 1970s, the percentage of women faculty in higher education rose from 23 to 29 percent. Furthermore, the momentum of this change persisted. The next four years (1979–83) witnessed the addition of 20,000 male faculty members and 29,000 women. From 1969 to 1983 the proportion of African-American faculty members rose from 2 to 4 percent.[40]

These changes were obtained by instituting a pervasive tilt in the recruitment of faculty. With the affirmative action scorecards being carefully toted, individuals from the favored categories were deliberately recruited, hired, and promoted. For critics, these special efforts implied that some favored individuals were less qualified than majority males who were passed over. This point, however, is a moot one. Qualifications, at least for entry-level faculty, are imperfect approximations of potential for achievement. But fulfillment of potential requires an institutional locus for a career. What actually occurred was that, given the surplus of qualified aspirants in most fields, women and minorities were differentially awarded the relatively scarce opportunities for academic careers. Once in those careers, they had positive incentives in terms of recognition and reward to develop their academic potential. White males with good academic skills, on the other hand, faced disincentives to pursue academic careers. The result was the outcome that prevailing egalitarian values had sought: greater ethnic and sexual diversity on university faculties. What was not achieved, however, was the original liberal ideal of a color-blind and gender-blind evaluation of accomplishments and provision of subsequent rewards. That liberal ideal was soon regarded as antediluvian. Instead, the categories of ethnicity and gender became entrenched on university campuses and continued to exert a significant influence on the politics of the curriculum and faculty selection—a preoccupation reflecting the connection between these policies and the disillusionment toward academic norms that existed at the end of the 1960s.

The disenchantment with research universities evident on campuses and in federal policy had a counterpart on the state level. Although policies varied enormously across the fifty state systems of higher education, three kinds of developments affected research universities adversely. In a few states, legislatures reacted vindictively to punish universities for their failure to control the student rebellion. Second, and more widespread, changes in state control over higher education lessened the autonomy of flagship campuses. Third, constraints in the funding of universities were commonplace, whether related or not to the other two developments.

In 1970 the California legislature voted a 5 percent cost-of-living raise for all state employees, including nonacademic university staff, but denied the raise to the faculty of the California state college and university systems.[41] This was one of the few overtly punitive acts taken by state governments in response to campus disorders. Proposed legislation to punish student dissidents or cut university support were far more common, but the enactment of such benighted retaliation was nearly always avoided. State research universities nevertheless suffered a decline in esteem and influence from a tangled combination of effects. Student unrest definitely tarnished their image; the change in prevailing ideologies put them on the defensive about their research mission as well as the sincerity of their efforts to conform with the new social demands; and with the tumult existing on campus, university leaders were in no position to assert the interests of their institutions forcefully in the political arenas of their states. The state politics of higher education was given scant attention during the 1960s, when all eyes were focused on Washington, D.C.; however, the power of states to shape and control systems of higher education quickly became a preoccupation of the 1970s.[42]

State coordination of higher education actually grew substantially during the 1960s. Particularly significant was the adoption at the beginning of the decade of the tripartite California Master Plan, which defined the separate missions and governance of the University of California, the California state college system, and the state's two-year community colleges. Far from being pernicious to the university, the Master Plan is generally credited with protecting that sector and allowing it to develop into a system of unparalleled scope and eminence.[43] The Master Plan was overseen by an advisory board with the capacity to plan, while implementation was left to the different systems. In the classic study of coordination done at the end of the decade, Robert Berdahl identified two stronger forms of state control: coordinating boards with regulatory powers and consolidated governing boards. During the 1960s, Berdahl found, the number of states using advisory boards increased from 5 to 13, those with coordinating boards from 5 to 14, and consolidated governing boards (often states with very small systems) from 16 to 19.[44]

The burgeoning of public higher education in the 1960s was the direct stimulus for greater coordination. Faced with the competing demands of different campuses, legislators needed assistance in order to rationalize and regularize these claims. Coordination in the sixties did not generally impede the research universities. The competition for resources was less intense in the era of the rapidly expanding pie, and the prestige of flagship universities remained high through most of the decade. Conditions were different during the next wave of coordination that occurred at the beginning of the 1970s. Universities were under a cloud, and coordination was advertised as a way of saving taxpayers' money.

Much depended on circumstances in each state. In North Carolina, for example, a consolidated board of governors was given control in 1972 over all four-year public colleges and universities. This new entity, however, was an expansion of the body that had formerly governed the two principal universities, the University of North Carolina and North Carolina State. Under the presidency of the former UNC president, William Friday, the new board catered to the academic ambitions of the state's two public research universities.[45] The political tide seemed to run against flagship universities, however, in the Midwest and along the Pacific Coast where the principal public research universities were located.

Events in Illinois well illustrate the three perils that universities faced in the early 1970s: attacks from state politicians, regulatory interference, and fiscal stringency. Illinois established a Board of Higher Education in 1961 to coordinate the rapid expansion of higher education in the state. Although conflicts were muted during the growth era, it soon became apparent that the Board and the University of Illinois were in competition for power: "in order to establish a position of power for itself . . . , [the Board had to] decrease the status of the major university."[46] In 1969 a new director with political ties to the governor was appointed and the staff was greatly enlarged. In the name of cutting costs and promoting efficiency the board assumed a more active role in the internal operations of universities. The governor also identified himself with halting the growing costs of public higher education. In 1971 he made this a political issue, first clashing with the legislature and finally slashing the higher education budget with line-item reductions. The changing priorities in higher education are evident in the year-to-year figures. In a statewide allocation to higher education that was equal to the year before, the University of Illinois was reduced by $7 million, Southern Illinois University by a like amount, and the other eight state institutions by $10 million. State aid to private institutions (mostly medical) increased by $10 million, state support for community colleges rose by $7 million, as did student aid (which was intended to compensate for higher tuition). Although these developments were detrimental to the University of Illinois's ability to maintain its stature as a research university, they were far more damaging to the developing state universities with immature programs and less tradition.[47]

Events in Ohio paralleled those in Illinois. There a statewide Board of Regents was created in 1963, and the initiative for setting public policy in higher education shifted from the university presidents to the chancellor of the board.[48] By the early 1970s President Harold L. Enarson of Ohio State, for one, was alarmed by the drift of events. He perceived a tendency to treat state universities like "simply another agency of state government," and thus "to convert relatively free-standing, self-directing institutions of higher education into homogenized state systems." These efforts, he felt, were counterproductive: the promised economies from tighter control never materialized, nor was teaching or research furthered. Instead, "the impact of multiple sources of regulation on the university is to discourage flexibility, cripple initiative, dilute responsibility, and ultimately to destroy true accountability."[49] These fears may appear exaggerated in retrospect, but they were quite real at the time. In Michigan, for example, the universities had to defend their constitutional autonomy in court against the aggrandizement of the State Board of Education.[50] Homogenization was carried furthest, however, in Wisconsin.

At the urging of Democratic governor Patrick Lucey, legislation was enacted in 1971 that merged the four campuses of the University of Wisconsin with the nine-campus Wisconsin State University system. The governor claimed that the move would save money through greater administrative and fiscal efficiency, but he was also, in all likelihood, seeking political favor by diminishing the special status of the protest-ridden Madison campus. He could also argue, with considerable validity, that the existing coordinating council had failed to resolve competition between the two systems.[51] None of these were particularly good justifications for uniting fundamentally dissimilar types of institutions—as events would show.

The influence of the University of Wisconsin at Madison was undeniably diminished by the merger. Henceforth, it would have to maintain the trappings of a world-class research university amidst resentful 'peers' having less talented students and lower-paid faculty. The conflict that had previously existed between the two systems was now fully vented within the single supersystem. Any immediate cost-cutting was illusory. The governor in fact felt compelled to offer generous faculty salary increases to appease potential critics of the merger. State appropriations to higher education rose considerably during the merger years without any growth in enrollments—in marked contrast to the experience of most states (see below). But harder times would follow. In actuality, state spending for higher education was largely unrelated to the form of statewide coordination adopted.[52]

The amounts of direct appropriations supporting research universities varies considerably from state to state. In the most simplified terms, there are three distinct spheres for analyzing fiscal effort. First, the financial capacity of the state can be broken down into the economic wealth of the state and the relative tax burden imposed on its citizens. Second, the claims of higher education have to be weighed against the claims of other state services and obligations. Third, the needs of the research sector compete against those of other sectors of higher education. Since each of these factors varies more or less independently of the other, the year-to-year variation across the fifty states is enormous.

In the second decade after Sputnik, contrary to contemporary impressions, the relative commitment by states to support higher education did not diminish: both state revenues and appropriations for higher education increased by an identical 207 percent from 1968 to 1977. The central region of the country, which included the Big Ten universities, had the highest increase in tax revenues, but nearly the lowest growth in support for higher education. Within higher education, universities in this region lost the largest share of state appropriations to other sectors.[53] Clearly, the problem there was not financial capacity as much as it was competing demands for state funds. Relative claims are ultimately decided through the political process, and governors in several of these states took public stands against the high costs of public universities. During these years the changing priorities in higher education also worked against the universities. Nationwide, their share of state appropriations declined from 54 to 46 percent, while support for community colleges rose from 10 to 17 percent (1968–77). State colleges lost 2 percent (28 to 26%), while that much was gained by aid to students or private institutions (6 to 8%). The efficiency-promoting state boards and agencies claimed an additional percentage of total appropriations for themselves (2 to 3%).[54]

Overall, state support for universities declined relative to state revenues and to other institutions of higher education. There was considerable variability

TABLE 23. Funding Changes for State Higher Education, 1968–1978[55]

	FTE Enrollment		Funding for All Higher Education		Funding for Research Universities	
	1968–73	1973–78	1968–73	1973–78	1968–73	1973–78
California*	41%	27%	36%	41%	17%	35%
Illinois	55	9	31	0	8	−3
Indiana*	26	10	8	20	−11	2
Michigan*	32	−9	33	2	13	1
Minnesota	20	2	32	15	19	15
N. Carolina*	31	16	60	70	35	49
Ohio	35	10	46	22	30	12
Texas*	n.a.		42	56	27	45
Washington	44	10	16	23	−4	22
Wisconsin	21	3	51	−1	41	0
U.S.	42	17	39	21		

*Two or more research universities in Table 16

from state to state, however, where the actual effects were felt. Table 23 provides relevant data on the ten states that possessed the most prestigious state research universities in the mid-sixties.

The experiences of these states varied widely, but several patterns are nevertheless evident, as well as some special circumstances. The reduced priority of research universities is evident in that the growth of their appropriations was almost always less than that of state appropriations to higher education. The slowing of enrollment growth in the mid-seventies is also apparent in each of these states, but it seems to have had little effect on funding. The most significant development mirrored in these figures is the relative weakness of Big Ten states, as well as Washington, in comparison with those of the Sun Belt, especially in the latter period.

Indiana, Washington, Illinois, and Michigan show the weakest funding for their universities from 1968 to 1973. The first two could at least plead poverty: both Indiana and Washington had previously supported higher education at levels well above the national averages, but during these years they experienced negative real growth in state revenues. Disenchantment was evident as well, however: the University of Washington had $10 million, or 14 percent, slashed from its appropriation in 1971, while a like amount was added to experimental Evergreen State College and the community colleges.[56] Illinois, and to a lesser extent Michigan, had growing revenues, but chose not to devote these additional funds to higher education. The healthy increases in Ohio and Wisconsin should be seen in a longer perspective: Ohio was raising one of the country's lowest bases of support for higher education. Wisconsin spent heavily before and during the merger, but not afterward, as faculty salaries at Madison slipped to the lowest in the Big Ten.[57] Only Minnesota had both a fairly prosperous treasury and a willingness to support its university.

The disparities between the Big Ten and the Sun Belt states was more marked for the mid-seventies, as university support in North Carolina, Texas, and California far outdistanced that in the Midwest. This pattern was just a partial indication of a larger shift of the university research system. The universities that were able to advance in academic standing and research volume during the 1970s were predominantly from the South and West, as will be seen in the next chapter.[58] The universities of the Big Ten remained distinguished, but the weakness in public funding eventually translated into a relative loss of academic stature. When graduate departments were rated at the beginning of the 1980s, the most prestigious Big Ten universities, as well as the University of Washington, all fell in rank—except for Minnesota, which remained the same. Conversely, North Carolina, Texas, and UCLA advanced, while Berkeley remained at the top.[59]

It is apparent from these developments that political unpopularity and fiscal stringency ultimately translated into academic weakness, at least in relative terms. Those states that continued to back the missions of their research universities, on the other hand, saw quality enhanced. Behind this superficial relationship, however, lay a deeper and more subtle lesson that only slowly emerged in the course of the 1970s. Just as the private universities realized in the early 1970s that they could no longer hope that the federal government would fulfill their growing needs, so the state universities gradually learned that they could expect little additional help from state legislatures. Higher education in the 1970s became a mature industry which, like most other agencies of state government, had to be maintained within fiscal limitations. But, as educators like Harold Enarson were at pains to point out, universities were intrinsically different from state bureaucracies. They not only needed autonomy to manage their own affairs, but to retain their vitality they also needed to grow. They had to keep enlarging their activities if they were to keep abreast of the expanding frontiers of knowledge and evolving opportunities to serve society. But state governments, even those well-disposed toward universities, could not in the long run be counted on to provide ever-higher levels of resources. For immediate relief state universities raised tuition, like their private counterparts; but even large percentage increases in their comparatively low fees produced small absolute gains.[60] Over time, state universities too became more dependent on tuition fees, but such revenues did not resolve their problems. Essentially, they needed to find additional ways to be useful to and garner resources from society.

This realization struck private universities sooner and with greater urgency. For state universities, the financial crisis developed somewhat later, and then its immediate cause seemed to lie with state government.[61] But since states for the most part lacked the financial capacity or will to enlarge university budgets, universities were increasingly thrown back upon their own devices. In this respect, however, they were inhibited by the very malaise that was in part responsible for their predicament. The loss of trust in universities had led many states to hamstring their autonomy with constrictive regulations. When universities most needed to exercise their own initiatives they were least able to do so. On campus, the dominant polity held that the university should function as a critic of society rather than as an constructive component. Universities still worried that involvement with the productive economy would compromise their supposed aloofness and moral superiority. Private universities were afflicted with federal regulation and a similar campus sentiment, but out of necessity they responded more pragmatically to address their financial woes. State universities, on the whole, were more lethargic. Not until the 1980s would they regain the self-confidence to once again assert their role.

That the decade after Sputnik had been an ephemeral golden age for research universities was apparent only in retrospect. Beginning in 1968, that comfortable world was progressively dismantled. The student rebellion, the financial squeeze, the regulatory assault—these were all calamities that could be endured. More difficult was adjusting to the pervasive change in ideology. The faith in basic research that had provided the underpinning for the post-Sputnik expansion was discredited, and in the process the fundamental mission of research universities was devalued. Ascendant now were values predicated on egalitarianism and social justice. This new standard affected universities obliquely: it made the operations of research universities more costly and more cumbersome, but it also made the institutions diffident about their *raison d'être*. By the middle of the 1970s, the research universities faced a need to articulate a fresh and compelling rationale for their basic role as guardians of advanced knowledge and rational inquiry.

9

Surviving the Seventies

1. The State of Universities in the Mid-1970s

The mid-seventies was a time for taking stock in higher education—for attempting to come to terms with the tangible and intangible factors causing the pervasive malaise. The journal *Daedalus,* ever attuned to the intellectual pulse, devoted two volumes to "American Higher Education: Toward an Uncertain Future."[1] The contributors were distinguished representatives of the academic community, including many presidents of leading research universities. A wide spectrum of opinions was offered in the 81 pieces, but the overall tone was pessimistic. Clark Kerr summed up these sentiments when he averred, somewhat hyperbolically, that higher education had passed from its Golden Age to an Age of Survival.[2] The threat no longer came from students; in fact, the volumes are sprinkled with harsh judgments of the unruly students who had embarrassed many of the same writers just short years before. Several of the presidents nevertheless identified difficulties posed by the egalitarian legacy of the protest years.[3] The main sources of worry, however, were the growing intrusions of government and persistent financial pressures.[4] These common themes emanating from some of the most knowledgeable members of the university community thus reflected the preoccupation with present rather than future issues.

When these same minds turned to the future of higher education, there was virtually no convergence of views. Indeed, their diverse ideas projected the disunity that some of the contributions remarked upon.[5] The concerns about government regulation tended to be couched in terms of highly normative conceptions of the university. Although such thoughts may have been comforting, they foretold little of future events. Ideas for eluding the financial crisis all too often looked again to the federal government. Seen in retrospect, it is remarkable how little of the future development of American higher education these wise heads actually divined.[6] Their gaze was largely focused on matters involving the linkages between higher education and American society—regulation, financial support, public confidence, and, the function the public most related to, undergraduate education. As important as these matters were in steering developments in higher education, they had largely been factored into present concerns. The trends of the future, on the other hand, were inchoate within universities—the product of each institution's efforts to cope with the very conditions that preoccupied these writers.

Just after the *Daedalus* collection appeared, the National Science Foundation and the Association of American Universities sponsored another kind of stocktaking. Investigators led by Bruce Smith and Joseph Karlesky conducted an empirical canvass of the university research system in 1975 and 1976 to gauge the "State of Academic Science." While scarcely cheerful about the long-term prospects, their conclusions reflected the strengths of research universities as well as their problems. Smith and Karlesky found that "the continued scale, vigor, and creativity of American science in virtually all fields of research endeavor can be termed outstanding."[7] On the most important measure, significant scientific advances, they reported exciting progress in each major discipline. This conclusion should not be surprising. The university research system shaped by the post-Sputnik expansion had actually changed little at the level where research was conducted. In real terms, expenditures for research had been on a plateau since 1968. Enormous forward momentum had been created by training large numbers of scientists, granting them lifetime employment, and providing them with the resources to pursue research: the ongoing productivity of the university research system was the natural result.

Some things had changed, however, and for the worse. The withdrawal of federal support for graduate students, plus the stagnant market for new faculty, combined to depress the numbers and the quality of graduate students.[8] The curtailment of special support for facilities and instrumentation was already inhibiting some lines of research. The principal danger facing university research, the authors speculated, was that this momentum would be lost. A massive new investment would then be required to reinitiate forward progress.

The effects of this weakening were visible at the departmental level. What Smith and Karlesky observed was an apparent contraction of the system toward the departments of recognized quality. Those departments had less difficulty securing research funding; they continued to appoint some junior faculty; and, they had first call on the diminished cadres of new graduate students. One drawback to heightened competition was detected: more difficult funding and placement conditions had seemed to make scientists and their students more cautious. Sticking to the tried and true seemed to be the best course for guaranteeing grants, publications, and faculty appointments.

Below the most distinguished departments, problems were apparent. Departments were often saddled with faculty who no longer received research support. A dearth of graduate students had a negative effect on research and sometimes on departmental resources. And aging equipment was often inadequate. The situation seemed to be worst in physics, the postwar darling that was now plagued by shrinking research support from NASA and the DoD, as well as changing priorities in federal energy programs. However, the authors also observed ways in which some departments were adapting to the new environment. Instead of trying to cover every field, departments were specializing in order to emphasize their strengths and enhance their visibility. The shortage of graduate students could be countered by utilizing more technicians and postdocs, in effect operating more like an *institute*. In addition, some departments admitted moving into applied research when funding for basic research was not forthcoming.

The authors attempted to extrapolate the experiences of departments to the level of institutions, foreseeing a concentration of research in the strongest universities. This prospect raised the issue posed in the Seaborg Report some seventeen years before. One of the collaborators on the study bluntly stated, "the country does not need as many universities emphasizing research and graduate education as aspired to that status a decade ago."[9] By this juncture it was already clear that a number of institutions had dropped out of the race. Wesleyan University, for example, which then had the highest per-student endowment in the country, decided in 1971 that it was not wealthy enough to be a research university and opted instead to make liberal education its top priority. Brown, which in 1960 was considered poised to join the first-tier of research universities, made a similar commitment to emphasize undergraduate education. New York University, another promising candidate of 1960 and recipient of a Ford Challenge Grant, was derailed by one of the more severe institutional financial crises. Nor were state universities immune. Rutgers, which had consciously set out to become a research university, experienced at full force all of the calamities described in the previous chapter, leaving its research aspirations seriously compromised by the early 1970s.[10]

The State of Academic Science identified at least two dynamic elements that were largely ignored in the *Daedalus* volumes. The first, just indicated, was the concentration of university research. The creation of additional research universities had been an objective of public policy during the previous decade and a large, decentralized, and competitive university research system was felt to be the key to American scientific leadership. Smith and Karlesky were of the opinion that those qualities could be preserved in a system having somewhat fewer research universities than then existed. More interesting, however, what they thought they were observing was not in fact occurring. The postwar secular trend of deconcentration apparently slowed from about 1969 to 1974, but an actual change of direction toward the hypothesized *reconcentration* never took place.[11] This misperception was no doubt influenced by the prevailing mood. Obscured by the preponderance of negative publicity surrounding the research universities and their mission was the continued incremental development of some institutions, particularly in the Sun Belt states. Smith and Karlesky, in fact, held open this possibility with one shrewd observation:

> Any university with access to even moderate amounts of discretionary funds will now have a distinct advantage in attracting outstanding faculty, in entering new fields of investigation, [and] in setting its own priorities. . . .[12]

Indeed, as will be seen, there were in fact institutions that still found the ideal of a research university attractive.

The second dynamic element identified by the authors was the discernible beginnings of a closer relationship between universities and industry. Much of the initiative seemed to be coming from university faculty and administrators, "especially," they wrote, "in the most prestigious universities, at which anti-industry protests and attitudes were strongest in the late 1960s." In part, such ties held promise for providing some additional funding for research. More was at stake, however: reaching out to industry implied a break with the cloistered mentality that had flourished in the 1960s. At the time they wrote, though, the authors were well aware that such attitudes still impeded closer cooperation.[13]

The sections that follow address these two issues. Detailed attention will first be given to two institutions that possessed some crucial discretionary resources and used them to advance significantly as research universities. The final section will trace the rapprochement between universities and industry from its beginnings in the seventies through its efflorescence in the 1980s. Both the emergence of new research universities and the changing attitudes toward ties with industry and programmatic research not only helped research universities survive the seventies, but also laid a foundation for renewed progress in the next decade.

2. The University of Arizona

The University of Arizona in some ways might stand for many state institutions that slowly were transformed into research universities. It was well behind the others, however, in the postwar and Sputnik eras, but this relative backwardness turned into an advantage in the 1970s.

In the aftermath of World War II the University of Arizona was a provincial outpost of sorts, one of many state land-grant colleges whose existence was still closely tied to the land. It was woefully underfunded by the state, and was gradually instituting 'reforms' that were taken for granted at other universities.[1] On the eve of Sputnik, the university had just two doctoral programs in arts and sciences, and it conducted less than $1 million of separately budgeted research. Thus it was in no position to be an immediate beneficiary of the burgeoning research economy. By the end of the post-Sputnik expansion, Arizona had advanced sufficiently to become a fledgling research university, but it ranked only 68th as a recipient of federal research dollars. By the end of the 1980s, however, Arizona had joined the top twenty performers of academic research—becoming *ipso facto* a major performer. In part this rise reflected some advantages of residing on a late-developing frontier, as well as a frontier-like pragmatism in the pursuit of academic advancement. On the other hand, the rise of Arizona also revealed some of the forces affecting university research in the 1970s. The same factors that have been identified in the advancement of other research universities—establishing centers of research excellence, academic leadership, and the availability of resources—were vital to Arizona as well.

The University of Arizona is the senior of three institutions governed by the Arizona Board of Regents. Before the 1970s it would be fair to say that regental concerns about the university centered on its predominant service role, lodged chiefly with the professional schools. The College of Agriculture worked closely with commercial agriculture in the state, and the Experiment Station had a larger research budget than the university itself until 1960. Similarly, the College of Mines was structured to serve industrial needs, and even included the state Bureau of Mines as an affiliated unit. The Business College was a third powerful school having an active outside constituency; until 1966 it included the department of sociology, and it continues to house economics—both anomalous arrangements. One of the few units dedicated to pure research was the Laboratory of Tree-Ring Research (dendochronology), which traced its antecedents to 1906.

When Richard A. Harvill became the fourteenth president of the university in 1951, it enrolled about 6000 students and was oriented toward a fairly narrow conception of service to the state. Harvill himself was a product of this milieu. He came to the university in 1934 as an instructor of economics and served as dean of both the graduate school and the College of Liberal Arts. When he retired in 1971, the university was in a much different state—enrollments exceeded 18,000 and it had earned a growing regional reputation for research. Just what ambitions Harvill nurtured for the institution are unclear. He was a remote and autocratic leader, who did not share his intentions even with close associates. Most certainly, he acted to protect the preponderant interests of the professional schools. He also waged a never-ending struggle to accommodate rising student enrollments. But he was alert to opportunities for research too. Shortly after Sputnik he stated that Arizona's role in the expanding research economy would be to concentrate on fields in which it possessed some natural advantage.[2] Indeed, opportunism and natural advantage would account for the initial building blocks for the university's research role.

The first of these building blocks was the Institute for Atmospheric Physics. The Institute's creation in 1954 was a rather serendipitous development, but it was to have great influence on the subsequent growth of research. The southern Arizona region is at once critically dependent upon a fickle rainfall and also an ideal environment for observing atmospheric processes. Some initial efforts at rain-making and the intervention of a prominent citizen lay behind the establishment of the Institute.[3] Originally, it was established as a joint venture with the University of Chicago, which had a mature program in meteorology, but it soon became solely an Arizona enterprise. The Institute was founded with university funds and a grant from the Sloan Foundation. Under its resourceful director, A. Richard Kassander, who later would become the university vice-president for research (1972–81), the Institute immediately became more than just a center for research. When the NSF designated atmospheric research as one of its early areas of emphasis, recurrent support for the Institute became available. The Institute thereby became an important source of contact between the university and federal science agencies. In addition, the Institute had the flexibility and the foresight to facilitate the founding of several other important organized research units (ORUs).

In 1958 the Rockefeller Foundation made a grant to the university to establish the Laboratory for Arid Land Research. As the university is fond of pointing out, some 30 percent of the earth's surface is found in arid or semi-arid climates. Arizona provided an ideal setting to study such environments, and research in this field still flourishes. In 1958 the Laboratory found its first home with the Institute rather than the commercially oriented College of Agriculture (which it joined only in 1982). The Laboratory then helped to provide the critical mass of scientific activity that permitted the school (later college) of earth sciences to disengage itself from engineering studies in the College of Mines (1963). Later, the Water Resources Research Center and the Solar Energy Research Laboratory would follow similar paths, first being shepherded by Kassander in the Institute and eventually becoming independent ORUs. The department of geosciences within the new school of earth sciences provided an anchor of sorts for environmental studies. It covered a broad area from paleontology to economic geology and, in combination with these ORUs, formed an active center of research.[4]

The most powerful concentration of research developed in and around astronomy. In this case several disparate developments were needed for the university to capitalize on the natural advantage of its clear skies. The first was the decision by the NSF to locate an optical observatory at Kitt Peak, just fifty miles from Tucson. Arizona was not included as a charter member of the consortium of universities that managed the observatory because it lacked a doctoral program in astronomy. This lacuna was soon rectified (1961), and proximity to Kitt Peak then aided further development of the department. In addition, the university was given its own site on the mountaintop where it soon installed a telescope.[5]

In 1960 the country's foremost lunar astronomer unexpectedly expressed an interest in joining the university. Gerard Kuiper was director of the University of Chicago Yerkes Observatory, but he had reached an impasse of sorts there: rising interest in the space program had created a great demand for further knowledge of the moon, but the facilities at Yerkes were strained to the limit. Moreover, Kuiper had to contend with the disdain of 'real' (i.e. trans-solar-system) astronomers for his study of lunar and planetary subjects. Considering the alternatives before him, and assured of comfortable federal support, Kuiper decided that Arizona would be the optimal location for the large-scale lunar and planetary studies that he envisioned. President Harvill greeted this possibility enthusiastically, but then encountered an obstacle. His own 'real' astronomers, having just attained the facilities needed for their research, had no interest in having their telescope preempted for lunar observations. Harvill then turned to Kassander, who was pleased to take Kuiper and his entourage into the Institute for Atmospheric Physics. The Institute, in fact, had more substantive interests in common with Kuiper than did the astronomers (e.g. planetary atmospheres). The Lunar and Planetary Laboratory thus began its existence under the wing of the Institute. It subsequently became independent and flourished as a close accomplice of NASA and the space program.[6]

The research complex in astronomy was further enriched by the establishment of the Optical Research Center in 1964. This, only the second center of specialized optical research in the U.S., was the personal project of Aden Meinel, who had directed both the Kitt Peak and the University of Arizona observatories. His wish to establish optical research in Arizona found ready support in Washington, first from the ARPA and then from the Air Force. Meinel's chief interest was in building better telescopes, and one of the Center's accomplishments was to design a novel "multi-mirror telescope," which had greatly enhanced light-gathering power. The field of optics, however, soon came to include much more. The military held great interest in looking down at the earth from the sky. With the development of lasers, further opportunities for research and application abounded. The Optical Science Center soon became a national leader on one of the most fruitful frontiers of basic and applied research.[7]

Another building block of research emerged in the department of anthropology. It capitalized upon the rich archaeological treasures of the region and the proximity of Native Americans of the Southwest and Mexico. In contrast to those natural-science fields just discussed, anthropology developed with considerable local assistance from the Bureau of Ethnic Research, the Arizona State Museum, and the Archaeological Field School before many federal dollars were available. Anthropology built upon these opportunities and succeeded in becoming, with astronomy, the first Arizona departments to receive national recognition in reputational ratings (1966)[8]

The establishment of these different research centers followed a pattern. First, from the study of Native-American culture, to paleontology and arid lands, to geology, the planets, and intergalactic space—there existed a natural advantage to studying these phenomena in southern Arizona. Second, the subjects in which the university rose to prominence were somewhat off the beaten academic paths. (Astronomy was shaped by the existence of special facilities.) These were specialties in which Arizona did not face inordinate competition from wealthier and more prestigious universities. Third, achieving these pockets of research excellence had far-reaching effects on the rest of the university. It overcame a kind of defeatist attitude that was prevalent on the campus—an assumption that Arizona could never hope to attract first-rate scientists. Furthermore, these research centers provided leadership for subsequent advances. The key role of Kassander's Institute for Atmospheric Physics in encouraging other centers has been noted. These units also established regular links between the university and NASA and the NSF. Finally, the Arizona research centers were for the most part genuinely interdisciplinary before that became fashionable, a factor that helped to spread their influence within the university. The achievement of this kind of research presence, nevertheless, was only a beginning. For the university to develop further as a research university, it felt the need to cultivate greater strength within the core disciplines on which these interdisciplinary efforts to some extent depended. Accomplishing this would be an extended process.

Arizona's rise to become a research university was aided by being named as one of the first recipients of a NSF University Science Development grant. Arizona well fit the geographical and developmental criteria of this program, as discussed in Chapter 6. Of key importance, however, was the criterion of supporting institutions that had "developed significant strength in at least one field of science."[9] For Arizona the successes in astronomy were critical. The grant and its renewal brought the university $7.2 million over five years for the strengthening of Astronomy, Chemistry, Mathematics, and Physics. These funds had the direct effect of compressing the development time of these fields by enlarging the departments and providing additional facilities.[10] Indirect effects were probably just as important. Being a first-round winner in this competition improved morale within the university and caused positive recognition nationally. Both these attitudinal effects made it easier for the university to attract the kind of productive scientists that it sought. The application process also forced the institution into a form of long-range planning, and particularly the identification of qualitative, research-related goals. In financial terms, the university had to commit itself to a commensurate investment in these departments in the short term, and the maintenance of these costly commitments over the longer term. The NSF Science Development grant thus tended to crystallize an ambitious research agenda for the university.[11]

The institutionalization of significant research programs constituted a marked change from former conditions. In the late 1950s there was virtually no research in either physics or chemistry. The head of the chemistry department saw little need for research or a doctoral program. The head of physics was opposed in principle to any dealings with the armed services, and as a result the department received almost no external funding. In 1956 the department obtained its first typewriter and a half-time secretary.[12] The aspirations of the department were raised when Albert Weaver, a Chicago-trained physicist, became head in 1958. He quickly brought expansion, outside research funds, and a doctoral program. But it was difficult to build from such a weak base. With four new positions to fill in 1960, the department received 60 applications, made 15 offers, and had zero acceptances.[13] In his first four years, Weaver was nevertheless able to double the physics faculty and build outside funding above $250,000; but the Arizona physics department was still a neophyte when it received the NSF Science Development grant.

The university was able to take advantage of one other natural advantage to further its academic development—the attractiveness of Tucson as a retirement community. Productive scientists who reached mandatory retirement age were often eager to continue their careers there, and in the early days this attraction was perhaps the only means for securing individuals with national reputations. During the 1960s Larry Gould, a famed Antarctic explorer who had also been president of Carleton College, was added to the geology department, against its wishes, by President Harvill. Gould wrote an evaluation of this whole subject area that prompted the creation of the School of Earth Sciences. Another retiree, George Gaylord Simpson, established Arizona in the forefront of paleontology. Similarly, the renowned organic chemist, Carl 'Speed' Marvel, provided the Arizona chemistry department with much needed leadership after retiring from Illinois.[14] All three men were active at Arizona for fifteen or more years. Well-known scientists like these brought an easy familiarity with research-funding networks, while helping to attract and to develop the young faculty upon whom the departments would ultimately depend. They also provided the academic leadership at the departmental level that was often lacking among existing senior faculty. All these things were important contributions to the advancement of the university.

The Arizona faculty had little authority or influence during the Harvill presidency. If they had, it is unlikely that they would have favored research, as the examples of Gould and the geology department or Kuiper and the astronomy department suggest. The university-wide Senate was dominated by administrators, but important decisions in any case devolved upon the president. It is unclear to what extent Harvill fathomed the ramifications of making Arizona into a research university. He clearly welcomed the recognition that research brought, and he furthermore discovered that indirect cost reimbursements could place appreciable funds at the president's discretion.[15] He accordingly gave full rein to those units trying to expand research, without necessarily imposing the research imperative upon the entire the university. One of his major accomplishments, for example, was the establishment of a medical school during the 1960s. The delicate task of justifying the large expenditures required was couched in terms of meeting the health-care needs of the state's population. The dean's foremost responsibility was cultivating political acceptance of the new school, and as a consequence research was slow to develop.

By the late 1960s, Harvill had effective academic leaders in the key administrative posts: Albert Weaver was vice president for academic affairs, and John Shaefer, a young chemist, was dean of the College of Liberal Arts. Under their stewardship research activity expanded rapidly. If existing structures presented obstacles, new and more accommodating arrangements were devised (which accounts for the bewildering changes in nomenclature and affiliation of the units described above). In one case, when a building was needed to house the Optical Sciences Center, the university borrowed money privately from the University of Arizona Foundation—a move of dubious legality—with the understanding that overhead from an Air Force contract would cover repayment.[16] The Harvill administration did what it needed to do to further its goals with little worry about internal or external scrutiny.

Autocratic leadership may indeed have been the only feasible means for institutional advancement given the relative paucity of resources. In 1960 real instructional expenditures at Arizona were considerably below what they were at established state research universities (cf. Table 20). During the next decade the university grew from 9,000 to 18,000 full-time students, and real instructional spending per-student increased by 58 percent. The university remained comparatively poor, but growth was a great asset. Because large numbers of faculty were being added, it had the opportunity, if it hired wisely, of significantly improving its research capacity. Still, in 1970 the student-faculty ratio was about 20:1, and the average professorial salary was 14 percent below the national average. In addition, the institution was chronically starved for capital. Classes had to be conducted from 7:30 a.m. to 10:30 p.m., and space off campus still had to be rented.[17] For a university thus handicapped to compete in the research economy required selective commitments not easily made in a democratic manner.

When Richard Harvill stepped down from the presidency in 1971, Arizona was a regional research university undergoing rapid development. The progress that had been achieved, however, was fragile. Research was not the generalized commitment of the institution, but rather the preoccupation of several salient groups within it. Academic leadership to assure that forward momentum would be sustained was precarious. Other uncertainties loomed. The Harvill autocracy had somehow been unscathed by the student rebellion of the 1960s, but the new regime would clearly require a different style of governance. Finally, while Arizona could still count on considerable future growth, it remained resource-poor for an aspiring research university. These issues may well have been addressed in the search for a new president, but the process became mired in a political deadlock which eventually alienated most of the candidates.[18] In the end, the regents chose the thirty-six year-old dean of the College of Liberal Arts, John P. Schaefer—a choice that assured an unequivocal commitment to advancement as a research university.

Schaefer brought to the presidency a clear vision that foresaw the University of Arizona attaining a stature comparable to the major public research universities of the Big Ten and the Pacific Coast.[19] He also brought an aggressiveness and directness to this aspiration that may have reflected his relative inexperience. He differed markedly from Richard Harvill in being highly accessible to the university community, and in delegating powers extensively to his chief officers. But his was also a strong administration, and one that shared the president's vision. With considerable unevenness in the level of academic development across departments, firm administrative direction was needed to produce progress. Specifically, this required selective treatment of departments and sufficient discretionary funds to allow the administration to place its bets.

The basic strategy of the Schaefer administration, which was widely understood, was to support those departments that possessed the capacity and the initiative to upgrade themselves.[20] Arizona thus implemented its own version of the 'steeples' approach. The key element of this strategy was that positions were not awarded to departments by formula, but rather through competition. In this way the administration could support and reward those departments that were 'doing the right things.' In practice this meant continued support for the proven winners, like astronomy and anthropology; but other enterprising departments, notably philosophy and sociology, were given the faculty positions that allowed them to build national reputations.

This strategy was predicated to some extent upon the existence of discretionary funds at the disposal of the president. Schaefer considered such funds to be the real power base of the president, since the ability to effect a program required the freedom to commit funds. He was fortunate that growing state appropriations, expanding voluntary support, and the ability to retain some indirect cost reimbursements, all gave the president a considerable war chest during the 1970s. Some of these funds were utilized for pet projects, like establishing the Center for Creative Photography. More generally, available funds allowed the Arizona administration to move quickly when opportunities presented themselves to obtain distinguished faculty.[21]

The hiring of senior stars was only one part of the department-building strategy. The Schaefer administration was explicit that these recognized scholars were not an end in themselves, but rather a means. Quality departments could only be developed through good junior faculty. Senior faculty had a key role to play in selecting, attracting, and guiding the professional growth of younger scientists and scholars. In practice, the administration treated departments with great flexibility, in keeping with their uneven levels of development. Mature, established departments could be counted upon to sustain their stature because good scholars wished to join them; in recently upgraded departments, however, a few key appointments might be of crucial importance for maintaining quality; some other subjects were favored because it was felt that they had the potential to develop—an expectation that was sometimes disappointed; and some units were regarded as basically teaching departments with little potential for advancement.

It was indispensable for department building that a rigorous process for evaluating promotion and tenure decisions be established. Characteristically for the old regime, no university-wide policy existed prior to 1971. Decisions were erratic across schools and departments and tended to reflect personal factors. An important element of the new procedure was utilizing reviewers from outside the university. This step was critical for departments that aspired to national reputations, and also for evaluating scholars of higher attainments than those already on board. Perhaps of equal importance was maintaining an objective and self-critical attitude. The university seems to have largely avoided the trap of complacency as it rapidly improved during the 1970s. The administration was fully aware of departments that did not meet expectations and of areas, like the biological sciences, that lagged the pace-setting departments. The presence of late-coming senior stars may have helped in maintaining an objective view. When one department head became effusive in an annual report, claiming a status in the top ten or even five departments, a senior faculty member appended a demurrer to the report.[22]

The overt emphasis given to research at Arizona could not have been sustained without clear presidential leadership. Schaefer took a number of steps that contributed directly to the enlargement of research capacity. He began a policy of returning 25 percent of research overhead reimbursements to the departments that generated them. This provided a fluid research fund for initiating projects and assisting junior faculty, as well as an incentive to get additional grants. He also made the development of the library a major commitment of his administration. During the 1970s it was transformed from an obviously inadequate facility to the fifteenth largest academic collection in the country.[23] The president also had to communicate the value of research to the external constituencies of the university. The regents and the Arizona public comprehended little of research, but they understood economic development. Schaefer had estimates made of the economic impact of sponsored research, and then publicized the findings: by this reckoning, each $1 million in research support for the university purportedly generated $1.046 million in economic activity for the Tucson area and created 86 jobs.[24] The continual education of the regents and the public was necessary to generate support for the research role of the university, and thus to encourage the state to maintain the flow of resources on which university development depended.

The general stagnation in the university research system did not affect the University of Arizona. During the 1970s enrollments grew by 27 percent, but state appropriations, buoyed by a strong state economy, increased by 79 percent. As a result, the university was able to sustain approximately the same level of growth, as measured by real instructional expenditures per full-time student, as in the 1960s—56 percent versus 58 percent. During the Schaefer administration the number of senior faculty increased by 116. Furthermore, the AAUP rating for professorial salaries advanced from 4 (below average) to 2 (above average).[25] Unlike the 1960s, Arizona was upgrading departments when most other research universities were not. In 1972, for example, the biology department reported a "buyer's market" in the biological sciences, and the philosophy department received 700 applications for the two positions it advertised.[26] Such conditions produced a 'trickle-down effect,' by which graduates from the most prestigious graduate schools were obliged to accept positions in lesser ranking schools.[27] Universities like Arizona that were still adding faculty benefited greatly from this situation.

During the 1970s Arizona continued to put resources into its 'steeple' departments, but the university also accepted the conventional view of the importance of strengthening the core disciplines. Not only did fields like engineering and astronomy depend to some extent on chemistry and physics for support, but there was also a conviction that a first-rate university could not neglect basic areas of learning like mathematics, history, and the humanities and social sciences generally. In these core disciplines, however, Arizona had no natural advantages; and national reputations proved far more difficult to establish.

Albert Weaver, who oversaw academic development as vice president during these years, initially concentrated on the natural sciences because he felt that reputations there were more certain and more visible. But he confronted an obstacle that was rooted in the intellectual structure of the disciplines. Good experimentalists were relatively easy to hire and would contribute to the university's strength in a particular specialty. But distinguished theoreticians were decidedly scarce; yet, they had a wider impact on their field and greater stature across the entire discipline. Theoreticians consequently tended to be monopolized by the established departments.[28] The head of the physics department explained the situation in which the department found itself in 1972: the Roose-Anderson study had ranked the department as 49th; he felt that improvements since then had raised the department to 32nd: it was 2nd–3rd in atomic physics; the nuclear group stood near 20th; solid state would rank from 28 to 35; however, with no large accelerator, the weakness in high-energy physics weighed down the department's overall standing.[29] One might add that peripheral fields like optics, atmospheric physics, or astrophysics seemed to contribute little or nothing to national reputations.

This situation can be cautiously generalized. Late-developing research universities like Arizona typically found opportunities to advance in expanding specialized research areas, which were often outside of the mainstream of the discipline. Such fields might generate substantial research funds, but they contributed less to academic prestige. Advancing into the front ranks was particularly difficult in the very large, competitive disciplines like chemistry, physics, psychology, or economics. In light of these constraints, Arizona's accomplishments were creditable.

The Schaefer years roughly spanned the interval between the 1970 Roose-Anderson ratings and the 1982 *Assessment*.[30] In the former study, Arizona was given a national ranking in just two departments—anthropology and astronomy; and just three other departments were rated as good (2.5–2.9 raw score). In the latter study Arizona was rated as strong ($\geq$ 3.0) in six departments—anthropology (ranked 6), geosciences (15–22) philosophy (12–13) physics (37–43), sociology (9–10), and zoology (20–22). (Astronomy was omitted from this study.) Another six departments were rated as good (2.5–2.9). In addition, many of the Arizona departments were recognized for above-average improvement during the previous five years.[31]

When John Schaefer left the presidency in 1981 to become the head of the Research Corporation, he left an institution that had been substantially strengthened. In just a decade it had advanced from the status of a regional research university to one of national stature. Moreover, that accomplishment showed every sign of enduring. A number of solid departments had been built that could be counted on to sustain themselves. The research imperative had to a considerable extent been generalized across the campus. The university had also become one of the top twenty-five performers of research, with active programs across the spectrum of academic fields. Arizona may well have achieved its ambition of joining the top ten public research universities, although such a distinction would depend on how one kept score. What is beyond cavil, however, is that Arizona's stature is remarkable for a state that is 27th in population, 24th in total tax revenues, and 38th in potential tax revenues per student (1985).[32]

The apparent stability of Arizona's academic standing assumes particular importance in light of the circumstances that the university faced during the 1980s. After about 1982 the growth in the Arizona state economy slowed appreciably, producing recurrent fiscal crises that directly diminished the university budget. Overall, from the 1981 to the 1986 academic years the university's instructional budget increased by 16.5 percent in real terms while enrollments rose slightly. The heady expansion of the 1960s and 1970s gave way to a period of consolidation. In addition, the ineluctable bureaucratization of university governance seemed finally to have reached the Arizona frontier. The university's budget became a public document in 1979, making it more difficult for the president to sequester funds for discretionary purposes. The capacity to act swiftly and decisively when opportunity presented itself, which was crucially important for Harvill and Schaefer, had in all likelihood lessened. In addition, as happened elsewhere in the 1970s, the Arizona Board of Regents in the 1980s became more active in determining university policies across the state. The prospects for the University of Arizona were nevertheless not bleak. It could probably look forward with greater confidence than most state research universities to maintaining the momentum of its recent development.

Trends for potential student enrollment, state population growth, and economic development generally continue to be better for Arizona than for most other states. The amount of funded research at the University of Arizona has been rising faster than the national averages, and the potential has scarcely been exhausted. After having faced the constraint of inadequate physical capital for its entire postwar history, the university received the authority to issue bonds for construction in the 1980s. A building boom ensued that significantly enlarged research capacity. Invigorating research in the life sciences was also made a top university priority. After being comparative laggards, the medical school became more active in research, and a concerted effort was undertaken to strengthen the basic biological sciences.[33] Arizona has also been in the forefront in industry-sponsored research. On the whole, the academic advancement of the University of Arizona represented a rather traditional approach. For other ambitious research universities, getting ahead after the golden age required less orthodox means.

3. Georgia Institute of Technology

In the 1989 ranking of research performers, Georgia Tech stood in nineteenth place, just above Arizona, with almost identical spending for research. Its ascent to become a major research university, however, was even more abrupt than Arizona's. Tech awarded its first doctorate in 1950, and twenty years later it ranked near 100 as a recipient of federal research funds.[1] But like Arizona, Georgia Tech launched a determined effort of academic advancement during the early 1970s, when few other institutions were willing or able to do the same. The distinctive research capabilities that Georgia Tech possessed then found favor in the research economy of the late 1970s and 1980s. In many ways this development was unanticipated. In the mid-1960s, no less an authority than Allan Cartter stated that Georgia Tech "would not ordinarily be thought of" as among "the most prominent institutions for national recognition."[2] Rather, Tech in its evolution had conformed to a highly specialized niche in higher education—a Southern, public, non-land grant engineering school. Tech was considered to be the finest of its type; but by this narrow specification it was also one of a kind.

The Georgia School of Technology was founded in 1885 in order to contribute to the economic regeneration of the 'New South.' At that time, thinking on engineering education was divided between proponents of "school culture" and "shop culture." The former, best exemplified by MIT, advocated the teaching of higher mathematics and basic science to prepare graduates for engineering analysis and design. The latter sought to reproduce actual shop conditions in order to train machinists and foremen ready to enter the workplace. The new school in Atlanta embraced a strident version of shop culture, even though this approach was then being superseded in the North. For its first eight years (1888–

96), for example, it housed commercial shops where students performed contract work for local businesses. The curriculum would modernize in accordance with the overall evolution of engineering education, but the shop-culture legacy of training practical engineers for industry would long remain a Tech signature.[3]

Unlike land-grant institutions, Georgia Tech was devoted single-mindedly to engineering. Exceptions, like the School of Commerce started in 1913, merely aimed to serve the industrial economy in yet another way. The institution basically prospered in this specialized role, but how its achievement was assessed depended on whether one took a Southern or a national perspective. Georgia Tech soon became recognized as the premier engineering school in the South. It had the largest engineering enrollments in the region and consistently garnered regional distinctions—e.g. the only Guggenheim Fund grant for aeronautical engineering (1930), the first Naval ROTC unit (1926), the first national recognition of a department of architecture (1926).[4] Such accomplishments, however, at best matched the attainments of the better engineering colleges in the North. In other, more fundamental respects, Tech could scarcely compete. It was woefully supported by the state of Georgia and as a result could not hope to attract top-flight faculty. Graduate education was virtually nonexistent; nor was appreciable research undertaken in its departments.

Most research instead was located in a separate, related unit—the Engineering Experiment Station. Authorized by the Georgia legislature in 1919, it only came into being fifteen years later as a result of the interests of a few Tech faculty. The Station was then given a state appropriation and a mandate to investigate matters of regional economic interest. By 1940 it was conducting contract research for industrial firms as well. The war brought a considerable expansion of externally supported research from industry and, in the late stages, OSRD. Still, the Experiment Station's totals remained quite modest. The research lines established in the last years of the war nevertheless gathered additional momentum in the postwar environment. It was eager to undertake the kind of narrowly programmatic research sought by the armed services, including classified projects disdained by other universities. Research was performed for operating divisions of the armed services—the Navy Bureau of Ordnance and the Army Chemical Warfare Service—rather than the academically oriented ONR. By the Korean War, the Experiment Station resembled an independent research institute, like SRI or Battelle Institute. Some faculty and graduate students were involved with its projects, but the bulk of its activities were conducted by a staff of full-time researchers. The largest number of contracts was for military electronics research.[5] In research as in instruction Georgia Tech pursued a practical course.

The compartmentalization of research, as well as its applied bias, reinforced the pattern just noted: Georgia Tech was the largest and in some ways most advanced engineering school in the South, but it was an also-ran in national terms. Tech admirably fulfilled its mandate to educate large numbers of practical, job-ready engineers. It also, by emphasizing football and extracurricular life, fulfilled Southern expectations for the collegiate social experience. Increasingly in question, however, was the extent to which this congenial and functional institutional configuration could be adapted to the changing imperatives of the postwar university research system.

In this respect, the difficulties faced by Georgia Tech were those confronting Southern universities in general. To a large extent, higher education below the Mason-Dixon Line had been insulated from developments in other regions from the mid-nineteenth century until World War I. Subsequent advances had been led by a few state universities—those in North Carolina, Virginia, Texas, and Florida—and the handful of relatively wealthy private institutions, particularly Duke and Vanderbilt. Progress was nevertheless slowed by the prevailing intellectual myopia of the region, by a preoccupation with the social aspects of college, and by the persistence into the 1960s of racial segregation.[6] The emphasis on research and graduate education after Sputnik, in addition to the turmoil over desegregation, tended to make the contrast between the South and the rest of the nation more glaring. This issue of Southern backwardness was consequently of increasing concern by the mid-1960s, when a study by Allan Cartter sought to define and measure the problem.[7]

Cartter's study fully documented the gap between the South and the rest of the country. But even though fewer students went to college and less was spent on their instruction, Cartter felt that these discrepancies represented a time lag that might soon be closed. He sensed a willingness in the South to undertake quantitative expansion of higher education; what was lacking, however, was the will to promote qualitative improvement. Yet, Cartter believed that investments in quality were ultimately more critical for spurring economic growth—and thus for attacking a root cause of Southern backwardness.

The failings of Southern universities in this respect were fully evident. According to his own survey of graduate departments, one in three rated departments across the country were deemed good-to-distinguished, but only one in ten of those in the South. Most graduate programs there were also far below optimal size. With the federal government explicitly underwriting the diffusion of academic research capacity, now was clearly the moment to address these problems. Cartter, for his part, was quite specific about how this could be done. First, there was need to close a salary gap of approximately 20 percent between Southern and non-Southern institutions in order to attract and retain promising young scholars. Second, graduate education needed to be strengthened and expanded, not everywhere, but particularly in those institutions capable of cultivating high standards. Third, Southern educators had to raise their level of aspiration to match the standards of excellence prevailing elsewhere. The next ten years, Cartter warned, would be crucial for the advancement or stagnation of Southern universities: "in an age of national rather than regional competition—for faculty, students, foundation support and government contracts—Southern higher education must become quality conscious or be left behind."[8]

Both this diagnosis and prescription fit Georgia Tech. In terms of the product it was most known for—undergraduate engineers—Tech was a Southern institution; but the medium in which it dealt—engineering and technology—knew few regional boundaries. For the quarter-century after World War II, the history of the institution could be written in terms of the opposing pull of its traditional, regional role and the rapidly advancing national university system.

The president who led Georgia Tech through the postwar era, Colonel Blake Van Leer (1944–56), possessed a vision of creating a technological university and succeeded in taking some initial steps in that direction.[9] He established the first doctoral programs, changed the name from 'School' to 'Institute,' and offered rudimentary encouragement of academic research. But his control over events was tenuous at best. Research in the Experiment Station, for example, proceeded according to its own dynamics. More detrimental, important matters of policy were decided by the state Board of Regents. Georgia had created a unified university system in 1931 so that, as in Arizona, one board of regents governed all higher education. Unlike Arizona, a powerful chancellor presided over the Georgia system. This arrangement had little to recommend it for Georgia Tech: as a distinctive institution it might have benefited from a board that identified with its mission. Instead, it was a perennial second fiddle to the flagship university in Athens. During the Van Leer years the regents allowed Tech to grow, but in other respects the state leadership was concerned with such things as keeping faculty workloads high, loyalty tests, and preserving racial segregation. Internal administration depended heavily on personalities. When Van Leer attempted to modernize the administrative structure by creating vice presidents, the reform foundered on regent distrust of the individuals involved. The penurious attitude of the regents was also an obstacle to improving the faculty: in 1952–53, for example, fifty-two faculty members left the institution, largely because of low salaries.[10] Provincialism remained ascendant during these years, but the balance began slowly to shift after Sputnik.

The beginnings of a qualitative upgrading at Georgia Tech, such as Allan Cartter had urged, began to be evident during the presidency of Edwin D. Harrison (1957–69).[11] Steps taken early in his administration moved Tech closer to national norms. Of particular importance, Tech peacefully integrated in 1961, the first public university in the South to do so without a court order. Academically, admission standards were raised and the engineering curriculum was revised in keeping with nationally recommended guidelines. Harrison deliberately sought to raise salaries and improve working conditions for the faculty. Graduate education was expanded, aided by a grant from the Ford Foundation Engineering Program (1961). By the mid-1960s the balance had clearly shifted in terms of faculty qualifications, as more than half the Tech faculty now held doctorates. Its own Ph.D. output reached upwards of fifty per year. An important step in defining research at the Institute was taken in 1964. Hitherto, all research funds were administered through the Experiment Station, but now grants for basic research would go directly to academic departments, while the Station would continue with contract research for clients.

In connection with the modernizing effort, Georgia Tech undertook an extensive self-study in the early sixties. When the faculty was polled on the mission of the institution, however, a sharp polarity was revealed. Nearly half felt that the traditional emphasis on practical undergraduate engineering education ought to be preserved, while only a slight majority advocated an enlargement of purpose toward becoming a university of science and technology. The modern version of the 'shop-culture' mentality was particularly strong in the College of Engineering, where Dean Jesse Mason resisted any dilution of the practical, 'hands-on' approach to engineering. In 1965 the popular Mason was ousted from his powerful position through a wrenching administrative reorganization. The modernizing forces appeared triumphant; however their victory proved to be a Pyhrric one. The conflict between local traditions and national aspirations remained unresolved at the departmental level. This uncertainty, combined with other complications, seemed to check further progress for a time at Georgia Tech.

A new factor entered the equation in 1965, when George L. Simpson, Jr., was appointed chancellor of the University System. Having served as director of the North Carolina Research Triangle and as a high administrator at NASA, he was a strong supporter of research and graduate education. Simpson was determined to upgrade higher education in Georgia to national standards, beginning with the University and Georgia Tech. Although this aim seemed complementary to Harrison's goals, the two soon became antagonists. Simpson apparently thought that Tech ought to be moving ahead more rapidly, while Harrison resented Simpson's intrusions into Institute affairs. In 1968 they reached an impasse over the hiring of a new vice president, and Harrison resigned (effective the next year).

The next four years were discouraging for Georgia Tech. By virtue of being Southern and catering almost exclusively to engineers and business majors, Tech was doubly insulated from the student protests that wracked other campuses. But it was difficult to establish a clear direction for the future. Harrison's successor, after a brief interregnum, was Arthur G. Hansen (1969–71), the dean of Engineering, who had come to Tech from the University of Michigan to replace Jesse Mason.[12] Young, vigorous, and moderately liberal on the social issues of the day, Hansen was clearly in the modernizing camp. In some ways he set the stage for future advancement, particularly through appointments; but he was soon at loggerheads with traditionalists over a proposed change in the status of the Experiment Station (see below). In 1971 he abruptly resigned to take the presidency of his alma mater, Purdue.

Other trends seemed to be turning against Tech in these years. Chancellor Simpson had greatly expanded public spending on higher education, with the University of Georgia being the first and principal beneficiary. When Tech's turn for budget expansion came, however, fiscal conditions had worsened and funds were no longer available for a similar boost in state support.[13] Tech continued to have a weak funding base for an institution devoted to science and technology. National developments were scarcely more encouraging. The end to the post-Sputnik boom hit Tech harder than most institutions, since the declines in defense and aerospace research were particularly marked. Engineers were suddenly in ample supply, and enrollments weakened. Prospects were far from bright when Joseph M. Pettit, dean of engineering at Stanford, agreed to become Tech's eighth president (1972–86).

The Georgia Tech that Pettit headed differed in one important respect from the internally divided institution of the 1960s: the leadership was now drawn mainly from the national engineering community. This change had been a gradual but deliberate process, in which Simpson's influence was evident. The recruitment of Hansen as dean of engineering was an initial step. Before Hansen was elevated to the presidency, a concerted attempt had been made to entice a national figure—the dean of engineering at MIT—to that position. As president, Hansen recruited deans from outside the Institute. Most critical, once again, was the dean of engineering. This position was confided to Thomas G. Stelson, who had made a career at Carnegie-Mellon University. That institution, like Georgia Tech, was a hybrid of an engineering school and an institute for applied research. The most important national figure, nevertheless, was Pettit himself.

Joseph Pettit was one of the leading engineering educators in the country. He had recently been an author of an influential national report on the subject and, unlike anyone at Georgia Tech, he was a member of the National Academy of Engineering. Even more significant, he was a protégé—indeed, virtually an understudy—of Frederick Terman. Pettit had done his doctoral work in electrical engineering at Stanford with Terman, joined him for wartime research at Harvard, worked with him as a faculty member, and then succeeded him as dean of engineering.[14] Only a few years earlier, it would have been rather unlikely for Georgia Tech to attract someone of Pettit's stature; the MIT dean had, after all, declined this opportunity. But the world was changing rapidly in those hectic times.

The melding of military, industrial, and academic research that Terman and then Pettit had cultivated at Stanford had come under intense attack since 1969. The Stanford Research Institute, which in some ways resembled Tech's Engineering Experiment Station, had to sever its ties with the university. The occupation by students of the Applied Electronics Laboratory, which was under Pettit's jurisdiction, brought mounting pressures against classified and military-sponsored research. Pettit was one of the few at Stanford to defend working with the Pentagon, since it was the principal source of funds for engineering research. Moreover, the applied laboratories were an important nexus in nurturing the technological community that had developed in Silicon Valley.[15] Georgia Tech, on the other hand, seemed to possess all the ingredients for the fruitful interaction of academic, industrial, and military research—the very amalgam that seemed to be disintegrating at Stanford. Pettit consequently came to the Institute as a national and modernizing figure, but also as one who wished to build upon Tech's traditional strengths.

Pettit conceived of the president's function as "creating and maintaining . . . the organizational setting in which teaching and research can best occur."[16] The setting for most research at Georgia Tech was the Engineering Experiment Station, but it had recently lost much of its vigor. As a unit devoted to applied research and technical assistance, the Station was out of harmony with the sixties ideology of basic research. It received an appropriation from the state of Georgia that covered much of its operating costs, while the bulk of its research was under contract with the military. Given these comfortable arrangements, the Station had exhibited little initiative in seeking a larger role. At the beginning of the 1970s, however, military research was dwindling and the state appropriation was substantially reduced. There was considerable dissatisfaction with the narrowness of the Station's role as well as its marginal contribution to academic life. President Hansen's proposed solution was to integrate the Station into the academic departments of the Institute. Such an approach was consistent with the 'ivory-tower' views prevalent throughout the country, which sought to restrict university research within academic spheres. Such a merger, however, was vehemently opposed at the Station. Countervailing sentiments were voiced for complete separation, as had happened with SRI and the Draper Labs.[17] Perhaps neither alternative was realistic, but the unsettled conditions at the Station had to be addressed.

Pettit had disapproved of the separation of SRI from Stanford, and was not disposed to allow the Station to be lost from Georgia Tech. The solution seemed to lie in bringing it under tighter administrative control, while encouraging more vigorous solicitation of research. "Client-oriented" was the telling phrase for this new approach. Such an attitude was rare on university campuses in 1972, although characteristic of the successful independent research institutes. The key individual in the reorganization of the Station was Thomas Stelson. His responsibilities had been enlarged in 1971 to include the coordination of research activities. In this capacity he oversaw the reduction of Station personnel and instilled a new emphasis on serving clients in research. It nevertheless took time for the new approach to begin showing results. Stelson himself directed the Station on an interim basis in 1975, and during that time reorganized the Station into eight separate laboratories. This decentralization allowed each division more autonomy to develop their particular capabilities and clienteles. The permanent director appointed the following year was Donald J. Grace, another electrical engineer from Stanford, who had extensive experience with defense electronics. A protégé of Pettit in some ways, Grace had risen to the position of associate dean of engineering at Stanford. At this juncture the revitalization of the Station began to be apparent.[18]

On the academic side of the Institute, research was conducted both in the departments and in special centers. In the 1960s interdisciplinary research centers had been established for Water Resources (1963) and Bioengineering (1969). In order to encourage such approaches, an office of Interdisciplinary Programs was established in 1973. The conduct of most basic research nevertheless still fell within the academic departments, but this area had been a longstanding weakness of Georgia Tech. At the end of Harrison's tenure only three departments—chemistry, aeronautical engineering, and physics—performed more than $100,000 in sponsored research. The paucity of research activity was also a handicap to the doctoral programs. The only remedy for this deficiency was to strengthen academic departments—a lengthy and costly undertaking.

Joseph Pettit began this process by strengthening the administrative structure. Coming from Stanford, one of the most advanced research universities in terms of its internal organization, to relatively backward Georgia Tech, he found much room for improvement. For research, the reorientation of the Station and the establishment of the Office of Interdisciplinary Programs were preliminary steps. In 1974 all facets of research were consolidated under Thomas Stelson in a new office of Vice President for Research. Stelson shared Pettit's views on the complementarity of applied and basic research in a technological university. By stressing the importance of both, they largely transcended the longstanding split between the shop-culture and school-culture mentalities that had plagued the Institute. The clear intention was that the Station, the centers, and departmental faculty would all pursue their respective tasks.

A similar administrative rationalization was needed in faculty matters. Recruitment of faculty was haphazard. The tenure system was in such disarray that the status of some individuals was uncertain. Expectations for promotion were confusing as written and were poorly understood among faculty. Participation of faculty in institutional governance, finally, was slight. Faculty were perceived as apathetic by the administration, while themselves feeling that they were not adequately consulted.[19] During the early years of the Pettit administration definite policies were established to deal with each of these situations. By the late 1970s, the faculty of Georgia Tech were being treated in a manner that was comparable to their counterparts at other research universities. As Georgia Tech overcame the vestiges of past parochialism, it began to make great strides in research.

The organizational changes that created the proper environment for research were the prelude to the actual expansion of research. From 1968 to 1974 expenditures for research were stagnant at the Engineering Experiment Station, while shrinking appreciably in real terms. Research in the academic units appeared to double, but only from a small base. Electrical engineering was the only department to expand its research to a significant size (over $1 million in 1976).

The upsurge in research at Georgia Tech was led by the Engineering Experiment Station. During the last half of the 1970s its research grew by an average of 30 percent per year. From near parity with the academic units in 1976, it managed to double their total research by 1980. Afterward, both grew at comparable rates. The Station had compensated somewhat for the drought in defense research by entering the growing environmental fields, particularly solar energy. The real take-off in research was nevertheless principally the result of renewed research spending by the military. The Station also worked to expand its service to the economy of Georgia. In this respect it took particular pains to cultivate greater interaction with industry. Overall, the remarkable jump in research at the Station propelled Georgia Tech from 70th place among research universities in the mid-1970s to 27th place in the mid-1980s.[20]

The other face of research at the Institute, that done in departments, made

TABLE 24. Research Income at Georgia Tech, 1968–1988 ($ millions)[21]

	1968	1970	1972	1974	1976	1978	1980	1982
Academic units	1.9	2.5	3.0	4.1	7.3	11.9	13.7	16.8
Experiment Station	5.0	4.8	4.8	4.9	8.1	15.7	27.1	51.5
Total	6.9	7.3	7.8	9.0	15.4	27.6	40.8	68.3

notable progress in the 1970s, but only against persistent fiscal constraints. The 1975–76 academic year typified the situation. While research vice president Stelson exulted in "another record-breaking year for research at Georgia Tech," Vernon Crawford, the academic vice president, pronounced it "the most difficult year" in his 26 years at Tech.[22] The state appropriation for that year was $1.5 million less than the year before. Raises that had been promised to the faculty were rescinded by the Georgia legislature and then, after a lawsuit, reinstated by the Supreme Court. Only special assistance from the Georgia Tech Foundation allowed many normal needs to be met—the library to maintain subscriptions, federal equipment grants to be matched, and faculty to travel to professional meetings. Even so, the shortfalls hurt. The year saw a record number of faculty resignations.

The 1975–76 year culminated more than a half-decade of disappointing budgets, largely due to weaknesses in the economy and state tax revenues. The years that followed brought a brief reprieve in the form of 10 percent increases, but the early 1980s renewed the laments of fiscal neglect. Georgia Tech thus remained under budgetary strain during the very years that its research volume was soaring. Enrollments too increased by about 3000 during the late 1970s, from the 8000 to the 11,000 range, and the quality of Tech students rose as well. At the start of the decade it enrolled about one of every two freshman applicants, but just one of four was admitted by decade's end. Graduate enrollments climbed by 500 to nearly 2000, helped in part by the growth in research. Faculty positions, however, increased by only 11 percent during the first decade of Pettit's presidency. Georgia Tech thus faced the formidable task of developing research in the academic departments without appreciable new positions, with salary levels that were well below national norms, and with increasing teaching burdens.[23]

The Pettit administration took what steps it could under the circumstances to improve faculty quality. It tightened lax recruitment practices, such as retaining Tech graduates or hiring handy regional candidates, and instead insisted upon national searches to fill positions. Pettit actively sought to enforce higher standards for appointment and promotion. The redefinition of tenure policies gave additional scope for raising expectations. Such expectations were carried through to the departmental level by appointing new heads. These efforts resulted in a house cleaning of sorts, so that there were a relatively large number of positions to fill. In chemistry, for example, only two of thirty faculty members remained five years after a new head was appointed. Insofar as it was possible, Pettit tried to employ Terman's 'steeples' principle, the favored departments in this case being electrical and mechanical engineering.[24]

But such actions, even coupled with a judicious choice of replacements, were scarcely capable of producing significant increases in quality by themselves. In fact, when the national assessment of graduate programs was made in 1980, Georgia Tech had made no discernible progress during the decade. Just four departments were rated above the median as 'good'—chemistry and civil, electrical and mechanical engineering. Computer science and chemical engineering were 'adequate plus'; while math and physics were merely 'adequate.'[25]

There are plausible reasons for this result. Much of Tech's hiring had necessarily been at the junior-faculty level; salaries and other conditions remained below research university standards; and reputations in any case are slow to build. But there is a more fundamental explanation for this phenomenon, having to do with the very nature of the institution. Productive faculty who found the Georgia Tech milieu congenial tended to value its distinctive features, particularly the ready access to applied and interdisciplinary research in the Engineering Experiment Station and the centers. Georgia Tech had a special character as a research university. As Thomas Stelson put it, "we are not a great basic research university, but we are a great technological university."[26]

Georgia Tech in the 1980s had clearly fulfilled Colonel Van Leer's aspiration to become a technological university. Tech was above all a focused institution. On the academic side, its make-up was heavily weighted toward engineering where 70 percent of the students matriculated and about the same proportion of research was done. In addition, the programs in the sciences had a heavily applied cast; and the technological thrust was further supported in the colleges of architecture and management. Both instruction and research were thus closely linked to the world of business and practical application. This propinquity was mirrored in an entrepreneurial culture among faculty that favored independence and initiative, especially in working with outside sponsors. The structure of programs at Georgia Tech in fact permitted faculty to find appropriate homes for their research interests outside of academic departments.

By the mid-eighties there were more than twenty interdisciplinary research centers. Each was predicated on the collaboration of at least three academic units and assurance of regular outside support. Some centers had research faculty of their own, but overall the centers depended on the voluntary participation of departmental faculty. Centers might represent generic areas. For example, the Microelectronics Research Center was established in 1981 in order to coordinate existing programs across the campus. Three years later some 35 researchers from at least six departments were active there. At this juncture a $30 million expansion was announced, half provided by a special allocation from the state of Georgia and half to be raised privately. The Center thus became a magnet for a substantial investment that promised to make Georgia Tech one of the leading universities in semiconductor materials among other areas of microelectronics.[27] Other centers at Tech were highly focused on client needs. The Center for Rotary Wing Aircraft Technology essentially conducted research on helicopters for the U.S. Army; and the Materials Handling Research Center, launched with a grant from NSF, allowed its research program to be guided by its industrial affiliates. These very diverse centers had one thing in common: they represented fairly substantial investments in highly focused areas. Georgia Tech generally sought to be a major presence in selected fields rather than to strive for broad or comprehensive coverage.

Faculty could also participate in research at the Engineering Experiment Station on an individual basis. The Station, which was renamed the Georgia Tech Research Institute (GTRI) in 1984, was nevertheless a self-contained unit with its own staff and distinctive mission. It presented itself to clients as offering the best of both worlds: "the distinct advantage of being an aggressive, full-time research organization, while still being an integral part of a prestigious university."[28] That is, the professional staff at GTRI could devote themselves fully to the needs of their clients, while still having access to specialized academic expertise. GTRI itself had nearly 600 professional staff in the mid-eighties. Most possessed a master's degree, but fewer than one in five held doctorates. For at least three decades the Station had specialized in research on defense electronics and various radars for the Pentagon. The DoD supported more than 80 percent of GTRI research in the early 1980s, although that figure declined thereafter. Tech was one campus where the military could comfortably conduct classified research on sensitive topics like target recognition, radar countermeasures, or the Strategic Defense Initiative. Other units at GTRI contributed to the Institute's multiple contacts with industry. GTRI also cultivated its original mission of providing economic development services to Georgia, which included maintaining field stations throughout the state and offering programs in industrial education.[29] All told, GTRI accounted for two-thirds of Tech's research in the 1980s. Since the lean years of the early 1970s, it had clearly tapped into a wellspring of demand for its services, but these tasks were for the most part well removed from academic engineering.

Every evaluation of the Institute and the Station/GTRI over the years made the same point—that closer interaction between the two was desirable. The overlap of tasks was nevertheless inherently limited. Typically, some academic faculty participated in projects at GTRI, while a few of the latter's professional staff taught courses for departments. GTRI laboratories also cooperated with various centers, particularly Microelectronics. Another form of interaction occurred through students. In the late 1980s more than 100 graduate students were employed at GTRI, while a like number of its staff was enrolled in graduate degree programs. Although these links might be enlarged somewhat, the divergence of purpose was inescapable. If the mission of the academic units, in order of importance, would be instruction, research, and service, then the mission of GTRI was just the reverse.[30] The success of GTRI in cultivating this service role was in a sense responsible for propelling Georgia Tech into the ranks of the major research universities. But in consequence, the volume of research at Georgia Tech tended to be relatively unrelated to traditional notions of academic quality.

Georgia Tech thus represented a distinctive model of a research university, far more programmatic than even MIT. It essentially consisted of two complete systems—the instructional units organized along disciplinary lines and GTRI organized by functional area—with the interdisciplinary centers intended to cut across both. If this model was far removed from the university ideal of the 1960s, it nevertheless proved exceptionally apt for the conditions of the 1980s. Its strengths included a broad constituency of supporters to which to appeal for private funds; an embedded commitment to 'technology transfer'—one of the preoccupations of the decade; and a longstanding working relationship with the Department of Defense.[31]

During the 1980s Georgia Tech continued to complain that its basic instructional mission was underfunded by the state. Appropriations were consistently disappointing, and the state seemed to foreclose other alternatives. Tech was prevented from raising tuition as much as it would have liked, and it complained that all overhead reimbursements from its growing research volume had to be devoted to covering the operating budget.[32] On the positive side, the Institute was able to derive badly needed funds from voluntary support. Georgia Tech had one of the highest percentages of alumni donors among public institutions, but its overall development efforts were not systematically organized. Alumni gifts had conventionally been sought for buildings, for maintaining the campus, and especially for athletic facilities. During the 1980s, gifts began to make a greater contribution to academics. Tech's first endowed professorship, in microelectronics, was given by the Schlumberger corporation in 1981. A decisive step in this same direction occurred in the middle of the decade, when Tech launched a $100 million campaign to commemorate its centennial. This campaign was its first since the 1920s, and it required an upgrading of the fund-raising organization. The proceeds were also devoted substantially to building endowment and long-range program development.[33] Georgia Tech found other creative ways to tap private funds in lieu of unavailable public support. Major research buildings were financed by an independent foundation using tax-exempt industrial revenue bonds, and then leased to Georgia Tech on advantageous terms. Such methods allowed the Institute to meet many of its growing needs during the decade despite the inadequacy of its core support.

'Technology transfer' was a basic mission of Georgia Tech since its inception—long before the current phrase was coined. For that reason, it was early to institutionalize many of the characteristic forms. Its patent policy was instituted in 1978; a corporate liaison program was established, modeled after that at MIT; and joint university-industry ventures were cultivated at the interdisciplinary centers. The 1980s brought state assistance in this area predicated explicitly on expectations of stimulating economic development. In 1980 a business incubator for technological firms, the Advanced Technology Development Center, was established on the Georgia Tech campus with state funding. By the end of the decade, one hundred companies had benefited from the Center, producing an undoubted economic impact. The state's large investment in the Microelectronics Research Center was motivated by similar economic considerations, and it was followed by similar investments for manufacturing and paper technology. Georgia Tech thus had somewhat better success in justifying public support for its service role than for instruction.

In research, Georgia Tech was in the forefront of all the growth areas of the 1980s, save biotechnology. It was the third largest recipient of funds from the Department of Defense. It was also third in R&D expenditures in engineering. Until the end of the decade, Tech was the second largest recipient of research funds from industry. This last connection was especially productive, since industry was also the largest source of voluntary support to Tech during the decade.[34]

As Georgia Tech celebrated the one hundredth anniversary of its founding in 1985, it could take satisfaction in having overcome most of the handicaps of Southern insularity described just two decades earlier by Allan Cartter. It had certainly arrived as a research university, although it preferred the term 'technological university.' As it contemplated its past, however, it also looked ahead to the future in an exercise of long-range planning. This effort exposed the tensions still existing between its aspirations for future development and the realities of current limitations. Interestingly, these tensions focused most insistently on the theme that Cartter had stressed—the need for improvements in quality.[35]

In this respect Georgia Tech had made strides, even since the 1970s. The most important objective according to President Pettit was attracting and retaining excellent faculty, and he now felt that the Institute was doing this. Progress should have been possible in this area. During the 1980s Tech, like Arizona, managed to raise its faculty salary rating to the second highest quintile—after being in the bottom quintile two decades earlier. The persistent problem nevertheless was that there was not enough faculty. In order to achieve a satisfactory student-faculty ratio, 350 additional regular faculty were needed. In qualitiative terms, a goal was envisioned of raising each of Tech's ranked departments into the top twenty in the nation. The expansion of doctoral programs was also foreseen as an important component of quality enhancement. The expansion of faculty and doctoral programs were longstanding desires at Georgia Tech, but equally venerable institutional constraints impeded the realization of these goals.

At the end of the 1980s Tech still had some 530 academic faculty, barely changed from the start of the decade. It awarded nearly 100 Ph.D.s, compared with about 60 ten years before. Perhaps its four engineering departments might aspire to top-twenty status, but the competition in the scientific disciplines was in all likelihood too stiff for the Tech departments to rise that far. The pursuit of academic quality is nevertheless an enduring attraction because, as Vice President Stelson put it, "research is an elitist activity."[36] High stature and national recognition are not merely sought for bragging rights, but because they are factors that actively advance the effectiveness of teaching and research. The route taken by Georgia Tech in its advancement emphasized expanding the volume of research by meeting the programmatic needs of sponsors. Success in this endeavor created one kind of quality. According to Stelson, Georgia Tech's competitive advantage lay in this focused emphasis—in having "a fairly small number of large programs."[37] This achievement has also provided Tech with a large base of activity on which to build. In doing so, Georgia Tech has amply fulfilled at least one of Allen Cartter's admonitions—to set a high level of aspiration.

The late development of Georgia Tech and the University of Arizona as research universities does much to refute the canards about the insuperable advantage of established institutions and the immutability of the university hierarchy.[38] The two institutions certainly differed by their nature and their experiences. Arizona conformed to the traditional pattern of a comprehensive university, and it placed high value on enhancing the stature of the basic academic disciplines. It was more fortunate than Georgia Tech in this respect by having an expanding budget during the buyer's market of the 1970s. Tech's development was led by the rising volume of client-oriented research in the Engineering Experiment Station, although it too eventually expressed aspirations for high academic stature. The common elements in their experiences nevertheless seem more significant than these differences.

As late-comers both institutions consciously sought to exploit their own comparative advantages in the university research system. These advantage were important for each institution in developing significant national roles. For Arizona, its natural setting encouraged research linked with astronomy or arid climates. Tech's forte of applied technology stemmed from its Engineering Experiment Station and made it a valued contractor of the Army and Air Force. Both institutions resided in milieus where research was little understood or appreciated; they consequently adopted the mantle of regional economic development to justify a part of their activities. In order to implement these strategies, they needed internal administration that was flexible and receptive to innovation. Both managed to achieve such adaptability during their most dynamic periods of development, despite the constraints of statewide systems of university governance. The opportunism of their approach was evident in their research profiles: both received a less-than-average proportion of funds from the federal government, and both performed proportionally more research for industry. There are other consequences as well.

Georgia Tech and the University of Arizona were able to expand the volume of research far more readily than they were able to raise themselves in the peer-ranked hierarchies of the disciplines. Although both exhibited some frustration with that fact, it was a natural consequence of the approach that they had perforce adopted. Seeking competitive advantage carried them into the unfilled niches of the research system, rather than the prestigious, theoretical mainstream. Whether this meant doing programmatic research for clients or developing subspecialties within or between disciplines, these endeavors carried less recognition than mainstream accomplishments. While academic stature remained an ineluctable lure, there were at least two consolations for their relative lack of recognition. For the institutions, a large volume of research carried its own rewards—thorough involvement in the research process for faculty and graduate students; substantial additional resources in the form of overhead payments, equipment, and gifts; and the maturation of some specialized fields into eventual prominence. For the research system as a whole perhaps the payoff is even greater. Relatively underdeveloped institutions, eager to accept the opportunities present in the environment, constitute a significant force for innovation and adaptation. Certainly compared with the post-Sputnik era, when the only client was the federal government and a narrow conception of academic prestige predominated, the stagnant seventies and the new era of the 1980s provided more incentive and more scope for such institutional initiatives. And in no single area was this difference more stark than in the renaissance of university interaction with industry.

4. Private Industry and University Research

When Smith and Karlesky wrote in the mid-seventies, the beginnings of closer relations between industry and university research were just becoming apparent. This tentative rapprochement was then—and has remained—controversial and misunderstood. Controversy inheres in the divergent natures of the two sectors; misunderstanding consistently arises from viewing this relationship solely from the perspective of the universities. Since industry is the purchaser of research from universities, its needs tend to be the paramount factor shaping the relationship. Accordingly, developments within industry during the latter 1970s set the stage for a major extension of industrial links with universities in the 1980s.

Research in industry and research in universities comprise two separate and autonomous traditions that overlap to a relatively minor extent. Interaction between the two systems began in earnest after World War I and took several forms. Industry originally looked to universities chiefly for the scientists to staff its own laboratories. After World War I many believed that universities might serve industry, as they did agriculture, through special engineering research stations. Expectations of federal legislation and support account for the origin of the Engineering Experiment Station at Georgia Tech and similar units elsewhere. Although no such program was enacted, special institutes that provided industry with applied research and development services flourished in many institutions during the 1920s.[1] By the 1940s, however, a different kind of relationship had emerged as the central paradigm of research ties between universities and industry: large and successful firms in technology-based industries like chemistry, pharmaceuticals, and telecommunications found it advantageous to perform the work most closely related to product development within their own laboratories. They looked to universities largely for more generic or theoretical knowledge that would supplement and enrich their own internal investigations. The current pattern of industrial R&D reflects these same inherent tendencies—the internalization of product development coupled with reliance on academic science for more general, basic research findings:[2]

Industrial Spending for R&D, 1980 ($ millions)[3]

	Basic	Applied	Development
Within industry	1,035	6,550	22,891
In universities & nonprofits	237	145	56
Percent within industry	81.4%	97.8%	99.8%

This point is borne out in the figures above, which show that interaction between these two sectors involves research and not development. (Hence, any discussion of this topic based on combined R&D data is rather misleading.) Also apparent is that externally supported research complements a very large basic and applied research effort within industry. Industry, in fact, pays for more research with its own funds than is supported in universities.

For a private firm, research is a costly form of overhead that must be oriented toward developing revenue-producing products. Industrial research nevertheless has striking achievements to its credit, including recent Nobel Prizes. There are also substantial areas of common interests among academic and industrial scientists.[4] University science is nevertheless nearly the obverse of the industrial effort: academic scientists collectively maintain broad coverage of all scientific fields and are primarily motivated to advance knowledge. These qualities give academic science the inestimable value of keeping abreast of the expanding research frontiers of virtually every field. When industrial scientists turn to university research, they predominantly seek to tap precisely those qualities—the things that university scientists in fact do best. Contact with university research can complement industrial efforts by providing a window onto research frontiers; it can furnish the expertise for a firm to catch-up with or enter into new fields; it can supplement and broaden the generic knowledge with which industrial scientists work; and it can be used to keep industrial scientists up-to-date with the larger field.[5] Benefits flow the other way as well; however, the interests of industry chiefly determine the dynamics of this relationship.

While research may be an imperative in many industries, interaction with academic scientists depends on recursive judgments. The general purposes indicated above might be accomplished in different ways—through consultants brought into industrial laboratories, for example, or by contracts with nonprofit laboratories, like SRI International. There is thus a degree of substitutability in industrial utilization of university research. As a result, the receptivity of universities and their faculty toward working with industry has constituted an additional factor in determining the degree of interaction. This receptivity operates at two levels. All ties rest on the willingness of individual faculty to work with companies. The critical motivation is usually intellectual interest in the scientific problems at issue. At the level of the school or university, steps are sometimes taken or policies formulated to accommodate the needs of industry. Variations in all these factors have played a role in the postwar evolution of this relationship.

Industry's total investment in research rose substantially from the 1950s to the 1960s, and that effort was sustained throughout the decade. The conventional view of the estrangement of universities and industry during the 1960s nevertheless appears correct. Industry was apparently crowded out of universities by the abundance of more attractive federal funding for research. This situation was particularly evident in biomedical research because of the copious

TABLE 25. Basic and Applied Research Supported by Industry[6]

	A National Total (mil. 1982$)	B A as % of GNP	C % of Univ.Res.	D % of A in Univs.	E % of A in Univ. & Nonprof.	F Univ.Share (D/E, %)
1955	2,850	0.19	8.1	3.1	6.6	47
1960	5,061	0.30	6.0	2.4	4.8	49
1965	6,263	0.30	2.8	1.8	4.2	44
1970	7,262	0.29	2.5	2.2	4.4	42
1975	7,180	0.26	3.3	2.5	5.0	51
1980	9,322	0.29	3.9	2.8	4.8	58
1985	13,127	0.35	5.7	3.4	5.5	65
1989	14,094	0.34	6.5	4.8	7.1	67

patronage of NIH.[7] The proportion of research purchased outside of industry (column E) declined 12.5 percent from 1960 to 1965, while that going to universities (column D) fell by 25 percent. During the last part of the decade industry utilized nonprofit institutes considerably more than universities (Column F).

The conventional view also holds that universities and university scientists became more receptive to industrial research early in the 1970s, after federal funding had been curtailed. This rapprochement was a slow process, however. During these years real industrial support for research was in decline. The overall effect was that universities in the first half of the 1970s managed to claim a somewhat larger share of a stagnant industrial research budget. After 1975 industrially funded research began to grow once more and virtually all additional external spending went to universities. By 1980 industrial support for research was little different from 1960 in relation to GNP and external spending, but universities now performed more industrial research than nonprofits.

The most striking changes in this relationship occurred during the 1980s. Industry's investment in research experienced a quantum increase in the first half of the decade. During the next four years total spending for research kept pace with the economy (i.e. GNP), but external spending registered an unprecedented rise and almost all of the additional research funds went to universities. These increases suggest important developments on both sides of this relationship—in the needs of industry as well as with the receptivity of universities. Taken together, the two developments constitute a major alteration in the university research system. The great changes of the 1980s were nevertheless impelled by forces that had taken shape previously, during the preceding decade.

At the beginning of the 1970s programmatic research in general was in retreat across American higher education. National reports called upon institutions to reduce their commitments to research, limiting them to those endeavors closely linked with teaching and academic inquiry.[8] As individual universities formulated policies for research in response to student protests they generally included the same strictures. These injunctions were principally directed toward military research, but they were equally applicable to research for industry. Indeed, prevailing opinion foresaw a diminished role for universities in the nation's research effort.[9]

One reason for such an attitude was the decided change in national expectations about research that had taken place. According to Harvey Brooks, attention had rapidly shifted from the problems of generating knowledge to those of linking knowledge with action, of applying it to the intractable problems that now confounded American society.[10] This impulse produced various responses. The Nixon Administration, through the NIH, declared the War on Cancer and then pressured the NSF into establishing a program on Research Applied to National Needs (RANN).[11] In the universities, the potentially conflicting demands for purity and relevance were reconciled by focusing on a by-now standard list of topics—poverty, race, urban problems, and environmental protection. No proponent of social responsibility yet argued that conducting research for industry would serve a useful social purpose, that the development of new products or the improvement of manufacturing techniques had a bearing on the public weal. The chasm between the campus and industry was so wide that the *Chronicle of Higher Education* could casually describe it in the language of the Cold War: "Academe and Business Explore Road to Detente."[12]

A kind of bedrock of ongoing research relationships nevertheless persisted, with little visibility, for the most part between corporations and departments of chemistry or schools of engineering. It was on this foundation that research relationships between the two sectors began to be enlarged. In one of the first pleas for greater cooperation in research (1972), a materials scientist estimated that "perhaps a quarter of our major institutions have the philosophy, willingness, and performance necessary for interacting with industry. To invest initial money outside these groups would be to invite failure."[13] That list would include late-starting, aggressive institutions like Georgia Tech and Arizona, institutes of technology generally, and selected schools within the major research universities.[14] These institutions comprised the institutional base for cultivating the rapprochement with industry.

That same year (1972) changed attitudes at the federal level became visible. Guy Stever assumed the directorship of the NSF after a long career at MIT and seven years as president of Carnegie-Mellon University—two of those institutions that were comfortable interacting with industry. Stever was strongly committed to lessening the gulf between universities and industry, but even so the contributions that the Foundation was able to make were comparatively modest. One small part of RANN promoted cooperative research, and Stever encouraged some redirection of graduate science and engineering programs toward industrial employment.[15] NSF also established three "technology innovation centers" at the University of Oregon, MIT, and Carnegie-Mellon. Despite such encouragements, government efforts to promote university-industry interaction appeared to a knowledgeable observer as "rather unstructured, unfocused, and uncoordinated." The difficulty stemmed from the fact that efforts to achieve the transfer of technology through such linkages "depend most on the two partners' own incentives to promote the flow of people and ideas."[16] Indeed, such incentives prompted the most remarkable coupling of the first half of the decade.

In 1974, after lengthy negotiations, the Harvard Medical School and the Monsanto Corporation quietly concluded a contract worth $23 million over twelve years.[17] The agreement was only made public by the press in February of the next year, and two years later the principals were still reluctant to disclose the details. Essentially, Monsanto provided funds for endowment, research support, and facilities for a pair of Harvard scientists. In return the company was promised the patent rights to any discoveries that resulted from their research. These were unprecedented actions by both parties. For Harvard the uncharacteristic secrecy was a sure sign that a negative reaction was expected from the academic community. More significantly, Harvard abandoned a longstanding policy that all patents in health fields must be dedicated to the public, allowing the future rights to be assigned instead to Monsanto. Harvard thus risked public opprobrium on several fronts in order to secure attractive long-term research support. For Monsanto, the size and the longevity of the contract were far outside industry standards. Also unusual was the freedom granted the scientists to pursue and publish basic research. This arrangement nevertheless held the possibilities for two kinds of payoffs. The Harvard research team was engaged in a line of research that might prove fruitful in developing cures for certain cancers. Patents derived from this work could be of considerable value.[18] But beyond this, the company sought an entree into biological research as part of a long-range repositioning of the company in pharmaceutical and agricultural products. Unable to hire top biologists away from universities, it sought close cooperation in part to build up its own internal research capacity.[19]

The Harvard-Monsanto agreement was a harbinger for the next decade. When it was signed, overall university investments in basic research—the principal point of contact with universities—were shrinking toward a nadir. Real industrial spending for basic research in 1975 was actually lower than it had been in 1962. From that low point, such spending doubled in the next ten years. This increase reflected the emergence of powerful incentives in both camps. The most fundamental changes occurred within industry, where the two most dynamic areas were microelectronics and biotechnology. In the former, industry was substantially ahead of university capabilities throughout the 1970s. University departments were in fact sorely deficient in both faculty expertise and the expensive equipment needed for many lines of research. But the fierce competition in this field eventually exhausted existing engineering know-how, producing a situation in which academic research in complementary fields became more relevant. After 1980, computer and semiconductor manufacturers had increasing recourse to university-based research for assistance. Biotechnology represented a different and ultimately more revolutionary pattern. Not only did expanded research activities in this field by chemical and pharmaceutical companies add greatly to the volume of industry-sponsored academic research, but scientific breakthroughs also led to a transformation in university attitudes toward these links.

Biotechnology, most simply, is the applied science of molecular biology. The fundamental discovery that made it possible occurred just two decades after James Watson and Francis Crick had established the basic structure of DNA and the method by which it replicated. In 1973 Herbert Boyer of UC San Francisco and Stanley Cohen of Stanford discovered a technique for splicing genetic material and inserting it into another organism. Most important, the foreign genes performed their previous function in their new host: genetic engineering thus became possible. A second key discovery emerged from immunology when Georges Kohler and Cesar Milstein produced single-purpose or monoclonal antibodies. Here was a technique for producing in quantity very specific antibodies that could be used for experiments, diagnostics, and possibly therapies.[20] Both accomplishments were fundamental scientific breakthroughs (the latter earned a Nobel Prize in 1984), and as such opened pathways for much further research. But they equally opened the possibilities for important applications. Developing those applications, however, was no simple task. Only the scientists who were familiar with the arcana of molecular biology, immunology, virology, and other related specialties possessed the expertise to guide such work. Then, a long and costly regulatory process stood between any product and the market. In fact, it would take almost a decade before the first genetically engineered substance was approved for sale (1982). The inescapable consequences of the biotechnology revolution were nevertheless, on the epistemological level, the confounding of basic and applied research; in practical matters, academic expertise was now confounded with the development of products for market.

The scientific community that initiated and experienced the biotechnology revolution transcended universities proper. In the United States this community was heavily dependent on the NIH, and particularly the National Cancer Institute. Besides maintaining its own laboratories, NIH supported researchers in university biological departments, in medical schools, and in teaching hospitals. In addition, independent research institutes, especially those devoted to cancer research, formed another institutional arm of this same community. Molecular biology, with its assorted subspecialties, was one of the purest wings of biomedical science. Unlike some other areas of basic science, it was prospering in the early 1970s under a second wind of funding from the War on Cancer. Throughout the 1970s these scientists had little reason to consider alternatives to their existing settings.

The institutions that should have had greatest interest in biotechnology were the large, multinational pharmaceutical firms. They knew the value of research, performed large amounts in their own laboratories, and also maintained ongoing relationships with academic scientists. Their entrenched modes of research, however, were not easily reconciled with the new science. Their principal research technique was to screen thousands of exotic compounds for various desired traits. Once identified, long development work was required to turn them into effective and usable drugs. This latter stage was an extended exercise in organic chemistry, and it was largely to aid this effort that the drug firms maintained regular relationships with university chemists. This empirical approach to drug development was effective without recourse to molecular biology, and the multinational drug firms were largely ignorant of the field.[21]

Although the large, technology-based corporations were the principal industrial funders of university research, they were not the only conduits for commercializing scientific discoveries. Another model was the small, high-technology company in which the founder(s) and other high corporate officers were themselves scientists or engineers, sometimes from Academe. There were several species in this genus. After World War II university scientists were instrumental in setting up numerous electronics firms. Such companies often had a symbiotic relationship with the Department of Defense. Research for the military would fund the development of important new technologies on which the new firms were based. Demand for military products then largely determined the market that these companies addressed. A second type of high-tech company emerged in the computer industry in the 1960s and 1970s. The entrepreneurs in this case tended to be engineers from larger firms and, despite the legend of Silicon Valley, academic connections were less critical in this industry. Once production was begun, these science-based firms tended to become more distant from university laboratories. Academic consultants might remain important, and access to talented graduate students was always desirable, but they preferred to spend their research budgets within the firm. For the most recent species of high-tech firm, the biotechnology startups, ties with academic science would be more fundamental and enduring.

The paradigm for the new biotechnology firms was set by Genentech, the first firm to be based explicitly on genetic engineering.[22] The initiative for forming the corporation in 1976 came from a venture capitalist, Robert Swanson, who was fishing for a way to tap the commercial possibilities of recombinant DNA. He negotiated an agreement with Herbert Boyer who, unlike other molecular biologists, had an interest in finding applications for this new technology. Boyer and his lab at the UC San Francisco were also at the cutting edge of recombinant DNA research. When he and Swanson agreed to form Genentech, Boyer already knew what research needed to be done and was in touch with scientists who could do it. Without ever leaving his academic post, Boyer assembled a team of academic researchers for Genentech. In just two years they succeeded, ahead of other teams of university scientists, in synthesizing the human gene for insulin.[23] This striking scientific achievement had well-understood commercial value. Genentech immediately licensed its discovery to the Eli Lilly Co., the dominant American manufacturer of insulin. Genentech thus validated the idea that genetic engineering could produce valuable commercial products and gave rise to a groundswell of anticipation about the miracles that might be worked by biotechnology. These expectations set the stage for the company's spectacular public debute.

On October 14, 1980, Genentech stock was offered to the public at an initial price of $35. Within minutes the stock was bid up to $89, and it finished its first day of trading above $70. This single event was in many ways the culmination of developments that had been building throughout the last half of the seventies; it transformed perceptions of the relationship between capitalism and university research on the part of all the principal actors. Most immediately affected were venture capitalists and molecular biologists, but universities and pharmaceutical corporations were implicated as well.

Venture capitalists were naturally the first to respond to the spectre of riches conjured up by Genentech.[24] They began canvassing the biological research community for scientists who possessed the crucial expertise and who were willing to join a commercial venture. They soon found the individuals they sought. Although each deal was unique, venture capitalists were in a position to offer academic scientists the best of both worlds. Scientists could usually remain in their academic posts and continue to conduct basic research in their specialties, but they would now receive an infusion of private funding. When they were induced to leave academic settings, they were able to reproduce the atmosphere of the academic laboratory within the new firms. In either case, they were able to continue path-breaking scientific research, but with the additional goal of patenting their findings. They would also receive an equity stake in the enterprise: if it became a commercial success the scientists would become rich.

Approximately 200 biotech firms were founded between 1980 and 1984.

Half of all the venture capital raised by 1988 for biotechnology was committed in the two years following Genentech's debut (1981–82).[25] Initially, venture capitalists sought out university scientists, but that situation was soon reversed. Relatively few biologists were able to found companies, but those who did had a wide impact on the scientific community. Research in this industry was inherently interdisciplinary and was conducted by teams of researchers. It was necessary to maintain broad contacts across several fields. Most of the firms had Scientific Advisory Boards comprised of eminent scientists who functioned as more-or-less permanent consultants. They often did research for the company and usually received an equity stake. The new firms also used regular consultants, and the larger of the firms granted research contracts to university scientists. After a few years, affiliation with a company was considered the norm in molecular biology departments. The new biotechnology firms, in short, were rooted in the core of academic biology.[26]

The multinational drug firms soon faced the challenge of tapping into that core. They were interested in products, not scientific breakthroughs, and they had an exceedingly long time-horizon. But the firms realized that they would have to begin investing in the new technology if they were to utilize it in the succeeding decades. Ultimately that would mean developing in-house capabilities, but in the meantime they could gain access to the new science through either the universities or the startup biotech firms. In fact they did both. One of the surest methods of developing expertise in this field was to conclude long-term research contracts, as Monsanto had done with Harvard. In just three years starting in 1981, at least eleven multi-year, multi-million dollar contracts for research in biotechnology were concluded between universities and chemical or pharmaceutical firms. In the largest, for $70 million over ten years, the German firm Hoechst supported the formation of a genetics department at Massachusetts General Hospital (affiliated with the Harvard Medical School). Monsanto continued its earlier strategy by entering into a long-term working relationship with its neighbor in St. Louis, Washington University.[27] These large corporations also had recourse to their traditional methods of tapping academic expertise, through consultancies and research contracts. Except for the long-term contracts, these relationships fit the dominant paradigm for research linkages.

University-industry relations in biotechnology thus presented two different faces. The new start-ups were an emanation of academic science and still intimately connected with university departments in the conduct of research and the affiliations of scientists. They provided some support for university laboratories, but the chief nexus was the equity stakes that gave scientists a vested interest in the success of the company. In terms of financial support for university research, however, the large corporations provided far greater resources. By one estimate, industry support for biotechnology in universities totaled $120 million in 1984.[28] If correct, that figure would comprise 42 percent of all industry-supported university research, and would clearly account for a major portion of the notable increase in such support. Related estimates further indicated that five-sixths of that $120 million came from large (i.e. Fortune 500) corporations. The two patterns of collaboration with industry presented universities with different kinds of opportunities—and problems.

At the height of the biotechnology boom the research universities found themselves pulled by two contradictory currents. The first arose from a global shift in attitudes toward interaction with industry that had begun at the end of the 1970s. The overriding concern behind this shift was the apparent declining competitiveness of American industry in world markets. Since the 1960s American corporations had been underinvesting in fundamental research and losing contact with academic research. Now, as universities were increasingly pressed for resources, the two sectors appeared to need each other. With growing frequency, calls were heard for efforts to provide greater resources for university research, to orient that research toward areas relevant to industry, and to promote mechanisms for conveying discoveries to industry for commercial development.[29] Economic competitiveness and technology transfer became the cornerstones of an emerging consensus on university research. The opposite of a grass-roots movement, this consensus crystalized on the level at which leaders of industry, universities, and government interacted. On campus the consensus was not shared by the majority of faculty and students, who were uninvolved with and antipathetic toward industry. Support for these ideas in high places nevertheless assured that something would be done.

In Washington, NSF began providing joint funding for university-industry collaboration, and in 1980 the National Science Board made this topic the focus of a special study. That same year Congress amended the patent law so that universities, rather than the federal government, could own title to inventions made with federal research funds. The next year the tax laws were changed to provide greater incentives for industry to support university research.[30] Corporate and university executives had already joined together in the Business–Higher Education Forum (f. 1978) in order to bring about closer cooperation and understanding between the two sectors.[31] A number of cooperative research programs were established, initially by those institutions like MIT and Stanford that had maintained close relations with industry. Large corporations, for their part, proved willing to join such partnerships.[32] Contacts between universities and corporations were thus expanding in areas other than biotechnology.

Biotechnology nevertheless became the principal focus for an opposing current of opinion concerned with the alleged dangers of university collaboration with industry. The tumult of the biotech boom quite naturally spread apprehension about the compatibility of free-wheeling capitalism and the mores of the academy. In 1981 and 1982 these same fears provided the focus for hearings in which congressmen assumed the posture of defenders of academic values.[33] The ire of Representative Albert Gore, Jr., co-chairman of the hearings, was particularly raised by the Hoechst contract. Such long-term arrangements appeared to allow a private firm to set the research agenda for academic departments. Moreover, it apparently aimed to appropriate the fruits of biomedical research that had been nurtured by NIH through an enormous investment of public funds.

Worst of all, Hoechst was a German firm and potential competitor to American industry. Congressman Gore did manage to resolve some of these issues by forcing the public disclosure of the Hoechst contract and the adoption of accounting procedures that assured no federal funds would be used to further research for the firm.[34] The fundamental issues, however, could not be so readily dispelled.

Did the influence of industry steer biological research from pure to applied topics? Was the free flow of information impeded? Were academic norms violated through conflicts of interest? Could faculty commit themselves to their companies while also being good citizens to their departments and universities, good colleagues to their fellow faculty, and mentors to their students? These important questions were being raised in countless forms, but applied across thousands of research settings they admitted of no simple answers.

The first two issues bore an underlying similarity to the problems introduced by federal funding of academic research after World War II. They were matters of degree, resistant to sweeping generalizations. There could be little doubt that, after the spectacular achievements of basic research which inaugurated the biotechnology revolution, the imperatives of commercialization induced a drift toward more programmatic work. But federal policy had been trying to push academic research in that direction for a decade. As for secrecy, it was inescapable in an industry that was based on patenting. Corporate sponsors were accorded as a matter of course the right to review and possibly delay articles before publication. More insidious was the indeterminable extent to which the free flow of information among scientists was inhibited.[35] In this and the other issues anecdotes provided the stuff of arguments, and what were undoubtedly exceptional cases conveyed the most damaging impressions. In a few situations conflict of interest was sufficiently apparent that professors were asked to choose between their university appointment and their biotech companies. In other cases allegations that scientists had exploited students warranted investigation.[36]

With respect to fulfilling faculty roles, there was also evidence for both sides. Entrepreneurs were among the most talented and energetic of faculty, and thus usually capable of juggling different roles. But they were also for that same reason especially valuable to their universities, and involvement in start-up firms seemed inescapably to diminish their academic roles. President Donald Kennedy of Stanford captured the essence of this situation when he expressed concern about "the loss of parts of people."[37]

A final question raised at this juncture was to what extent the university could be trusted to oversee these obviously delicate relationships? Confidence in this role was thoroughly shaken when, at the time of the Genentech debut, Harvard contemplated getting into the business itself. The conjuncture of a valuable patent by a Harvard biologist and interest from venture capitalists presented Harvard with a unique opportunity to found a biotech firm in which the university would have substantial equity.[38] The lure was one that enticed many universities: how to claim a share of the wealth that was being generated within their laboratories? As Derek Bok later wrote, the millions that might be gained from Wall Street "stir the blood of every harried administrator struggling to balance an unruly budget."[39] When the Harvard plan was reviewed by the national press, however, it became apparent how damaging such a step would be to the university's credibility and image. Harvard soon rejected the idea, but the research universities in general still faced an urgent need to address the issues raised by biotechnology. Officially and publicly, they had to develop sound institutional policies concerning such things as secrecy, conflict of interest, and faculty responsibilities; and by doing so to dispell any public suspicions of impropriety. Privately, they may have been concerned to forestall congressional intervention. Furthermore, there was still the puzzle of finding suitable means for universities to garner a share of the riches.

Immediately after the first congressional hearing on biotechnology, President Donald Kennedy summoned several of his peers for a kind of summit on university-industry relations. As his letter explained, "the problem is getting larger faster than we are coping with it, so I think some haste is desirable."[40] In March of 1982 the presidents of Harvard, MIT, Caltech, and the University of California, each accompanied by a small group of high administrators, faculty, and businessmen, joined President Kennedy and the Stanford contingent at Pajaro Dunes. The fact of this meeting was more significant than any outcome. It was ample testimony to the importance and urgency of the problems posed by the biotechnology revolution. The meeting (which was closed to the public and roundly condemned for that reason) was credited with producing frank and useful exchanges, but the universities could agree about little beyond the desirability of formulating policies that would protect academic values and reassure the public. When it came to specifics like contract disclosure, patent licensing, or defining conflict of interest, their differing practices could not be reconciled with the high-minded principles they espoused. In the end they had no recourse but to leave matters to the "special circumstances and traditions" of each university.[41]

The year 1982 marked a watershed for university involvement with biotechnology and with industry in general. With the second round of congressional hearings on the topic in the summer, and another university summit of sorts at the end of the year, the issues were thoroughly aired, if not resolved.[42] Within the biotechnology industry, however, the chaotic formative phase had nearly run its course. Founding companies became more difficult as the industry itself became more competitive.[43] The situation that had alarmed Donald Kennedy was now largely reversed; that is, universities began coping with the situation faster than it grew. Most importantly, after 1982 the new consensus linking American economic competitiveness and technology transfer was firmly in the ascendancy. A text for this new faith was appropriately supplied by the Business–Higher Education Forum: "America's Competitive Challenge" presented a world-view in which industrial competitiveness was crucial to the nation's well-being and university research was an indispensable input. The message, interestingly, favored retaining the university's emphasis on basic research: "the health of American basic research," it announced, "is critical in an era when international competition increases industry's need for scientific advance."[44] This was a message that universities yearned to hear: a quarter-century after Sputnik the research universities had found a new rationale for their distinctive mission.

The revolution in biotechnology appears to have been the critical factor in the growing acceptance of university-industry cooperation. Like atomic physics a generation before, it supplied the irrefutable example of how the purest of academic research could have profound practical consequences. The molecular biologists, moreover, had developed an extraordinarily effective means of technology transfer, which in turn promised international leadership to American companies. This experience once again validated the national investment in academic research, but in this case the lesson was given a distinctive twist. For the purposes of aiding industry, it was now held, university research should focus on 'generic' science and technology—the general kinds of knowledge underpinning the special techniques and applications that industry employs to develop products. Such generic research was more likely to be basic than applied in character, but this distinction was not crucial. Rather, like the predominant cast of academic research after World War II, industry-oriented research in the 1980s was programmatic in nature.

After 1982, a new landscape for university research quickly became visible. After a muddled start, the Reagan Administration in 1983 strongly endorsed greater support for basic research as well as defense-related research.[45] A new orientation to federal research policy also became evident, especially at NSF. Erich Bloch became the first director of the foundation appointed from private industry (1984-90). He immediately implemented a 1983 recommendation from the National Academy of Engineering to establish Engineering Research Centers at universities, designed to further cooperation between industry and academic researchers and to advance generic knowledge in economically relevant fields. During Bloch's six-year tenure, engineering was elevated to a status commensurate with science in NSF, and the mission of contributing to national industrial competitiveness became the principal rationale for requesting additional funding.[46] Federal policy since the middle 1980s has thus been explicitly intended to enhance university contributions to economic development through greater interaction with industry.

For its part, industry became increasingly receptive to such cooperation. Within a large, variegated field, two important patterns stand out. In engineering generally, and microelectronics in particular, firms proved willing to invest in cooperative research enterprises. Generic knowledge played an important role in these fields, while patenting had less competitive significance. In such a situation the economics of cooperative research were appealing, especially where costly facilities were publicly subsidized. The NSF Engineering Research Centers were just one of a number of types of cooperative ventures.[47]

In the biotechnology industry, where the crucial role of patenting precluded much cooperation, a sorting process continued throughout the decade. The insuperable advantage of large multinational corporations in developing and marketing human health and agricultural products became increasingly evident. They had several options for tapping the innovative research emerging from start-up firms—research partnerships, licenses, part ownership, or outright acquisition—and all were exercised at one time or another. A transmission belt thus developed to carry the discoveries of the biotech start-ups to the products of the multinational firms. By the end of the decade the industry looked quite different from the beginning. Few of the promised products of bioengineering had yet emerged from the long, development-testing-approval pipeline. Without many products to sell, many of the biotech start-ups reverted to a status of "research boutiques,"—selling their expertise to the multinationals.[48] New start-ups continued to be formed, and a handful of the earlier biotech firms attained the production stage. But when the Swiss pharmaceutical giant Hoffman LaRoche acquired controlling interest of Genentech in 1990, it augured the pre-ponderance of the multinationals firms in this industry.

As the industry reverted back toward its more traditional form, so too did research relationships with universities. This was a positive development for universities (if not for faculty entrepreneurs). The large firms funded more university research in the normal way, which caused fewer problems of competition and divided loyalties; they also had the resources to assist universities through major gifts. The whole area of biotechnology remained intellectually and organization-ally dynamic, but the maturation of the industry provided universities with more direct research funding and less potential for embarrassment.

Across the research universities, those relatively few institutions that had maintained close ties with industry were, after 1982, increasingly joined by oth-ers who embraced the new consensus. This endorsement was not always widely shared on campus; it tended to coexist with a latent distrust of capitalism. But in practice, because of the natural compartmentalization of university activities, such antipathies had little consequence. One study found that 86 percent of industry research flowed into schools of engineering, medicine, and agriculture, units that harbored their own distinctive cultures.[49] More significant, the top administrators of research universities almost uniformly backed the new con-sensus. Always craving public approbation, they welcomed a role in remedying the national competitiveness crisis. But they perceived more to be at stake. Cor-porate connections, it soon became apparent, might alleviate some of the exigent financial problems still facing the universities. In the 1980s the industrial con-nection would expand beyond cooperation to commercialization as universities sought both to provide services and derive profits from their new economic role.

IO

The New Era
of the 1980s

1. Turning Outward

The research universities, together with the rest of American higher education, entered the 1980s with considerable trepidation. Amidst the accumulated plaints and grievances that had arisen during the previous decade due to financial stagnation, government regulation, and cultural alienation, there loomed in addition the three seemingly unalterable facts of demography, economics, and politics.

Demographically, the age of the steady state had arrived. Enrollments in higher education had essentially reached a plateau after 1975, but now for the first time in the history of American higher education there was the possibility of actual decline. The number of 18-year-olds peaked in 1979; during the next dozen years the succeeding cohorts would decline by 26 percent and along with them the size of the college-age population. The proportion of those cohorts attending higher education would largely determine actual enrollments, but there was little optimism on that score either. The earnings advantage of college graduates had shrunk markedly during the 1970s, reducing the economic incentives for attendance.[1] The research universities may have been well insulated against actual enrollment decline, but the situation had dire ramifications for their graduate students who hoped to enter the academic profession. For institutions, with no foreseeable enrollment growth to assist adaptation to changing conditions and changing demands, the possibility of further retrenchment loomed.

Economically, the universities faced a difficult environment. Persistently high inflation was their worst enemy, since they faced constraints in both raising tuition and reducing labor costs. This vise was reflected in the annual inflation-adjusted change in faculty salaries, a good barometer of the financial health of higher education, which was negative from 1973 to 1980. A severe recession at the beginning of the 1980s threatened to make the situation even worse. The financial pinch varied according to the circumstances of individual institutions, but was most painful for public universities in industrial states. The University of Michigan, a prime example, received no increase in state appropriations for three consecutive years (FY1981–83), and thereby endured nearly a 25 percent loss in the purchasing power of those revenues.[2] The research universities as a whole were cursed by the crisis of American industry that, according to the ideology of economic competitiveness, they were expected to help resolve.

The political pall hanging over higher education was personified by President Ronald Reagan. The universities had received a short-lived respite during the administration of Jimmy Carter in the form of additional research support, fairly generous provisions for student aid, and the promise (unfulfilled) of assistance for research infrastructure. The attitude of the new, conservative administration could be characterized as indifference toward basic research, reluctance to spend federal funds on universities, and hostility toward the social sciences and the arts for their suspected liberal proclivities.[3] In actuality, support for universities during the early Reagan years turned out to be dismal rather than disastrous, as had been feared. Funding for infrastructure, student aid, graduate study, and the social sciences were all scaled back; basic research barely held its own, and the conspicuous growth area was research support from the Department of Defense. The unambiguous message nevertheless was that universities could not look to Washington for relief from their ills.

In the new era of the 1980s, then, universities could no longer rely upon enrollment growth, state governments, or federal agencies to find the additional resources needed to accommodate the inherent expansiveness of their intellectual activities. With few other alternatives, universities increasingly turned to the private sector. Several inchoate developments improved the prospects for such a course.

The threats that had appeared so ominous in 1980 began to dissipate after 1982. Enrollments in higher education remained at their plateau levels, buoyed in part by steadily widening earnings differentials favoring college graduates.[4] More important for research universities, a pronounced pursuit of quality assured a robust demand for places at selective institutions in both the public and private sectors. The recession of 1981–82 was followed by sustained economic growth in succeeding years. Faculty salaries managed to beat inflation for those years, and then, from 1984 onward, registered their first substantial real gains since the 1960s. Universities took advantage of the opportunities that a healthy economy offered, which made the next half-decade the most prosperous interlude since the mid-1960s. In addition, the federal government showed renewed appreciation for academic research, if not for other university needs. During the two Reagan Administrations, real federal funding for academic research increased by 45 percent, while total research grew by 62 percent.[5] These figures reveal a healthy rate of growth for a mature research system, as well as relative shrinkage in the federal role. What these generally prosperous conditions masked was a second and somewhat paradoxical characteristic of the 1980s—the persistence of stress throughout the system. In fact these two conditions—prosperity and stress—stimulated universities to exploit available opportunities. Universities essentially turned outward as they sought to tap resources in the private sector, perform research for programmatic sponsors, and reap direct gains from their contributions to the economy.

Privatization. The growing reliance upon private sources of income to support higher education was a phenomenon that was not confined to the research universities or, indeed, the United States.[6] The following figures indicate the change in the proportion of private resources from tuition, gifts, and endowment earnings in relation to the basic expenditures of institutions:[7]

Funds from Private Sources, Percent of Basic Educational Expenses

	1975–76	*1980–81*	*1985–86*
Public institutions	23.2	24.0	28.0
Private institutions	82.5	83.3	86.0

Year-by-year data would indicate even more clearly that privatization was essentially a phenomenon of the 1980s. It continued through the last years of the decade and into the 1990s, when large tuition increases in public universities became commonplace. This development was rapid, considering the large sums involved. For example, the percentage changes indicated above shifted $2.3 billion onto private shoulders in the first five years of the 1980s. Moreover, privatization was more pronounced at research universities, which charged the highest tuition in both the public and private sectors and generally increased those charges more than the averages. Research universities were also among the largest recipients of gifts and the largest holders of endowments. They, along with selective liberal arts colleges, were thus in the best position to augment revenues from private sources.

Increases in student tuition brought the most additional revenues to universities in the 1980s. These increases were originally prompted by inflation, but persisted even after inflation subsided. The years 1979 through 1981 endured double-digit inflation that even growing tuition hikes could not match. But the situation was then reversed: in both the 1981 and 1982 academic years tuition was raised by roughly 14 percent, while inflation dropped to 9 and then 4 percent.[8] Universities readily justified such increases by their need to catch-up with inflated price levels. When these tuition hikes failed to generate a significant backlash, universities continued to raise tuition in order to address their accumulated backlog of needs. For the next four years tuition increases hovered around 10 percent, while inflation was less than 4 percent. This differential lessened at the end of the eighties, as private universities, in particular, reacted to increasingly voluble complaints.[9]

For the decade, average university tuition rose more rapidly in the private than the public sector. The pattern of increases was also more uniform there, with those institutions charging the ceiling level of tuition setting the pace. In the public sector, the level of tuition varied widely according to the funding traditions of individual states. Reliance on student tuition tended to be greatest in those states that had difficulty supporting their universities. At Michigan, for example, during the three years of flat state appropriations, income from tuition rose by 17, 14, and 17 percent. Since state appropriations and tuition account for most of the revenues for regular operations, the degree of privatization can be gauged by comparing these amounts:[10]

TABLE 26. State Appropriations per Dollar of Tuition Revenue, 1978 and 1986

	1978	1986	% Privatized*
University of Texas	$7.45	$4.42	7
University of Illinois	5.05	4.00	4
University of Arizona	4.57	3.58	4
UCLA	4.54	4.11	2
UC Berkeley	4.44	3.99	2
University of Washington	3.93	2.17	12
University of Minnesota	3.74	2.89	5
University of Wisconsin	3.08	2.55	4
Purdue University	2.41	1.76	7
University of Michigan	1.98	1.36	7
Penn State University	1.34	.91	9
University of Pittsburgh	1.31	.85	11

*Percentage of financial burden shifted to student tuition.

The uniformity of this development is striking. The increase in the burden of supporting the institution borne by students varied from a minor 2 percent in California to a substantial 12 percent in Washington. On balance, though, the growth of dependence on tuition at these universities exceeded the average for the public sector.[11]

In a longer perspective, the resort to higher tuition was a continuation, and indeed intensification, of tendencies that were present since the early 1970s (see Chapter 8). During that decade, however, the private universities worried about pricing themselves out of the market, while public institutions feared that high tuition would reduce access. In the 1980s, when these same institutions saw applications soar, such concerns carried less weight. High demand for admissions corresponded with greater student concern for worldly success in business or the professions. Quality education at the undergraduate level was perceived as a means of securing entrance to the highly selective professional schools that paved the way to such careers. Reaganomics, furthermore, helped to boost the disposable incomes of the affluent so that they might afford premium tuition rates. Institutions adjusted by substantially increasing their own student financial aid in order to maintain the best possible pool of applicants. Tuition increases at public universities were largely driven by the necessity of supplementing state appropriations that were inadequate to maintain accustomed academic standards. At private universities, tuition increases early in the decade served the same purpose of preserving standards against double-digit inflation. By mid-decade, however, the hikes tended to be justified in terms of preserving or extending excellence, which was what their clientele demanded. In either case, substantive institutional improvements could scarcely be financed through student charges alone. For this purpose, universities looked to voluntary support.

Giving to higher education had faltered in the late 1960s, declining by some 20 percent after inflation from the 1968 to the 1974 academic year. From that point it began a slow real rise that brought it back to its 1968 level by the end of the 1970s.[12] Once the economic difficulties of the early 1980s passed, higher education entered the most propitious period for raising funds since the early 1960s. From 1984 to 1986, annual increases in total gifts averaged 15 percent. Giving then remained high in spite of instability in the financial markets and discouraging changes in the tax laws.[13] Virtually all the research universities were sensitive to this trend and sought to exploit the opportunity.

Voluntary support for higher education during the 1980s enlarged pre-existing patterns of giving. As a result, the chief beneficiaries were those institutions that had well-established traditions of giving. This category included the wealthiest private universities, as well as certain state institutions such as Michigan and Minnesota. There were nevertheless some notable departures from this pattern. Among recipients, many public institutions that had previously lacked well-organized development efforts became aggressive fund-raisers during the decade. Both Ohio State and Penn State, which fit that description, concluded campaigns in 1990 that exceeded their goals of $405 and $350 million respectively. Georgia Tech's Centennial Campaign also places it in this group. Fund-raising campaigns became virtually ubiquitous: in 1990, 38 of the 55 AAU universities were either conducting or planning such campaigns and at least six envisioned billion-dollar targets.[14]

Probably more than any other single factor, philanthropy in the eighties allowed the research universities to expand without growing—to create new faculty positions, initiate programs, and generally keep abreast of dynamic intellectual fields. But systematic and aggressive fund-raising had more subtle influence on institutional development. As universities beat the bushes for donations, particularly large donations, donors more often designated the purpose of those gifts. Whereas in 1970 about one-third of gifts were unrestricted, less than 20 percent were in the late 1980s. For research universities the proportion was closer to 10 percent. Even though most restricted gifts were for essential university functions—research, student aid, buildings, or faculty chairs—such funds nevertheless fell unevenly across universities. Voluntary support played a visible role in determining where the incremental expansion of research universities would occur. Schools of Business were conspicuously well treated, and corporations were solicitous toward engineering. The overall effect was to provide additional vigor to those professional schools in closest contact with the corporate world. This development could not be attributed solely to voluntary support or isolated to any meaningful extent from other forces pushing in this same direction. The enhanced importance of voluntary support was nevertheless an integral part of the general turning outward of universities in the 1980s.

Programmatic research.   The balance between disinterested and programmatic academic research shifted markedly toward the latter during the 1980s. Interestingly, this shift was the corrective to the ivory-tower mentality that had been called for since the late 1960s. But throughout the 1970s, as described above, universities were unenthusiastic, federal programs were limited in scope and effectiveness, and industrial investment in research remained low. Each of these conditions changed in the next decade.

The most radical turnabout occurred as a result of the expansion of military research that was begun under President Carter and greatly accelerated by President Reagan. Only a small portion of these funds trickled down to support university research, but that trickle was enough to make the DoD the fastest growing source of federal support for academic research. Its total doubled from 1978 to 1983, exceeding that of NSF. On the whole, this support was more heavily programmatic than DoD support in the postwar and Sputnik eras. A congressional review of federal science policy at mid-decade found the shadow of the Mansfield Amendment still affecting DoD support for academic science. One of the recommendations was that the Department revert to its earlier role and shoulder a greater part of the burden of sustaining basic research in universities.[15] No such change occurred. By the end of the decade basic research supported by the Pentagon was shrinking, and with it the weighting of DoD research on campus. Still, this shrinkage by itself did not diminish the overall drift toward programmatic research.

At the end of the 1980s, NSF bid to expand its role in supporting academic research, and it did so, ironically, by becoming more programmatic. The sponsorship of programmatic research by NSF began in earnest earlier with the founding of Engineering Research Centers. This initiative aroused fears within the basic research directorates, the bastions of disinterested research, that such projects were funded at their expense. Substitution was clearly not the intention of Director Erich Bloch, who foresaw the Foundation's programmatic role as an addition to its primary mission. By 1987 fourteen Engineering Research Centers were operating. Their explicit purpose was to encourage working relationships between universities and industry and to cultivate interdisciplinary research on generic topics. Industry was required to contribute support, which quickly amounted to about a third of Center budgets.[16] Smaller programs for "Industry/University Cooperative Research Centers" and for "Science and Technology Centers" were aimed toward the same end. By the end of the 1980s these three kinds of Centers comprised 3 percent, and engineering 10 percent, of the NSF budget. Overall, federal support for engineering grew from from 9 to 17 percent of research funds between 1975 and 1986.[17]

The fastest growing component in the university research economy, support from industry, was also inherently programmatic. As discussed in the previous chapter, these funds jumped in the first half of the 1980s in line with the rapid growth of industrial research. In the following years, universities attracted an increasing proportion of industrial research expenditures largely due to the numerous steps taken on campus to attract industrial patrons.[18]

Universities demonstrated their willingness to perform research for industry by establishing organized research units expressly for this purpose. The salient areas in which ORUs were created—microelectronics, biotechnology, manufacturing processes, material sciences, and artificial intelligence—underline their programmatic emphasis.[19] The utilization of ORUs was accompanied by the establishment of industrial affiliate plans and research consortia. These arrangements reflected the research needs of industry and were sometimes made more attractive by the availability of government subsidies. The crucial factor, nevertheless, was the eagerness of universities to expand ties with industry. As one student of the subject put it, "while industry is receptive, it is clear that the university is selling, not receiving."[20] Universities that were not closely linked with industry took special measures to develop such relationships. Berkeley, particularly noted for its aloofness, was induced by financial stringency in 1979 to establish its first affiliate plan in engineering. This initiative subsequently grew into a large program with multiple plans. Industrially oriented institutions, such as Georgia Tech or Stanford, typically multiplied interactions. Stanford had 14 industrial affiliate plans operating at the start of the 1980s, but created 27 new ones during the decade.[21] The active efforts of universities largely accounted for the continued rise in industrially supported academic research into the 1990s.

The swing of the pendulum back toward programmatic sponsorship of academic research revived some of the concerns felt before Sputnik, but not others. The fundamental difficulty facing the university research system in the postwar era was the absence of sufficient funding for basic, disinterested research. Although the ascendancy of the ideology of basic research carried the system to the opposite extreme, the original complaint had been valid: universities in the 1950s had been capable of conducting far more high-quality basic research than funding then allowed. Just as the proliferation of basic research after Sputnik had been an accretion on the postwar system, the programmatic research of the 1980s was also an accretion on the system that had been erected in the 1960s and had survived the 1970s. While arguments were made that various disinterested fields deserved additional funding,[22] the fact remained that the extensive foundations of academic science not only remained intact, but served as the platform for supporting the growth of programmatic research.

Still, universities found their incomes falling behind their burgeoning needs and aspirations. In keeping with their general turning outward, universities sought additional financial resources from expanding and exploiting their newly sanctified economic role.

Entrepreneurship.   During the 1980s university attitudes toward commercial relationships changed markedly.[23] The chief arenas of opportunity for such relationships were the nurturing of nascent industries through research parks and business incubators, profiting from the patenting of faculty discoveries, and obtaining equity in start-up firms based on university research. None of these activities was really new, although the last appeared in a new light after the Genentech saga. Stanford had established the first university research park in 1951. University patenting goes back much further—to the founding in 1912 of the Research Corporation to administer university patents and the creation of the Wisconsin Alumni Research Foundation (WARF) in 1925 with income from the Steenbock patent of Vitamin D.[24] Before 1978, however, research parks were exceptional across American research universities and patenting was a minor concern. Ten years later both were pursued systematically by the majority of research universities. Two parallel motives were clearly at work. Universities sought to accentuate their role in economic development and largely justified such activities in terms of technology transfer; but they also saw the opportunity to enhance revenues, possibly in a major way. The greatest change of the 1980s, however, occurred in university attitudes toward standards of appropriate institutional behavior in commercial relationships.

Just ten university research parks were opened before 1975, but twenty-five more followed in the next decade. In the early 1980s it appeared that only about one in four of these parks was a success in terms of attracting industries. Yet, at mid-decade some forty more universities had research parks under development.[25] Research parks were long-term investments with uncertain payoffs; but they proved nearly irresistible for universities during the 1980s. Basically, institutions were lured by the promise of economic development, technology transfer, and increased interactions with industry. They also stood to benefit directly from any improvement in their immediate economic environment. Other benefits were expected to flow from "propinquity effects,"[26] that is, the proximity of industrial laboratories could lead to sponsored research for the university, shared equipment, or other scientific interaction. The extent to which these benefits would materialize depended on the nature of the tenants, the receptivity of university faculty, and other circumstances. Experience nevertheless suggested that propinquity effects, and indeed a successful research park, were unlikely to occur without continuous active management on the part of the university.[27]

University behavior changed most broadly during the 1980s in the area of patenting. Almost every research university reevaluated its policies on "intellectual property rights"—a telling phrase of recent currency—and established procedures to enhance the flow of potential patents. Prior to 1980, with few exceptions, university approaches to patenting were passive and conservative, but a change in federal law that year allowed them to retain title to discoveries made during federally sponsored research. One after another, universities became decidedly more aggressive in the three phases of the patenting process—encouraging faculty to disclose inventions, filing for patents, and marketing the licenses to those patents.[28]

Invention disclosures are the origins of the technology transfer process. Institutions wishing to expand patenting have had to 'educate' faculty to be more mindful of the commercial implications of their work. Such changes in faculty awareness generally produced significant increases in the number of disclosures. Prior to 1980, the vast majority of universities relied upon outside patent management corporations, like the Research Corporation, to file and manage patents, but since then many institutions have taken over these activities themselves. One motivation was to increase the number of patent applications resulting from disclosures. Given the high cost of patenting and the low likelihood of royalties, external patent administrators tended to be conservative, patenting only about one in ten disclosures. In contrast, universities with aggressive internal administration were patenting one in three disclosures at the end of the 1980s.[29] The key change of the 1980s was nevertheless in the role of marketing. The leader in this approach was Stanford, which somewhat precociously organized its Office of Technology Licensing in 1970 around the central notion of marketing its inventions. Stanford was rewarded by seeing its revenues from patents climb from near zero to the highest in the country. MIT imitated the Stanford approach when it reorganized its patent administration in the mid-eighties. In this way the notion of finding users for inventions—the essence of technology transfer and the source of income from patents—became the driving force behind the entire process.

Only a handful of universities have succeeded in generating substantial revenues from licenses and royalties. By one estimate just four universities received half of all university income from patents—Stanford, MIT, California, and Wisconsin. Stanford alone received over $9 million in 1988, up from $2 million five years before. But there were expenses as well. The University of California incurred deficits in patent administration for 1986 and 1987 despite royalties of $3.4 and $5.4 million those years. In 1988 royalty revenues rose to $6.8 million and the University was able to distribute $1.7 million of net income across seven campuses—a comparative pittance for the country's largest administrator of academic research.[30]

Aggressive patent administration clearly involved costs as well as potential profits. University revenues from this source expanded notably during the 1980s, largely because great strides could be made when initial marketing efforts were launched. The University of Washington, for example, by dint of such effort increased its income from patents from $35,000 to $798,000 (1984–88).[31] But net income, even for the few successful universities, remained a comparatively minor sum. Universities justified the new patenting practices as a means of technology transfer and a service to faculty and industry. They also envisioned patents as a source of supplemental income. Since years were needed to build an inventory of income-generating patents, the results of the 1980s investments in patent administration will not be known for some time.

Equity ownership was the facet of entrepreneurial activity where standards of appropriate university behavior changed most markedly. The difference could be symbolized by Harvard's apparent reversal of course: in 1988 it announced the formation of a limited partnership designed to commercialize discoveries in the medical school by forming start-up companies. Harvard maintained that its actions did not represent any change in policy from the time it backed away from forming a biotech company in 1980. Indeed, at least three factors made the second situation different. First, the new venture was carefully debated and elaborated over several years rather than being a reaction to a sudden and unanticipated opportunity. It thus met with the approval of the medical school faculty on whom it ultimately depended for invention disclosures. Second, the partnership was intended as a buffer between Harvard and the newly founded companies; Harvard would receive 10 percent of the profits from the partnership, but did not invest its own funds and would not hold equity in those firms. Third, by 1988 Harvard was no longer in the vanguard of commercialization, but was in fact replicating arrangements that were now widespread across research universities.[32]

Most universities sought to avoid direct investment in start-up firms associated with faculty. The preferred routes were to utilize buffer organizations and to acquire equity without investing university funds. The two-stage structure employed by Harvard resembled the Dome Corporation established by Johns Hopkins University. Case Western Reserve concentrated all its commercialization activities, from patenting to firm formation, in a non-profit subsidiary, University Technology, Inc. Michigan State used a grant from its university foundation to establish Neogen, a for-profit corporation intended to develop and commercialize agricultural products. MIT acquired equity in fledgling firms in return for licenses to its patents; and Rensselaer Polytechnic Institute received a small equity stake from each firm admitted to its business incubator.[33] Universities during the 1980s reconfigured themselves in a variety of ways to reap some of the benefit from the technology generated within their walls. This new entrepreneurial behavior can be viewed in a somewhat longer perspective.

With the revolution in biotechnology and the decided shift toward programmatic research, universities in the 1980s found themselves strategically placed at the fount of valuable knowledge and also encouraged by society to disseminate that knowledge as expeditiously as possible. This strategic placement was the key opportunity—the comparative advantage—that universities possessed as they entered commercial realms in which they had little experience otherwise—real estate development, patenting and marketing, and venture capital investment.[34] Such activities were also dissonant with academic norms. The means of avoiding both pitfalls was to create separate organizational structures, either within the university or somewhat removed, to conduct these tasks.

This situation was broadly analogous to the proliferation of sponsored research in separate units after World War II (see Chapter 2). Then universities were broadening the research role and, in effect, allowing it to acquire an existence autonomous from their academic mission. In the 1980s, much the same occurred with the service role. Here too there had been adumbrations—pure service entities for agricultural extension or technical assistance, for example. But now a panoply of new entities was added to research universities in the name of technology transfer and economic development. As with much organized research, the technology transfer superstructure was weakly related to the educational mission, primarily benefited only a handful of (albeit important) faculty, and transgressed certain academic norms. But, also like research, this service role was accepted because it was perceived to be valuable to society and because it was (more or less) self-supporting as well. Technology transfer thus claimed to enlarge the scope of university activities without burdening, and perhaps enriching, the university fisc.

An inherent tension nevertheless existed between the commercial activities into which universities ventured and the disinterested pursuit of teaching and learning for which they ineluctably stood. At its worst, this tension amounted to outright conflicts of interest that could impair the judgment of institutions and undermine public trust in their principal mission. In its more prevalent form, it consisted of acquiescence in practices that rubbed against the academic grain—secrecy or noncooperation in research; attempts to exclude foreign firms from technology transfer; suspicion of the misuse of graduate students; diversion of faculty time and effort from teaching and research. Universities learned from a succession of embarrassments to contain many of these problems. No doubt additional lessons await them. Almost uniformly, however, universities in the 1980s made the judgment that the inducements to commercial activities outweighed the possible risks to their core academic roles.

2. Research in the 1980s

The university's embrace of commercial endeavors typified a mode of behavior evident in many realms during the decade. The spirit of excess that characterized financial markets and personal consumption seemed to have an analog among research universities as well, which paid little heed to reservations that might formerly have restrained them. Broadened involvement with donors, industry, and commercial markets provided examples of consequential and most likely irreversible change. In a similar vein, universities experienced robust development in their professional schools, aided in part by external ties. Perhaps most significant, universities substantially expanded their distinctive mission of research.

Academic research grew more in the 1980s than in any previous decade—from nearly $7 billion to almost $12 billion ($1982).[1] This achievement was remarkable in itself and also impressive in relative terms. Academic research attained its largest share of G.N.P., for example, surpassing the levels attained in the late 1960s. This rise could not be fully accounted for by the ascendant ideology of economic competitiveness and the encouragement of programmatic research. Universities, after a decade of charges that they did too much research or the wrong kinds of research, received from American society clear signals of appreciation for their research role. They accordingly placed renewed emphasis on research, not just to assist the economy but more particularly to enhance their own academic standing. Still, much of the robustness of academic research sprang from science itself, from the major discoveries that propelled advancements in diverse fields.

No brief account can do justice to the enormous progress of basic academic science during the era of the 1980s. A wide range of technical and conceptual breakthroughs opened up entire fields of scientific inquiry. In optoelectronics the stage was set for utilizing photons instead of electrons to convey information. In materials science, the scanning tunneling electron microscope made it possible to see and manipulate matter at the atomic level. Superconductivity, another breakthrough of the 1980s, spawned a flood of basic research as a prelude to eventual applications. Advances in the power of supercomputers, as well as their availability through a network of national centers, enabled more complex simulations to be used in studying neural networks, fluid dynamics, molecular configurations, and rational design. In biotechnology, the decade witnessed a relentless pace of advancement following on previous breakthroughs. The 1980s set the stage for the mapping and sequencing of the human genome in the 1990s, which will provide the foundation for molecular biology in the twenty-first century.[2] This scientific work, of which these examples are but a sample, in some respects transcended the academy; but for the most part it was centered in university laboratories and contributed to the remarkable expansion of academic research. The chief point, all too often overlooked, is that the intellectual advances made by university scientists in this era were the single most important consequence of university research. The coeval difficulties with which academic scientists wrestled should be seen in light of these striking achievements.

The research universities themselves made a conspicuous contribution to the progress of research. Their enthusiasm in this respect stood in contrast to the previous era when research was crowded by other commitments. It also might be contrasted to the post-Sputnik era when efforts by universities to expand research were encouraged by government through explicit programs of science development. In the 1980s federal assistance for expanding research capacity was piecemeal at best. Special programs like the NSF Engineering Research Centers were designed for this purpose, but only affected a few institutions. The dominant pattern of the 1980s was for universities to look to the private sector for additional resources; many needed research facilities were thus erected wholly or partially with donated funds. Perhaps the most telling indication of the backing that universities gave to research was the increasing extent to which they employed their own general funds toward these ends—an increase from 12 to 18 percent of separately budgeted research.[3] Generally, though, universities found that enhancing their reputation for research paid dividends in terms of attracting better students, projecting a positive image of public service, and enlarging voluntary support.

Partially for that reason, the dispersion of academic research among a greater number of universities continued during the 1980s. When changes in institutional shares of research during the 1980s are compared, the evidence of dispersion is striking.[4] Of the 30 largest performers at the start of the decade, 19 saw their share decline by 1990.[5] The highest ranked universities also tended to experience relative decline rather than growth. Of the 24 institutions judged to have the most prestigious graduate departments in 1982, fifteen registered negative changes in their shares of research expenditures.

The universities that increased their shares, not surprisingly, often had particular capabilities in the expanding spheres of the research economy. Among patrons, industry and the Department of Defense most enlarged support. By fields of research, engineering grew more than any other general area, electrical engineering and computer science being particularly vigorous. Institutes of technology naturally thrived in this environment. Beyond them, the institutions that achieved above-average gains tended to be the smaller and more service-oriented public universities, especially those in Sun Belt states that had previously done comparatively little research.[6]

Financial factors help to account for only part of this pattern. The connection that was apparent in Chapter 8 between academic and financial strength still held for the major state universities. Those states that most increased the support for research universities in the 1970s also showed the best results for research funding through the mid-1980s—namely, Texas, North Carolina, and California.[7] States with middling levels of support (Ohio, Minnesota, Washington) had middling or slightly negative results. However, Illinois, Indiana, Michigan, and Wisconsin combined little or no increase in support with negative changes in research shares. Pennsylvania was an exception to this pattern, but its universities were also least dependent on state appropriations.[8]

In the private sector, where financial gains were widespread, there was no apparent connection between prosperity and change in research share. Harvard, Chicago, and New York University all improved their financial positions substantially, while experiencing some of the largest relative contractions of research. Apparently, most private universities chose not to employ their additional resources in ways that might have enlarged the volume of research. Several factors bear on this phenomenon. Biomedical research, for which funding was relatively stable, comprised a major portion of research for most private universities. In addition, they tended to emphasize the humanities and social sciences, where strength was not reflected in research expenditures. Similarly, they tended to place a higher value on the academic prestige of basic science departments, where growth in support was near average, than on research for programmatic sponsors. Since many of the private universities contained the most prestigious graduate departments, their behavior partly accounted for the previously noted disjunction between academic quality and increasing shares of research expenditures.

In essence, university research expanded substantially during the decade of the 1980s while the academic base on which it rested was fairly static. Few research universities increased their enrollments; graduate education rose moderately in professional fields, particularly engineering, but scarcely at all in arts and sciences. And research universities were quite conservative about adding regular faculty positions.[9] Much of the growth in research consequently took place outside of academic departments in separate ORUs.

The number of ORUs at research universities increased by 30 percent during just the first half of the 1980s.[10] The proportion of research funds expended by ORUs was on the increase as well at almost half the institutions. This phenomenon, in all likelihood, began in the late 1970s and continued through the last half of the 1980s. It was also consistent with other trends of this era. For universities eager to expand research, creating client-oriented ORUs to attract pro-grammatic funds was perhaps the most direct means. This approach, as already seen, was particularly used to foster greater interaction with industry. In addi-tion, the most dynamic fields of the 1980s tended to require special arrange-ments. Biotechnology was inherently multidisciplinary. Universities that wished to have a presence in this fast-moving field had little choice but to establish spe-cial ORUs. Microelectronics often utilized costly equipment, which required separate facilities and separate financing. Materials science was both multidis-ciplinary and utilized special equipment. Viewed as ideal types, the ORUs founded during these years resembled the *institutes* characterized in Chapter 2. That is, they were designed in large measure to be self-supporting and they tended to employ non-faculty professionals as permanent staff. Such a core of researchers was necessary to meet the needs of clients, to operate large-scale instruments, or to sustain research teams. The number of non-faculty research-ers doubled from the end of the 1970s to the end of the 1980s.[11] Entering the 1990s, one of every four academic scientists or engineers was being supported with 'soft money' from the research economy.

Despite the vigorous expansion of academic research, the 1980s ended with a sense of impending crisis. An overview of conditions published in *Science* reported that "everyone seems to agree that discontent is at an all-time high."[12] The problems facing academic science at this juncture were in one respect like those of two decades earlier—they stemmed essentially from the preceding years of expansion. Anxieties again focused on not just the level of resources needed to sustain the vigor of university research, but also on the state of the institutions conducting that research.

The issue of adequate funding for academic science was given prominence early in 1991 by Leon M. Lederman, Nobel laureate, former director of Fermi Lab, and at the time president-elect of the American Association for the Advancement of Science. After surveying a small sample of academic scientists, he composed a report gloomily echoing that by Vannevar Bush forty-five years earlier: *Science—the End of the Frontier?*[13] His central argument was that low morale among academic scientists resulted from inadequate federal support for research. Respondents to the survey complained that the difficulty of obtaining grants had constrained their work and that preparing multiple proposals con-sumed increasing time and effort. The outlook seemed to be particularly bleak for graduate students and junior faculty. The former were being discouraged from academic careers by the pressures of grantsmanship, while the latter faced formidable competition in establishing their own research programs. Lederman argued that federal support of academic research, adjusted for the inflation of R&D costs, has risen only 20 percent since 1968—the end of "the golden age of American science."[14] Over the same time, the number of doctoral scientists and engineers at work in colleges and universities had doubled. Meanwhile, the cost of doing research increased greatly due to a conjunction of factors, from more sophisticated instrumentation to higher overhead rates. Perhaps most important, science itself had greatly expanded, creating ever more topics to be profitably investigated. Lederman's case was largely corroborated by the actions of the principal supporters of science. NIH attempted to increase the size of its grants during the 1980s, but allowed the number of annual awards to fall by a third. NSF took the opposite tack, keeping the number of awards up, but letting their real size shrink, thereby squeezing support for equipment and graduate students out of research budgets. In order to restore the health of academic science, Lederman recommended doubling federal support within three years.

The reaction of members of the Washington science policy community to Lederman's manifesto went beyond skepticism to outright hostility. After coping for years with the deepening difficulties posed by the federal deficit, they apparently took umbrage at being upstaged by a proposal that was impressionistic and politically naive. In an era of limited government, policy priorities, and concern for economic relevance, Lederman had resurrected the 1960s ideology of basic research. He looked solely to the federal government for succor, recommended greater support for academic research across the board, and argued that basic research, by spawning critical technologies, was the key to improving the quality of life. More jaundiced critics suggested that technology could be developed directly instead of via basic research. From their point of view the funding problem was caused by too many academic scientists clamoring for support.[15]

Lederman's calculations of the dimensions of the funding crisis—both for past comparisons and future needs—could legitimately be questioned. Still, the issue of how much federal support was appropriate or optimal for academic research could not be easily dismissed.[16] Despite the declining federal share, many areas of basic science remained dependent on such funds, including some of the most fundamental and costly fields. Similarly dependent were fields where the benefits of research were primarily social, such as health care, the environment, or energy conservation. Most scientists believed that an abundance of exciting and fruitful lines of inquiry could be identified and should be investigated. The record of advances in the 1980s seemed to bear this out. Inadequate funding exacted a real, if indeterminate, price in terms of science not done. As competition for funds intensified beyond healthy levels, negative consequences became apparent: scientists inclined toward safer, less risky projects; young faculty were frozen out of support by more experienced grant writers; and talented students were discouraged from pursuing academic careers. Respondents to Lederman's survey reported all of these symptoms.[17]

The president of the National Academy of Sciences, on the other hand, stated that "no nation can write a blank check for science."[18] Overly ample support for research was not only wasteful, but counterproductive in other ways, as the record of the 'golden' 1960s might be read. Then, too little competition encouraged narrow specialization, remoteness from developments outside of universities, and the recruitment of researchers with middling skills and motivation. For the research universities in the 1990s, there seemed to be little danger that this scenario would recur. Rather, the challenge lay in avoiding the worst consequences of a constrained research economy. Pressure thus remained, as it had throughout the era of the 1980s, to enlarge the sources of support for research.

At the same time, the ability of universities to sustain their internal research capacity with adequate resources was again called into question.

Universities relied upon their own resources to provide many of the critical inputs to the research process. In most cases, the balance between external and internal resources varied. It was already remarked, for example, that universities increasingly employed their own funds to support the direct costs of research during the 1980s. Their chief indirect contribution to research capacity came through the support of regular faculty. Libraries were a vital component of research capacity, which were heavily supported with internal funds. The same could be said for the now indispensable campus computers. Since the termination of the government programs of the 1960s, facilities had been erected and refurbished for the most part with university-generated dollars. Graduate students in the natural sciences tended to be supported with research grants, but a significant part of the cost of graduate education was still borne by institutions. Similarly, universities largely maintained certain departments or programs, such as area studies, more for research than instructional purposes. Finally, instrumentation was particularly crucial to the research infrastructure of universities. Federal funds were inevitably required for the most expensive items, and industry sometimes assisted as well; but some of these costs still devolved on institutions.

At the beginning of the recent era, universities were badly squeezed for the resources needed to bolster research capacity. Through the middle of the 1980s a succession of official and semi-official reports called attention to different facets of this problem.[19] Interestingly, conditions had begun to improve even as these warnings were being issued. Then, the vigorous economy of the mid-1980s and the success of universities in tapping private sources of support for a time alleviated some of these pressures. By the end of the decade universities had managed to enhance their research capacities significantly along several dimensions.

The total number of faculty at doctoral institutions remained virtually constant throughout the era, but the per-faculty expenditures backing them registered substantial gains. In addition, the number of scientists and engineers (faculty and non-faculty) grew steadily, as did their compensation. Equipment and facilities, when measured against this same population, also rose appreciably.[20] At decade's end the facilities available for academic science seemed reasonably adequate, but instrumentation remained an unresolved problem. The deepening complexity of contemporary scientific problems were associated with devices of ever greater power and sophistication. Academic science faced a deficit of instrumentation not purchased during leaner times, plus the escalating costs of state-of-the-art equipment.[21]

Longer term, the challenge of sustaining university research capacities appeared to be without end. Entering the 1990s existing sources of university income held only slight possibilities for growth and no new sources were in sight. At the same time, the requirements for sustaining the health of research universities were daunting. To one university president, "ever more massive fund drives seemed to be needed simply to maintain existing programs at satisfactory levels of quality."[22] In an approaching environment of increasing constraint, a critical consideration became not just the level of resources that universities possessed but how they chose to apportion them between their research roles and their other activities.

3. Centrifugal Forces

Universities expanded their research in the 1980s by catering to the programmatic needs of sponsors, and for that reason many of the tasks they added were increasingly removed from their academic core. Such was the case with, for example, business incubators, research parks, and industry-supported centers. These additions contributed incrementally to the fragmentation of universities as institutions. This phenomenon was scarcely new. When the American university emerged in its characteristic form a century before, it reconciled disparate missions by separating them in insular compartments. The simultaneous cultivation of liberal learning, utility, and the advancement of knowledge, as well as the heavy emphasis placed on the proper socialization of undergraduates, developed to a large extent as separate spheres of activity. But this multiplicity of purpose, even then, had its drawbacks. The original American research universities lacked any single overriding mission, harboring instead a congeries of values appropriate to their multiple tasks.[1] During the era of the 1980s this fundamental process advanced yet another degree, further complicating university culture.

The arts and sciences, the intellectual core of universities, had been shrinking since the early 1970s. The proportion of bachelor's degrees in these areas fell from 45 percent in 1972 to 27 percent in 1988. Most of this decline occurred in the 1970s, with the humanities and social sciences affected far more than the natural sciences. The growing popularity of business accounted for much of the change. The proportion of bachelor's degrees in business almost doubled to reach nearly a quarter of college graduates. At the doctoral level the drop in arts and sciences degrees was somewhat smaller—from 48 to 37 percent—and felt almost entirely in the humanities and social sciences.[2] The powerful tide toward professional subjects that began in the 1970s persisted through the 1980s. Professional education had always been an essential component of the American university, but it also differed in character from the pure academic disciplines. Professional education looked outside the academy to the realm of praxis as well as inside for theoretical knowledge. The robust health of professional education in the recent era was thus another centrifugal force acting on universities.

As universities took more and more varied tasks upon themselves, the defining character of their basic educational mission appeared to be threatened. The growth of programmatic research and specially tailored ORUs lessened the connection between research and graduate education. While graduate study lost none of its close connection with research, much of the additional university research had little contact with instruction.[3] In the case of undergraduate education, where links with research were tenuous at best, complaints became increasingly common that the demands of research conflicted with teaching. A literature on 'teaching versus research,' exaggerated and anecdotal in character, flourished at the end of the 1980s.[4]

Derek Bok summed up the general situation when he called the university an "overextended organization": specifically, he wondered "how many more responsibilities universities and professors can take on without seriously overloading their administration and eroding the quality of their teaching and scholarship."[5] This problem, Bok made clear, stemmed from the very usefulness of universities—from precisely those attributes that allowed them to expand their research and their external involvements during the 1980s. But the time had come, he felt, for universities to reverse this drift by avoiding commitments that did not require their special qualities and benefit their central missions, by establishing closer control over the activities of their own professors, and by separating the service commitments they did undertake in organizational forms that were outside rather than inside the academic structure. Bok's diagnosis confirmed the organizational strains that had arisen from the fissiparous effects of multiple roles, but it did not instruct universities how to deny the supplications of outside parties or to resist their own incentives to acceed.

Universities had to contend with another source of divisiveness which, paradoxically, was linked with efforts to promote internal unity. At the center of this issue was the place of minorities on campuses. Policies adopted over the previous two decades to enhance minority representation were increasingly regarded in the 1980s as inadequate, and stronger measures were widely advocated. Beyond this particular grievance, other university groups sought to advance causes that were in some respects related. By the late 1980s, no less than a new ideology based on multiculturalism crystalized out of these several concerns. Universities henceforth operated under the sway of this new ascendant ideology, which was at best oblique to their research role and at times antagonistic toward it.

Like previous ideologies that colored the thinking and influenced the actions of universities, the ideology of multiculturalism also had its consecrating document. A blue-ribbon group, the Commission on Minority Participation in Education and American Life, in 1988 published a Report entitled *One-Third of a Nation*.[6] The general message of the Report was that the progress minorities had been making in education and employment had stagnated from the mid-seventies to the mid-eighties. More aggressive steps were consequently called for in order to raise "people of color," who might one day comprise one-third of the country's population, to conditions of parity with the majority. The report thus provided a compelling social rationale for undertaking extraordinary measures.

This message was directed, despite the Commission's broad title, especially toward American colleges and universities. Cornell president Frank Rhodes chaired the Commission, and he was joined by seven other academic heads. Sponsorship came from the Education Commission of the States and the American Council on Education. The latter organization provided subsequent backing for the Report by holding a conference and issuing a handbook to guide institutions. The most feasible recommendations of the Report were also aimed at colleges and universities. They were enjoined to make commitments to "recruit minority students more aggressively at every level. . .; create an academic atmosphere that nourishes minority students and encourages them to succeed; create a campus culture that values the diversity minorities bring to institutional life. . .: [and] place special emphasis on inspiring and recruiting minority candidates for faculty and administrative positions. . . "[7] Each of these admonitions was more easily stated than accomplished. In the recruitment of minority students and faculty, in particular, institutions had long-established policies that had been frustrated to some extent by limited pools of qualified applicants. Campus culture and atmosphere, however, constituted a sphere for much potential innovation. Here in particular, the Report served its purpose to galvanize universities into action.

The problem addressed by *One-Third of a Nation* was of grave importance to American society. That gravity was implicitly conveyed to the reforms urged upon universities, even though, as with previous ideologies, the connections were tenuous.[8] The largely unchallenged nature of the purposes undergirding this ideology gave it considerable influence in campus deliberations, justifying intensifications of the already extensive efforts to recruit minorities as well as new initiatives to alter the campus atmosphere. University presidents found this document of their peers to be a useful talisman for demonstrating their sympathy with multiculturalism to internal and external constituencies. Interested groups within the university also utilized these arguments to provide backing for their programs.[9] Although the ideology of multiculturalism was ostensibly aimed at helping blacks, Hispanics, and American Indians, the cause was energetically supported on campus by the women's movement and the gay and lesbian communities. Each group had a vested interest in changing the culture and atmosphere of campuses in ways that would support feminism and discourage homophobia. Women, in particular, had an explicit interest in strengthening the levers of affirmative action. Together, these groups constituted a potent coalition for exerting pressure in favor of what was generally called *diversity*.

In most basic terms, diversity referred to the officially recognized presence on campus of minorities, feminists, and homosexuals. Multiculturalism seemed to become the preferred euphemism over time, but both terms primarily encompassed the same categories (and concealed indifference toward cultures outside the diversity coalition). Each of these groups defined itself as being oppressed or victimized by American society. Each also could claim that its distinctive culture and its viewpoints were neglected in course offerings or, for that matter, in the scholarship of academic disciplines. In making claims for greater inclusion, these groups were all able to unite against a common enemy—the existing university courses that they charged were dominated by a white male "Eurocentric" outlook. The effort to instill diversity on campuses thus became in part a *Kulturkampf* centered on the curriculum.

The entire conflict surrounding diversity was obfuscated by the fact that the intellectual positions advocated by the groups within the diversity coalition were not unitary, but rather represented a considerable range of views. Each group championed moderate stands that fell well within the campus consensus—affirmative action and cultural recognition for minorities, equality of treatment for women, and toleration for gays and lesbians. Some members of each group also expressed views that were more extreme. Blacks were prone to make exaggerated accusations of American racism, or to claim that only "Afrocentric" perspectives adequately conveyed their culture. Feminists went further in some ways, constructing a demonology that condemned the nuclear family, portrayed women as a class, and sought the elimination of gender differences.[10] Gays and lesbians derided mere toleration without acceptance of the moral equivalence of homosexuality as "heterosexism."

Although ranges of interpretation exist in any field, these "cultural studies" had a dynamic that was peculiarly their own. The mainstream of thought in these fields probably lay closer to the extremist than the moderate pole. Given the insurgent status still felt by most adherents, moderates were reluctant to criticize more zealous colleagues, such criticism being considered disloyal to the movements.[11] In appealing for wide acceptance, proponents of cultural studies tended to invoke consensus arguments, such as those publicized in *One-Third of a Nation;* however, the actions taken to alter the culture or the atmosphere of campuses generally incorporated the outlooks of the more extreme factions. Furthermore, those outlooks included as central components the repudiation of values that have been fundamental to universities. Heated attacks were directed against the "canon" of works felt to embody the Western tradition because they failed to convey the approved notions of race, gender, ethnicity, and class.[12] Rationality and objectivity were condemned as "male modes of thought."[13] Instead, a highly relative approach was favored in which the nature of knowledge was assumed to be determined by the race, sex, or ethnicity of the person propounding it. If all knowledge was relative, then each racial, sexual, and ethnic groups could claim representation in the curriculum. The insertion of cultural studies into the curriculum was nevertheless a two-stage process.

First, cultural studies were incorporated as specialized offerings during the 1970s and 1980s. Much like other specialized fields, they staked their own territories within the fragmented university curriculum. Most degree programs in Black/African-American studies and Latin American studies were founded in the early 1970s, and by 1990 they had been accumulating a specialized knowledge base and literature for almost two decades. Women's studies, which defined itself as treating topics from a feminist perspective, expanded steadily, adding more than one hundred degree-granting programs during the 1980s. By 1990, Afro-American studies had some 350 programs and Women's studies at least 500.[14] Gay and lesbian studies was a comparative newcomer in 1990, bidding to follow the path of the established studies programs. In this process of creating a body of academic knowledge and implanting it in the university, women's studies was by far the most successful. Many of the growing number of women faculty employed feminist perspectives in their own disciplines and participated in women's studies programs. These activities produced a substantial body of academic writings and a commensurately large representation in university courses.

The second stage, occurring late in the 1980s, was a product of the diversity *Kulturkampf.* Compulsory courses were proposed as a means for exposing all undergraduate students to viewpoints associated with diversity, and thereby

making the campus climate more hospitable for those groups. Student popula-
tions tended to divide into those who enrolled in and heartily supported cultural
studies and those who were indifferent or unsympathetic. The same dichotomy
might be made for any field of study, but the non-participating students in this
case were regarded as being 'insensitive' toward those in the diversity coalition
or, worse yet, responsible for perpetuating racism and sexism on campus. By
1991, approximately half of all colleges and universities had established some
requirement for students to take courses that treated material from the perspectives of race, gender, or (often) social class. Nearly two-thirds had imposed multicultural additions to disciplinary courses.[15] These numbers were indicative of
the extent of sympathy with the aims of diversity, but not necessarily the extent
of change in the curriculum. Faculty reservations and differing interpretations of
goals sometimes diluted the ideological intent of such measures. Course requirements, however, were not the only means employed to change attitudes on campus.

From the point of view of those seeking to advance diversity, universities were
rife with hostile attitudes and behaviors. To rectify this situation, alternative
modes of speech, belief, and behavior were posited that were intended to be
sensitive to the self-styled oppressed groups. These dictates appeared narrowly
doctrinaire and constraining to many academics, and perhaps somewhat puz-
zling to outsiders. They came to be dubbed "political correctness" by opponents—a sarcastic reference to adherence to the party line by American communists in the 1930s. Pressures to conform focused on some relatively
innocuous matters, such as the attempt to neuter the English language by proscribing, among other things, words ending in -man (e.g. freshman, chairman).
More notorious was the establishment of speech codes at numerous universities.
Supposedly aimed at suppressing 'hate speech,' the codes' vague provisions could
have been used to punish many types of expression. For that reason, they were
found in more than one case to be in violation of the First Amendment.[16] In a
more alarming development, a few faculty members were harassed or discouraged from teaching because their views about minorities or women were at odds
with the conventions of political correctness.[17] Both speech codes and infringe-
ments of academic freedom were subsequently disavowed by some influential
proponents of diversity, but damage had already been done. The American public took notice that universities seemed to have abandoned basic values for
which they ostensibly stood.

During 1991 universities received an inordinate amount of public attention
for their apparent zeal in the cause of diversity. President George Bush used the
Commencement podium at the University of Michigan to condemn the threat
to free speech posed by political correctness on campus. Legislation was introduced in Congress (but not enacted) to withhold federal funds from universities
having repressive speech codes.[18] Attention was drawn to this entire subject by
the publication of Illiberal Education: The Politics of Race and Sex on Campus
by Dinesh D'Souza, an Indian immigrant whose own political past was decidedly
illiberal. Although this work was clearly tendentious, its extended critique of the
diversity movement was both lucid and well documented, and all the more con-

vincing coming from a "person of color."[19] While many academics denounced the book, it made a powerful impression on newspaper editors, columnists, and even the television news.[20] A wave of writings followed which sought to fathom this peculiar phenomenon that had engulfed the universities.

Political correctness was often likened to McCarthyism in the inhibitions it imposed on freedom of expression in and out of the classroom. The analogy was inexact, however. McCarthyism reflected a powerful anticommunist consensus in American society which was largely shared in the academy. The persecution of dissident views was nevertheless widely opposed and resented on campuses. Political correctness, by way of contrast, was largely a campus phenomenon. In this respect, a better analogy might be made with the conditions that prevailed during much of the Vietnam War. Then too, only one side of the issue was effectively heard on campus; dissent from that view was discredited as stemming from the financial interests of the miscreant individuals, or through name-calling ("fascist pig" being a rough equivalent to the later "racist, sexist"); moderates, who had compelling arguments to offer on specific issues, were largely drowned out by extremists, whose overriding objective became the transformation of American society. In the Vietnam era and again in the early 1990s, universities sought to lead the country along a course that, on the whole, it did not wish to follow. Perhaps most telling, in both cases conservative presidents appealed to the majority of the American people against apparent excesses on the campuses.[21]

By no means should universities be hostage to the views of elected officials, but they flout public values and open themselves to political attack at their peril. The ideology of multiculturalism in its basic tenets represented an attempt to come to terms with an important social phenomenon. In that respect, it resembled the ideology of economic competitiveness that it superseded, but did not displace. That both outlooks coexisted was indicative of the state of the contemporary university. Each largely pertained to different sectors of the university and different tasks; each delivered a different set of instructions for university policies; and each was predicated in a different way on service to American society. Entering the 1990s, American universities were perhaps more fragmented and overextended than ever before. Yet they continued to draw strength from the stability of their core purpose and its continuing relevance to the rest of society.

4. Research Universities and American Society

The American university discovered at the outset of the twentieth century that a meaningful research role could not be supported through internal resources alone. This dependency on external support for research was superimposed upon existing dependencies on student clienteles and on different forms of subsidization for its educational role. The university's multiple points of contact with society thus arose from its multiple purposes. This interaction produced a complex and segmented institution, defined primarily by its social functions.

Among these functions, research for the advancement of knowledge occupied a special place. It was informed by a single, unequivocal idea—what Robert K. Merton defined as the "scientific ethos," or what Talcott Parsons and Gerald Platt called "cognitive rationality."[1] This ideal might be questioned philosophically, but it remained axiomatic in actual scientific investigation and among communities of scholars. But if this spirit of unfettered and systematic inquiry was the fixed point in the research role, much else was variable within the organizational framework of a modern university. While such a spirit should in theory inform instruction, its intensity in actuality varied across institutions, by level of study, as well as among subjects. The amount of investigation that a given university could sustain also varied, being determined in part by the level of institutional resources and in part by competing claims for those resources. Topics of investigation were sanctioned by the support provided by outside patrons, as well as by the curiosity of academics. The research role might lie at the heart of the modern American university, but internally it was constrained and often contested, while its content was shaped appreciably by external forces.

Universities, as they evolved, shed few of their multiple tasks. Their histories, especially since World War II, have rather been chronicles of more or less continuous expansion—the inertia of established tasks being supplemented by the incremental acquisition of new ones. The incremental growth of universities, in turn, was shaped to a significant degree by prevailing sets of ideas about the proper role and the most urgent tasks of universities—by the succession of ascendant ideologies that have been described in this study. Thus, the dynamism of research universities has been governed by a complex interaction of internal purpose and external influence.

The proliferation of university activities is striking testimony of the value to society of the culture of learning and inquiry that universities nurture. This proliferation is also evidence that, regardless of the idiosyncratic behavior of any single institution, the American university system adapted over time to what was expected from it by American society. As universities were impelled forward, undertaking more and more varied tasks, they faced a continuous challenge both to sustain the vigor and integrity of academic culture and to maintain a semblance of balance among their manifold roles.

The challenge was imposed in unique terms with the onset of World War II. In one of the most stark adjustments in their history, American universities were enlisted to perform research that would aid in winning the war. This responsibility persisted after the end of hostilities chiefly due to the indispensability of science-driven technologies like atomic energy and radar. The assumption by universities of a permanent role in conducting federally supported research, however, was accompanied by a magisterial justification—Vannevar Bush's *Science—the Endless Frontier*. The postwar system of academic research that evolved in the latter 1940s often invoked the ideals of the Bush report, but differed greatly from its prescriptions in being dominated by mission agencies. After 1950 the departure became even more glaring. The full impact of the Cold War imposed a rather different, clearly understood mission on research universities. Programmatic research for the Defense Establishment coexisted uneasily with the pure-science ideals of the Bush report through most of the 1950s.

Universities were fearful that the massive support provided for programmatic purposes would distort their research, displacing the cultivation of disinterested academic inquiry. Certainly, institutions that wholeheartedly embraced this mission, like MIT, ceded some control over their own course of development. But any institution that wished for the sake of purity to stand aside was doomed to be left behind in the onrushing progress of the natural sciences. Over time it became apparent, however, that there was no dilemma here. Universities could use research support from the Pentagon to build academic distinction. The military and the AEC were in most respects benign patrons. The National Science Foundation then emerged as the champion of academic science, and private foundations took responsibility for furthering academic social science. By the end of the postwar era, the new university research system was proving remarkably congenial to research universities. Their preponderant responsibilities for undergraduate education were little changed once the dislocations associated with the GI Bill had passed. Demand for admission caused standards to ratchet upward, a phenomenon that quickly became a point of pride. Graduate education in the sciences was closely linked with research, and thus with support for research. Both were associated with academic distinction. The rise of UC Berkeley symbolized the emergent harmony between academic ambition and service to the federal patron.

The post-Sputnik era witnessed the triumph and even hypertrophy of this marriage of ambition and service in the ideology of basic research. Universities received a mandate to make American science pre-eminent in the world and to train vastly more Ph.D.s. The enormous resources that the federal government poured into this effort allowed universities to accomplish both purposes. They also did much more. The top tier of established research universities was able to expand their faculties, graduate enrollments, and the volume of research as never before. In a veritable "academic revolution" the pattern of behavior and values that they exemplified was transposed to scores of aspirant institutions. The very success of these efforts, however, affected the internal ecology of universities.

The founding of Students for a Democratic Society foreshadowed the alienation from, as well as the fixation with, the university on the part of one group; the critique of the university that accompanied the Free Speech and antiwar movements gave these sentiments wide currency.[2] Soon, the political-cultural schism of the late sixties turned these discontents into the clichés of the student rebellion. Behind the hyperbole, the source of alienation was real. Universities had abandoned, largely unconsciously, the moral and cultural stewardship of undergraduates. The end of *in loco parentis* was an outward manifestation of the end of attempts to mold the character of college graduates. In the curriculum, students were offered increasingly erudite and recondite specialties, which were a far cry from the liberal education universities still professed to offer. University acquiescence to student demands considerably exaggerated both these developments. In addition, even the ascendant research role came under strain. Ph.D.s went suddenly from under- to over-supply; and supporters of research began to demand 'relevance' from university research, although by this they meant something quite different from the slogans of students. At the end of the 1960s the research universities faced the need to reshape relations with American society.

A new ideology of egalitarianism and social responsibility set the terms for universities. During the 1970s the additional social resources devoted to higher education were directed at expanding access rather than bolstering research. University leaders exuded zeal for innovation. Almost unanimously they upheld that, if university education was the key to the good life in America, it should henceforth be equitably available to minorities, women, and the socially disadvantaged. Determined constituencies on campus united with federal regulators toward forwarding this same end. Universities were left to reconcile the means required for acceptable results with their own standards of merit, but in this process their sphere of autonomy was ineluctably narrowed. Throughout this period, the research role of universities provided an element of stability. In spite of somewhat diminished resources, the legacy of the bountiful 1960s remained in youthful, well-trained faculties, in up-to-date research facilities, and for the most part in continuing support. In terms of students, though, the story was different. Undergraduate and doctoral students shifted commitments away from academic disciplines and toward professional subjects. Once more the university research system adapted incrementally to new demands.

In the new era that began at the end of the 1970s, the research universities continued to develop along the two paths already marked—one for research and another for social responsibility. Their research role received a new ideological validation as an asset in the national struggle for economic competitiveness. Support for research registered impressive growth, and its sources diversified as well. Academic distinction was again recognized and rewarded by society—in increased demand for high-cost/high-quality education and in an upsurge of giving to universities. These developments were complemented by the great vigor of professional education—as instructional units of universities, as fields of research, and as pathways for individuals to lucrative careers. Just as in the post-Sputnik era, universities accomplished what was asked of them. Alone they could not reinvigorate the economy but, entering the 1990s, university research was probably more responsive to American society than at any time since World War II.

In the domain of social responsibility, by way of contrast, a new ideological mandate for American universities only became fully evident late in the 1980s. Still confounded by the problem of achieving adequate representation of minorities on campus, universities intensified recruitment efforts and sought to alter the culture and atmosphere of the campus. Differing interpretations over the nature and extent of the problem, as well as the appropriateness of some of the attempted remedies, made this issue divisive on campuses. The underlying ideology of multiculturalism nevertheless remained clearly in the ascendancy.

The research role of universities and their contested social roles coexist in comparative isolation within an organization that has grown in size and complexity in response to successive conceptions of its principal purposes. In addition to vastly expanding its core tasks of cultivating, advancing, and disseminating knowledge, the American university of the late twentieth century also elaborated fairly autonomous roles in research and service. These same institutions nevertheless tend to picture themselves in unitary and rather special terms—as communities of scholars, free and ordered spaces, dedicated to the unfettered pursuit of teaching and learning. Such an idealized view has some validity, but it fails to account for the actual behavior of American universities. Nor can it explain the real nature of their specialness.

The mainspring of the contemporary university, as Parsons and Platt emphasized, is cognitive rationality.[3] The application of systematic, rational inquiry does not in itself produce wisdom, sagacity, or liberal learning, but rather yields increasingly specialized knowledge. Scientists and scholars endeavor to discover all that they can about bewildering varieties of topics—arcane or mundane. The synthesis of knowledge naturally is required as well; in fact the most highly valued contributions are those of greatest generality. But the essential process of advancing knowledge is at bottom one of relentless specialization. This very process accounts for those distinctive conditions that universities require. The unique terms of faculty employment are predicated on selecting and guaranteeing tenure for one-of-a-kind specialists.[4] The complementarity of instruction permits their continuous employment and hence long-term concentration on a particular area. Academic freedom permits investigators to determine the most promising lines of inquiry.

As a result, the contemporary university constitutes, above all, a kind of warehouse of specialized knowledge. Its professors are able to disseminate their expertise to students at varying levels of advancement. They also constitute a valuable resource for society, to be called upon as needed for expert advice. When viewed from this perspective, some of the paradoxical features of the contemporary university are clarified.

In the most recent era American universities have been more willing than ever before to make their expertise available to outside parties. This openness, above all, has been responsible for the considerable enlargement of their research role. Unbridled specialized inquiry feeds upon itself, ever seeking greater depths in analysis and finding further topics to scrutinize. The growing size and high ambitions of the academic research community have thus produced an insatiable appetite for support.[5] Such support is negotiated with different constituencies of American society. It represents in part backing for the work that scientists believe to be most important for the progress of basic knowledge, and in part the purchase of knowledge needed by society. The growth in funding for academic research, as well as its notable achievements, are both testimony to the value to the country of this repository of specialized expertise.

In other respects, the relentless application of cognitive rationality has served universities less well. An inherent tension exists between their wealth of specialized knowledge and the kind of general knowledge that students require as a base for advanced learning or to understand the world about them. An inescapable epistemological basis thus exists for the elusiveness of liberal education, as well as for the ongoing tension between the instructional and research roles. Similarly, those responsible for the actual application of knowledge complain, as they always have, that university scientists are too specialized or too deeply committed to their disciplines. Yet, that is the proper role of university professors, their special niche in the ecology of knowledge. With respect to the internal conflicts of universities, specialization of knowledge is a precondition rather than a solution. Since the modern university has been all-inclusive in its applications of cognitive rationality, it has lacked any recognized, consensual basis for choosing among its numerous specialties. The university can no longer state with any logical conviction either what students ought to learn, or what might be inappropriate for inclusion in the curriculum.

The implacable specialization that lies at the intellectual heart of the contemporary university is nevertheless a source of enormous resiliency. The reservoir of expertise and basic knowledge that universities represent is an inherent component of an advanced industrial society, and the continual expansion of that reservoir through research is indispensable for its future. Advanced education is the second element buttressing the stability and continuity of the university. The transmission of sophisticated understanding and technique is an equally indispensable task for sustaining the production of goods and services on which society depends. Thus, the assertion made decades earlier that universities were central institutions to post-industrial society seems belatedly validated.[6] Indeed, this contention rests mainly on their vital role of discovering and disseminating knowledge of the objective world. In this respect the record of the research universities has been superb. When dealing with knowledge of human affairs, however, the recent record of universities inspires less confidence.

The march of specialized knowledge in the humanities and social sciences has tended to atomize former certainties without providing new truths to replace them. The result has been to dissolve any reliable link between the study of human affairs and guidance for human action. The academic disciplines most concerned with the human condition are those most plagued by such nihilistic symptoms. Thoughtful appraisals of these disciplines have reached strikingly pessimistic conclusions: history as a community of discourse has "ceased to exist"; possibilities for a scientific sociology have become more remote, as has the likelihood of serving "the intellectual needs of large audiences in American culture"; psychology presumes to advise, but is actually "too primitive a discipline to help . . . much in solving even simple social problems, let alone complex ones"; and in literary studies, the least constrained and most politicized of academic fields, literature itself has been desiccated by arid literary theory, i.e. "inquiry into assumptions, premises, and legitimating principles and concepts."[7] It is not that these disciplines are foundering: on the contrary. History, for example, is "hopelessly fragmented," but "the fragments were doing very well indeed."[8] The same is largely the case in the other disciplines. Rather, there is considerable irony in the fact that contemporary universities have been eager to assume a mantle of leadership on social issues when the academic knowledge of human affairs rests on such a parlous foundation.[9]

Contemporary American research universities are sustained by society more for the usefulness of their educational and research roles than for any claims to moral leadership. If in this respect they seem to resemble other major institutions of society, they also differ from the others in claiming a substantial degree of autonomy and internal freedom as precondition to fulfilling those roles. Universities are also distinguished by a residual idealism associated with the pursuit and discovery of knowledge. Autonomy, freedom, and idealism are indispensable for universities in their mission of advancing and disseminating knowledge. The extent to which such conditions are actually realized, however, may well vary according to the two diverging paths that contemporary universities have followed—one dealing with things and the other concerned with people. For the first path—investigating the objective world—universities have been accorded great autonomy and internal freedom. Cognitive rationality reigns supreme in this domain, and American society expects continued usefulness from university teaching and research. For the second path—that dealing with human affairs, whether through those particular academic disciplines, liberal education, or social involvement—the university faces a far more difficult challenge in nurturing disinterestedness and impartiality. In precisely this realm of human affairs are autonomy, freedom, and commitment to rationality most needed, and it is here that they are most difficult to sustain. Specialized inquiry in these domains may provide no new, overarching certainties, but the process itself, when undertaken with a commitment to objectivity, in the longer run contributes toward an unfolding but never completed understanding. As the American research university enters the second century of its existence, its scientific and technical roles seem destined to flourish even while the endeavor to elucidate the human condition remains approximate, contested—and vital to a free society.

Notes

Preface

1. The Carnegie Foundation classified 70 institutions as "Research I" and 34 as "Research II" universities: Carnegie Foundation for the Advancement of Teaching, *A Classification of Institutions of Higher Education* (Princeton: 1987). For the purpose of this study, being a "research university" implies both the conduct of significant amounts of research and self-identification with the research role. The membership of this category is hence ambiguous at the margins, and varies over time.

2. Daniel Bell, *The Coming of Post-Industrial Society: A Venture in Social Forecasting* (New York: Basic Books, 1973).

3. Burton R. Clark, ed., *The Research Foundations of Graduate Education: Germany, Britain, France, United States, Japan* (Los Angeles: University of California Press, 1993).

4. Roger L. Geiger, *To Advance Knowledge: The Growth of American Research Universities, 1900–1940* (New York: Oxford University Press, 1986).

5. I.e., fraud in science is a rare and self-defeating aberration; most universities tend to understate their indirect costs, which in any case are lower than those of other research performers; students have sought admission to research universities in growing numbers and have departed, for the most part, highly satisfied; and for most subjects universities offer a forum to air and debate a wide range of views.

Chapter 1. Origins of the Federal Research Economy

1. The Organization of Research for War

1. James B. Conant, *My Several Lives: Memoirs of a Social Inventor* (New York: Harper & Row, 1970), 236; Vannevar Bush, *Pieces of the Action* (New York: Morrow, 1970), 38–39; A. Hunter Dupree, "The 'Great Instauration' of 1940: The Organization

of Scientific Research for War," in Gerald Holton, ed., *The Making of Modern Science* (New York: Norton, 1972), 443–67.

2. Roger L. Geiger, *To Advance Knowledge: The Growth of American Research Universities in the Twentieth Century, 1900–1940* (New York: Oxford University Press, 1986), 95–101; Daniel J. Kevles, *The Physicists: A History of a Scientific Community in Modern America* (New York: Random House, 1979), 102–38. Contemporaries judged the wartime accomplishments of American science to be anything but modest: Robert M. Yerkes, ed., *The New World of Science* (New York: 1920); and Ronald C. Tobey, *The American Ideology of National Science, 1919–1930* (Pittsburgh: University of Pittsburgh Press, 1971).

3. Geiger, *Advance Knowledge,* 97–100; Kevles, *Physicists,* 148–54.

4. Geiger, *Advance Knowledge,* 255–64; Robert Kargon and Elizabeth Hodes, "Karl Compton, Isaiah Bowman, and the Politics of Science in the Great Depression," *Isis* 76 (1985): 301–18.

5. National Science Foundation, *Science—The Endless Frontier* (Washington, D.C.: NSF, 1960), 86.

6. Conant, *Several Lives,* 207–33;' Bush, *Pieces,* 32–33.

7. Bush, *Pieces,* 33.

8. Ibid., 34–35; A. Hunter Dupree, *Science in the Federal Government* (Cambridge: Harvard University Press, 1957), 365; Nathan Reingold, "Vannevar Bush's New Deal for Research; or, the Triumph of the Old Order," idem. *Science, American Style* (New Brunswick: Rutgers University Press, 1991), 284–333.

9. Not everyone concurred with Bush's plans. There was opposition in the Navy, in particular to the intrusion of civilian scientists, who were considered impractical and security risks; but such resistance was decisively overruled: Harvey M. Sapolsky, *Science and the Navy: The History of the Office of Naval Research* (Princeton: Princeton University Press, 1990), 15–18.

10. Dupree, "Great Instauration"; Irvin Stewart, *Organizing Scientific Research for War: The Administrative History of the Office of Scientific Research and Development* (Boston: Little, Brown, 1948).

11. Stewart, *Organizing Scientific Research,*

12. James P. Baxter, 3rd, *Scientists Against Time* (Boston: Little, Brown, 1946).

13. Dupree, "Great Instauration," 454.

2. Universities and War Research

1. Irvin Stewart, *Organizing Scientific Research for War* (Boston: Little, Brown, 1948), 191–99; F. Leroy Foster, *Sponsored Research at MIT, 1900–1968:* vol. 2, *1941–46* (typescript, MIT Archives and Special Collections), 22–26.

2. Emilio Segre, *Enrico Fermi: Physicist* (Chicago: University of Chicago Press, 1970), 97–116; Leo Szilard, "Reminiscences," in Donald Fleming & Bernard Bailyn, eds., *The Intellectual Migration: Europe and America, 1930–1960* (Cambridge: Harvard University Press, 1969), 94–151.

3. A. Hunter Dupree, "The Great Instauration of 1940: The Organization of Scientific Research for War," in Gerald Holton, ed., *The Making of Modern Science* (New York: Norton, 1972), 455–57.

4. James B. Conant, *My Several Lives* (New York: Harper & Row, 1970), 274–85; Arthur Holly Compton, *Atomic Quest: A Personal Narrative* (New York: Oxford University Press, 1956), 45–64.

5. Compton, *Atomic Quest,* 67–145; Conant, *Several Lives,* 286–304; Segre, *Fermi,*

117–32; J. L. Heilbron, Robert W. Seidel, & Bruce R. Wheaton, *Lawrence and His Laboratory: Nuclear Science at Berkeley, 1931–1961* (Berkeley: Office for History of Science and Technology, University of California, 1981), 30–41.

6. Richard G. Hewlett & Oscar E. Anderson, Jr., *The New World: A History of the United States Atomic Energy Commission* (Washington, D.C.: AEC, 1962), 53–226.

7. E. Mendelsohn, M. R. Smith, and P. Weingart, eds. *Science, Technology and the Military* (Norwell, Mass.: Kluwer, 1988), esp. S. S. Schweber, "The Mutual Embrace of Science and the Military: ONR and the Growth of Physics in the United States after World War II," 1–45; Peter Galison, "Physics Between War and Peace," 47–86; Paul K. Hoch, "The Crystallization of a Strategic Alliance: the American Physics Elite and the Military in the 1940s," 87–116.

8. Daniel J. Kevles, *The Physicists*, 303–8.

9. James R. Killian, Jr., *The Education of a College President: A Memoir* (Cambridge: MIT Press, 1985), 22–23.

10. Roger L. Geiger, *To Advance Knowledge: The Growth of American Research Universities in the Twentieth Century, 1900–1940* (New York: Oxford University Press, 1986), 177–83.

11. Foster, *Sponsored Research*, 1–6;

12. Killian, *College President*, 24, 55.

13. John Burchard, *O.E.D. M.I.T. in World War II* (New York: John Wiley & Sons, 1948), 215–42; Karl L. Wildes & Nilo A. Lindgren, *A Century of Electrical Engineering and Computer Science at MIT, 1882–1982* (Cambridge: MIT Press, 1985), 190–209.

14. The MIT Rad Lab also spawned a few satellite laboratories. Radar countermeasures were located at Harvard, and a team was placed at Columbia: John S. Ridgen, *Rabi: Scientist and Citizen* (New York: Basic Books, 1987), 133–45.

15. Clayton R. Koppes, *JPL and the American Space Program: A History of the Jet Propulsion Laboratory* (New Haven: Yale University Press, 1982), 18–29; Joseph C. Boyce, ed., *New Weapons for Air Warfare* (Boston: Little, Brown, 1947); John E. Burchard, ed., *Rockets, Guns and Targets* (Boston: Little, Brown, 1948).

16. Boyce, *New Weapons*, 90–93; James P. Baxter, 3rd, *Scientists Against Time* (Boston: Little, Brown, 1946), 169, 176, 256–59.

17. Stewart, *Organizing Scientific Research*, 7–97.

18. Bush, *Pieces*, 31–33; Conant, *Several Lives*, 242–43.

19. E. C. Andrus, *Advances in Military Medicine*, 2 vols. (Boston: Little, Brown, 1948); Stewart, *Organizing Scientific Research*, 98–101; Bush, *Pieces*, 42–49. In metallurgy as well the NDRC operated through existing NRC committees: Nathan Reingold, "Vannevar Bush's New Deal for Research," 24–26.

3. Postwar Federal Science Policy

1. Admiral J. A. Furer, "Post-War Military Research," *Science* 100 (1944): 461–64; Daniel J. Kevles, "Scientists, the Military, and the Control of Postwar Defense Research: The Case of the Research Board for National Security, 1944–46," 20–45.

2. Carroll Pursell, "Science Agencies in World War II: The OSRD and Its Challengers," in Nathan Reingold, ed., *The Sciences in the American Context: New Perspectives* (Washington, D.C.: The Smithsonian Press, 1979), 359–77; Daniel J. Kevles, "The National Science Foundation and the Debate over Postwar Research Policy, 1942–1945: A Political Interpretation of 'Science—The Endless Frontier,'" *Isis* 68 (1977): 5–26.

3. Bush's concern to insulate the world of science from the supposed perils of big government has been admirably portrayed by Nathan Reingold, "Vannevar Bush's New Deal

for Research: or, The Triumph of the Old Order," in *Science, American Style* (New Brunswick: Rutgers University Press, 1991), 284–333; Bush's 1943 views were expressed in "The Kilgore Bill," *Science* 98 (1943): 571–77.

4. Reprinted in *Science—the Endless Frontier* (Washington, D.C.: National Science Foundation, 1960). All further references are to this edition.

5. The committee reports are reprinted in *Science—the Endless Frontier*. On Bowman, see Robert Kargon and Elizabeth Hodes, "Karl Compton, Isaiah Bowman, and the Politics of Science in the Great Depression," *Isis* 76 (1985): 301–18.

6. Reingold makes it clear that Bush's concern for postwar science were far larger than just basic research; however, the emphasis on basic research in *The Endless Frontier* is consistent with his underlying aim to minimize government intrusions in science: "Vannevar Bush's New Deal for Research."

7. Reingold concludes: "Bush did not see the [national research] foundation as primarily, let alone solely, a means of funneling federal dollars to the universities for the support of pure research"; and, "lumping medical and military research with the more general basic investigations was Bush's contribution, his particular vision. Whether intended or not, that made his proposed foundation look like a peacetime version of OSRD": "Vannevar Bush's New Deal for Science," 306, 307.

8. *Science—the Endless Frontier*, 32, 79, 81.

9. The Medical Advisory Committee recommended the creation of a separate "National Foundation for Medical Research," completely severed from the Public Health Service or any other governmental agencies with "special interests." They proposed that a presidentially appointed board of trustees be responsible for the foundation, and that it would appoint both a technical board, which would supervise research matters, and an executive director. The Bowman Committee wanted the national research foundation's independence to be guaranteed by its own $500 million endowment. It proposed that the governing board of trustees be appointed by the President from a list drawn up by the National Academy of Sciences: ibid. 62–66, 115–17.

10. The lone dissenter was Frank Jewett, whose attitudes and influence are analyzed in Reingold, "Vannevar Bush's New Deal for Research"; the legislative history is presented in J. Merton England, *A Patron for Pure Science* (Washington, D.C.: NSF, 1982), 25–44.

11. Dael Wolfle, "Making the Case for the Social Sciences," in Samuel Z. Klausner and Victor M. Lidz, eds. *The Nationalization of the Social Sciences* (Philadelphia: University of Pennsylvania Press, 1986), 185–96.

12. England, *Patron for Pure Science*, 36–42; An interesting contemporary analysis of the political factors underlying this split was provided by Talcott Parsons: "very broadly speaking, this was a division between an inner group which had played the leading role in the work of the Office of Scientific Research and Development during the war and were [sic] associated with the institutions where the bulk of that work had been done and, on the other side, a much broader group of scientists all over the country": "National Science Foundation," *Bulletin of the Atomic Scientists* 2 (Nov. 1, 1946): 7–9.

13. Bush, "Kilgore Bill."

14. Quoted in England, *Patron for Pure Science*, 30.

15. id., 45–60. Scientists supporting this legislation held Bush fully responsible for its failure: Howard A. Meyerhoff, "Obituary: National Science Foundation, 1946," *Science* 104 (1946): 97–98.

16. On the establishment of the AEC, Richard G. Hewlett and Oscar E. Anderson, Jr., *The New World, 1939–1946: A History of the United States Atomic Energy Commission* (Washington, D.C.: AEC, 1972), I:482–530; on its impact on science legislation, Alice

Kimball Smith, *A Peril and a Hope: The Scientists' Movement in America: 1945–47* (Chicago, University of Chicago Press, 1965), 437–44.

17. Stephen P. Strickland, *Politics, Science and Dread Disease: A Short History of United States Medical Research Policy* (Cambridge: Harvard University Press, 1972), 36–45. An additional bill to provide $100 million for cancer research in NIH was narrowly defeated on July 26, 1946: E. V. Cowdry, "Financing Cancer Research," *Science* 104 (1946): 53–57.

18. Agricultural research was unaffected by the currents surrounding the new postwar channels of federal research support: Richard G. Axt, *The Federal Government and Financing Higher Education* (New York: Columbia University Press, 1952), 94–96.

4. The Postwar Federal Research Economy

1. Robert W. Seidel, "Accelerating Science: The Postwar Transformation of the Lawrence Radiation Laboratory," *Historical Studies in the Physical Sciences* 13 (1983): 375–400; Daniel S. Greenberg, *The Politics of Pure Science* (New York: New American Library, 1967), 100–102. Compton's efforts to advance Chicago physics during the wartime emergency were widely resented: Nathan Reingold, "Vannevar Bush's New Deal for Research; or, the Triumph of the Old Order" in idem. *Science, American Style* (New Brunswick: Rutgers University Press, 1991), 284–333.

2. Robert W. Seidel, "A Home for Big Science: The Atomic Energy Commission's Laboratory System," *Historical Studies in the Physical Sciences* 16 (1986): 135–75; Greenberg, *Politics of Pure Science*, 133–37, 212–15; Seidel, "Accelerating Science," 388–92.

3. Richard G. Hewlett and Francis Duncan, *Atomic Shield, 1947–1952: A History of the United States Atomic Energy Commission*, vol. 2 (University Park: Pennsylvania State University Press, 1969), 33–35, 79–84, 222–27; Seidel, "Home for Big Science," 137–41. For the Los Alamos attempt to attract university scientists, see "University Affiliations Conference," reprinted in Manhattan District History, *Project 'Y': The Los Alamos Story* (Los Angeles: Tomash, 1983), 380–429.

4. Hewlett and Duncan, *Atomic Shield*, 249–51.

5. Ibid. 222–60.

6. Ibid., 82–83.

7. Ibid. 252.

8. Ibid., 251–60.

9. National Science Foundation, *Federal Funds for Scientific Research and Development at Nonprofit Institutions, 1950–51 and 1951–52* (Washington, D.C.: NSF, 1953).

10. Reprinted in Seymour Melman, *Pentagon Capitalism: The Political Economy of War* (New York: McGraw-Hill, 1970), 231–34.

11. F. Leroy Foster, "Sponsored Research at MIT, 1900–1968" (unpub. ms., MIT Archives and Special Collections).

12. For a useful overview of from the military side of this complicated topic, see Herbert F. York & G. Allen Greb, "Military Research and Development: a Postwar History," in Thomas J. Kuehn & Alan L. Porter, ed. *Science, Technology, and National Policy* (Ithaca: Cornell University Press, 1981), 190–215. The Air Force differed from the Army, and was highly innovative, in the manner in which it sought civilian advice on strategy and planning, e.g., by creating RAND: Bruce L. R. Smith, *The RAND Corporation: Case Study of a Nonprofit Advisory Corporation* (Cambridge: Harvard University Press, 1966); RAND, *The RAND Corporation: Its Origin, Evolution, and Plans for the Future* (Santa Monica: RAND, 1971).

13. Nick A. Komons, *Science and the Air Force: A History of the Air Force Office of Scientific Research* (Arlington, Va.: U.S. Air Force Office of Aerospace Research, 1966), 4–5; S. S. Schweber, "The Mutual Embrace of Science and the Military," in E. Mendelsohn et al., eds. *Science Technology and the Military* (Norwell, Mass: Kluwer, 1988), 1–45 [41–42]. T. von Karman authored the report, *Toward New Horizons* (1945), which was specifically intended to rebut *Science—the Endless Frontier* on the issue of civilian control, which von Karman felt could only "injure progress in Air Force research." This view was apparently influential within the Air Force, but not elsewhere since it was a classified document until 1960! Theodore von Karman with Lee Edson, *The Wind and Beyond* (Boston: Little, Brown, 1967), 294, 291.

14. Richard G. Axt, *The Federal Government and Financing Higher Education* (New York: Columbia University Press, 1952), 100–101.

15. Ibid., 101.

16. The authoratative work on the Office of Naval Research is Harvey M. Sapolsky, *Science and the Navy: the History of the Office of Naval Research* (Princeton: Princeton University Press, 1990), esp. 37–56.

17. The 'Bird Dogs,' "The Evolution of the Office of Naval Research," *Physics Today* (Aug. 1961), 30–35. The 'Bird Dogs' were actively involved in research during World War II; they had also participated in a "Navy system of postgraduate study in various universities which had developed in many officers an understanding and appreciation of science": ibid., 32. Harvey M. Sapolsky, "Academic Science and the Military: The Years Since the Second World War," in Nathan Reingold, ed., *The Sciences in the American Context: New Perspectives* (Washington, D.C.: The Smithsonian Press, 1979), 379–99; Harold G. Bowen, *Ships, Machinery and Mossbacks: The Autobiography of a Naval Engineer* (Princeton: Princeton University Press, 1954), 182–89, 350–54; "Science Dons a Uniform . . .," *Business Week* (Sept. 14, 1946).

18. Sapolsky, "Academic Science and the Military," 386; 'Bird Dogs,' "Office of Naval Research," 34–35.

19. Daniel J. Kevles, *The Physicists* (New York: Random House, 1979), 354–55.

20. Sapolsky, *Science and the Navy,* 45–46. Precise figures for the support of academic research do not exist for the 1940s: see *ibid.,* 131–33; and National Science Foundation, Division of Policy Research & Analysis, *The State of Academic Science and Engineering* (Washington, D.C.: National Science Foundation, 1990), 57–58.

21. John E. Pfeiffer, "The Office of Naval Research," *Scientific American* 180, 2 (Feb. 1949): 1–15.

22. Sapolsky, "Academic Science and the Military," 386–90. See below, Chapter 2.

23. David K. Alison, "U.S. Navy Research and Development Since World War II," in Merritt Roe Smith, ed., *Military Enterprise and Technological Change: Perspectives on the American Experience* (Cambridge: MIT Press, 1985), 289–328, esp. 296–97.

24. Sapolsky, *Science and the Navy,* 71, 132.

25. Alan T. Waterman, "Government Support of Research," *Science* 110 (1949): 701–7 (quote p. 703).

26. Much of this criticism appeared or was reprinted in *The Bulletin of the Atomic Scientists* (f. 1945); in particular, see Louis N. Ridenour, "Military Support of American Science, A Danger?" [negative], and the numerous replies [mostly affirmative]: reprinted from the *American Scholar,* ibid. 3 (1947): 221–30.

27. Waterman, "Government Support"; Sapolsky, "Academic Science and the Military," 394n; Komons, *Science and the Air Force.*

28. Stephen P. Strickland, *Politics, Science and Dread Disease: A Short History of*

United States Medical Research Policy (Cambridge: Harvard University Press, 1972), 15–31; Donald C. Swain, "The Rise of a Research Empire: NIH, 1930 to 1950," *Science* 138 (1962): 1233–37.

29. The AMA supported Bush's science foundation with the proviso that it "must avoid the bureaucratic domination of research" (Strickland, *Politics, Science and Dread Disease*, 21). Strickland wonders why "broad, solid experience seems not to have triumphed over preconceived, personal fears. At the end of the war, many scientists whose personal and professional sustenance had been provided by government suddenly again distrusted government—and vice-versa" (ibid., 42–43). Reingold, in effect, provides an answer in terms of Vannevar Bush's aversion to the New Deal's erosion of the spheres of private volition: "Vannevar Bush's New Deal for Research."

30. Strickland, *Politics, Science, and Dread Disease*, 32–54.

31. Ibid., 76.

32. Swain, "Rise of a Research Empire," 1236.

33. Stella Leche Deignan and Esther Miller, "The Support of Research in Medical and Allied Fields for the Period 1946 through 1951," *Science* 115 (1952): 321–43; Kenneth M. Endicott and Ernest M. Allen, "The Growth of Medical Research 1941–1953 and the Role of Public Health Service Research Grants," *Science* 118 (1953): 337–43; Frank W. Reynolds and David E. Price, "Federal Support of Medical Research through the Public Health Service," *American Scientist* 37 (1949): 578–86. The useful data in the last two citations would seem to be part of a public relations effort on the part of the PHS, in keeping with their desire for legitimacy.

34. J. Merton England, *A Patron for Pure Science: The National Science Foundation's Formative Years* (Washington, D.C.: NSF, 1982), 61–82; Don K. Price, "The Deficiencies of the National Science Bill," *Bulletin of the Atomic Scientists* 3 (1947): 291–94.

35. England, *Patron for Pure Science*, 83–106.

36. Pfeiffer, "The Office of Naval Research," 15; Waterman, "Government Support of Research," 705–6.

37. England, *Patron for Pure Science*, 113–28; John T. Wilson, *Academic Science, Higher Education, and the Federal Government, 1950–1983* (Chicago: University of Chicago Press, 1983), 10–11. The biological section of ONR, in particular, followed Waterman to NSF.

38. Waterman, "Government Support of Science."

39. National Science Foundation, *First Annual Report, 1950–51* (Washington, D.C.: NSF, 1952), viii.

40. James B. Conant, "Foreward" in National Science Foundation, *First Annual Report, 1950–51*, viii; *Science and Common Sense* (New Haven: Yale University Press, 1951), 317–24.

41. NSF, *Science—the Endless Frontier*, 40.

42. Axt (*Federal Government and Financing*, 93) provides the following estimate for federal support of academic science in 1950:

Large AEC projects	$58 million
Other large defense projects	$29
Agricultural Extension Stations	$12
Public Health Service research	$11
Small projects in natural science	$30
Total	$140 million

Chapter 2. Universities in the Postwar Era, 1945-1957

1. From War to Peace to Cold War

1. Karl L. Wildes and Nilo A. Lindgren, *A Century of Electrical Engineering and Computer Science at MIT, 1882-1982* (Cambridge: MIT Press, 1985), 243-45; and see below, Chapter 3.

2. Peter Galison, "Between War and Peace," in *Science, Technology and the Military,* E. Mendelsohn, M. R. Smith, and P. Weingart, eds. (Norwell, Mass.: Kluwer, 1988), 47-85.

3. James Phinney Baxter, 3rd, *Scientists Against Time* (Boston: Little, Brown, 1946), 456.

4. Galison, "Between War and Peace," 50-62; William H. McNeill, *Hutchins' University: A Memoir of the University of Chicago, 1929-1950* (Chicago: University of Chicago Press, 1991), 123-24.

5. See below, Chapter 3, Chapter 5.

6. John S. Ridgen, *Rabi: Scientist and Citizen* (New York: Basic Books, 1987), 178-92; Judith R. Goodstein, *Millikan's School: A History of the California Institute of Technology* (New York: Norton, 1991), 271-73.

7. Michael Bezilla, *Penn State: An Illustrated History* (University Park: Pennsylvania State University Press, 1985), 212-14; Robert W. Seidel, "A Home for Big Science: The Atomic Energy Commission's Laboratory System," *Historical Studies in the Physical Sciences* 16:1 (1986): 135-75 [139-40]: Chicago also threatened to break its ties with the Argonne Lab, but subsequently became part of a consortium of managing institutions; Clayton R. Koppes, *JPL and the American Space Program: A History of the Jet Propulsion Laboratory* (New Haven: Yale University Press, 1982), 24-29; Michael Dennis, "Reconstructing Technical Practice: The Johns Hopkins University Applied Physics Laboratory and the Massachusetts Institute of Technology Instrumentation Laboratory After World War II," ms.

8. The "defense establishment" was defined by Harvey Brooks as the Department of Defense, the AEC, and (later) NASA: "Impact of the Defense Establishment on Science and Education," *Hearings on National Defense Policy,* House Committee on Science and Aeronautics (Washington: 1970), 931-63.

9. Stuart W. Leslie, "Profit and Loss: The Military and MIT in the Postwar Era," *Historical Studies in the Physical and Biological Sciences* 21 (1990):59-85 [60-66]; Leslie. "Playing the Education Game to Win: The Military and Interdisciplinary Research at Stanford," ibid. 18 (1987): 55-88. Similar electronics labs were supported from the end of the war at Harvard and Columbia: Paul Forman, "Behind Quantum Electronics: National Security as Basis for Physical Research in the United States, 1940-1960," ibid. 18 (1987): 149-229 [204-05].

10. Seidel, "Home for Big Science," 137-41. S. S. Schweber, "The Mutual Embrace of Science and the Military: ONR and the Growth of Physics in the United States After World War II," in Mendelsohn, et al., *Science . . . Military,* 3-45 [7, 38n].

11. Leslie, "Profit and Loss," 73-78.

12. Richard G. Hewlett and Francis Duncan, *Atomic Shield: A History of the United States Atomic Energy Commission, 1947-1952* (University Park: Pennsylvania State University Press, 1962), 246-47, 435.

13. Dan Kevles, "Cold War and Hot Physics: Science, Security and the American State, 1945-56," *Historical Studies in the Physical and Biological Sciences* 20 (1990): 240-64; Forman, "Behind Quantum Electronics," 157-59.

14. See below, Chapters 3 and 5; Herbert F. York, *The Advisers: Oppenheimer, Teller and the Superbomb* (San Francisco: Freeman, 1976), 121–35.

15. From 1951 to 1958 R&D expenditures at AEC laboratories more than tripled, from $51 to $166 million, and employees grew by 50 percent (Seidel, "Home for Big Science," 162).

16. Harvey M. Sapolsky, *Science and the Navy* (Princeton: Princeton University Press, 1990), 57–81.

17. Schweber, "Mutual Embrace," 23.

18. For specific critical fields, see Bernard Cohen, "The Computer: A Case Study of Support by Government, Especially the Military, of a New Science and Technology," in Mendelsohn et al., eds., *Science . . . Military,* 119–54; and Forman, "Behind Quantum Electronics."

19. Kevles, "Cold War," 246–47.

20. Especially germane in the large literature on this subject is York, *The Advisers.*

21. The General Advisory Committee's Report is reprinted, ibid. 150–59.

22. James G. Hershberg, "'Over My Dead Body': James B. Conant and the Hydrogen Bomb," in Mendelsohn et al., eds., *Science . . . Military,* 379–430.

23. Among the vast literature on Oppenheimer and his trial, Barton J. Bernstein, "'In the Matter of J. Robert Oppenheimer'," *Historical Studies in the Physical Sciences* 12 (1982): 195–252. York, *Advisers,* clarifies many of the technical issues.

24. Paul Hoch, "The Crystallization of a Strategic Alliance: The American Physics Elite and the Military in the 1940s," in Mendelsohn et al., eds., *Science . . . Military,* 87–116 [107–10]; Seidel, "Home for Big Science," 145–48.

25. On the general phenomenon of McCarthyism, most comprehensive is David Caute, *The Great Fear* (New York: Simon & Schuster, 1978); most thorough on academic McCarthyism is Ellen W. Schrecker, *No Ivory Tower: McCarthyism and the Universities* (New York: Oxford University Press, 1986).

26. David P. Gardner, *The California Oath Controversy* (Berkeley: University of California Press, 1967), vii, 245–46.

27. Jane Sanders, *Cold War on Campus: Academic Freedom at the University of Washington, 1946–64* (Seattle: University of Washington Press, 1979).

28. Mary Ann Dzuback, *Robert M. Hutchins: Portrait of an Educator* (Chicago: University of Chicago Press, 1991), 200–201.

29. Schrecker, *No Ivory Tower,* 217–18.

30. Ibid., 219–33; Caute, *Great Fear,* 417–18. Schrecker reports that one dismissed individual, Mark Nickerson, was tenured; Caute calls him untenured. Tenure, in any case, was no defense in itself against dismissal in these cases.

31. Schrecker, *No Ivory Tower,* 260–64; Caute, *Great Fear,* 410–14. Harvard has congratulated itself for its principled stand in opposition to McCarthyism, and in this respect its record is far better than most contemporary universities: Schrecker, *No Ivory Tower,* 202–4; Seymour Martin Lipset and David Riesman, *Education and Politics at Harvard* (New York: McGraw-Hill, 1975), 179–97. One of those dismissed, Sigmund Diamond, has disagreed: "Veritas at Harvard," *New York Review of Books* (April 28, 1977).

32. Schrecker, *No Ivory Tower,* 340.

33. Besides the numerous examples given in Schrecker, *No Ivory Tower* and Sanders, *Cold War,* see the autobiography of Martin D. Kamen: *Radiant Science, Dark Politics: A Memoir of the Nuclear Age* (Berkeley: University of California Press, 1985).

34. Gardner, *California Oath,* esp. 228–29.

35. Howard R. Bowen, *Academic Recollections* (Washington: ACE, 1988), 25–36.

36. Robert A. McCaughey, *International Studies and Academic Enterprise: A Chapter in the Enclosure of American Learning* (New York: Columbia University Press, 1984), 141–65.

37. Peter Novick, *That Noble Dream: The "Objectivity Question" and the American Historical Profession* (New York: Cambridge University Press, 1988), 281–319; even deeper involvement of historians came through espionage: Robin W. Winks, *Cloak and Gown: Scholars in the Secret War, 1939–1961* (New York: Morrow, 1987).

2. The Burdens of Finance

1. Richard G. Axt, *The Federal Government and Financing Higher Education* (New York: Columbia University Press, 1952), 122–27.

2. Keith W. Olsen, *The G.I. Bill, the Veterans, and the Colleges* (Lexington: University of Kentucky Press, 1974), 103.

3. Roger Geiger, *To Advance Knowledge: The Growth of American Research Universities, 1900–1940* (New York: Oxford University Press, 1986); enrollment data from *Biennial Surveys of Education.*

4. H. K. Allen, *State Public Finance and State Institutions of Higher Education in the United States* (New York: Columbia University Press, 1952), 49; UC income from Verne A. Stadtman, ed., *The Centennial Record of the University of California* (Berkeley: University of California Press, 1967); Olsen, *The G.I. Bill,* 88.

5. Allen, *State Public Finance;* John D. Millett, *Financing Higher Education in the United States* (New York: Columbia University Press, 1952), 254–68, 324–30.

6. Yale University, *Treasurer's Reports.* Much of the shrinkage of real income was absorbed by shrinkage in real salaries of faculty. Thus, purchasing power may have been less adversely affected than CPI figures would indicate. This situation, however, was untenable for long: see below, Chapter 4.

7. President's Commission on Higher Education, *Education for American Democracy,* 6 vols. (Washington, D.C., 1947).

8. The Commission on Financing Higher Education, *Nature and Needs of Higher Education* (New York: Columbia University Press, 1952), vi–x. The more factual Staff Report of the Commission is, Millett, *Financing Higher Education.*

9. Millett, *Financing Higher Education,* 307.

10. Ernest V. Hollis, "Federal Aid to Higher Education," *School and Society* (1949): 20–23. Tuition charges from American Council on Education, *American Universities and Colleges,* IV, VI.

11. Millet, *Financing Higher Education.*

12. Commission, *Nature and Needs,* 168–76, 179–84; F. Emerson Andrews wrote, "During the last twenty-five years it has been widely proclaimed that the day of creating large foundations was over. In the first part of this period, the depression was wiping out all great fortunes; later, high taxes were alleged to be making substantial accumulations impossible." But by 1956 it was becoming apparent that "the facts scarcely support these opinions": *Philanthropic Foundations* (New York: Russell Sage Foundation, 1956), 334. See also, Peter Dobkin Hall, "A Historical Overview of the Private Nonprofit Sector," in *The Nonprofit Sector: a Research Handbook* (New Haven: Yale University Press, 1987), 3–26.

13. F. Emerson Andrews, *Corporate Giving* (New York: Russell Sage Foundation, 1952), 199–219. Business corporations were allowed a tax deduction for charitable contributions in 1936, but the legality of such contributions (vis-à-vis shareholder suits) was not settled until the A. P. Smith case in 1954: Merle Curti and Roderick Nash, *Philan-*

thropy and the Shaping of American Higher Education; Harvard University, *President's Report,* 1949–50, 17–18; for the MIT campaign, see Chapter 3.

14. John Price Jones Company, *American Philanthropy for Higher Education, 1957–58* (New York: Inter-River Press, 1959).

15. Commission, *Nature and Needs,* 157–65.

16. Geiger, *To Advance Knowledge,* 233–40.

17. Millet, *Financing Higher Education,* 399–411; Allen, *State Public Finance,* 167–68.

18. The states mentioned in this paragraph, plus Ohio, were alone in providing more than $15 million for higher education in 1950, with the exception of Wisconsin ($13.1 million): Millet, *Financing Higher Education,* 329. Also, Jane Sanders, *Cold War on Campus* (Seattle: University of Washington Press, 1979), 6–14.

19. Source: ACE, *American Universities and Colleges,* VII, VIII.

20. George B. Darling, "Can We Pay for Our Medical Schools?," *Atlantic* (June 1950): 38–42.

3. Organized Research in Postwar Universities

1. "Funds Available in 1920 for the Encouragement of Scientific Research," *Bulletin of the National Research Council,* no. 9 (1921).

2. James B. Conant, "Foreword" in National Science Foundation, *First Annual Report, 1950–51,* viii; see also, *Science and Common Sense* (New Haven: Yale University Press, 1951), 317–24.

3. Robert K. Merton has identified such disinterestedness as one of the four components of the 'ethos of science': *The Sociology of Knowledge,* ed by Norman Stoner (Chicago: University of Chicago Press, 1973), 267–78.

4. Paul Forman explicated this point at length, without employing Conant's term 'programmatic': "in truth, only a small fraction of . . . R&D funds labeled basic research went to support investigation that could reasonably be called fundamental": "Behind Quantum Electronics: National Security as Basis for Physical Research in the United States, 1940–1960," *Historical Studies in the Physical and Biological Sciences* 18 (1987): 149–229, quote 216.

5. Different typologies are offered by Stanley O. Ikenberry & Renee C. Friedman: *Beyond Academic Departments* (San Francisco: Jossey-Bass, 1972), which focuses on institutes, and Carlos E. Kruytbosch, *The Organization of Research at the University of California: The Case of Research Personnel* (Ph.D. diss. University of California, Berkeley, 1970), 65–75.

6. Harvard University, *The Behavioral Sciences at Harvard: A Report by a Faculty Committee,* June 1954 (Cambridge: Harvard University, 1954), 283–89.

7. Verne A. Stadtman, *The University of California, 1868–1968* (New York: McGraw-Hill, 1970), 369–70. Although Birge was out of step with the times in this respect, his point cannot be entirely dismissed. The physicist Philip M. Morse decades later complained: "by the late sixties, it was almost necessary to describe what one expected to discover and when, and then prove the expected discovery's practical value, before one would be granted the funds": *In at the Beginnings: A Physicist's Life* (Cambridge: MIT Press, 1977), 286.

8. *Behavioral Sciences at Harvard,* 287.

9. Harvard University, *President's Report,* 1962–63, p. 8.

10. John W. Gardner to Clyde Kluckhohn, 9/8/47, Clyde K. M. Kluckhohn Papers, Harvard University Archives.

11. Harvard University, Russian Research Center, *Five Year Report and Current Projects* (1953). The Carnegie Corporation made a second five-year grant after just three years, after which the Center's principal patron became the Ford Foundation. It also performed a major project for the Air Force (see below).

12. Russian Research Center, *Five Year Report.*

13. Clyde Kluckhohn, "Russian Research at Harvard," *World Politics* I (1949): 267–72; Carnegie Corporation of New York, *Annual Report,* 1948, 20.

14. Harvard University, *Russian Research Center, Ten Year Report and Current Projects, 1948–58* (1958).

15. "Report of the Reviewing Committee of the Russian Research Center" (6/6/52), in Clyde K. M. Kluckhohn Papers, Harvard University Archives.

16. *Behavioral Sciences at Harvard,* 302. At some universities area studies programs were elevated to departmental status; however, even in such settings "faculty members were careful to maintain their disciplinary base as well. Similarly, graduate students . . . took their degrees in a specific discipline": Robert A. McCaughey, *International Studies and Academic Enterprise: A Chapter in the Enclosure of American Learning* (New York: Columbia University Press, 1984), 221.

17. Russian Research Center, *Ten Year Report.*

18. McCaughey, *International Studies,* 212.

19. Many of these points are discussed by Ikenberry and Friedman, since *institutes* correspond with what they term a "standard research institute": *Beyond Academic Departments.*

20. Jean M. Converse, *Survey Research in the United States: Roots and Emergence, 1890–1960* (Berkeley: University of California Press, 1987), 239–57.

21. *Regents Proceedings,* 1945–48, 522; Walter A. Donnelly, ed., *The University of Michigan: An Encyclopedic Survey,* 4 vols. (Ann Arbor: University of Michigan Press, 1941–1958), 4:1549–60.

22. Converse, *Survey Research,* 340–78.

23. University of Michigan, *Reports to the President,* 1951–52, pp 429–48; idem. *Institute for Social Research, 1946–1956* (Ann Arbor: University of Michigan, n.d.); idem. *Institute for Social Research, 1952* (Ann Arbor: University of Michigan, 1952).

24. The Bureau traces its origins to the Office of Radio Research, established at Princeton with Rockefeller Foundation support in 1937, and transferred to Columbia in 1940. Lazersfeld was the guiding force throughout these years: Paul F. Lazersfeld, "An Episode in the History of Social Research: A Memoir," in Donald Fleming and Bernard Bailyn, eds., *The Intellectual Migration: Europe and America, 1930 1960* (Cambridge: Harvard University Press, 1969), 270–337. Also see, Converse, *Survey Research,* 267–304.

25. "BASR: Report to the SSRC" (first draft: 12/8/46), Paul F. Lazersfeld Papers, Box 6, Rare Book & Manuscript Library—Columbia University. The acceptance of the Bureau at Columbia coincided with the appointment of a committee chaired by Elliot Cheatham (1944) to consider whether or not Columbia ought to engage in contract research.

26. Charles Y. Glock, "Organizational Innovation for Social Science Research and Training," in Robert K. Merton, James S. Coleman, and Peter H. Rossi, eds., *Quantitative and Qualitative Social Research: Papers in Honor of Paul F. Lazersfeld* (New York: Free Press, 1979), 23–36.

27. James S. Coleman, "Autobiographical Sketch," ms. (2/27/85); Columbia University, Bureau of Applied Social Research, *Twentieth Anniversary Report* (New York: author, 1957).

28. Samuel D. Sieber, "The BASR—a Status Report and Evaluation" (Nov. 1960),

Lazersfeld Papers, 6; idem. *Reforming the University: The Role of the Social Research Center* (New York: Praeger, 1972); Allen H. Barton, "Paul Lazarsfeld and Applied Social Research: Invention of the University Applied Social Research Institute," *Social Science History* 3 (1979): 4–44.

29. Converse notes that "the [sociology] department was wary of the 'laboratory' tail wagging the departmental dog"; and more generally, "the Bureau achieved eminence *in spite of* Columbia administrators and other scholars": *Survey Research,* 279.

30. Barton, "Lazarsfeld and Applied Social Research."

31. Ibid.; Sieber, "The BASR—a Status Report."

32. The contradictory facets of the Bureau were in fact embodied in Lazarsfeld himself, who could with equal zest sell survey research to prospective patrons and give theoretical guidance to other social scientists. Still, the Bureau remained more academic than ISR or the National Opinion Research Center in that it did not employ a national battery of interviewers: Converse, *Survey Research,* 270–72, 280–81.

33. Foundations played an important role in the lives of both ISR and the Columbia Bureau by alleviating the pressures of doing applied research for clients and allowing them to pursue more academic topics. Ford Foundation support for the Detroit Area File after 1951 permitted ISR to expand its links with departmental graduate training. At Columbia foundation support was behind Bureau investigations of methodological issues of mathematical sociology and the study of socialization in medical schools. For social science institutes generally the foundations played a vital role at this juncture in facilitating disinterested research.

34. Michael A. Dennis, "Reconstructing Technical Practice: The Johns Hopkins University Applied Physics Laboratory and the Massachusetts Institute of Technology Instrumentation Laboratory after World War II," ms. My thanks to the author for a prepublication copy.

35. Clayton R. Koppes, *JPL and the American Space Program: A History of the Jet Propulsion Laboratory* (New Haven: Yale University Press, 1982), passim.

36. Koppes, *JPL,* 240; Dennis, "Reconstructing Technical Practice."

37. Robert W. Seidel, "A Home for Big Science: The Atomic Energy Commission's Laboratory System," *Historical Studies in the Physical Sciences* 16 (1986): 135–75; Morse, *Beginnings,* 220.

38. NSF, *Federal Funds for Scientific Research, 1950–51 and 1951–52.*

39. In 1957, for example, the number of federal research centers managed by nonprofits had risen to 34. University research centers received 49 percent of federal funds for extramural research (1955): NSF, *Federal Funds for Science,* 1955–1957, and 1957–58. In the mid-sixties the number of centers was back to 25: NSF, *Federal Support to Universities and Colleges, 1963–1966.*

40. University of Michigan, *Reports to the President,* 1951–52.

4. An Autonomous Research Mission and Its Discontents

1. For example: for Columbia, see above 2.3, note 25; for MIT, see below, Chapter 3 (Lewis Report).

2. Carlos Kruytbosch, "The Organization of Research in the University: The Case of Research Personel" (Ph.D. diss., UC Berkeley, 1970); William G. Bowen, *The Federal Government and Princeton University* (Princeton: Princeton University, 1962); Harold Orlans, *The Effects of Federal Programs on Higher Education* (Washington, D.C.: The Brookings Institution, 1962).

3. American Council on Education, *Sponsored Research Policy of Colleges and Uni-*

versities (Washington, D.C., 1954), 60–66; John D. Millet, *Financing Higher Education in the United States* (New York: Columbia University Press, 1952), 356–58; Bowen, *Government and Princeton,* 62–92; Orlans, *Federal Programs,* 221–35.

4. Vannevar Bush, *Science—the Endless Frontier* (Washington: GPO, 1945), 26.

5. S. S. Schweber, "The Mutual Embrace of Science and the Military" in *Science, Technology and the Military,* E. Mendelsohn, et al., eds. (Norwell, Mass.: Kluwer, 1988), 1–45 [26].

6. ACE, *Sponsored Research Policy,* 79–81; Harvard University, *President's Report,* 1946, p. 10. It soon became evident that there existed a large 'grey' area of classified research: work that required access to classified material; work that needed security clearance before being published; and work publishable after certain delays. These were generally not considered to be 'classified,' and hence were usually permissible on campus.

7. For example, Bowen, *Federal Government and Princeton,* 236–62.

8. "Report of Reviewing Committee," loc. cit.

9. W. Albert Noyes, "Is Sponsored Research a Danger to the Academic Tradition?," *Journal of the Association of American Universities* 51 (1950): 37–47.

10. Dan Kevles, "Cold War and Hot Physics: Science, Security, and the American State, 1945–1956," *Historical Studies in the Physical and Biological Sciences* 20 (1990): 239–64; Allan A. Needell, "Preparing of the Space Age: University-based Research, 1946–1957," ibid. 18 (1988): 89–110; Sapolsky, *Science and the Navy,* 62–66.

11. For example, Whitney Griswold, "Survival Is Not Enough," *Atlantic* 187 (April 1951): 25–29; Ellen W. Schrecker, *No Ivory Tower: McCarthyism and the Universities* (New York: Oxford University Press, 1986).

12. Commission on Financing Higher Education, *Nature and Needs of Higher Education* (New York: Columbia University Press, 1952), 157–58.

13. Ibid.

14. The issue of federal control became acute in the 1970s, under circumstances unrelated to research: see below, Chapter 8.

15. "Effects of Gifts and Contracts from Foundations, Government Agencies and Industry on the Administrative Integrity of the University: A Statement of Propositions," Seven Universities Meeting (1/28/59), Frederick E. Terman Papers (III, 48, 5), Stanford University Archives. The seven universities were Chicago, Columbia, Cornell, Harvard, Princeton, Stanford, and Yale.

16. Morris Bishop, *A History of Cornell* (Ithaca: Cornell University Press, 1962), 581.

17. Constance Reid, *Courant in Göttingen and New York: The Story of an Improbable Mathematician* (New York: Springer-Verlag, 1976), 284–85.

18. A similar point about loss of administrative control to faculty is made by Richard M. Freeland, *Academia's Golden Age: Universities in Massachusetts, 1945–1970* (New York: Oxford University Press, 1992), 167–68.

Chapter 3. The Development of Universities in the Postwar Era

1. The Massachusetts Institute of Technology

1. "Summary of Discussion on the Needs of the Physics Department" (12/5/56), Julius C. Stratton, Chancellor's Papers, Box 4: Physics, Institute Archives and Special Collections [IASC], MIT Libraries, Cambridge, Mass.

2. Roger L. Geiger, *To Advance Knowledge: The Growth of American Research Universities, 1900–1940* (New York: Oxford University Press, 1986), 177–83; MIT, *Annual*

Reports, 1940, "Registrar." For the overall development of MIT, see Richard M. Freeland, *Academia's Golden Age: Universities in Massachusetts, 1945–1970* (New York: Oxford University Press, 1992), 123–78.

3. MIT, *Annual Reports,* 1947, "Treasurer."

4. "Report of the Task Force on the Evolution of Interdisciplinary Forms" (March 1979), IASC. The histories of several of these units, including RLE, are presented in Stuart W. Leslie, "Profit and Loss: The Military and MIT in the Postwar Era," *Historical Studies in the Physical and Biological Sciences* 21 (1990):59–85.

5. MIT, *Annual Reports,* 1948, "Treasurer"; "Summary . . . Physics Department": the budget for general expenses and special research is arbitrary in that it was a partial contribution toward actual costs.

6. MIT, *Catalogue,* 1946, 1956; Physics Department Memo, "Teaching Loads" (4/25/52), Stratton Papers, 4: Physics. Since most MIT undergraduates were required to take two years of physics, the department had a heavy teaching load.

7. MIT, *President's Report,* 1948, 11–12; "President's Papers, Compton-Killian" AC-4, 238–39, IASC; "MIT-CIT Conference" (Spring 1956), Stratton Papers, 1: Caltech. Among other things, the oil companies were offered discounts on overhead in future research contracts. Companies participating were Standard Oil of New Jersey & Indiana, Texas Oil, Socony, Cities Service, and Humble Oil. See also, James R. Killian, Jr., *The Education of a College President: A Memoir* (Cambridge: MIT Press, 1985), 255–58; and Leslie, "Profit and Loss," who points out that the initial appeal to industry was unsuccessful and the Lab was initiated with a Navy contract (pp. 74–75).

8. MIT, *President's Report,* 1947, 19; 1948, 9–10; "MIT-CIT Conference"; Killian, *Education,* 253–54, 258–65.

9. Warren K. Lewis, Chairman, *Report of the Committee on Educational Survey* (Cambridge: Technology Press, 1949); Killian, *Education,* 79–82.

10. *Lewis Report,* 49, 61–64.

11. Ibid., 62–63.

12. Jerome B. Wiesner, "The Communications Sciences—Those Early Days," in *R.L.E.: 1946 + 20* (Cambridge: Research Laboratory of Electronics, 1966), 12–16. See also, Karl L. Wildes and Nilo A. Lindgren, *A Century of Electrical Engineering and Computer Science at MIT, 1882–1982* (Cambridge: MIT Press, 1985), 242–79; and Leslie, "Profit and Loss," 60–66.

13. Objectives of RLE as set forth by joint-military-MIT founding committee, quoted in Henry J. Zimmermann, "Research and Education," in *R.L.E.: 1946 + 20,* 17–21.

14. Albert G. Hill, "Why the Military?," ibid., 7–11.

15. Ibid.; Killian, *Education,* 63–67. In addition, each of the services had a scientific or technological advisory board, on which MIT's scientific leaders, together with those from other universities, invariably sat. The key figures at MIT, then, were involved in all stages of defining and fulfilling the military's scientific needs.

16. For the alacrity with which so major an undertaking was accepted, see Leslie, "Profit and Loss," 66.

17. Hill, "Why the Military?"; Killian, *Education,* 71–73.

18. "Report on the Evolution of Interdisciplinary Forms," 57–70; *R.L.E.: 1946 + 20,* 24–27.

19. Wiesner, "The Communications Sciences"; Norbert Wiener, *Cybernetics* (New York: Wiley, 1948). The complex interaction of Wiener and his ideas at MIT and the RLE defy brief description: for the ideas, see Wildes and Lindgren, *Century of Electrical Engineering,* 252–67; for Wiener himself, see Steve J. Heims, *John von Neumann and Norbert Wiener: From Mathematics to the Technologies of Life and Death* (Cambridge:

MIT Press, 1980). As explained by Heims, Wiener was opposed to postwar military research at MIT and refused any direct participation.

20. Wiesner, "Communication Sciences"; Morris Halle, "Linguistic Research in R.L.E." in *R.L.E.: 1946 + 20, 39–44.* Many important intellectual developments involved the interaction of more than one MIT lab. For example, some significant linguistics work took place in the acoustics lab.

21. Hill, "Why the Military?," 11.

22. Research Laboratory of Electronics, "Twelve Years of Basic Research, 1946–1958" (RLE: 1958), IASC.

23. "Report of the Evolution of Interdisciplinary Forms," 34–37 (quote p. 37); Killian, *Education,* 65–67.

24. Center for International Studies, *Annual Report,* 1957–58. Much of what follows draws upon "Report of the Evolution of Interdisciplinary Forms," 33–56.

25. E.g.: "we cannot amass a large amount of information on such a subject without the risk of being called upon to advise in the decision-making process itself": Stratton to Burchard (8/6/53); Killian to Stratton (9/28/56), Stratton Papers, "CIS."

26. "Memorandum for Robert A. Lovett on the Center for International Studies Visiting Committee, held May 1957" (9/30/57), Stratton Papers, "CIS."

27. One of the leading architects of that policy was W. W. Rostow, a charter member of CIS. Ithiel de Sola Pool and Lucien Pye of the Center were generally known for their defense of American policy.

28. During the 1970s the Center became much like similar centers at other universities: a home for visiting scholars and political science graduate students, a device for integrating scholars from several departments, and a holding company for faculty research grants: "Report on the Evolution of Interdisciplinary Forms," 55–56.

29. Michael A. Dennis, "Reconstructing Technical Practice: The Johns Hopkins University Applied Physics Laboratory and the Massachusetts Institute of Technology Instrumentation Laboratory after World War II," ms.

30. John Burchard, *Q.E.D.: MIT in World War II* (New York: Wiley, 1948); Killian, *Education,* 34–36.

31. "Memo on Instrumentation Lab" (1/12/55); "Memorandum for File [after conversation with C. S. Draper]" (9/5/56), Stratton Papers, "Aeronautical Engineering".

32. In 1967–68 the I-Lab paid $42,000 in faculty salaries, or 20 percent of salaries in the Aeronautics Department; It provided $111,000 for graduate assistants. From 1945 to 1969 987 student theses were related to I-Lab projects, not including 19 current Ph.D. theses in progress: from Instrumentation Lab, *Annual Report,* 1969, given in Dorothy Nelkin, *The University and Military Research: Moral Politics at M.I.T.* (Ithaca: Cornell University Press, 1972), 51.

33. "Memorandum for File" (9/5/56), Stratton Papers, "Aeronautical Engineering."

34. Nelkin, *Moral Politics at M.I.T.,* passim; see below, Chapter 8.

35. Specifically, Lincoln Lab had a more highly educated professional staff that spent more time on research and published more scientific papers. It also involved more MIT faculty as consultants: ibid., 136–37.

36. For some of the fruits of MIT research, see Wildes and Lindgren, *Century of Electrical Engineering,* passim. MIT research also helped to spawn the growth of the electronics industry along Route 128 around Boston: Christopher Rand, *Cambridge, U.S.A.: Hub of a New World* (New York: Oxford University Press, 1964).

37. MIT advertised its wartime research activities with an entire volume: Burchard, *Q.E.D.: MIT in World War II.* Freeland discusses President Compton's ambitious expansion policies: *Academia's Golden Age,* 131–36.

38. James R. Killian, Jr., and Arthur D. Hill, "For a Continental Defense," *The Atlantic* 192 (1953): 37–41.

39. During the 1920s negative feedback in this sense, specifically a snub by the Rocke-feller Foundation, was an important goad to diminishing the heavy reliance upon applied industrial research at MIT: Geiger, *To Advance Knowledge,* 180–81. MIT employed a system of visiting committees for each department or unit, thus generating considerable feedback. Committee members, however, were often from within the Tech orbit, and tended not to offer sharp criticism.

40. "Report on the Institutional Structures," 54, 65–66; Nelkin, *Moral Politics at M.I.T.,* 42–45.

2. The University of California, Berkeley

1. Clark Kerr, interview with author (11/20/86).

2. David P. Gardner, *The California Oath Controversy* (Berkeley: University of California Press, 1967); Verne A. Stadtman, *The University of California, 1868–1968* (New York: McGraw-Hill, 1970), 319–39; Hayward Keniston, *Graduate Study and Research in the Arts and Sciences at the University of Pennsylvania* (Philadelphia: University of Pennsylvania Press, 1959), 119.

3. In addition, Berkeley was favored in its postwar development by several back-ground factors: the pleasant climate and surroundings; the development of efficient coast-to-coast airline travel; private voluntary support, particularly from the Bay Area; the pro-pinquity of Stanford, which enlarged the academic community.

4. Stadtman, *California,* 257–80; Roger L. Geiger, *To Advance Knowledge* (New York: Oxford University Press, 1986), 211–13; J. L. Heilbron and Robert W. Seidel, *Lawrence and His Laboratory: A History of the Lawrence Berkeley Laboratory,* vol. 1 (Berkeley: University of California Press, 1990), 208–10.

5. Sproul to unit heads (10/25/43), CU-5, Box 1187, University of California Archives, Bancroft Library.

6. Verne A. Stadtman, ed., *Centennial Record of the University of California* (Berkeley: University of California Press, 1967). Real spending per student calculated from Annual Treasurer's Reports.

7. J. H. Cowley, "Post-War Building Priorities: A Report to the Regents" (2/24/50), CU-5, Box 1187, UC Archives.

8. C.f. John D. Millet, *Financing Higher Education in the United States* (New York: Columbia University Press, 1952), 329.

9. Carlos E. Kruytbosch, "Themes in the Legislative Analyst's Reports on the Budget of the University of California, 1947–1967," Space Sciences Laboratory, Restricted Series A-3 (April 1967) (My thanks to the author for providing this paper.) Stadtman, *California,* 374–75; Kerr interview (11/20/86).

10. Formulation of a postwar research policy at the University of California was orig-inally stimulated by ONR contracts (W. C. Pomeroy to R. G. Sproul [1/19/46], CU-5, Box 1190, Part III, UC Archives); organized research was endorsed by the University of California All-University Faculty Conferences, tentatively in 1949, and strongly in 1954 (*Proceedings . . . 4th Conference* [1949: 20–29]; . . . *9th Conference* [1954: 28–37]; in 1953 Sproul provided a strong endorsement of sponsored research in a major report to the Regents (4/30/53: CU-5, Box 1191, Part IV, CU Archives). A later positive endorse-ment of the university research role: "The Research Function of the University," *Pro-ceedings of the UC 15th All-University Conference* (University of California: 1960)). For an overview of the issues raised, focusing on the Berkeley case, see Carlos E. Kruytbosch,

"The Organization of Research in the University: The Case of Research Personnel," Ph.D. diss., UC Berkeley, 1970.

11. Stadtman, *California,* 371–73; Stadtman, ed. *Centennial Record,* 382–83; Kruytbosch, "Legislative Analyst's Report"; University support for research units in California might be contrasted with the stipulation of the Michigan Regents that the Survey Research Center be self-supporting (Chapter 2).

12. Berkeley's distinctiveness in this respect is, of course, a matter of degree: most universities espoused this same philosophy, but Berkeley seemed to come closer to fulfilling it. Exceptions could certainly be cited. In particular, E. O. Lawrence's was accustomed to pleasing patrons in order to get resources. Before the war he sought support by assisting medicine (below n.13), and afterward he continued applied research for the Manhattan Project and the AEC. Later, weapons-related research was diverted to Livermore: John L. Heilbron, Robert W. Seidel, and Bruce R. Wheaton, *Lawrence and His Laboratory: Nuclear Science at Berkeley, 1931–1961* (Berkeley: University of California, History of Science and Technology, 1981), 62–75.

13. Glenn T. Seaborg, ["autobiography"] in Irving Stone, ed., *There Was Light: Autobiography of a University: Berkeley: 1868–1968,* (Garden City, N.Y.: Doubleday, 1970), 49–72.

14. Glimpses of Lawrence's postwar laboratory may be found in Herbert F. York, *Making Weapons, Talking Peace: A Physicist's Odyssey from Hiroshima to Geneva* (New York: Basic Books, 1987), 30–42.

15. Robert W. Seidel, "Accelerating Science: The Postwar Transformation of the Lawrence's Radiation Laboratory," *Historical Studies in the Physical Sciences* 13 (1983): 375–400; Glenn T. Seaborg, "Nuclear Research and National Science Policy," Oral History, History of Science and Technology Project [HSTP] (1984), Berkeley: Bancroft Library, 174ff.

16. Manhattan Project director General Leslie Groves provided support for the projects listed below. Lawrence did not receive, however, the nuclear reactor that Seaborg had wanted; in fact, he had to support the lab he had promised Seaborg by redeploying the earlier Rockefeller Foundation grant: Seidel, "Accelerating Science," 379–84.

17. Ibid.; Heilbron, Seidel, and Wheaton, *Nuclear Science at Berkeley;* National Research Council, *Doctorate Production in United States Universities, 1936–1956* (Washington, D.C.: NRC, 1958).

18. A 1948 organizational chart for the Rad Lab is reproduced in Seidel, "Accelerating Science," 390–91; William Brobeck, "Engineering and Big-Machine Physics at the Radiation Laboratory," Oral History (HSTP, Berkeley, 1982).

19. The following material on Calvin is drawn chiefly from Melvin Calvin, "Chemistry and Chemical Biodynamics at Berkeley, 1937–1980," Oral History (HSTP, Berkeley, 1984). Berkeley may have had the finest department in physical chemistry in the country before the war. Calvin characterized the attitude toward research under G. N. Lewis: "that was the only thing you should do. That was the prime task." For an appreciation of the pressures in the department, see Martin D. Kamen, *Radiant Science, Dark Politics: A Memoir of the Nuclear Age* (Berkeley: University of California Press, 1985), 134–36.

20. Producing radioactive isotopes for medical research and cancer therapy had been a fundamental justification for funding E. O. Lawrence's cyclotrons before the war, and he clearly thought in those same terms immediately after the war, i.e., before the largesse of Groves and the AEC. In 1940 this concern had caused Lawrence to assign a research program to Martin Kamen that led directly to the discovery of Carbon-14: Kamen, *Radiant Science,* 127–32.

21. In light of the criticism persistent in the postwar research system that contract research had destroyed the flexibility needed for science (and formerly available through 'fluid' research funds), it is noteworthy that large operaters like Calvin and Lawrence re-created needed flexibility through a multitude of grants or contracts, and the leeway in shifting funds that these permitted.

22. "I had set out to . . . understand molecules, and I was doing it. The price was to serve medical physics": Calvin, "Chemistry and Chemical Biodynamics," 181: see also, 133.

23. Gardiner, *Oath Controversy,* 251.

24. Stadtman, *California,* 336–39; Kerr interview (11/20/86).

25. The following is drawn chiefly from Kerr interview (11/20/86); also see Stadtman, *California,* 376–99.

26. Margaret T. Hodgen, "The Department of Social Institutions, 1919–1946" (1971), ms. UC Archives; Reinhard Bendix, *From Berlin to Berkeley: German-Jewish Identities,* (New Brunswick, N.J.: Transactions Books, 1986), 229–40; "Special Problems: Social Institutions," Cu-5, Box 1197, UC Archives. Teggart could inspire strong loyalties in his students: Robert A. Nisbet, ["autobiography"], in Stone, ed., *There Was Light,* 293–310.

27. Edward Strong to A. R. Davis (11/21/47); Reinhard Bendix, interview with author (11/21/86).

28. Herbert Blumer, "Department of Sociology and Social Institutions: Plan of Development (5 Years)" (1/19/53), Sproul Presidential Papers, Sociology and Social Institutions: 1952, UC Archives; departmental membership can be traced in the University of California, *Catalogue;* Kerr interview (11/20/86); Bendix interview (11/21/86); Kenniston, *Graduate Study;* Allen M. Carrter, *An Assessment of Quality in Graduate Education* (Washington, D.C.: ACE, 1966).

29. "An Academic Plan for the Berkeley Campus, University of California (June 1957), UC Archives.

30. The College of Letters and Sciences were to receive the bulk of the new positions (cf. Engineering, +85%; Professions, +68%; within the College the departments designated for 100% increases or more were: Anthropology (216%), Mathematics (204%), Physics (183%), Philosophy (177%), Chemistry & Chemical Engineering (152%), History (130%), Zoology (127%), Sociology and Social Institutions (119%), and Psychology (100%).

31. Seaborg, "Nuclear Research and National Science Policy," 245–48.

32. Master Plan Survey Team, *A Master Plan for Higher Education in California, 1960–1975* (Sacramento: Assembly of the State of California, 1960); Neil J. Smelser and Gabriel Almond, eds., *Public Higher Education in California* (Berkeley: University of California Press, 1974), 28–32 & passim.; and, retrospectively, OECD, *Review of Higher Education Policy in California* (Paris, OECD, 1989).

33. E.g. Talcott Parsons and Gerald Platt, *The American University* (Cambridge: Harvard University Press, 1973).

3. Yale University

1. Yale University, "Reports to the President, 1950–51": Graduate School, 2; Yale College, 20: Yale University Archives (hereafter YUA).

2. Charles Seymour, Presidential Papers, YUA, YRG 2-A-15, [series] I, [box] 59: [folder] 518.

3. Yale University, *Treasurer's Report,* 1940, 1947, 1954.

4. Yale University, "Reports," 1949–50: Graduate School, 2; Brooks Mather Kelley, *Yale: A History* (New Haven: Yale University Press, 1974), 436.

5. Seymour Papers, YUA, YRG 2-A-15; I, 59: 518. This ranking must be regarded as somewhat anomalous, not just because it was the only one ever to rate Yale number one. 1946 was hardly a propitious moment, since the changes wrought by the war could not yet be adequately assessed. Several universities, including Michigan and Stanford, refused to participate. The departments that were rated tended to favor Yale's strength in the humanities, while engineering departments were not included.

6. Yale University, *President's Report,* 1946, 18–19; Rebecca S. Lowen, "Strategies for Supporting the Sciences: Yale and Stanford in the 1950s," ms. Yale University Program on Nonprofit Organizations (Aug. 1986). My thanks to the author for sharing this draft.

7. Kelley, *Yale,* 415–18.

8. Yale University, *President's Report,* 1949, 25; 1950, 12.

9. Yale University, "Reports," Yale College, 1951; Sheffield Scientific School, 1952; University Council Committee on the Division of the Sciences, Draft Report (5/10/54), A. Whitney Griswold Presidential Papers, YUA, YRG 2-A-16, 218: 2022; Roger L. Geiger, *To Advance Knowledge* (New York: Oxford University Press, 1986), 203–7.

10. Sheffield Scientific School, Administrative Records, YUA, YRG 31-B, III, 49: 534.

11. Loc. cit. Other physicists apparently under consideration were Nobel Laureate Carl Anderson of Caltech and Lee A. Dubridge of Rochester University.

12. Yale University, "Reports," Sheffield Scientific School, 1950, 1952. Breit received a named chair in 1957 and became an emeritus professor in 1968.

13. Yale University, "Departmental Reports: Physics, 1948" Office of the Secretary, YUA, YRG-4-A, IV, 343: 773.

14. Yale University, "Departmental Reports: Physics, 1953," Office of the Secretary, YUA, YRG-4-A, IV, 347: 806.

15. Yale University, "Reports," Graduate School, 1948, 7.

16. Yale University, "Departmental Reports," Physics, 1952, YUA, YRG-4-A, IV, 346: 801; Physics, 1953, loc. cit.

17. Yale University, "Reports," 1953, Yale College, 2.

18. Yale University, "Departmental Reports," Physics, 1953, loc. cit.

19. University Council Committee on the Division of the Sciences, "Report for 1956," A. W. Griswold Presidential Papers, YUA, YRG 2-A-16, 218: 2022; Hayward Keniston, *Graduate Study in the Arts and Sciences at the University of Pennsylvania* (Philadelphia: University of Pennsylvania Press, 1959), 141.

20. W. W. Watson to A. W. Griswold (5/25/59), Griwold Papers, YUA, YRG 2-A-16, 184; 1667.

21. President's Committee on the Natural Sciences and Mathematics, "Interim Report" (Sept. 1959), Griswold Papers, YUA, YRG 2-A-16, 184: 1667.

22. Yale University, "Departmental Reports," Economics, 1945–46, Office of the Secretary, YUA, YRG 4-A, IV, 343: 768. The development of the economics department is also described in the memoirs of John Perry Miller: *Creating Academic Settings: High Craft and Low Cunning* (New Haven: J. Simeon, 1991), 39–42, 61–65.

23. Yale University, Departmental Reports," Economics, 1947–48, loc. cit. 344: 776.

24. "Statement Concerning Texts Currently Being Used in Economics 10 and Elementary Economics at Yale," and Reynolds to Griswold (3/3/52), Griswold Papers, YUA, YRG A-16, 83:747; University Council Committee, "Report on Department of Economics" (1/21/52), and University Council, "Interim Report of the Committee on

the Social Sciences" (5/4/51), Griswold Papers, YUA, YRG A-16, 218: 2023; Lloyd G. Reynolds, "The State of Economics at Yale," *Yale Alumni Magazine* (Nov. 1951), 18–20.

25. "Departmental Reports," Economics, 1952–53, loc. cit. 346: 803; William F. Buckley, *God and Man at Yale*.

26. "Department Reports," Economics, 1951–52, 1953–54, loc. cit. 346: 796; 155: 10; Keniston, *Graduate Study*, 129.

27. Keniston, *Graduate Study*, 127, 146: Chemistry ranked a strong sixth; sociology a poor tenth. Yale had revitalized Chemistry by bringing in a renowned chemist, John Kirkwood, to rebuild the department (he died suddenly in 1959); with sociology a strategy of surrounding the department with strength had proven ineffective: "Reports," Yale College, 1950–51; 1954–55, 1957–58.

28. Kelley, *Yale*, 425–61. John Perry Miller, interview with author (9/29/86). The disdain for institutes was widespread at Yale: President Seymour allowed the renowned Institute of Human Relations (1929–49) to expire by not seeking continued funding.

29. The forced migration of the Institute of International Relations is documented in Joseph H. Willits, *Diary, 1950–51*, Rockefeller Archive Center: quotes pp. 17, 13. Willits is discussed below in Chapter 4.

30. Willits, *Diary, 1950–51*, 13, 19, 110–11, 118.

31. Ibid., 13, 44–48; quotes pp. 47, 48.

32. Ibid., 110–11; John S. Brubacher, *The Department of Education at Yale University, 1891–1958* (New Haven, 1960), YUA.

33. Yale University, *President's Report*, 1952, 8–11; 1957, 30–31. Griswold's views—pro-business, but anti-industrial research—are documented in Lowen, "Strategies for Supporting the Sciences."

34. John Perry Miller writes: "In retrospect it seems to me that . . . Yale missed an opportunity to mount a distinguished program in International Relations in the ensuing decades. Despite many efforts Yale was never able to recoup its losses" (*Creating Academic Settings*, 65).

35. Keniston, *Graduate Study*, 120–23. The Yale Library housed humanistic ORUs in the Boswell Papers, the Walpole Papers and the Benjamin Franklin Papers. The Institute of Human Relations was allowed to expire in 1949, doomed essentially by the absence of university backing.

36. Yale University, "Reports," Yale College, 1957.

37. Yale University, "Reports," Graduate School, 1960, 1961. Miller interview (9/29/86).

38. "President's Committee on Natural Sciences, "Interim Report," loc. cit.

39. Kelley, *Yale*, 447.

40. Miller, *Creating Academic Settings*, 93–126.

41. Seymour B. Sarasohn, *The Making of an American Psychologist: An Autobiography* (San Francisco: Jossey-Bass, 1988), 230.

Chapter 4. Private Foundations and the Research Universities, 1945–1960

1. Foundations and Academic Social Science

1. Roger L. Geiger, *To Advance Knowledge* (New York: Oxford University Press, 1986).

2. Ford Foundation, *Annual Report*, 1960; Francis X. Sutton, "The Ford Foundation: The Early Years," *Daedelus* 116 (Winter 1987): 41–91.

3. Stella L. Deignan and Esther Miller, "The Support of Research in Medical and Allied Fields for the Period 1946 Through 1951," *Science* 115 (1952): 321-43.

4. There was virtually no provision of federal support for social scientific research in universities after World War II. Social science was originally excluded from the purview of the new National Science Foundation: Samuel Z. Klausner, "The Bid to Nationalize the Social Sciences," in *The Nationalization of the Social Sciences,* Samuel Z. Klausner and Victor M. Lidz, eds. (Philadelphia: University of Pennsylvania Press, 1986), 3-40.

5. "Grants—by Categories, 1928-1955," Carnegie Corporation Archives [CCA]; Rockefeller Foundation, *Annual Reports;* Carnegie Corporation, *Annual Report,* 1943, 14.

6. Keppel, Dollard, and Gardner are characterized in Ellen Condliffe Lagemann, *The Politics of Knowledge: The Carnegie Corporation, Philanthropy, and Public Policy* (Middletown, Conn.: Wesleyan University Press, 1989), 100-22, 158-60, 182-86.

7. Charles Dollard, "Note" (12/7/45): "Policy and Program, 1943-1946," CCA.

8. John W. Gardner, "A Program for the Carnegie Corporation" (7/3/46): "Policy and Program, 1943-46"; Devereux C. Josephs, "A Long Term Program" (9/17/46): "Policy and Program, 1943-46," CCA.

9. Josephs, "Long Term Program" (9/17/46); John Gardner, "A Survey of CC Fields of Interest" (9/49): "Policy and Program, 1947-55," CCA; in the postwar decade the Carnegie Corporation grants were classified as follows:

International Affairs	$13.1 million
Social Sciences	6.0
Education	19.7
TIAA & Misc.	9.6
other	4.1

Source: "CC Grants—1946-55" (n.d.): "Grants—by Categories, 1928-1955," CCA. Education became a major emphasis of the Carnegie Corporation under John Gardner (1955-65): Lagemann, *Politics of Knowledge,* 182-215.

10. Gardner, "Program" (7/3/46) CCA.

11. On the Russian Research Center, see above, Chapter 2; also Lagemann, *Politics of Knowledge,* 172-75.

12. Carnegie Corporation, *Annual Reports,* 1947, 1948.

13. Josephs, "Long Term Program" (9/17/46) CCA.

14. "Discussions of DCJ and Dr. Robert T. Crane on General Questions Connected with Social Science Projects and on Carnegie Corporation's Place in the Picture" (10/23/45): "Program and Planning, 1943-1946," CCA.

15. Ibid.; Beardsley Ruml's key role in developing social science in the 1920s is explained in Geiger, *To Advance Knowledge,* 149-60; and, Joan Bulmer and Martin Bulmer, "Philanthropy and Social Science in the 1920s: Beardsley Ruml and the Laura Spelman Rockefeller Memorial, 1922-29," *Minerva* 19 (1981): 347-407.

16. Gardner, "Survey of CC Fields of Interest" (9/49) CCA; also see *Annual Reports.* Earlier, the Carnegie Corporation had sponsored Gunner Myrdal's classic study, *An American Dilemma:* Lagemann, *Politics of Knowledge,* 136-46.

17. "For the Information of the Trustees" (10/21/48): "Policy and Program, 1947-1955"; "Request for 5 year Renewal Grant" (3/8/52): University of Michigan—Center for Japanese Studies, CCA; Gardner, "Survey of CC Fields of Interest."

18. [John Gardner], "JG's Visit to Center" (10/27/49); [William Marvel], "WM Memo" (2/18-19/53); [idem.], "WM Memo" (11/18/55): University of Michigan—Center for Japanese Studies," CCA.

19. "Memo" (2/25/52); [Caryl P. Haskins], "CPH Memo on Institute of European Studies" (3/7/52): Columbia University—Institute for European Studies," CCA. Also not recommended for renewal were the centers at Johns Hopkins, Minnesota, Wisconsin, North Carolina, and Texas: "Request" (3/8/52).

20. Carnegie Corporation, *Annual Report,* 1949, 23; "Survey of CC Fields of Interest" (9/49).

21. Lagemann, *Politics of Knowledge,* 165–72.

22. Marvel, "WM Memo" (11/18/55).

23. The Corporation possessed some social science expertise in Pendleton Herring (Ph.D., political science, Johns Hopkins, 1928), who was on the staff immediately after the war but left to become Director of the SSRC in 1947; John Gardner (Ph.D. psychology, Stanford, 1935) had been a college teacher, somewhat disillusioned with his subject, and Charles Dollard had been an administrator at Wisconsin (see note 6, above).

24. Carnegie Corporation, *Annual Report,* 1954, 29–30.

25. Joseph H. Willits, "Social Implications of Atomic Energy to the RF" (12/5/45); Willits to Chester I. Barnard (3/21/46); Rockefeller Foundation Archives [RFA] R.G. 3, series 910: box 1, folder 7, Rockefeller Archives Center.

26. Rockefeller Foundation Social Science Division appropriations by field for 1939–49 were as follows:

Functioning of political democracy	$1.5 million
Functioning of economy & econ. history	6.3
International relations	3.7
Development of social sciences in Europe	1.7
Interpersonal/intergroup relations	1.3
Other	0.6
Research and training agencies	1.7
Fellowships	2.0
Grants in aid	2.2
Total	$22.0 million

"Appropriations Data—SS Program, 1939–1949": RFA 3, 910: 3, 18.

27. Willits wrote that the majority of social scientists "are narrow men: and the improvements of the last 30 years [in s.s. education] have been, for all their value, narrowing in their influence": Willits to Barnard (3/21/46); RFA, R.G.3, Series 910, Box 1, Folder 7.

28. On Willits's full list were: Food Research Institute, Stanford; National Bureau of Economic Research; Russian Institute, Columbia; Institute of International Studies, Yale; Center for Studies in Communications, Yale; Industrial Research Department, Wharton School; Sociology Department, Chicago; Industrial Relations Center, Chicago; Harvard Business School (Human Relations in Industry); Population Research, Princeton; Research Center in Entrepreneurial History, Harvard; Bureau of Business and Economic Research, California; Scripps Foundation, Miami Univ. "JHW Memo" (1/31/49), RFA, R.G. 3, Series 910, Box 1, Folder 8.

29. J.H. Willits, "Future Program in Light of Reduced Budget, 1948–49" (1/24/49), RFA, R.G. 3, Series 910, Box, 3, Folder 18. The Ford Foundation would later sponsor institutional self-studies similar in spirit to Willits's idea: see below.

30. See above, Chapter 3 (Yale).

31. Joseph H. Willits, *Diary, 1950–51* (May 10, 1951), 164–65; RFA.

32. J.H. Willits, "Social Science Program," Trustees Meeting, 12/7/49. RFA, R.G. 3, Series 910, Box, 3, Folder 18.

33. Norman S. Buchanan, "Notes on Rockefeller Foundation Program in the Social Sciences" (Aug. 1955). RFA, R.G. 3, Series 910, Box 3, Folder 19.

34. For the origins of the Ford Foundation, see Francis X. Sutton, "The Ford Foundation: The Early Years," *Daedalus* 116 (1987): 41–92; the classic account remains Dwight Macdonald, *The Ford Foundation: The Men and the Millions* (New York: Reynal, 1956); see also Waldemar Nielson, *The Big Foundations* (New York: 1976). For the politics of the Board, see Donald K. David, "Oral History" (3/14/72); and Waldemar Nielson, "Oral History" (10/5/72), Ford Foundation Archives [FFA].

35. "Report of the Study for the Ford Foundation on Policy and Program" (Detroit, Mich.: Ford Foundation, Nov. 1949); Donald G. Marquis, "Oral History" (10/27/72), FFA, 1–7; Sutton, "Ford Foundation."

36. Robert A. McCaughey, *International Studies and Academic Enterprise* (New York: Columbia University Press, 1984); Ralph L. Nelson, "The Production and Use of Economic Knowledge: Economic Research Sponsored by Private Foundations," *American Economic Review, Papers and Proceedings* 56 (May 1966): 519–29.

37. Marquis, "Oral History," 8–9; Bernard Berelson, "The Ford Foundation Behavioral Sciences Program: Final Report, 1951–57" (Sept. 1957), FFA: 002074, p. 4.

38. The Ford Foundation Behavioral Sciences Program, "Proposed Plan for the Development of the Behavioral Sciences Program" (Dec. 1951), FFA: 002072, pp. 2, 11–16.

39. Ibid., 16–19; Berelson, "final Report"; William McPeak, "Behavioral Sciences Program (1951–1957): Report and Appraisal," (Dec. 1961), FFA: 003156, quote p. 2.

40. McPeak, "Behavioral Sciences Program," 6–7, 16.

41. Ibid., 4–7; Bernard Berelson, "Oral History" (7/7/72), FFA, 19–28. Among the controversies, a proposed new edition of the *Encyclopedia of the Social Sciences,* which was rejected by the Board because some of the multitude of authors were sure to have past connections with the Communist Party: Berelson, "Oral History," 23.

42. Bernard Berelson, "Ford Foundation Behavioral Science Program: Final Report, 1951–57," (Sept. 1957), FFA: 002074, p. 20; Berelson, "Oral History," 32–46.

43. Bernard Berelson, "Five Year Report on Program V" (Aug. 1956), FFA: 010420, 3–4.

44. Ford Foundation, *Annual Report,* 1953, 71; W. Allen Wallis, "The 1953–54 Program of University Surveys of the Behavioral Sciences" FFA: 002918, 2–3.

45. "University of Chicago Survey of the Behavioral Science" (1954), FFA: 53–91; *The Behavioral Sciences at Harvard: Report by a Faculty Committee* (June 1954) (Cambridge: Harvard University, 1954); "The Stanford Survey of the Behavioral Sciences, 1953–54," FFA, 53–93. At this time, in an unrelated decision, the Center for Advanced Study in Behavioral Science was placed at Stanford on land donated by the University: Berelson, "Oral History," 49–53.

46. Wallis, "University Surveys," 43; interview with Dr. Francis X. Sutton (4/6/87).

47. Ford Foundation, *Annual Report,* 1955: Chicago received a separate $1 million grant for research on law and the behavioral sciences; Berelson, "Final Report," 3.

48. Wallis, "University Surveys," 4–5.

49. "Proposed Plan" (12/51), 45. Some early fellows did bring students with them: e.g. Seymour Martin Lipset, "Socialism and Sociology" in Irving L. Horowitz, ed., *Sociological Self-Images: A Collective Portrait* (Beverly Hills: Sage, 1969), 159.

50. Wallis, "University Surveys," 36–38. This same conclusion surfaced in the deliberations of both the Carnegie Corporation and the Rockefeller Social Science Division; it was indeed productive, but represented the antithesis of "good foundation practice," i.e. program-directed grants, strategic intervention, and limited involvement.

51. Berelson, "Five Year Report," 2–3. As for the other three "particularly good" programs, the Chicago law program was basically an application of the behavioral sciences

to topics of legal concern; the mental health program seems to have been straightforward academic research; and a grant to Johns Hopkins assisted the creation of a social relations department, largely to be a combination of sociology and public health, while support for MIT went toward building conventional departments.

52. Francis X. Sutton, "American Foundations and the Social Sciences," *Items* 39 (Dec. 1985): 57–64.

53. A full breakdown of social science grants to leading universities, by foundation and triennia, appears in Roger L. Geiger, "American Foundations and Academic Social Science, 1945–1960," *Minerva* 26 (1988): 315–41, [333–35].

54. Geiger, *To Advance Knowledge*, 161.

55. Sources: Annual Reports of the Carnegie Corporation, Rockefeller Foundation, and Social Science Research Council; data provided by the Ford Foundation Archives; National Research Council, *Doctorate Production in American Universities, 1936–1956* (Washington, D.C., 1958); Hayward Keniston, *Graduate Study and Research in the Arts and Sciences at the University of Pennsylvania* (Philadelphia: University of Pennsylvania Press, 1959).

56. Steven Schlossman, Michael Sedlak, and Harold Wechsler, "The 'New Look': The Ford Foundation and the Revolution in Business Education," *Selections* 3 (Winter 1987): 11–30.

57. Ibid.; *Behavioral Sciences at Harvard,* passim; Paul A. Samuelson, "Economics in a Golden Age: A Personal Memoir," in *Twentieth-Century Sciences: Studies in the Biography of Ideas,* Gerald J. Holton, ed. (New York: Norton, 1972), 155–70; Benton Johnson and Miriam M. Johnson, "Integrating the Social Sciences: Theoretical and Empirical Research and Training in the Department of Social Relations at Harvard," in *Nationalization of the Social Sciences,* 131–40; and above, Chapter 2.

58. For sociology, see Edward Shils, "Tradition, Ecology"; and above, Chapter 2.

59. Alexander G. Ruthven, *A Naturalist in Two Worlds: Random Recollections of a University President* (Ann Arbor: University of Michigan Press, 1963), 118–19; "University of Michigan Survey of the Behavioral Sciences" (7/1/54), FFA: 53–92, 145–46, 230–31.

60. A high Ford Foundation official commented on a different matter: "I have reluctantly come to the conclusion that most people at Yale University tend to look inward in connection with problems which affect education, rather than looking outward. In other words, there is a sort of self-satisfaction about Yale": Thomas H. Carroll, "Memorandum Re: Technical Development of the Behavioral Sciences Under Ford Foundation Auspices" (n.d. [1952?]), FFA: 010586, 3.

61. E.g., A glimpse inside Minnesota's seventh ranked sociology department may be had from Don Martindale, *The Romance of a Profession: A Case History in the Sociology of Sociology* (St. Paul, Minn.: Windflower Pub., 1976).

62. McCaughey, *International Studies.*

63. Schlossman et al., "The New Look." The effort to upgrade business schools was renewed in the 1960s after two critical reports: R. A. Gordon and J. E. Howell, *Higher Education for Business* (New York: Columbia University Press, 1959); and F. C. Pierson, *The Education of American Businessmen* (New York: McGraw-Hill, 1959).

64. Edward Shils, "Tradition, Ecology, and Institution in the History of Sociology," *Daedelus* 99 (1970): 760–825, esp. p. 795. Also, George C. Homans, *Coming to My Senses: The Autobiography of a Sociologist* (New Brunswick, N.J.: Transaction Books, 1984), 303–5.

65. Nicholas C. Mullins, *Theory and Theory Groups in Contemporary American Sociology* (New York: Harper & Row, 1973), 105–28.

66. Shils, "Tradition, Ecology," 796–97; above, Chapter 3.

67. Karl W. Deutsch, John Platt, Dieter Senghaas, "Conditions Favoring Major Advances in Social Science," *Science,* 171 (1971): 450–58.

68. Idem. Letter, *Science,* 172 (1971): 1192.

2. Foundation Support for University Advancement

1. Carnegie Corporation, *Annual Report,* 1956.

2. James W. Armsey, "Special Program in Education" (3/15/60), FFA: 010417A, 1.

3. Sources: Ford Foundation, *Annual Reports,* 1957–1966.

4. Francis X. Sutton, "The Ford Foundation: The Early Years," *Daedalus* 116 (Winter 1987): 41–92; Ford Foundation, *Annual Reports,* 1955, 1960.

5. A riposte from the foundation world: Carnegie Corporation of New York, *Comments upon Recent Congressional Investigations of Foundations* (Aug. 1955) (New York: Carnegie Corporation, 1955).

6. Ford Foundation, *Annual Report,* 1957; technical institutes like MIT were excluded from accomplishment grants.

7. Waldemar Nielson, *The Big Foundations* (New York: Columbia University Press, 1976); Macdonald, *The Ford Foundation.*

8. Yale University, *Treasurer's Report,* 1957.

9. The presidency of Henry Heald, generally, was noted for largesse to the universities: Nielson accused him of regarding the foundation as "a kind of banking partner to higher education": *Big Foundations,* 92.

10. John Price Jones Co., *Surveys.* Cf. below, Table 6.

11. James W. Armsey, "Special Program in Education: Assumptions" (3/15/60), FFA, 010417.

12. F. C. Ward to McGeorge Bundy (8/30/68), FFA, 002379; "Special Program in Education: HTH Notes, March 1960 Trustees Meeting," FFA, 010417.

13. "HTH Notes, March 1960"; for Stanford, see below, Chapter 5.

14. Clearly the Ford Foundation had felt pressured to expand the Challenge Grants Program: Ward to Bundy (8/30/68), 3. For that reason Ward felt that the two desiderata of high selectivity and high visibility were incompatible: "the conspicuousness and symbolic weight of major support from the Ford Foundation, as part of an announced program for which many institutions are theoretically eligible, makes it very unlikely that the Foundation would find it possible to confine the program to steady, recurrent general support of a very limited number of institutions over a substantial period of time. The record of diffusion during the Special Program [i.e. Challenge Grants] is not auspicious in this regard": ibid., 5–6.

15. Armsey, "Special Program" (3/15/60); Ward to Bundy (8/30/68), 3–4.

16. Ward to Bundy (8/30/68), 3–4.

17. Ibid., 6–7.

18. Ibid.

19. Sources: John Price Jones Co. *Surveys;* Council for Aid to Education, *Voluntary Support of Education, 1985–86* (New York: CFAE, 1987).

Chapter 5. University Advancement from the Postwar Era to the 1960s

1. Stanford University

1. Ray Lyman Wilbur, *Memoirs, 1875–1949* (Stanford: Stanford University Press, 1960); J. Pearce Mitchell, *Stanford University, 1916–1941* (Stanford: Stanford University

Press, 1958); Edith R. Mirielees, *Stanford: The Story of a University* (New York: Putnam's, 1959).

2. "Mark X" (1/21/60), Box 23, J. E. Wallace Sterling Papers, Stanford University Archives and Special Collections. These concerns were of long standing and had been the focus of a meeting of Stanford leaders in 1941: Rebecca Lowen, "'Exploiting a Wonderful Oportunity': Stanford University, Industry and the Federal Government, 1937–1965" (Ph.D. diss., Stanford University, 1990), 12–22.

3. "Faculty-Staff—Prospective, 1950–51," Box 15, Sterling Papers; Frank A. Medeiros, "The Sterling Years at Stanford: A Study in the Dynamics of Institutional Change" (Ph.D. diss., Stanford University, 1979), 96–97.

4. Frederick Emmons Terman, "Oral History" (History of Science and Technology Program, U.C. Berkeley Bancroft Library, 1984), 115.

5. Stuart W. Leslie and Bruce Hevly, "Steeple Building at Stanford: Electrical Engineering, Physics and Microwave Research," *Proceedings of the IEEE* 73,7 (July 1985): 1169–80; quote p. 1176 [1943].

6. For the development of electronics at Stanford see, ibid.; and Stuart W. Leslie, "Playing the Education Game to Win: The Military and Interdisciplinary Research at Stanford," *Historical Studies in the Physical and Biological Sciences* 18,1 (1987): 55–58. The Microwave Laboratory is also treated in Lowen, "Exploiting," 77–103.

7. At the end of the war, ties with industry were seen by Stanford leaders as a source of research funds, and thus a partial solution to the university's predicament. This line of thought lay behind several important institutional decisions (the Microwave Laboratory, the Stanford Research Institute), and remained important even after the federal role in the postwar research economy became evident: Lowen, "Exploiting," 50–51 & passim.

8. Leslie, "Playing the Education Game," 73.

9. Terman, "Oral History," 127–28; Medeiros, "Sterling Years," 106–14.

10. The Stanford Research Institute was envisaged as having a closer relationship with the university than it subsequently did, since applied work for the military strongly influenced its evolution: Lowen, "Exploiting," 50–76.

11. Terman, "Oral History," 120, 138–42.

12. Leslie, "Playing the Education Game," 73. Also see Robert Kargon, Stuart W. Leslie, and Erica Schoenberger, "Far Beyond Big Science: Science Regions and the Organization of Research and Development," in Peter Galison and Bruce Hevly, eds., *Big Science: The Growth of Large-Scale Research* (Stanford: Stanford University Press, 1992), 334–54.

13. Robert Richardson Sears, "Oral History" (Stanford Oral History Project, Stanford Libraries, 1984), 29–31.

14. At issue was the status of associate professors, who were technically term appointments, but treated in practice as tenured: "Memo to J.E.W. Sterling: Procedures for Senior Academic Appointments" (10/31/56); "F. E. Terman to J.E.W. Sterling" (11/5/56), Frederick E. Terman Papers, III, 43, "Rhinelander, Philip: 1956–61," Stanford University Archives and Special Collections.

15. Quoted in Medeiros, "Sterling Years," 122.

16. "Report of the Planning Committee for the Ford Foundation Grant" (9/8/51); "Five Year Program, '55–56," Box A12; Donald C. McKay, "Survey of the Behavioral Sciences" (3/21/54), Box 49, Sterling Papers.

17. "Report of the Planning Committee for the Ford Foundation Grant" (9/8/51), Box A12, Sterling Papers; "Sociology, 1955–58," III, 48, Terman Papers; "Memo, Ernest R. Hilgard to J.E.W. Sterling" (1/4/55); and "Ernest R. Hilgard to Bernard Berelson" (1/6/55), III, 4, Terman Papers.

18. Sears, "Oral History," 34, 57.

19. McKay, "Survey"; "Report of the Visiting Committee" (Sept. 1954), *The Stanford Survey of the Behavioral Sciences, 1953-1954,* 53-93, Ford Foundation Archives.

20. "Commission on Financing Higher Education, 1950-53," Box 12, Sterling Papers.

21. Medeiros, "Sterling Years," 101-22; sources of voluntary support to Stanford are given in Council for Financial Aid to Education, *Voluntary Support of Education* [title varies] (1957-).

22. "J.E.W. Sterling to R. Gaither" (1/16/50), Box 49, Sterling Papers.

23. "William W. McPeak to J.E.W. Sterling" (Aug. 1951), Box 49, Sterling Papers.

24. Steven Schlossman, Michael Sedlak, and Harold Wechsler, "The 'New Look': The Ford Foundation and the Revolution in Business Education," *Selections* III,3 (Winter 1987): 11-27.

25. Sterling had wooed Dean William C. DeVane of Yale—an ambitious and unsuccessful gambit: "J.E.W. Sterling to W. C. DeVane" (7/6/51), Box 15, Sterling Papers.

26. Sears, "Oral History," 41.

27. "Biology—Dept. Head: Dept. Reappraisal," III, 4, Terman Papers.

28. Quoted in Medeiros, "Sterling Years" 125.

29. "F. E. Terman to J. J. Corson" (3/12/58), III, 13, Terman Papers.

30. Terman, "Oral History," 124.

31. Terman, "Oral History," 122; Sears, "Oral History," 52; "R. R. Sears to F. E. Terman" (8/27/65); and R. R. Sears to J.E.W. Sterling" (6/15/65), III, 4, "Biology," Terman Papers; Lowen, "Exploiting," 201-18.

32. "FET Notes on PHR (basis for discussion with WS)" (Summer 1961), III, 43, Terman Papers. "Memo, F. E. Terman to P. H. Rhinelander: Provost's activity in filling vacancies" (2/28/58), III, 43, Terman Papers.

33. Rhinelander was caught between Terman and the political science department in a dispute over the appointment of a professor with leftist views in 1958. He took the part of the department and thus angered Terman, who ultimately rejected the appointment: Lowen, "Exploiting," 206, 229n.

34. "A Program for Faculty Planning" (Oct. 1967); "Draft—Faculty Planning" (9/25/69), III, 64, Terman Papers.

35. Kenneth M. Cuthbertson, "Long-Range Financial Planning," in *Long-Range Planning in Higher Education.* ed. Owen A. Knorr (Boulder: Western Interstate Commission for Higher Education, 1965), 66; Medeiros, "Sterling Years," 177-86.

36. "Stanford's Minimum Financial Needs in the Years Ahead" (10/10/59), XIV, 18, Terman Papers.

37. Cuthbertson, "Long-Range Financial Planning," 67.

38. "Background to Faculty and Staff: Ford $25 million grant offer" (9/23/60), III, 25, Terman Papers. Voluntary support totals from Council for Financial Aid to Education, *Voluntary Support for Education.*

39. Sears, "Oral History," 44-45, 60-63.

40. "Stanford's Minimum Financial Needs, 17-19; Medeiros, "Sterling Years," 218-19.

41. Sears, "Oral History," 60.

42. Leslie, "Playing the Education Game," 59-60.

43. Medeiros, "Sterling Years," 214-17. The median Scholastic Aptitude Test Scores for freshmen entering Stanford increased from 533/533 (verbal/math) in 1954 to 661/665 in 1963; and Stanford rose to third in the number of National Merit Scholars: Kenneth Cuthbertson, "The Case for Plant Funds at Stanford" (5/11/64), Box 15, Sterling Papers.

44. From 1953 to 1963 applications to graduate standing increased from 1586 to 7588, and Stanford went from ninth to fourth place in the number of NSF Fellowship Holders, and eleventh to fourth place in the number of Woodrow Wilson Fellowship Holders: Cuthbertson, "Case for Plant Funds"; costs of instruction were monitored by Terman: "Direct Costs of instruction/student credit hour," III, 79, Terman Papers. Also see below, Chapter 7, for data on Stanford's growth.

45. National Science Foundation, *Federal Support for Academic Science, Fiscal Years 1963–66* (Washington, D.C.: 1967).

46. "Draft—Faculty Planning" (9/25/69), III, 64, Terman Papers.

47. Daniel S. Greenberg, *The Politics of Pure Science* (New York: New American Library, 1967), 224–36; Leslie, "Playing the Education Game," 80–87.

48. "Report of Staff Meetings of Feb. 7–8, 1958" III, 13, Terman Papers.

49. These cases are detailed in Lowen's valuable study: "Exploiting," 201–18. She concludes that the Stanford Administration took the part of outside sponsors of research and thus became "a proxy for those sponsors" (277). This is no doubt true; however, universities can ignore societal support for new and innovative fields of research only at their intellectual and financial peril.

50. Sears, "Oral History," 35.

51. John Walsh, "Stanford's Search for Solutions," in *Academic Transformations*, David Riesman and Verne A. Stadtman, eds. (New York: McGraw-Hill, 1973), 303–22; Medeiros, "Sterling Years," 229–31.

52. Lowen, "Exploiting," 236–64; Leslie, "Playing the Education Game," 80–84; Peter Galison, Bruce Hevly, and Rebecca Lowen, "Controlling the Monster: Stanford and the Growth of Physics Research, 1935–1962," in Galison and Hevly, eds., *Big Science*, 46–77.

53. "A Program for Faculty Planning" (Oct. 1967), III, 64, Terman Papers.

54. The 1982 *Assessment of Quality in Graduate Education* accorded Stanford a place with Harvard and MIT, although just below UC Berkeley, at the pinacle of the academic hierarchy. Stanford has remained one of the leaders in research expenditures, with a disproportionate amount of this funding coming from the federal government. Its endowment surpassed $2 billion in 1990, inferior only to those of Harvard, Yale, and Princeton.

2. The University of California, Los Angeles

1. The origins and development of UCLA are sketched in Verne A. Stadtman, *The University of California, 1868–1968* (New York: McGraw-Hill, 1970), 213–35, 266–70, and passim; factual material has been taken from Verne A. Stadtman, ed., *The Centennial Record of the University of California* (Berkeley: University of California, 1967).

2. Moore feared that there was "a communist behind every bush"; he also opposed appealing to Los Angeles business leaders for support because they might "take over [his] university": "The Godfather of UCLA: Regent Edward A. Dickson," 2 vol. Oral History Program, UCLA (1983), UCLA Special Collections, 308–9, 544.

3. Ibid.

4. Dickson typically opposed this constraint: Ibid., 267–68; Clark Kerr, Personal communication, (1/4/91).

5. James H. Corley, "Serving the University in Sacramento," UCLA Oral History (1969), 49–50. Kerr has noted that Sproul was always in charge, but often let others be blamed for unpopular decisions: op. cit.

6. Paul A. Dodd, "Oral History," UCLA Oral History (1985), 280. Neil H. Jacoby,

"The Graduate School of Management at UCLA: 1948–1968," UCLA Oral History (1974), 97.

7. Dickson was also chair of a special committee of southern regents and considered himself tantamount to president of UCLA: Kerr, op. cit.

8. Richard C. Maxwell, "Law School Modernizer," UCLA Oral History (1983), passim; Dodd, Oral History, 257–61; Verne O. Knudson, "Teacher, Researcher, Administrator," UCLA Oral History (1974), 1078–80.

9. Stafford L. Warren, "An Exceptional Man for Exceptional Challenges," 3 vol. UCLA Oral History, 1031–35 & passim.

10. Ibid., 1025–26.

11. Ibid., 1047, 1052, 1202.

12. Ibid., 1035, 1055; cf. also "Comparative Analysis: UCLA School of Medicine—UCSF School of Medicine" (11/18/55), Record Group 3, Series 1, Box 408: 1955: 1—Medicine, UCLA Archives.

13. Warren, Oral History, 1047; "Comparative Analysis," loc. cit.; University of California, *Treasurer's Report*, 1958.

14. Jacoby, Oral History.

15. Ibid., passim.

16. Kerr, op. cit.

17. Ibid., 193–200; in recent years, voluntary support from Los Angeles has greatly assisted the UCLA professional schools.

18. William G. Young, "Building the UCLA Chemistry Department," UCLA Oral History (1984), 64–5, 122–23.

19. Ibid., 111–22.

20. Willard F. Libby, "Nobel Laureate," UCLA Oral History (1983), 136–57.

21. Jane Sanders, *Cold War on the Campus: Academic Freedom at the University of Washington, 1946–64* (Seattle: University of Washington Press, 1979); Ellen W. Schrecker, *No Ivory Tower: McCarthyism and the Universities* (New York: Oxford University Press, 1986), 95–112.

22. John S. Galbraith, "Academic Life and Governance in the University of California," UCLA Oral History (1982), 39.

23. "Deans' Estimates of the Level of Distinction of Their Schools" (8/20/58), Record Group 3, Series 1, Box 392, UCLA Archives. Knudson, by way of contrast, was more realistic about UCLA's standing: ibid.

24. For the expansion and planning of higher education in California, see Stadtman, *University of California*, 339–62, 376–99.

25. "Excerpt from Transcript of Meeting of Committee on Education Policy" (8/15/57), Record Group 3, Series 1, 1957: Schools & Colleges, UCLA Archives.

26. These changes were implemented with variable haste: the College of Applied Arts dropped several programs and was transformed into the College of Fine Arts (1960); physical education became for a time a department of kinesiology (1962); and undergraduate business was the last vocational subject to be dropped in 1965.

27. "Confidential Memorandum of a Conference between R. B. Allen and B. L. Johnson" (8/19/57), Record Group 3, Series 1, 1957: Schools & Colleges, UCLA Archives.

28. Galbraith, Oral History, 60.

29. Kerr, op. cit.

30. Academic Senate Committee on Educational Policy, "Report on Educational Policy and Program at Berkeley and UCLA" (5/19/58), Record Group 3, Series 1, 1958: Education Policy and Program for Berkeley and UCLA, UCLA Archives.

31. "Regents' Minutes Excerpts" (7/18/58), Record Group 3, Series 1: 1958: Education Policy and Program at Berkeley and Los Angeles, UCLA Archives.

32. E.g., research at UCLA was placed under the same policies as Berkeley; overscale appointments became equally available for both campuses; and, perhaps most controversial, a university-wide library plan accorded UCLA equal treatment: Kerr, op. cit.

33. Stadtman, ed., *Centennial Record,* 10–11.

34. Galbraith, Oral History, 61ff.; Jacoby, Oral History, 217–18; Gustave O. Arlt, "Dean of Graduate Deans: Champion of Arts and Humanities," UCLA Oral History (1978), 145–46; interview with Allen Barber, UCLA, 6/1/88. Knudson had a qualified opinion of Murphy, considering him too heavy on promotion and not strong enough on faculty recruitment: Knudson, Oral History, 1291–92.

35. Negotiations undoubtedly occurred over what equal treatment meant in terms of appropriations. Murphy is credited at UCLA, for example, for accelerating the schedule for building up the library.

36. Jacoby, Oral History, 57–61. Construction at UCLA in FY 1964 consisted of 46% of the University's nine-campus total, and 29% of that under construction—both figures highest for any campus: University of California, Report of the President, "Values and Visions: A Report of Six Years of University Growth, 1958–64," (University of California, 1964), 22.

37. Galbraith, Oral History, 62–83 (quote p. 62).

38. "Academic Plan for the University of California, Los Angeles" (3/15/62), UCLA Archives.

39. Young, Oral History, 136.

40. Ibid., 137. Steeple building was not evident in the departmental projections for the 1967 plan: "Academic Plan for the University of California, Los Angeles, 1967–1975" (Revised: Aug. 1967), UCLA Archives.

41. "Academic Plan for the University of California, Los Angeles" (Aug. 1974), UCLA Archives.

42. From "Academic Plans," 1962, 1967, 1974, op. cit.

43. One interpretation of the *Assessment of Quality in Graduate Education* (1982) places UCLA together with Michigan and Wisconsin at the top of the 'second tier': David S. Webster, "America's Highest Ranked Graduate Schools, 1925–1982," *Change* (May/June, 1983): 14–24.

3. The University of Pittsburgh

1. Robert C. Alberts, *Pitt: The Story of the University of Pittsburgh, 1787–1987* (Pittsburgh: University of Pittsburgh Press, 1986), 247. This book provides the fullest account of the Litchfield administration and utilizes restricted sources. Also insightful is Daniel S. Greenberg, "Pittsburgh: The Rocky Road to Academic Excellence," *Science* 151 (1966):549–52, 658–62, 799–801.

2. University of Pittsburgh, *University of Pittsburgh, 1945–1955* (Pittsburgh: University of Pittsburgh, 1955); Edward H. Litchfield, "Toward Higher Ground: A Five-Year Report on Progress of the University of Pittsburgh" (9/17/62); idem. "The University of Pittsburgh, 1955–65: A Report to the Community," University of Pittsburgh Archives; Alberts, *Pitt,* 210–19.

3. Greenberg, "Rocky Road"; Alberts, *Pitt,* 204–9, 244–52.

4. Greenberg, "Rocky Road"; Alberts, *Pitt,* 247–55.

5. Litchfield's predecessor, Rufus H. Fitzgerald, was pressured to resign by the trust-

ees, who had higher ambitions for Pitt. The means they used, ironically, was an outside study that criticized Fitzgerald's administration of the university, and particularly recurring budget deficits: Alberts, *Pitt*, 229-32.

6. Edward H. Litchfield, "Organization in Large American Universities: The Faculties; The Administration," *Journal of Higher Education* 30 (1959): 353-64, 489-504.

7. "Financial Development Program of the Academic Disciplines (1960-65)," Papers of Charles H. Peake, Vice-chancellor, Academic Disciplines (1959-67), FF3, UP Archives.

8. Litchfield, "Five-Year Report"; Alberts, *Pitt*, 257-58.

9. Alberts, *Pitt*, 279-83: this gift appears to have been a result of Litchfield cashing in on promises made when he assumed the chancellorship.

10. Litchfield, "Five-Year Report"; Alberts, *Pitt*, 262-66. The university's real estate ventures generated hard feelings in the community.

11. Herman B. Wells, Chairman, "The University of Pittsburgh: A Selective Review with Proposals for Future Paths" [Wells Report] (Jan. 1966), UP Archives.

12. Alberts, *Pitt*, 300-323.

13. Pennsylvania has historically provided aid on a selective basis to private colleges and universities for programs in the public interest: Carnegie Council for Policy Studies in Higher Education, *The States and Private Higher Education* (San Francisco: Jossey-Bass, 1977), 146-50.

14. Wells Report: this conclusion was probably more just for graduate/professional programs than for the academic disciplines, and thus reflected the intended expansion.

15. Memo from Edward Litchfield to Charles Peake (4/9/63), Peake Papers, FF20, UP Archives.

16. Memo from Edward Litchfield to Lawrence L. Monnett, Jr. (8/29/63), Peake Papers, FF20, UP Archives.

17. Wells Report, 13.

18. National Science Foundation, *Federal Funds for Academic Science, 1963-1966* (Washington, D.C., 1967).

19. Allan M. Cartter, *An Assessment of Quality in Graduate Education* (Washington, D.C.: ACE, 1966); Alberts, *Pitt*, 282-83.

20. "An Analysis of the Implications of the 1967-68 Budget Decision for the Academic Disciplines" (11/14/66), Peake Papers, FF16, UP Archives.

21. Ibid.

22. University of Pittsburgh, *Treasurer's Report*, 1957-64; memo of Charles Peake (2/19/63), Peake Papers, FF3, UP Archives.

23. "Report to the Faculty Senate, University Administration, and Board of Trustees of the Ad Hoc Committee to Evaluate the Wells Committee Report" (2/3/66), UP Archives.

24. Alberts, *Pitt*, 334-35; Wells Report, 18.

25. Quoted in Alberts, *Pitt*, 319.

26. Council for Financial Aid to Education, *Voluntary Support for American Colleges and Universities, 1957-1965*.

27. Alberts, *Pitt*, 279.

28. Memo from Lawrence L. Monnett, Jr. (3/12/63), Peake Papers, FF20, UP Archives.

29. Pitt received $9.7 million from the Ford Foundation from 1956 to 1970. Aside from the 1956-57 capital grants, given to all colleges and universities, most of these funds came in small to medium grants for specific projects. The only "program-building" sup-

port was for international studies ($1.5 million in 1964) and support for a primate center: information supplied by the Ford Foundation Archives.

30. Charles Peake made this same point, that fund-raising responsibilities could not be delegated: "The Number One Person must go": Alberts, *Pitt,* 279.

31. Memo from Edward Litchfield to Charles Peake (11/20/62), Peake Papers, FF20, UP Archives.

32. Peake Papers, FF113, UP Archives: Pitt received a Center of Excellence award for physics/chemistry/crystallography in 1969.

33. Litchfield, "The University of Pittsburgh, 1955–65."

34. Wells Report, 25.

35. Alberts, *Pitt,* 328–49. Pitt had implicitly assumed a responsibility for providing higher education for western Pennsylvania when it established a satellite campus in Johnstown in 1927. Three more centers were added during the Litchfield years.

36. National Science Foundation data.

Chapter 6. The Transformation of Federal Research Support in the Sputnik Era

1. The 1950s Research Economy and the Rise of NSF

1. National Science Foundation, *Scientific Research and Development in Colleges and Universities: Expenditures and Manpower, 1954* (Wasington, D.C.: NSF, 1956).

2. James B. Conant, *Science and Common Sense* (New Haven: Yale University Press, 1951), 323.

3. Merle A. Tuve, "Technology and National Research Policy," *Bulletin of the Atomic Scientists* 9 (1953): 293–93

4. Julius A. Stratton, "Research and the University," *Chemical and Engineering News* 31 (1953): 2581–83.

5. Tuve, "Technology and National Research Policy," 292.

6. The concern for the unfettered freedom of the individual scientist is a kind of litmus test for coming to terms with the federally funded research system. To have funded individuals on the basis of their supposed creativity, as advocated by Conant and others (*Science and Common Sense;* Curt P. Richter, "Free Research versus Design Research," *Science* 118 (1953): 91–93) would in practice have been highly restrictive. On the other hand, these critics were objecting to real limitations inherent in project funding. Princeton president Harold W. Dodds, for example, "chastised "projectitis" as "an unhappy addiction to limited objectives, perhaps at the very moment at which the individual should [have] . . . freedom for roving speculation in an atmosphere unencumbered by the pressures of problem-solving commitments to external agencies": *Physics Today* VII, 1 (1954): 4–5.

7. Lee A. DuBridge, "Science and Government," *Chemical and Engineering News* 31 (1953): 1384–90.

8. For the early history of the NSF, see J. Merton England, *A Patron for Pure Science: The National Science Foundation's Formative Years, 1945–57* (Washington, D.C.: NSF, 1982); and Milton Lomask, *A Minor Miracle: An Informal History of the National Science Foundation* (Washington, D.C.: NSF, 1976).

9. National Science Foundation, *Annual Report,* 1950–51, 2.

10. Lomask, *Minor Miracle*, 91–110; England, *Patron for Pure Science*, 148–50, 181–202.

11. NSF, *Annual Report*, 1950–51, 23–24; Merton, *Patron for Pure Science*, 113–20, 130–51.

12. From 1952 to 1958 sixteen research universities received $25.4 million or 43% of total NSF research grants:

1.	California, Berkeley (est.)	$2,595,292
2.	Chicago	2,239,500
3.	Harvard	2,158,240
4.	M.I.T.	2,005,150
5.	Michigan	1,872,800
6.	Wisconsin	1,805,920
7.	Columbia	1,749,000
8.	Yale	1,638,600
9.	Illinois	1,531,000
10.	Cal Tech	1,235,650
11.	Pennsylvania	1,154,600
12.	Johns Hopkins	1,113,350
13.	Minnesota	1,111,630
14.	Purdue	1,073,400
15.	Cornell	1,062,550
16.	Indiana	1,016,700

England, *Patron for Pure Science*, 259.

13. NSF, *Annual Reports*, 1950–51, pp. 3–12; 1951–52, pp. 5–7; 1952–53, pp. 1–8; Alan T. Waterman, "Research for National Defense," *Bulletin of the Atomic Scientists* 9 (1953): 36–39.

14. Charles C. Grant & Bertha Rubinstein, "Funds for Science: The Federal Government and Nonprofit Institutions," *Science* 117 (1953): 669–76 (quote p. 676).

15. Quoted in *Physics Today* (July 1953), 19. Wilson credited this observation to Charles F. Kettering. Interestingly, Wilson was named to the original National Science Board, where he would have been an iconoclastic presence, but he never attended.

16. England, *Patron for Pure Science*, 152–60; Lomask, *Minor Miracle*, 79–82.

17. England, *Patron for Pure Science*, 216–22.

18. Ibid., 353–55.

19. NSF, *Scientific R&D in Colleges and Universities*, 1954, 1958.

2. Sputnik

1. Barbara B. Clowse, *Brainpower for the Cold War: The Sputnik Crisis and the National Defense Education Act of 1958* (Westport, CT: Greenwood Press, 1981), 5–16; Walter A. McDougall, . . . *the Heavens and the Earth: A Political History of the Space Age* (New York: Basic Books, 1985), 141–56; Homer E. Newell, *Beyond the Atmosphere: Early Years of Space Science* (Washington, D.C.: NASA, 1980), 55–57.

2. McDougall, . . . *the Heavens and the Earth*, 148–56.

3. Enid Curtis Bok Schoettle, "The Establishment of NASA," in Sanford A. Lakoff, ed., *Knowledge and Power: Essays on Science and Government* (New York: The Free Press, 1966), 162–270; McDougall, . . . *the Heavens and the Earth*, 157–76.

4. Schoettle, "Establishment of NASA," 217–20, 261–62; McDougall, . . . *the Heavens and the Earth*, 172–75; Newell, *Beyond the Atmosphere*, 87–90.

5. National Science Foundation, *Federal Funds for Research, Development, and Other Scientific Activities, Fiscal Years 1964, 1965, and 1966* (NSF, 1965); (on NACA) Newell, *Beyond the Atmosphere*, 90–91.

6. Janet Kerr-Tener, "From Truman to Johnson: Ad Hoc Policy Formation in Higher Education" (Ph.D. diss. University of Virginia, 1985), 131–210.

7. Kerr-Tener, "Ad Hoc Policy Formation," 163–74; Clowse, *Brainpower for the Cold War*.

8. Clowse, *Brainpower for the Cold War*, 162.

9. Lawrence E. Gladieux and Thomas R. Wolanin, *Congress and the Colleges: The National Politics of Higher Education* (Lexington, Mass.: D.C. Heath & Co., 1976), 11.

10. Data from NSF.

3. The Politics of Academic Science

1. Charles S. Maier, "Science, Politics, and Defense in the Eisenhower Era," introduction to George B. Kistiakowsky, *A Scientist at the White House* (Cambridge, Harvard University Press, 1976), xiii–lxvii; James R. Killian, *Sputnik, Scientists, and Eisenhower: A Memoir of the First Special Assistant to the President for Science and Technology* (Cambridge: MIT Press, 1977); John S. Ridgen, *Rabi: Scientist and Citizen* (New York: Basic Books, 1987), 247–51. For the decline of this system, David Z. Beckler, "The Precarious Life of Science in the White House," *Daedalus* 103 (Summer, 1974): 115–34; Bruce L. R. Smith, *The Advisers: Scientists in the Policy Process* (Washington, D.C.: the Brookings Institution, 1992), 169–79.

2. Killian, *Sputnik, Scientists*, 110.

3. For the multiple roles and positions through which scientists like Bethe and Rabi coordinated the scientific establishment, see Daniel S. Greenberg, *The Politics of Pure Science* (New York: New American Library, 1967), 140–41; also, Ridgen, *Rabi*, 232–54. PSAC membership as of Dec. 1, 1957, from Killian, *Sputnik, Scientists*, 277–79.

4. Maier, "Science, Politics, and Defense," xxi–xxix, lv–lvi; Killian, *Sputnik, Scientists*, 112–16.

5. Cf. National Science Foundation, *Basic Research, a National Resource* (Washington, D.C.: GPO, 1957).

6. Robert N. Kreidler, "The President's Science Advisor and National Science Policy" in *Scientists and National Policy-Making*, Robert Gilpin & Christopher Wright, eds. (New York: Columbia University Press, 1964), 124–25.

7. President's Science Advisory Committee, *Strengthening American Science* (Washington, D.C.: GPO, [Dec. 27,] 1958).

8. PSAC, *Education for the Age of Science* (Washington, D.C.: GPO, [May 24] 1959).

9. Dael Wolfle, ed., *Symposium on Basic Research* (Washington, D.C.: American Association for the Advancement of Science, 1959). Dissenters from this consensus are noted by Nathan Reingold, "Physics and Engineering in the United States, 1945–1965, a Study of Pride and Prejudice," in *American Science in the Age of Michelson, 1870–1930*, Stanley Goldberg and Roger H. Stuewer, eds. (New York: American Institute of Physics, 1988).

10. Ibid., 133–42. For the political history of SLAC, see Greenberg, *Politics of Pure Science*, 224–37.

11. PSAC, *Scientific Progress, the Universities, and the Federal Government* (Washington, D.C.: GPO, [Nov. 15] 1960), 2, 5, 10–11, 13. An additional PSAC Report in 1962, known as the Gilliland Report, advocated the expansion of graduate education: see below, Chapter 7, Section 4, n. 10.

12. Don K. Price, "The Scientific Establishment" in Gilpin & Wright, *Scientists and*

National Policy-Making, 19–40; and more generally, *The Scientific Estate* (Cambridge: Harvard University Press, 1965).

13. Greenberg, *Politics of Pure Science,* 141.

14. Ken Hechler, *Toward the Endless Frontier: History of the Committee on Science and Technology, 1959–79* (Washington, D.C.: GPO, 1980); Jeffrey K. Stine, *A History of Science Policy in the United States, 1940–1985,* House Committee on Science and Technology, Science Policy Study Background Report No. 1 (Washington, D.C.: GPO, 1986), 43.

15. Stine, *History of Science Policy,* 44–45.

16. Kenneth Kofmehl, "COSPUP, Congress, and Scientific Advice," *The Journal of Politics* 28 (1966): 100–120.

17. Kofmehl, "COSPUP, Congress," 105; Greenberg wrote, "to the extent that there could be a single voice for the amorphous body known as the scientific community, it was COSPUP's": *Politics of Pure Science,* 160.

18. Kofmehl. "COSPUP, Congress," 111; Greenberg, *Politics of Pure Science,* 160–61.

19. National Academy of Sciences, *Federal Support of Basic Research in Institutions of Higher Learning* (Washington, D.C.: NAS-NRC, 1964).

20. National Academy of Sciences, *Basic Research and National Goals: A Report to the Committee on Science and Astronautics* (Washington, D.C.: GPO, 1965), 1.

21. Ibid., 3–24. Daniel Greenberg noted that until 1967, "15 per cent [annual growth] was the magic number, generally accepted by all who had a hand in science policy": *Politics of Pure Science,* 166n.

22. William W. Lowrance, "The NAS Surveys of Fundamental Research 1962–1974, in Retrospect," *Science* 197 (1977): 1254–60.

23. National Research Council [NRC], *Physics: Survey and Outlook* (Washington, D.C.: NAS-NRC, 1966); NRC, *Ground-Based Astronomy: A Ten-Year Program* (Washington, D.C.: NAS-NRC, 1964); NRC, *The Plant Sciences: Now and in the Coming Decade* (Washington, D.C.: NAS-NRC, 1966); NRC, *Chemistry: Opportunities and Needs* (Washington, D.C.: NAS-NRC, 1965).

24. Greenberg, *Politics of Pure Science,* 167–69; Lowrance, "NAS Surveys," 1257, 1260.

4. Federal Support and the Golden Age of Academic Science

1. National Science Foundation, *Scientific Research and Development in Colleges and Universities: Expenditures and Manpower, 1958* (Washington: NSF, 1962); *Scientific Activities at Universities and Colleges, 1964* (Washington: NSF, 1968); *Federal Support to Universities, Colleges and Selected Nonprofit Institutions, Fiscal Year 1983* (Washington: NSF, 1985).

2. National Science Board, *Science Indicators, 1987* (Washington: NSF, 1988); *Federal Support, 1983.* Total real expenditures for academic R&D remained fairly constant through the early 1970s and did not significantly surpass 1968 until 1976 (+8%); federal support for academic research exceeded 1968 levels in 1977; NSF appropriations made a new peak in 1985; and academic R&D attained its highest proportion of GNP in 1987. The 1960s peaks for percentage federal funding and percentage basic research have not been equaled.

3. COSPUP, *Basic Research and National Goals* (Washington: GPO, 1965), 24. Several months after this report was published, NSF Director Leland Haworth would use similar language in testifying before the House Subcommittee on Science, Research, and

Development: *Government and Science: Review of the National Science Foundation* (Washington: GPO, 1965), 87, 980–82.

4. Dorothy Schaffter, *The National Science Foundation* (New York: Praeger, 1969), 116–24.

5. National Science Foundation, *Annual Reports*, 1960, 1966. Data of science support excludes budget items for science education, information, and operating expenses.

6. Daniel Greenberg, *The Politics of Pure Science* (New York: New American Library, 1967), 170–206; Milton Lomask, *A Minor Miracle: An Informal History of the National Science Foundation* (Washington: NSF, 1976), 167–95.

7. Harold Orlans, *The Effects of Federal Programs on Higher Education* (Washington: Brookings, 1962), 135–86.

8. Lomask, *Minor Miracle*, 132; *Review of the NSF*, 1134.

9. *Science* 132 (Aug. 12, 1960): 405; NSF, *Annual Report*. 1962, p. 64; *Review of the NSF*, 93–96.

10. *Review of the NSF*, 1044.

11. J. Merton England, "Investing in Universities: Genesis of the National Science Foundation's Institutional Programs, 1958–1963," *Journal of Policy History* 2 (1990): 131–56.

12. National Science Foundation, *Science Development Program for Colleges and Universities, 1964 and 1965* (NSF, 1964). See also Howard Page, "The Science Development Program" in *Science Policy and the University*, Harold Orlans, ed., (Washington: Brookings Institution, 1968), 101–13; David E. Drew, *Science Development: An Evaluation Study* (Washington: National Board on Graduate Education, 1975); NSF, *The NSF Science Development Programs: A Documentary Report* (Washington: NSF, 1977).

13. NSF, *NSF Science Development*, 17–20, 68–69.

14. Lyndon Baines Johnson, "Strengthening Academic Capability for Science Throughout the Country," in James L. Pennick, et al., eds., *The Politics of American Science: 1939 to the Present*, Rev. ed. (Cambridge: MIT Press, 1972), 333–36; NSF, *NSF Science Development*, 15–17.

15. The following table depicts the incidence of Science Development grants to the 100 academic institutions receiving the largest amounts of federal R&D funds, FY 1966, by decile:

Decile	USDP	SSDP	Dept.SDP	TOTAL
I	0	0	0	0
II	3	0	2	5
III	6	0	3	9
IV	7	1	1	9
V	3	1	2	6
VI	2	3	3	8
VII	3	0	1	4
VIII	2	1	4	7
IX	3	1	4	8
X	0	1	5	6
Total	29	8	25	62

This distribution shows that the Science Development funds went roughly where they were intended to go: half of the USDP awards went to institutions in the top four deciles, while departmental grants went predominantly to weaker institutions in the lower deciles. It is also apparent that most eligible institutions got something from the programs. Sixteen institutions appear to have been too good to qualify; some other institutions appeared in the top 100 by virtue of narrow research activity in medicine or agriculture. Of the remainder—NSF's real target group—probably more than 80 per cent received some award.

16. Drew, *Science Development,* 163–66.

17. NSF, *NSF Science Development,* 33–51; Memorandum to the Director from Program Officer, SDP (July 18, 1975), "Briefing on the Science Development Program (1965–72, 115 grants to 102 institutions, $233 million." I thank J. Merton England for bringing this document to my attention.

18. Subcommittee on Science, Research and Development of the House Committee on Science and Astronautics, *Review of the National Science Foundation,* 2 vols. (Washington: GPO, 1965).

19. Lomask, *Minor Miracle,* 199–213.

20. National Science Foundation, *Report on Funding Trends and Balance of Activities: National Science Foundation, 1951–1988)* (Washington: NSF, 1988).

21. Ibid., 7, 22.

22. NSF data.

23. Quoted in Stephen P. Strickland, *Politics, Science, and Dread Disease: A Short History of United States Medical Research Policy* (Cambridge: Harvard University Press, 1972), 192.

24. Greenberg, *Politics of Pure Science,* 279.

25. Before Shannon, the Director of the Public Health Service, which housed NIH, had been the foremost spokesman for medical research; but with the rise of the NIH empire, Shannon's post was made directly responsible to the Secretary of Health, Education & Welfare: Strickland, *Politics, Science, and Dread Disease,* 226–28 & passim.

26. Appropriations data for NIH from: *NIH Factbook: Guide to National Institutes of Health Programs and Activities* (Chicago: Marquis Academic Media, 1976); data on university expenditures from NSF sources.

27. For a full account of the medical research coalition and its political history, see Strickland, *Politics, Science, and Dread Disease.*

28. Testimony of Alvin M. Weinberg, *Review of the NSF,* 265. This was also the view of the Wooldridge Committee which reviewed the NIH: NIH Study Committee, *Biomedical Science and Its Administration: A Study of the National Institutes of Health* (Washington, D.C., 1965).

29. Testimony of James A. Shannon, *Review of the NSF,* 1258, 1241; see also 394–95. In Shannon's first year as Director he changed the name of the Institute of Microbiology to the Institute of Allergy and Infectious Diseases because, it was remarked, "whoever died of microbiology?": Strickland *Politics, Science, and Dread Disease,* 192.

30. Testimony of James A. Shannon, *Review of the NSF,* 1245; NSF, *Scientific Activities, 1964.*

31. *Review of the NSF,* 1043–46.

32. Numerous medical schools were established during the 1960s; however, it generally took several years for new schools to develop extensive research programs, and the NIH Advancement Program did not aid these institutions (see next note).

33. NSF, *NSF Science Development: Documentary Report,* 10, 60–63. Awards were made to Cornell, Purdue, Vanderbilt, Washington, Rice, and Duke universities, and the universities of Virginia, Oregon, Colorado, Kansas, and California-Davis.

34. NSF, *Scientific Research and Development in Colleges and Universities, 1953–54* (Washington, 1959); NSF, *Federal Support to Universities and Colleges* (Washington; 1967).

35. A fourth major change, less germane in this context, would be the complex interrelationship that has evolved between the medical schools and their teaching hospitals.

36. National Academy of Sciences, *The Life Sciences* (Washington, D.C.: NAS, 1970), 307.

37. National Research Council, *Chemistry: Opportunities and Needs* (Washington, D.C.: NAS, 1965), 170; Behavioral and Social Sciences Survey Committee, *The Behavioral and Social Sciences: Outlook and Needs* (Washington, D.C.: NAS, 1969), 236.

38. Strickland, *Politics, Science, and Dread Disease,* 184–232; James Walsh, "NIH: Demand Increases for Applications of Research," *Science* (July 8, 1966), 149–52.

39. Response by James A. Shannon, *Review of NSF,* 1245.

40. Richard A. Rettig, *Cancer Crusade: The Story of the National Cancer Act of 1971* (Princeton: Princeton University Press, 1977).

41. NAS, *Life Sciences,* 311.

42. NSF, *Scientific Research,* 1958; *Scientific Activities,* 1964: totals do not include the Department of Agriculture.

43. Harvey Brooks, "Impact of the Defense Establishment on Science and Education," in *Hearings on National Science Policy,* Subcommittee on Science, Research, and Development, House Committee on Science and Astronautics, 91st Congress (Washington, D.C.; 1970), 931–63.

44. Task Force on Science Policy, House Committee on Science and Technology, *Science Support by the Department of Defense,* Science Policy Study Background Report No. 8 (Washington, D.C.; 1986), 136.

45. Robert W. Seidel, "A Home for Big Science: The Atomic Energy Commission's Laboratory System," *Historical Studies in the Physical Sciences* 16 (1986): 135–75.

46. "Prepared Statement of the Atomic Energy Commission": Subcommittee on Employment and Manpower, Senate Committee on Labor and Public Welfare, *Impact of Federal Research and Development Policies on Scientific and Technical Manpower* (Washington, D.C.; 1965), 569, 605.

47. Greenberg, *Politics of Pure Science,* 207–88; Donald R. Fleming, "The Big Money and High Politics of Science," *Atlantic* (August 1965): 41–45; Seidel, "Home for Big Science," 168–73.

48. Harold Orlans, *Contracting for Atoms* (Washington: Brookings Institution, 1967), 185–87.

49. Glenn T. Seaborg, "Statement," *Hearings on National Science Policy,* 661–69; "The Government-University Partnership in Graduate Education," in *Centralization of Federal Science Activities,* Subcommittee on Science, Research, and Development, House Committee on Science and Astronautics (Washington: 1969), 494–505. Seidel credits Seaborg with helping the national laboratories withstand widespread criticisms and enlarging their budgets in the 1960s: "Home for Big Science," 167.

50. Seaborg, "The Government-University Partnership," 502; AEC, *Impact of Federal Research,* 575, 625–30.

51. Orlans, *Contracting for Atoms,* 127–28.

52. AEC, *Impact of Federal Research,* 584.

53. David Dickson, *The New Politics of Science* (Chicago: University of Chicago Press, 1988), 138–40.

54. NASA head James E. Webb intended, somewhat unrealistically, to use NASA grants to universities to promote cooperation with local governments and industry. The absence of any discernible progress in this area eventually soured him on the Sustaining University Program: Homer E. Newell, *Beyond the Atmosphere* (Washington, D.C.: NASA, 1980), 232–36.

55. Subcommittee on Space Science and Applications, House Committee on Science and Astronautics, *1966 NASA Authorization* No. 2, Part 3 (Washington, D.C.; 1966), 581–620; NSF, *NSF Science Development,* 8–9, 53–55.

56. Willard F. Libby, "Nobel Laureate," UCLA Oral History (1983), 157–58; Newell, *Beyond the Atmosphere,* 227.

57. Earl D. Hilburn, "Prepared Statement," *Impact of Federal Research,* 775.

58. Ibid.; the listed institutions all received substantial grants from NASA to construct research facilities, and such grants were invariably accompanied by research and training grants: *1966 NASA Authorization,* 599.

59. NASA had to go to extraordinary lengths to attract the very top scientific talent. The creation of the Institute for Space Studies in New York City was such an attempt, designed to facilitate at least temporary participation from the area's leading scientists: Newell, *Beyond the Atmosphere,* 238–39.

60. Herbert F. York and G. Allen Greb, "Military Research and Development: A Postwar History," *Bulletin of the Atomic Scientists* 14 (Jan. 1977): 13–26; House Committee on Science and Technology, *Science Support by the Department of Defense,* Science Policy study Background Report No. 8 (Washington, D.C.; 1986), 52–54; Charles S. Maier, "Science, Politics and Defense in the Eisenhower Era," in George B. Kistiakowsky, *A Scientist at the White House* (Cambridge: Harvard University Press, 1976), lx. The DoD also created the Jason group in 1958 to tap the ideas of top scientists in annual brainstorming sessions.

61. Eric J. Lerner, "Technology and the Military: DOD's DARPA at 25," *IEEE Spectrum* 71 (Aug. 1983); *Science Support by the DoD,* 101–8.

62. Brooks, "Impact of the Defense Establishment," 944, 952–54.

63. James Botkin and Dan Dimancescu, "The DARPA Exception," in *The Militarization of High Technology,* John Tirman, ed. (Cambridge: Ballinger, 1984), 222–25.

64. Chalmers W. Sherwin and Raymond S. Isenson, "Project Hindsight: A Defense Department Study of the Utility of Research," *Science* 156 (1967): 1571–77; Jeffrey K. Stine, *A History of Science Policy in the United States, 1940–1985,* Science Policy Study Background Report No. 1, House Committee on Science and Technology (Washington, D.C.; 1986), 59–60.

65. Harvey M. Sapolsky, *Science and the Navy: The History of the Office of Naval Research* (Princeton: Princeton University Press, 1990), 77–81.

66. Karl Kreilkamp, "*Hindsight* and the Real World of Science Policy," *Science Studies* 1 (1971): 43–66.

67. Illinois Institute of Technology Research Institute, *Technology in Retrospect and Critical Events in Science (TRACES),* 2 vols. (Washington, D.C.: NSF, 1968); Stine, *History of Science Policy,* 60–61.

68. James L. Penick, Jr., et al., *The Politics of American Science, 1939 to the Present,* Rev. ed. (Cambridge: MIT Press, 1972), 333–36.

69. Lt. Gen. William T. Ely, "Statement," *Impact of Federal Research and Development,* 444–45.

70. Penick, *Politics of American Science,* 336–38; *Science Support by the DoD,* 147; NSF, *Science Development Program,* 9, 56–59. Even THEMIS could not escape antiwar hostility to all military programs: Elinor Langer, "Themis: DOD Plan to Spread the Wealth Raises Questions in Academe," *Science* 156 (1967): 48–50.

71. Quoted in Brooks, "Impact of the Defense Establishment," 950.

72. *Science Support by the Department of Defense,* 136–40. See below, Chapter 8.

73. Ibid., 140–46. In the case of ROTC, real changes were more widespread, with many universities ceasing to allow it as an academic program.

74. The DoD spent $34 million on research in the social and behavioral sciences in 1966, and that figure was projected to rise to $51 million in 1969. About 60 percent of these outlays went for relatively noncontroversial research concerning human perfor-

mance, selection, and training. At issue were spending on "cultural and social factors," and "policy planning studies." The former were conducted largely in universities ($5.1 million); while the latter were done almost entirely by nonprofit organizations like RAND and IDA ($6.1 million): "Statement by John S. Foster," *Defense Department Sponsored Foreign Affairs Research*, Senate Committee on Foreign Relations (Washington, D.C. ; 1968), 7.

75. Brooks wrote of this: "DoD support could have the . . . effect of arming the supporters and disarming the critics of American policy"; and "because of the generally conservative bias of the military, the suspicion is bound to arise of the possible use of unique information obtained under military sponsorship to further the suppression of social change in foreign areas on the unproved assumption that it is inimical to U.S. interests": "Impact of the Defense Establishment," 953–54.

76. *Defense Department Sponsored Foreign Affairs Research*, 1, 18.

77. Military Authorization Act of Fiscal Year 1970 (Public Law 91-121, Section 203): *Science Support by the Department of Defense*, 141.

78. Sen. Mike Mansfield, "Rechanneling the Public Resources for Basic Science Through the Civilian Agencies: A New Goal for National Science Policy," *National Science Policy*, 604–9, quote 608; reprinted in Pennick, *Politics of American Science*, 338–49.

79. Sapolsky writes that the Mansfield Amendment had an impact at the operating level: "defense research agencies were reminded once again of the political risks involved in supporting fundamental work. Ever more elaborate reviews were required to gain approval for such projects": *Science and the Navy*, 75.

80. *Science Support by the Department of Defense*, 135, 147.

81. See Brooks, "Impact of the Defense Establishment," passim.

82. Sapolsky, *Science and the Navy*, 72.

83. Mansfield, "Rechanneling," 608; Brooks, "Impact of the Defense Establishment," 945.

84. The materials research laboratories were switched from ARPA to NSF in 1972, but few other programs changed sponsorship.

85. John Walsh, "Project Themis: Budget Cuts, Critics Cause Phase Out," *Science* 169 (1970): 749; Sapolsky, *Science and the Navy*, 74–76.

86. For example, Stuart W. Leslie, "The Military and the Shaping of University Teaching and Research," paper presented to the workshop "Research Perspectives on Research Universities," Pennsylvania State University, April 14–15, 1989; This issue is discussed further in Roger L. Geiger, "Science, Universities, and National Defense, 1945-1970," *Osiris* 7 (1992): 94–116.

87. Dickson, *New Politics of Science*, 28–29.

88. Maier, "Science Politics, and Defense," lx.

89. *Impact of Federal Research and Development Policies*, 949, 4.

90. Pennick, *Politics of American Science*, 335.

91. *Science* (July 8, 1966); 149–50.

92. Fleming, "Big Money and High Politics of Science"; Greenberg, *Politics of Pure Science*, 281.

93. The principal legislation: the Higher Education Facilities Act of 1963; the expansion of the National Defense Education Act of 1964; and the Higher Education Act of 1965: see Congressional Research Service, *Reauthorization of the Higher Education Act: Program Descriptions, Issues, and Options*, Senate Committee on Labor and Human Resources (Washington, D.C., 1985).

94. Cf. Greenberg, "Postscript 1970," in *Politics of Pure Science*, 290.

Chapter 7. The Golden Age on Campus: The Research Universities in the 1960s

1. The Evolving University: Contemporary Perceptions

1. *Digest of Educational Statistics, 1985-86,* 110.

2. Carnegie Commission on Higher Education, *Sponsored Research of the Carnegie Commission on Higher Education* (New York: McGraw-Hill, 1975); contemporary crisis literature is mentioned in Clark Kerr, *The Great Transformation in Higher Education, 1960-1980* (Albany: State University of New York Press, 1991), 163-64.

3. Charles V. Kidd, *American Universities and Federal Research* (Cambridge: Harvard University Press, 1959); The Carnegie Foundation for the Advancement of Teaching, *Annual Report, 1962-63,* 9-70; Harold Orlans, *The Effects of Federal Programs on Higher Education: A Study of 36 Universities and Colleges* (Washington: Brookings Institution, 1962).

4. Kidd, *American Universities,* 212.

5. William G. Bowen, *The Federal Government and Princeton University* (Princeton University, 1962), 93-107, 174-87; Kidd, *American Universities,* 211; Orlans, *Effects of Federal Programs,* 44-78.

6. Orlans, *Effects of Federal Programs,* 205-20, quote 219; Kidd, *American Universities,* 147-49.

7. Kidd, *American Universities,* 119-22; Orlans, *Effects of Federal Programs,* 280-92.

8. CFAT, *Annual Report, 1962-63,* 32-34, 66-68; Kidd, *American Universities,* 54-60, 83-102; The fullest discussion of this issue is in Bowen, *Government and Princeton,* 35-124.

9. Orlans, *Effects of Federal Programs,* 178-86; Kidd, *American Universities,* 59-60; CFAT, *Annual Report, 1962-3,* 66-68.

10. Clark Kerr, *The Uses of the University* (Cambridge: Harvard University Press, 1963), 46-84, quotes, 69, 51.

11. Evidence of this consensus is drawn from the following works; Christopher Jencks and David Riesman, *The Academic Revolution* (Chicago: University of Chicago Press, 1968; 1977); William G. Bowen, *The Economics of the Major Private Universities* (Carnegie Commission on Higher Education, 1968); Jacques Barzun, *The American University* (New York: Harper & Row, 1968). Each of these works was largely prepared, or finalized, in 1967, i.e. before the events of 1968 that considerably polarized sentiments about higher education. By 1969 a far more cynical attitude seemed to prevail, which is discussed below; also, Jencks and Riesman, "Preface to the Second Edition," xiv-xvii, dated January 1969.

12. Jencks and Riesman, *Academic Revolution,* 541, xiv.

13. Ibid., 244-50, quote p. 250.

14. Ellen Condliffe Lagemann, *The Politics of Knowledge: The Carnegie Corporation, Philanthropy, and Public Policy* (Middletown, Conn.: Wesleyan University Press, 1989), 226-30.

15. Bowen, *Economics,* passim.

16. Barzun, *American University,* 10-33.

17. Ibid., 34-62, 171-206; quotes, 54, 181.

18. For example, Jencks and Riesman advocated more applied and interdisciplinary subjects, as well as greater emphasis on teaching (513-38); Bowen underlined the public value of private universities (57-62); and Barzun offered 68 suggestions, the last of which being "the university should not be afraid of its own dignity" (285).

2. Changing Patterns of Research and New Research Universities

1. President's Science Advisory Committee, *Scientific Progress, the Universities, and the Federal Government* (Washington, D.C.: GPO, 1960); see above, Chapter 6.3.

2. Prewar research universities are examined in Roger L. Geiger, *To Advance Knowledge: The Growth of American Research Universities, 1900–1940* (New York: Oxford University Press, 1986); 1957 ratings are given in Hayward Keniston, *Graduate Study and Research in the Arts and Sciences at the University of Pennsylvania* (Philadelphia: University of Pennsylvania Press, 1959), 119.

3. Efforts to draw qualitative distinctions among a larger group of institutions were attempted, but were crude: Bernard Berelson, *Graduate Education in the United States* (New York: McGraw-Hill, 1960), 124–28, 280–81; Albert Bowker, "Quality and Quantity in Higher Education," *Journal of the American Statistical Association* 60 (March, 1965): 1–15.

4. From NSF series on Federal Support to universities, variously titled, 1954–1989.

5. Compiled from NSF series on Federal Support to Universities, FY 1963 & 1964, 1972 & 1973.

6. See above, Chapter 4 and Chapter 6.

7. Ibid.; David E. Drew, *Science Development: An Evaluation Study,* Technical Report No. 4, National Board on Graduate Education (Washington: National Academy of Sciences, 1975); and above, Chapter 4.

8. Data from Ford Foundation Archives and *Annual Reports;* National Science Foundation, *The NSF Science Development Programs, A Documentary Report* (Washington, D.C.: NSF, 1977).

9. See above notes 5 and 7.

10. Adapted from H. W. Magoun, "The Cartter Report on Quality in Graduate Education," *Journal of Higher Education* (37 (1966): 481–92.

11. Discussed below, Chapter 9.1.

3. Academic Quality and Institutional Development

1. Bernard Berelson, *Graduate Education in the United States* (New York: McGraw-Hill, 1960), 96.

2. David S. Webster, *Academic Quality Rankings of American Colleges and Universities* (Springfield, Ill.: Charles C. Thomas, 1986), 33–39.

3. Raymond M. Hughes, *A Study of Graduate Schools of America* (Oxford, Ohio: Miami University Press, 1925); *Report of the Committee on Graduate Instruction* (Washington: ACE, 1934).

4. See above, Chapter 3.3: Yale, note 5.

5. In 1991 a decision was made to replicate the 1982 *Assessment*. This step was provoked in part by continual unsystematic rankings of institutions by popular news magazines!

6. Heyward Keniston, *Graduate Study and Research in the Arts and Sciences at the University of Pennsylvania* (Philadelphia: University of Pennsylvania Press, 1959).

7. Allan M. Cartter, *An Assessment of Quality in Graduate Education* (Washington, D.C.: ACE, 1966).

8. When the Cartter ratings appeared, H. W. Magoun asserted that institutional rankings were of concern to "central administrative officers" who would wish to improve their institution, and also to the "communities and regions" which have come to depend upon

graduate schools for "intellectual and economic well-being": "The Cartter Report on Quality in Graduate Education," *Journal of Higher Education* 37 (1966): 481–92 (quote p. 483).

9. Kenneth D. Roose and Charles J. Anderson, *A Rating of Graduate Programs* (Washington, D.C.: ACE, 1970).

10. Only four years after the well-received Cartter ratings (cf. Note 8, above), Roose and Anderson admitted to "serious misgivings about the apparent endorsement a study of this kind gives to the primacy of the university and, more particularly, to a hierarchy of university prestige and influence": Ibid., 24.

11. *Rating of Graduate Programs,* 9–19.

12. Cartter, *Assessment of Quality,* 8–9, 106–17, 124–25.

13. David A. Garvin discusses some of these variables in terms of a "utility maximization model" for universities: *The Economics of University Behavior* (New York: Academic Press, 1980), 21–39. A National Science Foundation study examined the relationship of these and other variables with university prestige: *Graduate Education: Parameters for Public Policy* (Washington, D.C.: National Science Board, 1969).

14. Data from various sources, including the NSF Policy Research and Analysis Division CASPAR data; *American Colleges and Universities;* and institutional archives. Sources were chosen to provide the greatest consistency, with institutional sources preferred.

15. Willard Thorp, Minor Myers, Jr., and Jeremiah S. Finch, *The Princeton Graduate School: A History* (Princeton: Princeton University Press, 1978), 213–24; William G. Bowen, *The Federal Government and Princeton University* (Princeton: Princeton University, 1960), 188–224.

16. Princeton's overall rank was sixth in the 1925 Hughes rating and sixth in the 1982 *Assessment,* and there was little variation in between: David S. Webster, "America's Highest Ranked Graduate Schools, 1925–1982," *Change* (May/June 1983), 14–24.

17. John A. Hannah, *A Memoir* (East Lansing: Michigan State University Press, 1980); Paul L. Dressel, *College to University: The Hannah Years at Michigan State, 1935–1969* (East Lansing: Michigan State University Press, 1987).

18. Department building at Michigan State was inhibited by a distinctive curriculum that featured mandatory courses for freshmen and sophomores in special interdisciplinary departments. This scheme placed large numbers of faculty in non-research departments.

19. Cf. the desire of UCLA to shift toward greater graduate enrollment, above, Chapter 5.

4. Graduate Education in the 1960s

1. All data on doctorates from American Council on Education, *American Universities and Colleges,* vol. 7–12 (1956–83).

2. Doctorates awarded in 1987–88 barely exceeded those for 1972–73, and the totals have risen gradually since then. A far larger percentage of doctorates are now foreign nationals.

3. National Education Association, "Teacher Supply and Demand in Universities, Colleges, and Junior Colleges," published biennially, 1955–65 (Washington, D.C.). The crisis literature is discussed in Allan M. Cartter, "A New Look at the Supply of College Teachers," *Educational Record* 46 (1965): 267–77.

4. Berelson, *Graduate Education,* 69–80; quote p. 79.

5. Cartter, "Supply of College Teachers"

6. Allan M. Cartter, *Ph.D.s and the Academic Labor Market* (New York: McGraw-

Hill, 1976), 11-23 (quote p. 18); "Scientific Manpower for 1970-1985," *Science* 172 (1971): 132-40; also, "The Supply of and Demand for College Teachers," *Journal of Human Resources* I (1966): 22-38. Lewis B. Mayhew, *Graduate and Professional Education, 1980: A Survey of Institutional Plans* (New York: McGraw-Hill, 1970), 1.

7. These figures, derived from doctoral data in *American Universities and Colleges,* are for colleges, universities, and institutes of technology, but do not include professional schools. The latter are marginal for producing Ph.D.s, but comprise approximately 20 percent of institutions that award the doctorate.

8. Stephen H. Spurr, *Academic Degree Structures: Innovative Approaches* (New York: McGraw-Hill, 1970), 142-48; John M. Howell, "A Brief against the Doctor of Arts Degree," *Journal of Higher Education* 42 (1971): 392-99.

9. Berelson, *Graduate Education,* 96-109; See also Cartter, *Assessment,* 119-21.

10. *Science* 125 (1957): 730; John J. Scanlon, "The Ford Foundation and Higher Education: A Review of the Higher Education and Research Program," Nov. 1, 1973, Ford Foundation Archives: 003496, pp. 37-41. Because of the accompanying institutional grant, Woodrow Wilson Fellowships effectively supported 2000 students per year.

11. President's Science Advisory Committee, *Meeting Manpower Needs in Science and Technology* (Washington, D.C.: GPO, 1962); *Science* 138 (1962): 1314-16.

12. *Science* 139 (1963): 23-24; 474-75; National Science Foundation, *Annual Reports;* National Board on Graduate Education, *Federal Policy Alternatives toward Graduate Education Board,* Report No. 3 (Washington, D.C.: National Academy of Sciences, 1974), 117.

13. J. Merton England, *A Patron for Pure Science* (Washington, D.C.: NSF, 1982), 231. The number of Woodrow Wilson Fellows enrolled by institution were as follows:

Harvard	1321	Princeton	497	Johns Hopkins	195
Yale	932	Stanford	491	MIT	183
Columbia	818	Wisconsin	342	Pennsylvania	182
Berkeley	682	Michigan	328	Indiana	167
Chicago	509	Cornell	299	North Carolina	162

David W. Breneman, "Efficiency in Graduate Education: A Report to the Ford Foundation" (Jan. 1977), p. 17. I would like to thank the author for making this report available to me.

14. National Science Foundation, *Graduate Student Support in Graduate Science Education* (Washington, D.C.: NSF, 1968).

15. James W. Armsey, "Some Thoughts on Graduate Education," August 1977, Ford Foundation Archives: 008212, 4; Berelson, *Graduate Education,* 119-24. David W. Breneman, "The Ph.D. Production Process: A Study of Departmental Behavior" (Ph.D. diss.), University of California, Berkeley, 1970).

16. Hayward Keniston, *Graduate Study and Research in the Arts and Sciences at the University of Pennsylvania* (Philadelphia: University of Pennsylvania Press, 1959), 91; Berelson, *Graduate Education,* 144.

17. Berelson, *Graduate Education,* 149.

18. Ibid., 146-50.

19. Robert Dubin and Frederic Beisse, "The Assistant: Academic Subaltern," in *The State of the University: Authority and Change,* Carlos E. Kruytbosch and Sheldon L. Messinger, eds. (Beverly Hills: Sage Publications, 1970), 271-94.

20. Adapted from David W. Breneman, *Graduate School Adjustments to the 'New Depression' in Higher Education* (National Board on Graduate Education, Technical Report No. 3, Feb. 1975), 28-34.

21. William G. Bowen, *The Federal Government and Princeton University* (Princeton University, 1962), 189–90.

22. E.g., University of California, Berkeley, Academic Senate, *Education at Berkeley: Report of the Select Committee on Education* (University of California, Berkeley, 1966), 159–71; Ann M. Heiss, *Challenge to Graduate Schools* (San Francisco: Jossey-Bass, 1970); W. Gordon Whaley, *Problems in Graduate Education* (Washington, D.C.: National Association of State Universities and Land-Grant Colleges, 1971); Christopher Jencks and David Riesman, *The Academic Revolution* (Chicago: University of Chicago Press, 1968); and generally, Lewis B. Mayhew, *Reform in Graduate Education* (Atlanta: Southern Regional Education Board, 1972).

23. Specifically concerned with attrition are: Breneman, "Ph.D. Production Process"; and Joseph D. Mooney, "Attrition Among Candidates: An Analysis of a Cohort of Recent Woodrow Wilson Fellows," *The Journal of Human Resources* 3 (1968): 47–62. This subject has been updated in William G. Bowen and Neil L. Rudenstine, *In Pursuit of the Ph.D.* (Princeton: Princeton University Press, 1992).

24. Ford Foundation, "Discussion Paper: A Program in Graduate Education" (Sept. 1966), Ford Foundation Archives: 002453.

25. Breneman, "Ph.D. Production Process," above, note 15. This study was published as three papers of the Ford Foundation Research Program in University Administration, University of California: "An Economic Theory of Ph.D. Production: The Case at Berkeley" (June, 1970); "The Ph.D. Production Function: The Case at Berkeley" (Dec. 1970); and "The Ph.D. Degree at Berkeley: Interviews, Placement, and Recommendations" (Jan. 1971). I would like to thank the author for making these available to me.

26. Breneman, "Ph.D. Degree," 36.

27. Mooney, "Attrition."

28. Ibid.

29. I.e. language requirements were perfunctory; examinations were early and focused; information about completion was open; and dissertation topics arose naturally from lab work: Breneman, "Ph.D. Degree," 17–20.

30. Breneman, "Efficiency," 78.

31. The following account draws upon: James W. Armsey, "The Anatomy of a Major Program: A Report to the Ford Foundation on an Effort to Reform Graduate Education in the United States" (March 1977), Ford Foundation Archives: 008211; "Some Thoughts on Graduate Education" (Aug. 1977), Ford Foundation Archives: 008212; and David Breneman, "Efficiency in Graduate Education: An Attempted Reform."

32. While Berelson's general views may have inspired the Ford Foundation Graduate Program, his advice was not followed in important details. Berelson believed that graduate students should finish their degrees on their own money—through loans—which undoubtedly would have provided a goad to finish: Breneman, "Efficiency," 5–6, 11; Berelson, *Graduate Education*, 242–44.

33. The ten principal recipients were: Berkeley, Chicago, Cornell, Harvard, Michigan, Penn, Princeton, Stanford, Wisconsin, and Yale. Columbia, which ranked in the top ten, was bypassed because its doctoral candidates took especially long (but see note 37, below). Smaller grants were given in 1968 and 1969 to Denver, Emory, Johns Hopkins, MIT, Minnesota, Rice, SUNY Buffalo, and Washington U.: Armsey, "Anatomy," 61.

34. Breneman, "Efficiency," 90–91.

35. Breneman, "Economic Theory," 21–29.

36. Breneman in fact predicted that additional funding for graduate study would not lessen the time to the doctorate: "Ph.D. Production Function," 38. Other literature supporting this view: Mooney, "Attrition"; Kenneth Wilson, *Of Time and the Doctorate* Monograph No. 9 (Atlanta: Southern Regional Education Board, 1965).

37. The Ford Foundation Graduate Program seems to have been motivated in part to compensate leading institutions for the loss of Woodrow Wilson Fellowships. The recipients were in fact those schools that attracted the largest number of Woodrow Wilsons, (above, note 13), except for Columbia, which had just received a huge Challenge Grant: Breneman, "Efficiency," 10–12.

38. Scanlon, "Ford Foundation and Higher Education; also see above, Chapter 4.

39. These smaller grants, which were focused on special programs in selected departments, appeared to be generally successful. One striking difference was the commitment of faculty to the ends of these programs: Breneman, "Efficiency," 103n.

Chapter 8. Dissolution of a Consensus

1. The Student Rebellion

1. Seymour Martin Lipset and Sheldon S. Wolin, *The Berkeley Student Revolt: Facts and Interpretations* (New York: Anchor Books, 1965); Michael V. Miller and Susan Gilmore, *Revolution at Berkeley: The Crisis in American Education* (New York: Dell, 1965); Max Heirich, *The Beginnings: Berkeley* (1968). The protesters' view of the FSM has been admirably captured in the documentary film by Mark Kitchell: *Berkeley in the Sixties* (San Francisco: California Newsreel, 1990).

2. David Riesman and Verne A. Stadtman, *Academic Transformation: Seventeen Institutions Under Pressure* (New York: McGraw-Hill, 1973), passim; "United States of America: Derangement from Coast to Coast," *Minerva* 7 (1969): 822–63.

3. Events and circumstances at Columbia are presented in the Cox Commission, *Crisis at Columbia* (New York: Random House, 1968); but this crisis is usually interpreted as a turning point for the New Left: Kirkpatrick Sale, *SDS* (New York: Random House, 1973), 439–41; Allen J. Matusow, *The Unraveling of America: A History of Liberalism in the 1960s* (New York: Harper & Row, 1984), 335.

4. Irving Louis Horowitz and William H. Friedland, *The Knowledge Factory: Student Power and Academic Politics in America* (Chicago: Aldine, 1970), 220–80—a tendentious but detailed account of events at Cornell; Lawrence E. Eichel et al., *The Harvard Strike* (Boston: Houghton Mifflin, 1970); Zelda F. Gamson, "Michigan Muddles Through: Luck, Nimbleness, and Resilience in Crisis," in Riesman and Stadtman, *Academic Transformation*, 173–98.

5. Philip G. Altbach, "The Champagne University in the Beer State: Notes on Wisconsin's Crisis," ibid., 383–408; *The Report of the President's Commission on Campus Unrest* (Washington, D.C.: GPO, 1970).

6. The stages of student revolts are analyzed in John R. Searle, *The Campus War: A Sympathetic Look at the University in Agony* (New York: World Publishing, 1971), 5–38; also insightful is Martin Trow, "Conceptions of the University: The Case of Berkeley," in *The State of the University: Authority and Change,* Carlos E. Kruytbosch and Sheldon L. Messinger, eds. (Beverly Hills: Sage, 1970), 27–44.

7. Neil J. Smelser, "Berkeley in Crisis and Change," in Riesman and Stadtman, *Academic Transformation*, 51–70.

8. Hence the bitter accusations of cowardice: e.g., Allen Bloom, *The Closing of the American Mind* (New York: Simon & Schuster, 1987); for one explanation of faculty ineffectiveness, see Searle, *Campus War,* 18–22, 122–51.

9. Burton R. Clark, "The Wesleyan Story: The Importance of Moral Capital," in Riesman and Stadtman, *Academic Transformation,* 367–82.

1 0. Edward Shils, "The Hole in the Centre: University Government in the United States," *Minerva* 8 (1970): 1–7. Martin Trow in a similar vein described a basic weakness of the multiversity (or the absence of moral capital) as "the lack of a central widely shared sense of the nature of the institutions and a weakness in its capacity to gain the loyalties and devotion of its participants": "Conceptions of the University," 36.

1 1. Sale, *SDS,* 5 1–5 4; *Port Huron Statement*

1 2. Edward Shils, "Observations on the American University," *Minerva* 1 (1963): 1 8 3–93; Clark Kerr, *The Uses of the University* (Cambridge: Harvard University Press, 1 9 6 3), 64–6 5.

1 3. Sheldon S. Wolin and John H. Schaar, "The Abuses of the Multiversity" [from *The New York Review of Books,* March 1 1, 1 9 6 5] in Lipset and Wolin, *Student Revolt,* 3 5 0–6 3, quote p. 3 6 1.

1 4. University of California, Berkeley, Academic Senate, *Education at Berkeley: Report of a Select Committee on Education* (March 1 9 6 6); Princeton University, Faculty Advisory Committee on Policy, *Students and the University* (1 9 6 8); Stanford University, *The Study of Education at Stanford* (1 9 6 7–6 8).

1 5. At several universities T.A.s succeeded in unionizing after staging strikes. These efforts were largely motivated by issues of compensation and job security, as well as the desire to gain greater voice in university governance: Andrew Hamilton, "Wisconsin: Teaching Assistants' Strike Ends in Contract Signing," *Science* 1 6 8 (1970): 345–49; "Harvard Teaching Assistants Strike," *Science* 1 7 6 (1972): 1 4 8.

1 6. Christopher Jencks and David Riesman, *The Academic Revolution* (Chicago: University of Chicago Press, 1 9 6 8), 2 3 6–5 0.

1 7. Roger L. Geiger, "The College Curriculum and the Marketplace: What Place for Disciplines in the Trend Toward Vocationalism?" *Change* (Nov.-Dec. 1 9 8 0), 1 7–2 3.

1 8. Mario Savio, "An End to History"; Wolin and Schaar, "Multiversity"; Clark Kerr, "Reply to Wolin and Schaar," in Lipset and Wolin, *Student Revolt,* 2 1 6–1 9, 3 5 0–6 3, 3 6 4–6 6.

1 9. Burton R. Clark, "The New University," in Kruytbosch and Messinger, *State of the University,* 1 7–2 6.

2 0. Wolin and Schaar, "Multiversity," 3 5 5; Clark Kerr, "The Frantic Race to Remain Contemporary," in *The Contemporary University: U.S.A.,* Robert S. Morison, ed. (Boston: Beacon Press, 1 9 6 4, 1 9 6 6), 1 9–3 8, quote p. 2 8.

2 1. Sale, *SDS,* 8 4–8 6 & passim; Matusow, *Unraveling,* 3 1 9–3 5.

2 2. [Mark Rudd], quoted in Matusow, *Unraveling,* 3 3 4.

2 3. *Education at Berkeley,* 6 3.

2 4. The essential conservatism of universities arose, according to Martin Trow, from "an intricate network of understandings and arrangements among participating interest groups . . . [which] provide the framework for the coordination of the multivaried functions of the university": "Conceptions of the University," 3 8.

2 5. Jencks and Riesman, *Academic Revolution,* 3 5–5 0.

2 6. D. Parker Young, "The Legal Aspects of Student Dissent and Discipline in Higher Education," University of Georgia, Institute of Higher Education (1970); *Science* 1 6 6 (1 9 6 9): 486–88.

2 7. E.g., "American universities are absolutely central components of the social system of technological warfare-welfare capitalism. The functions, goals, structure and organization of the universities are directly and indirectly determined by the needs and perspectives of that system"—statement of Harvard radicals, quoted in Eichel et al., *Harvard Strike,* 3 9.

2 8. D. S. Greenberg, "IDA: University-Sponsored Center Hit Hard by Assaults on Campus," *Science* 1 6 0 (1 9 6 8): 7 4 4–4 8.

29. Paul Sigmund, "Princeton in Crisis and Change," in Riesman and Stadtman, *Academic Transformation*, 249–70.

30. *The Cox Commission Report: Columbia at Crisis* (New York: Random House, 1968), 89–95; Greenberg, "IDA."

31. Harold Orlans, *The Nonprofit Research Institute: Its Origin, Operation, Problems, and Prospects* (New York: McGraw-Hill, 1972), 148.

32. *Science* 164 (1969): 1039–41.

33. Dorothy Nelkin, *The University and Military Research: Moral Politics at M.I.T.* (Ithaca: Cornell University Press, 1972), 127. See also, "M.I.T.: Panels on Special Labs Asks More Nondefense Research," *Science* 164 (1969): 1264–65; "M.I.T.: March 4 Revisited Amid Political Turmoil," *Science* 167 (1970): 1475–76.

34. Victor K. McElheny, "MIT Administration Makes Public Its Intentions on Disposition of Draper and Lincoln Laboratories," *Science* 168 (1970): 1074–75; Nelkin, *Moral Politics*, 125–45, 178–84. The Lincoln Laboratories continued to be an FFRDC administered by M.I.T.

35. Horowitz and Friedland, *Knowledge Factory*, 281–342.

36. John Walsh, "Stanford Research Institute: Campus Turmoil Spurs Transition," *Science* 164 (1969): 933–36.

37. Steve Weissman [Stanford activist], quoted in John Walsh, "Confrontation at Stanford: Exit Classified Research," *Science* 164 (1969): 536.

38. Ibid., 534–37; Walsh, "Stanford Research Institute." At the University of Michigan continual protest against military research eventually led to the separation of the Willow Run Laboratories, an off-campus facility devoted to military reconnaissance and surveillance. The flavor of this confrontation may be had from, Ann Arbor SDS, "Strung Out: A Report on the Relationship between the University of Michigan and the Military," pamphlet, n.d. [1971] Michigan Historical Collections, Bentley Historical Library.

39. Quoted in Walsh, "Confrontation at Stanford," 536.

40. Searle, *Campus War*, 129–40.

41. Quoted in Walsh, "Confrontation at Stanford," 536. There is some irony in Panofsky's pious stance: short years earlier his own physics department had wished to exercise 'collective moral restraint' in opposing the Stanford Linear Accelerator Center which Panofsky directed: Rebecca Lowen, "'Exploiting a Wonderful Opportunity': Stanford University, Industry, and the Federal Government, 1937–1965," Ph.D. dissertation, Stanford University, 1990, 236–51.

42. David R. Goddard and Linda C. Koons, "Intellectual Freedom and the University," *Science* 173 (1971): 607–10.

43. The student rebellion in Europe achieved, through government assistance, official representation on university governing bodies for students and often staff *(Drittelparitat)*: see Hans Daalder and Edward Shils, *Universities, Politicians and Bureaucrats: Europe and the United States* (Cambridge: Cambridge University Press, 1983).

2. The Financial Crisis of the Research Universities

1. William G. Bowen, "Economic Pressures on the Major Private Universities," in *The Economics and Financing of Higher Education in the United States* (Washington, D.C.: GPO, 1969), 399–439, esp. 400.

2. From *American Universities and Colleges* (1960, 1968).

3. From American Association of University Professors, "Reports of the Economic Status of the Profession" [annual] in *A.A.U.P. Bulletin*. Average faculty salaries increased more rapidly than per capita personal income from 1957 to 1963, about the same from

1964 to 1967, and then less than personal income after 1967: "Economic Status of the Profession, 1970-71," *A.A.U.P. Bulletin* 57 (1971): 228.

4. William G. Bowen popularized the argument that "in every industry in which increases in productivity come more slowly than in the economy as a whole, cost per unit of product must be expected to increase relative to costs in general": *The Economics of Major Private Universities* (Berkeley: Carnegie Commission on Higher Education, 1968), 16.

5. Ibid., 26.

6. Jacques Barzun, *The American University* (New York: 1968): see above, Chapter 7.

7. The "ceiling tuition" is here calculated as an average of undergraduate tuition at Yale, Harvard, and Columbia College. Seymour E. Harris, *Higher Education: Resources and Finance* (New York: McGraw-Hill, 1962), 41-168, esp. 101-2.

8. For analysis of differences in state funding of higher education, see ibid., 325-420.

9. Selma J. Mushkin, "A Note on State and Local Financing of Higher Education," in *Economics and Financing of Higher Education,* 530-40.

10. Janet H. Ruyle and Lyman A. Glenny, *State Budgeting for Higher Education: Trends in State Revenue Appropriations from 1968 to 1977* (Berkeley: Center for Studies in Higher Education, 1978), 32.

11. Voluntary support data from Council for Aid to Education, *Voluntary Support of Education, 1986-87* (New York: CFAE, 1988).

12. Earl F. Cheit, *The New Depression in Higher Education* (New York: McGraw-Hill, 1971), 7-10; annual inflation is reported annually in "Economic Status of the Profession," *A.A.U.P. Bulletin.*

13. NSF annual series, *Federal Support to Universities, Colleges, and Selected Nonprofit Institutions* (Washington, D.C.: NSF).

14. Robert L. Farrell and Charles J. Anderson, "General Federal Support for Higher Education: An Analysis of Five Formulas" in *Financing Higher Education: Alternatives for the Federal Government,* M. D. Orwig, ed. (Iowa City: American College Testing Program, 1971), 219-68; Clark Kerr, "Federal Aid to Higher Education Through 1976," in *Economics and Financing of Higher Education,* 599-617. Gladiaux and Wolanin, *Congress and the Colleges.*

15. All of the following financial data for Yale is taken from the annual *Report of the Treasurer* for the years indicated.

16. *Report of the Treasurer,* 1967, p. 17; *Report of the President,* 1964, pp. 13-14.

17. *Report of the Treasurer,* 1966, 1967; *Science* 158 (1967): 1658-59. The Yale 'drive' was not a formal campaign and appears to have been forgotten rather than having a definite terminus.

18. *Report of the President,* 1971, p. 2.

19. *Report of the Treasurer,* 1971, p. 3; *Report of the President,* 1971, 15. *Plus ça change, plus le même chose:* in January 1992 Yale was again planning a restructuring to reduce its cost base. A special committee recommended reducing the faculty by 10.7 percent over the next decade: *Wall Street Journal,* Jan. 17, 1992.

20. *Report of the Treasurer,* 1972, pp. 1-6; 1973, pp. 2-4.

21. Ibid., 1974, p. 9; 1975, p. 6.

22. *Report of the President,* 1973, p. 11.

23. Dorritt Ann Cowan, "Single-sex to Coeducation at Princeton and Yale: Two Case Studies" (Ed.D. diss., Teachers College, Columbia University, 1982).

24. Gardner Patterson, "The Education of Women at Princeton: A Special Report," *Princeton Alumni Weekly* 69, 1 (Sept. 24, 1968): 4-56.

25. Ibid., 54.

26. Kingman Brewster alluded to the financial benefits of admitting women: "coeducation was not a financial burden, rather the opposite": *Report of the President,* 1973, p. 7. I would like to thank William G. Bowen (at the time, Provost of Princeton and member of the Patterson Committee) for alerting me to the financial importance of the coeducation decision: (New York City, 19 April, 1989).

27. "Economic Status of the Profession," *A.A.U.P. Bulletin,* 1970, 1972, 1976.

28. *Report of the Treasurer,* 1971, pp. 12–14; 1973, pp. 8–9; D. Bruce Johnstone, *New Patterns for College Lending: Income Contingent Loans* (New York: Columbia University Press, 1972), 52–55, 178–84.

29. *Report of the President,* 1969; 1974; John Perry Miller, *Creating Academic Settings: High Craft and Low Cunning* (New Haven: J. Simeon Press, 1991), 211–26.

30. Ibid., 1968, pp. 27–29; Miller, *Creating Academic Settings,* 173–210.

31. David S. Webster, "America's Highest Ranked Graduate Schools," *Change* (May/ June 1983), 14–24.

3. A Deeper Malaise

1. Seymour Martin Lipset and David Riesman, *Education and Politics at Harvard* (New York: McGraw-Hill, 1975), 240; Richard E. Peterson & John A. Bilorusky, *May 1970: The Campus Aftermath of Cambodia and Kent State* (Berkeley: Carnegie Commission on Higher Education, 1971).

2. Philip W. Semas, "The Student Mood"; "Student Activism Shows New Sophistication"; "Student Protest, 1975: Stress on Economic Issues," *Chronicle of Higher Education* (April 26, 1976); 7–8; (May 3, 1976); 3–4; (June 9, 1975); 3.

3. Attitude surveys by Marshall W. Meyer, reported by Lipset and Riesman, *Education and Politics at Harvard,* 252–54.

4. Lewis B. Mayhew, *Legacy of the Seventies* (San Francisco: Jossey-Bass, 1977), 222–25, quote p. 2.

5. For example, tenure is an easy target to attack, but compare the defense offered by Henry Rosovsky: *The University: An Owner's Manual* (New York: Norton, 1990), 177–89; or Michael S. McPherson and Gordon C. Winston, "The Economics of Academic Tenure: A Relational Perspective," in *Academic Labor Markets and Careers,* David W. Breneman and Ted I. K. Youn, eds. (New York: Falmer Press, 1988), 174–99.

6. Semas, "Student Protest, 1975"; Gael M. O'Brien, "Student Protests: Cutbacks, Tuition Hikes Are Among Targets," *Chronicle of Higher Education* (April 19, 1976), 2.

7. Lipset and Riesman, *Education and Politics at Harvard,* 237–43, quote p. 239; Marshall W. Meyer, "After the Bust: Student Politics at Harvard, 1969–72," in *Academic Transformation,* David Riesman & Verne A. Stadtman, eds. (New York: McGraw-Hill, 1973), 127–54.

8. Under pressure from black students, the Harvard faculty voted in 1969 to create the Afro-American Studies Program: Lipset and Riesman, *Education and Politics at Harvard,* 240–241, 350–51; Rosovsky, *The University,* 264.

9. Derek Bok, *Beyond the Ivory Tower: Social Responsibilities of the Modern University* (Cambridge: Harvard University Press, 1982), 299.

10. Ibid., 103, 115, 292, 305–9, passim.

11. Frank Newman et al., *Report on Higher Education* (Washington: GPO, 1971); Assembly on University Goals and Governance, "Theses," *Daedelus* (Winter 1975); 322–46 (first published January 1971).

12. Newman, *Report,* 4–16; Assembly, "Theses," 327–30.

13. Newman, *Report,* 33–43, 76–78; Assembly, "Theses," 331.

14. Newman, *Report*, 82–86; Assembly, "Theses," 337–38.

15. Newman, *Report*, 44–56, 84–86; Assembly, "Theses," 326–34.

16. Carnegie Council on Policy Studies in Higher Education, *Making Affirmative Action Work in Higher Education* (San Francisco: Jossey-Bass, 1975), 97–112; Walter C. Hobbs, ed., *Government Regulation of Higher Education* (Cambridge: Ballinger, 1978); Hugh Davis Graham, *The Civil Rights Era: Origins and Development of a National Policy, 1960–1972* (New York: Oxford University Press, 1990).

17. Nancy Gruchow, "Discrimination: Women Charge Universities with Bias," *Science* 168 (1970): 559–61, quote p. 561.

18. Ibid.; Robert J. Bazell, "Sex Discrimination: Campuses Face Contract Loss over HEW Demands," *Science* 170 (1970): 834–35; Deborah Shapley, "Sex Discrimination on Campus: Michigan Wrestles with Equal Pay," *Science* 173 (1971): 214–16.

19. Deborah Shapley, "University Women's Rights: Whose Feet Are Dragging?" *Science* 175 (1972): 151–54.

20. Caspar Weinberger, "Regulating the Universities," in *Bureaucrats and Brainpower: Government Regulation of Universities* (San Francisco: Institute for Contemporary Studies, 1979), 47–70.

21. By the late 1970s affirmative action pressure on universities lessened for several reasons: it became evident that the applicant pools of qualified minorities and women were smaller than had been assumed; the high cost of the plans retarded implementation; HEW was overwhelmed by the paperwork it had required; and several court decisions gave credence to the notion that reverse discrimination might not be legal: see Miro M. Todorovich, "A Road to Stalemate—the Current State of Regulations," in *Bureaucrats and Brainpower*, 95–112. On the other hand, the courts, which had been reluctant to intervene in internal university personnel decisions during the first part of the decade, abandoned that reluctance by decade's end. A University of Georgia professor was even jailed for refusing to reveal how and why he had voted in a tenure committee: Malcolm Moos, *The Post-Land Grant University: The University of Maryland Report* (University of Maryland, 1981), 40–44.

22. Cf. Hobbs, *Government Regulation*, 52–53.

23. *Making Affirmative Action Work*, 105–7.

24. Robert L. Sproull, "Federal Regulation and the Natural Sciences," in *Bureaucrats and Brainpower*, 71–94; Cheryl M. Fields, "Can Scientists Be Trusted on Hazardous Research?" *Chronicle of Higher Education* (Aug. 2, 1976), 4–5.

25. The Buckley Amendment was offered and enacted on an impulse, without benefit of prior public hearings to determine if a problem existed and if it was one of federal concern. In fact, institutions had long-established policies on access and confidentiality of files that were widely assumed to be adequate: Estelle Fishbein, "The Academic Industry—a Dangerous Premise," in *Government Regulation*, Hobbs, ed., 57–64.

26. Richard W. Lyman, "Federal Regulation and Institutional Autonomy—a University President's View," in *Bureaucrats and Brainpower*, 27–46, esp. 41–42. In keeping with this pattern of growing intrusion, the Office of Management and the Budget in 1980 required that "every federal grant recipient . . . account for 100 percent of his or her working time, dividing it into time spent on research, teaching, administration, and other duties. This resulted from an audit which showed that *one-quarter of one percent* of the research funds were being improperly charged": Moos, *Post-Land Grant University*, 45 [emphasis in original].

27. Ernest Gelhorn and Barry B. Boyer, "The Academy as a Regulated Industry," in *Government Regulation*, Hobbs, ed., 25–56, quote 29.

28. Nathan Glazer, "Regulating Business and Regulating the Universities: One Problem or Two?," in *Bureaucrats and Brainpower*, 113–40.

29. E.g. [Traditionalist] Edward Shils, "Great Britain and the United States: Legislators, Bureaucrats, and the Universities" in *Universities, Politicians, and Bureaucrats: Europe and the United States,* Hans Daalder and Edward Shils, eds. (Cambridge: Cambridge University Press, 1982), 437–80; [Proponent] U.S. Commission on Civil Rights, *The Federal Civil Rights Enforcement Effort—1974* III (Washington, D.C.: GPO, 1975), 275–308; [Pragmatist] Lyman, "Federal Regulation and Institutional Autonomy."

30. For the specialized nature of faculty positions, see McPherson and Winston, "Economics of Academic Tenure," 179–91.

31. Weinberger, "Regulating the Universities," 59–60.

32. This situation seemed inescapable, since there was in fact no pool of unemployed women or minorities that had been denied employment in higher education, and thus readily available for appointments.

33. "The Criteria of Academic Appointment in American Universities and Colleges: Some Documents of Affirmative Action at Work," *Minerva* 14 (1976): 97–117.

34. *Making Affirmative Action Work,* 136–45.

35. Cheryl M. Fields, "Women Hit 'Conciliation' Pact by Berkeley and Civil Rights Unit," *Chronicle of Higher Education* (March 11, 1974); 1, 6. *Federal Enforcement Effort—1974,* 298–305.

36. *Making Affirmative Action Work,* 140–41.

37. Lyman, "Federal Regulation and Institutional Autonomy," 40.

38. Theodore Caplow and Reece J. McGee, *The Academic Marketplace* (New York: Basic Books, 1958).

39. Neil Smelser and Robin Content, *The Changing Academic Labor Market: General Trends and a Berkeley Case Study* (Berkeley: University of California Press, 1980). This is an account of a search for three entry-level positions in the Berkeley Department of Sociology under affirmative action pressures. Widely advertised, the search elicited 286 applications, which brought in more than 1000 letters of recommendation, as well as other materials. The three appointees (1% of applicants) were from Harvard and Chicago— institutions that would have been canvassed under the old-boy system. One was a women, who was selected by the department in a close vote, but without outside pressure. In the absence of affirmative action, one might wonder if that vote would have been different.

40. *Digest of Education Statistics,* 1975, 1988.

41. Earl F. Cheit, *The New Depression in Higher Education* (New York: McGraw-Hill, 1971), 17.

42. Samuel K. Gove and Barbara Whiteside Solomon, "The Politics of Higher Education: A Bibliographic Essay," *Journal of Higher Education* 39 (1968): 181–95; Joseph B. Tucker, "The Politics of Public Higher Education," *AAUP Bulletin* (Autumn 1973), 286.

43. Organization for Economic Co-operation and Development, *Review of Higher Education in California: Examiners Report and Questions* (Paris: OECD, 1989).

44. Robert O. Berdahl, *Statewide Coordination of Higher Education* (Washington, D.C.: American Council on Education, 1971), 35.

45. Hugh Davis Graham, "Structure and Governance in American Higher Education: Historical and Comparative Analysis in State Policy," *Journal of Policy History* 1 (1989): 80–107, esp. 89–90.

46. Samuel K. Gove and Carol Everly Floyd, "The Politics of Public Higher Education: Illinois," *AAUP Bulletin* (1973); 287–92, quote 290.

47. Ibid.; M. M. Chambers, *Higher Education and State Governments, 1970–1975* (Danville, Ill.: Interstate, 1974), 84–95.

48. Joseph B. Tucker, "The Politics of Public Higher Education: Ohio," *AAUP Bulletin* (1973): 310–23.

49. Chambers, *Higher Education and State Governments,* 202–3.

50. Ibid., 128–32.

51. Allen Rosenbaum, "The Politics of Public Higher Education: Wisconsin," *AAUP Bulletin* (1973); 298–310.

52. Ibid., 307, 310; Graham, "State Policy," 90–91; Chambers, *Higher Education and State Governments,* 265–71.

53. Janet H. Ruyle and Lyman A. Glenny, *State Budgeting for Higher Education: Trends in State Revenue Appropriations from 1968 to 1977* (University of California Berkeley: Center for Studies in Higher Education, 1978).

54. Ibid., 32.

55. Ibid., 152–57.

56. Chambers, *Higher Education and State Government,* 259–61.

57. "By 1984, faculty salaries for full and associate professors had fallen to last place in the Big Ten, and prestige universities began raiding its best research faculty": Graham, "State Policy," 91.

58. See Jennifer R. Krohn, "Advancing Research Universities: A Study of Institutional Development, 1974–1986" (Ph.D., Pennsylvania State University, 1992).

59.

Ranking:	1970	1982
Illinois	9	13
Indiana	18	21 tie
Michigan	4	8tie
Michigan State	24tie	n.r.
Minnesota	16	16tie
Ohio State	22 (1966)	n.r.
Washington(Seattle)	13	19
Wisconsin	6	8tie
UC Berkeley	1	1
UCLA	10	8tie
UC San Diego	n.r.	21 tie
North Carolina	24tie	20
Texas	17	16tie

David Webster, "America's Highest Ranked Graduate Schools," *Change* (May/June 1983); 14–24.

60. For example, in 1969 tuition at 113 institutions belonging to the National Association of State Universities and Land-Grant Colleges increased by an average of 16.5 percent; in 1970 the University of California imposed tuition for the first time in its history; in 1973 the University of Michigan substantially raised tuition and began charging different rates for underclassmen, upperclassmen, and graduate students: Cheit, *New Depression,* 13; Chambers, *Higher Education and State Governments,* 136.

61. William J. Baumol and Maryse Eymonerie, "Rising Costs and the Public Institutions," *AAUP Bulletin* 56 (June 1970): 174–86.

Chapter 9. Surviving the Seventies

1. The State of Universities in the Mid-1970s

1. *American Higher Education: Toward an Uncertain Future* 2 vol. *Daedalus* (Fall 1974 & Winter 1975).

2. Clark Kerr, "What We Might Learn from the Climacteric," ibid., II: 1–7, esp. 1.

3. Martin Meyerson, "After a Decade of the Levelers in Higher Education: Reinforcing Quality While Maintaining Mass Education," ibid., 304–21; Richard W. Lyman, "In Defense of the Private Sector," ibid., 156–59.

4. John G. Kemeny, "The University in Steady State," ibid., 87–96; Robin W. Fleming, "Reflections on Higher Education," ibid., 8–15; Martin Trow, "The Public and the Private Lives of Higher Education," ibid., 113–27.

5. Daniel P. Moynihan, "The Politics of Higher Education," ibid., 128–47; W. Allen Wallis, "Unity in Higher Education," ibid., 68–77; Kerr, "Climacteric," 2–3.

6. Several authors made prescient observations: Richard Lyman foresaw the greater adaptability of private institutions ("Defense"); Patrick McCarthy signaled that the coming challenge would be to achieve expansion without growth ("Higher Education: Expansion Without Growth," ibid., 78–86); and Clark Kerr observed that "the moods of higher education seem to swing farther up and farther down than reality fully warrants" ("Climacteric," 7).

7. Bruce L. R. Smith and Joseph J. Karlesky, *The State of Academic Science: The Universities in the National Research Effort* (New York: Change Magazine Press, 1977), 227.

8. Ibid., 185–89, 86–158. A background paper by David Breneman, however, concluded that "the serious threat to vital and productive research capacity in the universities lies not in the domain of graduate education per se but rather in the limited number of openings for younger faculty": "Effects of Recent Trends in Graduate Education on University Research Capabilities in Physics, Chemistry, and Mathematics," in *The State of Academic Science: Background Papers*, Bruce L. R. Smith and Joseph J. Karlesky, eds. (New York: Change Magazine Press, 1978), 133–62, quote p. 158.

9. Dael Wolfle, "Forces Affecting the Research Role of Universities," ibid., 17–60, quote p. 56.

10. Robert L. Jacobson, "Retrenchment, Campus Sale Brings Optimism at Shaky New York U.," *Chronicle of Higher Education* 7 (Oct. 10, 1972): 5; Burton R. Clark, "The Wesleyan Story: The Importance of Moral Capital"; and Richard P. McCormick, "Rutgers, the State University," in *Academic Transformation: Seventeen Institutions Under Pressure*, David Riesman and Verne A. Stadtman, eds. (New York: McGraw-Hill, 1973), 367–82, 271–86. Rutgers suffered from prolonged student activism, administrative acquiescence to student demands, a divided faculty that eventually unionized, and close state regulation. The university employed discretionary resources largely to expand access, and followed current fashions by founding a new college focused on urbanization and racism.

11. Smith and Karlesky, *Academic Science*, 40–45, 229–35.

12. Ibid., 234.

13. Ibid., 70–75.

2. The University of Arizona.

1. For example, in 1947 the university established a retirement plan for faculty and won the right to pay the expenses of faculty attending academic meetings: Douglas D. Martin, *The Lamp in the Desert: The Story of the University of Arizona* (Tucson: University of Arizona Press, 1960), 220–39.

2. University of Arizona, *President's Report* 1958–59.

3. Martin, *Lamp in the Desert*, 252–54; Louis J. Battan, "A Brief History of the Institute of Atmospheric Physics and the Department of Atmospheric Sciences" (1984), University of Arizona Archives [UAA]; interview by author with A. Richard Kassander, Tucson, 1/19/89.

4. John Williams Anthony, "Georeminiscences" (1985) UAA; Battan, "Atmospheric Physics"; University of Arizona, *President's Report: A Decade of Progress, 1963-1973* (1973), 55-58. The Institute of Atmospheric Physics spawned a teaching arm, the Department of Atmospheric Sciences in the College of Liberal Arts.

5. J. Merton England, *A Patron for Pure Science: The National Science Foundation's Formative Years, 1945-57* (Washington, D.C.: NSF, 1982), 290-92; *Decade of Progress,* 56-57; University of Arizona, *President's Report,* 1985, 32-35.

6. Ekwen A. Whitaker, *The University of Arizona's Lunar and Planetary Laboratory: Its Founding and Early Years* (1985), UAA.

7. University of Arizona, *President's Report,* 1982, 27-29.

8. Allan M. Carrter, *An Assessment of Quality in Graduate Education* (Washington, D.C.: ACE, 1966): anthropology was ranked 12th and astronomy 6th.

9. National Science Foundation, *The NSF Science Development Programs* (Washington, D.C.: NSF, 1977), 13.

10. Interview by author of John P. Schaefer, Tucson, 1/19/89. In addition, in 1968-69 an award of $600,000 over three years to support atomic physics was received from the Defense Department's THEMIS program: "Annual Report of the Department of Physics, 1968-69," UAA.

11. NSF, *Science Development Programs,* 33-36; Howard E. Page, "The Science Development Program," in *Science Policy and the University,* Harold Orlans, ed. (Washington, D.C.: Brookings Institution, 1968), 101-19.

12. Leon Blitzer, "Skeletons Out of the Closet: An Anecdotal History of the UA Physics Department" (1985), UAA; Kassander interview.

13. "Annual Report of the Physics Department," 1960-61 & 1961-62, UAA.

14. Anthony, "Georeminiscences," 63-64; University of Arizona, *President's Report,* 1980, 47-48; Kassander interview.

15. Kassander interview; Schaefer interview.

16. Kassander interview; *President's Report,* 1982, 27.

17. John L. Carpenter, "Interview with Richard A. Harvill," *The Phoenix Gazette* (Oct. 20-24, 1969), (UAA). Annual department reports from the mid-sixties complain that low faculty salaries are a problem for recruitment: e.g. History, Philosophy, Chemistry, 1965-66.

18. Interview by author of Albert Weaver, Tucson, 1/20/89.

19. This goal became defined as becoming one of the top ten public research universities. This select group was defined as the most prestigious Big-Ten universities (Michigan, Wisconsin, Illinois, Minnesota), Berkeley, UCLA, and Washington on the West Coast, and the University of Texas. Schaefer considered it a great boost to Arizona when it was included in the Pac-10 Athletic Conference in 1978. The importance was in the associations it created (Schaefer interview). The first official Pac-10 activity was to host a conference of deans (interview by author of Paul Rosenblatt, Tucson, 1/19/89).

20. The following account is largely based upon interviews with Kassander, Schaefer, Rosenblatt, and Weaver, which provide a consistent picture of the steps taken during the Schaefer years to further the academic advancement of the university.

21. Dean Paul Rosenblatt relates one incident in which he learned of the possible availability of a prized scholar, confirmed his interest in Arizona, then received authorization from the president and made a firm offer, all within 90 minutes. See also, the account of the hiring of Andrew M. Greeley: *Confessions of a Parish Priest: An Autobiography* (New York: Simon & Schuster, 1986), 422. This same procedure was used for purposes of affirmative action. It was a general policy that any department that discovered a desirable minority candidate would be given an additional line to hire him or her. Such

policies have become standard practice (see Chapter 8.3), but generally are embodied in official procedures, rather than as an understanding with the president: Rosenblatt interview.

22. "Annual Report, Department of Sociology," 1975–76, UAA.

23. Association of Research Libraries, "ARL Library Index, 1981–82."

24. University of Arizona, *President's Report,* 1977–78.

25. Instructional expenditures from annual *Financial Reports,* UAA.

26. "Annual Reports, Department of Biology, Department of Philosophy, 1971–72," UAA.

27. John A. Muffo & John R. Robinson, "Early Science Career Patterns of Graduates from Leading Research Universities," *Review of Higher Education* 5 (1981): 1–14.

28. Weaver interview.

29. "Annual Report, Department of Physics, 1971–72," UAA.

30. Kenneth D. Roose & Charles J. Anderson, *A Rating of Graduate Programs* (Washington, D.C.: ACE, 1970); Lyle V. Jones, et al., eds., *An Assessment of Research-Doctorate Programs in the United States,* 5 vols. (Washington, D.C.: National Academy Press, 1982).

31. E.g., Arizona's history department received the highest rating on improvement: *Assessment: Social and Behavioral Sciences,* 90–91.

32. Kent Halstead, *State Profiles: Financing Public Higher Education 1978 to 1987* (Washington, D.C.: Research Associates of Washington, 1987).

33. Interview by author of Michael Cusanovitch, Tucson (1/19/89).

3. Georgia Institute of Technology

1. Research data from NSF: *Selected Data on Academic Science/Engineering R&D Expenditures, FY 1989; Federal Support to Universities, Colleges, and Selected Nonprofits, FY 1970.*

2. Allan M. Cartter, "Qualitative Aspects of Southern University Education," *Southern Economic Journal* 32 (July, 1965): 39–69, quote p. 68.

3. Robert C. McMath, Jr., et al; *Engineering the New South: Georgia Tech, 1885–1985* (Athens: University of Georgia Press, 1985), 8–11, 52–58.

4. Ibid., 168–71.

5. Ibid., 186–87, 212–17, 258–70.

6. No synthetic history of the desegregation of Southern universities exists, but appreciation of this momentous development can be gained from the experiences of individual institutions: Thomas G. Dyer, *The University of Georgia: A Bicentennial History, 1785–1985* (Athens: University of Georgia Press, 1985), 303–34; Paul K. Conkin, *Gone With the Ivy: A Biography of Vanderbilt University* (Knoxville: University of Tennessee Press, 1985), 539–80.

7. Cartter, "Qualitative Aspects of Southern University Education."

8. Ibid., 69.

9. McMath, *Engineering the New South,* 235–301.

10. Ibid., 290–91.

11. Ibid., 301–70.

12. Ibid., 373–81.

13. In 1967 the University of Georgia was allocated a $30 million budget increase which led to the addition of 450 faculty members: Dyer, *University of Georgia,* 344–45; McMath, *Engineering the New South,* 403–5.

14. Ibid., 409–19; Ben Moon, "Dr. Joseph M. Pettit—a Man of Convictions with No Fixed Notions," *Tech Alumnus* (Fall 1971), 7–9.

15. See above, Chapter 8; McMath, *Engineering the New South*, 412–15.

16. Bill Seddon, "The President and His Men: Facing the Problems of the 70's," *Georgia Tech Alumni Magazine* (1973), 5–9, quote p. 9.

17. McMath, *Engineering the New South*, 398–401; Donald J. Grace and Frederick A. Rossini, "Georgia Tech Research Institute: An Interdisciplinary Perspective" (GTRI, 1986); Engineering Experiment Station, "Self-Study—1973": Georgia Institute of Technology Archives [GITA].

18. McMath, *Engineering the New South*, 418–20; "New Director Brings Wide Experience to EES," *Georgia Tech Alumni Magazine* (Nov. 1986), 23–24.

19. Georgia Institute of Technology, "Self-Study—1973," 29–41: GITA.

20. Jennifer R. Krohn, "Advancing Research Universities: A Study of Institutional Development, 1974–86" (Doctoral diss., Pennsylvania State University, 1992)

21. "Report of the Institutional Self-Study Committee on Research—1973," 459; GIT, "Self-Study—1983," 551: GITA. Income constitutes "Total earned income from sponsored research" and is less than research expenditures reported to NSF.

22. GIT, "Annual Report, 1975–76," 209, 1: GITA.

23. GIT, "Annual Report of the President, 1979–80": GITA.

24. "Self-Study—1983," 36–37, 45–46; McMath, *Engineering the New South*, 420; interview with Robert C. McMath, Jr., Nov. 2, 1989; Krohn, "Advancing Research Universities," 164–65.

25. Lyle V. Jones, et al., *An Assessment of Research-Doctorate Programs in the United States* (Washington, D.C.: National Academy Press, 1982).

26. "Long-Range Planning at Georgia Tech" (Fall, 1986): GITA: quote: VP/RES (6/1/86), p. 6.

27. J. M. Pettit, "Memorandum to the General Faculty on the Microelectronics Center" (Nov. 18, 1981): GITA; "Tech Plans $30 Million Expansion of Microelectronics Research Program," *Metropolitan Atlanta Business Report* (Aug./Sept. 1985), 6–7.

28. "Long-Range Planning": quote: GTRI (6/1/86), p. 1.

29. Ibid.; GIT, *1988-89 Georgia Tech Fact Book* (Atlanta: GIT, 1989), 129–33; GTRI, *Annual Report, 1989;* interview with Donald J. Grace (Nov. 3, 1989).

30. "Long-Range Planning"; GTRI, *Annual Report, 1989.*

31. See below, Chapter 10.

32. GIT, *President's Report, 1980-81.*

33. McMath, *Engineering the New South*, 450; *President's Report, 1981–82;* Karen Buttermore, "Heeman's Goal: Make Tech the Best," *Georgia Tech Alumni Magazine* (Oct. 1979): 19–21.

34. NSF, *Selected Academic R&D, 1989, Academic Science/Engineering Funds, FY 1987* (NSF, 1989); *Federal Support to Universities, Colleges, and Selected Nonprofit Institutions, FY 1986* (NSF, 1987). Voluntary support from industry from Council for Financial Aid to Education, *Voluntary Support of Education* [annual] (New York: CFAE).

35. "Long-Range Planning."

36. Ibid.: quote: VP/RES, p. 1.

37. Ibid.: quote: VP/RES, p. 1.

38. See below, Chapter 10; Krohn, "Advancing Research Universities," chap. 2.

4. Private Industry and University Research

1. David C. Mowery and Nathan Rosenberg, *Technology and the Pursuit of Economic Growth* (Cambridge: Cambridge University Press, 1989), 21–97; Roger L. Geiger, *To Advance Knowledge: The Growth of American Research Universities, 1900-1940* (New York: Oxford University Press, 1986), 174–91; David F. Noble, *America by Design: Sci-*

ence, Technology, and the Rise of Corporate Capitalism (New York: Alfred Knopf, 1977).

2. Roger L. Geiger, "The Ambiguous Link: Private Industry and University Research," in *The Economics of American Higher Education,* William E. Becker and Darrell Lewis, eds. (Hingham, Mass.: Kluwer, 1992), 265–98; Richard R. Nelson, "What Is Private and What Is Public About Technology," *Science, Technology, and Human Values* 14 (1989): 229–41.

3. National Science Foundation, *National Patterns of R&D Resources: 1989* (Washington, D.C.: NSF, 1989). Further references to university and industrial research expenditures will be from this source unless otherwise indicated.

4. Nelson, "What Is Private?," 237–38. E.g., the 1988 Nobel Prize for Medicine was awarded to three pharmaceutical researchers for discoveries made in industrial laboratories.

5. Government-University-Industry Research Roundtable, *Industrial Perspectives on Innovation and Interactions with Universities* (Washington, D.C.: National Academy Press, 1991), 8–10; Lois Peters and Herbert Fusfeld, "Current U.S. University-Industry Research Connections," in National Science Foundation, *University-Industry Research Relationships* (Washington, D.C.: NSF, 1982), 1–162, esp. 34–35.

6. Adapted from NSF, *National Patterns of R&D*

7. Eli Ginzberg and Anna B. Dutka, *The Financing of Bio-medical Research* (Baltimore: Johns Hopkins University Press, 1989), 22.

8. The Assembly on University Goals and Governance, "Theses," *Daedalus* (Winter 1975): 337–38; Harold Orlans, *The Nonprofit Research Institute: Its Origin, Operation, Problems, and Prospects* (New York: McGraw-Hill, 1972), 141–44.

9. Orlans, *Nonprofit Research Institute,* 144–57; David Z. Robinson, "Will the University Decline as the Center for Scientific Research?," *Daedalus* (Spring 1973), 101–10. Both authors, after acknowledging the conventional wisdom about research leaving the university, report that the university is far more resilient than such a view holds.

10. Harvey Brooks, "Knowledge and Action: The Dilemma of Science Policy in the '70's," *Daedalus* (Spring 1973): 125–44.

11. Strickland, *Politics, Science and Dread Disease;* Milton Lomask, *A Minor Miracle: An Informal History of the National Science Foundation* (Washington, D.C.: NSF, 1976), 237–50.

12. *Chronicle of Higher Education* (Dec. 24, 1973), 6.

13. Rustum Roy, "University-Industry Interaction Patterns," *Science* 178 (1972): 255–59.

14. Peters and Fusfeld, "Current University-Industry Research," 63–66.

15. Lomask, *Minor Miracle,* 254.

16. Walter S. Baer, "The Changing Relationships: Universities and Other R&D Performers," in *The State of Academic Science: Background Papers,* Bruce L. R. Smith and Joseph J. Karlesky, eds. (New York: Change Magazine Press, 1978), 61–104, quote pp. 99–100.

17. Barbara J. Culliton, "Harvard and Monsanto: The $23 Million Alliance," *Science* 195 (1977): 759–62.

18. It took ten years just to isolate the tumor angiogenesis factor, the main object of the research, but other patents were derived from this work: Martin Kenney, *Biotechnology: The University-Industrial Complex* (New Haven: Yale University Press, 1986), 58–59.

19. Ibid., 194–95, 199–200; Jack R. Kloppenburg, *First the Seed: The Political Economy of Plant Biotechnology, 1492–2000* (Cambridge: Cambridge University Press, 1988), 208–9.

20. Robert Teitelman, *Gene Dreams: Wall Street, Academia, and the Rise of Biotechnology* (New York: Basic Books, 1989), 18–20; Stephen S. Hall, *Invisible Frontiers: The Race to Synthesize a Human Gene* (New York: Atlantic Monthly Press, 1987), 55–65.

21. Teitelman, *Gene Dreams,* 122–52; Peters and Fusfeld, "Current University–Industry Research," 62–63; Office of Technology Assessment, *Commercial Biotechnology: An International Analysis* (Washington, D.C.: OTA, 1984), 99–110.

22. Kenney, *Biotechnology,* 132–89.

23. Hall, *Invisible Frontiers.*

24. Kenney, *Biotechnology,* 132–75; Teitelman provides a detailed case of this process at one firm: *Gene Dreams.*

25. Office of Technology Assessment, *New Developments in Biotechnology: U.S. Investment in Biotechnology* (Washington, D.C.: OTA, 1988), 78–87. It is almost self-defeating to assess this fast-moving industry at any single point in time. Although investments in biotechnology companies peaked first in 1983 and then again in 1986–87, they surged once again in 1991.

26. A survey conducted by the Office of Technology Assessment found "47 percent of biotechnology faculty reported consulting with an outside company, and 8 percent reported holding equity in a firm whose products or services are directly related to their own university research": *New Developments,* 119. These figures are indeed high, and justify somewhat the impressions reported in Kenney, *Biotechnology,* 96–100.

27. Kenney, *Biotechnology,* 55–72, esp. 56; Bernard D. Reams, Jr., *University-Industry Research Partnerships: The Major Legal Issues in Research and Development Agreements* (Westport, Conn.: Quorum Books, 1986).

28. David Blumenthal et al., "Industrial Support of University Research in Biotechnology," *Science* 231 (1986): 242–46.

29. This was the theme of the 1979 presidential address to the American Association for the Advancement of Science: Edward E. David, Jr., "Science Futures: The Industrial Connection," *Science* 203 (1979): 837–40; David Dickson, *The New Politics of Science* (Chicago: University of Chicago Press, 1984), 65–72; Derek Bok, *Beyond the Ivory Tower: Social Responsibilities of the Modern University* (Cambridge: Harvard University Press, 1982), 136–68.

30. OTA, *New Developments,* 101–8.

31. Sheila Slaughter, *The Higher Learning and High Technology: Dynamics of Higher Education and Policy Formation* (Albany: SUNY Press, 1989).

32. Peters and Fusfeld, "Current University-Industry Research," 48–49; Mowery and Rosenberg, *Technology and the Pursuit,* 238–73.

33. U.S. House of Representatives, *Commercialization of Academic Biomedical Research* (Washington, D.C.: GPO, 1981); *University/Industry Cooperation in Biotechnology* (Washington, D.C.: GPO, 1982).

34. *Commercialization,* 87–96; Kenney, *Biotechnology,* 61–64.

35. Bok, *Ivory Tower,* 163; Kenney, *Biotechnology,* 121–31.

36. *University/Industry Cooperation,* 65–66, 122–30.

37. *Commercialization,* 21.

38. Kenney, *Biotechnology,* 78–83; Bok, *Ivory Tower,* 136.

39. Bok, *Ivory Tower,* 141.

40. Quoted in Kenney, *Biotechnology,* 84.

41. Quoted in Barbara J. Culliton, "Pajaro Dunes: The Search for Consensus," *Science* 216 (April 9, 1982): 155–58.

42. Thomas W. Lanfitt et al., eds., *Partners in the Research Enterprise,* [A National Conference on University-Corporate Relations in Science and Technology, held at the

University of Pennsylvania on 14–16 December 1982] (Philadelphia: University of Pennsylvania Press, 1983).

43. OTA, *New Developments*, 77–87; cf. Teitelman, *Gene Dreams*.

44. Business–Higher Education Forum, *America's Competitive Challenge: The Need for a National Response* (Washington, D.C.: 1983), 9. Mowery and Rosenberg present an informed argument that changes in the economic and technological environment now require firms to invest more heavily in cooperative research, especially with universities: *Technology and the Pursuit*, 205–37.

45. Bruce L. R. Smith, *American Science Policy Since World War II* (Washington, D.C.: Brookings Institution, 1990), 129–33; Also see below, Chapter 10.

46. George T. Mazuzan, *The National Science Foundation: A Brief History* (Washington, D.C.: NSF, 1988), 26–29; National Science Foundation, *Long-Range Plan, FY 1989–1993* (Washington, D.C.: NSF, 1988).

47. United States General Accounting Office, *Engineering Research Centers: NSF Program Management and Industry Sponsorship* (Washington, D.C.: GAO, 1988); Mowery and Rosenberg, *Technology and the Pursuit*, 257–73.

48. Teitelman, *Gene Dreams*, 208. This conclusion is shared by Kloppenberg for the agricultural industry: *First the Seed*, 223–41. However, a few young biotech firms have evolved into substantial corporations with commercial products, which indicates that this industry is too dynamic and diverse for sweeping generalizations.

49. Peters and Fusfeld, "Current University-Industry Research," 20.

Chapter 10. The New Era of the 1980s

1. Turning Outward

1. Carnegie Council on Policy Studies in Higher Education, *Three Thousand Futures: The Next Twenty Years of Higher Education* (San Francisco: Jossey-Bass, 1980), 152–201. Richard B. Freeman, *The Overeducated American* (New York: Academic Press, 1976).

2. University of Michigan, *Financial Report, 1984, 7*.

3. Gilbert S. Omenn and Denis J. Prager, "Research Universities and the Future: Challenges and Opportunities," in *Research in the Age of the Steady-State University*, Don I. Phillips and Benjamin S. P. Shen, eds. (Boulder, Col.: Westview, 1982), 21–36; John T. Wilson *Academic Science, Higher Education, and the Federal Government, 1950–1983* (Chicago: University of Chicago Press, 1983), 71–103; David Dickson, *The New Politics of Science* (Chicago: University of Chicago Press, 1984), 44–50.

4. Kevin Murphy and Finis Welch, "Wage Premiums for College Graduates: Recent Growth and Possible Explanations," *Educational Researcher* 18, 4 (May 1989): 17–26; idem, "Wages of College Graduates" in *The Economics of American Higher Education*, William Becker and Darrell R. Lewis, eds. (Norwell, Mass.: Kluwer, 1992), 121–41.

5. "The Annual Report of the Economic Status of the Profession, 1990–1991," *Academe* 76 (March-April 1991); National Science Foundation, *Selected Data on Academic Science/Engineering R&D Expenditures, FY 1989* (Washington, D.C.: NSF, Oct. 1990).

6. Roger L. Geiger, *Privatization of Higher Education: International Trends and Issues* (Princeton: ICED, 1988).

7. Adapted from *Digest of Education Statistics, 1988*.

8. Ibid.

9. Private universities in the 1990s felt that they were testing the limits of tuition

increases. They generally attempted to limit annual hikes (not always successfully) to inflation plus 1 or 2 percent; and they placed great emphasis on controlling costs—even to the point of cutting core faculty positions.

10. Calculated from NSF Computer Aided Science Policy & Analysis [CASPAR] database.

11. California raised university tuition substantially in 1991, thus falling more in line with other states.

12. This and all subsequent data on voluntary support from the annual reports of the Council for Aid to Education, *Voluntary Support of Education.*

13. Voluntary support for higher education declined 3.5 percent in 1987-88, which seems minor considering changes in the tax laws that encouraged giving in 1986 as well as the market crash of October 1987.

14. Survey by the Office of University Relations, Pennsylvania State University (5/11/90). My thanks to Roger Williams for providing these data.

15. U.S. House of Representatives, Committee on Science and Technology, *American Science and Science Policy Issues: Chairman's Report* (December 1986), 50-57.

16. National Science Board, *The Role of the National Science Foundation in Economic Competitiveness* (Washington, D.C.: NSF, 1988); National Science Foundation, *Long-Range Plan, FY 1989-1993* (1988); U.S. General Accounting Office, *Engineering Research Centers: NSF Program Management and Industry Sponsorship* (August 1988).

17. Frederick Betz, "Partnerships for Research: Lessons from Experience" in David R. Powers et al., *Higher Education in Partnership with Industry* (San Francisco: Jossey-Bass, 1988), 281-327; National Science Foundation, "Budget Summary, Fiscal Year 1991" (n.d.).

18. Roger L. Geiger, "The Ambiguous Link: Private Industry and University Research," in Becker and Lewis, eds., *Economics of American Higher Education,* 265-97.

19. Robert S. Friedman and Renee C. Friedman, "Sponsorship, Organization and Program Change at 100 Universities," Pennsylvania State University, Institute for Policy Research and Evaluation (June 1986).

20. Herbert I. Fusfeld, "Overview of University-Industry Research," in *Partners in the Research Enterprise,* Thomas W. Langfit, et al., eds. (Philadelphia: University of Pennsylvania Press, 1983), 10-19; quote 14. See also, Government-University-Industry Research Roundtable, *Industrial Perspectives on Innovation and Interactions with Universities* (Washington, D.C.: National Academy Press, 1991), 13-14.

21. Gary Matkin, *Technology Transfer and the American Research University* (New York: Macmillan, 1990), 179-81.

22. For example, U.S. Congress, Office of Technology Assessment, "Proposal Pressure in the 1980s: an Indicator of Stress on the Federal Research System" (April 1990).

23. Geiger, "Ambiguous Link."

24. Matkin, *Technology Transfer,* 56-63; David Blumenthal, Sherrie Epstein, and James Maxwell, "Commercializing University Research: Lessons from the Experience of the Wisconsin Alumni Research Foundation," *New England Journal of Medicine* 314 (1986): 1621-26; Charles Weiner, "Patenting and Academic Research: Historical Case Studies," *Science, Technology, and Human Values* 12 (1987): 50-62.

25. David R. Powers and Mary F. Powers, "Making Partnerships Work" in Powers et al., *Higher Education in Partnership,* 3-242, esp. 86; Lois Peters and Herbert Fusfeld, "Current U.S. University-Industry Research Connections," in National Science Foundation, *University-Industry Research Relationships: Selected Studies* (Washington, D.C.: NSF), 7-162, esp. 107; Matkin, *Technology Transfer,* 255-67.

26. Geiger, "The Ambiguous Link," 281–89.

27. Matkin, *Technology Transfer*, 315–18.

28. The following discussion draws on, and simplifies, the analysis by Matkin, who discerns eleven phases of patent administration: *Technology Transfer*, 81–145.

29. Ibid., 110–20.

30. Ibid., 88, 127.

31. In 1976–80 U.S. universities were awarded 1,739 patents; in 1986–90 the comparable figure was 4,664 patents: National Science Board, *Science and Engineering Indicators, 1991* (Washington, D.C.: NSF, 1991), 390; Irwin Feller and Sudi Seshadri, "The Evolving Market for Patent Rights," Pennsylvania State University, Institute for Policy Research and Evaluation, 1990.

32. Eliot Marshall, "Harvard Tiptoes into the Market," *Science* 241 (1988): 1595; Matkin, *Technology Transfer*.

33. Government-University-Industry Research Roundtable, *New Alliances and Partnerships in American Science and Engineering* (Washington, D.C.: National Academy Press, 1986); Association of American Universities, *Trends in Technology Transfer at Universities* (Washington, D.C.: AAU, 1986); Matkin, *Technology Transfer*, 159–61.

34. Geiger, "Ambiguous Link," 288–92.

2. Research in the 1980s

1. National Science Foundation, *National Patterns of R&D Resources: 1989* (Washington, D.C.: NSF, 1989).

2. E.g., Elizabeth Culotta, "Hot Fields," *Science* 252 (1991): 1118–20; Frank Press, "Science and Technology Policy for a New Era," Speech to National Academy of Sciences (April 27, 1992).

3. Government-University-Industry Research Roundtable, [GUIRT] *Science and Technology in the Academic Enterprise* (Washington, D.C.: National Academy Press, 1989), 1–8. Internal direct support for research at public universities averaged more than twice the level of private universities.

4. The following discussion draws on data from Jennifer Krohn, "Advancing Research Universities: A Study of Institutional Development, 1974–1986," (Ph.D. diss., Pennsylvania State University, 1992); and analysis of CASPAR data in progress.

5. Research performed by the Applied Physics Labratory has been excluded. This unit, which performs almost 3 percent of academic R&D, was a separately budgeted Federal Research Center until 1978; since then it has been included in the research totals of Johns Hopkins University.

6. Krohn, "Advancing Research Universities."

7. See Table 23.

8. These patterns are confirmed by data on institutional finances in Krohn, "Advancing Research Universities."

9. GUIRT, *Science and Technology*, 11–48.

10. Robert S. Friedman and Renee C. Friedman, "Sponsorship, Organization, and Program Change at 100 Universities," Pennsylvania State University, Institute for Policy Research and Evaluation (June 1986).

11. Constance Holden, "Career Trends for the 1990s," *Science* 252 (1991): 1110–17.

12. Ibid., 1111.

13. Leon M. Lederman, *Science—the End of the Frontier?*, Supplement to *Science* (Jan. 1991).

14. Ibid., 5. In converting to constant dollars, Lederman used the R&D deflator, which reflects the fact that R&D costs have risen more rapidly than the consumer price index. By the latter measure, real expenditures for academic research increased by 60 percent from 1968 to 1988: Joseph Palca, "Leon Lederman's Quest: Double Science Funding," *Science* 251 (1991): 153–54.

15. Holden, "Career Trends," 1111, 1116.

16. GUIRT, *Fateful Choices: The Future of the U.S. Academic Research Enterprise* (Washington, D.C.: National Academy Press, 1992).

17. Lederman, *Frontier?*; Office of Technology Assessment [OTA], *Federally Funded Research: Decisions for a Decade* (Washington, D.C.: GPO, 1991), 65–66.

18. Quoted in Palca, "Lederman's Quest," 154.

19. *Research Universities and the National Interest: A Report of Fifteen University Presidents* (New York: The Ford Foundation, 1978); Sloan Commission on Government and Higher Education, *A Program for Renewed Partnership* (Cambridge, Mass.: Ballinger, 1980); Robert Rosenzweig, *The Research Universities and Their Patrons* (Berkely: University of California Press, 1982); John Brademas, *Signs of Trouble and Erosion: A Report on Graduate Education* (New York University, 1984); Don Fuqua, *American Science and Science Policy Issues: Chairman's Report to the Committee on Science and Technology* (Washington, D.C.: GPO, 1986); White House Science Council, Panel on the Health of U.S. Colleges and Universities, *A Renewed Partnership* (Washington, D.C.: GPO, 1986).

20. GUIRT, *Science and Technology*, I–12, II–48–51; National Science Foundation, Division of Policy Research and Analysis, *The State of Academic Science and Engineering* (Washington, D.C.: NSF, 1990), 133–39.

21. NSF, *The State of Academic Science*, 126–33; OTA, *Decisions for a Decade*, 178–81.

22. Derek Bok, *The President's Report, 1989–1990* (Harvard University, 1991).

3. Centrifugal Forces

1. Laurence Veysey, *The Emergence of the American University* (Chicago: University of Chicago Press, 1965).

2. *Digest of Education Statistics, 1990*.

3. GUIRT, *Science and Technology in the Academic Enterprise* (Washington, D.C.: National Academy Press, 1989), I–9.

4. E.g., Paul von Blum, *Stillborn Education: A Critique of the American Research University* (Lanham, Md.: University Press of America, 1986); Charles J. Sykes, *Profscam: Professors and the Demise of Higher Education* (New York: Regnery Gateway, 1988); Page Smith, *Killing the Spirit: Higher Education in America* (New York: Viking, 1990).

5. Derek Bok, *President's Report, 1989–1990* (Harvard University, 1991), 6.

6. *One-Third of a Nation: A Report of the Commission on Minority Participation in Education and American Life* (Washington, D.C.: American Council on Education, 1988).

7. Ibid., 22.

8. *One-Third of a Nation* invoked factors from pre-natal care to the budget deficit to account for the statistical underachievement of minorities. Clearly, such arenas as pre-collegiate education and labor market conditions were more determinative than higher education. The demographic analysis behind this document is highly suspect; for example, from 1920 to 1990 the black population increased from 10 percent to 12 percent of the U.S. population: Stephan Thernstrom, "The Minority Majority Will Never Come," *Wall Street Journal* (July 26, 1990).

9. *One-Third of a Nation* appeared at a time of considerable turmoil on campuses over minority issues: e.g., Duke University at this juncture made an unrealistic commitment to have a black faculty member in each department; Penn State promised under pressure to elevate Black Studies to a department, create a high administrative position for minority issues, and meet higher recruitment goals.

10. Arthur M. Schlesinger, Jr., *The Disuniting of America: Reflections on a Multicultural Society* (Knoxville, Tenn.: Whittle, 1991)—a critique of racial separatism. For the distinction between "liberal" (i.e. moderate) feminism and "gender" (i.e. extremist) feminism, and the dominance of women's study by the latter, see Scott Jaschik, "Philosophy Professor Portrays Her Feminist Colleagues as Out of Touch and 'Relentlessly Hostile to the Family'," *Chronicle of Higher Education* (Jan. 15, 1992), A1, A16–18.

11. Extremism is undoubtedly encouraged by the deliberate isolation of cultural studies, which stems in part from their rejection of academic disciplines and normal standards (like objectivity) of academic discourse. John Searle noted that statements presented "in the cozy and somewhat self-congratulatory atmosphere of a conference that one of the principals described as a 'rally of the cultural left'" became somewhat embarrassing when repeated in a national journal: "The Storm over the University: An Exchange," *New York Review of Books* (Feb. 19, 1991), 48.

12. Roger Kimball, *Tenured Radicals: How Politics Has Corrupted Our Higher Education* (New York: Harper & Row, 1990), 1–33. The battle over the 'canon' was fought most explicitly at Stanford University: "The Discussion About Proposals to Change the Western Culture Program at Stanford University," *Minerva* 27 (1989): 223–411.

13. Judith Harris, JoAnn Silverstein, and Dianne Andrews, "Educating Women in Science," in *Educating the Majority: Women, Challenge Tradition in Higher Education,* Carol S Pearson, Donna L. Shavlik, and Judith G. Touchton, eds. (New York: ACE-Macmillan, 1989), 294–310, quote p. 299. According to one observer, skeptical of both women's studies and research universities, "the older notion of 'objectivity' has gone by the board completely in Women's Studies. There is no pretense that the instructors have objectivity or even impartiality or 'judiciousness' as a goal.... It is difficult to overemphasize the importance of women in undermining the academy's notion of 'objectivity'.... They are the last utopians; they have revived the dream of a better, more humane society, not to be achieved by the science of reason or objectivity, but by the keener sensibilities and nobler character of women": Page Smith, *Killing the Spirit: Higher Education in America* (New York: Viking, 1990), 289, 292.

14. Change Trendlines, "Signs of a Changing Curriculum," *Change* (Jan. 1992): 52; Dinesh D'Souza, *Illiberal Education: The Politics of Race and Sex on Campus* (New York: Free Press, 1991), 204.

15. Arthur Levine and Jeanette Cureton, "The Quiet Revolution: Eleven Facts about Multiculturalism and the Curriculum," *Change* (Jan. 1992): 25–29; Denise K. Magner, "Difficult Questions Face Colleges that Require Students to Take Courses that Explore Issues Relating to Race," *Chronicle of Higher Education* (March 28, 1990): A19–21. E.g., idem., "Faculty Members at Berkeley Offer Courses to Satisfy Controversial 'Diversity' Requirement," *Chronicle of Higher Education* (March 11, 1992), A-1, A-16–17.

16. The speech code at the University of Michigan was struck down in 1989; that for the University of Wisconsin was declared unconstitutional in 1991. Efforts to devise and impose a constitutional speech code have persisted at both institutions: Jennifer Silverberg, "MSA Opposes Anti-Harassment Policy," *Michigan Today* 24 (Feb. 1992): 4; "Campus Life," *New York Times* (March 22, 1992): 39.

17. E.g., D'Souza, *Illiberal Education,* 194–203; Anthony DePalma, "Hard-Won Acceptance Spawns New Conflicts Around Ethnic Studies," *New York Times* (Jan. 2, 1991), B8.

18. "Text of Remarks by President George Bush at the University of Michigan Commencement," *Michigan Today* 23 (May 1991): 9–10; Thomas J. DeLoughrey, "Controversial Amendments to Higher-Education Bill Expected in Senate," *Chronicle of Higher Education* (Feb. 19, 1992), A24.

19. D'Souza, *Illiberal Education*, above, n.17. One review explores D'Souza'a past association with right-wing campus groups, the one-sidedness of his arguments, *and* the validity of his critique: Louis Menand, "Illiberalism," *New Yorker* (May 20, 1991), 101–7.

20. The McNeill-Lehrer News Hour of Public Television devoted an unprecedented solid week of programming to political correctness in the summer of 1991. Judging solely from the sanitized views expressed there, one would never know what the fuss was about.

21. Above, n. 19. President Richard Nixon left the harshest criticism of students to Vice President Spiro Agnew, who called student demonstrators, among other things, "nattering nabobs of negativism." Governor Ronald Reagan also gained political capital by bashing students in that era.

4. Research Universities and American Society

1. Robert K. Merton, *The Sociology of Science,* ed. by Norman Storer (Chicago: University of Chicago Press, 1973), 267–78; Talcott Parsons and Gerald M. Platt, *The American University* (Cambridge: Harvard University Press, 1973), 47.

2. See above, Chapter 8: "The Student Rebellion."

3. Parsons and Platt, *American University.*

4. Michael S. McPherson and Gordon C. Winston, "The Economics of Academic Tenure: A Relational Perspective," in *Academic Labor Markets and Careers,* David W. Breneman and Ted I. K. Youn, eds. (Philadelphia: Falmer Press, 1988), 174–99.

5. A principal argument in, Office of Technology Assessment, *Federally Funded Research: Decisions for a Decade* (Washington, D.C.: GPO, 1991).

6. Daniel Bell, *The Coming of Post-Industrial Society: A Venture in Social Forecasting* (New York: Basic Books, 1973).

7. Peter Novick, *That Noble Dream: The 'Objectivity Question' and the American Historical Profession* (Cambridge: Cambridge University Press, 1988), 628; Stephen Park Turner and Jonathan H. Turner, *The Impossible Science: An Institutional Analysis of American Sociology* (Newbury Park: Sage, 1990), 196; Joseph Adelson, "Politically Correct Psychology," *The American Scholar* (Autumn 1991), 580–83, quote p. 583; Gerald Graff, *Professing Literature: an Institutional History* (Chicago: University of Chicago Press, 1987), 252.

8. Novick, *That Noble Dream,* 592.

9. Academic leadership of this nature is often proffered in a diffuse form, as in *One-Third of a Nation.* Internally, Derek Bok has warned, "universities are not very good at passing collective judgments on political issues in the outside world. Their decisions often reflect the strong convictions of strategically placed minorities. . . . When political issues are at stake . . . discussions quickly become partisan, demogogic, and filled with inaccuracies and exaggerations. Such debates do not produce wise conclusions, nor are they worthy of the university's commitment to thoughtful, dispassionate analysis": *President's Report, 1989–90* (Harvard University, 1991), 3–4.

Index

405

CPSIA information can be obtained at www.ICGtesting.com
Printed in the USA
LVOW131802250113

317296LV00001B/252/P